Robert De Niro
Untouchable

Unauthorised

Andy Dougan

For Christine, Iain, and Stuart, and once again to the memory
of my parents, Andrew and Winifred Dougan

First published in Great Britain in 1996 by
Virgin Books
an imprint of Virgin Publishing Ltd
332 Ladbroke Grove
LONDON W19 5AH

A catalogue record for this book is available from the British Library.

ISBN 1 85227 537 5

Phototypeset by Intype London Ltd
Printed and bound by
Mackays of Chatham PLC, Chatham, Kent

Contents

Robert De Niro: Untouchable

Author's Note and Acknowledgements

This is, as the title says, an unauthorised biography. Robert De Niro has not co-operated in any way in the writing of this book, although he was aware that it was being written.

I have taken the utmost care to source and check the material. A great many people have helped me in my endeavours, and I would like to thank them publicly for their efforts.

My thanks first of all go to two people who took a chance – my agent Jane Judd and Mal Peachey of Virgin Publishing. I trust that their faith and confidence will be vindicated by what you find in these pages.

I am enormously grateful to all of those who agreed to be interviewed. Some of the material comes from interviews I had conducted previously. However a number of people agreed to specific follow-up interviews and my thanks go to – in no particular order – Diane Ladd, Roger Corman, Ron Howard, Brian Grazer, Kurt Russell, Addison Arce, Barry Norman, Gilbert Adair, Cathy Moriarty, Lorenzo Carcaterra and Chazz Palminteri.

My thanks also to the publicists and agents who helped set up the interviews, including Claire Thornton, Debbie Turner, Kate Farquhar-Thompson, Peter Scott, Kate Lee, David Smith and Peter Dunne.

A number of friends and colleagues were kind enough to offer advice, encouragement, support, and access to their interviews. This book would not have been possible without the help of Maureen Beattie, Marianne Gray, Allan Hunter, Garry Jenkins, Anwar Brett, Chris Boyce, Alison Webb, Quentin Falk, Sara Dickerman, Russell Kyle, Kevin Bourke, Sue Greenway and Fraser Massey. I am also grateful to Bob Shelton for his invaluable advice and supportive friendship.

In compiling the material I spent a long time in various archives. I would like to acknowledge the enormous contribution made by the library staff at the British Film Institute, the Museum of Modern Art in New York, the *Los Angeles Times*, the *New York Daily Times*, and *Village Voice*. I would especially like to thank the indefatigable Faigi Rosenthal at the *Daily News* and the equally tireless Greg McNulty at *Village Voice* for their efforts on my behalf.

For technical help with pictures I am grateful to Karen Arch at MOMA, Jim Connor, John Young and Ian Blackley. And finally, for her invaluable help in photographic research, I would very gratefully like to acknowledge the contribution of Jennifer Sym.

'I Don't Want To Reincarnate Any More'

So many lives
Laid end to end
Like a river
At each bend

Am I really all these faces
Tattered vestiges one traces

Let me curb my temper
Quietly sit and fast
Hoping that tomorrow
It's all past

From *A Fashionable Watering Place*, written and published by
Robert De Niro Snr, 1976

Illustrations

Prologue

After the United Artists logo – the blue steel one with the serrated 'A' – fades, the screen is black for a full fifteen seconds. Five seconds into the darkness there is the faint sound of music. A solo violin plays a vaguely recognisable classical piece.

The music continues to grow in volume and becomes more recognisable. White letters on the black background announce 'A Robert Chartoff–Irwin Winkler Production', by Hollywood standards a modest billing. This in turn is followed by another equally discreet title: 'A Martin Scorsese Picture'. Finally we have 'Robert De Niro in . . .' There is another second of darkness before the screen fills abruptly with a hazy monochrome image.

A boxing ring before a fight. It is clouded with the smoke of too many cheap cigars and cigarettes. In the left-hand corner of the ring there is a fighter shrouded in a hooded leopard-skin robe. He is shadow-boxing, punching at no one in particular and lost in concentration. The camera shot from outside the ring frames him perfectly between the ropes. He is like an animal in a cage trapped by the top and bottom rope, the middle rope neatly bisecting him at the waist.

The music swells and becomes instantly recognisable. It is the intermezzo from Mascagni's *Cavalleria Rusticana*. As the full string section joins in, the title of the film appears in lurid Michael Powell red between the top and middle rope: *Raging Bull*. It will be the only splash of colour in the next 119 minutes.

The fighter continues his shadow-boxing. The lush strings give his single-minded concentration a balletic grace. The combinations are coming thick and fast as he gets up on the balls of his feet. The crowd at ringside watch rapt, but the fighter does not even dignify them with so much as a glance. He drops his head and right shoulder and begins a fast and furious tattoo of punches to a phantom solar plexus. He is compact now but powerfully built. Anyone on the end of even one of those blows would be doubled over for a week. The screen flares briefly as a flashbulb pops somewhere in the stalls. It is a futile gesture by the unseen photographer. The fighter has his back to the crowd; he will not show his face.

The combinations are finished. Once again he is up on the balls of his feet, bouncing in place, a model of controlled fury. He breaks step and starts to stride across the ring, his boxing boots making his steps absurdly flat-footed. In five steps he lumbers across to the near ropes, his hands no longer throwing punches but still held guardedly at chest height. At the near side of the ring he starts prancing again, up on his toes, anything to keep the energy focused. All the while he has not even looked at the crowd. This man could be on Mars for all the attention he is giving to his surroundings. Back and forth across the ring he paces; you can almost feel the adrenalin pouring out of him. His gloves are pressed together, his strength is focused, his concentration complete.

Eventually he settles back in the corner where we first saw him. The music ends, the man still throwing punches. The scene changes.

This is the public perception of Robert De Niro – a man outside the system, existing in isolation, throwing phantom punches at an unseen enemy.

1 Greenwich Village People

THE STREETS OF GREENWICH Village are not particularly mean. Not compared to other parts of New York.

Greenwich Village is a polyglot melting-pot located towards the southernmost tip of Manhattan. For years it has been the haunt of some of America's finest artistic temperaments – Edgar Allan Poe, Nathaniel Hawthorne and Bob Dylan are a few of the many who have found a creative wellspring for their talents as they passed their days in its coffee houses, bars, and cafés. Greenwich Village is actually two communities which sprawl west, east and south around Union Square Park, roughly divided by Lafayette Street as it runs into Fourth Avenue. The East Village borders on Little Italy and Chinatown and, despite recent attempts at gentrification, remains the less salubrious of the two. The West Village, on the other hand, is a haven for artistic souls. Property values are high, streets are safe, and the atmosphere is one of a discreet lack of inhibition.

It was to Greenwich Village that a 24-year-old Berkeley student named Virginia Admiral was headed in January 1940. The Village was a different place in those days – for one thing it was much smaller and more self-contained. The two sub-communities of SoHo and NoHo, situated respectively SOuth and NOrth of HOuston Street which sprang up as a result of seventies yuppification, were in those days still largely industrialised collections of factories and warehouses. Virginia's immediate aim was to study at Hans Hofmann's School of Fine Arts. She had been born in The Dalles in Oregon on 4 February 1915, and had spent most of her childhood in Iowa and the northern timber town of California and Washington State. A bright student and a gifted painter, at the age of seventeen she had had the opportunity to go to Paris to study and paint but had turned it down. Instead she went to the University of California. At Berkeley she had found friends who would go on to make their own mark on the world – men like the poet and illustrator Robert Duncan and women like the poet and painter Mary Fabilli, her sister Lili and Pauline Kael, who would become the definitive film critic of her generation.

The Berkeley campus in the late thirties was fiercely political. Spain had been devastated by the Civil War and the rest of Europe was about to become engulfed in the Second World War. The combination of the two circumstances was raising political consciousness all round. Virginia Admiral's friends in the Berkeley Young People's Socialist League were Trotskyites and, she remembered in a later article, 'a voice crying in the wilderness, for the campus was almost entirely Stalinist'. Like all good students they lived in a garret which also housed the YPSL mimeograph machine from which would be fired the latest shots in the propaganda war with the campus Young Communist League. As they sat and listened to Duncan recite his poetry, the world must have seemed a fairly uncomplicated place in February 1938. They moved around like vagabonds during those pre-housing-shortage days – all the while enjoying the delights of each others' company. In an article for a retrospective of Duncan's illustrations, Virginia Admiral remembers it as 'a very happy time' while her own mother described it as a mutual admiration society. 'As if there were something wrong with that,' as Admiral would write later.

In 1939 the war in Europe loomed closer, and Virginia and her friends spent more and more of their time at meetings, going to demonstrations, and printing and handing out their own leaflets. The Trotskyites were becoming the Fourth International and splitting into the Shachtmanites and the Cannonites. Meantime the Berkeley YPSLs, who had been thinking more along the lines of the sixties New Left, were dismissed as 'poets and dilettantes, not fit to form underground cadres'. Virginia Admiral had by this time already received a BA degree in English Literature and had been working on the Federal Arts Project in Oakland. The time had come, she decided, to head for the Hofmann School and a waitressing job in Greenwich Village.

Virginia's mother, herself a teacher of English and Latin, was obviously alarmed at the prospect of her daughter setting her sights on such an insecure lifestyle. She made Virginia promise to live at International House and go to teacher training college at Columbia to get a masters degree in Art Education. To this end she borrowed money from her own father, but by the end of Virginia's first semester the money had run out. Early in the summer of 1940 she went to nearby Woodstock to visit Robert Duncan, who was writing, printing, and publishing his own literary journals – something he and Virginia had done at Berkeley. After visiting Duncan she spent six weeks teaching at a summer camp in Maine. Then it was time once again to set her sights on Greenwich Village.

She quickly found the perfect studio, a loft on East 14th Street which had enormous windows allowing the north light to flood in, with the added bonus of a glorious view of Union Square. It may have been the perfect studio but it left something to be desired as a dwelling. For one thing it had no bathroom and the rent was $30 a month, much more than Virginia could afford on her own. She managed to find two friends to share the apartment, and Robert Duncan used it as one of his many crash-pads on his trips from Woodstock to New York.

Duncan remembers Virginia and the studio fondly in his notebooks of the period. An entry written not long before America entered the war, from a 1941 journal in the Bancroft Poetry Archive, paints a particularly vivid picture.

'Virginia's studio opens out,' it begins. 'We stand in the shadows above the lights of fourteenth street. The paintings move back into the walls like mirrors of our dreams – the dark stage of gathering forces. This is our last nursery – this is today's, 1941's projection of a Berkeley Paradise where we go over again drawings by Virginia, by Mary, by Lillian, by Cecily, by me from the golden age – where I sit reading to Virginia and her fellow students.'

By the autumn Hofmann had given Virginia a scholarship and she had given up all thought of completing her master's degree and was instead devoting herself to her painting. And there was now another interest in her life. In 1941 a former student had left a full scholarship at Black Mountain College to return to the Hofmann School. Within a few months he and Virginia were sharing the loft at 30 East 14th Street. His name was Robert De Niro.

De Niro was born in 1922 in Syracuse in upper New York State to an Irish mother and an Italian father. He grew up in a predominantly Irish neighbourhood. He showed artistic talent from the age of five and with it a marked single-mindedness about his art for one so young. So much so that when he started taking formal art classes at the University of Syracuse at the age of eleven, they soon had to provide him with a studio of his own in which to paint. His teachers at Syracuse recognised and encouraged a burgeoning talent, as did Hans Hofmann, who regarded De Niro as among the best and brightest of his students. A dynamic painter with a strong sense of colour, De Niro has been compared to the Fauves, including Matisse. He has also been described by the *New York Times* as 'the archetypal Expressionist, whose emotions must be as fully engaged as his eyes in order to work at his best'.

A handsome man with a shock of wavy hair, Robert De Niro's features were defined by deep-set, soulful dark eyes under a heavy brow and a strong jawline that must indeed have made him seem a singularly single-minded child. He was not exceptionally tall at five feet ten, but his soft-spoken manner and intense charm made an impression on everyone who knew him. Coupled with this outward charm was an inner fire. De Niro set impossibly high standards for himself and was his own harshest critic. Contemporaries recall his being frequently frustrated by his own efforts, and these frustrations would occasionally manifest themselves in violent outbursts. These would take the form of tempers and rages directed at what he perceived to be his own shortcomings rather than physical violence.

One of his friends described his involvement with art as a matter of life and death. His determination to create art in its purest form drove him to paint over work again and again in a quest for, if not perfection, then at least satisfaction. In 1958 the influential New York magazine *ARTnews* carried an article on De Niro with the intention of showing the artist at work. The work in question was a crucifixion, and De Niro's progress was tracked for a little more than two years.

'... but due to his restive dissatisfaction with each start,' recalls the catalogue from the retrospective exhibition held in 1995, two years after his death, 'his painting and repainting and moving from canvas to canvas, the final essay is an account of frustration as each version of the subject underwent continual metamorphosis and ultimate rejection until at the end only one gouache survived.'

Although he was a contemporary, albeit a younger one, of Abstract Expressionists like Mark Rothko and Jackson Pollock, Robert De Niro's painting clung on tenaciously to the moods and styles of the European Expressionists. He painted from classic subjects – studio models, jugs and vases – and frequently from photographs of places he had never seen for himself. His paintings have a strong Mediterranean sensuality to them in terms of both colour and atmosphere. He was briefly and justifiably lauded in the forties and fifties but – aided by his own intransigence as far as selling to collections and galleries was concerned, and the increasing trendiness of the art world itself – after his return from France in the early sixties he became known as a painter's painter. He was enormously respected by the cognoscenti but almost unknown to anyone outside that charmed circle. After his death in 1993 a sheet of paper was found in his studio on which he had scribbled down a quotation from the journals of the French artist Eugène Delacroix.

'Really to live in my way,' it said, 'that is to say, through the feelings and the heart, I am obliged to seek my enjoyments in painting and to seize them from there.'

All of this was still to come, however, when Robert De Niro and Virginia Admiral met at the Hofmann School. Within a few years both would have exhibited at Peggy Guggenheim's Art of This Century, and Virginia would have sold one of her paintings, *Composition*, to the Museum of Modern Art in New York, becoming the first of her contemporaries to do so. The painting sold for $100, which was not a large amount, but Admiral had been advised by Peggy Guggenheim that since it was going to a museum, and since it was her first sale, she should not hold out for a larger sum.

Admiral and De Niro were an odd couple, he a volatile Irish-Italian, she an intellectual and fiercely independent. But oddly matched or not, they were a golden couple at Provincetown – or 'P-town', as Hofmann's students referred to it. They were among the best in the school, attracting attention in an atmosphere where painters either excelled or were ignored completely. Fellow students recall a tangible aura of potential greatness around this couple who had the respect of their teachers and their peers.

But whatever aura of greatness surrounded them, it would not last long.

2 Chelsea Mornings

THE AMERICAN CENTURY HAS been defined as much by its places as its people. Ronald Reagan's Washington and its politics defined the eighties, the climax of the West Coast-led anti-war movement set the tone for the highly politicised seventies, and for the sixties it was the summers of peace, love and LSD which emerged from San Francisco. But there is no doubt that in the period immediately following the Second World War, American society took its lead from New York and particularly from Greenwich Village.

America had been at war for almost two years when Robert De Niro was born. It would be another two years before the dropping of the atomic bombs at Hiroshima and Nagasaki brought an uneasy peace that ushered in the atomic age and the nascent Cold War. The end of the war also brought a new excitement and vitality to America, which was finally and irrevocably about to assume its role as the world's policeman. These were exciting times in which to be alive and to be American. There was, it seemed, nothing that America could not do and, by extension, nothing to which the ordinary American could not aspire. This was the philosophy and the guiding light of those born immediately after the war, the generation that became known as the Baby Boomers. De Niro was born two years too early to be an official Baby Boomer, but he was shaped by the same social climate and conditions.

Robert De Niro Snr was just nineteen when America entered the war. With the anxiety of the draft hanging over them, De Niro and Virginia Admiral decided, in January 1942, to get married. Their financial position was parlous to say the least. Admiral had been doing occasional typing for writers, and in their first summer in Provincetown they picked blueberries to make money. De Niro also worked briefly in a fish factory. Back in New York they each got a $15 cheque for art materials every month from Hilda Rebay, director of the small Guggenheim Museum. In the autumn of 1942 Rebay gave De Niro a black suit and a job at the museum, where he would sit at a desk and answer questions from visitors for a few hours a day. This paid $35 a week, about three times what they had been living on up till then, so their financial worries were over. De Niro arranged for Jackson Pollock and several other painters to share the job and once a week they would take turns sleeping over at the museum to guard the paintings.

Babies were something of an unknown quantity in the circles in which De Niro and Admiral moved, and the furthest thing from anyone's mind. However, in October 1942 Virginia Admiral looked after a new-born nephew for a few days and marvelled at the child, especially its apparently miraculous energy. Her maternal instincts were roused, and ten months later – on 17 August 1943 – she gave birth to Robert De Niro Jnr.

Meanwhile De Niro and Admiral had found, for the princely sum of $22 a month, a whole top floor in a three-storey building at 200 Bleecker Street – between McDougal Street and Sixth Avenue – across the road from the San Remo Café. The apartment is now part of New York's famous Little Red Schoolhouse. After a wall had been taken down there were two large studios and a bedroom. They bathed in a laundry tub in the kitchen and – since the flat had no heating – they installed two large heaters, one in each studio.

What they lacked in central heating they more than made up for in *joie de vivre*. The apartment was brightly painted throughout and the baby De Niro was surrounded by the great and the good of New York's cultural and artistic élite as he crawled around their feet. There were always people around and there was always coffee on the go, even if it had to be drunk out of old mayonnaise jars. A visitor to the top floor of 200 Bleecker Street in 1943 might have run across artist Marjorie McKee, or art critic Clement Greenberg, or indeed Robert Duncan, who remained a friend.

The baby Robert De Niro grew into an ebullient, even charismatic, toddler. In nearby Washington Square Park people would always turn to see what he was doing and follow his exploits when he was out. At the nearby Greenwich House nursery school he was enthusiastic and fearless – and by far the youngest child to go down the playground slide. However, at the age of two, his life was turned upside down when his parents separated. Neither Robert De Niro Snr nor Virginia Admiral has ever talked on record about the split which does not appear, initially at least, to have been an amicable one. It was suggested by the *Observer* newspaper in London, in a 1977 article which quoted an unnamed source, that their split was caused by the intervention of a psychiatrist who was himself a frustrated artist. This appears not to have been the case, since the man involved was a Freudian and as such would not have sought directly to influence anyone he was treating. Whatever the reasons, neither De Niro nor Admiral wanted them made public.

For some months the baby De Niro lived with his grandparents in Syracuse while custody arrangements were worked out. It was while he was with his grandparents that he was baptised a Roman Catholic, against his parents' wishes. His father had left the Church at the age of twelve and his mother, while raised a Presbyterian, was by now an atheist. The separation of the golden couple caused something of a scandal in their tightly knit artistic community, but it was made final with a divorce in 1953. Given the climate of the times – it was almost impossible for a woman successfully to sue for divorce, adultery being the only possible grounds – we must assume that De Niro eventually agreed to an arranged divorce in which he would not contest an accusation of adultery.

For Robert De Niro Snr painting was everything. He would do whatever he had to do to provide for his art. He had lived in a tent, he had worked on a coal barge, he had even done the obligatory stint of waiting on tables – Tennessee Williams was a waiter in the same restaurant. It was taken for granted that Admiral would assume total financial and moral responsibility for their son. But some years later, when De Niro received $1000 from the Gloria Vanderbilt Foundation for a painting, he gave all the money to his ex-wife. After they split up there was a period of estrangement between the parents but Virginia Admiral did not deny her son access to his father; she actually encouraged the boy to spend time with him. For his part Robert De Niro continued to occupy studios in the Greenwich Village/SoHo area which were within walking distance for his son.

Robert De Niro saw his father frequently as he grew up, spending many hours at his studio. When he was still small enough he would sit on his father's knee as the elder De Niro worked away at his easel, watching as his father set himself near-impossible standards with his art, observing him revise painting after painting in his search for perfection. He would see at first hand the man whose emotions must be as fully engaged as his eyes to work at his best, and would carry that memory with him into later life.

Father and son would often spend their afternoons and evenings at the movies together. Doubtless it was his father who introduced the young De Niro to the charms of the enigmatic Greta Garbo, an actress to whom he would be compared in later life in terms of his fanatical desire to be left alone. Robert De Niro Snr was obsessed with Garbo; indeed, one of his most famous series of paintings was inspired by the Swedish star in her famous role as Anna Christie. A sculptor and poet as well as an artist, he

10

also produced busts of Garbo as Christie and wrote poems about her. His son has often stated that Garbo is one of the actors he found most influential in his career.

After a year or so in an unheated top-floor tenement at 521 Hudson Street – painter friends of Admiral rented other apartments in the building as studios – Virginia Admiral and her son moved to a relatively elegant top-floor studio at 219 West 14th Street. It had huge closets, a functioning heating system, parquet flooring and a large bedroom for Bobby, as he was known to his parents and everyone in the neighbourhood. But it also cost $50 a month.

Virginia Admiral had had to put her painting on hold and devote herself full time to providing for herself and her son. She had been working in a picture-framing shop for the going rate of $1.25 an hour, the minimum wage at that time. She then acquired a job with another picture-framing company which paid a little more, although still only $1.50 an hour. She would turn her hand to anything. In fairly quick succession she worked for a textile designer and a jewellery designer; she was a temporary secretary; she was even assistant editor of *Underworld Detective* and *Detective World*, two magazines that seem to have catered to the lunatic fringe. Little Bobby meanwhile was spending his days at the Greenwich House nursery school. This was a major help to his mother since, under a government programme designed to encourage mothers to take on war work in defence plants, it cost her only $1.25 a week. Later, when he was at primary school, he would continue going after school to Greenwich House, where he is remembered as an 'unusually creative' child.

Virginia Admiral was quickly coming to the conclusion that she needed to find a way to work at home. She began typing and editing for two foreign writers, Ladislas Farago and Maria Piscator, but most of all she would type dissertations for Columbia University students and PhD candidates. This was successful up to a point, but the work was too seasonal to depend on. Eventually she acquired a varitype machine and an executive typewriter and set up her own cold-type service, mostly for printers. The company, called Academy, operated out of the apartment on West 14th Street for a time before she moved it in 1957 round the corner to an office at 68 Seventh Avenue. By the time of the move she had built it into a company with ten employees and her own printing press. One of the reasons for the move apparently was that the young De Niro was so annoyed by the sounds of the typewriters and typesetting machines that he threatened to throw them out of the window. Admiral's political instincts were undimmed, and one of the firm's sidelines was typesetting and printing pamphlets and leaflets for the Socialist movement. In 1964

Admiral moved out and gave the studio on West 14th Street to her son, who continued to live there until the early seventies, when he eventually let it go.

Even though his parents were separated and then divorced, De Niro managed to live a reasonably normal childhood. He would spend Christmas Day, for example, with his mother and her relatives, and the following day he and his father would go to Syracuse to see his grandparents. Likewise his summers tended to be spent in upstate New York where he would stay for six weeks in Syracuse. The arrangement of spending time with his father continued until at fifteen De Niro attended a going-away party on board the ship on which his father sailed for France, where he had decided to live and paint. The party and their parting must have been a poignant moment for both of them.

The young De Niro first went to school at PS41, which is situated on West 11th Street, although the building has been replaced since De Niro's time. The school faced Greenwich Avenue, and indeed the façade of the old building has been incorporated into the new one and can be seen from the playground. De Niro would walk the few blocks from his home to the school, where he was an unremarkable student. Although other accounts of his childhood frequently feature contemporaries claiming De Niro was never without a book in his hand or stuffed into his pocket, the truth is that he did not have a lot of time for books. He taught himself to read largely through comic books which in those days, as with television today, were considered a bad influence on young people. These were not the flimsy excuses for comic books than exist today – this was the end of the Golden Age of comic books when they were 64 pages thick and 'all in color for a dime'. The young De Niro would lose himself in this four-colour world of thrills and adventures. Doubtless his teachers frowned on his passion, but his reading skills jumped several years in one summer.

Whether Virginia Admiral approved or disapproved of her son's reading material, she was not very likely to have done anything about it. Like her own mother, Virginia Admiral was an admirer of John Dewey's theory of permissive education, which was fortunate given the constant pressure of Academy's deadlines. The absence of discipline does not appear to have corrupted the child – the young De Niro was not a troublesome boy. While it is true that he and his friends would sometimes fill balloons or paper sacks with water and drop them down on 14th Street, or go the wrong way on escalators, he was basically a trustworthy child who was simply never asked to clean his room.

De Niro left PS41 at the end of sixth grade. There was concern in the neighbourhood about the level of violence in the local junior high school which De Niro and his friends were due to attend. There was a certain amount of delinquency and rumours about knife-wielding gangs so rather than transfer to IS71, as he was supposed to, De Niro instead went to a private school. Elisabeth Irwin High School in Charlton Street, New York, was a forward-thinking and enlightened educational institution with very liberal views – it was the high school of the Little Red Schoolhouse which now occupied De Niro's first home in Bleecker Street.

A rare picture of De Niro at this period can be found in *Glamour* magazine, a New York publication. A photographer who was a friend of a friend of Virginia Admiral asked to photograph her son to illustrate an article on state versus private schools. Although he was at a private school, De Niro's picture was chosen to represent a typical state school pupil. The tow-headed De Niro clad in a worn biker jacket and jeans stares out of the photograph. He would have been no more than thirteen at the time, but already there is a strong hint of self-awareness and self-determination in this young boy's eyes. Interestingly enough he also seems as dubious about having his picture taken here as he would in later life when the paparazzi would dog his every move.

Robert De Niro's time at Elisabeth Irwin was not terribly successful. The school's liberal leanings meant that with the advent of McCarthyism, the launch of Sputnik, and the beginnings of the Cold War, the school's only defence against accusations of 'pinkness' would be its academic record. As a consequence it tried to get as many of its students into Ivy League colleges as possible. This is where Robert De Niro struck his first educational problem. His grades were affected, ironically, by an excessive perfectionism. This would drive him, for instance, to spend hours copying and recopying a single composition to avoid blots – a reflection of those long hours spent on his father's knee, watching him paint over his work time and time again. The boy's attitude to his school essays was a manifestation of the dedication and drive for perfection that would eventually make him the greatest actor of his generation. Nonetheless, at that time his school grades were not up to Ivy League standard, and after completing seventh and eighth grades at Elisabeth Irwin, De Niro was told to apply for a scholarship to the High School of Music and Art.

De Niro had always been largely responsible for his own upbringing. As he began venturing further afield and making friends with kids from Little Italy, so he would spend more time out of the house and on the streets. But it was definitely not the existence of a pre-pubescent Travis Bickle. De Niro was not prowling the streets as an isolated loner. He acquired a great deal of self-awareness and self-possession at a very early age, but he was never without his friends as they sampled the delights of

Greenwich Village and Little Italy street life. And in the fifties, these streets were among the most exciting places in the world.

A generation of Americans had come back from the war with a new world view and a new outlook on life. This manifested itself in a magnificent outpouring of creativity in literature, music, theatre, and in film. And at the heart of this was Greenwich Village. The café society of the thirties and forties, much beloved by columnists like Walter Winchell, had given way to a vibrant new outpouring. The Village in the fifties was a melting-pot where the six-storey brownstones with their skeletal fire escapes provided the crucible in which the voice of a new generation was forged. In 1956, when De Niro was barely in his teens, Allen Ginsberg wrote 'Howl', the pioneering beat poem that was a rallying call to a new breed. Ginsberg and fellow revolutionaries like Jack Kerouac, Neal Cassady and William Burroughs had been gathering an exciting and increasingly vocal following in the cafés and coffee bars of Greenwich Village for several years before this. This was the era of Charlie Parker and Elvis Presley; it was also the era of the man who became a spokesman for his generation. Bob Dylan was discovered at Gerde's Folk City on West Third Street in Greenwich Village. Two years earlier, Joan Baez, the artist who latterly became known as a distaff Dylan, had also been discovered in the Village. This rich kaleidoscope of sights and sounds presented itself daily and nightly for the delectation of the young De Niro, who drank it all in as he moved through the streets of the Village.

De Niro talks about his teenage years only in the vaguest terms. In public he begs off, allegedly for fear of embarrassing his pals. This in itself appears to be something of an attempt at reinventing himself. De Niro's early screen image is of a tough loner walking down the mean streets of New York's East Side. In fact he was born and raised in a relatively genteel part of the more up-market West Village. Even when he moved with his mother to West 14th Street, this was actually in Bohemian Chelsea rather than in Greenwich Village itself. There was no Cagneyesque rough-and-tumble about the neighbourhood. This was not *Angels with Dirty Faces*, and De Niro was no latter day Bowery Boy. His worst indiscretion involved being a 'steerer' for would-be buyers of fire crackers in Little Italy – hardly likely to get him on the FBI's Ten Most Wanted list.

Having obtained the scholarship, De Niro only stayed at the High School of Music and Art for a few days. He was appalled by fellow students he saw 'wearing sandals and playing guitars in Washington Square Park' and he wanted to go to 'a normal junior high school'. So he finally wound up at IS71, Charles Evans Hughes junior high. His mother has been quoted as saying that her son's idea of school was 'not turning up'.

This is not strictly true. De Niro was responsible enough to realise that his mother had been paying for his education. As long as it was costing her money he would go to school religiously, but the moment he returned to the state system he started skipping classes. The petty tyrannies of the state education system could not have been easy for him to take. The more enlightened system that prevailed at home probably meant he was a good deal more mature than his peers. This, after all, was a child who had been responsible for buying his own clothes from the age of ten. The frustrations boiled over one day when De Niro was threatened with suspension and even expulsion for raising his hand to a teacher. No blow was struck and the circumstances of the incident are not recorded, but it was a serious challenge to the school's authority and plainly De Niro could not remain there. His mother read between the lines and realised that it was simply not going to work out at IS71, no matter what happened, and she put him into McBurney, another private high school. Once again she was paying for his education and once again De Niro responded with diligent attendance. His previous truancy had taken its toll, however, and he was put into a class a couple of years behind his contemporaries. At the end of his first year at McBurney he was also told he would have to go to summer school if he was to go back for a second year. De Niro felt he had shown willing by working harder than he had ever done before and categorically refused to go, in the belief that he was being unfairly treated. Instead he announced to his mother that he would spend the summer of 1960 on his previously planned vacation trip across the United States to visit some of her relatives in California. He promised two things on his return. The first was that he would tell her what he was going to do with his life, the second was that she would be pleased with his choice.

At Maria Piscator's Dramatic Workshop, at the age of ten, Robert De Niro trod the boards for the first time as the Cowardly Lion in a production of *The Wizard of Oz*. Although he did not realise it at the time, he was hooked. Even now he cannot put his finger on what made him want to become an actor.

'Acting', he once said, 'is a cheap way to do things that you would never dare to do yourself.'

It is something about which he remains intensely curious, but he claims to have known that even from around the age of nine or ten this was what he wanted to do with his life. It may seem that De Niro simply wanted what every actor wants – to be someone else. He frequently describes himself as an outsider and, if he genuinely believes that, then acting gives him the perfect opportunity to be in the spotlight instead of on the outside. If no one paid attention to him on the street or in the classroom then they had to pay attention when he was on the stage. One of his earliest acting tutors asked him why he wanted to be an actor and De Niro told him he didn't know. The teacher told him that he wanted to be an actor to express himself. It was a remarkably prescient observation about a man who has seldom, if ever, expressed himself in his own words on anything significant. De Niro has continually chosen to express himself through the mouths of others. Screenwriter Paul Schrader would later accuse him, not unkindly, of coming alive in other people's bodies. It seems likely that De Niro chooses which bodies to inhabit in terms of what they will allow him to express about himself. Travis Bickle in *Taxi Driver* or Jake La Motta in *Raging Bull* express his internal rages and frustrations, while Michael Vronsky in *The Deer Hunter* allows him to make a political statement. All his roles provide De Niro with maximum deniability. If pressed he can always claim – whether it is true or not – that he is simply playing a part.

Although the images he created at Greenwich House were bold and artistic and his colouring books showed a Bonnard-like sense of colour, especially one memorable effort involving a circus cart with, of all things, a salamander inside. Robert De Niro was never told by his parents what to do with his life. Like everything else he had done, and would do, he figured it out for himself. Nonetheless, his parents were very supportive of his chosen career, even if his father's support was confined to moral rather than financial backing.

'They would never tell me no,' recalls De Niro. 'My mother worked for a woman named Maria Ley-Piscator who with her husband founded the Dramatic Workshop. This couple had come out of Germany and the guy went back but his wife stayed on and ran the workshop. My mother did typing and proofreading and stuff for her and as part of her payment I was able to take acting classes there on Saturdays when I was ten. It was a big school with a lot of actors, some of whom were able to study acting on the GI Bill. Marlon Brando and Rod Steiger went there in the generation before me.'

As an adult, De Niro's devotion to subsuming himself totally in the roles he plays is his trademark. One of the earliest signs of this total immersion came on the streets of New York when he was fourteen. De Niro was still at Elisabeth Irwin at the time, and the children there were being victimised by Italian kids from a nearby school who were in the habit of threatening them and stealing their lunch money. Whether he felt there was safety in numbers, or whether, since he loved gangster movies, he was simply childishly impressed by their behaviour, De Niro 'became' an Italian after he left Elisabeth Irwin. His absorption in the role was total. He started to affect silk suits and would even get up early to go to Mass with his new friends. He spent his time watching and doubtless admiring the 'made men' who hung out on Mott Street in Little Italy, observations that would serve him well in later life when playing such men would make him an international star. For De Niro and his friends their kingdom was the area bounded by Kenmare Street, Mulberry Street and Elizabeth Street – the nexus of an area where Little Italy, Chinatown, and Greenwich Village all run together.

Although he was dignified with a nickname – 'Bobby Milk' on account of his pale complexion – it would be something of an exaggeration to class De Niro and his new friends as a gang in the way we now understand the term in these days of drug-running and drive-by shootings. His father was less than thrilled, but the crowd his son ran with hardly constituted a serious threat to public order. The lasting perception of De Niro having been 'a nice kid' in the memories of everyone who talks about this time would seem to undermine the actor's own attempts to make his teens appear more interesting. The gang, it seemed, gave him a much-needed sense of identity and accounted for some of his lasting friendships. He is still close to Clem Caserta with whom he ran then, but most notably it was on his visits to Mott Street that he first encountered his artistic alter ego in the shape of Martin Scorsese.

Acting also gave him a sense of identity, albeit a borrowed one, and would soon once again exert a hold on the growing boy. De Niro had promised his mother an answer after he had made his trans-continental odyssey. When he returned, having turned seventeen on the trip, he announced that he was going to be an actor, and that he would study at the Stella Adler Conservatory. When it was pointed out to him that Stella Adler would not take him without a high-school diploma, De Niro had a solution already worked out. He would go to Adler's conservatory during the day and high school at night to get his degree.

De Niro had first encountered Stella Adler when she taught some of his Saturday classes at the Dramatic Workshop. She was the foremost exponent of the Stanislavsky Method. When he started attending her famous Conservatory of Acting in Greenwich Village De Niro would unconsciously be following in the footsteps of Marlon Brando, who had also been an Adler pupil. Adler ran a tight ship, and in an establishment devoted to the encouragement of uninhibited creativity discipline was strict and protocol rigorously adhered to. There was a dress code for both sexes: for boys, white shirts with dark, pressed trousers and black shoes; for girls, skirts, high-collared blouses, heels, and hair tied back off the face. When Adler made her entrance students were required to stand and recite in unison, 'Good morning, Miss Adler. We are pleased to meet you and look forward to embarking with you on our journey to discover our art.' Adler would then proceed, as the *New York Times* memorably put it, to 'curse, cajole, rage, roar, and from time to time even compliment her students'. She preferred to teach the use of what she called creative imagination in her version of the Stanislavskian method of learning a role from the inside out. Her views on teaching acting were as rigid and uncompromising as her methods. De Niro found himself in a similar situation to his parents in their days at the Hoffmann School, where failure was not an option – he would either shine or be ignored.

'The teacher has to inspire,' Stella Adler once said. 'The teacher has to agitate. You cannot teach acting. You can only stimulate what is already there.'

Nonetheless she realised what she had on her hands with the teenage De Niro. She described one of the scenes he performed in her class as the best she had ever seen. In the end he made good only on one part of his promise to his mother. Although he did go to school at night, he never actually graduated from high school. Ironically his grades at Rhodes were very good and the decision not to graduate was his and his alone. He was three credits short in his final year – amounting to a single course – when he decided that he would not take the vital last subject. It appears to have been a declaration to himself that he now knew what he would do with his life. He would not need a high-school diploma. It was the sort of action that would become a typical De Niro way of making a point. One person who knew him at the time claims he wanted people to know that he was aware that the whole business didn't actually mean anything. He could have graduated if he had wanted to; he simply did not want to.

The decision not to graduate is the first example of something that would become increasingly evident throughout his life. Robert De Niro is essentially his own creation. As a child he would watch his father dedicate himself to painting and his mother work round the clock at times to support them both. He had two shining examples of dedication and hard work. These became the two guiding principles of his life and sustained him through the early part of his career.

With his mother's agreement, De Niro took the money he would have spent on college fees and put it towards his acting career. Having grown up around single-minded people he found himself admiring Stella Adler's conviction that hers was the way the Stanislavsky Method should be taught. But a few years later he decided to sample the techniques of the other exponent of the Method and sought out Lee Strasberg at his famous Actors Studio. He attended as an observer and never auditioned for Strasberg himself. He did, however, take part in a great many workshops with the actors, some of whom, like Sally Kirkland and Diane Ladd, became close and lasting friends.

Strasberg's way of teaching was much less rigorous than Adler's. There was no dress code at the Actors Studio and the relaxed atmosphere brought the best out of the students. The fact that Studio alumni are reckoned to have won something like 60 per cent of all the acting awards presented in America since the studio was set up speaks volumes for the merits of Strasberg's teaching system. Although De Niro was only an observer, he made an impression at the studio, but even he could not have dreamed that years later he and Strasberg himself would star in a movie together.

'Bobby was one of the prime representatives of the Actors Studio,' says Diane Ladd. 'He got the same training that I got, the same training that Sally Kirkland – who is a great actress – also got. He follows in the tradition of Geraldine Page, Maureen Stapleton, Shelley Winters, Joanne Woodward, Paul Newman, Marlon Brando, and Jimmy Dean. They all came out of that place.

'You just need a place where you can go and do your work and not be judged too harshly,' she says in an attempt to explain the success of Strasberg's establishment in producing some of the finest actors seen on stage or screen. 'An actor needs a place where they can fail without being condemned – a place without a guillotine – because an actor is a species which lives between chance and oblivion. In order for them to grow in those circumstances, which are challenging enough on their own, they have to have a place which is not there to judge them. The Actors Studio is not there for results; you cannot be result-minded when you are acting any more than a surgeon can be result-minded when he is performing an operation. You should just be thinking about the moment, the second, and that's what the Actors Studio encourages. It's like making love. You shouldn't be thinking about results when you are making love, it should be all about the moment. And creativity and love are the same thing.'

3 Sally and Shelley

ROBERT DE NIRO'S FONDNESS for sharp Italian suits was a momentary aberration. Once he started at Stella Adler's and Lee Strasberg's schools he quickly dedicated himself whole-heartedly to acting. He also began to look more like a drama student. The Italian tailoring quickly reverted to the less modish but more practical leather jacket and jeans as worn in his 'modelling assignment' for *Glamour* magazine.

Although he was still a teenager, De Niro took the craft of acting as seriously then as he does now. Visitors to the apartment he shared with his mother in West 14th Street recall that at times it resembled a theatrical costumier's. The two large walk-in cupboards in the apartment were both crammed with old jackets, coats, and hats. De Niro was noted for raiding thrift shops and old clothes stores for material that would come in handy at some future date. It would be convenient to assume that this was some early attempt literally to lose himself in other people's characters by wearing their clothes, but the real explanation is depressingly mundane. In common with the other actors at the Studio, De Niro was responsible for providing his own props, it was an aspect of the emotional attachment to the role that is part and parcel of the Method. De Niro was simply filling the flat with costumes and other miscellaneous items of wardrobe that might come in useful to help him get into a character. He seldom wore any of the clothes for normal day wear, with the exception of the hats, for which he had a real passion. He boasted a large collection, and these he would wear out, the style of headgear varying as the mood took him. Within a few years one of these hats would come in very useful (if you call establishing him as the most exciting actor of his generation useful).

One of the more frequent visitors to West 14th Street in those early sixties days was Sally Kirkland, whom De Niro had met at the Actors Studio. Kirkland would go on to make a name for herself with a number of controversial nude appearances on stage and through her work with Andy Warhol. Later in her career she would receive a well-deserved Academy Award nomination for Best Actress for playing a Polish woman in the 1987 film *Anna*. While they were both at the Actors Studio, Kirkland and De Niro would go to his apartment to rehearse theatrical pieces from class, as well as others they would improvise themselves. Kirkland recalls that De Niro was determined to establish himself and the vast collection of wardrobe items was to help.

'He would go to auditions,' she remembers. 'Every time he went he would take with him a portfolio of about twenty-five pictures of himself in various disguises to prove that he wasn't just an ethnic actor.'

Another contemporary recalls that when they went to have their photographs taken for agents and casting calls, De Niro was unique. While everyone else would go for the standard eight-by-ten glossy head-shot, De Niro ordered what is known as a 'composite shot'. This is an eight-by-ten divided into four quarters, each showing a shot of the actor in various characters. They are more frequently used by character actors. Young men setting out in the business normally want to be seen as leading men, hence their preference for the solo head-shots.

De Niro has never had what anyone would describe as leading-man looks. As he got older his face became more interesting and acquired a certain dramatic weight, but he has never been conventionally handsome. The frailty that marked him from the days when he was known as Bobby Milk would take some time to fade away, and in his late teens he was still as thin as a whip.

But De Niro seems never to have been interested in being a leading man or being famous simply for its own sake.

'Bobby was hell bent on being a success but not as a movie star,' says Diane Ladd. 'He didn't want to be a star, he wanted to be an actor, and that's why he was with Lee Strasberg at the Actors Studio, to be an actor.'

For all his desire he was also a pragmatist. He believed in his talent and friends like Sally Kirkland also believed in it. But De Niro knew there was a world of difference between believing you could play the part and actually landing the part. He, along with thousands of others in a profession where fewer than 5 per cent are in work at any given time, would spend his days making the rounds of auditions and casting calls. Looking back, he can afford to be philosophical.

'As an actor who's starting out you can't say, "Hey, I'm too good for this",' he recalls. 'You've got to do it because people see you and your name gets around and it has a cumulative effect. Auditions are like a gamble. Most likely you won't get it but if you don't go you'll never know if you could have got it.'

For a brief time during this period De Niro was also known as 'Robert De Niro Jnr' out of deference to his father's fame, which was much greater than his at that point in their respective careers. However, after a while, and certainly before making his film debut in 1963, he had resorted to dropping the qualification.

The exact date of Robert De Niro's film debut is a matter of some argument for film purists. The facts appear to be these. In 1965 he was seen on screen for the first time with a brief walk-on part as an extra in the film *Trois Chambres à Manhattan*. He was cast presumably because, having spent some time in France with his father, he at least understood the language. The film was directed by the French film-maker Marcel Carné, whose career was on the wane after the peak of his 1942 classic *Les Enfants du Paradis*. As a consequence of Carné's fading reputation the film was scarcely seen. However, before *Trois Chambres à Manhattan* was released, De Niro had already made a movie. In 1963 he teamed up with an equally inexperienced Brian De Palma to make a film called *The Wedding Party*, which also featured another newcomer, Jill Clayburgh.

De Palma, like De Niro, was a native New Yorker. In 1963 he was working towards a post-graduate degree at Sarah Lawrence College in Bronxville. *The Wedding Party* would be the struggling young director's degree movie, and he was directing it along with two other people, Cynthia Munroe and Wilford Leach. De Palma advertised for actors who would be willing to work for next to nothing. De Niro got to hear about it and turned up for the open-call audition, as he would have done for so many before. De Palma remembers that he started off inauspiciously and finished up sensationally.

'He was very mild, very shy, and very self-effacing,' he says 'Nobody knew him, he was only a kid of about nineteen. We held open auditions and Bob came in about nine or ten at night. We gave him some material to read. He did it well and then we asked him to improvise and he was extraordinary. Then he said he had something else he wanted to show us, something he was working on. He left the room and was gone about twenty minutes. We thought he'd changed his mind and gone home. Then the door flies open and he bursts in from nowhere and he does a scene from a play by Clifford Odets. It was like watching Lee J.Cobb. Personally De Niro may be shy and soft-spoken but in character he could be anybody.'

De Niro's perception of events was that he had completely blown the first part of the audition when he read from the script. Asking to do the improvisation was something of a panic measure. Nonetheless it paid off because he got the part, and with it his first professional movie fee, the princely sum of $50, considerably less than he would get for his multi-million dollar cameo as Al Capone in De Palma's version of *The Untouchables* some fifteen years later. De Palma remembers that he and Munroe and Leach were all so impressed with De Niro's audition that they agreed he had to be in the film. No one was quite sure what he would play, but all three knew he had to appear.

'I also got a percentage which of course I never saw,' says De Niro wryly of his *Wedding Party* fee. 'I thought I was getting fifty dollars a week but my mother read it and said, 'No, it's just fifty dollars.''

Virginia Admiral had to sign the contract because De Niro was too young to sign it himself. She had some experience of contracts from her own business dealings, which is why she quickly spotted that it was a one-off fee. De Niro was further disillusioned when he discovered that he would once again have to supply his own props out of his $50. De Palma's production was as financially strapped as all the other theatrical pieces De Niro had done for Adler or Strasberg. One of the props the actor acquired was a suitcase. He was less than pleased when he discovered it was going to be thrown from a car, damaging it irreparably.

The Wedding Party is the story of three guys trying to deal with the fact that one of them is about to get married. The future groom, Charlie, was played by Charles Pfluger. De Niro ended up playing Cecil, one of Charlie's two pals who are trying desperately to stop him tying the knot. The other pal, Baker, was played by John Quinn. Together they try to convince Charlie that life with bride-to-be Clayburgh is not a good idea. They should stay together they argue, and continue with the adventures they planned for themselves before settling down to married life.

Some reviewers were kind to *The Wedding Party* but most dismissed it as a talky and tiresome romantic comedy. The show-business newspaper of record, *Variety*, did at least concede that 'Robert De Nero' – as he was billed – was one of the few who made an impression in this film. The film did not find a distributor when it was released in 1965, and two years later an attempt to acquire the rights failed because De Palma and the others couldn't afford a showcase run in a Manhattan cinema for which they would have to meet all publicity and marketing expenses, as well as provide a house guarantee. It was eventually released in 1969, the year after De Niro and De Palma would get together again for *Greetings*, a much more successful endeavour. The 1969 release still had De Niro's name mis-spelled, an error that would not be corrected until 1982 when Lloyd Kaufmann of exploitation kings Troma Films acquired the rights to the movie on the strength of the combined box-office value of De Niro,

Clayburgh and De Palma. Not only had the spelling been corrected but De Niro also received co-star billing status along with Clayburgh, while the publicity stills made it appear that they were the happy couple to be.

Although it would be a long time before he was to become a household name, De Niro's career was about to step up a gear. Having made his first two films with Carné and De Palma – albeit with a walk-on part on one and the other unreleased – he was about to land his first substantial stage role. He was also about to meet a woman who would arguably play the most significant role in his career.

De Niro and his friend Sally Kirkland had gone to a bar on Eighth Avenue called Jimmy Ray's. It was there that Kirkland introduced him to a friend of hers and a fellow Actors Studio alumnus, Shelley Winters. Winters was a major Hollywood star who had built a career on playing earthy sexy roles in films like *Winchester 73* and *A Place in the Sun*. In the fifties she had bravely chosen to study under Strasberg, a move that turned her career around. No longer the girlfriend or the hooker with a heart of gold, she embarked on a series of character parts that would bring her a Best Supporting Actress Oscar in 1959 for *The Diary of Anne Frank* and another in 1965 for her marvellous performance in *A Patch of Blue*. If De Niro was star-struck by meeting a major Hollywood player in the flesh, he certainly didn't show it.

'Bobby was around nineteen,' according to Winters. 'He was skinny and very gentle with dark watchful eyes. He didn't say much. He had very little money at that point and he used to ride around town on a rickety old bike.'

Winters was intrigued by De Niro and the feeling appears to have been mutual. They would share an abiding friendship which reportedly bordered on romance for a time. And during that period, with some discreet help from Winters, De Niro's career would move on to the launching pad to prepare for blast-off.

The long hours spent cycling around Manhattan from audition to audition with hopes constantly raised and dashed finally paid off for De Niro when he was cast in the off-Broadway production *Glamour, Glory and Gold*. This play by Jackie Curtis opened at Bastiano's Cellar Studio on 7 August, 1968. Sub-titled 'The Life and Legend of Nola Noonan: Goddess and Star', the play was about the rise and fall of a movie diva. It appears to have featured just about everything from small-town rape to a Hollywood comeback, all in two acts and a coda! Curtis herself played the lead role of Nola, while De Niro appeared in a number of parts as the men in her life. Jean Richards and Candy Darling also starred. *Glamour, Glory and Gold* appears to have been an indifferent play but De Niro found himself getting the first good notices – actually the first notices of any kind – of his career.

'The nicest acting,' wrote the *Village Voice* newspaper two weeks after the play opened, 'came from Jean Richards as a dumb, good-hearted, timid girl friend of Nola's, and, especially, from Robert De Niro in a variety of Nola's boy friends and leading men. De Niro made clean, distinct character statements in a series of parts which many actors would have fused into a general mush. De Niro is new on the scene and deserves to be welcomed. The other actors tended to grab onto one or two character elements and to play them straight, hard, and loud.'

Sally Kirkland went along to see the play and afterwards offered an analysis that would prove to be tellingly prophetic.

'He played five parts and I'd never seen anything so brilliant,' she says. 'I went backstage and told him, "Do you know that you are going to be the most incredible star?" He was unbelievably shy. I thought perhaps I was embarrassing him but I could tell that, more than anything, he wanted to believe it.'

People were starting to sit up and take notice of Robert De Niro. By this stage he was 25 and beginning to feel that his career ought to have been gathering some momentum. One of his earliest advocates was Brian De Palma, who was trying to get the money together for another movie. *Greetings* was to be an unconventional film which De Palma and his producer Charles Hirsch hoped would do for American cinema what Truffaut and Godard had done for Europe with the *nouvelle vague*. Hirsch was working as a talent executive at Universal Studios and his job was to seek out and encourage exciting young directors like De Palma. *Greetings* was to have been studio-funded, but Universal balked at a story about three hippies trying to dodge the draft. In the end De Palma and Hirsch raised $43,000 themselves and shot the film in thirteen days on location in New York.

De Palma had been impressed by Robert De Niro's performance in *The Wedding Party* which, although shot five years previously, still languished on the shelf awaiting theatrical distribution. He was keen to work with him again, and felt he would be perfect for one of the roles. De Niro ended up playing Jon Rubin, a voyeur and cinematic peeping Tom who enjoys filming other people making love. The two other roles in this free-wheeling, anarchic comedy – also known as *The Three Musketeers* – were taken by Jonathan Warden and Gerritt Graham. The film received a mixed reception. Younger critics more in tune with the mood of America at the time tended to love it. Older, more Establishment-oriented reviewers either didn't like it or simply didn't get it. Although all of the actors were praised by those who enjoyed the film, none of them was singled out for special attention.

Despite the fact that it was made a year before *Easy Rider, Greetings* did catch enough of the mood of American youth to cover its costs and go on to make a small profit. It may not have launched a new wave, as De Palma and Hirsch had hoped, but it certainly played its part in the development of the independent American cinema. It was also successful enough to encourage them to make a sequel, and in the process provide Robert De Niro with his first starring role.

4 Bobby's Bloody Mama

N HIS EARLY TWENTIES Robert De Niro was still in the same position as all struggling young actors. He was at the stage where the work was choosing him, and it would be some time yet before he was able to choose the work. There was also no hint yet of the obsessive desire for truth in his performances which would characterise his later work. There was as yet no Robert De Niro 'style'. Those audiences who saw him in *The Wedding Party* or *Greetings* would not know enough of him to be aware of whether or not he was in character or whether what they were seeing on screen was what he was always like.

De Niro was having trouble dealing with life in general at that time, and had begun to see a therapist. The therapy, which he has referred to obliquely in only one interview, indirectly related to the separation of his parents. De Niro may not actually have been aware of this at the time but he was certainly aware of feelings of frustration and confusion and at the centre of these feelings was his relationship with his mother.

After Virginia Admiral had left his father she began to resume a normal life, which inevitably involved seeing other men. Her son resented this greatly and the resentment manifested itself in simply trying not to be around whenever his mother's boyfriends were in the house. What De Niro did not appear to realise at the time was that his mother had no intention of remarrying, and even if she did it would surely only have been to someone of whom he approved. Since he did not approve of any of her boyfriends the matter was therefore completely out of the question. Things appear to have come to a head with a relationship with the film critic, painter and essayist Manny Farber.

De Niro, who could be quiet almost to the point of diffidence, and the wild, volatile Farber simply did not get on. Farber did not like children in any event and he was particularly hard on De Niro. He seems, however, to have been genuinely fond of Virginia Admiral, but in the end the relationship foundered when she would not choose him over her son. De

Niro's antipathy is easy to understand – he was fond of his father and would find it difficult to relate to anyone he perceived to be supplanting his father's place in the home and in his mother's affections. It was later reported in *Redbook* magazine that some years after Farber and Virginia Admiral had split up the two men met at a party. Farber allegedly introduced himself effusively and reminded De Niro of how he had been his mother's boyfriend. He then told him that he looked much more like his father than his mother. The mention of his father by Farber – a man De Niro plainly felt was not good enough to lace his father's shoes – was too much. De Niro, it is claimed, ran out of the room without looking back.

This is a potentially fascinating story but, unfortunately, according to those close to De Niro, it is completely apocryphal. Certainly it does not stand up to scrutiny. Why, for example, would De Niro not recognise a man who had made life so difficult for him?

For a long time De Niro was not adequately able to deal with his feelings towards his mother and her boyfriends. His love for Virginia Admiral was unqualified, but at the same time he seems to have been tainted by a great anger that she had not effectively gone into purdah when she and his father separated. He never, one assumes, paused to reflect how strange it might have been if she had. How different De Niro might have been both as a man and as an actor if he had grown up as a mummy's boy, with her sacrificing every aspect of her life for him.

Did he choose parts like Travis Bickle, Michael Vronsky and Jake La Motta, or did they choose him? They are all men who carry an enormous amount of pain and anger around with them. Does that pain make it easier for De Niro to play them? Does he identify with them because of his own inner rage? Or do the roles provide him with a catharsis for his own anger? It is a question he has never adequately answered.

It would seem that these film roles did provide some kind of release for his inner anger. The therapy sessions alone seem not to have helped, and those who know him best suggest that he has only recently, with the maturity of age rather than the help of a therapist, been able to deal completely with his feelings. But when he was 23 the solution to finding himself was much simpler.

'I left New York and hitched all over Europe for four months,' he says. 'I'd been there before to visit my father when he was in Paris. I lived in hotels on the Left Bank but they were a bit funny, they kept throwing me out. Anyway, I finally found one that would have me in Montmartre. I went to the Alliance Française and met a lot of expatriates. The French are very hard to meet. They're very private. But it's a great experience to do something like that when you're young.'

On his trip round Europe, De Niro also got some sense of his place in the world and the legacy of his parents. During his meanderings through Italy he came across one of his mother's paintings in the Peggy Guggenheim Venetian Collection. The young actor was inordinately proud of his mother's achievement.

He returned to New York with his batteries recharged after his Continental sojourn. He was, however, still living at the whim of casting directors and agents, just another of the thousands of hopefuls who merge into one generic face at any one of hundreds of open casting calls. In 1969 he appeared in a movie called *Sam's Song*, a tiresome, pretentious drama about a film editor's weekend in Long Island. De Niro played the eponymous Sam. The film was almost unreleasable when it was made. However, like *The Wedding Party*, which had finally been released the previous year, someone would eventually see its potential. By 1981 the rights to the film had been acquired by the then up-and-coming Vestron Home Video. An entirely new plot was constructed around some of the 1969 footage and new actors came in to augment the cast. The long-winded navel-gazing of the original was transformed into an equally tiresome *film noir*.

Anthony Charnotta had been drafted in as Sam's elder brother Vito. The action now allegedly takes place ten years after the original, and Vito becomes obsessed with finding out who killed his brother. He is racked by guilt because he was supposed to look after his younger sibling but has failed him. De Niro appears only in a pre-credits sequence and then in a couple of sequences that are shown as flashbacks as Vito continues his obsessive search. Vestron, whose brief existence owed much to their marketing skills, were not about to let that put them off. The film was retitled *The Swap* and De Niro featured prominently in the advertising as the star of the movie. Later still *The Swap* was retitled *Line of Fire* for another video rerelease, with De Niro's presence once again heavily touted.

'I've been in bad films but they had good intentions,' De Niro would say later in his career. Even the most generous soul would be hard pressed to find the good intentions behind *Sam's Song*, no matter what it was titled.

During the difficult years, when money was hard to come by, De Niro also made a living on the dinner theatre circuit. This form of bread-and-circuses entertainment is frowned on by some sections of the theatrical world. De Niro had no qualms whatsoever.

'Dinner theatre was looked down on by some actors because you had to wait on tables too,' he agrees. 'But for me it was good experience at a time when I wanted as much experience as I could get. A lot of actors felt it was beneath them but I made enough in tips to get by without worrying when I wasn't working.'

The years spent being raised by his mother had instilled in De Niro a sense of thriftiness and self-determination. Unlike other young actors, he was not about to hand over a share of what little money he made to an agent. In the early days he made all his own decisions, as he still does.

'When I was about twenty-five I really committed myself,' he recalls. 'I started to look for stuff. I would go out on auditions, I would send résumés, the whole thing.'

Apart from a brief appearance in the soap opera *Search for Tomorrow* and a couple of commercials, De Niro avoided television, preferring to seek his fortune on the stage.

'Usually someone is shooting someone else or someone is following someone else,' he said scathingly of television. 'And no one is doing it well enough to make you put down what you are doing to watch it.' Plainly his view changed some years later when he produced his own anthology series for television under the banner of his TriBeCa production company.

De Niro had remained friendly with Shelley Winters after their first meeting in Jimmy Ray's. She had kept an eye on his career and seemed simply to be waiting for her opportunity to step in and intervene. By this stage she had seen him on stage in *Glamour, Glory and Gold* and the experience had galvanised her.

'When he moved across the stage it was like lightning,' she recalled. 'It gave me tingles. I hadn't felt or seen anything like that since the forties when I saw Brando in a four-performance flop.'

Winters always seemed to encourage a gaggle of theatrical waifs and strays, but De Niro appears to have been one of her favourites. She recognised his potential and was able to provide him with the two biggest breaks of his career up to that point.

Roger Corman was the king of the 'B' pictures in the sixties, although not an Ed Wood figure who would get the shot in one take, good or bad, and sail blithely on. He was, and remains, an urbane and intelligent man who was able to make highly entertaining films for amounts that would not pay the salaries of a single star in any other production. His series of Edgar Allan Poe movies for American International Pictures made him an international name. They also made Vincent Price's name synonymous with horror and revived a career that showed signs of flagging.

Corman's greatest gift is his ability to spot and encourage talent. Directors like Francis Ford Coppola, James Cameron, Peter Bogdanovich and Jonathan Demme owe their careers to his willingness to take a chance on them. Actors like Jack Nicholson and more recently Bill Paxton also began their careers with Corman at AIP. Now it was Robert De Niro's turn.

Corman's other knack was the ability to spot a trend and cash in on it before the market cooled. Arthur Penn's *Bonnie and Clyde* had been a huge hit in 1967 and the audiences seemed ready for gangster movies. If the audience wanted gangster films, then that's what Corman was going to give them. He would make a movie based loosely on the exploits of Kate 'Ma' Barker and her murderous brood, who terrorised the mid-West in the thirties. The script was knocked out fairly quickly after the success of *Bonnie and Clyde*, but by the time it was ready to shoot the mood of the country had changed. The assassinations of Robert Kennedy and Martin Luther King encouraged Corman to believe that America would not enthusiastically embrace a film with the lurid title *Bloody Mama*. The film was put on the shelf to be revived at some future date.

By 1969 Corman felt it would be politic to go ahead with the picture. The intervening period had also convinced him that it should be shot on location, and by the standards of AIP movies be a fairly lavish event.

'It was a four-week picture and that was long for me,' says Corman. 'I don't think I'd ever done one before that which ever required more than a three-week shoot. But I had looked at the script and I said, "Hey, look. I've brought everything in in three weeks up to now but we're going to do this one on location in Arkansas. This is going to be very tough. We're filming all over the state. We're going to be up in the Ozarks in northern Arkansas then we're going to be filming around Little Rock and various other places. I really need four weeks." And they gave them to me.'

Corman always knew that Shelley Winters was going to play Kate Barker. But he had also decided that she would have an input in casting her four screen sons. Don Stroud played Herman, Clint Kimbrough played Arthur, and Robert Walden played Fred. That only left Lloyd, the psycho-pathic, drug-abusing son. Winters had absolutely no hesitation in recommending Robert De Niro for the role.

'The first time I met Bobby was with Shelley,' recalls Corman. 'What struck me most at the time was his intensity. He was a very intense and dedicated actor whose life seemed to be centred more around acting than most actors I had met. He didn't seem interested in the glamour or the publicity and he didn't feel inclined to go and play golf in his spare time or anything like that. He was very much centred on acting. I had no problem with casting him because I had seen the films he had done for Brian De Palma by this stage and again they impressed me with his level of concentration and the way he seemed to be totally into the work.'

Either by chance or design Corman ended up with a cast of principals who were all trained in the Method. From Winters to De Niro, they were all Stanislavskian. As it happened, Corman too had trained in the Method as an actor. He was able to put that shared experience to good use. On the sort of budget he had to work with there would have been simply no chance of De Niro, for example, using the multiple-take method he became used to later in his career. However, Corman recalls that, like the rest of the cast, De Niro worked very well under his system.

'We resorted to our Method training,' he remembers. 'We discussed the backgrounds of the various characters and then we read the script. After that we improvised some scenes from the picture as well as improvising some scenes which were not in the picture but which might have taken place between the characters. After we had done all that we sat down to actually block out the scenes. I had blocked them out in advance in my head and in sketches, which is the way I always do it, but I indicated loosely to them what I was looking for from them. I only gave them a very vague indication because I wanted to see what they would do, providing it was broadly along the lines that I had been thinking on. Then I could modify my sketches or modify their performances to make the best of what my original blocking had been. What they brought to it, of course, could only make it better, because it came from inside the actor, but it also saved us an awful lot of actual shooting.'

De Niro responded to Corman's way of working. It gave him the opportunity to take a character off the page and mould it into his own image. To play Lloyd Barker, he decided that he would starve himself to look properly gaunt and emaciated. His near-starvation diet caused a considerable amount of alarm to Winters and Corman, who feared their brightest prospect might pass out at any moment. Shelley Winters recalls that De Niro drank only water. Corman remembers that in addition to the water he took a little food as well as vitamin pills to maintain his vitamin and mineral balance. After they had both spoken to him and voiced their concerns, De Niro did concede the point and eased up a little. Even so he lost around 30 pounds during the shooting of the picture.

It was the first time he had been seen on screen as a character rather than simply Robert De Niro, actor.

'He stayed in character as Lloyd Barker for the whole day,' says Corman. 'After the day's shooting, towards dinner, he'd gradually come out of it, but by the time you called him in the morning he'd be Lloyd Barker again and he would stay that way for the entire day's filming.

'He was reasonably gregarious with the other actors. He'd be with them and they'd talk about the picture and they would hang out together in the evening after dinner. He got along well and there were no problems because everyone on that film was a dedicated actor.

'At the end of the four weeks I got the feeling that I had come to know him within the confines of his work as an actor. As for his personal life or anything else, I wouldn't know, he was really closed off about that.'

Like all Corman's American International movies, *Bloody Mama* made money for the company. However, it has acquired something of a life of its own in the intervening years. Owing partly to the presence of De Niro, partly to Shelley Winters and partly to the energy and vitality of Corman's direction, the film has acquired cult status. It is a popular favourite on the campus and film society circuit, as well as being a late-night television mainstay all over the world.

A number of myths and legends, for want of a better term, have grown up surrounding the film, and more especially surrounding De Niro in the intervening period. Some, like De Niro's starvation diet, are true, but Corman insists that most of them aren't and have simply grown in the telling.

Shelley Winters has said that De Niro was so keen to be in the film, and so absorbed by the part, that he didn't even know how much he was being paid. She claims that, at one point, he wasn't even receiving expenses until she intervened.

'He did get expenses,' says Corman confidently. 'These stories just build over the years. AIP was signed up to the Screen Actors Guild agreement. As I recall what he got would be the SAG minimum – I don't remember what that was at the time – but it would be the normal rate for that period. He would have got that plus his transportation and daily expenses as per the Screen Actors Guild agreement.'

The other story that sounds too good to be true concerns De Niro's funeral scene. Lloyd is the first of the brothers to die in the movie. He is a drug addict and his habit increases throughout the movie until he eventually dies of a self-inflicted overdose. The funeral scene, as Ma Barker weeps for her baby boy, would be a moving sequence in any film, regardless of its budget. It is one of Shelley Winters' biggest moments in the movie, and she pulls out all the stops to wring every ounce of emotion from it. However, it has also been suggested that De Niro actually put himself into the open grave to lend an air of authenticity to the scene.

'That was really all to do with Shelley,' says the director. 'At the burial sequence we had a couple of shots to do before Shelley was needed. She had already told me that she wanted to come straight to the set and play the scene and that was fine by me. What I didn't know was that she had asked for a funeral home in Little Rock to be opened up for her early in the morning and she went there in full make-up and wardrobe. So we called her there. To be honest I didn't know where she was at the time. I just told the assistant director, "Okay, we're going to be ready in about half an hour. Call Shelley and tell her what time we'll need her for the scene."

'So they picked her up from the funeral home and she came running out of the car straight down this hill to the side of the lake where we were shooting the scene. All the time she's screaming, "My son. My son is dead. You can't do that. Don't put him in the ground." I was completely taken aback and I started to say, "Shelley, Shelley, those aren't the lines." But Bobby Walden came up to me and said, "Be very careful, she's in the part. Don't do anything that might take her out."

'It was one of the more extreme examples of Method acting I had seen but Bobby Walden was right. So I just quietly said a few things to modify what she was doing so she would turn in relation to the camera position. I have to say Shelley was absolutely brilliant.

'But it was us who put Bobby in the grave. I told him that if Shelley was going to play it that way then he should just lie there so she could see him. So we did put him in the grave.'

Whether or not it had the desired effect we'll never know. Shelley Winters' reaction when she saw him lying there was typical. She told him to get out straight away before he was either smothered by earth or caught his death of cold.

If Shelley Winters took Corman by surprise with her preparation for the funeral scene, then De Niro's commitment to the film and his dedication to the character of Lloyd Barker gave him another nasty turn in one of the big action set-pieces. He wanted to film the Barkers as they made their getaway with guns blazing from their runabout. He had asked De Niro to drive with Shelley Winters firing salvoes from the back window towards their pursuers.

'Bobby was driving and we were coming down a dirt road on this steep hill,' says Corman, taking up the story. 'Shelley and Bobby Walden and I think Bruce Dern, who was also in the movie, were in the back of the car. Shelley was supposed to be firing this machine-gun out of the back of the car. The cameraman was tied to one fender in the front of the car and I was tied to the other so we could see what was going on.

'Bobby came screaming down the road at a terrific speed and he was bouncing all over the place, on and off the road. When we got to the bottom and the car stopped I said, "That was really great, Bobby, but it looked to me like you might have lost control once or twice. I'm not certain that we've got it all on camera. Let's do it one more time." And he looked at me and I'll never forget the look on his face. He said, "Sure I lost control once or twice. I've never driven before. I'm from New York. I don't have a driver's licence. I don't need one!"

'So I said, "Tell you what, Bobby, let's just print this take. We don't need another one." '

5 A Blazing Talent

FTER HE HAD COMPLETED his work on *Bloody Mama* De Niro went back to the stage, but not in New York. He spent the 1969/70 theatrical season in Boston as a member of the Theatre Company of Boston, a repertory company that did the usual round of such popular fare as *Cyrano de Bergerac*, *Compulsion* and *Long Day's Journey into Night*. He remained close to Shelley Winters throughout this period. They must have made a curious couple, De Niro skinny and quiet, Winters earthy and independent and a Hollywood star. It was already being suggested that their relationship was based on more than just career advice. Recalling the time on the set of *Bloody Mama*, Roger Corman said he had been aware of hearing things from various people.

'I always prefer not to go into that,' he says. 'I prefer to stay away. But it would certainly be fair to say that Shelley was a major guiding influence on Bobby, very much so.'

Actress Diane Ladd is a close friend of Shelley Winters, who is godmother to her daughter Laura Dern. She is also close to Sally Kirkland and became friendly with De Niro.

'Shelley did help Bobby,' she says adamantly. 'She helped a lot of actors, but she was always more prone to help the actors than she was to help the actresses. I tell her that to her face.'

Winters has written two best selling volumes of a marvellous showbiz memoir. Her other famous lovers are mentioned freely but, if they were lovers, then De Niro is conspicuous by his absence. The only hint of their relationship comes in an interview she gave to Guy Flatley of the *New York Times* in November 1973 for a profile of De Niro, one of the first major pieces written about the actor, who by then had become a fast-rising star.

According to Flatley, De Niro had affectionately tagged Winters as 'his Jewish mama', but she took exception to this.

'I'm his Italian mama,' she told Flatley, before changing her mind. 'Well, maybe I am his Jewish mama, but if I am then he is my Jewish son.

'Bobby needs somebody to watch over him; he doesn't even wear a coat in the wintertime. Do you know that when we did *Bloody Mama* in the Ozarks he didn't even know how much money he was getting? When I found out how little they were paying him I demanded they give him something for his expenses at least. Bobby was broke, but of course he will never borrow. So you have to find ways of giving him money without letting him know you're giving it to him.'

Corman has already offered his opinion on De Niro's remuneration on *Bloody Mama*. But now Flatley was approaching what was the sixty-four-thousand-dollar question. Did Winters, he wondered, also find a way, as well as giving him cash, of giving him a little more than motherly affection?

Flatley's article describes the Oscar-winning actress purring at the other end of the phone before answering.

'Listen,' she told him, 'let's put it this way – I had a bigger romance with Bobby than with any of my lovers. Better change that to any of my husbands,' she suggested, before going back on herself again. 'No,' she continued, 'I guess lovers sounds all right. The truth is, I feel very close to Bobby.'

She then went on to make one more astonishing claim later in the interview.

'Bobby will never talk about what made him the way he is,' she offered. 'But I suspect he must have been a lonely kid. I suspect that somewhere along the line he was brutalised.'

It must be said that there is nothing to suggest that De Niro suffered either direct physical or emotional abuse while he was growing up. All the signs are that he grew up with two parents who each loved him but simply could not live together. However, any child must go through some kind of trauma when a family breaks up, albeit indirectly, especially at such a young age. Although there were times when, for one reason or another, De Niro did not want his father around, there is no doubt that the absence of his father marked the boy. So much of what he did is informed by his father – from the endless copying out of essays, to the films they saw together where he grew to admire actors like Brando and Montgomery Clift, to his own inexplicable rages, even to the film he would make himself as a director – that the impression of Robert De Niro's absence can be seen upon his son.

Shelley Winters' statements to Guy Flatley were typically bold and forthright. A number of people were surprised, not least Virginia Admiral and De Niro himself. A source close to the family describes Admiral as being shocked when she read the article. Winters and Admiral had already met at the Actors Studio and neither appears to have been especially impressed with the other. Admiral felt that Winters had overstepped the mark with her comments. Her view, according to friends, was that Winters had read too much into her son's friendship and was assuming more to their relationship than was actually there. De Niro was also surprised by the article. He is notorious for never reading his own interviews, but he was told about the piece by friends. He was grateful then and remains grateful now to Shelley Winters for everything she did for him, but their friendship cooled noticeably after the article appeared.

Guy Flatley's article also makes reference for the first time to a De Niro girlfriend. From Flatley's description and the timing of the interview we must assume that this is Diahnne Abbott whom he would later marry. They met when he was a struggling actor in the Village and she was an actress-singer who was filling in between jobs as a waitress. Winters goes on to wonder aloud whether De Niro's apartment was tidy or not and assumes that, if it was, Abbott must have been picking up after him. Since he had grown up without ever being asked to tidy his room, this was not a habit the actor was likely to develop in later life. His attitude seemed to be to let things lie where they fall; he had more important things to do with his life than clean up rooms.

Meanwhile, De Niro was about to continue another long-running creative relationship in the early part of 1970. He was about to do a third film with Brian De Palma. The director and actor felt comfortable together and responded well to each other. This was a precursor of the relationship that De Niro was shortly to embark on with Martin Scorsese – a relationship that would be the defining creative force of his career. De Palma, on the other hand, was about to give him his first starring role.

Greetings had made enough money to encourage the film company to bankroll a sequel. Producer Charles Hirsch was this time given $100,000 – more than twice the budget of the first movie – on condition that the film be shot non-union and in New York. The result was *Hi, Mom!*, in which De Niro reprised his role of Jon Rubin, the first and to date the only time he has ever played a character more than once. *Greetings* had ended with the voyeuristic Rubin himself becoming the subject of someone else's camera as he was caught on TV footage slogging through the jungles of Vietnam. In *Hi, Mom!* – the film takes its title from De Niro's enigmatic last line – Rubin has returned from Vietnam as a much more hard-line, right-wing figure than when he left. He is, however, still addicted to voyeurism, and spends much of his time filming the three girls in the apartment opposite in various stages of undress. (One of the girls, incidentally, is played by Jennifer Salt, who had also appeared in *The Wedding Party*.)

Rubin also becomes involved with a radical theatre group and gets roped into their experimental revue. They need a military type and Rubin, with De Niro looking remarkably like a young Travis Bickle from *Taxi Driver*, fits the bill. The film then devolves into a dark and sinisterly anarchic satire which ends with the black theatre group being gunned down by the white residents of Rubin's apartment building. Rubin then blows up the building and, as he sits in the rubble, he is asked by a roving TV news crew if he has anything to say to America. 'Hi, Mom!' he says with the lop-sided grin that fans would come to know and love over the years.

Although none of the three principals of the first film was singled out for praise, De Niro, who was this time the star of the movie, found himself almost universally admired for his performance. The *Hollywood Reporter* still had trouble with his name, referring to him as 'Nero' in an otherwise positive review. The praise was not unanimous. The *New Republic*, a liberal magazine that really ought to have found some sympathy at least with the film's political perspective, described De Niro as the weakest point in the film. It pointed out that he was very good as part of the ensemble of three in the first film, 'but lacks the range and appeal to sustain a film more or less by himself'.

Shelley Winters, meanwhile, was stretching her creative wings by writing a play. Her time at the Actors Studio had developed her talent and her confidence. She had also been working with the civil rights movement, and that too had helped her self-esteem. She was now at the point where she was about to commit some of the experiences of her rich and turbulent life to paper. The play actually began as a series of workshops at the Actors Studio. It was originally cryptically entitled *The Gestation of a Weatherman*, but by the time it made it off-Broadway to the Actors Playhouse the title had changed to *One Night Stands of a Noisy Passenger*.

The show was basically three one-act plays. The first act took place during the Second World War in New York. Sally Kirkland played the actress – the 'noisy passenger' of the title – while Richard Lynch played the man responsible for her political awakening. The second play was set in Paris and took place against the backdrop of the Korean War and the Hollywood blacklist. This time the actress was played by Joanna Miles and Will Hare played the Hollywood producer with whom she was now involved. The final play took place after the actress has won her Oscar. Called 'Last Stand', Diane Ladd was playing the noisy passenger by this time. There was really only one person who could play her brash young one-night stand – Robert De Niro.

'We were the longest of the three acts,' says Diane Ladd. 'Ours was the big one, it lasted about forty-five minutes as I remember, and the whole show was based on incidents in Shelley Winters' life.

'Our play was about a woman who finally wins an Oscar and she meets this kid at the Oscar party. Everybody's kiss-assing her and she finally realises how invalid all of this is; she sees in those moments of success how alone you are unless you have someone. And this woman has no one. The people who are intelligent enough to realise this are afraid to talk to her, but this kid isn't afraid because he isn't smart enough to be scared. He just starts talking to her and they sit and talk and end up going for a drink. Then he slips her some dope without her knowing and they end up back in his apartment for a one-night stand.'

Diane Ladd is one of America's finest actresses. She was once described by *Time* magazine as one of the ten best actresses in the world. She has won a great many honours and she and her daughter Laura Dern share the distinction of being the only mother and daughter to be nominated for Oscars in the same year. Both were nominated for their performances in *Rambling Rose*, Ladd for Best Supporting Actress and Dern for Best Actress. She remembers De Niro then as a struggling actor living in a one-room walk-up apartment and putting glue on his windows in a desperate attempt to keep out the icy blast of a New York winter. He kept himself to himself, but he spoke frequently and with great affection of his father. But like almost everyone who worked with the young De Niro, Diane Ladd also recalls his fire and his dedication to his craft, although there were occasions when that fire needed to be stoked.

'Bobby is a couple of years younger than me,' Ladd continues. 'But I had to pretend to be ten or twelve years older than him to make him constantly look up to me. Shelley kept saying, "Don't tell him your age. I have to make him think you're older." "Jesus," I said. "We're actors, Shelley." But she said "I don't care. He's got to look up to you. He's got to adore you." '

As he progressed in his career, the one word that would follow De Niro doggedly is 'disciplined'. There isn't an actor or a director who has worked with him who would not, no matter what else, praise his discipline and his dedication. But that was something that had to be acquired over the years. And, as Diane Ladd remembers, it was a lesson that sometimes had to be learned the hard way.

'I found Bobby a little undisciplined when we worked together,' she says. 'I remember one scene where we have to wake up in bed together with no clothes on and I have to get dressed in front of the audience. On one occasion Bobby decided the set needed a little something and being true products of the Actors Studio we used to bring our own props. I had to get into a dress which was sequinned all round and trimmed with fur on the sleeves.

'Bobby had forgotten to tell me that he thought we needed more candles on the stage, but he had lit some candles and put them on the bureau. So I'm moving toward the bureau while I'm talking to him and I don't know that these candles are there. I heard the audience gasp and then I felt the heat and when I turned round my sleeve was going up in flames. I put it out with my hand – it's amazing the adrenalin rush you get on stage – I just slapped it out with my hand and went on with the play. However, out of the corner of my eye, I could see Shelley running up the aisle absolutely thunder struck. I also remember when I came off stage Shelley was horrified because I think she thought I was going to walk out of the play.

'I told her, "I want a meeting tomorrow morning," and then went to my dressing room.

'The following morning the three of us – Bobby, Shelley, and I – met at Shelley's house. Straight away Shelley started saying "Now, Diane, these things happen. Things just happen."

'And I said, "You sit down and shut up, just shut your mouth. When you were our age if a young actor had done to you what Bobby did last night – which may well have been an accident – nevertheless you would have cut his head off, set it on a stump, and walked away saying prayers and never looked back. So shut your mouth." And she did. She just sat there.

'So I turned to Bobby and said, "Bobby, don't you ever put anything on stage without telling your fellow actors because if you do, and I hear about it, I'm going to come and beat the living shit out of you." I don't think Bobby has ever forgiven me for that. But no matter how brilliant an actor he is, he could have taken my life that night.'

Diane Ladd's assessment of De Niro as 'brilliant' was shared by almost every reviewer who saw *One Night Stands of a Noisy Passenger*. The *Village Voice*, which had highlighted his performance in *Glamour, Glory and Gold*, was equally generous in its review of his performance in the Winters' play. Although the piece is somewhat equivocal about the play as a whole, reviewer Arthur Sainer had no doubts about De Niro, describing his performance as 'stunning'.

Despite generally good reviews, *One Night Stands of a Noisy Passenger* only lasted a week. It opened on 30 December and closed after only seven performances. Shelley Winters believes the show was under-funded and never had the opportunity to find its target audience. She was particularly upset that De Niro's performance did not perhaps get the appreciation it deserved in terms of the numbers who saw it.

Regardless of the show's capitalisation, its run would also not have been helped by an actors' strike which hit off-Broadway productions during this period. The actors' union was looking for an increase in the off-Broadway rate, which at that time was $65 a week.

'Bobby had some great lines in this play and the audiences loved it,' says Diane Ladd. 'But the truth is we got struck just after opening night. Geraldine Page, who was one of the leaders of Equity at that time, prom-ised they would not strike on opening night but they did. Laura was only a baby at that time and I ended up losing my home because of that strike. First of all I turned down a movie to do the play which cost me money because of what they were paying off-Broadway. You cannot collect unem-ployment while there is a strike, you cannot take another job, and I could not pay my way. It was a disaster. Eventually Joanna Miles said, "To hell with it," and she went and took another job. That was the final straw. That put the whole play down the tubes because we had only one day to rehearse a new actress before we went back and we couldn't do it in the time available. The whole thing was a disaster.'

One Night Stands of a Noisy Passenger may have been a disaster for Diane Ladd but it was a godsend for Robert De Niro. It had given him the best reviews of his career and convinced him that he could succeed in his chosen profession.

6 Gathering Momentum

D E NIRO HAD PAID his dues in off-beat films like *Greetings* and *Hi, Mom!* and plays like *Glamour, Glory and Gold* and *One Night Stands of a Noisy Passenger*. He had been generally praised but not many people had seen his performances. Praise does not pay the rent and at the start of 1971 he was still a young actor with a growing reputation and a diminishing bank account. The one film that had been seen by significant numbers of people, *Bloody Mama*, had not provided much in the way of financial security, depending on whether you believe Roger Corman's or Shelley Winters' version of events.

But De Niro was beginning to get noticed, and he was about to step up to the big league with parts in major Hollywood productions. At the start of 1971 there was no Hollywood movie bigger than *The Godfather*. Peter Bart, then an executive at Paramount where he was in charge of creative affairs and now editor-in-chief of *Variety*, had discovered author Mario Puzo. He had set him up with an office at the studio to allow him to finish his epic novel about Mafia life, and so it was inevitable that the film version of his by now bestselling book would go to Paramount. Among the directors who were on the studio's hit-list were major names like Fred Zinnemann, Arthur Penn, Costa-Gavras, Peter Yates, Richard Brooks and Sidney J. Furie. All of them passed on the project for one reason or another. Eventually the producer, Fred Roos, and his line producer, Gray Frederickson, offered it to the young Francis Ford Coppola – the 32-year-old director was their thirteenth choice and it turned out to be lucky thirteen for all concerned. At that stage, however, Roos and Frederickson were only interested in the fact that Coppola was used to low budgets – he started with Roger Corman, after all – and he had never had a hit and would therefore work cheap. If he happened to be Italian, then so much the better.

The casting of *The Godfather* was almost as much of an epic as the movie itself. The key role was not that of the patriarchal Don Corleone, which would eventually be played by Marlon Brando, but of his son Michael. Although he was nominally the 'white sheep' of the Corleone family, circumstances would force war hero Michael to step into his father's shoes and take over the family business. Paramount wanted Robert Redford for the role; others were lobbying for Warren Beatty, Ryan O'Neal or Jack Nicholson. Even Rod Steiger allegedly expressed an interest at one point. It seems that at one stage almost every Italian-American actor under pensionable age tested for this movie. Among them was Robert De Niro. Coppola was interested but he was not convinced that De Niro would be right for the role of Michael. The most promising test came from Al Pacino, but he was initially rejected as 'too Italian'. The other front-runner as Michael was James Caan. Eventually the producers decided after all that the role should go to Pacino, which meant that a role then had to be found for Caan who, to his credit, had also been lobbying strongly on Pacino's behalf.

Although Coppola was not convinced that De Niro was right to play Michael, he did think he looked more interesting as Sonny, Don Corleone's wild eldest son. But out of the running as Michael, Caan was then offered the role. He took it and in the process became one of the biggest box-office stars of the seventies.

But what of De Niro? He was eventually given the role of the traitorous Paulie Gatto. It was a supporting role but he was happy to take it. But when the chance of a leading role in a major movie came along he dropped out of *The Godfather* and signed on to play in *The Gang That Couldn't Shoot Straight*. Just to complete the round of musical casting chairs, the actor who gave him his chance by dropping out of *The Gang That Couldn't Shoot Straight* was none other than Al Pacino, who was going in the opposite direction. Judging by the relative performances of the two films, De Niro may have felt at the time that his choice was not the best. He had, after all, had a shot at playing three roles in what would be the most successful movie ever made to that date, and he had finished up with nothing. However, years later he would realise that if he had stuck with playing Paulie Gatto then he would have been killed off in the first film and someone else would have had to play the role of young Vito Corleone in *The Godfather Part II*. If nothing else, that would have left De Niro with one award less in his trophy cabinet.

The very process of being tested for so many roles in *The Godfather* created a buzz around the young De Niro, and he quickly found himself involved in two other major studio projects. *Jennifer On My Mind* was one of United Artists' prime projects for 1971. They had paid $50,000 for the rights to the novel on which it was based; Erich Segal, who was currently hot in Hollywood terms after the success of *Love Story*, was writing the script; and the film had a budget of $2 million. Michael Brandon and Tippy Walker would play the leads, two bored and disaffected rich kids who turn to drugs through a lack of familial affection. The cast was also peppered with a host of promising young actors like Jeff Conaway, Barry Bostwick, and Chuck McCann. And nineteenth on the cast list was Robert De Niro.

Ironically, in light of his subsequent fame, De Niro was actually cast as a gypsy taxi driver called Madrigian. It is an appearance befitting someone who is nineteenth in the cast list. De Niro could do nothing more than provide a rather exaggerated cameo with the few lines he was given.

The film was an unmitigated disaster and one of the biggest money-losers of the year for United Artists. The company quickly realised that their hoped-for controversial love story was a major bomb, and the film was barely released. For De Niro, however, it was at least a glimpse into the world of big-budget film-making that previously had been foreign territory to him. And again the reviews were kind. The *Hollywood Reporter*, which had championed him in *Hi, Mom!*, again singled him out as the one memorable original character in the whole movie. But even though the industry trade paper was consistently proving his strongest advocate, it still couldn't get his name right. After referring to him as 'Nero' in *Hi, Mom!*, the *Hollywood Reporter* review for *Jennifer On My Mind* lavishes its praise on 'Robert Deniro'.

De Niro was now approaching his 28th birthday. He had been acting for more than twelve years waiting for the elusive break to come along, and although it was certainly closer, success was not exactly knocking his door down. Fortunately for him the one thing about which he seems never to have been uncertain is his own talent. Virginia Admiral says her son has become successful through sheer 'force of will'. This was the force of will he had acquired from her and his father as he watched their dedication and perseverance, and it was this force of will which was sustaining him now. He knew that the important thing was to keep working. He knew he had not yet earned the right to say no. The vital thing was to maintain forward momentum. Don't stop. Take the parts and make the best of them that you can. Above all learn from the experience. De Niro has never been a great conversationalist and is seldom the life and soul of any gathering. He is, however, a great listener and a great observer, and he learns and draws from almost every experience in his life. This would be no exception.

After the disaster of *Jennifer On My Mind* he found himself cast in another drugs movie. *Born to Win* looked highly promising on paper, but then so did *Jennifer*.

Born to Win starred George Segal, then an 'A' list actor, and was directed by Ivan Passer, who was being seen as a hot new director. Segal plays Jay Jay, a formerly trendy hairdresser who is reduced to hustling and petty crime on the streets of New York to maintain his $100–a-day heroin habit. He is continually harassed by De Niro's policeman, who is determined to arrest him. Although he has very little dialogue, De Niro is always lurking in the background in this impressive film. The rest of the quality cast was rounded out by Paula Prentiss, Karen Black, Hector Elizondo, and Burt Young.

Born to Win is an uncomfortable mixture of comedy and horror and United Artists, who had produced it, became scared the moment they saw it. It was far too depressing for them and they ordered it recut to play up the comedic elements and play down the tragedy of Jay Jay's life. Even so, they barely released the film. Film reviewer Pauline Kael says 'they didn't open it; they just let it out'. Although *Born to Win*'s lack of release was another setback for De Niro's burgeoning career, the real victim in this case was Segal. This unjustly neglected and cruelly treated film contains what is probably his best performance in a career which, although long, has never quite reached its fullest potential. It is a harsh but not uncommon twist of fate that his finest work should come in a film that hardly anyone saw. Its chances were improved slightly in the video boom of the early eighties. It was retitled *The Addict* and repackaged with De Niro's name first in the cast list. Then in 1994 it was repackaged again and released with *The Swap* – formerly *Sam's Song* – as a 'Robert De Niro double bill'.

Real success was proving tantalisingly elusive for Robert De Niro. It seemed that no matter what he played, his part was doomed never to find an audience.

The Gang That Couldn't Shoot Straight, the film for which he had dropped out of *The Godfather* was not much of an improvement. The original novel by New York newspaper columnist Jimmy Breslin is a very funny story based on a gang of small-time incompetent Mafia types. The film version is a clumsy and in hindsight frequently racist film that is woefully short on laughs. Again, however, the prospects were good on paper. The original book had sold well, Waldo Salt was an Oscar-winning screenwriter, and director James Goldstone was a well regarded film-maker. But once again it simply failed to come off the page. It remains interesting in the De Niro canon, however, because this was the first time that he went to extremes to get into his character. He plays Mario, a kleptomaniac who falls for Angela, played by Leigh Taylor-Young. When he learned that he had got the part, De Niro travelled to Sicily with a tape recorder to absorb the local dialect, so that his character would sound authentic. Fellow New York actor Danny Aiello, who saw De Niro for the first time in this picture, recalls that at the time he thought he was seeing 'an Italian actor straight off the boat'.

Most of the actors in the cast were criticised for their dreadful accents, but De Niro was universally exempted. Once again he found himself a good actor in a bad film, but the critics were starting to pay attention. Bruce Williamson in *Playboy* magazine described De Niro as 'an amiably handsome recruit from the New York theatre scene who contributes a socko performance as Mario'. De Niro and Leigh Taylor-Young were also praised by Jay Cocks of *Time* magazine for bringing a small degree of charm and reality to the lamentable goings-on. Neither Cocks nor De Niro could have known at that stage that in just over a year the critic was about to play the most important role in De Niro's career.

After his movie excursions De Niro went back briefly to the theatre. It is probably safe to say that his run in *Kool Aid* was a whole lot briefer than he intended. The play opened and closed within five performances at the Repertory Company of Lincoln Center. The play was in two acts, the first called 'Three Street Koans', the second 'Grail Green'. De Niro was back in *Noisy Passenger* territory here, playing another pair of stoned rebels. The play was not a success, and perhaps fortunately for all concerned it does not appear to have been reviewed favourably or otherwise.

7 Breakthrough

MARTIN SCORSESE ARRIVED IN Hollywood at the beginning of 1971. He was an eager but raw product of the New York University film school. He had made a number of impressive student films like *It's Not Just You Murray!* and *Who's That Knocking at My Door*. No matter how impressive those films were, Hollywood was managing to find the film-making talents of the young New Yorker eminently resistible. Scorsese was also a skilled and gifted editor, earning the affectionate nickname 'The Butcher' for his work in assembling other people's footage. While he was waiting for his own big break he worked as an editor on such films as *Woodstock, Elvis on Tour* and *Minnie and Moskovitz*. But even though he was working, times were hard for Scorsese. He actually lived on the set of *Minnie and Moskovitz* while he was working on the film. But he endured, and with fellow young Turks Brian De Palma and George Lucas – who were also working at Warner Brothers – he dreamed of the day when he would finally make his breakthrough.

One of the first people he had met when he came to Hollywood was Roger Corman. Scorsese and Corman met at the William Morris Agency with a view to Scorsese doing a sequel to *Bloody Mama*. Scorsese has an encyclopaedic knowledge of film and could see in Corman's movie the energy and vitality that had been the hallmark of the early Warner Brothers gangster pictures. Corman promised that the script would be ready in six months and they parted amicably with Scorsese less than optimistic of ever hearing from Corman again. In the meantime Scorsese had begged work from John Cassavetes, who hired him as a sound editor on *Minnie and Moskovitz*, a position Scorsese would later describe as '$500 a week for doing nothing'.

When the call came from Corman, Scorsese was as surprised as anyone. The sequel to *Bloody Mama* was not actually a sequel at all. *Boxcar Bertha* was, however, broadly in the same genre, and Scorsese was more than happy to be directing his first mainstream film. Barbara Hershey and Keith Carradine were the stars of the movie, with Hershey in the title role of a woman who lived the life of a hobo, riding the rails during the Depression. Scorsese was given a script, a budget of $600,000, and told he could do what he liked providing he didn't go over budget and maintained the required amount of nudity or implied nudity which American International Pictures required. Scorsese and his cast and crew went off to Arkansas for the six-week shoot, then returned with the footage to Los Angeles for mixing and editing.

Boxcar Bertha is a remarkable piece of work. It does what it sets out to do in that it performs admirably well as part of a drive-in double feature. At the same time, Scorsese's skill and mastery are evident in every shot. Much of *Boxcar Bertha*, especially the climactic crucifixion sequence in which Carradine is nailed to a railcar for his union beliefs, is a forerunner of Scorsese's later work. It contains the familiar themes of sin and redemption as well as a great deal of religious symbolism. The director was justifiably pleased with what he had done. There was one acid test remaining.

'I showed a rough cut of the film to John Cassavetes,' recalls Scorsese. 'After he'd seen it he took me into his office. He stood for a moment and he embraced me. "You're a good kid," he said, "but you just spent a year of your life making a piece of shit. You're better than that stuff. Don't do it again. It's a nice picture for what it is, it's rotation, but you don't want to get hooked doing that stuff. Don't you have something that you want to do for yourself? Don't you really have something you want to do?" he asked me. And I said I had. "Get it made," he said. "It needs rewrites," I told him. "So rewrite it," he said.'

While Martin Scorsese was in Arkansas making *Boxcar Bertha*, Robert De Niro was further south touring the rural byways of Florida. He had been cast in a film called *Bang the Drum Slowly*, along with another up-and-coming actor, Michael Moriarty. De Niro plays Bruce Pearson, a slow-witted catcher on a baseball team who is the butt of everyone else's jokes. His only friend on the team is Moriarty's Henry Wiggens, an All Star player with a big-money contract.

The film begins at the Mayo Clinic where Pearson learns that he has Hodgkin's disease – a form of cancer – and has a year to live. This will be his final season. Only Henry knows, and he decides to do all he can to make his friend's final months as comfortable as they can be. He attempts to make sure that Bruce manages to die with as much dignity as he can muster. The other major player in the equation is coach Vincent Gardenia, who is aware that there is something being kept secret between Bruce and

Henry without actually knowing what it is. Not that he cares too much because Henry is showing the form that made him an All Star, and even Bruce is playing like he never played before. The team, the New York Mammoths, win the title, Pearson dies, and Wiggens is the only representative of the team at his funeral.

Bang the Drum Slowly – the title comes from the country and western ballad 'The Streets of Laredo' – had originally been performed as an American television drama shortly after Mark Harris wrote it in 1956. Paul Newman took the Moriarty role with Albert Salmi playing De Niro's part. When the television version was made for the Playhouse 90 series neither Newman nor Salmi was as well known as either of them would become. The producers of the film wanted the same effect for their version – two men who were talented enough to play the parts but sufficiently unknown for the audience to be able to relate to them as real people. Both Newman and Salmi got rave reviews from the critics but neither of them would bring to the part anything like the authenticity for which De Niro strove. *The Gang That Couldn't Shoot Straight* may have been a dreadful film but it was an important turning point for De Niro. It was the first time he had begun to submerge himself in the character; for *Bang the Drum Slowly* he went even further.

'I think the way you look has a lot to do with the way you act,' he said. 'That's why I start with a character's looks. When I got the part of Bruce I learned he was from a small town in Georgia. So I went to Georgia and stayed in a small town. I found an old-fashioned country store and I bought the kind of clothes Bruce would buy. I wore them all around. Then I started with the way that Bruce would talk. The people in the town were really nice and they didn't mind me copying the way they talked. In fact they would even correct me if I started to sound too much like a New Yorker. After a while I began to move like Bruce and I began to feel like him.'

But there is more to playing a baseball player than a southern accent and some ill-fitting clothes. If that were all it took then everyone would make the World Series every October. De Niro did have some problems in mastering the sport itself. Not much of an athlete, he had never played baseball before, and his childhood sporting activities were confined to the odd game of stickball on the streets as he grew up. Along with Hancock, Moriarty and the rest of the crew he went through the equivalent of spring training as everyone spent two hours a day playing baseball before shooting started. With that and the further background of reading books, watching players and studying films, he was eventually able to pass muster.

One other aspect of the ball player's life almost eluded him: chewing tobacco made him sick as a dog, according to John Hancock.

Chewing tobacco and spitting are as much a part of America's national pastime as hot dogs and singing 'Take Me Out To The Ballgame' during the seventh-innings stretch. For De Niro it was almost a chaw too far. But to his credit, says Hancock, he never gave up.

'It was a bad experience,' remembers De Niro. 'Somebody told me to mix the tobacco with chewing gum but that only made me sticky and sick. Finally a doctor told me that chewing tobacco would make my teeth white and that gave me the courage to keep chewing. I got to the point where I could look like I was enjoying chewing. But it didn't do a thing for my teeth.'

Bang the Drum Slowly was shot in and around New York, which meant that De Niro was able to stay at home and hang out with his old friends like Sally Kirkland, Gerrit Graham and, of course, Diahnne Abbott. As 1972 drew to a close he was beginning to feel good about himself and his career. The advance word on *Bang the Drum Slowly* was good, and there was every prospect of being able to parlay that into bigger and more satisfying roles in major productions. He had also become friendly with *Time* magazine film critic Jay Cocks, the man who had been so prescient in singling him out of the mire that was *The Gang That Couldn't Shoot Straight*. Cocks's wife Verna Bloom was an actress, and she and De Niro had worked together. When Cocks and his wife were throwing a dinner party that Christmas, De Niro was on the guest list, as was their mutual friend Brian De Palma, who had cast De Niro in *The Wedding Party*, *Greetings*, and *Hi Mom!*

De Palma had a friend of his, another young director, with him at that dinner. De Niro thought he knew him from somewhere. The feeling was mutual – the other man was sure he knew the actor too.

'Hey, I know you,' said De Palma's friend.

De Niro wasn't sure but seemed to register assent. That was enough for the other guest to press home his advantage.

'Didn't you used to hang around Hester Street? Kenmare Street?' he persisted.

De Niro grinned. The game was up. He had been found out. Brian De Palma then formally introduced him to Martin Scorsese.

'I knew it was him,' Scorsese would later recall. 'I just hadn't seen him for fourteen years. He used to hang out with a different crowd of people over on Broome Street while we were on Prince Street. We had seen each other at dances and said hello. He had liked my film *Who's That Knocking at My Door* and felt, like many, that it was the only accurate portrayal of life on the Lower East Side to date.'

'Sometimes when we were kids we'd meet at the dances at a place on Fourteenth Street,' says De Niro in his version of one of the most important introductions in American cinema. 'It was just an Italian-American dance place. I saw Marty round there and we knew each other. Friends of his, from his group, would sometimes change over into our group. We had like a crossover of friends.

'I had ideas about being an actor when I was ten or eleven, but no real interest. At about sixteen I started becoming interested. Marty and I didn't talk about this but we had a mutual friend who Marty had directed. When I saw *Who's That Knocking at My Door* I said, "He did this about the neighbourhood, and he really understands it." It was very, very good.'

When they met at Jay Cocks's party Martin Scorsese was working on a project that would be a sequel of sorts to *Who's That Knocking at My Door* and the third part of a trilogy. This was the script he had mentioned obliquely to John Cassavetes when he was on the receiving end of the most constructive dressing down he would ever have. It was called *Season of the Witch* when Scorsese told Cassavetes it needed rewrites. He had taken his mentor's advice and had had it rewritten. The title had also changed. It was now called *Mean Streets*.

Martin Scorsese had made *Who's That Knocking at My Door* as a student film. He started it in 1965 and it was finally premièred at the 1969 Chicago Film Festival under the title *I Call First* before reverting to its current title. It was the second part of a proposed trilogy which Scorsese saw as an anthropological look at life on the streets of Little Italy – real life with real people, not the Hollywood versions that had been foisted on audiences up till then. The first part has never been filmed. It was a forty-page treatment called *Jerusalem, Jerusalem* and dealt with a group of young men on a weekend at a Catholic retreat house. The central character in *Jerusalem, Jerusalem*, as he had been in *Who's That Knocking at My Door*, was J.R. In many ways J.R. was a Scorsese alter ego. In *Who's That Knocking at My Door* he was a young Italian-American man struggling with his attraction to the blonde Protestant girl of his dreams.

Scorsese had restructured *Season of the Witch* with Mardik Martin, a screenwriter friend from NYU. He and Scorsese wrote what was to become *Mean Streets* as they drove round the streets of Little Italy in Martin's old car.

'We would park wherever we could find a spot,' recalls Martin, 'mostly in Manhattan, around the neighbourhood. *The Godfather* was a big book at the time but to us it was bullshit. It didn't seem to be about the gangsters we knew, the petty ones you see around. We wanted to tell the story of real gangsters. Marty could relate to a gangster as well as to a man like me. What this film is, is Marty's vision of a way of life, of people that he saw better than anybody. My job was to make a story of it.'

In the rewrite J.R. had become Charlie, but he was still effectively a Scorsese doppelganger. The new title came from a Dashiell Hammett quote – 'Down these mean streets a man must go' – suggested by Jay Cocks. Scorsese privately felt the title was rather corny and hoped that something better might turn up, but in the end it grew on everyone. *Mean Streets* begins where *Who's That Knocking at My Door* ends, with Charlie in church holding his hand in the flame of a votive candle. The pain must be intense, but Charlie reminds himself that the fires of hell burn hotter. Scorsese once said that all his films are about sin and redemption, but none is more so than *Mean Streets*. Even the tag-line in the film's poster – 'You don't make up for your sins in church. You do it in the streets' – is a distillation of the message in Scorsese's movies.

Charlie is keen to repent, to do the right thing by God and by himself. He asks for a sign which is duly delivered in the shape of Johnny Boy, a mercurial loser. Johnny Boy is the mirror image of Charlie's mafioso wannabe. He is a slob, a gambler, irresponsible, and he believes the world owes him a living. Johnny Boy will be the cross that Charlie will have to bear. By sorting out Johnny Boy, Charlie will do physical penance for his sins and earn spiritual atonement. Charlie's Uncle Giovanni is the local made man, literally the neighbourhood Godfather in Johnny Boy's case. Even Giovanni has washed his hands of his wastrel godson. He tells Charlie to cut his ties with this loser, but Charlie prevaricates, torn between his loyalty to a friend and his fealty to his family. Johnny Boy makes life even more difficult by refusing to pay off a local loan shark and then rebuffing Charlie's attempts to mediate. Eventually Charlie and his girlfriend Teresa decide to smuggle Johnny Boy out of the neighbourhood, but they are pursued by the loan shark's gunmen, who hand out a vicious lesson in one final, bloody confrontation.

Finding the finance for *Mean Streets* had not been easy. Scorsese had approached a number of sources without success. Roger Corman and his brother Gene had been willing to put up $150,000 to make the movie with a non-union crew, but only if Scorsese would change the script to make the characters black to cash in on the current trend for blaxploitation movies. Scorsese didn't dismiss the idea right away, but soon realised that the film's Catholic imagery and religious convictions wouldn't sit well with Afro hairstyles and an Isaac Hayes soundtrack.

'I just couldn't see those black guys in church, or at confession,' he admitted later. 'It just wouldn't work. The plot didn't really mean anything, it was the characters that mattered, so I stuck to my guns.'

Funding eventually came from an unlikely source. Verna Bloom introduced Scorsese to Jonathan Taplin, formerly road manager for The Band, and Bob Dylan, who wanted to branch into movie production. It was Taplin who eventually came up with the $300,000 to make the film. Scorsese brought in Paul Rapp, Corman's associate producer, who had guided him through *Boxcar Bertha*, as well as the rest of the *Boxcar Bertha* crew, and he was ready to go.

By the time he and De Niro met at that Christmas dinner, shooting had already begun. Scorsese had approached Jon Voight to play Charlie, but he had dropped out at the last minute. He then approached Harvey Keitel who, as J.R. in *Who's That Knocking at My Door*, had effectively played the role before. Scorsese and Keitel had gone into the streets of Little Italy with a small crew during the feast of San Gennaro in October to grab what footage they could. After their meeting Scorsese invited De Niro to audition for the movie. He duly went along, and the habits of a lifetime got him the part. De Niro's search for realism in costume and character had made him an inveterate scavenger of thrift shops in the search for coats and hats. For his audition he wore a crumpled creation that may have started out as a pork-pie hat but had definitely seen better days.

'When I saw that crazy hat,' Scorsese remembers, 'I knew he would be perfect.'

De Niro had some reservations. He had by now acquired a certain status, and he also knew that *Bang the Drum Slowly*, although as yet unreleased, was going to do great things for him.

'He offered me four parts,' he says, 'not Charlie, that was Harvey's part, but four others. I didn't know which one to do. I was kicking them around and talking with Marty and trying to decide. I saw interesting aspects in each one. Then I ran into Harvey on the street. I told him that maybe at this stage of my career I ought to hold out for something else. I felt the logical part for me was Harvey's part, but he already had it. On the other hand I also wanted to work with Marty.

'One day Harvey said, "I can see you doing Johnny Boy." I hadn't thought of playing him at all. I had picked a role, and it wasn't Johnny Boy. I said "I'm going to do this one", but Harvey somehow made me see it another way. I couldn't see Johnny Boy at first but in a way that was a good thing.

'When you play a role you don't see yourself doing at first, you can get things from yourself that you ordinarily wouldn't get. I didn't see myself as Johnny Boy as written, but we improvised in rehearsal and the part evolved. We would find a structure for the improvisations and figure out how to pace it. It's not just freewheeling, it has to have a structure. Then we'd tape what we'd do. It had to build. Working this way takes a lot of personal stuff.'

Scorsese was keen to allow De Niro and Keitel and the other key cast members, David Proval and Richard Romanus, to improvise and develop their parts. On the other hand he was also aware that money was very tight. He had a budget of just $300,000 and only 27 days of shooting. The budget had already forced him to make one major concession. Paul Rapp had told him that the film could not be made entirely in New York for the money they had available. Scorsese was dumbstruck. But, according to Rapp's calculations, they could not afford to pay the Teamsters Union what it would cost to do the climactic car-crash sequence in New York. It would have to be shot in Los Angeles. Rapp did have a solution. Scorsese could go to New York, shoot four days of backgrounds, and then do the interiors in Los Angeles.

'We had only twenty-five or twenty-six days to shoot and we had no money,' says Scorsese. 'The first night of shooting Harvey Keitel had to get into a cab and drive around Greenwich Village. We got there and I had the whole crew waiting and I said to Harvey, "Okay, now hail a cab." And we hailed this guy and gave him twenty-five dollars for a few hours and then the engine started overheating and began to smoke. We ended up pushing it and the guy wasn't happy so we had to give him another couple of dollars.'

In the end Scorsese managed to stretch the Manhattan end of things to eight days' shooting, but it led to some curious anomalies. For example, in the scene where De Niro as Johnny Boy is firing a rifle from a window, the building is evidently in New York because you can see the Empire State Building in the background, but the actual window from which the shot was taken was an interior in Los Angeles. At times Scorsese was shooting anywhere between 24 and 36 set-ups a day to maximise his time in New York. Richard Romanus remembers the director wearing white cotton gloves to stop him biting his nails. He also called in favours from the neighbourhood, like shooting in the home of the mother of the man on whom De Niro's character was based, and drafting his own mother Catherine in as a cast member. She complains that Scorsese kept her up till two in the morning and made her do 20 takes of her big scene in the film where she comforts Teresa after an epileptic fit.

Scorsese could not fail to be aware during shooting that he was filming history. De Niro and Keitel give electrifying performances as Johnny Boy and Charlie, and the director was keen to harness as much of that energy as he possibly could.

'Much of the improvisation in this film was taped at rehearsal and then scripted from those tapes,' he says. 'A few scenes like the one in which De Niro and Keitel fight each other with garbage pails were improvised during shooting. I remember that at the end of one take, Bobby threw the thing at Harvey and Harvey threw it right back and I said, "Great, we'll do that in the next take." '

One of the key scenes in the film is where Charlie takes Johnny Boy into the back room of the bar to try to talk some sense into him. Richard Romanus as Michael the loan shark has already approached Charlie about Johnny Boy's bad debt, and Charlie is keen that his friend should do something. Inevitably Johnny Boy doesn't want to know, and the serious discussion degenerates into a near-comic double-talk routine.

'I thought it would be fun to improvise and show more of the characters,' says Scorsese outlining the thinking behind the sequence. 'We realised that we all liked Abbott and Costello a great deal, their language routines with inverted word meanings done with impeccable timing. We tried to keep as much of that as possible, though it had to be done very quickly. The result is so structured that if you only see that one scene you know more about their way of life from it than from anything else in the film. We see the shifting of trust, how Johnny trusts Charlie but he's got his problems, we see how Charlie trusts Johnny but he's using him. The scene was Bob's idea and since he and Harvey are not afraid to try things I said, "Why not?" When I shot it, it was about fifteen minutes long, hilarious, and clarified everything totally. It's like the betrayals of trust, one character taking advantage of another, that I enjoy in the Hope and Crosby movies.'

De Niro's first appearance in *Mean Streets* is literally explosive. We see him drop a bomb of some sort into a mailbox for the hell of it, and then run away exhilarated by his own sense of anarchy. De Niro stayed in character as Johnny Boy during the day's shooting, but on one occasion his feigned violence almost gave way to the real thing.

'We did the climactic scene where Bobby suddenly pulls a gun on Richard Romanus on the next-to-last day of shooting,' recalls Scorsese. 'Something had happened between Bobby and Richard because the animosity between them in that scene was real, and I played on it. They had got on each other's nerves to the point where I think they really wanted to kill each other. I kept shooting take after take of Bobby yelling all these insults while the crew was getting very upset.'

Richard Romanus was the outsider of the group in the *Mean Streets* cast. De Niro and David Proval, who plays Tony, the bar-owner, came from the neighbourhood, while Harvey Keitel is from Brooklyn, not a million miles away on the subway. Romanus, on the other hand, was a small-town country boy. He and De Niro also had very different acting styles in the movie. Romanus and Proval had made a conscious decision to be more laid-back in their characters, to provide a contrast to the high-energy performances of their co-stars. It is this divergence in styles which seems more than anything to have provoked the conflict between Romanus and De Niro.

'Working with Bobby De Niro was interesting,' says Romanus. 'It was my first movie and to watch Bobby take charge of his work was a great lesson for me. By taking charge I mean he would say, "Whoa, whoa, I want another take. I want to do this again." He put the responsibility for his own performance on his own shoulders. So he wasn't able at the end of the day to turn round to anyone and say, "I would have been better but for him."

'In the scene where Bobby insults me, where he tells me I was stupid to lend him the money in the first place, I started to laugh. Bobby got angry. He thought I should be angry, which I was, but by laughing I was saving face. He thought I should be fuming but he had no control over my reactions. If you're working correctly no one has control over anyone's reactions. Sometimes the reaction you get from your acting partner is not the one you want. Then you simply have to react off that. But in this scene I laughed organically. I thought Bobby was very funny when he was doing that stuff. And he looked ridiculous.'

The following day, shooting on *Mean Streets* was complete. Scorsese had everything he needed in the can and he had done it on budget and in 27 days. He had also laid the groundwork for the most important creative relationship between an actor and a director in the history of the cinema. He had found his imperfect twin. Before *Mean Streets*, Harvey Keitel had been the man Scorsese secretly saw when he looked in the mirror. Whether it was as J.R. or as Charlie, he was Scorsese's alter ego. But in *Mean Streets* De Niro supplanted Keitel in that role. Scorsese had found the actor who most mirrored and complemented his own sensibilities. For his part, De Niro had found a director whose sense of commitment and intensity of purpose matched his own. He had also found a soulmate who could express himself and control himself in ways in which the actor could not. *Mean Streets* began a run of films that would virtually define the benchmark against which American cinema would be judged for the next 20 years and more.

When Scorsese had his first assembly of the picture ready, he went back again to the man who had been indirectly responsible for the whole process.

'John Cassavetes saw the first rough cut of *Mean Streets*,' says Scorsese. 'After he had seen it he said, "Don't cut it whatever you do." I said, "What about the bedroom scene?" and he replied, "Oh yeah, you could cut that," because John didn't like nudity.'

Mean Streets was released in a special digitally restored souvenir video edition in Britain in 1993 to mark its 20th anniversary. The director summed up his feelings about the film in the accompanying brochure.

He said: 'Harvey Keitel, Robert De Niro and myself became part of each other with this film – checking in with each other every now and then for the past twenty years and I hope for many more years to come.'

8 The New Brando?

B
Y THE TIME HE had finished *Mean Streets*, De Niro's career was rather like a firework waiting to go off. The blue touchpaper had been lit and now everyone was standing back waiting to see some spectacular results. There are very few surprises in Hollywood. Long before films are screened for critics or the public the studios know exactly how good they are. There is a constant flow of information from all sorts of sources. From the labs printing the footage, from the crew watching the daily rushes, from the editing rooms and from the studio executives themselves, the word percolates out on a hot new movie or a hot new talent.

That is exactly the position in which De Niro found himself in the summer of 1973. Neither *Bang the Drum Slowly* nor *Mean Streets* had opened to the public yet, but as far as the industry was concerned De Niro had been anointed. He was the hottest talent in town and would soon be having to deal with reviews that were so good they were almost embarrassing.

Fame was still not going to his head. He was living modestly in West 14th Street between Greenwich Village and Chelsea paying $70 a month for a sparsely furnished fourth-floor apartment, although by now presumably he no longer had to put glue on the windows as a draught excluder. He was also contemplating a return to the stage. The few press reports that had appeared about him by this stage were already starting to tag him unfairly as 'the new Brando'. Their early careers had run in parallel inasmuch as they had both gone to the Dramatic Workshop and both had studied under Stella Adler and Lee Strasberg, but this was more by accident than design. Although De Niro does cite Brando along with James Dean and Montgomery Clift as actors he admired growing up, he is much too single-minded to have allowed any actor to influence his own style. The 'new Brando' tag is simply publicity shorthand. As men they do share some common traits. Both are notoriously close-mouthed to the point of inarticulacy in public, and both have developed a lack of interest in the press which borders on contempt. Other than the suppressed rage of their performances, their acting styles are totally dissimilar. Brando did spend time in a wheelchair for his breakthrough role as a paraplegic in the film *The Men*, but his absorption in a part is nowhere near as intense as De Niro's. De Niro says he cannot fake acting while Brando, especially latterly, seems happy to do so. On the set of *A Dry White Season* he didn't even learn his lines; instead he wore a tiny earpiece and had an assistant read the lines to him off-set, and he would then repeat them. For Brando this provided spontaneity; one suspects De Niro would rather die than be that spontaneous.

The summer of 1973 could have provided an interesting opportunity to compare the two great Method actors of their generations. After making two films back to back, De Niro was returning to the stage. As it happened, the Lincoln Center in New York was reviving Tennessee Williams's *A Streetcar Named Desire*. De Niro wanted to play Stanley Kowalski, and was willing to work for the off-Broadway rate of $65 a week to do it. For reasons best known to themselves, the Lincoln Center decided that he was not the man for them and turned him down. Brando had set Broadway alight when he created the role of Kowalski on stage. The chance to compare the two at roughly the same age would have been tantalising, but doubtless if the Lincoln Center had cast him then De Niro would have spent the rest of his life tagged as 'the new Brando'.

After missing out on *Streetcar*, De Niro then appeared in an experimental one-act play at Stage 73 in the Manhattan Theatre Club, again for a fraction of his movie salary. He played a construction worker who falls for a preppy college student in *Schubert's Last Serenade*, a one-act play by Julie Bovasso. The play ran only for a week, but during rehearsals Bovasso wondered if she was making the right choice. All the action is set in a restaurant in which De Niro and his leading lady Laura Esterman are trying to have a romantic dinner.

'For the first week of rehearsals I thought, Oh, my poor play,' said Bovasso later in an interview with *Newsweek* magazine. 'Bobby arrives at his characterisations by what sometimes seems like a very circuitous route. He wanted to do one scene, for example, while chewing breadsticks. I was dubious but I agreed and for three days I didn't hear a word of my play – it was all garbled up in breadsticks. But I could see something happening; he was making a connection with something, a kind of clown element. Then at dress rehearsal he showed up without the breadsticks. I said, "Bobby, where are the breadsticks?" And he said simply, "I don't need them any more." '

The business with the breadsticks would make no sense to anyone but De Niro. But like Bruce Pearson's K-Mart clothes and Johnny Boy's hat, they were invaluable in helping to shape the character. De Niro was in the midst of exploring the whole process of acting. In a sense he was conducting his education in public by learning to turn a performance into more than just a series of skilful line readings. He was attempting to create a performance as an organic whole.

Because of his domestic circumstances, De Niro grew up faster than most children of his age. He was given trust at an early age and he responded to it. This left him with the invaluable traits of self-possession and self-awareness as a result of which he does not seem to need to be liked in the way that most of us do. De Niro became comfortable with his own company and appears to have mastered the art of being alone without being lonely. Like most self-educated people, he has an intuitive sense of self-protection, almost a cunning, which takes over from formal education. However, he does not convey his thoughts or feelings precisely unless he is in a film or a play where he can use the words of others to interpret his own emotions. Martin Scorsese has said that one of the reasons he and De Niro are so close is that they both see themselves as outsiders. In De Niro's case we have to assume that this is not an outsider in the sense of someone who is excluded, but rather someone who is an outsider because he has nothing in common with a group. This is a man who excludes himself by dint of his different experience. But by becoming someone else for two hours a night he ceases to be an outsider. He can express himself and we will either embrace that or reject it, but we will at least react to it.

'Of course you always bring something of yourself to a part but to me acting means playing different parts,' De Niro told the *New York Times* in his first major profile in 1973. 'You try to get as close as possible to the reality of a character. You learn his lifestyle, how he holds his fork, how he carries himself, how he talks, how he relates to other people. It's hard to do because it means you always have to keep looking.

'Some days you find nothing, other days you're inspired and you see lots that's exciting. That's why I like to travel before I do a part, so I can feel I've prepared as well as I can. I want to feel I've earned a right to play a person.'

In one of those quirks of timing unique to the film industry, *Bang the Drum Slowly* and *Mean Streets* were released almost simultaneously in the autumn of 1973. The releases were so close to each other that in some New York cinemas they were playing on different screens in the same theatres. *Bang the Drum Slowly* was released first and became an instant hit with the public and critics alike. The *New York Times* critic Peter Schjeldahl compared De Niro to a young Dustin Hoffman and suggested that he would have a great future as a 'character lead' who could play anything he was offered.

The release pattern of *Mean Streets* was a little more chequered. The film opened at the 1973 New York Film Festival to astonishing reviews. *Newsweek* suggested that De Niro's performance as Johnny Boy ought to be preserved in a time capsule. Pauline Kael, the doyenne of American film reviewers, said in the *New Yorker* that *Mean Streets* was 'a true original of our period, a triumph of personal film-making. If this picture isn't a runaway success the reason could be that it is so original that some people will be dumbfounded – too struck to respond.' Even Frank Rich, the notorious Butcher of Broadway, who was reviewing films at the time, found praise for De Niro, even though he was not wholeheartedly behind the picture.

As it turned out, Pauline Kael's review was right on the money.

'Because the picture did such good business in New York in the first couple of weeks,' recalls Martin Scorsese, 'our producer wanted to open the film in twenty-five cities just like *The Last Picture Show* and *Five Easy Pieces*. He went to Warner Brothers who said, "Do it because there's nothing opening in October except *The Way We Were* and that won't make a cent." Famous last words.

'We thought the New York Film Festival meant something in L.A. but nobody even knew about the picture. We had big full-page ads but the ads were not good. We had no idea how to sell the picture. How are you going to sell it? As *The Gang That Couldn't Shoot Straight*? This was our first concept – guys running around with shorts on and guns and hats, because Johnny Boy takes off his pants at one point. It would have looked like a comedy. In fact it is funny but it wasn't meant to be. We'd been advised to let it play in New York. That was probably right – we should have let it play in New York for a couple of months.

'But next thing I know, we opened in L.A., got nice reviews, did two weeks' business, and that was that. Every other city it was exactly the same thing.'

Warner Brothers had acquired distribution rights to *Mean Streets* for $750,000. They were also just about to release *The Exorcist* which had cost them $14 million. As Scorsese points out, they were hardly likely to throw away what they perceived to be good money after bad for a low-budget picture they hadn't even made themselves.

By the time *Mean Streets* was going on release across the country, De

Niro was off on another research trip. He was going back to Italy to brush up on his Sicilian.

After stating several times in public that he had no interest in making a sequel to *The Godfather*, Francis Ford Coppola was gearing up for *The Godfather: Part II*. Like Vito Corleone in the original, Paramount Pictures had made him an offer he couldn't refuse. They were giving him $1 million to write, produce and direct, and a 13 per cent share of the profits from the first dollar. He would also have full creative control, and Paramount had agreed that his latest movie, *The Conversation*, could be distributed by the company he had set up with fellow film-makers Peter Bogdanovich and William Friedkin. This company, called with blinding originality the Directors Company, was actually being bankrolled by Paramount in any event.

The only condition was that Paramount wanted a sequel and they wanted it quickly. Coppola had a scant three months to write it and put it straight into production.

'I was making a thirteen-million-dollar movie as if it were a Roger Corman picture,' said the former Corman graduate ruefully.

Coppola's intention was to make a film that would in effect book-end the first one. He did not believe a genuine sequel could be made from Mario Puzo's original, so he chose to film a prequel and a sequel in one. The second film would show Michael Corleone taking over the reins of power from his dead father, as well as revealing how young Vito Corleone had become Don Vito.

The film would begin in Sicily, showing how young Vito Andolini's life would be spared by the mafiosi who killed his father. Vito would then go to New York as a poor immigrant but would rise to a position of immense power, pausing only to return to his homeland to settle a debt.

Coppola wanted Marlon Brando to reprise the role of Vito Corleone. Brando wasn't sure whether he wanted to do the movie at all, far less go through the rigorous make-up that would be required if he were to play the young Vito. He also felt that Paramount had paid him poorly for the first one in the light of the money it had gone on to make. Paramount executives, for their part, were less than thrilled at the prospect of another appearance by Brando after he had caused chaos at the Academy Awards. Unlike George C. Scott, who had turned down his Oscar for *Patton*, Brando accepted but sent a Native American squaw to collect his Best Actor award and read out a statement about white exploitation of the Indians. The girl, Sacheen Littlefeather, later turned out to be an actress, but Paramount were still less than pleased.

A new actor would therefore be required to play Vito Corleone. Coppola had seen *Mean Streets* and was impressed not just by the film but specifically by the work of De Niro. Johnny Boy scored a big hit with Coppola, who remembered De Niro from all the tests he had done for the original film. He particularly remembered being struck by De Niro's facial resemblance to Brando.

Once he had decided to film the sequel, Coppola and his casting director and executive producer Fred Roos invited De Niro out to lunch. The actor thought it was a social call; he didn't know that Coppola and Roos were anxiously scrutinising every aspect of his face to see if he would make an acceptable Vito Corleone. Roos felt that because De Niro had only played 'goofballs and slightly comedic simpletons' he was an unconventional selection. Paramount were similarly inclined, but Coppola and Roos stuck to their guns and won the day, signing De Niro without so much as a screen test. After three years of tests and auditions, De Niro was finally going to appear in a *Godfather* movie.

He threw himself into the part. He and veteran make-up artist Dick Smith collaborated extensively in an attempt to find a make-up that would make him look like Brando. In the end they abandoned the notion and De Niro agreed to play the part without extensive make-up. He studied tapes and watched *The Godfather* again and again until he had got a general impression of how Brando moved and talked, especially in the much-impersonated hoarse whisper that had become his trademark in the film.

De Niro could not have been unaware of the irony of playing the role made famous by the man to whom he has most often been compared. But the situation was also fraught with pitfalls, which De Niro also recognised.

'I didn't want to do an imitation,' he told *Photoplay* magazine, 'but I wanted to make it believable that I could be him as a young man. I would see some little movements that he would do and try to link them to my performance. It was like a mathematical problem where you have the result and you try to make the beginning fit.

'There was a little pressure because I couldn't tell if the choices were good. I made them and I went with them because you've got to trust the director and trusting Francis is very easy. There is a thin line between identification and imitation. I wanted to seem like the young guy who ends up the older godfather. We couldn't look alike because my face is so different from his. Dick Smith and I experimented but it was his idea to go simple and I agreed. I feel it's better to do less than more.

'What I did was watch videotapes of Brando's scenes looking for gestures or movements to pick up. Or maybe just a variation on something he did.

The voice we tried at first. I thought we might be going too far and that it was too raspy. I think it turned out pretty good though.'

Filming began on *The Godfather Part II* on 1 October 1973. While Coppola and the rest of the crew were shooting the Lake Tahoe sequences, De Niro was getting into character. He had already taken a crash course in Italian at Berlitz and was going off to hone his accent – almost all his dialogue in the film is Italian – in preparation for the film. He began shooting the Little Italy sequences of the movie in January 1974 and finished off in Sicily from April to June. As he did for *Bang the Drum Slowly* he took a tape recorder and went to Palermo to seek out the relatives of the film's Sicilian consultant, Romano Pianti. De Niro had already been studying intensively with Pianti but he felt he needed to hear the living language for himself.

'I was always up front about what I was doing,' he said. 'I felt it would be underhanded not to say anything. I'm just an actor doing my work. I've found people enjoy helping you. If they understand what you're looking for you save a lot of time and unnecessary suspicion. Although they are very cordial to you as a tourist Sicilians have a way of watching without appearing to be watching. They'll scrutinise you thoroughly and you won't even know it.'

But even this scrutiny was useful. Many times in the Little Italy flashback sequences, De Niro is seen simply standing and watching, but no one in the audience can be in the slightest doubt that Vito Corleone is marking and memorising everything he sees. This remarkable stillness in De Niro's performance undoubtedly came from weeks of being an object of curiosity himself.

When he returned from six weeks in Sicily, he astonished Romano Pianti by how quickly he had picked up the language and the dialect.

'If you had asked me if it was possible that an actor could master a language like Sicilian in such a short time I would have said, "Never. Impossible," ' he said. 'But this De Niro has done it.'

De Niro, incidentally, is the only person in the *Godfather* films who utters the immortal phrase about non-refusable offers. 'I'll make him an offer he don't refuse,' he says to Bruno Kirby, discussing how he will deal with the local gangster boss. When Al Pacino as Michael relates Vito's negotiating ploy in the first film he says only, 'My father made him an offer he couldn't refuse.' De Niro's memorable line is one of only three lines of English in his whole performance.

It was Pacino who came up with the idea of casting De Niro's acting mentor, Lee Strasberg, as mobster Hyman Roth. The part was originally intended for director Elia Kazan but he turned it down. So although they had no scenes together, De Niro found himself in the same film as the man who was responsible for teaching him the craft of acting.

The annual awards season in Hollywood begins in December with the Los Angeles and New York Film Critics awards. It then gathers momentum with a succession of other ceremonies until it reaches a climax on the last Monday in March when the Academy Awards are handed out in front of a worldwide television audience running into billions.

Robert De Niro's double whammy as the slow-witted Bruce Pearson and the mercurial Johnny Boy had made him a serious contender in the awards stakes for the first time in his career. It was *Mean Streets* which had gathered most attention, but *Bang the Drum Slowly* also showed that he had range and depth. The combination of the two won him the Best Supporting Actor award from both the New York Critics Circle and the National Society of Film Critics. With those two high-profile awards in the bag the Oscars beckoned, but surprisingly De Niro didn't even rate a nomination.

A disgruntled 'New York trade veteran' told *Variety* De Niro had been passed over by the Actors' Branch of the Academy because *Bang the Drum Slowly* was 'a New York picture and they hate us out there.' One other factor which may have weighed heavily against De Niro is that not enough Academy members would have seen *Mean Streets* – undoubtedly the better of the two performances – to ensure that he was nominated. In the end his *Bang the Drum Slowly* co-star Vincent Gardenia was nominated in the Best Supporting Actor category for his performance as De Niro's coach. He lost out to the eventual winner and sentimental favourite, John Houseman. The former member of Orson Welles's Mercury Players had made a comeback to acting in *The Paper Chase* after ten years as a teacher.

If De Niro was disappointed at missing out on an Oscar nomination then he was too busy with *The Godfather Part II* to show it. In any event his disappointment would not last for long.

9 'And the Winner is . . .'

I N ORDER TO MAXIMISE its chances of Oscar success, and with that its box-office potential, *The Godfather Part II* was not due for release until December 1974. To qualify for an Academy Award a film has to play on one screen in Los Angeles or New York before the end of the Oscar year, which also corresponds to the calendar year. Coppola's film would open in New York – on the same five screens as *The Godfather* – on 12 December, 1974.

Meanwhile De Niro had succumbed to the lure of the Mediterranean and in the process made the first serious mis-calculation of his career. By the time filming on *The Godfather Part II* had ended in June, he had already agreed to star in an epic for the Italian director Bernardo Bertolucci. *1900*, also known under its Italian title of *Novecento*, had been a pet project of the maverick film-maker. It was originally conceived as a six-part mini-series for Italian television, and Bertolucci had hoped it would star Jack Nicholson. However, after the success of his controversial *Last Tango in Paris*, Bertolucci decided that it should be a film rather than a TV series. And not just a film, a great film, a film that would stand for all time as a monument to cinematic achievement. Anyone who proposes making a film with those criteria is almost certainly headed for disaster, and Bertolucci was no exception.

1900 is the story of two men born on the same day, one into a family of wealth and influence, the other into a family of peasants. The story covers 50 years of Italian history, with particular emphasis on the parallel growths of Fascism and Socialism in the thirties. The two central characters, the patrician Alfredo and the proletarian Olmo, are heavy-handed metaphors for the political process. Alfredo would be played by Robert De Niro and rising French star Gérard Depardieu would be Olmo. The cast would also include Sterling Hayden, Burt Lancaster, Donald Sutherland and Dominique Sanda, and the film would take the better part of a year to shoot.

'I realised while shooting the picture and especially while it was being edited that *Novecento* is constructed according to the principle of contradiction,' says Bertolucci. 'The contradiction between Depardieu and De Niro, between the peasants and the landowners, between the Hollywood stars and the real country people, between the most careful preparation and the most unruly improvisation, between archaic rural culture and a truly upper-class culture.'

Bertolucci was able to bring in his epic film for a relatively cheap $6.5 million. With *The Godfather Part II* not released yet, De Niro was still a relatively inexpensive proposition, while veteran actor Burt Lancaster was so keen to work with Bertolucci that he offered to do his three weeks on the movie for nothing. As ever the Hollywood studios had been seduced by the prospect of another happy marriage between artistic integrity and commercial success. It had worked with *Last Tango in Paris*, so why not now? Before Bertolucci had shot a foot of film *1900* had almost recovered its budget in distributors' advances.

'The first few days with De Niro were a nightmare,' said Bertolucci afterwards. 'He's a very sensitive and probably neurotic person. But if one has the patience it is probably worth it.'

De Niro for his part at least appreciated what his director was trying to do.

'Bertolucci is good,' he said. 'He's good with actors. He was an actor himself at one time. He's schooled.'

The relationship between Bertolucci and De Niro was certainly strained. This may simply have been due to a clash of styles. Bertolucci, like most Italian directors, knows exactly what he wants on set. Italians like Bertolucci, Zeffirelli and Sergio Leone are not noted for collaborating with actors. Up to this point, De Niro had been used to working with directors like John Hancock, Martin Scorsese and Roger Corman, who shared his New York sensibility and would allow him the opportunity of bringing the Method into play. It may also have been that De Niro's actor's instincts were beginning to develop to the point where he knew that the part of Alfredo was completely wrong for him. Alfredo is weak and vacillating while De Niro is strong-willed and single-minded. De Niro has never successfully played a weak character and he must have felt distinctly uncomfortable during the mammoth shoot. Characters like Bruce Pearson, Johnny Boy, and especially Vito Corleone had an inner strength that De Niro was able to exploit. With Alfredo there was nothing for him to work with.

1900 was filmed over 1974 and 1975 and finally made its debut at the 1976 Cannes Film Festival. In its original form it ran to a staggering five hours and twenty minutes of almost unremitting boredom. Bertolucci's grand plan to create a masterpiece had fallen flat on its face, taking De Niro with it. Presumably De Niro had been intrigued by the idea of working with a director of Bertolucci's reputation and wanted to see if he could stretch himself artistically with the role. The short answer was that he could not, and this was reflected in the reviews.

'A sober De Niro is somewhat overshadowed by a role condemning him to passivity,' said *Variety*. *Time* magazine went even further. 'Must he be so boring,' Richard Corliss's review asked of Alfredo. 'De Niro has played quiet characters before but there has always been a residue of strength, a hint of obsessiveness, a sense of personal pride. Alfredo has none of these qualities and De Niro has no hook to hang his own outsized but narrow-ranged talent on. His performance is as boring as his character.'

De Niro was not helped by Bertolucci's working methods. The Italian director allowed his cosmopolitan cast of French, Italians, Germans and Americans to deliver their lines in their own language so they could re-dub the lines into Italian later. In De Niro's case it was almost a year later before he looped his dialogue, which by this time had a pronounced and jarring American accent. Even more jarring is the fact that the inflection of the dubbed dialogue doesn't quite match the inflections of the original dialogue, leaving him distractingly out of synch.

Whether it was artistic curiosity or sheer vanity which convinced him he could succeed in a part so obviously unsuited to him, *1900* could have finished De Niro's career almost before it had begun. Fortunately the length of time it took to finish the film, coupled with endless rows over when it would be distributed, meant that he had completed two of the defining roles of his career before anyone ever got to see his Italian disaster.

The Godfather Part II was the most eagerly awaited film of 1974. In attempting to convince Francis Ford Coppola that he should do a sequel, Paramount boss Charles Bluhdorn had told him he knew it would be a success. 'You've got the formula for Coca-Cola!' he enthusiastically assured him. And he was right. The film was an instant success on its limited pre-Oscar release, and by the end of 1975 it had grossed almost $30 million in America alone. Even allowing for budget overruns and Coppola's percentage that would still translate into a healthy profit for Paramount.

The film was acclaimed by almost every critic in America, none of whom failed to point out that here was a rarity, a sequel that surpassed the original. Equally, none of them failed to single out De Niro for the quality of his performance. His Vito Corleone is a lean and hungry man who spends his life watching and waiting and quietly plotting until he sees his opportunity. De Niro's performance is both passive and commanding. The eye cannot fail to follow him in every scene he is in. Even while he is simply standing and watching he gives the impression of preparing his next move. 'Like Brando's Vito,' said Pauline Kael, 'De Niro's has a reserve which can never be breached. Vito is so secure in the knowledge of how dangerous he is that his courtliness is no more or less than noblesse oblige.' The *Los Angeles Times* described it as 'a sensational performance'. Reviewer Charles Champlin said De Niro does 'an amazing job of preparing us for the Brando we remember'.

It is worth remembering that at this stage De Niro was much better known inside the profession than out. Despite success with *Bang the Drum Slowly* and *Mean Streets*, these had been at best modest hits and his face was largely unknown to the movie-going public. Most of those who would see him in *The Godfather Part II* were seeing him for the first time. He was an actor's actor at this stage, but that very status is what would propel him into the next stage of his career.

The various Academy Award nominations are made by the respective branches of the Academy. Actors vote for actors, directors for directors, editors for editors, and so on. Only the Best Picture category is open for everyone to vote on. Given his reputation within the industry, and possibly since he was passed over the year before, De Niro seemed to be a certainty for a nomination this year. In the end Coppola's film and Roman Polanski's *Chinatown* were the front-runners with ten nominations each. Three of *The Godfather Part II*'s nominations were in the Best Supporting Actor category, where De Niro was up against his former mentor Lee Strasberg and Michael V. Gazzo, who had played Frankie Pentangeli. The other contenders were Fred Astaire with his only Oscar nomination for his straight dramatic role as an ageing conman in *The Towering Inferno* and Jeff Bridges for his role opposite Clint Eastwood in *Thunderbolt and Lightfoot*.

Bridges was deemed to be an instant outsider because of his youth and also because there was a perception that his nomination had been 'bought' by a huge advertising campaign. The sentimental favourites seemed to be Strasberg – bearing in mind John Houseman's win the previous year – and Astaire. The legendary dancer had made no secret of the fact that he was less than pleased that people who had worked with him, like partner Ginger Rogers and choreographer Hermes Pan, had won awards over the years while his trophy cabinet remained empty.

The Academy Awards are always a nervous time for nominees, especially those in the audience who have to look affable and generous as the cameras zoom in. For Best Supporting Actor candidates the ordeal is a little less painful since it is normally the first award to be given out. Traditionally it is presented by the winner of the previous year's Best Supporting Actress trophy. After the laborious reading of the rules, this year accompanied by a bizarre film on how the Academy votes, Tatum O'Neal, who had won the previous year for *Paper Moon*, stepped forward with her father Ryan. Four of the five nominees were in the audience at the Dorothy Chandler Pavilion that night. Only De Niro was absent, back home in New York, perhaps anticipating a sentimental result with a win for Astaire.

When the O'Neals opened the golden envelope and announced the magic phrase 'And the winner is Robert De Niro' the audience erupted into spontaneous applause. It was left to Francis Ford Coppola to bound on to the stage and accept on his behalf.

'I'm happy that one of my boys made it,' said an ebullient Coppola. 'I think Robert De Niro is an extraordinary actor and he's going to enrich the films that will be made in years to come. He is the most talented actor working today. I doubt if he knows how good he is.'

There was also praise from Lee Strasberg, the man whose teaching methods were partly responsible for De Niro having been in contention at all. Strasberg allowed that he would have liked to have won himself for his performance as Hyman Roth, but if anyone else had to win he was glad it was De Niro. 'Bobby deserves it,' he said simply.

De Niro's win kicked off an Oscar landslide for *The Godfather Part II*. It went on to win six Oscars on the night including Best Picture and Best Director for Coppola, who had been pipped by Bob Fosse two years previously. De Niro's win earned him two places in the footnotes of Oscar trivia. Given that Brando had won two years earlier it was the first time that an Oscar had been won by two actors playing the same part, and it was only the second time that an Oscar had been given to an actor for a subtitled role. The previous winner had been Sophia Loren for *Two Women* in 1961.

De Niro was not readily accessible to the press to react to what should surely be a high point in a young actor's career, even if only in terms of the effect on his earning potential. When the media did track him down two days later his reaction was equivocal to the point of being churlish.

'Well, lots of people who win the award don't deserve it,' he told *Women's Wear Daily*, 'so it makes you a little cynical about how much it means. Did it mean that much to me? Well, I don't know. It changes your life like anything that will change your life. People react to it. I mean, it's not bad winning it.'

10 God's Lonely Man

WORKING FOR BERTOLUCCI HAD not been a happy experience for De Niro. He returned to New York after his time in Italy disillusioned and dispirited by the whole experience. There was one man to whom he could turn – his new best friend Martin Scorsese. He and Scorsese were soulmates and kindred spirits.

'In Martin,' said Scorsese's second wife Julia Cameron, 'Bobby has found the one person who will talk for fifteen minutes about the way a character would tie a knot. I've seen them go at it for ten hours non-stop.'

Scorsese and De Niro agreed that they would film *Taxi Driver*, a script written by Paul Schrader back in 1972. Schrader originally wrote it for Brian De Palma who had directed his script for *Obsession*, but De Palma had passed. The script ended up with the production team of Tony Bill and Michael and Julia Phillips who between them had produced hits like *The Sting* and *Shampoo*.

Part Russian tragedy, part science fiction, *Taxi Driver* is the story of Travis Bickle, a Vietnam veteran who spends his life driving a cab through the seedy streets of New York. He prowls around 42nd Street and the New York Port Authority like an alien in a space capsule. Pauline Kael would describe it as a tabloid version of *Notes from the Underground*. By coincidence Scorsese has long wanted to film the Dostoevsky book.

Taxi Driver is the quintessence of the cinema of alienation. Screenwriter Paul Schrader describes Bickle in a quote from Thomas Wolfe as 'God's lonely man'. Travis observes without taking any part. He despises the pimps and the junkies and the prostitutes; he welcomes the rain that will sweep the city clean of their filth. But although he has the freedom to take his cab anywhere, at the same time he is drawn to them because they are freak-show outsiders like himself. He haunts the streets around Time Square as he begins a mesmerising descent into his own personal hell. Travis is drawn to two women in particular. There is Betsy, the unattainable blonde campaign worker for a presidential wannabe, and there is

Iris, a child whore who is in the thrall of a brutal pimp. Finally, like some perverse knight errant, Travis sets out to win over these women and at the same time atone for his sins in an orgy of violence. His original plan to kill the candidate is foiled by the Secret Service, so instead he descends into the squalor to redeem himself by rescuing Iris. In a blood-soaked finale, Iris is rescued and returns to her family, the media hails Travis as a hero, and he returns to his former life. In the final scene of the film he sees Betsy waiting in line for a taxi. Each of them ignores the other and life goes on as Travis drives away.

Paul Schrader wrote *Taxi Driver* when he was at his lowest ebb and much of its content reflects his own feelings about life at that period.

'At the time I wrote it I was very enamoured of guns,' he said. 'I was suicidal, I was drinking heavily, I was obsessed with pornography in the way a lonely person is and all of those elements are upfront in the script. Obviously some of them are heightened – the racism of the character, the sexism. Like every kind of underdog, Travis takes out his anger on the guy below him rather than the guy above.

'When they edited the film for TV I didn't mind so much having to lose the violence, but they had to remove huge sections of narration because of the virulent anti-black and anti-women characterisations. He appeared a very silly kind of guy because there was no edge to his anger; you just wanted to slap him in the face and say, "Come on, come on."

'In fact, in the draft of the script that I sold, at the end all the people he kills are black. Marty and the Phillipses and everyone I showed it to said, "No, we just can't do this, it's an incitement to riot." But it was true to the character.'

Having acquired Schrader's script, Tony Bill and Michael and Julia Phillips started to shop it around. Julia has contributed a fascinating account of the production process in her scabrous and vitriolic Hollywood memoir *You'll Never Eat Lunch in This Town Again*. She was not a fan of the script. She felt that 'Travis was a nut case, a valid nut case but a nut case. I thought Schrader was too.' Nonetheless a number of major directors expressed an interest in the script, including Irving Kershner, Lamont Johnson, and John Milius, but the year came and went with no one definitely signed. It began to look as though *Taxi Driver* would finally make it to the screen with Robert Mulligan directing Jeff Bridges. Then Martin Scorsese met Phillips at a party, according to her version, and asked if he could direct it. She was unenthusiastic because at that stage he had only directed *Boxcar Bertha*. However, agent Harry Ufland, who was acting for Scorsese and De Niro, persuaded Phillips to watch a rough cut of *Mean Streets*. By the time the film was halfway through she realised that Scorsese was right for *Taxi Driver*. He could direct the film on one condition; he had to get De Niro to play Travis.

De Niro said yes but even then the picture suffered interminable delays in finding studio finance. Warner Brothers, who had picked up distribution rights for *Mean Streets*, seemed most likely, but studio boss John Calley couldn't make up his mind. But after the initial success of *Mean Streets* he finally agreed to green-light the film if it could be made for $750,000. By this time Scorsese had already agreed to direct *Alice Doesn't Live Here Any More* for Warner Brothers. De Niro meanwhile had completed *Godfather II* and was off to Italy for *1900*. There was a further setback when, after *Alice*, Scorsese tentatively agreed to work with Marlon Brando on a film version of Dee Brown's bestseller *Bury My Heart at Wounded Knee*.

By the time that project had fallen through, and both Scorsese and De Niro were free, Warner Brothers had pulled out because, officially, they didn't believe the film could be made for less than a million dollars. Privately, like every other major studio, they were horrified by the level of violence in Schrader's script. In desperation Phillips arranged a meeting with her mentor at Columbia Pictures, David Begelman, to keep the project alive. Steven Spielberg, for whom she and her husband were producing *Close Encounters of the Third Kind*, was also at the meeting. As a gesture of good faith to his producer and to his friend Scorsese, Spielberg even offered to direct the film himself to keep the project up and running. Eventually Begelman and Columbia agreed to a deal where the film could be made for no more than $2 million. De Niro, Scorsese and everyone else agreed to modify their salaries accordingly to stay within budget. De Niro, for example, worked for only $35,000, a fraction of what he was being offered in the wake of his Oscar. So on a humid June night a yellow taxi cab emerged from a cloud of steam billowing up from a New York street and *Taxi Driver* finally got underway.

Travis Bickle is a man who is in emotional pain throughout the film. His Method training would have encouraged De Niro to bring his own pain to the part. The actor stayed in his trailer for most of the shoot, away from the rest of the crew. Even Scorsese asked permission before disturbing him. But De Niro still contributed a number of ideas to Bickle's character. The pain and isolation that lingered from his childhood and which the therapy had not been adequately able to deal with would manifest themselves in a portrayal that is as uncomfortable to watch as it must have been to play. His anger at his mother and her boyfriends may have led to De Niro's feelings of frustration around women when he was a young man. Shelley Winters recalls a party she gave which an actress

De Niro was keen on was due to attend. He was visibly on edge as the evening wore on and she had not appeared. When she did eventually arrive she scarcely looked in his direction. De Niro got up and fled into a bedroom. Winters followed and found him punching the wall in frustration. Having lived with that sort of emotional intensity for his whole life provided De Niro with a deep well of private anguish from which to draw the character of Travis Bickle. And since Bickle's relationships in *Taxi Driver* are almost exclusively with women, it seems logical to assume that his own emotions would have played a part in defining his role.

De Niro is always reluctant to discuss his characters and how he arrives at them. With Travis Bickle the reluctance borders on paranoia.

'There are underground things about yourself that you don't want to discuss,' he said obliquely when asked about Travis. 'Somehow these things are better expressed on paper or on film.'

The pain and torment that De Niro endures on screen as Travis appear to go beyond simply acting. Any therapist would confirm that to understand the pain and play it so convincingly De Niro would have had to have endured at least some of it. Travis Bickle is plainly the grown-up version of the boy from Greenwich Village, the boy who couldn't even go home to his father, and had no wish to turn to the man living with his mother. De Niro's cryptic comments certainly suggest that there are many hidden and tortuous depths to Travis Bickle.

Schrader had partly based his story on Arthur Bremer, the psychopath who stalked and finally shot Alabama Governor George Wallace in 1972. The Secret Service have since come up with a psychological profile of a would-be assassin which they refer to as 'the Bremer type'. To prepare for playing the role of Travis Bickle, De Niro had Schrader read Bremer's diary into a tape recorder. He would then play the tape over and over again. Schrader is at pains to point out that the Bremer diaries were published after he had written the script. De Niro also created his own costume for Travis, but this time the king of the thrift shops went to another source – he borrowed clothes from Schrader himself.

Apart from the clothes and the Bremer diaries, De Niro felt he had to earn the right to play Travis. He acquired a probationary taxi driver's licence, had his fingerprints taken by the police as the law required, and drove a cab on the New York streets for several weeks. Despite money not being important he managed to make 100 dollars a week, including tips. No one recognised him except a fellow actor who had innocently flagged down his cab.

'Jesus,' said the actor, according to Martin Scorsese, who tells the story with glee, 'you won the Oscar and now you're driving a cab again.' De

Niro explained that he was only doing research, to which his fellow thespian replied, 'It's okay, Bobby, I've been there too.' Whether he believed him or not, his former colleague gave De Niro a dollar tip for his trouble!

One of the problems in casting the film, according to Julia Phillips, came in choosing the right actress to play Betsy, Travis's obscure object of desire. Almost every actress in Hollywood had been seen, and the favourite was *Charlie's Angel* star Farrah Fawcett. Scorsese however went for Cybill Shepherd, a cool blonde and former top model who had made her name in Peter Bogdanovich movies.

In her book Phillips has accused Scorsese of misogyny in casting Shepherd. She says he fell into the classic sterotypical trap of an Italian-American male falling for a cute WASP blonde. The result, according to Phillips, was disastrous for all concerned. De Niro and Shepherd did not get on; he in particular allegedly disliked her intensely. Scorsese, says Phillips, had to give her line readings to get the performance he wanted. Phillips even accuses Scorsese of deliberately choosing unflattering shots of Shepherd and leaving them in when he came to cut the film.

The casting of Iris, the pre-teen hooker, also proved to be a major headache. Scorsese wanted Jodie Foster for the movie. Foster was as big a child star then as she is an adult star now. She was twelve and a half years old at the time, exactly the same age as Iris in the film, and had made her name in a series of children's movies like *Freaky Friday* for Disney and Alan Parker's *Bugsy Malone*. Initially she was not keen to play the role, even though she recognised it as a great part. She was concerned about what her friends might say. Her mother, who at that time played a much more active role in her career, had no such qualms. However, the Los Angeles Welfare Board, which is charged with looking after the morals of young actors, was not convinced. Brandy Foster was willing to take them on.

'I was determined to win,' she said later. 'Here was some board trying to tell me what was too adult for my own daughter.' Given that her daughter's first acting job was having her bikini bottom playfully pulled down by a dog in a Coppertone ad at the age of three, Mrs Foster plainly had been over this particular course before. The Welfare Board found they had picked a formidable opponent.

Eventually a compromise was reached in which Foster would be replaced in the more sexually explicit scenes by a body double – in this case her 20-year-old sister, Connie. Then, before she was able to join the crew in New York, there was a four-hour interview with a court-appointed child psychologist who had to rule that she was stable enough to take the part.

'There was a welfare worker on the set every day,' Foster told the *New York Times*. 'She saw the daily rushes of the scenes and made sure I wasn't on the set when Robert De Niro said a dirty word. Actually I think the only thing that could have had a bad effect on me was the blood in the shooting scene.

'It was really neat though,' she added with relish. 'It was red sugary stuff and they used Styrofoam for bones. And a pump to make the blood gush out of a man's arm when his hand was shot off.'

Foster also contributed a great deal to the morale of the shoot. One of the high spots came when she perfected an impression of De Niro as Travis. Martin Scorsese was highly amused and had it filmed and sent to his star. De Niro's response is not recorded.

The special effects that so impressed Jodie Foster in the final bloodbath were again the work of make-up man Dick Smith, who collaborated extensively with De Niro, as he had on *The Godfather Part II*, to make the scene look as authentic as possible.

Scorsese also cast himself in the film. He plays the man in the back of Bickle's cab who contributes a homicidal rant about what he would like to do to his unfaithful wife. He appears in by accident. His original choice for the role, George Memmoli, who started the pool-hall fight in *Mean Streets*, was unavailable after injuring himself in a stunt on another movie. Scorsese stepped in and found himself sharing one of the most powerful scenes in the film with De Niro.

'I learned a lot from Bob in that scene,' he admits. 'I remember saying the line "Put down the flag, put down the flag." De Niro said: "No, make me put it down." And Bobby wasn't going to put that flag down until he was convinced that I meant it. And then I understood. His move had to be a certain way and if he didn't feel it the move wasn't going to be right. For me, it was a pretty terrifying scene to do.'

There were other lessons to be learned for both De Niro and Scorsese in *Taxi Driver*. In the most famous scene in the film, the one that will be shown for years to come in Scorsese and De Niro retrospectives, Travis contemplates his arsenal before beginning his rampage. He is wearing faded combat fatigues and has designed a complicated holster contraption which will allow him to draw and fire even faster. He is surveying his handiwork in a full-length mirror.

'You talking to me,' he says as he spins and draws on a non-existent opponent. 'Are you talking to me!' he continues, savouring the moment. 'Ain't nobody else here so you must be talking to me.'

Robert De Niro: Untouchable

It is a picture of a man on the brink of the abyss which is both chilling and comical. It has been imitated by any number of impressionists. Michael J. Fox borrowed it in *Back to the Future III* and even Robin Williams's genie does a Travis Bickle in *Aladdin*. But the moment is entirely the creation of De Niro. Paul Schrader's script simply says, 'Travis looks in the mirror.' De Niro experimented with various line readings and Scorsese rolled the camera. It is lightning in a bottle, a moment of genuine movie magic. It was also a technique that De Niro would come to employ in later years when he would give reading after reading in search of the one that felt most truthful.

Taxi Driver had become a personal project for both De Niro and Scorsese. Although, as written, Travis is a mid-Westerner, both the actor and the director identified very closely with him. Scorsese went much further stylistically in this film than in any of his previous movies. Travis is an outsider and Scorsese reinforced this by story-boarding the film so that whenever he is in his cab or when other people are talking to him, Travis is in the frame by himself. Although he is in almost every shot of the film, he still exists in his own space as if it were a world of his own.

'The whole film is very much based on the impressions I have as a result of growing up in New York and living in the city,' says Scorsese. 'There's a shot where the camera is mounted on the hood of the taxi and it drives past the sign 'Fascination' which is just down from my office. It's that idea of being fascinated, of this avenging angel floating through the streets of the city, that represents all cities for me. The overall idea was to make it a cross between a Gothic horror and the *New York Daily News*.'

Although *Taxi Driver* was destined to become a cinematic oxymoron, an instant classic, it continued to be dogged by bad luck and misfortune. Julia Phillips remembers that the first try-out before a preview audience was a complete disaster. The film had been edited along the same lines as Schrader's script and was not playing well. One of the biggest problems came in the final scene in which Betsy and Travis meet again. She asks how he is and he says he doesn't get headaches any more. According to Phillips, that line – with the notion that mass murder can act as an analgesic – always received big but unintentional laughs, as did many others in the film. Scorsese recut the film again and again until finally he came up with a version that ignored continuity in favour of driving the story along.

Columbia Pictures had backed the film providing it was made for under $2 million. The final budget was around $1.3 million, but even so the studio was not prepared to embrace the film enthusiastically. They decided to open it in a low-profile Westwood art-house cinema in Los Angeles, much to Phillips's annoyance. The studio was queasy about the level of violence in the film, especially in Travis's final bloodbath. They were not the only ones to be concerned. The MPAA, which oversees America's film classification system, was also concerned, partly because of the violence and partly because of the presence of Foster. They wanted to give the film an 'X' rating, which would have been the kiss of death since no major theatre chain would book an 'X' film as a matter of policy. In the end Scorsese received an acceptable rating by the simple expedient of using a filter in the final sequence so that the blood did not appear so red on screen. One other stumbling block, the sound of Bickle's zipper being pulled down as an invitation to sex with Foster, was left uncut in the American version but cut from the British release.

When the film finally opened audiences loved it. Much to Scorsese's distress they cheered and applauded when Travis embarked on his orgy of destruction.

'I was shocked by the way the audiences took the violence,' he admits. 'Previously I'd been surprised by the audience reaction to *The Wild Bunch* which I first saw in a Warner Brothers screening room and loved. But a week later I took some friends to see it in a theatre and it was as if the violence became an extension of the audience and vice versa. I don't think it was all approval, some of it must have been revulsion.

'I saw *Taxi Driver* once in a theatre, on opening night, and everyone was yelling and screaming at the final shoot-out. When I made it I didn't intend to have the audience react with that feeling, 'Yes, do it. Let's go out and kill!' The idea was to create a violent catharsis so that they'd find themselves saying, 'Yes, kill'; and then afterwards realize, 'My God, no' – like some strange Californian therapy session. That was the instinct I went with but it was scary to hear what happens with the audience.'

De Niro remembers the shooting of those scenes as providing an entirely different catharsis. He and Scorsese were by this time developing a close relationship on set, and their shared off-beat sense of humour was manifesting itself.

'I once told Marty we should put together a movie of our out-takes,' says De Niro. 'For example, there are a lot of out-takes from *Taxi Driver* that I would use. When we were shooting that terrible bloody scene, ironically funny things happened.

'That wholesale slaughter scene at the end of the picture took us about four or five takes to shoot. Things went wrong technically. There are a lot of special effects and with those things something always goes wrong. You have this sort of very serious, dramatic kind of carnage going on and all of a sudden somebody drops something or the machinery breaks down. It just blows the whole thing and it turns out to be funny.

'Oddly enough in that sort of scene, I guess it's because it's so gruesome, everybody's ready to laugh. There was a lot of laughing and joking during the shooting between takes. I remember that. It was a lighter period even though the material was very heavy.

'The whole alienation thing probably affected people,' he says, addressing the film seriously. 'That's the thing with movies. You do them in a personal way and people are affected and you never know why.'

Taxi Driver was a watershed in the relationship between De Niro and Scorsese. With *Mean Streets* De Niro had found a soulmate, someone who shared his view of the world. At that stage Scorsese was definitely in charge, but with *Taxi Driver* the balance of power began to shift. De Niro felt confident enough to make suggestions; most of the characterisation of Travis Bickle derives entirely from his efforts and his ideas. Scorsese plainly respected De Niro's talent, and by leaving his star to himself in his trailer he was giving him the space he needed to play a difficult role, ceding control to him. Over the six other films they would make together the balance of power would swing back and forth. By *Raging Bull* and *King of Comedy* De Niro was plainly the dominant partner, coaxing and cajoling Scorsese. However, by the time of their later movies the collaboration would develop into an almost symbiotic relationship of two men who are closer than brothers.

Scorsese describes *Taxi Driver* as a labour of love for him, for De Niro, and for Schrader. But speaking to the *New York Times* before the film's release, he revealed a darker reason for making the film. A priest who is a close personal friend of the director saw the film and described it as 'too much Good Friday and not enough Easter Sunday'. With hindsight Scorsese would probably have to agree.

'I had to make that movie,' he said. 'Not so much because of the social statement that it makes but because of its feeling about things, including things I don't like to admit about myself. It's like when you're in therapy and the doctor takes a videotape of the session and then shows it to you. "Notice how you reacted to that question?" he says. "See how defensive you are?" Well, I'm not videotaping my life, but in a way I am trying to put certain things about myself on a canvas.

'I know this guy, Travis. I've had the feelings he has and those feelings have to be explored, taken out, and examined. I know the feeling of rejection that Travis feels, of not being able to make relationships survive. I know the killing feeling, the feeling of really being angry.'

Someone else shared Scorsese's feelings. But for John Hinckley, some five years later, *Taxi Driver* would not be a catharsis, it would be a signpost.

11 The Goodbye Boy

WHILE DE NIRO WAS roaming the seamier side of New York's dark underbelly in *Taxi Driver*, director Mike Nichols was engaged in a much lighter venture. Nichols, a sophisticated and intellectual director, had made six movies by the summer of 1975. They ranged from the hugely successful *The Graduate* to the quirky *Catch 22* with oddities like *The Day of the Dolphin* thrown in. His most recent film, *The Fortune*, had starred Warren Beatty and Jack Nicholson and had been described by one reviewer, much to Nichols' embarrassment, as 'the best motion picture comedy of the past 25 years'. That is an exaggeration, of course, but there is no getting away from the fact that Nichols was then, and is still, perceived by the studios to be a class act.

Nichols was preparing an original screenplay by Neil Simon. Few American comedy writers have been as consistently funny or as consistently successful as the Bronx-born playwright. Shows like *Barefoot in the Park*, *The Odd Couple* and *The Sunshine Boys* were major hits on Broadway and in the cinema. His original scripts like *The Heartbreak Kid* and *Murder by Death!* had met with similar success.

The creative teaming of Mike Nichols and Neil Simon seemed like a marriage made in heaven. Already producers were rubbing their hands with glee at the prospect.

The film they were preparing was an original screenplay from Simon called *Bogart Slept Here*. It was originally titled *Clark Gable Slept Here* but the title was changed because of the Gable and Lombard biopic that was also going into production. It would star his wife, the actress Marsha Mason, and Robert De Niro. On paper the film sounded like vintage Simon, and everyone believed it was simply a matter of sitting back and waiting for the money to roll in.

In June 1975, while he was still promoting *The Fortune*, Nichols was waxing lyrical to the *New York Times* about his enthusiasm for *Bogart*

Slept Here. Unlike a lot of Simon's work it was not, Nichols insisted, 'a wisecrack comedy'.

'The movie's about a slightly ageing off-Broadway actor with a wife who loves him and two little kids,' Nichols told the *Times.* 'He is struggling in New York. He is put in a movie and goes on struggling and then the movie comes out and all of a sudden he becomes a big star. Teenagers are ringing his door-bell. The subtitle of this movie could be "Getting there is all the fun".'

Nichols also stressed that the film was not about Dustin Hoffman, who had become a star overnight after appearing in *The Graduate.* Although he conceded that it was about an actor's problem, he said there were things in the script which had also happened to him and to Neil Simon as well as to Dustin Hoffman.

Bogart Slept Here began with the usual studio ballyhoo. But within two weeks of the film starting shooting things had turned very sour, and neither Nichols nor Simon and De Niro would be feeling particularly bullish about the turn of events.

For the first time in his life De Niro had been sacked from a film. The official reason given by Nichols was 'artistic differences,' but that seems to have been little more than a face-saving exercise. Neil Simon went further, telling reporters that 'Robert De Niro is a very intense actor. He doesn't play joy very well.' The more likely reason is that De Niro's punishing schedule in the past eighteen months, in which he had filmed *The Godfather Part II, 1900, Taxi Driver* and now *Bogart Slept Here,* had taken its toll, manifesting itself in a sub-par performance. De Niro also did not get along with Marsha Mason, and since Neil Simon has complete control over all of his films, including approval of the director and star, it seems pretty clear that he delivered an ultimatum to Nichols. The final factor in the equation may have been the back-to-back flops of *The Day of the Dolphin* and *The Fortune* – 'the best motion picture comedy of the last 25 years'. Nichols may have felt under pressure to play safe, to minimise the risk and give in to the playwright. Whatever the reason, it was De Niro's first taste of Hollywood power being wielded absolutely.

He has never spoken of this blot on his career other than to point out that the studio tried to get out of paying him for his work. He made sure he was paid and then moved on.

Whoever was responsible for the final decision, De Niro was out, though it beggars belief that he should ever have been in it the first place. De Niro's comedy experience was limited to the broad anarchic satire of *Greetings* and *Hi, Mom!,* nothing like the dry verbal by-play of a Neil

Simon play. What in the world convinced Nichols and Simon that a 32-year-old whose best work had been playing borderline psychotics could possibly be convincing as 'a slightly ageing off-Broadway actor' with a wife and two kids? Nichols and Simon's decision turned out to be a costly one. It was also a very public embarrassment since large ads had been taken out in trade papers announcing that shooting had begun with De Niro and Mason. Production was shut down after only two weeks at a cost of hundreds of thousands of dollars. Candidates as a possible replacement for De Niro included James Caan, Richard Dreyfuss, Tony Lo Bianco, Jack Nicholson and ironically Dustin Hoffman. He had to turn it down because he was already committed to *Marathon Man*.

Finally the producers had no option but to abandon the film altogether. For the sake of completeness it should be pointed out that in its own way *Bogart Slept Here* does have its part to play in movie history. After De Niro had been fired, Richard Dreyfuss came in and read with Marsha Mason for a week. He didn't get the part but Neil Simon was so impressed with the chemistry between them that he wrote *The Goodbye Girl* specifically with the two actors in mind. The film was a huge hit and Dreyfuss won his only Best Actor Oscar to date.

De Niro meanwhile had gone into hiding. His agent, Harry Ufland, stressed that there was no problem with his young star. He would still be starting work on 3 November as scheduled on *The Last Tycoon*, and would then go on to do another film with Martin Scorsese, *New York, New York*.

De Niro had been preparing for *The Last Tycoon* while he was filming *Taxi Driver*. The film was based on an unfinished novel by Scott Fitzgerald about a fictional Hollywood studio boss, Monroe Stahr. Fitzgerald's story was a barely disguised attempt at fictionalising the exploits of MGM boss Irving Thalberg, the legendary wonder-boy producer who died tragically young. De Niro was to play Stahr.

The script was written by celebrated playwright Harold Pinter, who spent eighteen months working on the project, dealing with constant demands for rewrites from producer Sam Spiegel, who was genuinely, as far as Hollywood was concerned, 'the last tycoon'. Pinter was working from a summary put together by Edmund Wilson from scraps of paper and notes left behind by Fitzgerald.

Hollywood is not a community blessed with any sense of irony, so no one would have turned a hair at the prospect of De Niro being directed again by Mike Nichols after the *Bogart Slept Here* débâcle. As it happened, Spiegel had indeed hired Nichols to make the movie, but the director became bogged down in editing *The Fortune* and could not begin preparations on *The Last Tycoon* on time. In the end the directing chores were handled by veteran film-maker Elia Kazan. The man behind films like *On the Waterfront* had not made a mainstream film since *The Arrangement* in 1969. However, the 66-year-old director had the unqualified admiration of the rest of his cast, which included Jack Nicholson, Robert Mitchum, Ray Milland, Jeanne Moreau and two 'newcomers', Theresa Russell and Ingrid Boulting. In fact Boulting was not as much of a newcomer as Paramount claimed her to be – she had already had an unsuccessful career in British films as 'Ingrid Brett'.

As always, De Niro was throwing himself into his preparation for the role. First of all he read everything he could about Thalberg, and then he set out on another regimen of strict dieting. Thalberg was a frail man with a rheumatic heart who died at the age of 37. Kazan became alarmed at how thin his star was becoming as he strove once again to earn the right to play his character. Kazan tempered his concern with an unstinting admiration for the lengths to which the actor was going.

Veteran actor Ray Milland was the only member of the cast who had actually worked in Hollywood in the golden age in which the film is set.

'De Niro is very much like Thalberg,' he said. 'Very meek, very quiet, and very thin.'

For Martin Scorsese, who was still making *Taxi Driver*, De Niro's preparation for this upcoming role was another revelation about the way actors work.

'Harry Ufland – who was my agent as well as Bob's – came by the set one day while we were shooting *Taxi Driver*,' he recalls. 'Bob had a suit on. He was between takes checking out a suit for the wardrobe of *Last Tycoon*. Harry didn't recognise him. For twenty minutes Bob wasn't Travis Bickle any more. He had become Monroe Stahr. It was amazing.'

Kazan and De Niro hit it off immediately. De Niro was so enamoured of the 66-year-old director that he got several copies of Kazan's monograph on directing, which he had read in preparing for the film, and had the director autograph them. De Niro then handed the pamphlets out to friends and colleagues.

'I sometimes see him as a parent who doesn't quite approve of his children or what they are doing,' he said warmly, attributing to the director a father-figure status. 'He can't relate to it but he still loves them.'

Kazan was equally taken with De Niro. He knew that this role was vastly different from anything the actor had done up till now, and he was prepared to give him all the considerable help at his disposal.

'Bobby has never played an executive,' explained Kazan. 'He's never played an intellectual. He has never played a lover. I had to find that side of him; it was unexplored territory.'

'The interesting thing about him,' says De Niro of Monroe Stahr, 'is that he is able to combine the artistic side of movies with the financial side. Usually they're in conflict. The dialogue is very spare. Harold Pinter himself has the constraint that we keep talking about in reference to the character of Monroe Stahr. Kazan has more feeling; he's more Mediterranean. He's always trying to play against Pinter's restraint. I think that makes for an interesting tension.'

The Last Tycoon is also interesting in that it provides the only opportunity to contrast De Niro in a head-to-head encounter with Jack Nicholson, this at a time when De Niro was the only serious contender from his generation for Nicholson's crown. Both of their careers had effectively been kick-started by Roger Corman, but they had gone about building their subsequent reputations differently. De Niro wanted to be an actor and proved himself in the theatre; Nicholson wanted to be a star and had ignited the screen with luminous performances in films like *Easy Rider, Five Easy Pieces* and the previous year's *One Flew Over the Cuckoo's Nest*. Likewise, while De Niro had been ill at ease and truculent with the press, Nicholson had been Mr Gregarious, conducting his life quite happily in the media spotlight. The confrontation was given added spice by the fact that Spiegel had wanted Nicholson to play Monroe Stahr while Kazan had gone for De Niro. Kazan resisted pressure from Spiegel right up to the first day of shooting, but as a concession to his producer gave Nicholson little more than a cameo role as a Communist union organiser. Nicholson's scenes with De Niro are fascinating. It is almost as if Pinter knew of their respective positions in the pecking order and played on it.

Mr Hollywood and the Crown Prince eye each other warily throughout their tantalisingly brief scenes together. As studio boss and union negotiator they are supposed to be antagonists, but even the most naïve viewer can see that there appears to be another agenda here. Territories are being staked out as they circle each other like wolves in a pack trying to determine who will be the alpha male. Monroe Stahr may have youth and vitality on his side but Nicholson's character – Brimmer – has stealth and cunning on his. In the end he wins when he literally knocks Stahr cold.

The cost of making movies these days means we are never likely to see Robert De Niro and Jack Nicholson on the same screen again, which makes their confrontation in *The Last Tycoon* all the more intriguing. Nicholson would deliver another knock-out blow in a few years when a poll of American critics would name him their 'Star of the Eighties'. In second place, just one vote behind, was Robert De Niro.

The last time De Niro had tried to stretch himself, in *1900*, the results had been disastrous. *The Last Tycoon* was a much more sensible move. He gives a performance of great poignancy and dignity and adds an appealing air of mystery to the character of Monroe Stahr, but the film was not a success. Like Kazan himself, the film is intelligent, witty, and elegant. Elegance had very little place in American cinema in the seventies – a period characterised by rage, violence, and volatility. It was a film out of its time and as such never quite found the audience it deserved.

12 A Star is Born

AMERICAN CINEMA AUDIENCES GOT a taste of things to come in the early part of 1976. As they settled into their seats and began to plough their way through their popcorn, they were given an ominous warning of what would be in store for them in the months ahead.

The 60-second trailer for *Taxi Driver* contained no hint of the violence in the film. Instead it consisted of a close-up of De Niro's face as Travis Bickle, while a disembodied voice sonorously read out previous reviews extolling the actor's skills. The only hint of what they might expect when they saw the film was a caption on the screen which read 'The most controversial film you will ever see.'

Taxi Driver was about to arrive in America riding a tidal wave of controversy and praise in equal measure. It had been a sensation at the Cannes Film Festival in May, where it had been given a standing ovation by some audiences. In the end the film won the supreme accolade at Cannes, the coveted Golden Palm. But the decision was not a unanimous one. Traditionally the deliberations of the various Cannes Festival juries are as secretive as the voting of the College of Cardinals on the election of a new Pope. This year, however, the silence was not so much broken as shattered by jury chairman Tennessee Williams. Although he did not mention *Taxi Driver* by name – conventions can only be broken up to a point, it seems – no one was left in any doubt about which film Williams was referring to when he read the Riot Act to a generation of up-and-coming directors.

Williams accused them of making 'serious films without hope, some of which reflected a violence seldom seen before. We are well aware that this violence and hopelessness reflect the image of our society. However, we fear that violence breeds violence and that, instead of being a denunciation, it leads our society to an escalation of violence.'

These were comments that Scorsese and De Niro would have to deal with whenever *Taxi Driver* was mentioned.

De Niro's relations with the press, always tenuous, had become almost non-existent. He was never one to court the media, and by this stage the media were starting to get a little tired of the situation. Film reviewers continued to heap praise on his performances but feature writers, columnists and profile writers were starting to pepper their pieces with phrases like 'Garbo-like disdain', as one *New York Times* columnist described De Niro's approach to interviews. All this was like water off a duck's back as far as De Niro was concerned. Like most actors he was first and foremost concerned with pleasing himself and then the audience. The media came a long way down the list of priorities. His celebrated coolness with the press has prompted speculation that he has something to hide. The more likely explanation is that he has nothing to say. Owing to the legacy of his childhood he does not feel any great need to share his feelings with the world, just as he has no great need or desire for the approbation of the world. He does as he pleases, providing he pleases himself. Whatever De Niro wants to communicate to the world can be safely expressed within the confines of a proscenium arch or a cinema screen.

De Niro went to Cannes to promote the film and Europe seemed to have a relaxing effect on him, perhaps as a result of the happy times he had spent there backpacking as a younger man, or indeed the time spent preparing for his role in *The Godfather Part II*. He did say once during the trip, possibly thinking aloud, that the last time he had been in the south of France he had been hitch-hiking. It had never occurred to him, he claimed, that he would travel through life in any other way. In any event he was almost in gregarious mood as he held court at Cannes. Most of the American media were still banned, much to their chagrin, although he was happy to speak to the European press. If the Americans were miffed at their exclusion, they were even more miffed about missing the big story. Robert De Niro had got married.

The actor had maintained a strict cordon of fiercely protective secrecy around his private life, as he still does. But in April 1976 he married actress and singer Diahnne Abbott. The ceremony, at the New York Ethical Culture Society, was attended by friends past and present. The guests included Scorsese, Paul Schrader, John Hancock, Shelley Winters, Julie Bovasso, Sally Kirkland and Harvey Keitel. The marriage could not have been a surprise to those who knew him, for he and Abbott had lived together for several years since just after he made *Mean Streets*. Although she did not mention her by name, Shelley Winters spoke warmly of her and the effect she had on De Niro in that first *New York Times* profile back in 1973.

'Was Bobby's apartment clean when you interviewed him?' she had asked Guy Flatley. 'It was? Then she must have cleaned it up for him. She's a beautiful girl and just right for Bobby because she allows him to concentrate on his work.'

De Niro had been concentrating on his work for the better part of two years non-stop. Now it was time for play, and although he was publicising *Taxi Driver*, Cannes would be something of a honeymoon for De Niro and his new bride. Abbott has a small part in the film – she plays the cashier in the ticket booth of the porno theatre to which Travis takes Betsy on a disastrous date. She was also a Greenwich Village native, having grown up around Washington Square Park not far from Bleecker Street where De Niro first lived. They met while she was a waitress trying to make her way in the world as a singer and he was a struggling actor. Abbott was and is a great beauty, while De Niro was still a quiet and gangly young man. The one thing they had in common was a supreme belief in his talent, although neither of them ever expected that he would be a star.

There is no disguising the fact that De Niro has had a fondness for black women over the years. Diahnne Abbott was described at the time as 'a mulatto'. In *The Last Tycoon* De Niro had just finished playing Monroe Stahr, the sort of studio boss who would not only have frowned on one of his stars being involved in a mixed-race marriage but would have actively discouraged it.

But De Niro does not give a fig for prejudice.

'I never thought it took a particular courage marrying a girl who is not white,' he told British reporters. 'Ten years ago maybe,' he conceded. 'Ten years ago this marriage couldn't have happened. When poor Lennie Hayton married Lena Horne he actually lost his job as musical director at MGM. But the studios don't work like that any more and I don't expect any trouble. I don't think about it at all. No one has said anything to me and if they thought about it they certainly didn't say it. Even if they did I wouldn't listen to them.

'Diahnne has beautiful features and we will have great-looking kids. I don't see why they should have any problems.'

Diahnne Abbott came with a ready-made family. She had a young daughter, Drina, from a previous marriage, and De Niro agreed formally to adopt her. Abbott also came with her own career, and she continued to pursue it both as a singer and actress while they were together.

By the time *Taxi Driver* opened at Cannes, De Niro was on his way to becoming the male star of the year. He had been obliged to abandon all notions of proving himself on stage as an actor – that time was past. Like it or not he was now a star. But, his disdain for the media apart, he did not behave like one.

He had moved to Hollywood but was living in a three-bedroomed house that was rented rather than owned. Likewise he drove a good-looking car, but that too was leased, he claimed, for tax purposes. His wardrobe was not packed with designer clothes. He owned very few clothes, and most of them were suits that had come from the wardrobes of films he had appeared in. The memory of a financially straitened childhood would shape his attitude to money for a long time. The screenwriter James Toback, for example, recalls sharing a taxi every day with De Niro when they were living in New York two years earlier. Toback had written a movie called *The Gambler* which was to be directed by Karel Reisz. De Niro wanted the title role and everyone thought he should get it. Everyone, that is, except Karel Reisz. Just as he had done in *The Godfather*, De Niro lost another role to James Caan. Toback's abiding memory of those cab rides is that every day De Niro would insist on paying, but would also insist on getting a receipt from the cabbie in order to keep track of his expenses.

De Niro must have sensed a breathing space at this point in his career, rather like that moment of uncanny stillness in Apollo space launches when the thrusters have ignited but the giant Titan rocket has yet to climb into the air and clear the gantry. Whether he was consciously aware of it or not, Cannes provided a window of opportunity through which he could take stock of his situation, a pressure-free moment that he would not have again for a long time to come.

'If it were all to go,' he says, explaining his lack of material goods, 'if I were to lose everything and not be able to work, I don't think I would be hung up with possessions. I have seen too many people overstep themselves in this business. When something bad hits them there is nothing they can do about it, but they have put their money into possessions that they don't really need.

'What I have learned and believe is that if you just keep on at doing what you want to do then you achieve something. They call me hot in Hollywood today but if that changes then I can go back to trying, just like I did when I was twenty and starting out in life. Except that then I needed an analyst to help me understand myself and now I don't.'

De Niro plainly claims to have worked out his problems, so perhaps Travis Bickle was a catharsis after all. But we may have to take his claims with a pinch of salt. One source who knows him well suggests that at this stage his deep-seated resentment of his mother's boyfriends had not even been confronted, far less dealt with.

Cannes gave De Niro a taste of the rough along with the smooth. Although he was being fêted for his work in the Scorsese movie, *1900*, the film he had made for Bernardo Bertolucci almost two years previously, had also opened. The response to the film's five hours and twenty minutes was one of at best indifference and at worst open hostility. Without a trace of irony, Bertolucci would later describe this version as 'a very good first cut'. For his part De Niro must have been counting his blessings that the post-production process had taken so long that he was able to establish himself in other work in the meantime. *1900* was a risk, and he conceded that risks have to be taken.

'I knew at the beginning that if I kept at it I would make it as an actor,' he went on. 'I never became disillusioned. I knew that if I kept at it I would at least make a living. If you are halfway decent at what you do, by the laws of averages in five or ten years you will make enough money to do what you want to do. That point came about three years ago. I haven't made as much money yet as you might think but of course it's on the way.

'If you are never going to try anything then you are never going to be disappointed, but I prefer to be a gambler. If you don't throw you'll never know, which is why I was maybe more often unemployed than employed.'

De Niro was indeed the hot ticket in Hollywood. One Oscar was already in his display case and his contemporaries were queueing up to pat him on the back. Directors were singing his praises, and even Jack Nicholson and Marlon Brando had marked him as a force to be reckoned with. For his part De Niro was not letting it turn his head.

'I find it flattering but I don't want to be a movie actor in the old-fashioned sense of the word. A Hollywood star is death as far as acting is concerned. You just end up playing the same part all the time and I happen to find it easy to say no. The atmosphere of money and status can make you lose your sense of why you are doing it. I don't need too much money anyway.

'I was offered a great deal of money to appear in one production but I refused. It wasn't right for me. I don't need money that badly. The thing is to press ahead and have fun doing work that is truthful and through which I can express myself.'

De Niro was in an uncharacteristically expansive mood as he sat at Columbia Pictures' expense in the rich man's playground of Eden Roc in the south of France. It would be a long time before he would relax that much with the press again. It was almost as if he knew that international stardom was just around the corner and he was making the most of his peace and quiet while he could.

He knew that he was about to lose his anonymity. He knew that whatever moments he had to himself from now on would have to be cherished. De Niro was well and truly on the Hollywood treadmill and his career was plotted out for the next two years, which he would spend working with Martin Scorsese. He was already taking saxophone lessons for his next film, *New York, New York*, and after finally convincing Scorsese that the autobiography of a failed boxer would make a good movie he was getting into preliminary training for the role of his career. He must also have known that, even while he was in France, his face was being screened in close-up in picture theatres across America, and he openly pondered that loss of innocence.

'I'm a New Yorker and I like to walk around and maybe get drunk once in a while without everyone knowing who I am,' he mused, although the notion of someone as controlled as De Niro allowing himself to get drunk in public is a bizarre one. It seems likely that he was being uncommonly accommodating in giving the press a decent line. 'I can still do that, but you know the day is coming when I won't be able to go into a New York bar and get drunk and get carried home without it being in the newspapers the next day.

'You just don't appreciate such a profound privilege as anonymity until you are about to lose it.'

De Niro's anonymity was not so much to be lost as to totally evaporate in the intense heat of the media spotlight that *Taxi Driver* would bring to bear.

America in the mid-seventies was at the heart of yet another debate on the place of the cinema as a guardian of the nation's morals. *Taxi Driver* was seized by both sides. Those who argued for greater censorship saw it as little more than an abomination, with the former seminarian Scorsese the nearest thing to the Antichrist in human form. Those who argued for greater liberalism hailed the film – correctly – as a masterpiece that proved what could be done when artists were allowed the freedom to create great work.

The debate would rage on for as long as the film ran, heightened by its problems with the classification authorities in the United States and in Britain. But ultimately the film was seen for what it was – a modern masterpiece in which Scorsese and De Niro once again set the standard for modern American cinema. The Cannes jury, although equivocal, were merely the first to heap honours on the film.

In *Newsweek* De Niro was described as 'the most remarkable young actor of the American screen'. In the *New Yorker* Pauline Kael placed him in exalted company when she said, 'Robert De Niro is in almost every frame; thin-faced, as handsome as Robert Taylor one moment and cagey like Cagney the next.' Roger Ebert, making the inevitable comparison, said, 'Robert De Niro, as Travis Bickle, is as good as Brando at suggesting emotions even while veiling them from us.'

As the award season drew round once again *Taxi Driver* was a hot if contentious favourite for most of the major trophies. De Niro was certain, it was argued, to get at least a Best Actor nomination, and even go one better than his previous Best Supporting Actor win. To add to his favouritism he was the comfortable winner of his second New York Critics Circle Award, this time for Best Actor.

The Academy Awards beckoned, but the performance that with hindsight is seen as one of the cinema's best ever would be overshadowed by a force of nature.

13 So Good They Named It Twice

THE ODDS IN THE 1976 Academy Awards race changed dramatically on the morning of 14 January 1977. The Oscars are awarded retrospectively, so that the ceremony held on the last Monday in March of one year honours films made in the previous year.

The Best Actor nominees that year were De Niro, with his first nomination in the blue riband acting category, for *Taxi Driver*, a previously unknown bit-part actor called Sylvester Stallone for *Rocky*, the Italian Giancarlo Giannini for *Seven Beauties*, and Peter Finch and William Holden for *Network*. Although *Network* and *Rocky* were front-runners with ten nominations each, it was generally agreed to be one of the most competitive Oscar races in years.

De Niro went into the Academy Award race with another New York Critics award behind him. His portrayal of Travis Bickle also received the nod from the Los Angeles critics and the National Society of Film Critics. His main rival was deemed to be Peter Finch, who was nominated in the Best Actor category because he refused to accept that his demented newsman Howard Beale was a supporting player in Paddy Chayevsky's satire on television news. Beale's catchphrase, 'I'm mad as hell and I'm not going to take it any more', swept through the chattering classes and he seemed to be the popular choice. Finch desperately wanted to win the Oscar and had given close to 300 interviews promoting the film and his performance. De Niro meanwhile had adopted the moral high ground and had not pushed himself forward.

Comparing two different performances by two different actors is a pointless exercise, but there is no doubt which of the two has been the more important and the more enduring. However, Finch's punishing interview schedule was winning over the hearts and minds of the Academy voters. On 14 January he was at the Beverly Hills Hotel to give another interview, this time a live insert into the ABC network's *Good Morning*

America, when he dropped dead of a massive heart attack in the hotel lobby. Finch's Oscar was assured almost before he hit the ground.

No one can be nominated posthumously for an Academy Award. In Finch's case the nomination ballots were already out and being returned, so there was nothing in the rules to prevent his name going on to the final ballot. On the night, as expected, actress Liv Ullman read out Peter Finch's name, and after a brief introduction from Chayevsky his widow Eletha stepped forward to receive the trophy.

So De Niro went unrewarded for one of the great performances in the American cinema. His only consolation may have been that he could have been a two-time loser. Another Oscar hopeful that year was Hal Ashby's *Bound for Glory*, a big-budget biopic of the folk singer Woody Guthrie. De Niro was one of several actors who turned down the role before it was eventually taken by David Carradine.

Meanwhile De Niro had been busying himself with yet another role for Martin Scorsese, this time in the musical *New York, New York* in which he would star opposite Liza Minnelli. Of the three of them, only Minnelli, an Oscar winner for *Cabaret*, would appear to have been an obvious choice for a musical. Scorsese, however, desperately wanted to do the movie. When producer Irwin Winkler announced that he was putting the film into production, Scorsese called his agent Harry Ufland and asked him to lobby on his behalf for him to direct the picture. For Scorsese it would be an evocation of his days back in New York when his parents would take him to ballrooms and dance halls like the Paramount and the Capital. The young Scorsese – he was born in 1942 – grew up to the sounds of Paul Whiteman, Xavier Cugat and Louis Prima.

New York, New York is the story of saxophonist Jimmy Doyle and vocalist Francine Evans. Jimmy is a tormented and frustrated musician who wants to come up with a new sound, ' a major chord', while Francine wants to be simply the best singer of her day. Their relationship is torrid and stormy. They cannot live with each other and they can barely live apart. They are each other's muse, and they do finally create one great song – provided in the movie by Kander and Ebb's title song – 'New York, New York'. But having created one moment of magic they cannot stay together and ultimately go their separate ways.

New York, New York was being hyped as one of the big hits of the year even before the cameras turned. The combination of the hottest male star in Hollywood and the greatest popular singer of her generation was considered to be money in the bank. If that were not enough, they were also shooting the movie at MGM, where Minnelli's mother Judy Garland had her greatest triumphs. For De Niro and Scorsese too the omens seemed right. Their friendship was growing, their artistic collaboration becoming even more intense – other actors would accuse De Niro of 'hogging' the director and vice versa – and both their wives were pregnant. (Julia Cameron's pregnancy was more advanced than Diahnne Abbott's. She was able to make a brief cameo in the movie singing 'Honeysuckle Rose'.)

Right from the start *New York, New York* was simply an accident waiting to happen. The opening scene, in which Jimmy spends ages trying to convince Francine to dance with him at a VJ Day celebration, took forever to film. There was no script to speak of. The actors were improvising everything and the scene took eight days to shoot, with thousands of extras waiting for hours while De Niro, Scorsese and Minnelli worked out what would happen next. One woman who worked on the film talks of extras being called at seven in the morning and waiting around until the scene was finally shot after midnight.

Screenwriter Mardik Martin, who had worked with Scorsese and De Niro on *Mean Streets*, knew that the film had serious problems. He could not come up with a satisfactory ending and spent many nights desperately writing material that was to be shot the following day. De Niro also knew that all was not well very early on in the production.

'They were having a lot of trouble with the script from the very beginning,' he remembers. 'A lot of time was spent on the script. Marty and Liza and I would get together and work on it. We'd all be trying to rectify things which were just not working. We were trying to shape it but because of the improvisation we were always trying to build on what had been shot before or to fit a scene in if we shot out of sequence. I think Marty would agree with me that you have to work those things out before you do it.

'It has to be in the script beforehand. You don't want to waste time figuring it out because it's very costly as you are shooting. We had a schedule and we were slowly getting close to the time where we had to finish the film. So we started before we really had the script in shape and did a lot of improvising.'

New York, New York was falling victim to the old maxim that 'if it ain't on the page, it ain't on the stage'. But Scorsese says there was another reason – good old honest-to-goodness hubris.

'By the time we started *New York, New York*, *Taxi Driver* came out and *Mean Streets* had had some nice reviews, and *Alice Doesn't Live Here Any More* had had nice reviews. Ellen Burstyn had won an Oscar for *Alice* and Bobby had won for *Godfather II*. *Taxi Driver* won the grand prize at Cannes and we started to get cocky,' he recalls. 'So throw away the script! We improvised a lot and we shot a lot of film.

'We got big heads and we felt that no script was good enough. For example, we shot for weeks on the opening scene where De Niro picks up Liza Minnelli and the original cut of this alone ran one hour. This was before *Heaven's Gate* when it was a case of giving the director everything he wanted – two brilliant actors, a thousand extras behind them, and ending up with a one-hour sequence.'

De Niro and Scorsese would spend long periods closeted together in intense discussion. Scorsese would always refuse to reveal to outsiders what had been discussed. One reporter visiting the set was told : 'The real stuff between Bob and me is private. Bob talks to me in private. He needs a lot of time. We need a lot of time.' It is moments like these which contribute to the perception that De Niro and Scorsese exist only for each other when they are shooting. De Niro monopolises Scorsese with his constant questions and Scorsese reciprocates by giving him the undivided attention that he seems to crave from a director.

On one occasion in the film, Jimmy Doyle breaks down in a fit of drunken fury and remorse at a night-club. De Niro had downed a few shots of bourbon to get ready for the role. Just before Scorsese could say 'action' he got up, put his arms out perpendicular to his sides and started spinning furiously like a top – it was a technique he had used before to make himself sick in *Bang the Drum Slowly*. By the time the cameras were turning over De Niro had stopped spinning and could then blunder drunkenly onto the night-club set. The crew burst into spontaneous applause when the scene was finished. Scorsese was ecstatic, but De Niro rushed over to him and there was another hurried, whispered conversation. Scorsese stopped applauding and told the crew they were going for another take.

De Niro cannot perform in a vacuum; he needs the co-operation of other actors. He will frequently do outrageous things to provoke his co-stars. This may discomfit them but it will give him the reaction he needs to fuel his performance. One man who has had a close insight into how De Niro works is his stand-in, Jon Cutler. He was on the set of *New York, New York* watching De Niro responding to a piano player who was supposed to be up-staging him as Jimmy Doyle. Cutler instinctively made an angry face which De Niro, the great observer, spotted out of the corner of his eye. He followed his stand-in to his dressing room and said: 'Jon, that piano player's no actor. Could you come back and react to me? I can't get anything off that guy.'

Cutler had more opportunity than most to study De Niro at close quarters; they had been together since *Bang the Drum Slowly*. It was on this film that he noticed something remarkable about the man for who he was deputising.

'I watched Bob at first off-camera from the sidelines,' he told the *New York Times*. 'He was totally unimpressive. Then, later on during the scene where he sits on his bed too weak to pull on his pants, I walked closer to the camera. Finally I was sitting under the camera, on the crab dolly. Crouching under the lens I discovered a fascinating fact. If I leaned my head three feet away from the lens I didn't see much coming out of De Niro. He looked boring. But if I put my head under the lens I was watching a genius. He was only brilliant when I sat under the lens. Bob is a guy the camera loves.'

Cutler has put his finger on the secret of De Niro's screen success. As with Gary Cooper or Katharine Hepburn or Marlene Dietrich, the camera is conducting a love affair with him on screen. The natural intensity of his performance is rendered luminous by the lens, and even unappealing characters like Travis Bickle or Jimmy Doyle are never less than fascinating. This love affair with the camera would, according to Cutler, have made De Niro a star in any era.

'It's spooky how much time he spends without speaking,' he said. 'Bobby is such a quiet actor. He's truly non-verbal. He would have been a great silent movie star.'

De Niro wasn't simply preparing to play Jimmy Doyle by drinking bourbon and spinning like a child in a playground. He had spent a long time with veteran swing musician Georgie Auld, who was teaching him the rudiments of saxophone playing. Even Georgie Auld was feeling the pressure, but only from his pupil's voracious appetite for information. Auld had led his own band and had played with Count Basie, Benny Goodman, Artie Shaw and Bunny Berrigan. But he had never come across anyone quite like Robert De Niro. He did once refer to him as a 'pain in the ass' on account of his constant questioning but there is no doubting his admiration for his pupil.

'It's incredible the way he learned,' Auld told the *New York Times*. 'I'll teach him something on a Friday – a difficult passage – and by Monday morning that son of a gun has learned it, he's got it down cold. He's got a little hideaway, and he practices until midnight. The kid plays a good tenor sax, and I mean it, and he learned it all in three months.'

For De Niro it was once again all about earning the right to play Jimmy Doyle. Not a note of his was heard on the final soundtrack – that was all recorded by Auld – but De Niro felt he had at least to understand Auld's arcane skills.

'My job is to create the feeling that I'm playing,' he told the *Times*. 'I play the same stuff that's in the movie. I have to synch it to what Georgie plays. It took a while to learn. I can't read music but I got a horn and Georgie taught me to play phonetically. I've learned phrasing and breathing the way Georgie does it.'

His new skill plainly tickled De Niro, and he was proud of the calluses on his thumb which he developed learning to play like Georgie Auld. He may like to effect an image of cool disdain, but months later, when the film was behind him, he was still offering, not entirely in jest, to play 'Tenderly' for journalists. No one appears to have taken him up on the offer.

Not all the problems on *New York, New York* were concerned with the script and the spiralling budget – the final cost was just over $9 million, some $2 million over budget, and the film finished seven weeks behind schedule. There were reports of cocaine use on the set and rumours were growing of an affair between Minnelli and Scorsese. The director's pregnant wife, Julia Cameron, was on the set constantly, and relations between her and everyone else were decidedly strained. Cameron would later cite her husband's drug use and his affair with Minnelli as reasons for her divorce.

New York, New York was dragging on and everyone was becoming increasingly edgy. On one occasion the pressure got to De Niro and Minnelli, and both of them ended up being injured.

'There was a scene with Liza where we had to have a fight in the car,' says De Niro. 'I thought it was funny to be so hopping mad that my head was sort of banging on the ceiling and I'd hit my hand somehow. I didn't get out of control, I just went a smidgen over, which can happen. Liza got hurt and I think I hurt my hand too. But we would try anything. So sometimes you can't predict the outcome.'

Some years later, during the filming of *Awakenings*, De Niro's co-star and good friend Robin Williams would find himself in a position similar to that of Liza Minnelli. This time De Niro would end up with a broken nose when the scene went wrong.

The *New York, New York* experience can be summed up in the treatment of the movie's show-stopping production number, 'Happy Endings'. The scene, a musical fantasy, cost $350,000 and took ten days to shoot. It was the first thing Scorsese filmed for the movie and it was one of his favourite sequences, recapturing everything he remembered and loved about the old MGM musicals. Two weeks before he was due to sign off on the movie, Scorsese dropped the whole sequence completely and turned in a cut that was four and a half hours long. He admits, with hindsight, that his judgement was off. The original cut of the film was reduced to a more commercially satisfying 153 minutes – 136 minutes after further cuts were made for a European release – but it was still not a success. Ironically, in 1981 a restored version of the movie which ran to 163 minutes with the 'Happy Endings' number received unequivocal praise on its re-release.

New York, New York was not the only De Niro film having problems at this stage. *1900*, which he'd made two years previously, had still not seen the light of day in America. The version shown at Cannes the previous year, at five hours 20 minutes, would not satisfy the American distributors, Paramount. They had a contract for a film running three hours and fifteen minutes. Producer Albert Grimaldi had delivered a film of that length to Paramount after cutting it without Bertolucci's consent. The director disowned that version and produced his own cut – running four hours and five minutes – which had its première at the 1977 New York Film Festival. No matter how much wrangling was involved, or which version was released, it did not change the fact that the film was still unutterably tedious and would bring De Niro the worst reviews of his career to date.

While he was promoting *Taxi Driver* in Cannes, De Niro had admitted to European reporters that he did have a house in Los Angeles. He said it was rented and described it as being in a 'fancy' part of town. Indeed it was. During filming for *New York, New York* De Niro was living in a palatial estate in Bel Air, a gated community for the Hollywood plutocrats. A little more than fancy and certainly not in keeping with the blue-collar image he was steadily acquiring and cultivating in the media.

It was here in Bel Air that he would play mine host to select dinner parties during shooting. He and Diahnne Abbott would entertain exclusive groups at weekends. Frequent guests would include Scorsese and Julia Cameron, and fellow director Brian De Palma. His *Taxi Driver* co-star Peter Boyle was another regular invitee.

He doted on Diahnne Abbott. One house guest told the *New York Times* he would sit next to her patting her back or stroking her leg as he listened to guests, describing him as 'possessive, almost jealous' of his wife, a trait not uncommon in Italian-Americans of De Niro's generation. Although he enjoyed the company De Niro would never be the centre of attention. His idea of a good time was to watch and listen and relax in the company of friends who were quickly taking on the status of a charmed circle. His friends are used to his silences and have come to indulge him over the years.

'It takes years to get to know Bobby,' says Brian De Palma. 'He's very bright but that intelligence comes like rare flashes of brilliant light and only after you've known him for years.'

Others who know and have worked with De Niro believe that the silence is a means to an end. It is a way of forcing other people to react and to do something. He may not be speaking but he is always watching and listening and every encounter becomes an opportunity to store up some trait or mannerism for a future performance. Actress Kathi McGinnis, who appears in *New York, New York*, believes there may be another reason for the famous De Niro silence.

'I think he's hiding something he thinks may be too weird,' she says. 'I mean he's protecting himself with all that silence. There's some part of him he can't show because he's afraid it's insane. Maybe it's only egomania, maybe it's not.'

14 In Country

D E NIRO HAD LOST 35 pounds to play Travis Bickle in *Taxi Driver*. The weight loss would add to Bickle's wasted, pallid look, making him appear even more like a creature of the night, a man who might wither away in the daylight.

His target at the beginning of 1977 was not so much to regain some of that weight as to get into shape. He had decided not to do another film until his boxing movie with Scorsese, at that stage still called *Prizefighter*. Mardik Martin was writing it as a play which would then be filmed – De Niro would take the role on stage and on screen. The weight loss did not bother him so much – it was after all bringing him down to his fighting weight – but when he wasn't practising saxophone he spent his spare time on the *New York, New York* set on road work and ringcraft to make sure he looked the part.

The actor had two other reasons for taking things easy in the early part of that year. In the first instance he had not had a reasonable break for almost three years and badly needed the rest. He had never intended to make so many films back to back, but the memory of the hungry years drove him on. He was in the predicament that many actors find themselves in when they make their breakthrough after years of struggling. They cannot quite believe that they have reached the position of being able to exercise their ultimate sanction, the right to say no. De Niro had now learned that not only was it acceptable to say no, it was almost advisable. The perverse nature of Hollywood is such that when an actor says no to one part he invariably finds himself being offered a bigger and better-paid one elsewhere.

His second reason for taking a break was much more compelling. He had become a father for the first time. His son Raphael was born in January 1977. De Niro apparently claimed that the child was named after the hotel in which it was conceived, which led Shelley Winters to quip, 'Thank God they weren't staying in the Algonquin.' De Niro obviously felt it was time to play the role of a doting dad. He would quickly have found that there is no way you can earn the right to play this character. Parenthood is not a vicarious experience, and no amount of research could prepare even Robert De Niro for his new vocation in life. He was nonetheless a proud father, and Raphael a happy child.

'He's been laughing since he was a month old,' the beaming father told one reporter who enquired after the boy.

De Niro's place in the stellar firmament of Hollywood was now assured, so he could afford to take the time off. Up to a dozen scripts a week were landing on Harry Ufland's desk from producers and directors who wanted the newly bankable De Niro to sign on for their projects. He passed on almost everything. He was already booked solid for two years, and if he had agreed to do everything that was offered to him Raphael would be in college before he ever saw him again. One script managed to make it through the net. In contrast to the Second World War there were no jingoistic, tub-thumping propaganda films made while America was fighting in Vietnam. Pragmatically you could argue that since the 10,000–day war was being seen live on television every night there was very little the film-makers could do to top that. Philosophically it was not a popular war – if there is such a thing – and America was losing. It would be a foolhardy producer who would gamble on the public slapping down their five dollars in large numbers to go and see a film in which their boys were coming second. The war ended in 1975, and by that time the mood of America had changed. The anti-war movement had convinced most people of the folly of the conflict, and the exposure of Richard Nixon as a cheat and a charlatan had deepened their sense of disillusionment. Towards the end of the seventies, after a little breathing space, film-makers were ready to provide America with a cathartic evaluation of the country's involvement in South-East Asia.

Michael Cimino was a screenwriter turned director with one film to his credit. He had made the Clint Eastwood vehicle *Thunderbolt and Lightfoot* for which Jeff Bridges had been nominated as Best Supporting Actor against De Niro in 1974. He had written a script about four friends from a predominantly Polish steel town in Pennsylvania, and the effect that Vietnam had on them and their community. The film was called *The Deer Hunter.*

'I liked the story and the dialogue,' De Niro said later, explaining why he had agreed to take on another project. 'It was very simple and it seemed very real to me.'

He had still not committed to the project but he was at least showing interest. With that behind him Cimino did a deal with EMI. The British company was making inroads into Hollywood at that time with an investment position in films like the Ryan O'Neal thriller *The Driver* and *Convoy*, a movie designed to cash in on the Citizens Band radio fad. EMI was interested for one very good reason. Unlike most American stars, De Niro had become bankable in overseas markets. At that stage there were only three genuinely internationally bankable stars – Robert Redford, Steve McQueen, and Clint Eastwood. These three could guarantee to open a film almost anywhere in the world. There were also about a dozen other stars whose films could be depended on to do good business in most territories. De Niro was one of them, as was the other emerging star of the seventies, Al Pacino.

It was Michael Deeley, joint managing director of EMI Films, who pointed out that De Niro's name would draw an audience in foreign territories much more easily than, say, Gene Hackman or Burt Reynolds. Deeley also underlined the fact that De Niro and Pacino had become international names virtually overnight, while people like Robert Redford had taken years to establish themselves.

'They don't seem as foreign to the rest of the world as classic, blue-eyed Americans,' he said, trying to explain the phenomenon. 'Blond, blue-eyed stars speaking in Portuguese present something of a credibility problem. Robert De Niro's name means a colossal amount abroad.'

With De Niro almost on board, Cimino had very little difficulty in hammering out a deal with EMI to finance the film. Deeley had also reasoned that since most of the film would take place in the Far East, the film would stand a good chance of penetrating the then notoriously difficult markets of Hong Kong, Singapore, Taiwan, and other oriental territories. EMI was so pleased with what they saw as a major coup for a British company that almost before the ink was dry on the contract they took out a huge ad in *Variety* promoting *The Deer Hunter* by showing De Niro in sunglasses and carrying a deer rifle, sitting on the bonnet of a truck.

The Deer Hunter was one of a clutch of Vietnam films either in production or about to be released. Others included Francis Ford Coppola's *Apocalypse Now*, *Dog Soldiers*, featuring De Niro's *Bang the Drum Slowly* co-star Michael Moriarty, *Coming Home* with Jane Fonda and Jon Voight, and *Rolling Thunder*, written by *Taxi Driver* screenwriter Paul Schrader. None of these films would have the effect on the American cinema-going audience that *The Deer Hunter* would have.

To prepare for his role, De Niro once again put on his vagabond shoes and started to travel. This time he headed for the steel mill towns of Steubenville and Mingo Junction in Ohio.

'I talked with the mill-workers, I drank and ate with them, and I played pool with them,' he said. 'I tried to come as close to being a steelworker as possible. I wanted to work a shift at the mill but they wouldn't let me.

'Acting isn't really respected enough as an art,' he continued, giving his most comprehensive analysis of his craft to date. 'An actor's body is like an instrument and you have to learn how to play an instrument. It's like knowing how to play the piano. There ought to be acting schools that take you in as small children, the way they do with music. A person doesn't need experience to learn technique. Technique comes first, then as you grow older and get experience you will apply it to what you know.

'Actors must expose themselves to the surroundings and keep their minds obsessed with that. Sooner or later an idea will creep into your head. A feeling perhaps, a clue, or maybe an incident will occur that the actor can later connect to the scene when he's doing it. I always look at everything. The important thing is to think it all out. Sometimes I write down my ideas. The main thing is to put in the time, even if it's boring. Then you know you've covered every possibility when you make your choices. Sometimes I practise the nature of a person's lifestyle and that's what I did with my characterisation of Michael in *The Deer Hunter*.

'You must keep practising and it's very tiresome to do that. If you don't practise, you don't know your subject and it can't be natural. People tend to take actors less seriously about that, and partially, it's the fault of the actors when they don't really do anything but play close to type. You've got to physically and mentally become that person you are portraying.'

Although he was raised in a political household and must have absorbed liberal views from his parents from an early age, De Niro was not a political activist. Unlike many other stars he has seldom loaned his name to political causes or fundraising movements. Significantly the only cause with which he has consistently been involved is the plight of the Vietnam veterans, and specifically the children of veterans. De Niro keeps his political persuasions as private as almost everything else in his life, but his feelings about Vietnam are on record. He was too old to be drafted, but that didn't stop him being against the war.

'I thought that the war was wrong but what bothered me most was that the people who went to the war became victims of it,' he said. 'They were used for the whims of others. I don't think that the policy-makers had the necessary smarts. I didn't respect their decisions or what they were doing. And it was a right of many people to feel "Why should I go and get involved with something that's unclear and pay for it with my life?" It takes people like that to make changes.'

Michael Vronsky, the character he plays in *The Deer Hunter*, was one of those victims. He goes to Vietnam to do what he believes is his duty to the country that has been good to him and his family. His spell in-country is so traumatic that when he returns he is a changed and deeply troubled soul. De Niro plainly felt strongly about the material and gives a performance of extraordinary power. Never one to blow his own trumpet, he did concede afterwards that his performance in *The Deer Hunter* was probably the best he had ever given.

De Niro and the other principals – Christopher Walken, John Savage, John Cazale, Meryl Streep and Chuck Aspegren – assembled in Follanbee, West Virginia and Cleveland, Ohio to film the American sequences which were being shot first because John Cazale, who was engaged to Streep, was suffering from terminal cancer. The studio wanted him out of the picture but Cimino insisted that he should do it. He then rearranged the shooting schedule, with Cazale and Streep's consent, so that he could film all his scenes first. Cazale completed all his own scenes but died before the film was finished.

The Vietnam jungle scenes and the Saigon city sequences were shot in Thailand. For the combat sequences De Niro and the other actors were keen to do their own stunts, but it almost killed them. In one sequence De Niro as Michael and John Savage as Steven have to jump from a helicopter as it approaches a bridge. The camera is so close to them that stunt doubles could not be used. They would hold on to the helicopter skids themselves and then drop some thirty feet into the River Kwai. Stunt co-ordinator Buddy Van Horn is one of the best in the business, and he had gone over it again and again, but when it came to the jump the two actors were on their own. They did the scene more than a dozen times over two days, but one take almost killed both of them and their director.

'The helicopter pilot didn't want to go too low because there were rocks on two sides and a narrow passage where the water rushed through,' recalls De Niro. 'The runners underneath the helicopter caught on the bridge's cable and without knowing it the pilot lifted the whole bridge and twisted it around while John and I were hanging from the helicopter.

'It was dangerous. I looked down and shouted "Drop!" and we just dropped. We came up out of the water and then I thought the helicopter was going to drop down on us. That happens in movies; you have to be very, very careful. Nobody plans an accident and, the thing is, sometimes the stunts don't even look like anything on film. Or the shot isn't even used. You could die doing one of these stunts and when people look at it they don't even know how dangerous it was.'

De Niro's words had a prophetic ring. Five years later actor Vic Morrow and two young children would be killed in a helicopter stunt on the set of *Twilight Zone: The Movie*.

The most controversial sequence in *The Deer Hunter* comes when De Niro as Michael and Christopher Walken as Nick are captured by the Viet Cong and forced to play Russian roulette while their captors gamble on the outcome. The film was attacked because there was no record of any such atrocity being perpetrated by either side. It was also criticised because the attack immediately preceding their capture seems to resemble the My Lai massacre perpetrated by the Americans in 1966, but in *The Deer Hunter* it is attributed to the Viet Cong. Director Cimino defended both incidents.

'I think that anyone who is a student of the war, or anyone who was there, would agree that anything you can imagine happening probably happened,' he said in a rather self-serving plea of mitigation.

'The film is not realistic – it is surrealistic. Even the landscape is surreal. The steel town which we call Clairton is composed of eight different towns in four states. You can't find that town anywhere – it doesn't exist. And time is compressed. In trying to compress the experience of the war into a film, even as long as this one, I had to deal with it in a non-literal way. I used events from 1966 like My Lai and from 1975 like the fall of Saigon as reference points rather than facts. But if you attack the film on its facts then you're fighting a phantom because literal accuracy was never intended.'

De Niro defended his director, but only up to a point.

'The Russian roulette thing is a metaphor,' he said. 'People said they didn't do that – but it had an effect. It shocked people in a way they wouldn't have felt if they had just seen another battle. What are you going to see, another battle scene? So you saw something else. You saw this metaphor and that made sense to me. It seemed valid.'

De Niro was less happy that their North Vietnamese captors were seen to be gambling on the outcome of the POWs' torture. He argued strongly against it with Cimino but in the end the director won.

'I had been reading a book at the time about POWs in Vietnam,' says De Niro. 'They were always being told to recant, to say they were wrong for invading Vietnam. It wasn't about money. That clutters it. It gets in the way. It was about ideas.

'It wasn't like Cimino said, "I disagree." I think he just thought it was part of the style of the movie. Directing a movie is very hard and it's easy to criticise. It was a slip. In the Saigon scenes it was a different story, you'd expect the money and the corruption thing. But out there in the Viet Cong strongholds if they'd told the prisoners "Just say you're wrong" or "Sign this paper" – something like that – I think it would have been more consistent. It would have elevated the movie.'

Arguments will continue to rage about the morality of Cimino's attitude to his story-telling, but there is no denying the ordeal that De Niro and Walken put themselves through to film the Russian roulette scene. They played the scenes in bamboo cages that had been assembled in the River Kwai. They were up to their shoulders in water and in a great deal of discomfort.

'The circumstances were real,' says Walken. 'It was hot, we'd been doing it a long time. We'd been tied up. There were mosquitoes. There were rats.'

Although he'd made half a dozen films before this, *The Deer Hunter* was Walken's first star turn in a movie. He was an accomplished and experienced stage actor but joked that in films he was rather like Blanche Dubois from *A Streetcar Named Desire*.

'In film, I have to depend on the kindness of strangers,' he told the *New York Times*.

One of those strangers was Robert De Niro. Walken had admired his work for a long time and he used that to create the character of Nick.

'My admiration for him is one of the things that shows in the film,' he says. 'It had some bearing on the characters. They're supposed to have been friends for twenty years, there's a powerful feeling between them. I think my feelings about Robert De Niro's work help create an impression of warmth and friendship.'

It was De Niro who suggested using one of his own acting tricks to provoke the necessary reaction in Walken during the torture sequence. His character is at first naturally reluctant to pick up the gun when he is forced to play the game. It was De Niro who suggested to Cimino that he should get one of the guards to slap Walken without letting him know it was going to happen.

'That scene was one of the many big moments I had in the film where I walked on the set thinking, "I wish I knew what I was doing", recalls Walken. But when somebody belts you fifty times, you don't have to fake a reaction. You don't have trouble shaking.'

Walkden continues: 'Robert De Niro is the most generous actor I have ever worked with. In the scene near the end of the film where I am in the gaming room for the first time, for instance, I have to pick up the gun and hold it to my head. He showed me how to do that.

'It's a very good moment for me, and I have to admit that it's stolen.'

15 The Phantom

A FUNNY THING HAPPENED on the way to one of the locations for *The Deer Hunter*. A group of students was gathered in the foyer of the Pittsburgh Holiday Inn taking a break from a conference on how to get jobs during the vacation. While they milled around the foyer, De Niro, the hottest star in Hollywood, came out of an elevator. He walked through the crowd and out through the door and not one of them recognised him.

This incident, recounted in *Time* magazine in the summer of 1977, was deemed bizarre enough for them to dub De Niro 'The Phantom of the Cinema' in their profile. They pointed out, quite correctly, that if any of his fellow luminaries like Redford, Pacino, Hoffman, or even Brando had been in that foyer, there would have been a near-riot. The audience of students should have been De Niro's people, but he went among them unnoticed.

With hindsight it is not so remarkable. De Niro is not physically striking in the way that Redford or Pacino or Hoffman is. His features are interesting rather than handsome. He looks like an ordinary guy, the epitome of a blue-collar American, the sort of man you would pass in the street without a second thought. It is this face, a tabula rasa, which allows De Niro to create some of his greatest roles. Bruce Pearson, Johnny Boy, Vito Corleone, Jimmy Doyle, and Michael Vronsky all look different. Their only common ground is that they are all moulded from the same physically unremarkable clay into something the camera turns into an extraordinary product. But without the camera, as his stand-in Jon Cutler points out, there is not much there. As *Time* commented, De Niro does not need to avoid the public because the public generally does not recognise him. At this stage there was no such thing as a 'Robert De Niro type' the way there was a 'Robert Redford type' or an 'Al Pacino type'.

Even his co-stars would agree that they never got to see the real Robert De Niro. While he was making *Taxi Driver*, Michael Moriarty stopped by the New York location. He was watching De Niro filming a scene inside a Manhattan coffee shop. One of the crew, recognising him and knowing he had starred opposite De Niro in *Bang the Drum Slowly*, went across and asked if he wanted to come over and say hello.

'No,' said Moriarty, 'don't bother. I don't know that guy at all. I knew Bruce Pearson. I don't know Travis Bickle or Bob De Niro.'

De Niro was now a seven-figure actor. He was able to turn down million-dollar salaries without turning a hair. He was financially secure and could do whatever projects his heart desired. Only one thing still troubled him. There was still, as he told *Time* magazine, the lingering fear of losing his edge. He was fuelled by the fires of anger and frustration; perhaps an overly comfortable life would dampen the flames.

'You know what I wonder about?' he asked *Time* correspondent Jean Vallely. 'Indecision. I think about it. There are so many alternatives one can take in life. I think about guilt. I wonder why people feel guilty about things they have nothing to do with. If I do something out of weakness I feel guilty. If it turns out bad, I feel guilty. If it turns out good, I feel guilty.'

It is an unusually expansive quote which involves the sort of self-analysis for which he had not previously been noted in public. It is also the sort of quote one might ascribe more readily to Scorsese, whose work deals almost universally with sin, guilt and redemption. Perhaps the collaboration was beginning to influence De Niro. Although he talks of 'guilt', perhaps what he really means is anger. Perhaps he is finally beginning to become aware of the reason for the childhood feelings of resentment. 'I wonder why people feel guilty about things they have nothing to do with,' he says. Is he blaming himself for the things he had nothing to do with, namely the end of his parents' marriage? Perhaps this unspoken guilt or anger is the factor that co-star Kathi McGinnis suggested might be a reason for his media silence?

Although he was able to command large salaries and pick and choose his projects, there was one thing that still eluded De Niro. He still had to win a Best Actor Oscar. Publicly he had made it plain that he had little interest in winning, as his rather churlish comments on receiving his Best Supporting Actor Oscar would seem to bear out. Privately – who knows? His closest collaborator, Martin Scorsese, so often unjustly passed over, makes no secret of the fact that he would now like a Best Director Oscar more than almost anything else. Whether De Niro felt the same is hard to say. What is certain, though, is that he had the best chance of his career with the performance that he himself had deemed to be his best ever in *The Deer Hunter*.

In 1979 it was a two-horse race between *The Deer Hunter* and another Vietnam film, *Coming Home*. Hal Ashby's movie starred Jane Fonda and Jon Voight and focused on the plight of returning veterans. The Academy was split in much the same way as audiences had been split. Many felt that *The Deer Hunter* was far too controversial and played fast and loose with the truth; others felt that *Coming Home* presented an idealised picture of life for the returning veterans.

The makers of *The Deer Hunter* had hired Allan Carr, former manager of Ann-Margret and the producer who had turned *Grease* into a $100 million hit. Carr had arranged for the film to open for one week only in New York and Los Angeles in December 1978. The idea was to make sure it qualified for the Academy Award nominations and the New York and Los Angeles critics awards. It was then taken off and would not go on release until February 1979. It played only eight shows in New York, each to 500 people. The buzz surrounding the film was phenomenal, and as Carr predicted it became the cocktail party circuit movie of the year. The producers hoped that by the time the film was eventually released in February it would be buoyed up at the box-office by a clutch of Oscar nominations. Normally box-office success encourages Oscar nominations; here they were hoping it might work the other way round. De Niro took very little part in all the hype. There were few interviews and even fewer television appearances. He had far more serious things to worry him at the beginning of 1979 than whether or not he might win another Oscar.

In March he announced that his three-year marriage to Diahnne Abbott was over. They had been married since 1976, but had been together for much longer. They were the perfect couple when they were both struggling, but the pressures of being a movie star and a movie star's wife seemed to be too much for either of them to deal with.

'I could have been just as happy without the fame,' a dejected De Niro told reporters ruefully. 'I would probably have gone on being an ordinary guy, living a simple life and nothing would have changed my marriage.'

De Niro and his wife had had an unusual marriage since they formalised their relationship in 1976. They maintained separate homes and at times separate lifestyles. They would go their own ways for a while but then they would come back together as if nothing had happened.

When the final split came, Diahnne Abbott remained in Los Angeles with two-year-old Raphael and her daughter Drina. She would pursue her own career independently of her husband. De Niro returned to New York. The two would remain friends and stay in almost constant touch.

'I miss Di and the kids terribly,' said De Niro, who could not have been unaware that he was putting his children in exactly the same position as his father had placed him. Those who do not learn from history are destined to repeat it, and De Niro seems to have sacrificed his marriage on the altar of his art, just as his father had done more than 30 years previously.

'They are always on my mind,' said the actor of his family. 'I want to be very close to my children, but because I am working and have to bring in an income it is impossible for me to be with them.'

There are two sides to every story and De Niro may simply have been dissembling when he blamed the pressures of stardom on his marital break-up. Helena Lisandrello, a singer who provided back-up vocals for Bette Midler, Bob Dylan and Elton John, claims that she and De Niro had begun an affair around the time the actor and his wife split up.

She would later tell her version of the story to *New York Post* columnist Cindy Adams.

'I'm driving down San Vincente Boulevard in L.A.,' said Lisandrello. 'This guy is cutting me off. I'd go fast, he'd go fast. I'd slow down, he'd slow down. This asshole kept following me. I didn't even know him. Finally he put his hands together in prayer position and said, "Pull over." So I stopped and he said, "Can we have lunch?" ' That was how Helena Lisandrello met Robert De Niro. She claims that at the time he was separated from his wife and living in the Chateau Marmont hotel off Sunset Boulevard.

'That night,' said Lisandrello, continuing her story, 'he called and took me out. He stayed the night and we slept together. From then on I'd go to his place or he'd be at mine.'

Lisandrello also claims De Niro once told her, 'Women throw themselves at me. That's just how it is.'

'His attitude would piss me off,' she said, 'but he thrives on turmoil. It feeds his artistic juices.'

Abbott may have been like many Hollywood wives, willing to turn a blind eye to a husband's extra-marital escapades up to a certain point. The line that had been tacitly drawn in the sand appears to have been irrevocably crossed in 1979. It would appear that De Niro's relationship with Lisandrello and the other women who allegedly threw themselves at him had become too much for his wife to ignore. So the couple went their separate ways. De Niro may regret the loss of his children but over the years to come he would have cause on many occasions to regret that lunchtime drive on San Vincente Boulevard. Helena Lisandrello was a thorn that would remain in his side off and on for the next fourteen years.

Even without the co-operation of an obviously preoccupied De Niro, Allan Carr's tactics paid off handsomely in the spring of 1979. By the time the Oscar nominations were announced, *The Deer Hunter* had nine nominations in all the major categories in which it was eligible. Its chief rival was *Coming Home* with eight nominations. On the night feelings ran high outside the Dorothy Chandler Pavilion, with demonstrators from the 'Hell No, We Won't Go Away' movement and Vietnam Veterans Against the War, thirteen of whom were arrested.

Inside the hall things were relatively tranquil, and by the end of the evening the awards were split between the two films. *The Deer Hunter* won five Oscars including Best Picture, Best Director and Best Supporting Actor. *Coming Home* won three but significantly it took both major acting awards for Voight and Fonda.

De Niro's consolation on the night was the heartfelt thanks of Michael Cimino who in his acceptance speech praised his star. 'I embrace Robert De Niro for his dedication and his dignity of heart,' he said as he picked up his Best Director statuette. A few moments later Cimino was back to collect the final award of the night for Best Picture, having beaten out *Coming Home* for the big prize. The only man in the room who couldn't have cared less which of the two won was ironically the man who handed over the Oscar – a painfully emaciated John Wayne, who was to die of cancer later that year.

Once again De Niro was not in the audience. Even though he wanted to stay out of the public eye because of the break-up of his marriage, he felt strongly enough about *The Deer Hunter* to consider attending. At one point he reportedly asked if he could sit out the ceremony backstage rather than wait in the auditorium with the rest of the nominees, pleading nerves. The Oscars do not make exceptions for anyone and producer Jack Haley let it be known that if he was going to show then he would show out front and not in the Green Room. In the end De Niro's nerves got the better of him and he stayed at home in New York.

For the second time in three years De Niro had missed out on an award that he ought to have won. Did he regret his comments on his first win? In spite of the advanced age of its membership at that time, the Academy had a long memory. De Niro's comments about the unworthiness of some of the previous winners may only have been articulating what almost everyone knew to be the case, but nonetheless they were hardly politic.

Although De Niro was publicly devastated by the break-up of his marriage it can hardly have come as a surprise to him. He would frequently spend long periods of time out of the family home staying in hotels like the Chateau Marmont. Since his childhood in Greenwich Village he has been entirely in charge of his own life and seemingly unwilling to make concessions to those on whose lives his impinges. He claims to be a man who needs his own space and says those who live with him need to get used to that. It is asking a lot of any woman, and was obviously asking too much of Diahnne Abbott.

The break-up does not appear to have dulled his appetite for work. In April 1979 he again sought refuge in the penthouse at the Chateau Marmont. He was just about to begin the movie that would give him the role of his life. Two years later his name would again be among the Oscar nominees; this time he would be at the ceremony himself and no one would deny him what was rightfully his.

16 The Bronx Bull

ALMOST AS SOON AS he had made his Hollywood breakthrough, Robert De Niro began to set in train the events that would turn him from an actor for hire into a major player. The journey that would ultimately end with the formation of his own TriBeCa film company and with him behind a camera on *A Bronx Tale* began in 1974.

He had made an incendiary impact with *Mean Streets* and was about to win his first academy award for *The Godfather Part II*. *Mean Streets* director Martin Scorsese, meanwhile, was working on his first major Hollywood movie, *Alice Doesn't Live Here Any More*. De Niro was now reaching that stage in his career which all actors crave; he was now able to choose the work instead of the work choosing him. One of the choices he made was to work with Scorsese again. De Niro visited Scorsese while he was shooting *Alice* and gave him a book he had been sent while in Sicily filming the *Godfather* movie. The book was *Raging Bull*, the autobiography of boxer Jake La Motta.

There are those who argue that, pound for pound, La Motta was one of the greatest fighters who ever stepped into the ring. Fighting as he did in the forties, his middleweight status kept him away from the stuff of legend – the heavyweight championship of the world, held then by the great Joe Louis. Nonetheless, he was in his day an awesome fighter. A violent man on either side of the ropes, his tactic was simply to rely on the sheer savagery of his punching and his ability to withstand more punishment than his opponent. He became involved with the Mob in order to get a shot at the title, which he won in 1949, but that involvement was the beginning of his downfall. Ultimately, after a spell in jail, La Motta ended up as a bloated parody of himself reciting Shakespeare in a night-club act. The autobiography written with Pete Savage and Joseph Carter is a rather self-serving piece in which he tries to justify the various reversals of his chequered life.

Nonetheless, the book appealed to De Niro, who felt there was potential there for a film.

'I had liked the book originally because it had some good scenes,' he recalled. 'A good scene is something that you think has a lot of dramatic possibilities and irony and humour and something that people can relate to, the way Marty and I relate to it. It could be the situation, the character in the moment. All these unexpected things. You just say "This is a great scene." You've never seen a scene like this. You want to do it. Or you have seen a scene like this, but you've never seen it done as well as it's done here. You can imagine it being done in a certain way. It could be terrific but then you have to worry about it being tied in to the rest of the film or the story.'

It is interesting that De Niro should reduce the triumphs and torments of Jake La Motta's life to 'a few good scenes'. Again it is an example of his single-mindedness. He did not really care about Jake La Motta as a person. When he refers to these few good scenes it is more likely that he sees the opportunity to express his own anger through them rather than sympathises with Jake's plight. Despite his assurances that the story had a few good scenes, and that La Motta was an interesting character, Scorsese could not see a movie in the book. He was not a boxing fan; indeed, he frequently said that the only approach to a fight which makes any sense is the Buster Keaton technique. In *Battling Butler*, Keaton goes into the ring with his opponent then promptly picks up a chair and hits him over the head with it.

The two men agreed to differ as far as *Raging Bull* was concerned. But over the years De Niro began to exert his influence on their creative partnership. He would not let go of the idea of turning this book into a film, nor would he let go of the idea of Scorsese directing it. A number of scripts were written but neither De Niro nor Scorsese particularly liked them. Four years after his initial overtures, De Niro made what was to be the decisive approach to Scorsese, who by this time was not in good physical, emotional or professional shape. De Niro, however, seemed to recognise in *Raging Bull* the potential to get his old friend back on his feet again, physically and creatively, by providing the sort of challenge he could rise to. Things were not going well for Scorsese. His personal life was in ruins, he had gone through a divorce, and his last film, *New York, New York*, had been slaughtered by the critics. His health was also suffering. The chronic asthma that had afflicted him since childhood now had him in hospital in Los Angeles. On Labor Day weekend in September 1978 De Niro went to see him. He was well aware of how Scorsese was feeling, and once again he broached the subject of the La Motta biography.

'You know, we can make this picture,' he told the director. 'Listen,' he continued, 'we could really do a great job. Do you want to make it?'

Perhaps unknown to De Niro, this time he had a powerful ally. Robbie Robertson, front man with the seminal rock group The Band was a close friend of Scorsese. The two men shared a house while Scorsese directed *The Last Waltz*, his epic documentary film of The Band's farewell concert. The two men had also travelled the world promoting the film at various festivals. It was, as Robertson recalls, 'a scary time', but they survived it and forged an unbreakable bond in the process.

'Marty was kind of teetering and on the line about doing *Raging Bull*,' says Robertson. 'He was just run-down, working and crazy, and running everywhere in the world. He was living with exhaustion and he got sick. I remember saying to him about *Raging Bull*, "Let's get off the fence on this thing. Are you passionate about this? Do you have to do this movie? Because if you don't have to do it, don't do it. Can you go on with your life without doing this?"'

This time when De Niro asked him, Scorsese was ready to say yes.

'Everything was very destructive and it was very bad for me,' he says. 'In the fall of 1978 everything clicked together and I kind of woke up and said, "This is the picture that has to be made, and I'll make it that way. These are the reasons why it has to be made." I understood then what Jake was, but only after having gone through a similar experience myself. I was just lucky that there happened to be a project there ready for me to express this.

'I had lived a crazy lifestyle for a couple of years before this movie, all of which culminated in *Raging Bull*. The understanding of why I was doing it found its way into Jake's character and I was able to deal with it on film. It's a tough picture and maybe it's not a movie that appeals to women as much as men. I don't know. I just made what I felt was right. I was able to survive a couple of crazy years and put it into this character and got to the point where Jake was able to sit in front of the mirror and be kind to himself at the end. That was what the lesson of the film was for me.'

Scorsese saw, possibly with De Niro's prompting, the real message in La Motta's book. La Motta is a primal force who is in the process of destroying himself and everyone around him, a situation possibly understood by De Niro himself. Finally he sees a glimmer of hope and in the process manages to make peace with himself and find a kind of redemption. Scorsese could read between the lines as well as anyone. He admits that he went into *Raging Bull* with the intention of using it to rehabilitate himself and then give up making films in America.

Scorsese's motives for taking on *Raging Bull* are clear. De Niro's are less so. Was it simply because the film contained a few good scenes? Or was it the chance to exorcise personal demons? Bearing in mind that he came across the book after *Mean Streets*, did he see in La Motta a chance to unleash the rage and frustration he had felt throughout his career? Was this the ultimate catharsis for the process of every few years watching a new man become his mother's boyfriend and replace his father in her affections? Whatever the reason, he shepherded this project through almost every stage of production. He brought the idea to Scorsese, he helped choose the cast, he helped write the script, he even used his muscle on the studio executives. Only when the cameras started turning did he step back and put himself completely in the hands of Martin Scorsese.

Throughout his discussions with Scorsese between 1974 and 1978, De Niro had always known what sort of story he wanted *Raging Bull* to be. It would not be the apology and justification for a life that the original book presented. One of the first things he did when he acquired the book was make a deal with screenwriter Mardik Martin, co-writer of *Mean Streets*, to turn it into a screenplay. At this stage the project was tentatively called *Prizefighter* and was originally to have been done on stage before being turned into a film. Scorsese, who at one point even considered doing the play at night and making the film during the day, had offered a number of opinions about what should and should not be in the story. Martin went away and worked on *Raging Bull* in between other projects. Eighteen months later he came back with a script. When he saw it De Niro did not like it and made his displeasure felt straight away to both Martin and Scorsese.

'What is this? What's going on here?' he asked them. 'This is not the picture we agreed upon.'

By this time Martin felt that the project was getting too much for him anyway and the two men parted company amicably. The writing then passed into the hands of *Taxi Driver* screenwriter Paul Schrader. The decision to take Mardik Martin out of the equation was an extremely painful one for Scorsese.

'Mardik Martin is like a brother to me,' he explains. 'We've known each other for more than twenty years. He is the person I've been closest to for twenty years. He has been with me through all my crises, all my good times, all my bad times. We started writing the script of *Raging Bull* during *New York, New York*. I just want to say for the record, the poor guy, I never gave him any direction. I was running around writing the script for *New York, New York* – the stuff we would shoot the next morning. Everyone was working on it – Earl Mac Rauch, the screenwriter,

Irwin Winkler, the producer, Julia Cameron, my second wife. I didn't want that to happen again but when Mardik came in with *Raging Bull* it was like *Rashomon*. He got twenty-five versions of the story because the characters were still alive. And I still hadn't made up my mind about directing the picture.'

According to Schrader neither he nor Scorsese was especially keen to make this picture. It was De Niro's persuasion that got Scorsese on board, then Scorsese joined De Niro in getting Schrader to do it. Scorsese admits, however, that after De Niro's reaction to Mardik Martin's script even he wasn't sure if he still believed in the picture. Although he concedes that this was probably due more to a lack of belief in himself than in the material.

Schrader went away and came up with a script which, although still very dark, was more acceptable to De Niro. This time, however, there were problems with United Artists, which was bankrolling the project. The studio was unhappy about a scene near the end of the film in which La Motta is jailed on a vice charge after allowing under-age girls into his Miami nightclub. The scene, as envisaged by Schrader, would be the high point of the film. Alone in his cell, La Motta begins to masturbate as he recalls all the women in his life. However, he loses his erection as he remembers how dreadfully he treated people. Faced with literal and metaphorical impotence, in the end he blames his hand and smashes it against the cell wall. For Schrader this three-page soliloquy is one of the finest scenes he has ever written. Neither De Niro nor Scorsese liked it. Schrader admits to being surprised, especially by De Niro's rejection. More importantly, the studio was horrified at the prospect of the scene being in the finished movie. United Artists could just about live with another scene in which a sexually aroused La Motta loses an erection by pouring iced water into his shorts so as to preserve his energy for the ring – apparently La Motta was prone to doing this in life – but the prospect of an Oscar-winning star masturbating in a prison cell was simply too much.

United Artists felt that there was no way the scene could be implied. It was either in the script or not. If it was in, then the film would almost certainly get an 'X' certificate in America, which would stop any major cinema chain from booking it and would effectively mean it would not be released. A meeting was arranged at Scorsese's apartment on 57th Street in New York between studio executive David Field, Scorsese and De Niro. Although neither De Niro nor Scorsese was aware of it at the time, this was in fact a crisis meeting that would decide the whole future of the picture. If Field was not convinced then United Artists would not be convinced and *Raging Bull* was dead in the water. With the costly failure

Left The house at 219 West 14th Street where Robert De Niro spent his childhood years

Right The house in Bleeker Street in the West Village where Robert De Niro was born. The De Niros' apartment (top right) is now part of the famous Little Red Schoolhouse

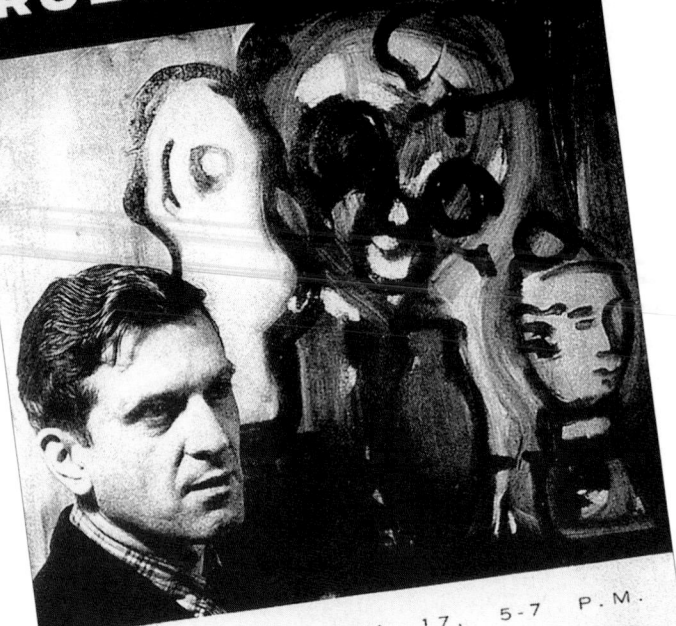

ROBERT DE NIRO

OPENING: JANUARY 17, 5-7 P.M.
JANUARY 17 TO FEBRUARY 4, 1967

ZABRISK

699 MADISON A

op left Robert De Niro Snr. The exhibition was his first major show when he
eturned from his European sojourn

ottom left A rare photograph of the young De Niro as he poses – albeit warily
to illustrate a magazine article on New York's school system

bove 'Composition'. The painting sold by Virginia Admiral – De Niro's mother
to the Museum of Modern Art for $1000

Above A shoulder to cry on. But was it more than just maternal affection? Shelley Winters and Robert De Niro in *Bloody Mama*, 1970

Left Alone in the locker room. Robert De Niro as the terminally ill Bruce Pearson in *Bang the Drum Slowly*, 1973

Right An offer he can't refuse. De Niro as the younger Vito Corleone ends Fanucci's career and begins his own in *The Godfather Part II*, 1974

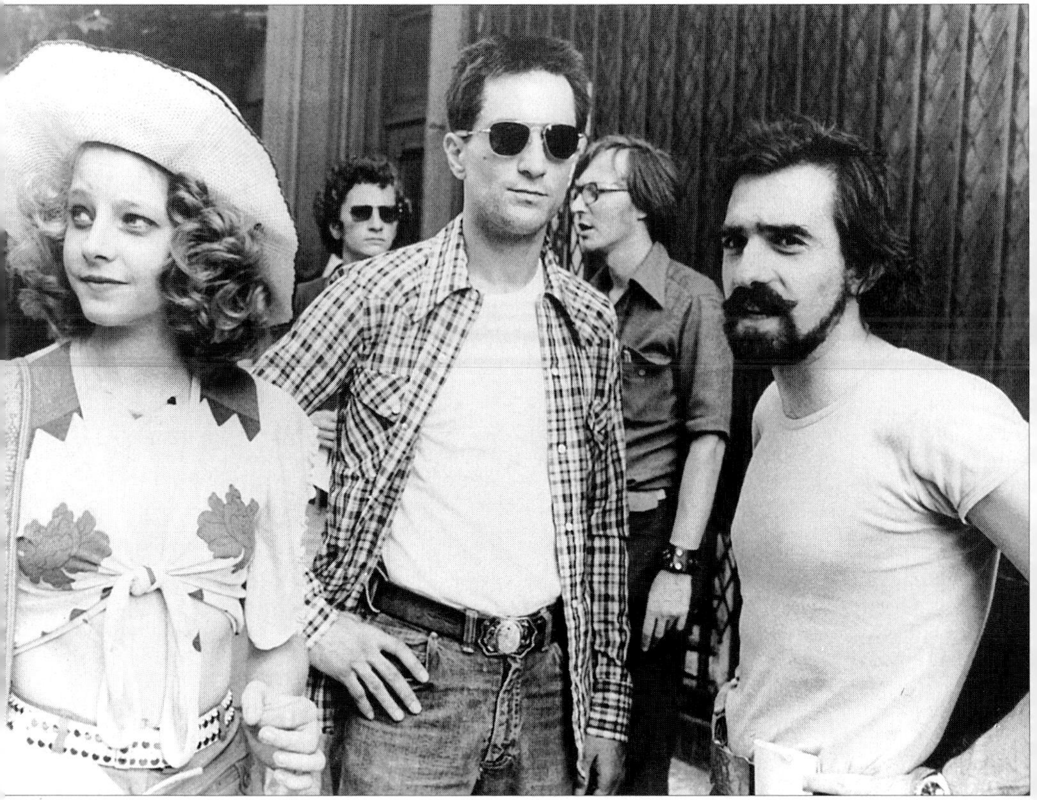

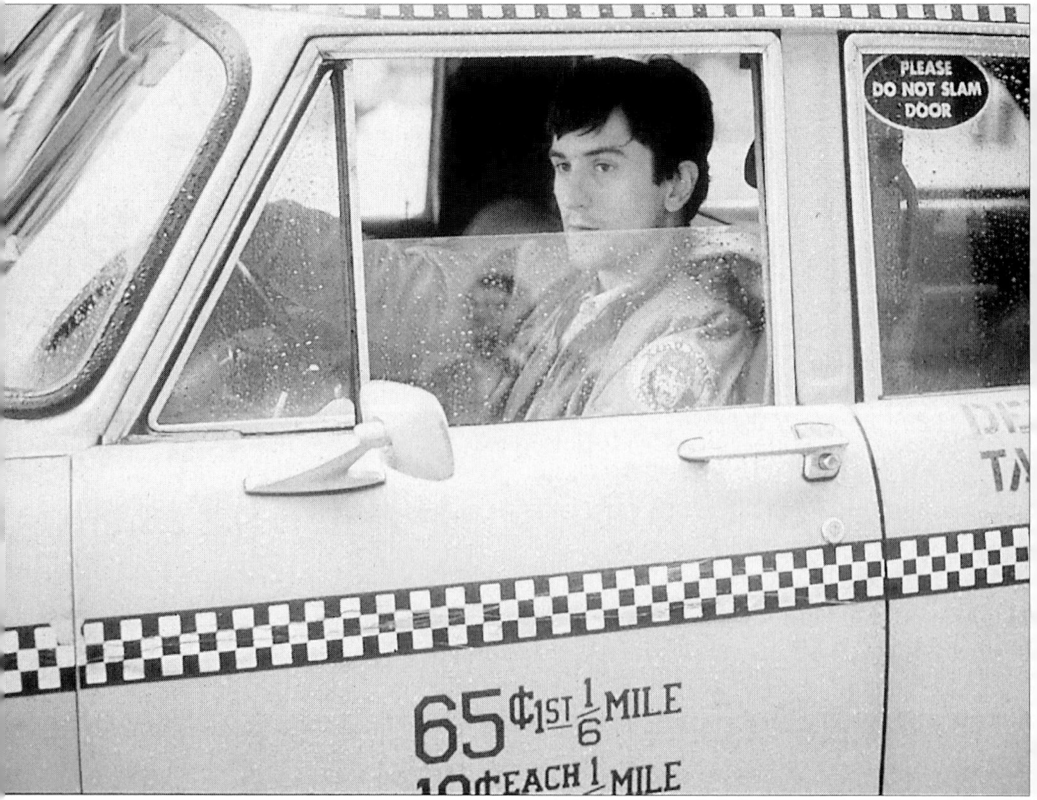
PLEASE
DO NOT SLAM
DOOR
65¢1ST 1/6 MILE

p left Jodie Foster, Robert De Niro and Martin Scorsese in a break from ~~~ooting during *Taxi Driver*, 1976

ottom left Travis Bickle roams the streets around Times Square in his cocoon- ~e cab. De Niro in *Taxi Driver*, 1976

bove A study in solitude. De Niro in his favourite role as Michael Vronsky in ~~e *Deer Hunter*, 1978

De Niro, as Jake La Motta, seeks redemption in the ring in *Raging Bull*, 1980

of *New York, New York*, Scorsese's stock was not at a particularly high premium in Hollywood. De Niro, however, was an Oscar-wining actor who was emerging as a fully blown movie star, his name was now enough to guarantee finance for a picture. When they got round the table in Scorsese's apartment, the director may have had the reputation, but De Niro was the one with the clout. De Niro remained silent for most of the meeting, listening quietly to the studio's concerns as articulated by Field. Most of the issues were dealt with agreeably, even the idea of filming in black and white. But Scorsese recalls that at one point Field asked why anyone would want to make a movie about a man who was such a cockroach.

De Niro broke his silence.

'He's not a cockroach,' he said simply.

The tone of his comment was flat and resolute rather than threatening, but the studio was left in no doubt about De Niro's commitment to the film, the subject, and the director. David Field left the meeting having agreed to underwrite a three-week trip to the island of St Martin in the Caribbean for Scorsese and De Niro to rewrite the script without the offending scene.

For Scorsese, whose idea of an island is Manhattan, the prospect of spending weeks in the Caribbean was anathema. De Niro convinced him, however. The actor virtually nursemaided his director through his anxiety about being away from his beloved New York. He would wake him at 7.30 every morning with coffee and the two men would then get down to serious work.

'Marty and I liked parts of Schrader's script but not others,' according to De Niro. 'We still had to make it our own. So we revised the script and went over every scene.

'We talked about how people had this kind of hippie attitude toward relationships. At the time people were saying "I don't care what she does," or "I don't care what he does," or "If you really love this person then you won't make demands." To me and to Marty that attitude was basically bullshit. It was ignoring basic emotions. It was saying that you have no right to feel them and, if you do, you're a jerk or you're not hip. It's a lot of bullshit. The fact is you're entitled to have those feelings. Some people may really feel they don't have them but they're unusual. Other people express them but in a hostile kind of way. I used to see people smiling and saying "Hi", like Hare Krishna types. They're smiling at me but they're really aggressive and hustling you to give them money.

'What we wanted with Jake was to have something that is very straight-out. Jake himself is primitive, he can't hide certain feelings. I worked with

Jake, the real Jake La Motta. I would pick his brain. There are a lot of things going on in there. I admired the fact that he was at least willing to question himself and his actions. But what's he going to do? Should he be like a college professor and try to say, "Well, I think the reason that I did that was because of so and so"? He tried to talk that way at times but he was more cunning. He'd look at you deadpan, or he'd laugh about certain things. He would protect himself sometimes, but then he would say, "Aah, I was a son-of-a-bitch." I always thought there was something very decent about him somewhere.'

At the end of three weeks on St Martin, De Niro and Scorsese had rewritten the entire movie. Characters had disappeared, others had been condensed, others still had been amalgamated. And, much to United Artists' relief, the masturbation sequence had disappeared. Neither De Niro nor Scorsese took credit for the rewrite. The script they delivered to United Artists had only their initials on the cover page. Final credit for the screenplay of *Raging Bull* still went to Paul Schrader and Mardik Martin.

From their first collaboration on *Mean Streets* to their most recent on *Casino*, the relationship between Scorsese and De Niro has been unique. No other actor and director trust each other so completely, and that trust was distilled into an unbreakable bond on *Raging Bull*. Creatively they were able to commend themselves into each other's hands. It is debatable whether any actor and director of their status have worked as closely as these two on this film.

'At times he'd say "Let me try something" and I would trust him and say "Go ahead," ' says Scorsese of De Niro. 'And I would generally like what he did so we would keep pushing each other in that way and it became that kind of collaboration. I knew that inevitably – especially if we were in a situation where we had to improvise something or we were in a situation and we had to roll with it and something happened by accident – I knew that he was the one person who would find the truth in the action.'

The relationship between Scorsese and De Niro goes beyond the creative. De Niro plays a very specific role in Martin Scorsese's personal demonology. It is a role that he plays for no one else, and no one else plays it for his director. They are mirror images, opposite sides of the same coin. The best work in each of their careers has been done in tandem. Together they appear to be much more than simply the sum of their parts, and the films they make separately often seem to be merely marking time until they can work together again.

'I think Bobby and Marty are like brothers,' says Steven Spielberg, who has known each man for a long time. 'There's something about Bobby being Marty's alter ego. Marty allows Bobby to do the violence, he allows Bobby to be the hitman so to speak. He allows Bobby to take the fall, lets Bobby go over the top and lose control so that Marty can remain in control. I think Bobby is just wonderful as a sort of extension of what Marty might have been if he hadn't been a film-maker.'

17 Jake and Vickie

APART FROM JAKE LA MOTTA himself, the two key roles in *Raging Bull* are those of Joey, Jake's brother, and Vickie, La Motta's second wife. The character of Joey is actually a combination of two people – Joey himself and Jake La Motta's childhood friend Pete Petrella, who took the pen name Pete Savage for the autobiography.

When they were looking for an actor to play the part De Niro remembered someone from a film he had seen on late-night television some time before. The film was a low-budget exploitation movie about the Mafia called *Death Collector*. It is one of those films that you may have seen without ever knowing it, since it is also variously known as *Family Enforcer*, *The Collector* and *The Enforcer*. This 1975 melodrama is instantly forgettable but for the performance of actor Joe Pesci in a supporting role. De Niro had decided he was perfect for Joey. The problem was that Pesci was no longer acting.

'I walked away from the business in '75 just after doing that movie, my first film,' he says. 'I did a lot of jobs after that. I went to Vegas, I was a labourer, then I went to the Bronx and ran a restaurant for some friends of mine for a while. That's where I got a phone call from Martin Scorsese asking me to be in *Raging Bull* and that's what brought me back into acting.'

Having seen Pesci in person both De Niro and Scorsese felt that he might be a little too old to play Joey. They asked him to come back several times. 'It's a good role, not a great role,' De Niro told him over one working dinner, as though he were already hedging his bets. Pesci, meanwhile, had told them that he was only interested in coming back to the business if he had a part that would prove he was good. In the meantime De Niro and Scorsese saw other actors, but they always came back to Pesci. For his part Pesci, who had started acting as a five-year-old, was sufficiently pragmatic not to get his hopes up.

'In the beginning I didn't really care because the part of Jake's brother was small and I figured they should give it to a working actor who really wanted it,' he says. 'I had got myself out of that place in Hollywood where you are at everybody's mercy all the time. You get to the point out there where you bump into walls and say "Excuse me" in case you might have offended someone who could get you a job. I wanted to get away from all that and get into a position where everybody treated you like a man. But when I met Marty and Bob I saw that working for them would be different.'

The casting of *Raging Bull* was starting to operate like a cinematic chain letter. While they were trying to make their minds up about Pesci as Joey, Pesci then recommended someone else for Vickie. Cathy Moriarty was a seventeen-year-old who had never acted before. By the time Pesci suggested her, casting director Cis Corman was almost at her wits' end. She had considered more than a hundred actresses, scoured Playboy clubs, and even checked out Florida resorts in the search for Jake La Motta's dream girl. Jodie Foster's mother had even had her daughter photographed, much to her embarrassment, in alluring swimsuit poses in the hope that she might get the part. But when Pesci showed her Moriarty's photograph she knew she had found her Vickie.

Cathy Moriarty is one of seven children born in the space of nine years. The Moriartys are a large but very close family who even now take a keen interest in each others' lives. It was Cathy's ambition to be an actress and follow in the footsteps of her heroine, Judy Holliday.

'I said to my mother when I was sixteen that I wanted to be an actress,' she says. 'She said, "That's really great, Cathy," but of course it was the last thing she wanted to hear. I really did want to be Judy Holliday. I was always putting on little plays and stuff and I have an active imagination. I did want to go to acting school but there just wasn't the money for that kind of stuff. With seven children my folks had other things to worry about than acting lessons for me. So I did the best I could; I was going to open auditions and that kind of thing.

'Then when I was seventeen I met Joe Pesci in a night-club. I wasn't old enough to be in the night-club but I was there anyway. I had never met him and I didn't know he knew me but apparently he had been watching me. Anyway he came up to me and said, "You know you resemble Vickie La Motta very much." At this stage he didn't even have the part yet. But I sent my picture down and I got a call and in October 1978 I went in and met Bobby and Marty.'

Both De Niro and Scorsese were immensely taken with this stunning newcomer and saw in her the potential to be Vickie La Motta. Moriarty had never acted before but the three of them worked together for three intensive months to school her in her craft.

'I never ever figured I would get the part,' Moriarty says now. 'I just figured I was getting free acting lessons. I had applied for a grant to go to acting school but back in 1976 when I applied they didn't consider acting to be a profession. So I was happy and delighted to be in Marty and Bobby's company and get my free acting lessons. When I actually got the part it was a bonus. When they told me I thought, Great. What else could I say? I didn't think I had a shot in hell at actually getting work out of this. After all, who was I? I was just a kid off the streets.'

Moriarty had been working with De Niro and Scorsese from November 1978 until the February of the following year. On 4 and 5 February they shot a two-day screen test on a sound stage on 5th Street in New York. Three scenes were shot in the test. There was a scene at the pool where Jake first sees Vickie, a fight scene between Jake and Vickie, and one of the most dramatic scenes in the film, where a marauding Jake breaks down a bathroom door to get to Vickie who has taken refuge inside. When they saw the results of the test they knew they had found the right woman. But there was still another snag. Moriarty was an untried non-professional, which raised problems with the American actors' union, the Screen Actors Guild. They were pressuring Scorsese to use a professional actress. Cis Corman solved the dilemma by going to the SAG with ten pictures of Vickie La Motta and ten pictures of Cathy Moriarty. Once they saw the resemblance the SAG agreed.

Looking back on those early days, Cathy Moriarty is still stunned by the whole experience. One regret now is that she never quite appreciated what was happening to her at the time.

'The first time I saw Robert De Niro in person I don't think I paid much attention to who he was. I know he wasn't this big movie star because he was so nice and regular to me. He was nice to my mother. He'd call on the phone and say "Hi!" He was just a regular guy. I remember one Christmas I got pneumonia and he called one Saturday after he had come back from Los Angeles. When he heard I had been sick he came over at Christmas and I remember he gave me a big kiss. And I thought Wow!

'He was an absolute gentleman to me. He was lovely, he was very concerned and caring. You have to consider that at this stage I was only eighteen years old. Here I was, an Irish-Catholic girl being pitched into this situation with these three single Italian men. But Robert De Niro and Martin Scorsese were so exceptionally lovely to me and so concerned and so caring that I will always be grateful to them.

'Off-set they are like a pair of kids, laughing and joking. It's like Dennis the Menace. But on the set it's very different. I didn't know then what I know now but they were incredibly professional and businesslike. They have a rapport between the two of them which is like a friendship which goes beyond friendship, and a professionalism which is almost unspoken. It's hard to describe what they have other than as a relationship that anyone would die for. I think that's why they work so well together.'

De Niro's courtliness towards Cathy Moriarty is something he would repeat with several young female co-stars – notably Uma Thurman – over the years. In these kinds of relationship he commands all the power and respect of the younger actress, so that he seems to control their perform-ance the way he likes to control his own life.

For much of the film Moriarty was a privileged spectator as De Niro and Scorsese held long conversations about the movie in general and Vickie La Motta in particular. There was, however, none of the macho posturing that had contributed, according to Julia Phillips, to making Cybill Shepherd's life a misery on *Taxi Driver*.

'The way the movie was shot I wasn't able to create my own character, I was playing somebody else,' Moriarty explains. 'I wasn't really playing Vickie La Motta, I was playing Jake La Motta's image of her, I was playing what Robert De Niro saw through his eyes. I was a little confused on that aspect and I didn't get a chance to meet her or anything like that when we were shooting. Then afterwards I did finally meet her and she was lovely.

'Bobby would do his homework and he would come to work and he would be in character and that would be it. Then when he goes home from work he is still in character. I was very fortunate to be the one that he taught how to do that. Learning acting from a genius like De Niro is like getting singing lessons from Pavarotti. You may think it difficult to teach what he does but to me he could. I was only eighteen, I was willing to learn, I was like a sponge. It was Bobby who taught me to always listen, always pay attention.'

The first scenes of *Raging Bull* to be filmed were shot in April 1979 on a California sound stage that was doubling for Madison Square Garden. The occasion was the 1946 contest between Jake La Motta and Sugar Ray Robinson, one of five epic encounters between the two deadly rivals over the years. The day's shooting had been prefaced by the arrival of a message for Scorsese from screenwriter Paul Schrader, whose script De Niro and Scorsese had rewritten. The telegram said, 'I did it my way, Jake did it his way, you do it your way.'

De Niro was in the best shape of his life. He had been working out for almost two years. Scorsese recalls that during the shooting of *New York, New York* in 1977 he would disappear into his trailer during breaks to work out and shadow-box. Once he got down to serious preparation he borrowed Sylvester Stallone's trainer to help hone his body into fighting condition. The fight scenes in *Raging Bull* are both extraordinarily brutal and extraordinarily poetic as both Scorsese and De Niro capture the spirit of Jake La Motta as a primal force punishing himself through his ordeals in the ring. Violence plays a very important and specific role in the films of Martin Scorsese. From *Mean Streets* to *Casino* his films examine violence as part of human behaviour, not for its own sake. Jake La Motta was the very quintessence of that philosophy, a man for whom violence was not so much an aspect of his behaviour but rather his natural state.

'The fight scenes would take some really critical physical stamina on the part of Bob and everyone else,' Scorsese recalls. 'They had to be shot over and over again. It would take patience too because very often you would get maybe two or three shots a day and that would be it. I remember talking to Bob two days in a row and he said to me, "What do I do in this shot?" and I said, "In this shot you get hit." And we went on to the next one. I got it all worked out and he said, "What about this one?" And I said, "In this one, you get hit!" It was really funny.'

The fight scenes also had to be shot in slow motion so that they would have as much impact as possible in the film. That required an additional discipline from De Niro. He came up with an idea that was as brilliant as it was simple. To shoot the fight scenes properly Scorsese had quartered the ring and would work in one section at a time. De Niro had a punch-bag put in one of the other corners of the ring. While Scorsese was setting up De Niro would be working up a sweat. When the time came to roll the cameras he would simply move to the spot where they were shooting, already looking as if he was in the middle of a title fight. For De Niro the scenes in the ring were rather like being at the Arthur Murray School of Dancing.

'In the fight scenes the punches are all choreographed,' he explains. 'Your opponent has to move his head in a certain direction when you hit him and the camera has to be at a certain angle so that it looks like he's been hit. Then you lay in the sound later. When I was alone in the ring, like in the opening scene, it wasn't a problem. I could do whatever I wanted, warming up, shadow-boxing and so on. But when there's another person there you have to rehearse so that nobody gets hurt accidentally. It's pretty specific. Once you do it, it's like learning lines – you know them, and then you just do them. It's all part of the rehearsing, the practising.'

All the while De Niro was being schooled by La Motta himself. The prime concern for any fighter, even above that of hurting the opponent, is to ensure that he does not get hurt himself. La Motta taught De Niro about defence and how to block. He also taught him his low-crouching, almost crab-like ring stance which made him so hard to hit and helped him soak up punishment. So effective a pupil was the actor that it wasn't long before he was inflicting on his teacher the sort of punishment he used to take in the ring. Apart from the black eyes, La Motta also claims that United Artists had to spend thousands of dollars on remedial dental work and surgery to his chin after his bouts with De Niro. He also fractured a rib but didn't claim for that, putting it down as an occupational hazard.

La Motta himself is convinced that De Niro, as he says in his final monologue in which he quotes Brando from *On the Waterfront*, 'could have been a contender'.

'Bobby's a main-event fighter,' he told the *New York Daily News* at the time. 'I'm not kidding. He's thirty-five, but he moves and hits like a nineteen-year-old. Any time he wants to quit acting I could easily make him into a champion. He's that good.'

But De Niro made it plain to others that he was not interested in fighting for its own sake. it was purely a means of preparing for this role.

'Don't make a meal of it,' he cautioned. 'I'm not one of those actors who goes around in private giving off that macho thing. I lead a low-profile life. The world is full of guys who can't wait to come up to you in a bar and show you how tough they are. What Jake taught me was how to take punishment, but I'm not anxious to prove a point.

'I know I'm supposed to be the actor who carries his role over into private life. There is a small spillage, but I don't flip out. I'm not eating glass for breakfast or beating up the wife as a result of getting inside Jake La Motta's skin.'

Earlier he had told *Newsweek* magazine that he didn't understand why a man would want to stand in a ring and take all that punishment. He speculated that perhaps there had to be some kind of guilt involved. The same argument might well be applied to De Niro himself. What guilt might he feel to punish himself with this kind of near-masochistic preparation? What pain has he gone through in his life that he can re-enact it so apparently effortlessly on screen?

De Niro's study of Jake La Motta was rapidly approaching the point of obsession. He almost moved in with him, spending the better part of two years virtually full-time at his apartment. When she sued for divorce, La Motta's wife Deborah claimed that the pressure of having the actor around so much undoubtedly contributed to the break-up of her marriage.

As his preparations grew more and more intense, De Niro became more and more like La Motta. Vickie La Motta, whom he visited several times in Florida, told *Playboy* magazine that he was so like her former husband that she wanted to sleep with him. An affair, she claimed, seemed like the logical step. De Niro, however, despite being in the process of separating from his wife Diahnne Abbott, apparently behaved throughout in a businesslike and professional manner, much to her disappointment. 'I should have just attacked him or something,' she said ruefully.

After spending time with Vickie, De Niro then used that to further hone and shape the performance of Cathy Moriarty. Her acting classes did not stop after the sessions leading up to the screen test.

'I was born at the end of the sixties, and when I took my screen test I had to play a woman from the forties and fifties,' she explains. 'First of all I was just a child, I didn't know anything about it. They gave me eyebrows and red lips and boobs and I'm thinking, My God, did people actually dress this way? But when I think back on it now I was able to fit into that era in a way that De Niro actually taught me. He spent lots of time with me and we had lots of coffees and talks together. I remember when I came to California in April 1979 he had me moved to his hotel because he was worried about me. He was very concerned and he would spend a lot of time with me. We would go over scrapbooks because he was so into his character. He also knew that I was playing a character who was seen through his character's eyes, and that I didn't have much choice in things. So he tried to teach me all of those things.'

Jake La Motta's jealousy was one of the prime destructive forces in his life. One of the key scenes in *Raging Bull* is the moment where Jake, consumed by his obsessive jealousy and his paranoid suspicions that Vickie is seeing other men, accuses Joey of sleeping with her. It begins innocently enough as the two men tinker with a television set in Jake's house.

'The scene with Jake La Motta fixing the TV is an example of a great scene,' according to De Niro. 'The domestic situation, fixing a TV, talking about something that has nothing to do with anything, and then finally just right to the point: "Did you fuck my wife?" We came up with that scene right on the set. We said, "How about fixing a TV?" Some stupid little domestic sort of thing where there is an incident waiting to happen. It just unleashes something that's always been there. It's just below the surface, you're living with it and all of a sudden this jealousy Jake had with his brother comes up.

'He has strong feelings about his wife and his brother that are close to the surface. So if he gets angry about something or he's not in a good mood or whatever, then whatever his brother says or does sets him off. Jake beats up his brother because he thinks he's been with his wife. And he happens to be right. And that's the whole thing in the TV scene about what's right, what's true, and what we perceive to be true. Maybe it's better not to know. On the surface nobody has seen anything or alluded to anything or shown anything that might have happened. But Jake's jealous of Joey and Vickie. Even though he hasn't seen anything, he knows something. It's like a sixth sense. A woman may ask her husband when he comes home late, "Where were you?" She knows something is up. She can't prove it and maybe she doesn't want to know. But Jake wants to know. Here's Joey and here's Vickie, maybe there's something. Jake's not sure. He's jealous on principle. So what does it mean? Does he have the right to pursue it? Maybe a person who is more middle-class, a refined type, someone not like Jake, would just let it go and not make a big deal about it. But Jake goes after his brother and he's right, his brother was with Vickie.'

Both Moriarty and Pesci, who played that scene with De Niro, are astonished by his claim that Joey and Vickie La Motta were actually unfaithful. For Pesci it is an example of Jake's paranoia manifesting itself in De Niro. But the actor did spend time with both Jake and Vickie La Motta and, given his passion for detail in the parts he plays, he must have asked the question at some time. It would seem that we have to give him the benefit of the doubt here.

The fight between Joey and Jake is one of several domestic confrontations in *Raging Bull*. The conflict in his private life is somehow legitimised in his conflicts in the ring. Once he is within the confines of the ropes La Motta is allowed to revert back to his primal instincts.

'I have felt personally embarrassed watching some of the scenes in *Raging Bull*, indeed in all of the Scorsese–De Niro collaborations,' says Steven Spielberg. 'I feel like I'm eavesdropping. I feel like I'm being a voyeur into a real situation with real people whose dignity and privacy I should respect. Marty has a way of bringing the audience into his scenes and starts to make you feel like you are an intruder in someone else's life.'

De Niro went from being in the best shape of his life to being in the worst shape of his life within six months on *Raging Bull*. The film captures the decline and ultimate redemption of La Motta, and it is therefore necessary to show him as the obese self-mockery of a man that he had become. When Goldie Hawn had to undergo a similar transformation in the film *Death Becomes Her* she used a blimp-like 'fat suit' to turn herself into an ice-cream-eating couch potato. De Niro was going to do it the hard way. He would simply put on the weight himself, and the shooting schedule was arranged to accommodate him.

The schedule originally called for five weeks of fight scenes, ten weeks of dramatic scenes, a two-month break, and then almost three weeks of 'fat' scenes. Because of the difficulties involved, the fight scenes ran over, and it was ten weeks before De Niro was able to start tackling the dramatic scenes. The final dramatic scene, a shot by the pool, called for De Niro as Jake in immediate post-retirement to be at an intermediate weight. He had to gain the weight for this scene during the ten weeks of shooting the initial dramatic sequences.

'I remember on the last month of shooting before we took the break,' says Cathy Moriarty. 'We would hang out together and I'd be sitting in his trailer watching him drink endless chocolate milk shakes and countless pieces of cheesecake. And he suffered for it too – he had constant heartburn.'

Once those scenes were shot, the production shut down for two months and De Niro went off to Europe to, in the words of Martin Scorsese, 'eat his way through France and Italy'.

'It's very hard,' he said at the time. 'You think the more you eat the more you're going to gain weight. But you have to do it three times a day. You have to get up in the morning and just eat. Eat that breakfast, eat those pancakes, eat lunch, eat dinner, even if you're not hungry. It's murder.'

By December 1979 De Niro was back on the set, having gained an astonishing 60 pounds on his European trip.

'Two months had passed and he knocked at my door and this whole different man came in,' says Cathy Moriarty of her first meeting with the new De Niro. 'He was a huge man and the weight made him snore loudly whenever he was in the make-up chair. Even though he had put on the weight he still had to go through a lot of make-up to make him look like Jake. He would lay down in this barber's chair to get all the latex and prosthetics put on him and all of a sudden you'd hear this big old snore. I had to keep poking him to wake him up. He was transformed into a whole different man. I think it is just incredible that, simply healthwise, anyone would put himself through that. I could hear him wheezing with all that extra weight. I was really concerned about him.

'But I could understand why he did it after working with him on this picture. He is probably one of the most disciplined actors I have ever met. He would go into the gym at lunchtime during the fight scenes. He is so disciplined with everything that when we would drive home together after filming he would get out two miles ahead of me and run the rest of the way home.'

Cathy Moriarty's concern for De Niro's health was shared by Martin

Scorsese. He was so alarmed by the condition of his star that he cut the scheduled two and a half weeks shooting back to ten days.

'Bobby's weight was so extreme that his breathing was like mine when I have an asthma attack,' he says. 'With the bulk he put on there was no more doing forty takes. There were three or four takes. The body dictated things. He just became that person.'

'I just can't fake acting,' said De Niro. 'I know movies are an illusion and the first rule is to fake it, but not for me. I'm too curious. I want to deal with all the facts of the character, thin or fat.

'As far as gaining weight the external speaks for itself. But the internal changes, how you feel and how it makes you behave – for me to play that character, it was the best thing I could have done. Just by having the weight on it really made me feel a certain way and behave in a certain way. You feel your weight on your back when you stand up. It was a little like going to a foreign land. A doctor was monitoring my health and he wasn't too happy about it. I had a little problem with my blood pressure.'

However, during a photo-shoot for *Life* magazine, the newly single De Niro revealed that gaining weight had not had any detrimental effect on at least one part of his life.

'It didn't interfere with my sex life,' he assured the magazine's readers. 'I mean, some women never give me a look unless they find out who I am. But believe it or not, some women liked me fat – they thought I was a big teddy bear.'

But the drawbacks more than outweighed whatever bonuses his extra weight may have provided in increased sex appeal.

'I reached the point where I couldn't tie my shoes and I was huffing and puffing and my breath started to sound strange. I was up at seven in the morning to start the day's eating. I really pigged out. My daughter didn't exactly ask me to stop picking her up from school but she quickly got to the point where she started to get embarrassed for her friends to see me. After all, I looked like an animal.'

That was exactly the look that both De Niro and Scorsese were seeking for in the climax of the movie. Jake was still in jail but, in contrast to Schrader's script, there was no masturbation. Instead he would pound his fists again and again on the cell wall, screaming, 'I am not an animal.' The drive for realism did not extend to using a real cell wall – a rubber section was substituted.

'I think of Jake as someone just battering along, doing all the wrong things, getting banged around. He made the wrong choices about things, sometimes for the right reasons, sometimes – maybe – just because he didn't want to be told what to do.

'In the end I think there was a lot of remorse with Jake, I think with his brother and his wife. He sort of takes it and he's sort of stoic. He takes the punishment. He created it so he has to live with it.'

In preparing and filming *Raging Bull*, De Niro and La Motta were virtually constant companions for two years. During shooting La Motta was on the set every day for the ten weeks it took to film the fight scenes. When the final shot was in the can the two men looked each other in the eye. Jake said, 'Yeah, I know. Goodbye.'

And De Niro said, 'That's right.'

18 'I Guess I Should Have Ducked'

OST PEOPLE THINK ABOUT dieting just after the Christmas holidays. For De Niro dieting was a major priority at the beginning of 1980, since he was still some 60 pounds overweight from playing Jake La Motta. He had embarked on the task of gaining weight with admirable single-mindedness, by simply eating from dawn till dusk and beyond. His solution to his burgeoning obesity was equally direct.

There was no miracle diet, no magic pill, no exotic regime. According to De Niro it was all done through simple willpower.

'I just ate less. That's all,' he said. 'It's not easy. I made myself do it. It's as bad as stopping smoking. I ate a little less of everything and cut out the milk and beer I had been drinking before.'

Almost everything in De Niro's life is a means to an end in terms of a part he is playing or might play in the future. Even the weight loss was factored into his next characterisation, in *True Confessions*, which he consciously started when he was about fifteen pounds above his regular fighting weight. He believed it would make his character look sleek and well fed. He and Robert Duvall play brothers who in 1948 become involved in a notorious Los Angeles murder. Duvall is the detective, De Niro plays a priest. His Monsignor Desmond Spellacy is a ruthless, upwardly mobile priest who has all but forsaken his vocation for the sake of influence and power. His main patron is the man who his brother Tom, played by Duvall, suspects of being heavily involved in the killing.

Duvall's investigation leads to the end of both of their careers. But De Niro's monsignor, relegated to an obscure desert parish away from the bright lights of the Los Angeles social scene, is at least redeemed by having rediscovered his vocation.

Members of the Catholic media and the Catholic hierarchy praised De Niro for his characterisation. They pointed out that Monsignor Desmond Spellacy was the most convincing cleric seen on screen in years. Given that De Niro had used his still-fleshy features to convey the impression of a 'fat cat' priest who has grown comfortable by paying more attention to his secular rather than his religious duties, it may not have been quite as much of a compliment as they thought.

True Confessions is a curiosity. Directed by the Belgian Ulu Grosbard, whom De Niro describes as one of his favourite directors, it is very much an actors' movie. De Niro gives a compelling performance, but it was plainly not the sort of role in which the public wanted to see him. The film died at the box-office with no better than moderate reviews.

While he was playing the priest on screen his off-screen sinning was continuing. He was still seeing Helena Lisandrello, who by this time claimed that she had become pregnant by accident, and that De Niro was the father.

'It happened at Chateau Marmont,' she told Cindy Adams of the *New York Post*. De Niro had taken up permanent residence at the exclusive Los Angeles hotel after moving out of the family home. 'I didn't have my diaphragm,' she continued. 'But I knew he didn't love me so I didn't tell him. I aborted. He never knew.'

Martin Scorsese, meanwhile, was frantically preparing *Raging Bull* for release. He was editing round the clock, which meant he wasn't seeing much of his new bride. He and the actress Isabella Rossellini, daughter of Ingrid Bergman and the Italian director Roberto Rossellini, had married in September 1979 while *Raging Bull* was still filming. The cutting of the film had not been going well, Scorsese becoming bogged down in the editing of the sound effects. Eventually producer Irwin Winkler stood over him and demanded a final print of the film so that it could go to the labs in time to be duplicated. Scorsese still wasn't happy about the sound of one line in the film and, obviously near the point of exhaustion, threatened to take his name off the completed movie. Winkler had the good sense not to take him seriously. *Raging Bull* finally opened in New York only four days after Scorsese had been prised away from editing it.

The reviews were ecstatic.

'De Niro's great performance captures the humanity in the bull and the tragic excitement in his rage,' said *Newsweek*. *Time* commented, 'De Niro is always absorbing and credible even when his character isn't.' Stanley Kauffmann of the *New Republic* said, 'Here they have found the best beast for De Niro in La Motta, best because free of patent psychopathy he is a 'normal' man capable of overpowering fury but still answerable to some social canons and therefore accessible to pathos rather than to clinical category.'

There were dissenting voices too, notably that of Pauline Kael, whose enthusiasm for De Niro had begun to wane noticeably over his past couple of films.

'De Niro wears scar tissue and a big bent nose that deforms his face,' she wrote in the New Yorker. 'It's a miracle that he didn't grow them – he grew everything else. He developed a thick muscled neck and a fighter's body, and for the scenes of the broken, drunken La Motta he put on so much weight that he seems to have sunk in the fat with hardly a trace of himself left. What De Niro does in this picture isn't acting, exactly. I'm not sure what it is. Though it may at some level be awesome, it certainly isn't pleasurable. He has so little expressive spark that what I found myself thinking about wasn't La Motta or the movie, but the metamorphosis of De Niro.'

Kael was a voice crying in the wilderness. Other critics were unanimous in their praise of De Niro as Jake. However, Kael does raise a valid point. Is what De Niro does acting or is it simply very detailed impersonation? He says he can't fake acting but, as Kael suggests, perhaps that's what acting is all about.

Although Kael caviled, the film was buoyed by other excellent reviews, but it was not a hit. Raging Bull had cost around $12 million to make and it recouped just over $10 million at the American box-office. By the time overseas revenues and ancillary sales to television, video and cable are added the film would have made a small profit for its backers. However, its critical acclaim and enduring fame – it was voted Best Film of the Eighties by America's film critics – will far outweigh its box-office returns.

After Raging Bull had opened in America, Scorsese, De Niro and editor Thelma Schoonmaker took the film on a gruelling round of international junkets and film festivals where it was greeted with universal acclaim. Harvey Keitel went with them, even though he wasn't in the film, so the Mean Streets trio was reunited. Scorsese is a big Sinatra fan and privately saw himself, De Niro and Keitel as a latter-day Rat Pack, unlikely as it may seem. The schedule also gave Scorsese the opportunity to lecture on film preservation, a subject close to his heart, but by the time they reached the Italian leg of the tour he collapsed with exhaustion. Whatever Rat Pack-style hi-jinks he might have planned had to be abandoned.

De Niro seems much more at ease in Europe than he does in America. He was much more accessible to the press and in Britain he even did television interviews and chat shows, something he shies away from whenever possible in America. Just as Taxi Driver had fallen foul of the British censors, so Raging Bull was running into difficulties in Britain. This time they came from the Rank cinema chain which was due to screen the film throughout the country but had decided that it was not suitable. Rank was unhappy about the level of profanity in the film and the première, which De Niro had gone to London to attend, had to be postponed for several weeks.

The actor was surprised by the ban but his public comments remained diplomatic.

'I did not know that Rank refused to release the film, so I can't comment on their attitude,' he told the *London Evening Standard*. 'But it is up to the individual to decide whether or not they like it. Swearing is in keeping with the lifestyle of the people portrayed in this film. Everyone knows there are certain cultures which speak that way. When you are playing that character the language is necessary.'

In the end *Raging Bull* was picked up by a rival cinema chain owned by veteran impresario Lord Lew Grade and, after a delay of a few weeks, played in Britain to great success and critical praise.

The difficulties with Rank were not the only problems on De Niro's European tour. On the Italian leg of the trip the actor was arrested as a suspected terrorist and held for 90 minutes by police while his identity was checked. After it had been discovered that he was indeed who he claimed to be, the Italian police apologised and allowed him to go on his way. They blamed the incident on a bad joke by the paparazzi who were following De Niro's car in the hope of getting a picture. When the police stopped their car the photographers claimed they were chasing an important gangster, and the carabinieri took things from there.

After he had been released with his apology De Niro failed to see the funny side.

'Those guys will do anything to get a picture,' he said, adding ominously, 'I'd like to get some of them inside a ring.'

The Academy Awards for 1980 were due to be held in the Dorothy Chandler Pavilion in Los Angeles on Monday 30 March 1981. In contrast to previous years there was no clear-cut front-runner, the nominations spread around a number of films including *Raging Bull, Coal Miner's Daughter* (a biopic of country singing star Loretta Lynn), David Lynch's *The Elephant Man*, and the directing debut of Robert Redford, *Ordinary People. Raging Bull* and *The Elephant Man* had eight nominations each while *Coal Miner's Daughter* had seven. The New York critics had given De Niro the edge going into the ceremony by naming him Best Actor once again. His *Raging Bull* co-star Joe Pesci, who was being sued for $2.5 million by the real Joey La Motta, was named Best Supporting Actor. However, it was Redford's story of upper-class family angst – cruelly dubbed *Ordinary Rich People* in some quarters – which took Best Picture in New York. Rising talent Jonathan Demme was named best director for his Howard Hughes road movie, *Melvin and Howard*.

De Niro was still favourite finally to pick up his first Best Actor Oscar. He had even decided that he would attend the ceremony this year. But there were still some dissenters who felt that Pauline Kael just about had it right. They included Italian superstar Marcello Mastroianni.

'By nature the actor is a kind of wonder who can allow himself to change personalities,' he said. 'If you don't know how to do this it's better to change professions. I think it's ridiculous to imagine that to play a taxi driver or a boxer you have to spend months and months 'studying' the life of cab drivers and the weight of boxers.'

Mastroianni's comments apart, De Niro still seemed the outstanding favourite. His rivals in the Best Actor category were Robert Duvall for *The Great Santini*, John Hurt for *The Elephant Man*, Jack Lemmon for *Tribute* and Peter O'Toole for *The Stunt Man*. Only Hurt, given the Academy's fondness for honouring actors who play disabled or disadvantaged characters, would appear to stand a chance against De Niro. The British actor's sensitive portrayal of the hideously deformed John Merrick had touched audiences and critics alike.

By the afternoon of 30 March, all bets were off. For the first time in their history the Academy Awards had been postponed and De Niro and Scorsese found themselves at the centre of an international controversy.

President Ronald Reagan had been leaving the Hilton Hotel in Washington on the afternoon of 30 March when a crazed young man opened fire, hitting the president and several of his aides. Reagan was taken to hospital, but although shot in the chest he was not seriously injured. 'I guess I should have ducked, honey,' the former Western star told his wife Nancy when she visited him. The gunman was taken into custody almost immediately by FBI and Secret Service agents. His name was John Hinckley and his motive was most unexpected.

Hinckley claimed to have shot Ronald Reagan to try to attract the attention of actress Jodie Foster. This deranged young man chose to act out a scenario from *Taxi Driver* in the hope of convincing one of the stars of the film that he loved her. In doing so he had cast himself in the role of Travis Bickle. Once he had been identified, FBI agents raided his home and discovered a letter from Hinckley to Foster. It was one of many he had written to the star.

'By sacrificing my freedom and possibly my life,' it said, 'I hope to change your life about me. This letter is being written an hour before I leave the Hilton Hotel . . .'

The shooting of the president, who had ironically taped an opening address to the Oscar ceremonies to show just how far an actor could go without one, sent shock-waves through America. The motive for the shooting shook Hollywood, and especially De Niro, to the core. The shooting had taken place late morning Los Angeles time, and by two in the afternoon, while the crowds of fans and onlookers were already gathering outside the Dorothy Chandler Pavilion, the Academy announced that the ceremony had been postponed. It would take place the following evening, by which time it had been confirmed that President Reagan was recovering and out of danger.

For the second time in 24 hours the great and the good in Hollywood clambered into their tuxedos and their little black dresses, got into their limousines, and prepared themselves for the gridlock that is the approach to the Academy Awards venue. Nerves or not, Robert De Niro, with wife Diahnne Abbott accompanying him, was one of the first to arrive. The event was being televised that year by ABC, and one of the first people to meet the actor was an ABC page, Thomas Rogers, who had been detailed to escort him from his car to the auditorium. In those pre-red ribbon days De Niro was struck by a green ribbon that Rogers was sporting on his lapel. He asked what it was for and Rogers told him it was to show sympathy for the wave of murders of black children which was currently taking place in Atlanta, Georgia. De Niro was plainly moved by this and asked Rogers if he had another. The page did not, so he took off the one he was wearing and gave it to De Niro. The actor then went inside.

With the president having been shot only 24 hours before, the normally strict security had become stringent. Given the circumstances of the shooting De Niro and Scorsese – Jodie Foster was still at college at Yale at this time – had been assigned special FBI protection, although neither of them knew it at the time. Even their limousine drivers were FBI agents.

'I'm a Catholic. It's easy to make me feel guilty,' says Scorsese when people ask him about the shooting.

'I only learned about the connection on the actual Academy Awards night, the day after the president had been shot. I'd been washing up and dressing. I'd been nominated for *Raging Bull* but I knew I wasn't going to get it. I knew I wasn't going to win but that was okay, I would go anyway. There were some pictures on TV of the president being shot the day before but I had the sound turned off so I didn't know any connection to *Taxi Driver* existed.

'Myself, Harry Ufland, De Niro and our wives were the first ones to be let in that night,' he recalls. 'I thought, This is great, this is terrific. Then I had to go to the men's room and these three big guys came with me. Three big guys with jackets with a lot of metal inside. I'm not kidding! I think they had radios, they had wires and things hanging out of their ears. I remember thinking, Gee, this security is incredible tonight. The security is remarkable.'

Scorsese was no stranger to this type of security. Previously, when both *Taxi Driver* and Foster had been nominated in 1976, he had received a death threat saying that if Foster won he would pay with his life for what he made her do. He spent that Academy Awards ceremony in the company of armed FBI agents as well. Foster lost out as Best Supporting Actress to Beatrice Straight in *Network*, so the threat, if it was ever genuine, came to nothing.

As the evening wore on De Niro sat uncomfortably in the audience watching the awards being given out. He had to watch as Scorsese, as the director himself had predicted, missed out again. The Best Director award went to Robert Redford. But when the previous year's Best Actress winner, Sally Field, read out the name of the Best Actor winner, it was De Niro who walked down the aisle and up the steps to collect the statuette. For a man who had been so churlish, albeit unintentionally, on his first Oscar win, his acceptance speech was a masterpiece of Oscar night clichés.

'I'm a little nervous,' he said with an astonished smile. 'I'm sorry, I forgot my lines so the director wrote them down.'

De Niro then went on to thank Jake La Motta, who was in the audience. He also thanked 'Vickie La Motta and all the other wives, Joey La Motta, even though he's suing us. I want to thank my mother and father for having me and my grandmothers and grandfathers for having them. I want to thank everyone else involved in the film and I hope that I can share this with anyone that it means anything to and the rest of the world, especially with all the terrible things that are happening.'

Still wearing Thomas Rogers's green ribbon, he concluded by saying, 'I love everyone.'

Martin Scorsese was sitting in the audience basking in De Niro's reflected glory, still unaware of the controversy raging over *Taxi Driver*. He was hustled out of his seat by FBI agents while the Best Picture award was being presented, going only under protest because he felt leaving early was an insult to presenter Lillian Gish. Although his own film was nominated, Scorsese was offered little consolation by the FBI man who told him there was no point in waiting since 'the Redford picture' was going to win anyway. He was right and Scorsese was left to go backstage to congratulate his star and put out some kind of joint congratulatory statement on their success.

De Niro had already completed the winners' obligatory round of the various press rooms to be interviewed by print and electronic media. He too appears to have been unaware of the Hinckley connection. When he was asked directly about the link between *Taxi Driver* and the assassination attempt he said, 'I don't know about the story.' He then insisted that he did not want to discuss the matter at that point – nor at any point in the future, as it turned out. When Scorsese arrived De Niro broke the news to him. The director was stunned beyond words and it was a very subdued party that went off to celebrate at the exclusive Ma Maison restaurant.

The affair simply wouldn't go away. Eventually Hinckley was put on trial and *Taxi Driver* was screened for the jury several times during the proceedings. Scorsese felt then, as he does now, that this was grossly unfair, especially to Jodie Foster.

'The film is a disturbing picture but we made it as a labour of love,' he argues. 'I really thought nobody would see that picture. Only Bob had a sense that the movie might be more successful than we thought. When he put on the Mohawk wig, he realised we had something special.

'But showing the movie at the trial was unfair.' Scorsese illustrates the point the only way he knows how, with a cinematic metaphor. 'It's like the end of *Fahrenheit 451* where the guy is chased and they just pick up anyone at random so they can tell people at home, "It's okay. We caught him. You can rest." It's okay; he did it because of our picture. Now you can all sleep.'

De Niro was deeply disturbed by the notion that a film he was involved in could provoke such an extravagant and inappropriate response as an assassination attempt on the president. His reluctance to speak of it since suggests that he has used his famed powers of concentration to try his best to block the whole episode from his mind. It is something that is never spoken of in interviews, other than to express his relief that Jodie Foster managed to overcome the stigma and the trauma of the incident.

One of his few public comments came some years later at a rare question-and-answer session at the National Film Theatre in London. De Niro was asked whether real-life events supposedly triggered off by the movie disturbed him.

'Well, it bothers me, sure,' he said, before adding cryptically, 'but kids who see *Superman* can put a towel round their necks and jump from a roof. It can happen with anything.'

De Niro was so appalled by the whole business that he could not bring himself to even think about work for six months afterwards. It would continue to prey on his mind and his reaction to John Hinckley would play a part in the film that would provide him with his last great leading role to date.

Jodie Foster was hardest hit. She continued to study at Yale and wrote an eloquent and moving first-person article for *Esquire* magazine about the Hinckley controversy. Her studies meant she had to take a three-year break from the film business. She came back with a maturity beyond her years and within a decade she would establish herself as a double Oscar winner and the most powerful actress in the film industry.

19 '. . . Heeeere's Rupert!!'

D E NIRO EFFECTIVELY PUT his career on hold after the moment of his greatest triumph. John Hinckley's actions the previous day had put an Oscar win in perspective. What did it really mean? Was any film worth it if it could cost a life? Was any film worth the economic and political turmoil that might have ensued had Hinckley been a better shot?

Putting the brakes on an actor's career is not as easy it appears. Actors, like opera singers and conductors, can be booked up years in advance. They also have the responsibility of knowing that, once they reach the position that De Niro had now reached, the moment they agree to do a picture they start to provide work for hundreds of other people. It is not then simply a question of De Niro deciding he had had enough and not showing up for work for six months. Actors can either be 'off' or 'off-off'. An actor who is merely 'off' will not be working but know that he has a film to start in three months, for example. Being 'off-off' is more difficult. It is rather like trying to stop an oil tanker; it requires a lot of time. For De Niro not to work for six months actually means that for months before that he will not even look at a script. So although he was too disturbed to think about work immediately after the Hinckley shooting, he didn't actually get the break he was looking for until much later in that year. Within a few weeks of winning the Oscar, he was back at work on another film with Scorsese.

As Tom Cruise is now, De Niro was then. He was the man every producer wanted to have attached to their movie. Even though he was not looking for work, that did not stop producers from claiming he was interested in their particular project. As the British Royal Family used to, De Niro kept himself above the fray and did not issue denials. This made him something of a soft target for anyone looking to make a fast buck.

That is how, in August 1981, De Niro came to be linked with an alleged film about one of Britain's most notorious serial killers, Peter Sutcliffe, the 'Yorkshire Ripper'. The story appeared in the *Daily Star*, then the most downmarket of Britain's tabloids. It claimed that De Niro was being tipped to play Sutcliffe and that he had described it as 'an interesting challenge'. The story was complete nonsense and had been planted by a man notorious for hoaxing the more gullible tabloids. Not surprisingly De Niro was not available for comment. The only comment came from a spokesman for the London office of the UK distributor of *Raging Bull*. Since they would have as much idea of De Niro's career plans as they would of flying to the moon, the comment was to say the least anodyne. Nonetheless, it was followed up by other newspapers and the unfortunate mother of one of Sutcliffe's victims found herself in the desperately cruel position of trying to organise a campaign against a movie that never existed in the first place.

De Niro has not spoken at any length in public about his reactions to the John Hinckley shooting. As always he chose to express himself on film, by going back to make *King of Comedy* with Martin Scorsese, a remarkably prescient choice as it turned out in the wake of events. He and Scorsese had now worked together four times since they met at Jay Cocks's Christmas party; this would be their fifth collaboration. Onlookers assume that because they are both Italian-Americans Scorsese and De Niro go together like pasta and Parmesan. In fact they are quite different. Scorsese is a stereotypically volatile, excitable, Italian thoroughbred. De Niro, on the other hand, is only a quarter Italian. He also has Irish, Dutch and French blood which makes him inclined to be more moody and less ebullient. De Niro is the watcher, Scorsese the doer. They complement each other, especially in their often childlike sense of humour and jokiness.

Generally speaking their films together have been a mutual collaboration. They each bring their own qualities to the films, and even if one of them is reluctant, as Scorsese was with *Raging Bull*, eventually they'll come around. That was not the case with their fifth outing, *King of Comedy*.

The film, written by former *Newsweek* movie critic Paul Zimmermann, is the story of Rupert Pupkin, a nightmarish blend of Walter Mitty and Andy Warhol, who believes he is entitled to his fifteen minutes of fame. Pupkin desperately wants to be a comedian. His problem is that he is the world's least funny human being. Rupert's idol is chat show host Jerry Langford. When he manages to do a favour for Langford he tries to parlay that into the friendship it has already become in his delusional version of reality. When Langford will have nothing to do with him, Pupkin and a fellow celebrity hound kidnap him. His ransom will be a five-minute comedy spot for Rupert on his coast-to-coast chat show.

Zimmermann had worked on a version of the script with director Milos Forman. When Forman dropped out Zimmermann then sent it to Scorsese whose cause, along with De Niro's, he had championed from the early days. Scorsese liked it but said that he and Jay Cocks were already working on a script about a comedian. Eventually the script found its way to De Niro, who fell in love with it. He met Zimmermann, they discussed the project, and he bought the script. De Niro had owned the script for some time before he decided the time was right to make the movie. In the time between buying it and putting it into production he had become a star. Like most movie stars, this most private of men had found himself fair game for the Rupert Pupkins of this world, most of them pleasant and well-intentioned, a few of them undoubtedly not. It can be argued that this is simply the price De Niro has to pay. If he did not want to be pestered he should have chosen another line of work. It was the Rupert Pupkins and all the other fans, after all, who put down their money to make him the box-office draw that he now is. Nonetheless, it can't be easy for him or for anyone in that position. On top of the day-to-day annoyances, John Hinckley had underlined what can happen when a Rupert Pupkin gets out of control.

'Bobby understood the bravery of Rupert Pupkin, his chutzpah, the simplicity of his motives,' says Paul Zimmermann. 'Bobby said he liked the single-minded sense of purpose. People speak of Bobby as an instinctive actor but he also understands these characters on an intellectual level. I think Bobby understood Rupert because he's an obsessive person himself.

'I knew Bobby when he was just beginning. Bobby was always full of dignity and full of ambition. Then and now, he seems to carry a larger world, an imaginative world, along with him. Sometimes when you're with him you feel part of him is living in that greater, instinctive world. Brando had that quality. Bobby could see Rupert as someone who would die rather than live anonymously.'

De Niro's public rationale for doing the film was much more simple.

'I liked the script for *King of Comedy*,' he said. 'I liked the character and I thought it was funny. We shot it on the streets of New York City and it gave us the opportunity to use things that we both knew happened there. There's a scene in *Raging Bull* where everybody is yelling. I was yelling at my wife, she was yelling at me, people were yelling in the building, in the alley. Those neighbourhoods were noisy. During shooting someone yelled from the street and I responded as Jake and the crew laughed and we kept it. We could use that kind of craziness on *King of*

Comedy. One time an old lady, just a regular person, came over. I was sitting down outside of the building waiting for Jerry to come out. She came over and started talking to me and she kissed me and said something to me. It was very cute and funny and everyone laughed. We'd use spontaneous things like that.'

Although De Niro was very bullish about *King of Comedy*, Scorsese was not. He was still feeling physically below par after having completed *Raging Bull* and his concert movie, *The Last Waltz*, with Robbie Robertson. But eventually he relented. As they had done with *Raging Bull*, De Niro and Scorsese took Zimmermann's original script and a novelisation he had already written and went off to Long Island to come up with a shooting script.

'*King of Comedy* was an uphill battle for me,' said Scorsese afterwards. 'It was more Bob's project than mine and I wasn't a big help at the time. The motives for making a film are very important to me. They have to be good motives. Mine weren't very clear when I started out on this picture.'

Scorsese's poor health was a recurring problem on the set. He had suffered from chronic asthma since he was a child, and whenever he became stressed or physically worn down the attacks would start again. His physical collapse in Rome while promoting *Raging Bull* had been brought on by a bout of pneumonia which had also taken its toll. Sometimes on this film, he was so weak and listless that they couldn't start shooting until mid-afternoon. This meant that they ran on into the evening and incurred hefty overtime and penalty payments for the crew.

The real problem with *King of Comedy* was that they had to start shooting far too early. A Directors Guild strike was looming and the only way a picture could continue shooting during the strike was if it had four weeks' worth of significant material in the can before the deadline. Consequently producer Arnon Milchan moved the start date up by a month. Scorsese was not convinced it could be done, but De Niro said it could and he eventually went along with that. Shooting began on 1 June, but Scorsese was clearly not relishing the task.

'I was so tired,' he recalls. 'I had to rush into the movie faster than I would have liked because of the threat of the strike. It became a chore. Production is always bad enough but you should never find yourself on a set saying, "Jesus, what am I doing here?"

'Originally I didn't like the film at all. I thought it was just a one-line gag. But then after making a few pictures and having a certain kind of success and being on both sides of that issue – part Rupert, part Jerry – I began to see both sides of it.

'It was a very interesting movie to direct but I had to keep reinventing reasons for doing it and caring about it. That can be dangerous. Imagine making a picture and not caring about it. What's it going to look like?'

Once again Scorsese dragooned his mother into appearing in the film as she had done in *Mean Streets*. In fact, Catherine Scorsese never actually appears on screen in *King of Comedy*. She is heard only as a disembodied voice, especially in one hilarious improvised scene in which she berates De Niro as Rupert for his obsession.

Obviously the character of Jerry Langford was modelled on Johnny Carson, the man who ruled as king of the nighttime talk shows in America for 30 years. Zimmermann originally wanted one-time Carson rival Dick Cavett to play the role. Scorsese saw Carson himself as Jerry but Carson wanted none of it. He was too long in the tooth to be swayed by Scorsese's assurances that he would only be required to do 'a couple of takes' of each scene. De Niro and Scorsese went through a number of potential choices. Orson Welles was considered and rejected, as was Frank Sinatra. But when they came to Sinatra they thought of his Rat Pack cronies including Dean Martin. And when they thought of Dean Martin they almost instantly made the intuitive leap to his old comedy partner, Jerry Lewis.

Jerry Lewis turned out to be an inspired choice as Jerry Langford – a potentially life-threatening one for Scorsese, who was frequently left wheezing and gasping for breath after being rendered helpless with laughter at Lewis's off-screen antics. Lewis had been a major star with Dean Martin in the fifties and as a solo comedian in the sixties. Now he was largely known for playing Las Vegas and for his annual charitable telethon for sick children. He was a star of the old school, and found De Niro's ways a little difficult to cope with at first.

De Niro had been spending months watching stand-up comedians at work to get the rhythm and timing of their performances just right. But when Lewis, one of the greatest stand-ups of his generation, invited him to dinner – the sort of courteous thing prospective co-stars did in his day – De Niro would not go.

'How could I,' he was quoted as saying, 'when in the film I am supposed to be at his throat and ready to kill him for my chance?'

Lewis was surprised but diplomatic in his response.

'De Niro has obviously never heard Noël Coward's advice to actors about remembering the lines and trying not to bump into the furniture,' he said. 'He just could not forget this part at the end of the day's work.'

The other key element in *King of Comedy* is Masha, the crazed autograph hunter and would-be Langford groupie who provides a sexual threat as she aids Rupert's kidnap attempt. De Niro was convinced that the role should be played by Meryl Streep with whom he had worked on *The Deer Hunter.*

'I asked Meryl to come in and meet Marty and talk about it because I thought she'd be terrific,' he says. 'She's very, very funny. She's a great comedienne. She came in but I don't think she wanted to do it, for whatever reason I never really knew. But I knew that she could do it.'

In the end the role went to up-and-coming comedienne Sandra Bernhard, who later confessed to being more nervous about meeting Jerry Lewis – 'he's just like somebody's dad' – than meeting De Niro and Scorsese. She too turns out to have been an inspired piece of casting as Masha.

'During the shooting the whole dynamic between me and De Niro happened naturally,' she says. 'He was such a total geek in that outfit. It was De Niro at his absolute most vulnerable. In a strange way he'd always been protected by his characters who were usually shut-off, deep, frustrated, angry people. But as Rupert, De Niro was out there. With his character and mine it was like the clash of two cuckoo birds.

'When we were shooting in the streets it was incredibly hot, ninety or a hundred degrees. New York in the summer with all these people around just felt out of control. With Marty there is always a sense of total freneticism, which he's controlling in his own way. I think Jerry Lewis found it difficult. I think he was uncomfortable and felt it was an unprofessional situation. He has directed movies himself. I think he felt it was too freewheeling and too improvisational.'

Like *New York, New York* and *True Confessions* before it, *King of Comedy* failed to find its audience. In commercial terms it was a complete disaster, taking only $1.2 million at the box-office against a budget of $19 million. De Niro's box-office record is not a good one. Of all the films he had done up to this point only *Taxi Driver* and *The Deer Hunter* can be considered genuine hits. *Taxi Driver* was made for less than $2 million and went on to take $12 million at the US box-office, *The Deer Hunter* went over budget but a returned a healthy $28 million. *The Godfather Part II* was also a success but can hardly be described as a De Niro film. There does not appear to be a large number of people who will throw the kids into the station wagon and rush out to the local multiplex for a De Niro movie. Yet for all that he was ranked number ten in the list of box-office draws in the United States as recently as 1977. His ranking reflects his standing in the industry rather than the actual cash returns he generates. His perception as an 'actor's actor', and an actor who will say 'no' more often than 'yes', gives him a certain cachet. He had always been a critics' favourite and producers are keen to cash in on that.

Even though *King of Comedy* died at the box-office, De Niro still received the sort of reviews an actor would sell his children for. *Vogue* hailed him as 'the greatest and most unsettling actor in movies today'. *Newsweek* said that De Niro had 'added another indelible portrait to his growing gallery', while the *New York Times* called it 'one of the best, most complex, and flamboyant performances of his career'.

De Niro's performance as Rupert Pupkin in *King of Comedy* is undoubtedly one of the best of his career. With his pastel blazers, his slacks, and his white penny loafers he is the picture of toe-curling embarrassment. The film is a comedy but it is not funny. It is not even black. This is the comedy of humiliation. The scene in which Rupert invites himself to Jerry's home is excruciatingly painful for the audience, all the more so because of Rupert's consummate insensitivity. His performance is not as flashy as his interpretation of Jake La Motta or as intense as his portrayal of Michael Vronsky, but it remains probably the single most underrated performance of his career. It would also bring to an end a string of extraordinary performances that redefined what screen acting was all about.

Up to this stage De Niro had always been a risk-taker. He was always likely to follow the path less travelled. But some years later, in a rare major interview with *American Film* magazine, he revealed that he felt he had taken risks that had not paid off in *King of Comedy*.

'I had certain ideas about him,' he said, 'and that's why it was fun. With Marty I can say, "Let's try this or that." Like the nerdy suit Pupkin wore. We just went into a store on Broadway and it was right on the mannequin, the whole outfit. It was just wrap it up and take it home, you know? The haircut might even have been a part of it too.

'With a character like that, sometimes you just take it, commit to something, and just do it. You might feel uncomfortable – it's not "you" – but that's the fun of it. Just take that chance. Eventually you have to make the choice and that's where interpretation comes in. It might not be right but it has to be a choice that personally you can commit to.'

20 Bobby and Bluto

I T WAS THE AFTERNOON of Friday 5 March 1982. De Niro was staying at the Chateau Marmont. His favoured room was number 64, one of the hotel's two penthouses. Although notoriously private, he had become friendly with another Marmont resident, John Belushi, one of the new breed of kamikaze American comedians who had rocketed to fame on the back of the cult hit *Saturday Night Live* comedy series. Belushi had charmed his way into De Niro's inner circle. Although he can dissemble and be as affable as the next man, De Niro does not make friends easily, and almost all his friendships are based on work. The people whom he admires or has enjoyed working with – Scorsese, De Palma, Elia Kazan, actors Harvey Keitel, Al Pacino and Peter Boyle, and producers like Art Linson – are the people whose company he seeks. De Niro and Belushi had not worked together but by this time it seems they had a common link through drug use. They had now become so close that the actor was in the habit of calling the comedian almost every day. On this particular day De Niro could not reach Belushi, who was in his usual suite, bungalow number three. The two had been together in the early hours of the morning but now De Niro could find no trace of his friend.

What he did not know was that Belushi was lying dead in the back bedroom of bungalow number three at the Chateau Marmont, a victim of a massive drugs overdose. He was 33 years old. Hotel staff tried to keep the news from De Niro. He insisted, however, that he wanted to speak to his friend. Eventually a senior member of the hotel management, a woman De Niro knew and trusted, came to the phone. She tried as best she could to break the news gently. Before she could tell him that Belushi was dead, De Niro guessed the seriousness of the situation for himself. He burst into racking sobs and put the phone down.

John Belushi was born in 1959 in Wheaton, Illinois, a town he quickly outgrew. His father owned two restaurants but had fallen on hard times and was forced to work as a barkeeper; his mother was a cashier in a local store. There were four children. John had one older sister, Marion, and two younger brothers – James, himself now an actor – and Billy. Belushi quickly rebelled at what he saw as the restrictive confines of growing up as the son of an immigrant family in a small mid-Western town. The chafing and the frustration he felt manifested themselves in two ways – comedy and drugs. Belushi's comic talent first started to show itself at high school where already his humour had a dark, anarchic side. A burly man with a boxer's nose and heavy jowls, his trademark was to explode in a frenzy of comedic action that dared audiences not to find him funny. Very few audiences could resist his singular charms. In 1971 Belushi joined Chicago's celebrated Second City Players. He quickly began to dominate the troupe and his mercurial nature, fuelled by his prodigious drug-taking, caused major concern among the other members of the company. Those who knew him were astonished at his intake. Bob Woodward's exemplary posthumous biography *Wired* has Belushi taking drugs with the enthusiasm and gusto of a child locked in a sweet shop.

There was one man in Chicago who did not share the other Second City Players' opinion of Belushi. Del Close was a former director of Second City revues and saw in Belushi the potential for a major comic talent. The last such talent Close had known was Lenny Bruce, who ironically was to die in similar circumstances. Close acted as Belushi's mentor and confidant, helping him hone his talent. After being spotted in an acclaimed comedy revue called *Lemmings*, Belushi was hired as one of the founder members of the cast of *Saturday Night Live*. At the beginning of 1975 NBC was looking for a fresh programming idea for its 11.30 p.m.–1 a.m. slot on Saturday nights. The network had been filling the gap with reruns of Johnny Carson's *Tonight* show, but network president Herbert S. Schlosser wanted something new and dynamic. The result was *Saturday Night Live*, and not since Sid Caesar's *Show of Shows* had a single television programme contributed so much talent from a single generation. The *Saturday Night Live* alumni rewrote the rule book of American comedy. Chevy Chase, Eddie Murphy, the late Gilda Radner, Dan Aykroyd, Belushi himself and many more owed their careers to this show. Even now, more than 20 years later, *SNL* – as it is now almost universally known – continues to launch a new generation of comedians like Mike Myers, Dana Carvey, Chris Farley and Adam Sandler.

Belushi's drug-taking was continuing unabated, and there were simmering disagreements with other cast members. The feuding was bitterest with Chevy Chase. The blue-collar Belushi particularly seemed to resent Chase's wealth and privilege as well as harbouring the suspicion that Chase might also have been plain funnier. However, Belushi's madcap characterisations on the show, including his samurai warrior and his 2000lb bee, had made him a firm favourite with audiences. Over the next two years he was fired and rehired several times by the show's executive producer, Lorne Michaels. But in the summer of 1977 both Belushi and Michaels were provided with a way out.

Director John Landis was making a film called *National Lampoon's Animal House*, a wild, anarchic low comedy set among the fraternity houses of an American college. The most disgusting character in the movie, Bluto, was written with Belushi in mind. Universal Studios were so determined that Belushi should appear in this film that they were prepared to withdraw the funding if Landis could not get him. As it turned out they need not have worried. After a desperately unhappy experience on his first film, *Goin' South*, Belushi was desperate to get to work for Landis. The movie was a sensation, and when it was released in the summer of 1978 it became the most successful comedy ever released to date. The beer-swilling, food-fighting, pantie-stealing, toga-clad Bluto became an instant role model as young America took the Kalashnikov comedian to its heart. Belushi believed he could do no wrong, but like so many before him he quickly paid the price for his hubris. One bad film followed another and none of them rekindled the box-office fire of *Animal House*. Even *The Blues Brothers*, now hailed as his definitive performance, was hammered by the critics when it was released in 1980, director Landis being singled out for his alleged self-indulgence in allowing the film to come in at $27 million – $11 million over its original budget.

By the time of his death two years later Belushi was in serious career distress. His self-destructive tendencies and his appetite for excessive drug use had left him a bloated, congested self-parody. Indeed his fame had waned to the point where one of the detectives investigating his death did not even recognise whose body it was until it was pointed out to him.

It was shortly after the critical and financial disaster of *The Blues Brothers* that John Belushi renewed his friendship with Robert De Niro. They met at a restaurant in Hollywood where Belushi had gone for a night out with a long-time friend, actress Carrie Fisher. Ironically Fisher, who played Belushi's fiancée in *The Blues Brothers*, was also one of the stars of *The Empire Strikes Back*, the movie that destroyed *The Blues Brothers* at the box-office. Belushi and Fisher were enjoying a quiet meal before he left for Colorado to star with Blair Brown in *Continental Divide*, a romantic comedy that he felt might change his fortunes. At one point De Niro too had been linked with *Continental Divide*. The idea was that he would star along with his former *Wedding Party* colleague Jill Clayburgh, but the project fell through. The comedian was in such an ebullient mood in the restaurant that afterwards he invited everyone back to On the Rox, a private celebrity club above the Roxy on Sunset Strip, which was one of his favourite haunts, so that the evening could continue.

Belushi's admiration for De Niro was total and unconditional. He referred to him ebulliently as 'Bobby D'. De Niro likewise, although some sixteen years older, was greatly taken by Belushi. Perhaps the highly controlled actor envied the comedian's wild, destructive, in-your-face attitude to life. It seems likely that the two first met around the end of 1972 when Belushi was living in Greenwich Village while performing in *Lemmings*, the satirical review that made his name. In *Wired*, Bob Woodward suggests that Belushi and De Niro had taken cocaine together. He cites Belushi's widow Judy as the source for a claim that the two had done drugs and De Niro had injured himself, requiring stitches. In a later interview De Niro does refer to having his nose broken at one stage, and this may have been the incident in question. In any event, Belushi certainly envied De Niro his reputation as the consummate Method actor of his generation. He admired his total dedication to his craft and his immersion in the role to the exclusion of everything else. As their friendship grew, he sought to enlist De Niro's support for what he had come to believe would be the part that would establish him as an actor just as De Niro had shocked critics and audiences as Johnny Boy or Travis Bickle only a few years before.

Tino Insana had been a friend and colleague of Belushi's since they first met at the comedian's Second City audition in 1971. They had collaborated on a number of projects and in the early part of 1982 they were working on a script from a treatment they had already written. With hindsight the story of the proposed film seems like extremely mawkish art prefiguring cruelly realistic life. Belushi was to play a straight advertising executive who questions his values when he meets a punk musician, Johnny Chrome, and his girlfriend. The ad man turns punk himself and when Chrome is found dead of an overdose in his apartment he delivers a toe-curling, self-serving rant eulogising the late great Johnny Chrome. Perhaps sensing that the real virtue of this untitled script would lie in its shock value rather than in its artistic merit, Belushi was planning the ultimate shock tactic. Only days before he died he was planning to convince Insana to include a scene in which heroin addict Chrome would persuade Belushi to shoot up. To cap the scene Belushi intended to dispense with the usual special effects and genuinely inject himself with heroin on screen.

Not surprisingly Insana was shocked and dead set against the idea, as was Belushi's wife Judy, even though Belushi promised he would have a doctor standing by if and when the scene was shot. Executives at Universal Pictures, who had seen the treatment, were equally horrified. Apart from the fact that what Belushi was planning to do was illegal, no insurance company would underwrite any film where there was a risk of the star dying by his own hand during the filming. Belushi was undeterred because he believed he had one important voice in his corner – Robert De Niro.

By this stage in Belushi's life the two had become close friends and were in almost daily touch. De Niro's most commonly stated maxim is that he cannot fake acting. He has never been required to inject himself on screen, but if he ever were it would doubtless present him with an intriguing ethical dilemma – to fake or not to fake? Having discussed the issue with the man he believed to be the greatest Method actor of them all, Belushi had reached the conclusion that De Niro would back him in his drive to live the moment on screen. As it happened the argument was resolved prematurely with an awful finality. Insana and Belushi parted company late on 4 March 1982, agreeing to work on the script the following day. Within hours John Belushi was dead.

De Niro is frequently characterised as the archetypal riddle inside an enigma wrapped in a mystery. Trying to pin him down is like trying to lift quicksilver with a fork. Nowhere is that more evident than in the connection between De Niro and Belushi in the final twelve hours of the comedian's life.

Not long after Insana had left, Belushi was in On the Rox with Cathy Smith. The two had met four days earlier when Smith had acquired some heroin for Belushi. Belushi, who had an aversion to injecting himself, had also persuaded Smith to shoot him up with a speedball, a cocaine-heroin mixture that would register on even his drug-inured senses. Thirty-five-year old Smith had made her way in the world by whatever means she could. She had dated musicians like Levon Helm and lived with the Canadian singer-songwriter Gordon Lightfoot for three years between 1972 and 1975. She sang backing vocals for Lightfoot as well as for country singer Hoyt Axton. Smith was a 'face'. She was one of those girls who were always able to find their way into the élite, private back rooms and upstairs bars like On the Rox because of the services they provided. In Cathy's case it was providing the drugs which gave her access to the rich and famous. By the end of the seventies, her short-lived music career behind her, she was dealing drugs to friends and friends of friends, like John Belushi.

The climate in Hollywood at that time was very different to the health-obsessed fitness culture that currently pervades in the movie capital of the world. Since about 1975, cocaine had been king in Hollywood. One publicity agent told the *Los Angeles Times* that it was 'the ambrosia of the gods'. In this case the gods were not those who lived on Mount Olympus but those who lived in Beverly Hills, Malibu and other starry enclaves. Hal Ashby, the acclaimed director of *Shampoo* and *Coming Home*, claimed that cocaine use was reaching epidemic proportions in Hollywood by that stage. He used it himself but says he stopped when it began to impair his judgement and made him snap at trusted friends. Publicist Al Ebner says that after only three weeks of shooting every bag sent to the Wyoming location of Steven Spielberg's *Close Encounters of the Third Kind* was stopped and searched because drugs were being sent to the set. Although illegal, the provision of cocaine was even used as a bargaining tool to encourage actors to sign on for particular films. The mid-seventies were characterised by a number of drugs cases against high-profile actresses who were arrested on suspicion of possession. In the case of Anjelica Huston, according to the *Los Angeles Times*, the charges were dropped in return for testimony against director Roman Polanski. Others, like Louise Lasser, Mackenzie Philips and Gail Fisher, were allowed to enter re-education programmes. Despite all this, cocaine remained the *narcotic du jour* for the new generation of movie-brat actors, directors, and producers who prided themselves on their ability to work hard and party harder. Those who could supply it quickly, efficiently and discreetly were guaranteed to be kept around. Nobody seemed to like Cathy Smith much, but she was certainly someone they wanted to keep around.

De Niro was one of those who did not like Cathy Smith. He thought she was a low-life and he seemed to resent the hold she had over his friend Belushi. When he arrived at On the Rox shortly after midnight on 5 March, Belushi called him over. De Niro had been trying to get hold of him earlier in the evening and had left a number of messages. Possibly because Smith was there, De Niro did not stay for long. Belushi, however, was keen to talk further about the heroin script, perhaps fearing that he might be losing ground in the argument with Insana and the studio. He asked De Niro to visit him in his bungalow after the club had closed for the night and the actor agreed. Also at On the Rox later that night was another acquaintance of Belushi, comedian Robin Williams. A superb improviser, Williams was at this stage undoubtedly America's finest stand-up comedian. He was also a household name after becoming an overnight sensation in the smash-hit television series *Mork and Mindy*. He had been performing at the nearby Comedy Store on Sunset Boulevard and headed for On the Rox when he had finished his set. Messages had been left at the club telling Williams that both Belushi and De Niro, an old friend, had been looking for him and had gone back to Chateau Marmont.

To this day Williams, who first met Belushi in New York some years previously, believes that there was an attempt to set him up that night, and possibly De Niro along with him. 'I was only in Belushi's room for five or ten minutes then I split,' he told *Rolling Stone* magazine in 1988. 'I saw him and split. He didn't want me there really, he obviously had other things he was doing.

'I do think I was set up in some way to go over there. A guy at the Roxy told me that John wanted me to stop by his bungalow. But when I went by he wasn't looking for me. He wasn't even there. When he arrived he said "What are you doing here?" He offered me a line of cocaine, I took it and then I drove home. If I had known what was going on, I would have stayed and tried to help. It wasn't like he was shooting up in front of me.'

The following afternoon, on the set of *Mork and Mindy*, Williams was stunned to be told by co-star Pam Dawber that his friend was dead.

De Niro meanwhile was also back at the Chateau. Williams had called him in his penthouse before going to Belushi's room, but according to the comedian he could hear women's voices in the background and did not pursue the matter. He then went to Belushi's room where another Belushi crony, Nelson Lyon, was waiting for the comedian. When Belushi returned with Smith and some cocaine, Williams accepted his hospitality and then left. He too was not enamoured of Smith, finding her frightening and out of step even with Belushi's excessive lifestyle. Williams was at Belushi's bungalow shortly after two in the morning. Not long after he had left, De Niro finally came downstairs. He had no time for Smith but he was interested in the cocaine. Smith later described both him and Williams as 'going at it with straws like a vacuum cleaner'. Belushi had little to say for himself and Smith was certainly not an inducement for De Niro to stick around. After snorting a few lines of coke he left and went back to his penthouse.

De Niro left Belushi's bungalow shortly after three in the morning. Some time later Smith mixed another speedball for Belushi and one for herself. She injected herself first and then attended to Belushi. As they lay in bed together Belushi complained of feeling cold. Smith pulled up the blanket and turned up the heating. She left Belushi's bungalow at around ten in the morning, noting that her friend had sounded congested and wheezy in the night. He was, she claims, all right when she left him but she never saw him alive again. Shortly after midday Bill Wallace, a personal trainer and bodyguard Belushi used on his periodic fitness jags, dropped by the Chateau and discovered his body. He called the emergency services but to no purpose – Belushi could not be resuscitated. Post mortem tests found massive amounts of morphine – which heroin becomes when injected into the body – and cocaine, which had accumulated over the final frenzied 48 hours of John Belushi's life.

He was pronounced dead at quarter to one in the afternoon of Friday 5 March 1982. Shortly afterwards, unaware of the tragedy that was unfolding downstairs, De Niro would be wondering why he couldn't get through to his friend.

21 In the Aftermath

T
HE CHATEAU MARMONT IS possibly the world's most luxurious Bohemian retreat. The great and the good can pay thousands of dollars to enjoy the simple life. It nestles grandly at the top of Marmont Lane off Sunset Boulevard gazing down on the comings and goings on the strip below.

The Chateau has been a Hollywood fixture almost since the days when the movie industry came west from New York. Opened in 1929, it was a visible manifestation of Hollywood's status as a boom town. Greta Garbo stayed there, as did Edith Piaf and Marilyn Monroe. Howard Hughes not surprisingly loved its seclusion. Jean Harlow honeymooned there. Boris Karloff lived at the Chateau for five years. De Niro lived there for two. And John Belushi died there.

When the Chateau opened for business in 1929 its original advertisements declared it 'fire and earthquake proof'. The events of 5 March 1982 showed that although the Chateau may have been proof against natural disasters, it could offer no protection against scandal.

Shortly after lunchtime on 5 March, Detective Addison Arce (pronounced Ar-SEE) was in court in downtown Los Angeles. Arce is now attached to the Robbery Homicide Division of the Major Crimes Section based at the headquarters of the Los Angeles Police Department at Parker Centre. In 1982 he was a detective in the homicide section of the Hollywood division of LAPD. While he was in court the 911 call came from the Chateau to summon the emergency services after Belushi's body had been discovered. Since the Chateau is in the Hollywood division it became the responsibility of their six-man homicide unit. In those low-tech days, before mobile phones and beepers, it was much more difficult to get hold of an officer once he was out and about unless he had a radio. Arce, being in court, was eventually contacted by phone and told to get back to the office. Making good time in the early afternoon traffic, he made his way to the Chateau Marmont where he remembers a 'tremendous amount' of police and media activity. The officer in charge of the Hollywood homicide unit was Detective Russell Kuster. He quickly ushered Arce into the back bedroom of bungalow number three. He pulled back the sheet and showed his partner the body. Arce did not recognise the prone figure but was told by Kuster that the victim was John Belushi.

Arce's view when he arrived was the same as that of the other detectives on the scene. They all believed they would be dealing with an accidental death, probably a drugs overdose. Indeed, one of the first police statements made to the gathering crowds of reporters said, 'This appears to be death by natural causes. The detectives at the scene found nothing to make it seem suspicious.'

'It was being considered as an accidental death pending the coroner's autopsy to make the final determination,' recalls Arce, a carefully spoken, phlegmatic police officer with, in 1982, fifteen years' experience on the force. 'A lot of times what we actually do is carry it as an undetermined death initially. Then once the coroner's findings are returned it could be an accidental death or an overdose or any of a number of things.'

That view seemed to be borne out the following day after an initial investigation by the deputy medical examiner. The preliminary conclusion from the autopsy was that John Belushi had died from a drugs overdose, confirming the detectives' view that they were almost certainly dealing with an accidental death.

Cathy Smith had returned to the Chateau about an hour after the police were called. She was not immediately told of Belushi's death but after being identified by a member of hotel staff as having been with the comedian earlier that day, she was handcuffed and taken to Hollywood police station. The homicide detectives were at the scene and at this stage their first priority was to search for evidence. While they were securing the crime scene, taking fingerprints, making drawings and taking photographs, other detectives were called in to assist with various aspects of the inquiry. One of those was Detective Richard Iddings, a robbery detective in the Hollywood division who was given the job of conducting the first interview with Cathy Smith after she had been taken to the Hollywood station. Although they were to become closer later, the first time Detective Arce saw Cathy Smith was as she was leaving the police station after that interview. When Smith first spoke to Iddings she was concerned because her initial thought was that Belushi had been arrested for possession of drugs and that she was going to be implicated. It fell to Detective Iddings to break the news of his death to her. Smith was stunned but insisted that Belushi had been all right when she had left him.

Although shaken, Smith was reasonably forthcoming during the interview. She told Iddings who they had been with the night before, mentioning Robert De Niro and Robin Williams by name. She also admitted using drugs herself. Police found a spoon and a needle – two of the requisite tools for mixing a speedball – in her handbag. Despite this she was not detained and she left the police station a confused young woman, passing Detective Arce on his way in.

Police have been criticised subsequently for not using the presence of the drugs paraphernalia to hold Cathy Smith, who would subsequently flee to Canada. At the time they had other priorities.

'There was some question about what we should do because of the hypodermic,' Arce recalls. 'But the decision was taken to release her. We had a statement from her about it in any case. At that stage the main object was to lock her into a time and place and establish what exactly the circumstances were when John Belushi was alive.'

There is no doubt that this was a high-profile case with a huge amount of media interest. But there was no question of Kuster, Arce or any of the others making any rush to judgement. There is a perception brought about by too many bad movies that police can be leaned on by the media to produce results. Certainly their superiors may feel some political pressure, but this seldom percolates down to the officer in the field. There may be more men assigned to the job as a consequence of pressure but the job remains the same. Every piece of evidence is catalogued and detailed, every witness is interviewed and every lead is followed until it either yields a new lead or peters out. The method is applied particularly rigorously in high-profile cases where the police are likely to be second- or even third-guessed by the media.

Addison Arce admits that covering all the bases is a lesson he learned the hard way in the Belushi case. While he and his colleagues were methodically sifting their way through the procedure, the case suddenly reared up and not so much bit them as almost devoured them.

Cathy Smith had accepted $15,000 from the weekly tabloid the *National Enquirer* for an interview about her version of events on the night of Belushi's death. She admitted mixing speedballs for herself and the star and told the newspaper that she had 'killed John Belushi'. She also named Robert De Niro and Robin Williams as having been with Belushi on the day he died. The *Enquirer* article, even though the information had been paid for and would therefore have to be suspect, suddenly put an investigation that was drawing to an orderly close back into the spotlight. Smith had made no mention to Detective Iddings about injecting Belushi or herself; she claimed in fact not to have taken any drugs for several days.

Now having gone public and 'confessed', the accidental death theory went out of the window.

'Once Cathy had talked to the *Enquirer* and made those incriminating statements we were dealing with a homicide inquiry," says Detective Arce.

And because of that both De Niro and Williams would have to be interviewed. At the time Deputy District Attorney Mike Genelin confirmed that, although neither man was a suspect, they would both be wanted for questioning. He told reporters in a brief statement that at the very least the two stars might be able to corroborate evidence.

Movie stars are used to circulating in their own orbit. They are not used to being questioned by anyone, let alone the police, so the detectives investigating what was now a homicide knew that life was not going to be easy.

'At some point we knew we were going to have to deal with their attorneys but we started with their publicists,' recalls Detective Arce. 'With Robert De Niro we were stonewalled right from the start. The publicists indicated that he was out of the country, in Italy as I recall. He had just left to shoot another movie and would not be available. Robin Williams was initially not available either but he eventually co-operated. We were told that his attorneys would contact us. It was eventually negotiated that we could indeed interview Robin Williams with his attorneys present but it was firmly indicated to us that Robert De Niro would not be able to return to the United States for an interview.'

By the summer of 1982 De Niro was indeed in Italy, where he was filming *Once Upon a Time in New York*. The police made a number of attempts to get in contact with him but were politely but firmly rebuffed at every turn. De Niro was in Italy and could not return and that, according to his minders, was that. It was obvious to the detectives that, from the point of view of the star's publicists, if they were to get a statement from De Niro then it would have to be obtained in Italy.

'It was determined by my superiors that I would not go to Italy and interview Mr De Niro on the grounds of cost and that's how it remained,' recalls Detective Arce. 'It was a matter of him being across the water and me being here. We never suspected him of being actively involved but his information could have been useful to us. He could have corroborated what Cathy Smith said or otherwise. He could have given me information which we did not already have and which might have led us in an entirely different direction. His statement may have been completely different from Cathy's.

'I did not give up trying to interview him because I knew in a case like this I was going to be second-guessed,' continues Arce, who was later peripherally involved in the O.J. Simpson case, which almost wrote the book on the police being pre-empted in their investigations by the media and the public. 'I knew I would be second-guessed in the Belushi case, no question about it, and that's why you want to cover yourself for everything. To me as an investigator cost is not a factor, but once it gets to my superiors, once it goes to anyone above the rank of lieutenant, then he has to decide whether or not it is pertinent.'

In the end Arce's superiors decided it was not pertinent. Matters would be very different more than ten years later when Arce would spend a week in the Bahamas chasing a minor lead in the O.J. Simpson trial and then face the prospect of being sent on to the Cayman Islands to check out a phone number!

With the Belushi case time was pressing because the media were having something of a field day. The decision was taken to go ahead with the case on the basis of the information provided by Cathy Smith and others. Robin Williams, unlike De Niro, was interviewed. The actor was at the height of his fame with *Mork and Mindy* and his attorneys obviously felt that he had an image to protect. Williams did sit down with detectives but his attorneys insisted that they should also be present and that he should only answer questions that they approved after they had been submitted in advance. Not surprisingly the interview was not one of the most probing the officers involved had ever conducted. Given Williams's co-operation and the closeness of De Niro's relationship with Belushi, it seems strange that De Niro would not want to help his friend. It may well be that – as is not uncommon – his minders were keeping information from him and simply turning down the police on his behalf without even letting him know. On the other hand it seems unthinkable that he and Williams would not at least have spoken on the phone, in which case Williams could presumably have told him how carefully any interview could be controlled. But by that stage, as we shall see, De Niro had other things on his mind.

After making her statement to the *Enquirer*, Cathy Smith had crossed the border and taken refuge in Canada. However, as a consequence of the article a grand jury was empanelled in Los Angeles in September 1982. There is no way to avoid giving evidence to a grand jury – it is an offence punishable in law to refuse their subpoena. Williams testified in person. De Niro also gave evidence but over the phone. Since grand jury proceedings are confidential no one knows what either man said. De Niro's testimony to the grand jury was obviously a source of frustration to Addison Arce.

'Sure it was,' he says. 'Not that I could probably have done any better but I would have liked to have locked him into a statement. I don't know whether he himself was ever aware that we wanted to speak to him or whether the publicists were acting on his behalf but I would have to say that Mr De Niro was conveniently unavailable. If the interview with Robin Williams was anything to go by I'm sure safeguards would have been built in if he had been interviewed. It would have been the same controlled situation. I have no problems with attorneys being in an interview but when they have me write the questions out beforehand then that's no interview.'

On 15 March 1983, a year and ten days after John Belushi died, the Los Angeles grand jury handed down its indictment and Cathy Smith was charged with murder in the second degree as well as sundry other drugs-related charges. She was still in Canada so extradition proceedings were initiated, with Smith and her lawyers determined to fight them every inch of the way. The charge of murder in the second degree means that Smith had killed Belushi without intending to. It was brought under the felony murder rule of California state law which allows for charges to be laid if someone is killed during the commission of a felony. For detectives the rule of thumb is summed up by the acronym BARROM.

'That stands for Burglary, Arson, Rape, Robbery and Other Mayhem,' explains Detective Arce. 'Suppose two people go off to commit a burglary and one has agreed to drive the car while the other goes into the house. While he's inside the eighty-year-old woman who lives there comes home and he pushes her down the stairs. Because she's eighty years old she dies. They flee and are later arrested and both are charged with murder in the second degree. That's the felony murder rule. If we apply this to Cathy Smith then she was committing a felony by injecting Belushi and as a result of that felony he died, so therefore it is a charge of murder. There is no specific intent. She did not intend to murder him, she accidentally murdered him. It's the same as this hypothetical burglary which those two guys just committed. The guy in the house didn't mean to kill the lady but he pushed her. He was committing a felony at the time and as a result of that felony somebody died so they can both be charged with murder.'

Under the felony murder rule Cathy Smith was the only one who needed to fear prosecution. Even if De Niro or Robin Williams or Nelson Lyon or anyone else was in the room when the injection was being administered, they could not be charged. Whether that was made clear to Williams by his lawyers and not to De Niro by his people is a point for conjecture. There is a possibility that someone in those circumstances could be charged as an accessory, but it would require an exceedingly zealous prosecutor to try to make it stick. The one other point worth making is one made by

Addison Arce himself to the district attorney before the decision was taken to charge Cathy Smith.

'What if it's John Doe living on the street who doesn't have a pot to piss in,' he maintained. 'He's got nothing to live for, he's been arrested forty times and you and everyone else know he's a fool. Then one day he gets his hands on some good dope, he goes over to a friend who's just as big a fool and he shoots him up and the friend dies. Are we going to file murder on him? There are people out there every day who can't shoot themselves, they just cannot do it, so other people shoot them up for them. But when they die do we charge some John Doe with murder? And the answer I got was that it would be done on a case-by-case basis. That was my answer. My gut feeling here is that this case went ahead because of who it was. Double standard? You bet!'

The one compelling reason for mounting this investigation and involving Williams, De Niro and everyone else was Cathy Smith's interview with the *National Enquirer*. Years later, when Gennifer Flowers accused then Presidential candidate Bill Clinton of adultery, no one took her seriously because the interview had been paid for. But in the early days of cheque-book journalism Cathy Smith's interview was given a lot more credence than it probably actually deserved. Neither De Niro nor Williams liked her, though given the fact that Belushi met her only a few days before he died they would have had little chance to show it. Did she simply name them to the *Enquirer* to spice up her story and provide value for money? Was she simply being mischievous and trying in some bizarre way to pay them back for their slights? Or, as Robin Williams has hinted, was there a plot to set them up for some extortion scam? Was Cathy Smith part of that plot?

Although millions read the *Enquirer* story only a few people have heard the tape of the interview. Addison Arce is one of them.

'By the time I got through listening to that tape it was obvious to me that they were getting her to say anything they wanted,' he remembers. 'It was almost like a controlled conversation to the point where the interviewer would be providing eighty-five per cent or even ninety-five per cent of the information and she would just be sitting there saying, "That's right." By the end of the conversation her voice was very slurred and her demeanour very casual. From that and the sucking noise during the inter-view it was obvious to me from working narcotics and being a policeman for so long that she was smoking a joint and enjoying a drink at the same time. It was a very relaxed atmosphere and they were having a conver-sation, but it was definitely a controlled environment.'

But even with their suspicion that a lot of the material in the article had actually been fed to Cathy, the police still had to take it seriously and go ahead with their investigation.

'Oh yeah,' says Detective Arce adamantly. 'Correct me if I'm wrong but she said, "When I got back with the cocaine" – I think it was in a bag around her neck – "and I took it off De Niro and Williams went at it with straws like a Hoover vacuum cleaner." That's not something I would come up with to plant in someone's head for her to say, "I agree." It was her statement so obviously she saw something.'

Cathy Smith was eventually extradited and served her time. She even managed to clean up her act and became a drugs counsellor herself.

'I was impressed by that,' says Arce. 'She wrote letters to me. They weren't solicited although we always had a good rapport. I had talked with her in Canada and I'll never forget that when the sentence came down I went over to wish her well and talk with her for a second. She told me then that she could have got the same sentence without having gone through the whole extradition thing, which I honestly believe. She wrote to me and told me she was a counsellor and had got her act together. But of course she went back and got arrested. It's very easy to get that sort of righteous mentality when you're in prison. They get religion or whatever and they get clean but once they get back out on the street again they have problems.

'If the likes of Robin Williams and Robert De Niro found her to be a low-life then by their standards she probably was. She was someone with easy access to drugs so they would keep her around. When they describe her as hard, well, her voice is very raspy. She's got a lot of miles on her with the booze and the narcotics. But if she was sitting here now she probably wouldn't come across that way to you or me.

'I think at the end of the day Cathy Smith was her own worst enemy. I think her mouth got her into trouble. I told her that. "Cathy," I said, "if you had never said anything you would never have got caught." And she did it for fifteen grand! Obviously the tapes were very important. Could she have got a better deal if she had stayed in Canada? Possibly. I don't think she got a raw deal. I think she was a victim of her own stupidity and her love for the bottle and the dope.

'Fifteen grand would have been gone in no time.'

22 Temptation

THE DEATH OF JOHN BELUSHI was a devastating blow for De Niro. For possibly the first time in his life he began to doubt himself and his chosen profession. He must have thought that nothing was destined to go right for him.

De Niro is not a man who forms attachments of any kind easily. He even has prospective directors checked out thoroughly before considering working with them. The sort of friendship he formed with Belushi and the speed with which it was formed, was an exception rather than the rule. For De Niro to have given of himself so openly in friendship and then to have lost his friend under such circumstances must have been a cruel blow. Never the most emotionally giving of men, he became even more introspective and contemplative.

He briefly considered giving up acting and effectively withdrawing from public life by turning to directing. There was talk of a musical that he would co-direct with music producer Quincy Jones. De Niro would do the dramatic sequences, Jones would handle the musical segments. The project eventually fell through without making much progress.

The timing of Belushi's death was crucial. All his life De Niro had believed in himself and his own ability, even when few others did. Then, when that belief was given the ultimate validation through a Best Actor Oscar, the moment was tarnished by the Hinckley assassination attempt. Then, as he attempted to come to terms with that, a man who became a dear friend was struck down – albeit by a self-inflicted wound – at what should have been the peak of his talent.

Trouble, they say, comes in threes. For De Niro the next part of this trinity of misfortune was just about to reveal itself.

He was still seeing Helena Lisandrello. At roughly the same time as he learned of the death of John Belushi, she told him that she was expecting his baby. She had become pregnant by him the previous year but had aborted without telling him. This time she was keeping the baby. In

Robert De Niro: Untouchable

September 1992 the newspapers announced that De Niro had become a father again by 'his mistress, the black singer Helena Springs'. (Springs was Lisandrello's professional name.) De Niro was of course still married at the time, although separated from Diahnne Abbott. His relationship with Abbott was still cordial – she had appeared on screen with him as Rupert's love interest in *King of Comedy*. He was also the father of Raphael, who was now five years old. According to the newspaper reports, while not exactly cramming cigars into the mouths of passing strangers, De Niro was delighted and had showered gifts on the child. It was also claimed that he had showered gifts on Lisandrello – including a sports car and a complete new wardrobe – when she had told him she was pregnant. The newspaper reports went on to say that De Niro and his mistress had named their new baby daughter Nina Nadeja. Ten years later, in the midst of a savagely fought paternity suit, Lisandrello would remember the circumstances somewhat differently when she spoke to Cindy Adams.

'This time I told Bobby,' she said, referring to the pregnancy she had hidden from him the previous year. 'He seemed to know what to do. He gave me a prescription of herbs. When that didn't handle it he became upset and went berserk for five days. He screamed at me and my sister made me hang up the phone. I got so nervous I jumped whenever the phone rang.

'He said "You can't have that fucking baby. What are your plans?" I said, "I will not have an abortion." He turned hateful and that began his ten years of cruelty to me. He was drinking and he never allowed me to be happy one moment. He'd say, "Your job is to fuck me between planes, bitch, not to get pregnant." It was mental abuse.'

It is important to remember that Lisandrello's comments were made in the heat of a bitter and acrimonious legal tussle to obtain maintenance for her child. It would be in her best interests to paint De Niro in as unfavourable a light as possible. Nonetheless, her allegations are shocking, and De Niro did not deny them other than to contest his paternity in court.

Helena claimed that it was De Niro who named the baby. It was his decision to call her Nina. She also claims that De Niro gave her $50,000 before the baby was born. She says he also had a room decorated for the child. Everything, however, was paid for in cash; there were no cheques and no records of any transactions. After the birth Lisandrello attempted to contact her lover to obtain details of his health background. De Niro, according to Lisandrello, flatly refused.

'He started to rant "You want my money," ' she told the newspaper. 'I said, "I'm making eighty thousand dollars a year. I can take care of my baby. I only want the information any mother wants." It was a nightmare. The man is a master manipulator.'

By the time the baby was born De Niro was in Rome making *Once Upon a Time in America*. It was from there that he gave his evidence to the Cathy Smith grand jury by telephone. In the circumstances his flight to Italy may simply have been the reaction of a man who was under a great deal of stress and wanted to get as far away from its source as possible. If that was indeed the reason, then he picked the wrong place. The film was not one of the easiest shoots he had ever been on.

Once Upon a Time in America is a gangster epic from Italian director Sergio Leone. By the time it came to start shooting in 1982, Leone had spent almost twelve years and large amounts of his own money getting the project off the ground. It is based on an autobiographical novel called *The Hoods*, written by small-time crook Harry Grey in Sing Sing prison when he was in his seventies. Leone went to New York to meet Grey and was impressed by his story. Although best known for Westerns like the *Dollar* movies with Clint Eastwood and *Once Upon a Time in the West*, Leone was drawn to the material in Grey's book. He claimed that Prohibition and the gangster era represented a 'second frontier' in American history.

Once Upon a Time In America is essentially the story of the rise and fall of two childhood friends, 'Noodles' and Max, as they make their way through gangster circles. Unlike *The Godfather*, Leone's movie is set against a backdrop of Jewish gangsterdom, leading to industry jibes about the 'Kosher Nostra'. The story, as it was initially conceived by Leone and his screenwriters, is told in an opium-induced flashback by an ageing Noodles. Originally Leone had intended to cast former big-name actors from gangster movies of the period in various supporting roles. Glenn Ford, Henry Fonda, George Raft, and Jean Gabin had all agreed to take part. However he finally decided to cast the film entirely with contemporary actors. Robert De Niro would play Noodles and James Woods would play Max. The cast was rounded out by Elizabeth McGovern, Treat Williams, Tuesday Weld, Burt Young, and Danny Aiello.

As written by Harry Grey, David 'Noodles' Aaronson was an amalgam of Bugsy Siegel and Meyer Lansky, two of the most influential figures in American gangsterdom. Siegel was the man who had the dream of building Las Vegas, the more prudent Lanksy the man who made the dream a reality. De Niro once again took his preparations seriously. He asked a disc jockey friend in Philadelphia, Jerry Blavatt, for help. Blavatt knew a gangster called Nicodemo 'Little Nicky' Scarfo. De Niro asked Blavatt to see if Scarfo would set up a meeting with Lansky, who was then still alive. Scarfo said no and De Niro did not pursue the matter.

'De Niro?' said Leone when he was explaining his casting. 'I don't consider Bob so much an actor as an incarnation of the character he is playing. Until he feels like that he can't go to the set. We have the same defects. We are precise in detail and share an obsession with perfection. In six months of casting the film I saw so many great actors. I was embarrassed when I finally had to make a choice. I find great spontaneity in American performers and no one is better than De Niro at being studied and spontaneous at the same time.'

Although he conceded that he shared many of the same characteristics as De Niro, Sergio Leone was less receptive to indulging his star than some other directors had been. Martin Scorsese and De Niro may spend hours discussing scenes but other directors are less inclined to do so. Francis Ford Coppola was driven almost to distraction at times by the younger De Niro's incessant questioning on the set of *The Godfather Part II*. Mike Nichols took the ultimate sanction and fired him from *Bogart Slept Here* when he could no longer deal with it. Leone handled things in his own way. His bear-like figure dominated every set he was on, and he was used to having things his own way. He could collaborate, but like most directors he would only collaborate on his own terms. He and Henry Fonda had had some celebrated set-tos on the set of *Once upon a Time in the West*. He was not about to go toe to toe with De Niro on this film, but there are still ways of making a point.

There was one reported occasion when Leone had gone to some trouble for a particular camera set-up. When he came on to the set De Niro then questioned some detail of Leone's work. Leone kept his head and invited the actor up on to the camera podium to take a look through the lens and see for himself. De Niro conceded that, in fact, Leone was quite correct.

'I'm glad you think so, Bob,' said Leone drily, 'since I am after all the director.'

'I'd sometimes say to him, "Show me how you would do it," ' recalls De Niro of working with Leone. 'If you hit the moment right then you get the language in a very organic way from the director. When he did that I'd say, "Okay, I've got it. You're not giving me the performance but I see the way you did it." After that, I had a way to do it.'

Through it all, however, Leone and De Niro maintained the greatest of respect for each other's work talent. When *Once Upon a Time in America* was completed they very much wanted to work with each other again. Leone died in April 1989, but he had spent the past five years of his life pouring much of his own money into a project about the siege of Leningrad during the Second World War in which De Niro had agreed to star.

The siege of Leningrad is an apt metaphor for what happened to Leone after he had completed *Once Upon a Time in America*. It had been part-financed with $10 million of studio cash from the Ladd Company – anywhere between a third and a quarter of the total budget, depending on who you believe. But American audiences simply did not take to Leone's 227-minute cut of the movie. There was a disastrous preview screening in Boston in February 1984 at which the audience was left angry and confused by the story. In fairness this says more about American audiences than it does about Leone's ambitious film. The Ladd Company say they were 'compelled' to step in and trim the film.

The trim amounted to 80 minutes, almost a third of the film's running time. Leone said *Once Upon a Time in America* had not been cut but 'barbarously massacred'. The influential *New York Times* critic Vincent Canby said the studio version of the film looked as if it had been 'edited on a roulette wheel'. Canby's review describes it as 'an inscrutable trailer'. The real tragedy of the studio version is that the emphasis of the film has been completely altered. The studio cut more or less rearranges the film in chronological order, destroying the elegantly constructed flashbacks of Leone's version. The director's version played in Cannes to rave reviews in 1984; it also opened in Britain and across Europe to exceptional praise.

'The main protagonist of this film is time,' said Leone. 'Time and memory. It was filmed in flashbacks to show the process of memory. It was never my intention to make a gangster film, but the American version looks like one because they have left only the squalid episodes, one after another. Many years ago, while it was still in manuscript, the head of Paramount, Charles Bludhorn, asked me if I wanted to do *The Godfather*. I turned it down because I didn't care to do a movie about gangsterism.'

There is still a third version of *Once Upon a Time in America*. This one was cut for Italian television and is far and away the best of the three versions. It is now regarded as the definitive version of the film and – despite some appalling ageing make-up – the quality and power of De Niro's performance comes through.

'He makes you feel the weight of Noodles' early experiences and his disappointment in himself,' said Pauline Kael, reviewing the long version of the movie. 'He makes you feel that Noodles never forgets the past and it's his all-encompassing guilt that holds the film's different sections together.'

De Niro was offered a choice of the two leading characters, Noodles and Max. In the end he went for Noodles, the man over-burdened by guilt. Guilt was becoming something of an obsession with him by this stage. Although he would have made the choice before Belushi's death and Lisandrello's pregnancy, it is interesting to speculate on his motives.

King of Comedy opened in New York on 9 February 1983 with De Niro still in Europe working on *Once Upon a Time in America*. Martin Scorsese, having had a dreadful time giving Rupert Pupkin his fifteen minutes of fame, was now preparing his next project with almost messianic fervour. His *Boxcar Bertha* star, Barbara Hershey, had given him a copy of *The Last Temptation of Christ*. The controversial novel by Greek writer Nicos Kazantzakis dealt with the life and Passion of Christ. The final temptation is offered to him by the Devil as he hangs on the Cross. It is the Devil who offers him the chance to come down from the Cross and live his life as a normal man with a wife and children into contented old age. Christ rejects the satanic blandishment and fulfils his predestined role.

The film was always going to be difficult to mount but Paramount Pictures had agreed to back it for a relatively modest $11 million. The major problem would be who to cast in the title role. With the exception of his documentary work, Scorsese's last four features had all starred De Niro. There was increasing speculation in the industry that he would once again ask De Niro to play the lead in *The Last Temptation of Christ*. He had optioned the book and asked Paul Schrader to write a screenplay. Schrader admits that he too had thought of De Niro in the title role. Scorsese duly hopped on a Concorde to Paris for a dinner with De Niro to discuss the project, among other things, but he claims that the actor's heart was never really in it.

'He explained to me that he really didn't want to do the project,' he recalls. 'Bobby knows that any script I have I'm going to change so it really wasn't the script. He said he couldn't see himself in robes and kept thinking of Paul Newman in one of his earlier movies, *The Silver Chalice*. It was one of my favourites but it's a terrible movie. He said, "It's just not one we should be together on." It would be hard to convince a guy to get up on a cross. You really have to want to do it.

'For De Niro to do a movie, he has to really be interested and he will start three years in advance. When we were doing *New York, New York* he was already practising at lunchtime for *Raging Bull*, though we didn't shoot *Raging Bull* until years later. But when he's really interested in something I know it. We always check in with each other, we always talk. With the religious film we never discussed it, we never had a meeting. It was kind of understood that I would give him the script and if he liked it, fine.'

For Scorsese, who had once harboured serious thoughts of being a

Catholic priest, there were compelling religious and theological reasons for making *The Last Temptation of Christ*. Despite their common background, De Niro does not share Scorsese's strong religious convictions. The Catholicism in his family comes from his grandmother but it was not strictly enforced, and there appears to be little room for formal religion in his life. But even without any overriding religious considerations, there was always friendship.

'I was not interested in playing Christ. It's like playing Hamlet,' he explained. 'I just didn't want to do it. Marty and I talked about it. We do things with each other because we like to work together, but also for our separate reasons. I have mine as an actor, he has his as a director. That's the best way.

'*Last Temptation* was something I was never interested in doing. But I did tell him, "If you really have a problem, if you really want to do it, and you need me, I'll do it. If you're against the wall and have no other way, I'll do it as a friend." '

Scorsese appreciated the gesture, but he also points out that when it was made De Niro had had his head shaved for a prosthetic that was required in *Once Upon a Time in America*. Both men probably knew in their hearts that the world was not yet ready for a balding Christ. In the end, after looking at several other actors, Scorsese settled on Aidan Quinn to play Christ. Harvey Keitel would play Judas, and the rock star Sting was in line to play Pontius Pilate. But after months of prevarication, and amid a growing wave of fundamentalist protests, Paramount boss Barry Diller eventually pulled the plug four days before Christmas 1983. By this stage Quinn, Keitel and Scorsese had all agreed to work for nothing. Scorsese had even offered to direct a sequel to Paramount's hit *Flashdance* for nothing, and the budget had been pared down to $6 million – including $4 million already been spent. Diller was unmoved and the project was officially dead in the water.

Scorsese would go on to establish himself as a safe pair of commercial hands with films like *After Hours* and *The Color of Money* before finally making *The Last Temptation of Christ* in 1989. Willem Dafoe played Christ and Harvey Keitel played Judas, as he was supposed to six years earlier. David Bowie took the role of Pilate and Barbara Hershey, who had started the ball rolling when she gave Scorsese the book, played Mary Magdalene.

De Niro was not approached; his offer made in friendship was not necessary this time around. After doing four films in a row, there would be an eight-year gap before De Niro and Scorsese worked together again.

23 Taking Stock

SINCE THE DEATH OF John Belushi, De Niro had been taking stock of his life. He was now, by the beginning of 1984, making anywhere between $2 million and $3 million per picture – not a superstar salary, but certainly enough to put him in the echelons of Hollywood's higher-paid stars. The money was largely as a result of his international popularity; he had not had a domestic hit for some time.

But even though he was now a millionaire the money itself meant nothing. A childhood where money was never in abundant supply had led him to a life of frugality. His one luxury was his Rolls-Royce; for the rest he lived modestly by film industry standards. He had just turned forty and was becoming disillusioned with Hollywood. He was never a party animal or a Hollywood schmoozer, and the death of Belushi had cast a pall over his old haunts and his old friends. Belushi's death was a wake-up call to Hollywood, which was no longer seeing booze and coke as the requisite trappings of a successful career. With middle age beckoning, De Niro also felt the need to take more control of his own career. He had moved from the stage where the work chose him to the stage where he chose the work, and now he was getting ready for the next stage – originating the work for himself.

More than anything else at the start of 1984, De Niro was tired. Twenty movies in fifteen years, many of them intensely physical parts like Jake La Motta or Travis Bickle, had taken their toll. He was physically and mentally weary and in need of a change. He may also have been feeling the need to go home. He had spent most of the past few years in Hollywood and now New York beckoned.

The means of getting him home was a script called *Falling in Love*. This first-time script from established playwright Michael Cristofer is the story of two married suburbanites who fall in love in New York. It would be directed by Ulu Grosbard, the Belgian film-maker who had directed De Niro in *True Confessions*. De Niro would take the lead role of Frank

Raftis, an honest, down-to-earth, happily married construction boss who is about to fall in love without being able to help himself. For Molly, the female lead, there was only one actress under serious consideration.

De Niro is on record as saying that Meryl Streep is his favourite actress. He respects her talent enormously and is personally fond of her. He was impressed with her courage and dignity in her relationship with the terminally ill John Cazale in *The Deer Hunter*. He had also been keen for some time to work with her again, having already suggested her to Scorsese for *King of Comedy*.

'I was always thinking of something I could do with Meryl, a play, a film, anything,' says De Niro. 'We had a reading and began to see possibilities in it. Then Ulu Grosbard seemed like the right director. Meryl and I had a wonderful time. I'd love to do a comedy with her one day; she has many more colours than people have seen. She's a great comedienne.

'In my opinion she's very beautiful and has a great deal of elegance about her. Usually a woman in that situation tends to be more concerned about how she appears because the beauty gets in the way. Meryl sort of goes against that, that's why she's terrific. The old movie stars of the thirties, some of them had more chutzpah, more than just being pretty and looked at. That's what Meryl has. She's really an actress.'

Streep's admiration for her co-star was no less forthright.

'We wanted something real, something awkward and crumpled,' she says, explaining the end result of their endless hours of drinking coffee and eating croissants in her SoHo apartment as they went over the script. 'He's incapable of making a false move. So when there was something wrong with the writing he just couldn't do it. Then everyone would realize that the scene was wrong and we'd fix it. He's infallible, like a compass. You're never adrift.'

Playing Frank Raftis was not so much a risk as a rest for De Niro. Raftis is a character without much of a back story. His reasons for falling in love are never quite explained – neither for that matter are Molly's. Raftis is the sort of man for whom any woman would trade her husband to marry. Likewise, Molly could be the ideal homemaker. Their respective spouses, played by Jane Kaczmarek and David Clennon, are equally appealing as sensitive souls and loving parents. Apart from appearing opposite Streep again, the prospect of a rest may have been the major factor for De Niro in taking this role.

'I was tired,' he said at the time. 'This script came along. It was a nice story, set here in New York. I thought I could concentrate on things other than what I usually concentrate on – make-up or whatever. I don't always have to do high-risk parts. I thought it was something different from anything I had done before and for that reason alone it seemed like a good idea to do it.'

Although he was not required to shave his head or put on weight, De Niro was not about to stint on his preparations. In hindsight, for a part that any actor worth his salt could have phoned in, De Niro appears to have gone over the top. For his telephone conversations with his screen wife he insisted that Michael Cristofer write her dialogue as well as his own, even though the audience would only ever hear his side of the conversation. He also had business cards printed as Frank Raftis. These were not used at any point in the film – De Niro simply carried them around with him. Like the breadsticks during rehearsals for Julie Bovasso's play *Schubert's Last Serenade*, the cards fulfilled a function so arcane that presumably they were of significance only to De Niro.

Despite how things might appear, De Niro insisted that playing Frank Raftis was every bit as difficult as playing Jake La Motta.

'It only appeared to be easier,' he maintained. 'You always have to worry. You always have to concentrate. It's just more deceptive when you are working on the surface. I did some research on being a construction foreman. But that didn't make the role any easier. He's still not me.'

Although the movie is called *Falling in Love*, Frank and Molly's relationship is exceedingly chaste. Although they plan romantic liaisons they are never consummated. De Niro is no one's idea of a romantic lead and had yet to play a major on-screen love scene. But he defended Frank and Molly's lack of physical intimacy.

'That's the nice thing about it, the non-consummating part,' he insisted. 'That's the whole point. Sex in a movie isn't that easy to do.'

Streep, not surprisingly, agreed with him.

'It's very sweet to know what's inside people's hearts instead of what's underneath their clothes, don't you think?' she asked one reporter rhetorically.

Frank Raftis may not have been consummating any relationships, but De Niro certainly was, at least according to British topless model Gillian De Terville. The young black model had started modelling as a way of helping out a friend who had a clothes business in the King's Road in London. But with the arrival of topless models on page three of Britain's daily tabloid newspapers, she soon found her niche in life. Gillian's ample charms made her one of the most popular of the page three girls.

De Niro had temporarily broken off his relationship with Helena Lisandrello and, according to De Terville, had begun what amounted to an eighteen-month transatlantic romance with her. The 41-year-old De Niro had obtained her number from a producer friend and called her at her parents' home in South London, according to the 24-year-old model.

'I couldn't believe my ears when he telephoned me,' she told a British tabloid. 'I was washing my car when my mum called from the window, "It's someone called Bob for you." I went to the phone and I could hear this American accent and I said I didn't know anyone called Robert. He said, "You know, Robert De Niro." We'd never met but he managed to convince me that it was him. He said he'd seen my picture and wanted to take me out for dinner. In the end I agreed to see him.'

According to De Terville, De Niro was staying at a London hotel and she agreed to meet him for a drink. She says she rang the hotel to cancel the appointment because she wasn't looking her best but he begged her to come along anyway. She agreed, and so began an affair that lasted for a year and a half in which they both jetted across the Atlantic for their romantic trysts.

'I love staying there,' said De Terville of De Niro's New York apartment. 'It's a big place with lots of paintings, large windows, and a big, round king-sized bed. There are all sorts of gadgets in the headboard for the radio and TV and that sort of thing.

'I suppose I see Robert about every six weeks. We both like eating good food and drinking good wine and often we just go out for a quiet dinner. He's very romantic and always holds my hand or puts his arm round me. Robert is very much the strong, silent type. He hates publicity and he's not flash. But sometimes we do go out with other stars.'

New York-born-and-bred De Niro was allegedly just as enamoured of life in Sydenham in South London as his new girlfriend was of life in New York. He was apparently fond of popping round to her parents' house when he was in London for a cup of tea and a chat.

'He's been round quite a few times,' says De Terville. 'He arrives in a cab and sits on the sofa and watches TV with the rest of the family. He gets on well with my dad and my younger brother. I don't think the neighbours even know it's him.

'I like him very, very much. When we're apart he phones me at home all the time and tells me he wants me to be with him. We have a proper relationship and we have a lot of fun together. I wouldn't like anyone to think he was whirling me around and paying for everything. It's not like that with me and Robert. Sometimes he pays my air fare because, obviously, he has a lot of money. But that's all.

'We haven't discussed marriage. We're just enjoying ourselves. There's so much I want to do before I even think of that.'

Gillian De Terville was plainly enjoying the new-look, kinder, gentler

De Niro, but cinema audiences were not. *Falling in Love* was another box-office disaster with audiences staying away in droves. Both De Niro and Streep were established as top-line actors rather than stars, and the combination singularly failed to set the box-office alight in a film that amounted to little more than a big-budget soap opera.

The reviews were not kind either.

'What a waste of talent,' opined Stanley Kauffmann in the *New Republic*. Pauline Kael, whose opinion of De Niro seemed irredeemably soured after *Raging Bull*, was equally scathing. 'Can a vacuum love another vacuum?' she enquired. 'That's the question posed by *Falling in Love*, a piece of big star packaging. They have nothing to say; each stares past the other into a separate space. The most compelling thing about them is the beauty spot-wart on De Niro's cheekbone: it has three dimensions – one more than anything else in the movie.'

'*Falling in Love* has a new De Niro,' director Ulu Grosbard enthused during shooting. 'Nobody has ever seen this De Niro before. He's funny. He's tender!'

But plainly movie-goers didn't have much interest in a funny, tender De Niro. They seemed to prefer a dramatic, violent De Niro.

24 A Mission from God?

F ALLING IN LOVE WAS THE beginning of a five-year trough in De
Niro's career. It was a period in which he would become lazy,
choosing parts that barely occupied him far less stretched him.
Previously the great strength of his performances lay in the fact
that you could scarcely imagine anyone else in the role. Now he was about
to embark on a series of films where almost anyone else could have played
his parts. In those five years he would have one big hit, a string of flops,
and in the process give his worst screen performance by a long way.

In that same period he would also discover that films did not have to
be creatively or artistically satisfying. They could be a means to an end.
The film that taught him that was Terry Gilliam's *Brazil*, a Kafkaesque
fantasy set in a dystopian future. Jonathan Pryce plays a humble clerk
caught up in the machinations of an unseen bureaucracy. De Niro makes
a brief cameo appearance as Harry Tuttle, a guerilla heating engineer who
turns up at Pryce's apartment one night. The role was not one that would
stretch De Niro. He knew that from the outset; he had taken it simply for
the chance to work with Gilliam, an eccentric and occasionally brilliant
film-maker. However, in the process he made himself $1 million for only
a few days' work. That was a lesson he would not forget and would soon
put to good use.

Goldcrest Films had made a huge impact on the world film market in
a very short space of time. The British company had burst on to the
international scene in 1981 with the success of *Chariots of Fire* which
went on to win four Academy awards. This was followed in 1982 by
Richard Attenborough's *Gandhi*, which swept the board that year with
eight Oscars. But by 1985 a combination of bad luck and poor judgement
meant that the company was in serious trouble. It had put all its eggs into
one basket and was depending on the release of three films over the next
eighteen months for its salvation. In the eyes of the media the future of

the British film industry rested on the success or failure of these three pictures.

The three eggs were wildly different. There was *Absolute Beginners*, a musical set in London in the fifties starring Patsy Kensit and David Bowie. It was directed by Julian Temple, a young man who had cut his teeth on rock videos. *Revolution* was comfortably the most ambitious and expensive British film made up to that point. Al Pacino, Donald Sutherland and Nastassjia Kinski starred in the story of a fur-trapper caught up in the American Revolution. The film was directed by Hugh Hudson, who had also been responsible for *Chariots of Fire*. Then there was *The Mission*, a period drama about politics and religion in the jungles of Central America, starring De Niro and Jeremy Irons with Roland Joffe directing. Joffe had been responsible the previous year for the critically acclaimed *The Killing Fields*, which had won three Academy awards.

Absolute Beginners and *Revolution* were unmitigated disasters. The pop musical cost Goldcrest £4.7 million and brought in only £1.8 million – a loss of almost £3 million. *Revolution* fared even worse. It had originally been budgeted at £16 million but ended up costing £19 million. Even though Goldcrest wasn't responsible for the whole budget it still ended up losing almost £10 million out of an investment of just under £16 million. Everything now depended on *The Mission*. The company's financial position was looking increasingly untenable, but if *The Mission* was reviewed well and performed well at the box-office it would perhaps stave off the inevitable.

The Mission is the story of how Spain and Portugal carved up Latin America in the eighteenth century. It is also the story of how the original spiritual intention of converting the heathen was subverted to commercial ends when the Jesuit missions in the rainforest were destroyed to allow commerce to take over. Jeremy Irons plays Gabriel, an idealistic Jesuit who has founded a Utopian community among the Indians of the rain forest. De Niro plays Mendoza, a former slaver and mercenary who has come to the mission to atone for killing his brother in a duel. When it becomes apparent that the mission cannot survive, these two men take different approaches to the problem. Gabriel puts his faith in prayer and cannot believe that his new oppressors will attack the mission; Mendoza reverts to his old ways and forms some of the Indians into a guerilla group, this time fighting for the Lord. Neither of them is proved right. Both men are killed, the mission is overrun, and the Indians are massacred.

Casting De Niro was a bold step. He was quintessentially a modern, urban actor and this was a period costume piece featuring the sort of robes he could not see himself in when Scorsese discussed *The Last Temp-*

tation of Christ. The suggestion was first made by Roland Joffe, who felt De Niro would be ideal for the role. Others disagreed, notably Goldcrest boss Jake Eberts and David Puttnam, who was co-producing the film. Eberts believed that De Niro was a wonderful actor but sincerely felt he was wrong for the part, that he would be out of place and audiences would no more accept him as an eighteenth-century missionary than they had accepted Al Pacino as a fur-trapper in *Revolution.* The Pacino experience had also taught Eberts to be wary of the effect, in financial and other terms, that having a major star can have on a production.

Puttnam shared many of Eberts's concerns and argued with Joffe over the choice. He subsequently stressed that it wasn't that he didn't want De Niro per se; he was simply concerned about the effect the actor might have on a tight schedule in a distant location such as Colombia, where the film was to be shot. Puttnam felt the role might have been better served by an unknown actor, one who might bring less baggage and fewer audience preconceptions to it.

Eventually the matter was settled late one night in De Niro's suite at Blake's Hotel. The exclusive South Kensington hotel had become his favoured London haunt and the three men – De Niro, Joffe, and Puttnam – met there to discuss *The Mission.* Puttnam told De Niro he was concerned about his reputation for demanding a great deal of rehearsal time and for multiple takes. He also pointed out that the problems inherent in the location and the limits of the budget simply would not allow for that. De Niro, who had already told Joffe that he was willing to reduce his fee to play the role, graciously said he appreciated the situation and guaranteed that he would not be responsible for delaying shooting in any way. Puttnam, perhaps feeling that his point had not been made sufficiently clearly, then told De Niro flat out that, in his opinion, he was wrong for the part.

De Niro was astonished. As he pointed out, no one had ever come out and said that to him in such a forthright manner. Puttnam, however, has never been one for calling a spade an agricultural earth displacer, and felt he had to speak his mind. If he was going to oversee a difficult shoot in a remote location, then the ground rules had to be established from the outset. De Niro, who remained courteous throughout what could easily have been a stormy exchange, again said he appreciated Puttnam's position. He pointed out, however, that while Puttnam was a producer, he was an actor, and he felt that he was right for anything he sincerely believed he could do.

In the end Puttnam was won over and De Niro signed on. Harry Ufland negotiated a reduced fee of $1.5 million in salary plus expenses, as well as 13 per cent of the net profits. Goldcrest approached Warner Brothers, their distribution partners, to help defray the costs. Warner agreed to pay $500,000, leaving Goldcrest to find the rest. It is worth noting that, even allowing for the fact that De Niro was working on a reduced fee, Goldcrest had spent the $1 million they had allocated for actors' salaries on one performer. And he would cost them more before the film was finished.

De Niro's participation in *The Mission*, along with other factors, meant that the original budget of £11.5 million had now spiralled to £15.4 million. On the plus side, his participation meant that there was a tremendous amount of interest in the film at the 1985 American Film Market, and it was pre-sold in a number of key territories.

Puttnam, however, plainly still had his doubts about De Niro's suitability. Liam Neeson, now a major star but then a virtual unknown, was signed on to play a young Jesuit who is fired up and inspired by Mendoza. It was commonly accepted that Neeson, whom Puttnam may have favoured for the role in the first place if it had been up to him, was also there to provide back-up should De Niro have been unable to fulfil the role for whatever reason. One potential problem was that De Niro felt uncomfortable with the subsequent casting of Jeremy Irons as Gabriel.

'It wasn't that he did or he didn't want Jeremy,' says Puttnam, 'but people tend to strike attitudes. He came round marvellously.'

For his part, Irons was unaware of De Niro's doubts. But as luck would have it he had already decided that, as part of his preparation for the role of Gabriel, he would steer clear of De Niro for a few weeks anyway.

'When we started on the film he was doing some of the earlier scenes as a slave-trader,' said Irons shortly after the film was completed. 'He was working very hard on his relationship with his brother, who was played by Aidan Quinn, while I was preparing with the Jesuit Father Daniel Berrigan, who had also been cast. It didn't seem to be useful to fraternize for those first four weeks. Then, during the area of the film where he becomes a Jesuit, we got to know each other much better. He's a very shy man and takes a lot of getting to know, so I suppose our off-screen relationship mirrored our on-screen one.

'Playing opposite Robert De Niro was a great learning experience too, as he works very differently from me. He's a very instinctive actor and he has an uncanny persistence in finding truthful moments. I think I'm quicker and have more technique because I'm more of a theatre actor. I'm used to working on the sort of pictures that don't have budgets that allow you to go again and again and again. Bob will tend to do a few takes but within them come up with extraordinary acting choices – very real choices. That was interesting to watch.'

Although De Niro had promised Puttnam and Joffe that he would not hold up the picture, he was having trouble with the script. *The Mission* was written by Robert Bolt, whose previous screenplays include *Lawrence of Arabia* and *A Man for All Seasons*. Bolt's intelligent and highly literate screenplay did not lend itself to De Niro's desire for improvisation, nor did the rest of the theatrically trained British cast find themselves inclined to deviate too much from Bolt's lines. De Niro eventually found his own solution.

'Bobby did improvise initially to find his character's expression,' explains director Roland Joffe, 'but essentially he had to deal with the text as written. I think he is superb in the part because he is relying on something other than what he has relied on before. He's holding his own in what is really quite a simple film – it's not a film about New York in which he can use his streetwise sense. I found him tremendously good to work with. I'd like to work with him on something modern where you don't have the constraint of having to say, "You can't use that dialogue, you have to use this, because this is the style of the film." '

Playing Mendoza, De Niro was once again dealing with a man who was trying to atone for his sins. Like Noodles Aaronson in *Once Upon a Time in America*, Mendoza was a man burdened by guilt – for a large part of the film he drags around a symbolic weight – who ultimately had to offer up his own life for his redemption. One cannot help but wonder what drove De Niro to these choices. Ironically, only a little more than a year after turning down the offer to play Christ for Martin Scorsese, he now found himself playing a Christ-like figure.

'I thought it was a really wonderful, meaningful story,' he would say later. 'The idea of this man changing appealed to me a lot. It was an amazing experience and I liked Roland Joffe a lot. He's a good director with a lot of heart. Some people thought it was ponderous but I thought it was a wonderful movie. I'm partial, and I don't usually say that, but I thought it was.'

Given the turmoil that had taken place in De Niro's life, this is a significant statement. Perhaps he saw the need for change himself. A fast-lane lifestyle had claimed the life of a good friend. He himself, a little disingenuously perhaps, had blamed stardom for the break-up of his marriage. He was clearly on the brink of some kind of epiphany and, in career terms at least, a conversation with David Puttnam would focus his attention even more clearly.

Filming of *The Mission* took place in the rainforests in and around Cartagena in Colombia over a fifteen-week period beginning in April 1985. Thanks to the professionalism of De Niro, Joffe and line producer

Iain Smith, the film proceeded without any major practical problems. There would, however, be one more confrontation between De Niro and Puttnam. As he had done with Sergio Leone on *Once Upon a Time in America*, De Niro questioned one of the scenes that was about to be shot. This was not one of his normal enquiries about the dialogue, but a serious disagreement with Joffe about the direction the scene should take.

That night he and Joffe and Puttnam discussed the situation over dinner in their hotel in Cartagena. De Niro again outlined his objections, which were principally to do with the way he felt the character ought to react, as opposed to the way in which he was reacting in the script. Puttnam listened politely and then laid down the law in a crowded restaurant in front of other diners.

'Well, Bobby,' Puttnam told him, according to his biographer, Andrew Yule, 'you may be right, but if you're not, we stand to lose a lot of money. We're walking into a brick wall here. If *The Mission* only takes as much as your last five films combined we are still going to lose a lot of money.'

No one had spoken to De Niro like that in a long time and he was less than pleased. When he asked Puttnam to explain, the producer continued.

'I'm saying that the real danger here is that what you've got is a pattern of films where you are quite wonderful, but somehow the film doesn't become the sum of its parts. They've been turned into De Niro vehicles. That's why we've got to make sure that you fit perfectly well in this picture with the overall.'

De Niro had plainly been given food for thought. Puttnam, of course, had put his finger on what was wrong with De Niro's career, and there was no arguing with the fact that he had appeared in flop after flop stretching back to *Raging Bull*. The offending scene was eventually played the way Bolt had written it and Joffe had envisaged it.

Creatively, De Niro may have had his problems with Puttnam and Joffe from time to time, but Puttnam was concerned about another effect he was having on the film. Puttnam was staying in constant contact with Sandy Lieberson who was now in charge of production at Goldcrest back in London. Within days of arriving on set in Colombia he had written to Lieberson outlining some of his more serious concerns about the effect De Niro was having on production. The letter is quoted at some length in Goldcrest chief executive Jake Eberts's account of the ill-fated company, *My Indecision is Final*.

'Without doubt,' the letter said, as it addressed the problem of casting De Niro and their ability to control personal expenses, 'as we discovered at the American Film Market, there are real advantages in the casting of "big names". However, sitting out here in Colombia, I am beginning to

ight Triumphant at
st. Robert De Niro
ceives his Oscar for
aging Bull, oblivious to
e John Hinkley
ntroversy which was
ging outside

elow De Niro and his
en wife Diahnne
bbott in a scene from
ing of Comedy, 1983

The Untouchable, 1987

lways a challenge for the director: With Martin Brest (*above*) in *Midnight Run*
nd Brian De Palma (*below*) in *The Untouchables*

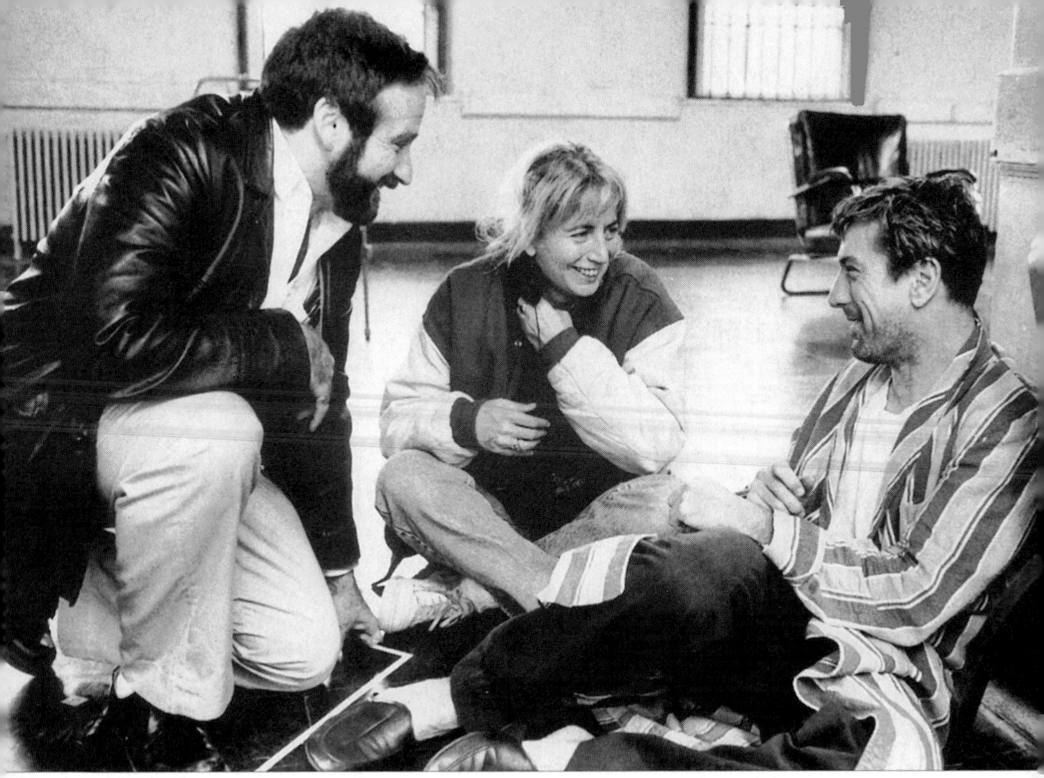

Above Old friends. Robin Williams, director Penny Marshall and De Niro share a joke on the set of *Awakenings*, 1990

Above Helena Lisandrello and her lawyer Marvin Mitchelson prepare for their decisive paternity hearing against Robert De Niro, 1993

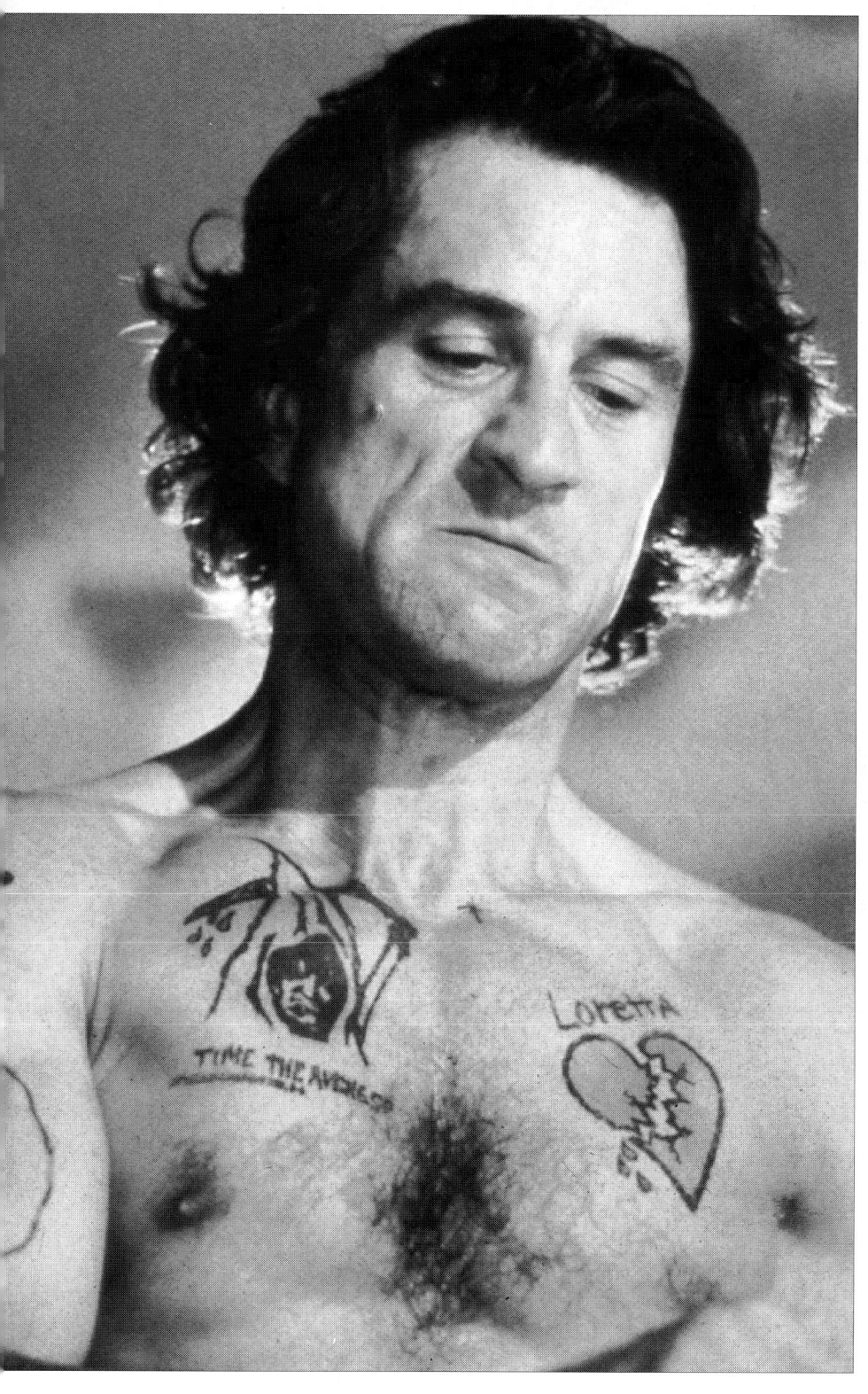

bove A force of evil. Robert De Niro as the fundamentalist psychopath Max
ady in *Cape Fear*, 1991

Above De Niro showing the fruits of make-up man Daniel Parker's endeavours in *Mary Shelley's Frankenstein*, 1994

Top right Robert De Niro (as Ace Rothstein) confronts the alluring Sharon Stone (as Ginger) about her infidelities in Scorsese's *Casino*, 1995

Bottom right The coffee shop scene from *Heat* with Robert De Niro as Neil McAuley and Al Pacino as Vincent Hanna, 1996

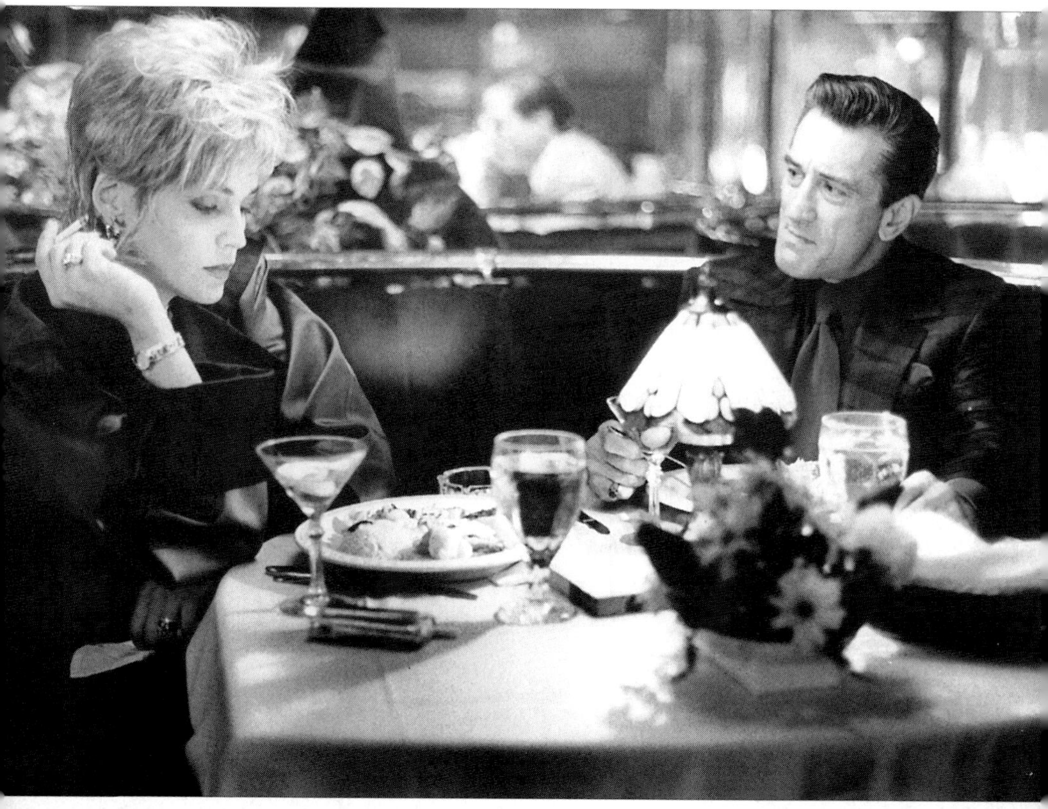

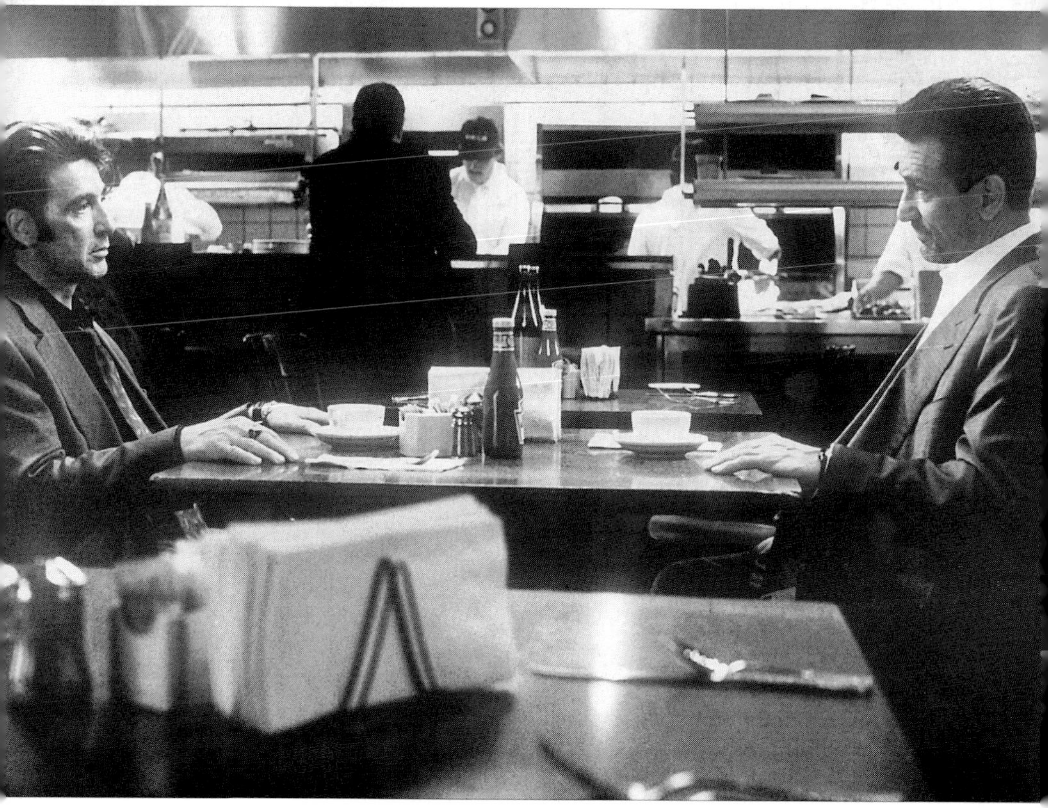

Robert De Niro's TriBeCa

come across the equally real disadvantages. First is the instinctive manner in which those departments which have to deal with him are understandably afraid and tend to overspend in order to be absolutely certain of meeting with his approval. This in turn also has an effect on Roland, and the net effect on the picture is that the focus is not consistently in the right place. Then there is the matter of cost. I have attached a schedule which shows you the add-on costs we have been forced to accommodate in the past month or so. All of which are outside our original expenses budget, and none of which on a major American movie would be regarded as unacceptable. I have to say that, in so far as I am concerned, they are! It is not just a question of De Niro himself but the fact that the other artists, including Jeremy Irons, all look to receive similar treatment. The net effect of that particular syndrome is at present unquantifiable.

' "This is not a moan," Puttnam concluded. "It is a factual rundown of the situation on the ground as opposed to the rather more mythological one which is liable to drift around the boardroom." '

The costs Puttnam alluded to were later revealed by Jake Eberts in his book. Estimated expenses for De Niro had been budgeted at £43,000. Instead they ended up totalling £103,000 and included air fares, living allowance, hotel accommodation, telephone, meals, physiotherapist and fencing instructor. Three weeks later, according to Eberts, De Niro's agent Harry Ufland submitted a further unspecified expenses claim which had also not been initially authorised.

One other expense which the producers did not complain about was the cost of providing bodyguards for De Niro. The American Drug Enforcement Agency was cracking down on the cocaine barons of the Colombian Medellin cartel. In retaliation the cocaine warlords had passed a death sentence on any and all Americans they found in Colombia. The thought of a major American star like De Niro being killed or – potentially more embarrassing for the Reagan administration – held hostage was simply too much to countenance. Iain Smith was able to pull some strings with the Colombians to get a couple of former Secret Service men to look after their star.

Death threats aside, there was plainly tension between De Niro and Puttnam on the set. It probably stemmed from that first meeting at Blake's at which Puttnam had decided to come clean with a few home truths. According to Jake Eberts, Iain Smith and Roland Joffe had nothing but praise for De Niro, claiming that whatever problems arose began only after Puttnam arrived in Colombia.

Puttnam insists, however, that by the end of the film they had parted on mutually respectful terms. In fact, when there was some doubt about the status of Puttnam's credit on the film, De Niro joined with Jeremy Irons and Roland Joffe in backing him. They insisted that if he did not get full credit as a co-producer they would take their names off the film.

At the end of the day, thanks to a co-operative effort from all concerned, *The Mission* actually came in slightly under budget. The final budget had been £17.5 million but it was brought in at £16.8, which is a remarkable achievement considering the difficulties it faced. It was not, however, well received. Reviews were mixed, pointing out, quite correctly, that the film has no central core. It is very difficult to sum up what *The Mission* is about or what is actually going on. De Niro's performance was in fact quite unremarkable, and the scenes between him and Jeremy Irons seem uncertain and strained.

Goldcrest had invested just over £15 million in *The Mission* and ended up losing almost £3 million. Proportionately this was nowhere near as bad as either *Absolute Beginners* or *Revolution*, but the damage was done. Goldcrest Films was grievously holed beneath the waterline and sank soon afterwards.

Meanwhile, De Niro would do what he had done several times before when he wanted to recover from a bad experience. He would seek the company of old friends. If there was another expensive cameo on offer as well, then so much the better.

25 Untouchable

THE SCENE IS THE Normandy Hotel in Deauville in November 1987. The French seaside town plays host to a festival of American films to which more and more major stars are being drawn. It will soon rival Cannes for star power if not prestige.

De Niro is in Deauville as a favour to his old friend Brian De Palma. He is here for the European première of De Palma's new movie, *The Untouchables*, in which he has taken another cameo role, this time as Al Capone. The film also stars Sean Connery, Charlie Martin Smith, newcomer Andy Garcia, and another promising young actor who is about to emerge as a fully fledged movie star – Kevin Costner. As well as supporting his friend, De Niro is here on more pleasant business. He has flown in from London to attend De Palma's birthday party. But all of that is in the evening to come. This afternoon De Niro is closeted in the Presidential Suite of the Normandy Hotel in Deauville, whiling away the hours until the big event.

There is a knock on the door. When the actor opens it he finds a young man in a bellhop's uniform. The young man has a silver salver on which he is carrying a bottle of Bollinger champagne and two glasses. He comes in, uncorks the champagne, and waits for De Niro to sign for it. The young man then takes a tip and leaves without saying a word.

That night, while De Niro is waiting with De Palma in the nearby Hotel Royal, the same young man approaches him. He reveals himself as the bellhop who brought the champagne. He then introduces himself as Lou Diamond Phillips, a rising star, in Deauville to promote his American hit *La Bamba*. Still barely able to speak, he tells a by now laughing De Niro that the only way he could think of meeting him was to borrow a bellhop's uniform and make a delivery to his room. Such is the esteem in which De Niro is held in some sections of the acting community.

It is a long way from the heat and humidity of Cartagena to the sea breezes of Deauville. In between De Niro had returned to the stage and made yet another brief but lucrative cameo appearance in a film. On a visit to Britain in 1985 he said that he was beginning to feel the need creatively to go back on stage. It had been ten years since his last appearance, and he was actively looking around for a project. He found one in the shape of *Cuba and his Teddy Bear*, which played for a sell-out six-week run on Broadway in 1986. De Niro played a drug dealer and Ralph Macchio, star of the *Karate Kid* series of movies, played his son. The sort of crowds he attracted during this run were very different from the select gatherings who had watched him in his experimental days in Manhattan. These were fans who had turned out to see De Niro, not necessarily to have a stimulating and challenging night at the theatre.

In the light of *King of Comedy*, De Niro must have been aware of the dangers of coming across a real-life Rupert Pupkin or a Masha. There were hundreds of autograph hunters, tourists, paparazzi and general rubber-neckers at the stage door every night. De Niro had his own solution for dealing with them. He would walk out with Macchio dressed in regular street clothes. Macchio, who would have been well used to demands for his own autograph, now found himself ignored. 'Where is De Niro?' is what everyone wanted to know. An amused Macchio would always tell the fans that De Niro was right behind. They would continue their vigil. In the meantime De Niro and Macchio would stroll off into the night. During the course of the play's extended three-month run De Niro was never spotted. It is impossible to think of another star of his stature having so little presence off screen. As Paul Schrader said years earlier, De Niro lives in other people's bodies. As a Latino drug dealer he is electrifying, but as himself he is inconspicuous to the point of insignificance – a man who apparently exists only in the moment, provided it is the moment of performance.

For whatever reason, De Niro was still not about to commit himself to another major project. His theatrical return had been strictly limited and his next film part was another cameo that barely stretched him.

Alan Parker's *Angel Heart* is a moody erotic thriller set against the backdrop of voodoo and the occult. Mickey Rourke is private eye Harry Angel, summoned by De Niro, in the guise of Lou Cyphre, to take on a missing person case. He is looking for a singer who disappeared, owing him a considerable debt. Lou Cyphre, of course, turns out to be Satan – surprise, surprise – and the debt is the soul the singer pledged to the Devil in return for showbusiness success.

De Niro has only four scenes in the movie. He does, however, manage to look suitably Mephisthophelean with his long hair, beard and impossibly long fingernails, which he drums on his malacca cane. The look of the character, he later revealed, was modelled on Martin Scorsese. The sardonic dialogue is delivered with a dry humour which barely hides his delight and astonishment that he is collecting a fat fee for work like this.

Alan Parker, a British director who at that time alternated between films like *Bugsy Malone, Midnight Express* and *Shoot the Moon* and TV commercials to keep his key crew together, wanted De Niro for the part. But by now De Niro was getting a reputation for being notoriously difficult in terms of committing to a project. He was in fact becoming like Brando, the man to whom he had frequently been unjustly compared. Now the comparison seemed more accurate to those who saw them both as lazy and squandering their talents. Alan Parker had originally offered De Niro the lead, which was eventually played by Rourke. When De Niro dithered he then offered him Cyphre, which he agreed to do because he felt he didn't want the responsibility of carrying a picture. *Angel Heart* was only two weeks away from the start of principal photography when De Niro finally made up his mind and chose the smaller role.

'I thought it would be fun to do,' he said later, 'not having to worry about the whole movie, you know, concentrating on those four scenes, and that's it. It worked out schedule-wise.'

'He was lovely only he wasn't definite,' says Parker. 'It took a lot of talking but in the end it was worth it. To see him working with Mickey Rourke, each the best of their generation, was like watching two gladiators. The thing is De Niro has made very few errors in any of his choices. That burden weighs heavily on him each time he has to decide what to do. Certainly he's extremely careful with someone like Roland Joffe or myself, directors he has never worked with before.'

There was no need to check out his next director. De Niro was going back to work with Brian De Palma, the man who had given him his first real movie job. In *The Wedding Party* De Palma had paid him only $50 for the whole movie. By the end of 1987 his asking price was around $3 million. Clearly there would have to be some negotiation.

De Palma was making *The Untouchables*, loosely based on the vintage 1963 television series. Set during the days of Prohibition it was the story of lawman Elliott Ness and his attempt to clean up Chicago. His hand-picked squad would not accept the bribes and kickbacks that were routine for some of their colleagues; they were 'Untouchables'. Their chief enemy was Al Capone, crime czar of the United States, who bestrode Chicago like a criminal colossus. Kevin Costner would play Ness but De Palma and producer Art Linson wanted De Niro to play his nemesis.

There was a problem. De Niro, through Harry Ufland, was asking for too much money, and wanted major changes in the shooting schedule to accommodate his own timetable. De Palma and Linson were reluctant to make any concessions and instead went ahead and signed English actor Bob Hoskins to play Capone. But the more they thought about it the more they were concerned that a quintessentially American story was becoming more and more European – Sean Connery had already been cast by this stage as a veteran Irish cop. Linson and De Palma knew they needed De Niro and negotiations were resumed. There was another worry for Linson in the shape of audience research conducted by Paramount Pictures, which was bankrolling *The Untouchables*. According to the surveys, audiences had no idea who Elliott Ness was, but they all knew Capone. This made the need for a recognisable and literally heavyweight Capone all the more pressing. With concessions on both sides, De Niro eventually signed on. Hoskins and De Palma parted amicably with an *ex gratia* payment of $200,000, and the British actor and De Niro remain friends. At the time Hoskins told De Palma that, with that kind of payday, if he had any other parts he didn't want him to play he had only to pick up the phone.

Art Linson's first meeting with the man he had just signed for a key role in his big-budget film was one he isn't likely to forget. Linson met De Niro for the first time the week before rehearsals were due to begin in Chicago. Up till then all the negotiations had taken place over the phone.

'He turned up around midnight and De Palma called me up to his room to meet him,' recalls Linson. 'He was thin, his face was gaunt. He was quiet and he looked so young. His hair was thick and low on his forehead and he wore a ponytail from the play he had just finished in New York. He didn't look anything like Capone. We had a brief, pleasant talk and I went back to my room. De Palma called and said, "What do you think?" I said, "If I didn't know that was Robert De Niro, I'd say we were doomed. Tell me we haven't made fools of ourselves." '

Linson's fears were allayed some three months later. All De Niro's scenes were filmed at the end of the shoot. He had stopped in only as a courtesy call for make-up and wardrobe consultations. After that he was off on a well-trodden path to Italy to put on the weight he would need to look like fat cat Capone.

'When he came back ten weeks later he was a different man,' says Linson. 'He had put on thirty pounds, he had had his hair plucked into position and he looked twenty years older. He went into wardrobe, got his hair right, did his make-up, had his nose done so it was broader, and when he came out he was Al Capone. It was breathtaking. There was a complete personality change. The shyness was gone. He was this flamboyant, bigger-than-life character. It was thrilling.'

De Niro's preparations for Capone were extraordinary. He looked at pictures, read newspaper clippings and studied library cuttings and watched as much newsreel footage of Capone as he could find. All this was for the interior man. His exterior preparations were equally meticulous, but none more so than his decision to have his hairline plucked, hair by hair, to match exactly Capone's own receding hairline. His clothes were designed by Giorgio Armani as an exact replica of what Capone would wear. The finishing touch was silk underwear from Sulka's, the New York men's outfitters that Capone himself used.

'I saw a lot of photographs,' says De Niro of his preparation. 'You can get a lot from those pictures and I saw all the movies that have been done about him and then I did it intuitively. Everybody knows that Al Capone was a robust, massive character so I had to gain weight. I could have worn a bodysuit but what would I have done with my face? So I did the weight thing again even though I didn't want to do it and, I promise you, I will never do it again.'

Playing Al Capone was something of a wake-up call for De Niro. It was technically a minor role – a little more than a cameo but a little less than a co-star's part – but he brought a power to his half-dozen scenes which critics feared might have been spent. There was no way that relatively inexperienced actors like Costner and Garcia were going to be able to stand up to this man. The forces of good were represented by Sean Connery, who was prepared to go toe to toe with De Niro in the scene-stealing Olympics. Connery just shades it by virtue of having won a Best Supporting Actor Oscar for his role as Jimmy Malone. Connery is a fierce and uncompromising judge of his fellow actors. He and De Niro did not meet until the final day of shooting when they shared their only scene together as Malone tries to restrain Ness from killing the arch-mobster.

'I like him,' says Connery unequivocally. 'There's often this tendency with actors when they're asked to play a villainous part to send little signals to the audience that say, "I'm not really like this." De Niro doesn't do that. He knows it's a performance so he can be as villainous as the part calls for. He appears very little in the film, but you always know he's there.'

Both *Angel Heart* and *The Untouchables* cast De Niro as out-and-out villains. These were men with few, if any, redeeming features. De Niro, however, chooses not to see things in such clearly defined terms.

'These characters are not simply bad or evil,' he says. 'They are people living at the edge. I prefer the so-called evil because it is more realistic. Good characters or characters who are only positive tend to be unbelievable and boring. I like to play more rounded characters but finally it depends on the script. A good writer describes realistic characters that are neither good nor bad. A rounded movie character comes into situations, into trouble, that forces him into making decisions. His decisions might sometimes not be the best but his reactions show the audience that they are not alone with their hopes and their problems. So the people can identify with that character. Characters who always react only positively are okay for fantasy films. I prefer realistic characters that are more believable.'

Al Capone was more like the De Niro of old. It was not a part in which he showed much of himself. Once again he was unrecognisable under thirty pounds of extra weight and a few pounds more of latex and pros- thetics. Hidden from view, he could come tantalisingly close to firing on all cylinders. There seems no doubt that De Niro was reluctant to commit himself to a full movie role at this stage. He had agreed to take the lead opposite Meryl Streep in the powerful and moving *Ironweed* as a man who becomes a hobo and a drunk after blaming himself for the death of his baby son. But when *The Untouchables* finally hove into view he left the project and the role was played, magnificently as it turns out, by Jack Nicholson. Perhaps David Puttnam's comments in Cartagena had stung him. The man who loved to gamble with roles appeared to have lost his nerve. If a movie was to fail – as they had all done since *The Deer Hunter* – then let it not be his fault; if he had only a minor part then the film could not reasonably be described as a De Niro film.

'Nothing had come along that seemed right,' he told *Rolling Stone* magazine two years later, a statement that seems to be at the very least economical with the facts in the light of the rejected lead in *Ironweed*. 'I liked the idea of doing a cameo, it's fun. You do these kinds of bigger- than-life parts or characters – mythical almost. I don't know what people's perceptions were but the main thing is you have to do it for yourself. If you please other people as well then that's good, but if not what are you gonna do? I just didn't want to have to carry a movie although doing *The Untouchables* was a lot like being a principal in a movie because of the preparation I had to do.

'But I enjoy doing cameos. I don't know how many more I'll do or when, but I did feel it was time to do a movie, you know, the whole thing.'

Like a runner in a long-distance race, De Niro had been doing little more than catching his breath with *Brazil*, *The Mission*, *Angel Heart* and *The Untouchables*. Now he was about to throw himself back into the race and surprise the whole industry by emerging as a serious box-office contender.

26 On the Run

N 1987 DE NIRO was in serious career distress. He had not had a
hit to his name for years and the pressure was starting to tell. *The
Untouchables* had been a commercial success but just as he could not
take the blame for the failure of his cameo films he was in no position
to take the credit for their success. *The Untouchables* was an ensemble
hit. Kevin Costner, Sean Connery and the memory of the Robert Stack
TV series all had as much to do with its popularity as De Niro.

His reputation was never founded on commercial success but even the
critical plaudits that had encouraged producers to scramble to hire him
were drying up. *The Untouchables* gave him his first overwhelmingly
positive reviews in years. Even so there were still 'Whatever happened to
Robert De Niro?' articles running in major newspapers and magazines. It
looked as if he might be reaching his sell-by date. When he made *The
Champ, Deliverance* and *The Odessa File* back in the seventies, Jon Voight
was briefly the world's number-one male star. Ten years later no one would
seriously consider him a major movie star. Other seventies names like Burt
Reynolds and Ryan O'Neal were going the same way. Even Al Pacino,
whose career had once so closely mirrored De Niro's own, was becalmed
in the eighties.

De Niro knew that he needed a hit and needed one fast. He flirted
briefly with the movie *Big*, a charming fantasy about a man who is
returned to his childhood while still remaining physically a man after a
close encounter with a penny arcade wishing machine. The role was
eventually to provide Tom Hanks with the stepping stone that would
propel him to superstardom. With hindsight, it is difficult to see De Niro
being even remotely convincing in the part. It is an angst-free joyous role
of a type he had never tried to carry off before. Nonetheless, he did
express an interest and the part was offered. The salary quoted was $3
million, but he turned it down after hearing that Warren Beatty had been
offered $6 million. Within a matter of days the story swept through the

industry that De Niro had come looking for the part and been turned down. Although it was completely untrue, the fact that the story was given credence and would continue to be mentioned for some time was an indication of where De Niro's stock was trading in Hollywood at that time. Perhaps the clearest sign that he knew he had to get his career back on track was that he allowed himself to be wooed by the all-powerful Creative Artists Agency. Under superagent Michael Ovitz, CAA had become pre-eminent in the Hollywood of the eighties, where 'the package' was everything. CAA offered one-stop shopping at its designer offices on Wilshire Boulevard. Once they had the concept they could then provide the writer, the director and, most importantly, the stars. All the studio had to do was put up the money.

De Niro's private life was equally turbulent at this stage. He was still technically married to Diahnne Abbott but had begun seeing the former model Doris 'Toukie' Smith. His love life has never been conventional. The one thing he appears to be totally unable to do is to make a commitment to a monogamous relationship. He would occasionally see Smith, the sister of the late fashion designer Willi Smith, and his 'wife' on the same night. Toukie Smith was a popular figure around the Manhattan social scene. She is everything that De Niro is not. With her dyed blonde hair and her trademark red dresses providing a dramatic counterpoint to her dusky complexion, she is guaranteed to stand out in a crowd. Smith is garrulous and gregarious, but De Niro appeared to have been both delighted and amused by her, and she has come as close as anyone to capturing his heart.

Meanwhile Helena Lisandrello maintains that she and De Niro met again during that period. She was living in Los Angeles and De Niro had by now moved to New York. They had seen each other backstage at a concert previously, but De Niro steadfastly avoided talking to her. But she claims that they started seeing each other again on his trips to the coast and that, she says, is when he met his daughter Nina Nadeja for the first time. Lisandrello's career had not been going well in the interim. The back-up singing and session work had dried up and by now she was working in a department store to keep her daughter fed and clothed. She says De Niro resumed his financial help but always in cash – no cheques, no money orders, no bank drafts. On a trip to Los Angeles, De Niro and Nina Nadeja spent several hours together.

'Bobby said, "I'm your daddy. Give me a kiss," ' Lisandrello told the *New York Post.* 'They spent the afternoon together.'

Lisandrello again pressed De Niro formally to acknowledge the baby as his. According to her he said he would acknowledge Nina when 'Toukie had her baby'. Although he and Smith wanted a child together they did not succeed, or at least not by normal means, and even then not for many years. De Niro was plainly close to Lisandrello. Although he never answers the phone himself (he is surrounded by a coterie of staff and friends who take his calls) she always knew how to get hold of him. She had his business and private numbers and the number of his personal answering service. In 1987 she married and contacted De Niro. Her husband was willing to provide for Nina Nadeja and wanted formally to adopt her. De Niro refused to give his consent and promised once again to acknowledge the girl, but it never happened.

There was more baby trouble for De Niro that year. This time it appeared to be a legacy of his Colombian location trip for *The Mission*. In December 1987 the *Observer* newspaper in London reported that two stars who had recently filmed in Cartagena were facing possible paternity suits. The Italian actor Franco Nero, who has appeared in films such as *Camelot* and *Die Hard 2*, had made three films in the region. He found himself vigorously denying allegations that he was the father of a child recently born to the housemaid of one of his friends. The paper also reported that a law firm in the nearby city of Barranquilla was preparing a suit against De Niro, who had filmed *The Mission* in the area two years previously. The woman involved was a young Indian who worked as an extra on the film and then gave birth to her child early in 1986. She claimed De Niro was the father. Despite the reports no suit was ever filed.

By the time Helena Lisandrello had contacted him about the proposed adoption, De Niro was finally getting himself back on course with his first leading role in four years. Ovitz and CAA had come up with a package for a movie called *Midnight Run*, an action-packed buddy comedy that was about as far away from the typical De Niro role as it was possible to get. The script was written by George Gallo, who had previously written *Wise Guys*, a crime comedy directed by Brian De Palma. *Midnight Run* is the story of a bounty hunter who has to bring back a mild-mannered accountant who has embezzled $15 million from his Mafia employers. With CAA in charge there was never any doubt that this was going to be a slickly packaged piece of Hollywood entertainment. They were the ones who came up with the package of Gallo as writer, another CAA client, Martin Brest – who had made Eddie Murphy a movie star in *Beverly Hills Cop* – as director, and CAA's newest client De Niro as bounty hunter Jack Walsh.

Even with CAA at the reins there were still doubts about De Niro's box-office clout, and given his track record and his lack of experience in this type of role they were entirely justified. When the project was taken to Paramount, studio boss Ned Tannen was happy to green-light the movie provided the budget was no higher than $20 million. When it crept beyond that and eventually soared to $31 million, Tannen had grave doubts about De Niro having the ability to carry a film like this on his own. He asked that the supporting role of the accountant be rewritten to accommodate Cher, who was currently on a roll after her Oscar win in *Moonstruck*. Cher, however, was unenthusiastic. If they were not prepared to rewrite quite so drastically then perhaps, Tannen suggested, the part could be tinkered with to make it more attractive to someone like Dustin Hoffman. Eventually the project ended up at Universal, who were not concerned about the cost and told Brest to pick whoever he wanted for the role of the accountant Jonathan 'The Duke' Mardukas. Robin Williams actively campaigned for the role opposite his old friend; he even offered to audition – an unheard-of gesture for someone in his position. Brest, however, chose Charles Grodin, a dry, cultured comedian with a proven theatrical background but a poor commercial movie track record.

The combination was an instant success. Grodin is a superb actor and De Niro responded to the challenge. Their scenes together are like a long sparring session. De Niro eventually emerges victorious thanks to one instinctive gesture. As they continue on their ever-more complicated journey back, Jack comes to realise that Mardukas is a patsy; he has been set up and is a victim of circumstance. The least he can do is allow him a few moments' grace to visit his ex-wife and see his kids. She is touched by the plight of her former husband and lends them her car to make their getaway. As Mardukas, still handcuffed, says goodbye, Walsh is about to close the car door. He notices that the Duke's coat is hanging over the sill and quickly bends to pick it up and pop it back into the car. It is a supremely humanising moment for Jack Walsh and the gesture is the mark of a consummate actor. This small piece of business is all the indication anyone needs to realise that at long last a film had De Niro's full attention. He was concentrating and giving it his very best.

The results were instantly apparent. *Midnight Run* is an unalloyed joy from start to finish and at the age of 45 De Niro found himself with his first certifiable hit. When it was released in July 1988 it made $5.5 million in its first weekend alone – more than *True Confessions* and *Falling in Love* made altogether. The film went on to be an international hit, raking in more than $100 million. De Niro found himself being hailed as a box-office star and made himself known to a whole new generation of admirers – the multiplex generation that made *Midnight Run* a hit had scarcely been born when he appeared in *Mean Streets*. The result was that he now found himself given the ultimate benediction – he was bracketed with Tom

Cruise as a potential co-star. The *Los Angeles Times* reported that the two men were allegedly to appear together in *Tour Mix and Pancho Villa*, with Dennis Hopper directing a mythical account about a meeting between the two men. Cruise was pencilled in to play the cowboy hero while De Niro would play the Mexican revolutionary, an intriguing partnership which, like so many Hollywood projects, never materialised.

Such was his commitment to *Midnight Run* that it extended to making himself available to the media again. Previously he had undertaken only four major interviews in eight years, but doubtless his new CAA minders would have advised him of the need to get out there and sell himself. Stars like Dustin Hoffman and Jack Nicholson, who were much more accessible to the media than De Niro had been, were having much more success. De Niro got the message, and although he was far from being 'hail fellow well met', he did at least consent to publicise his pictures from now on.

One interview shows just how aware De Niro was of the state of his career at the time. The image has been carefully cultivated of a man who cares more about art than commerce, who cares about the part rather than the box-office return. But De Niro is a shrewd operator who knows that you can only be blasé about commerce up to a point. You cannot ignore box-office returns because they are the very standard against which your ability to make your artistic choices is judged. So at Deauville in 1988, where he had been an interested bystander the year before at the première of *The Untouchables*, De Niro this time found himself working hard to talk to the European press. He also found himself desperately trying to convince them that he was not some kind of ogre. Friends insist that in private De Niro is a regular cut-up; Martin Scorsese and Brian De Palma claim he is downright hilarious. For the time being De Niro would be happy just to let people know that he was not all doom and gloom.

'*Midnight Run* I thought might lighten the image I've had of heavy dramatic pieces, you know,' he said tellingly. 'Then in the past couple of years I was only interested in cameo parts in some pictures. I've been kind of taking stock.

'I read the script of *Midnight Run* and was attracted to it straight away. What appealed was the humour. Everyone thinks that all I have is this dark side. I am a bit sick of always being taken so seriously. We were spending an awful lot of time trying to find the right person to play the other part. It had to match up. Casting is like ninety per cent of it to me. If you get the right people, you're OK.'

Although *Midnight Run* was a relatively lightweight project for him, De Niro did not take his preparations any less lightly. In interviews he revealed that he had accompanied on the police on raids and real-life bounty hunters in search of bail jumpers.

'Sure I went out a few times,' he said almost casually. 'The cops made me wear body armour and sign a waiver absolving the police department should anything unpleasant happen to me. Then when the raids happened they seemed somehow clumsy in real life. A door would be rammed, drug dealers would rush to hide their stuff and jump out of the windows – some die that way. It is different after the raids. Would you believe the guy in the handcuffs sometimes asked for my autograph?'

This new *entente* with the media was not as *cordiale* as it appeared to be. De Niro had stopped giving interviews because, as he told *Time* magazine, every time he gave an interview he then had to spend the next few interviews explaining what he meant. Given that he seldom finishes a sentence and appears to communicate in shrugs and gestures, he has to take some of the blame for that himself. He also said he became tired of being asked what he had for breakfast, so in future he would let the work speak for him. The problem was that, before *Midnight Run* at least, the work had not been so much speaking as mumbling diffidently. Hence the truce with the media. But in some quarters at least the barriers were still down. De Niro refused to co-operate with a *Vanity Fair* cover story which ended up becoming a profile from interviews with those friends who were willing to risk being branded disloyal by speaking to the magazine. A proposed *Playboy* interview turned out to be another disaster. The interview was supposed to run to coincide with the opening of *Midnight Run*. Instead De Niro dragged his feet so much that it finally appeared after the film had been released. On the other hand it did appear in *Playboy*'s 35th anniversary issue, which gave the magazine more of a coup than it actually intended. De Niro insisted that he was being forced to do the interview, though he never made clear by whom. Although he did co-operate, eventually, it might have been better for all concerned if he hadn't.

'This has nothing to do with you,' he began by telling interviewer Lawrence Grobel, 'it's just that I'm feeling angry about this. I'm being pressured into doing an interview and I resent that. I'm not good at editing how I feel, I'm only going to say some things. I'm not going to go into my life – that would be ridiculous.'

In the end De Niro's anger appears to have infected Grobel and the interview comes across as bitter and vindictive on both sides. Grobel, like anyone who has watched De Niro's movies, would not have been surprised to find himself dealing with an angry man. However, this is the first time De Niro even began to acknowledge that anger in public. It would not be long before the anger was not just spoken of but would also manifest itself in violence. Occasionally journalists less fortunate than Grobel would bear the brunt of it.

De Niro's new higher profile meant that once again the media began to take an interest in his private life. He had been linked romantically with the singer Whitney Houston, and had allegedly been showering her with gifts. But De Niro's blandishments appeared to have no effect, the fact that he was still married and seeing Toukie Smith notwithstanding. Houston announced her own engagement in March 1988 and that appears to have diminished De Niro's interest somewhat. The actor resumed his relationship with Smith and was then delighted to discover that she was pregnant. In contrast to his behaviour with Helena Lisandrello, De Niro made no attempt to hide the pregnancy. Both he and Smith were excited and delighted at the prospect of having a child together. Tragically Smith miscarried. She and De Niro then considered adopting an AIDS baby – Smith's brother had died of AIDS – but the adoption, of a two-year-old girl named La Toya, does not appear to have gone ahead. Despite their efforts and their obvious fondness for one another, they have never been able to cement their relationship by having a child in a conventional manner.

27 Never Mind the Quality

O NE OF THE MOST visible signs of the new improved media-friendly De Niro was his decision to go to Russia in 1987 to head the judging panel for the Moscow Film Festival. It was an extraordinarily public visitation – albeit in another country – for such an intensely wary man.

'I have come to Moscow,' he told a news conference, 'because I got nervous from the tensions between the USSR and the USA. I felt threatened, personally, that's why I engage myself in mutual understanding.'

Quite what part De Niro felt his mutual understanding might play in improving East-West relations is hard to decipher. Nonetheless in Moscow he was atypically gregarious. He had his eleven-year-old son Raphael and his adopted daughter Drina, who was nineteen, with him, and by all accounts he was the model ambassador. While in Russia he gave his first full-length interview in years. He fell in with a man called Wolfgang Wilke who told him he was an East German journalist. De Niro's latent left-wing sympathies were obviously engaged and in a gesture of solidarity he spoke at some length to Wilke. However, he had been taken in. Wilke was in fact an enterprising West German journalist who came up with the East German angle on the spur of the moment. His interview with De Niro was promptly sold around the world.

'I came to Moscow to see some movies that I would never have seen at home,' said De Niro, before going on to reiterate his concern about the tension between the Soviet Union and the United States. 'However, there are some similarities in both countries,' he conceded. 'We need more mutual information. Movies and personal contacts can help in this understanding.'

Wilke then went on to ask De Niro outright about his media shyness. He refuses interviews but a movie star has to publicise his movies. Has De Niro perhaps chosen the wrong profession?

'Why should I talk to journalists who put some stupid questions to me?' said De Niro, apparently missing the point. 'I do what I have to do and don't waste my energy by talking. People should go into the cinema, watch my movies and make up their own minds.'

Undoubtedly what Wilke did – posing as an East German – was unethical, but given De Niro's self-imposed media blackout and the occasionally absurd lengths he has gone to in order to avoid interviews, it is difficult to judge him too harshly. The interview did give one clear clue to the future direction of De Niro's career.

'I only go to Los Angeles when I'm paid for it,' he told Wilke in arguably the most significant section of the interview. His disaffection with Hollywood – the location rather than the film industry – was complete. He now saw it simply as a place of work. The idea had been forming in his mind for some time that he ought to be able to take more control of his career. After the success of *Midnight Run* he decided the time was right. He would move back to New York permanently and set up his own film company. He would be the master of his own destiny.

Setting up studios does not come cheap. It would require a considerable bankroll, so De Niro decided to go out and earn it. He had also just bought himself a base in New York. When his apartment building in Hudson Avenue became a condo, De Niro paid $875,000 for the flat he had been renting. The man who had made roughly a film every year and a half would make five films in the next two years. He flogged himself into the ground to raise the money to finance his dream. The films were a mixed bag. One performance was genuinely memorable, one verged on greatness, two were indifferent, and one was the worst screen performance he has ever given. While he was trying to put all this together, Sergio Leone came to America trying to raise money for the project he and De Niro had discussed. Leone was looking for funding for *The 900 Days*, the story of the siege of Leningrad. He said it would not be a war film but a love story set against that historical turning point, with De Niro playing the lead role of a journalist in his thirties. Leone diplomatically pointed out that by the time he raised the finance and wrote the script De Niro might in fact be too old to play the part. But given his own desire to raise money quickly for his studio it seems unlikely that De Niro would have committed himself to a year of shooting on a single film. In the end Leone died shortly after coming to America in 1989.

The success of *Midnight Run* had boosted De Niro's Hollywood stock. Thanks to a box-office hit and the negotiating power of CAA, he was now commanding between $4 million and $5 million a film. He was also once again an attractive proposition in any package presented to a studio.

Hence in the summer of 1988 he found himself co-starring with Jane Fonda in *Stanley and Iris*, to be directed by veteran film-maker Martin Ritt. De Niro is an illiterate blue-collar cook whose natural intellect and talent for invention are hampered by his lack of formal education. Fonda is a lonely widow who teaches him to read. Their relationship blossoms and they discover their potential together. It is worth noting that *Stanley and Iris* originally started life as a novel called *Union Street*, set in the gritty north-east of England with two decidedly unglamorous leading characters. But once Hollywood waved its magic wand it instantly became a suitable vehicle for Fonda and De Niro.

The two stars found themselves embroiled in a political row during shooting. Filming was to take place in the town of Waterbury, Connecticut, and the announcement had appeared in the local newspaper on 11 November, 1987 which, as it turned out, was Veterans Day. The city fathers' joy at the much-needed boost to the economy quickly turned into a major political headache. Waterbury is a rock-solid Republican town in which apparently a great many people had very long memories. They were unhappy with Fonda's 'Hanoi Jane' image from the Vietnam War, in which she had made anti-American broadcasts from Hanoi and been photographed with North Vietnamese troops. Veterans of Vietnam and the Second World War promised to protest against the film being shot in their town. The local council held an emergency meeting to vote on it. The decision was taken to allow shooting to go ahead. Filming proceeded without a hitch, but clearly some gesture of appeasement would be needed.

De Niro was against the Vietnam War but he keeps his politics to himself and made no comment on the Fonda row. At the time he was preoccupied with getting *Midnight Run* off the ground. However, in July 1988 he did join in a gesture of goodwill and solidarity with the people of Waterbury. The cast and crew of *Stanley and Iris* took part in a huge fundraising effort for the children of the victims of the Vietnam defoliant Agent Orange. The cause is one of the few for which De Niro actively campaigns, and he cheerfully took his place in a booth at the gala to pose for Polaroids at $15 each.

If he was going to make films at a faster rate than normal, then clearly something was going to have to give. De Niro had been acting long enough to no longer require the intensive periods of preparation he had undergone for his earlier films. He had found ways, like any other actor, of editing the process. With *Stanley and Iris* it was a question of expediency, but he would soon learn that it was a process he could put to good use in almost every film.

'I felt all right about it,' he told an interviewer at the time. 'I thought about it. I had averaged about a movie every eighteen months before this and I was ready for a faster pace. I'm at the age where I don't want to waste time. I want to do a lot of things.

'With *Stanley and Iris*, for example, I had a woman who interviewed and videotaped a lot of illiterates and spent a lot of time with them. I would just look at what she did instead of interviewing them myself. It was more helpful to me because I didn't have to spend all the time going through all the social stuff. I could just play it back and pick up all the nuances that way. It was at my leisure so I didn't have to worry and extend so much of myself.'

De Niro drew modest praise for his role but it was obvious that although he was engaging as Stanley it was not a part that occupied his full attention. The film is amiable enough, but neither De Niro nor Fonda had the star power to draw an audience, and this $20 million movie made less than $5 million at the American box-office.

De Niro had little opportunity to dwell on the failure of *Stanley and Iris*. Like a shark which has to maintain forward momentum he was already on to his next project. A little more than a decade after *The Deer Hunter* he was going back to Vietnam. In *Jacknife*, De Niro plays Joseph 'Megs' Meggesy, one of the walking wounded of the South-East Asian conflict. Megs is not physically wounded but he has been mentally scarred. He has been suffering from post-traumatic stress syndrome but appears to have conquered it. One day he turns up out of the blue at the home of his old Vietnam buddy, Ed Harris, who has never come to terms with life after Vietnam. De Niro attempts to force Harris to confront the reality of the situation and in the process begins to fall for Harris's sister, played by Kathy Baker.

There are no combat sequences in *Jacknife* but De Niro did spend time with Vietnam veterans before shooting began.

'I met a lot of guys when I was doing *Deer Hunter* but that was ten years ago,' he explained. 'The war was more immediate, it was closer to the end of the war so it was a different feeling. You never really talked with them about the pain and all that. That was something you just never talked about. You just talked about the bad scene, the experience, and how terrible it was. But nobody wanted to deal with the sense of rejection, like the country didn't care for them. It was like 'it happened, let's go on, let's forget about it'. But when I met the vets for this film they were more able to deal with things like that.'

Again De Niro adopted a high media profile for *Jacknife* giving a number of interviews to promote the film. It was, he claimed, a film that was very important to him and he wanted it to open well. Sadly he would be disappointed. Audiences stayed away from *Jacknife* in droves. The film had cost a relatively inexpensive $10 million but only took $2.2 million at the box-office. There was some consolation for De Niro, however, when on 25 May, 1989 Vietnam veterans awarded him their Vetty award for his artistic commitment and for speaking out about Agent Orange.

The lack of either critical or commercial success for his two films since *Midnight Run* must have been of some concern to De Niro and his people. There were already rumblings that *Midnight Run* might simply have been a flash in the pan. De Niro and Grodin might simply have been lightning in a bottle, and he might never have that clout again. His next choice would do nothing to damp down those fears. Before *Jacknife* was released there were strong suggestions that De Niro would appear in the screen version of David Mamet's incendiary play *Glengarry Glen Ross*. Ulu Grosbard, with whom he had worked on *True Confessions* and *Falling in Love*, was tipped to direct, with De Niro and Pacino starring. De Niro would have played failed real estate salesman Shelley Levine, with Al Pacino as Ricky Roma. The project, as it was conceived, came to nothing. It would be almost five years before the Mamet play came to the screen with Pacino as Roma but Jack Lemmon, not De Niro, as Levine. De Niro's next project would still involve David Mamet, but it would be light-years away in quality.

We're No Angels was a successful 1955 movie based on a stage play. Humphrey Bogart, Peter Ustinov and Aldo Ray played three escaped convicts from Devil's Island who take over a store and generally transform a small community. The film had been a favourite of De Niro's for some time, and he saw it as the vehicle he had been looking for to give him the chance to work with Sean Penn, an actor he admired greatly. De Niro and Penn then approached *Untouchables* producer Art Linson with the idea. Linson liked the notion and asked *Untouchables* screenwriter David Mamet to come up with a script. Neil Jordan, an Irishman who had made a name for himself in Britain but had had his first American film, *High Spirits*, savaged by the studio, was to direct.

Together they came up with a script that owed little more to the original than the title. De Niro and Penn play escaped convicts who take refuge in a small town. With their pursuers hot on their tail they are more than relieved when they are mistaken for eminent theologians and offered sanctuary in the local monastery. But with prison warder Ray McAnally still in town, they are forced to maintain their disguises.

'I think it was something he had wanted to do for a while,' says Jordan of De Niro's involvement. 'He was involved in the genesis of the script.'

In contrast to Mamet's other work there is very little of the quickfire dialogue that has become his trademark. *We're No Angels* is punctuated by long gaps which De Niro takes it on himself to fill with grotesque mugging that is almost embarrassing to watch. He goes well over the top in an attempt to milk a not very funny script of whatever laughs it might contain.

'There are a lot of spaces in David's dialogue,' says Jordan. 'Bob's performance was a combination of things. He's a very bold actor and I think characters develop in secret ways. We rehearsed rather briefly and as we went through it, as we began to explore the script, we decided to go for something that was quite broad in the characterisation. The writing is rather thin, though I think it is wonderful. I like dialogue where the characters don't always spell out their background and their history. There was a lot of room for the actors to develop, to actually fill in the characters for themselves.

'I don't think De Niro over-played. It was a conscious decision to go for something graphic and broad on Bob's part because the core of the film, the dramatic core of the film, is a farce. It's the comedy of mistaken identity. I think Bob is a great comic actor.

'He is an actor who has an incredible range and I like to have quite a bit of freedom to invent things. I found it very good working with Bob because he does like to expand the whole range of choices when he's actually acting. I valued that because the approach that Bob takes is basically what film-making at its best is about. The performance actually begins when the camera is there and you are surrounded by the environment, that is what you respond most directly towards. In Bob's case that leads to him giving a tremendous range of choices in the different takes that he does. Jim Clark the editor said when he was cutting, 'You don't cut De Niro, you mine him.' And he's right – you dig down through the different levels.'

De Niro had never been required to be funny on screen before. Although Rupert Pupkin in *King of Comedy* was nominally a comedian, the point of the film was that he was the world's most humorously challenged man. With Pupkin De Niro had to play it straight, but with Ned, his character in *We're No Angels*, he has to go for the laughs. The results are lamentable.

The *Village Voice* said that De Niro played 'by screwing up his face and bobbing up and down as if he's doing an oriental gentleman'; *Newsweek* talked of a 'heavily mugging De Niro'; for the *Wall Street Journal* De Niro was 'surprisingly inept, mugging throughout the movie with what he seems to think is a comical expression'; *Seven Days* magazine said, 'De Niro, as often when he is playing clods, is so excessively pleased with himself that he leaves the audience behind.'

Robert De Niro: Untouchable

The reviews were devastating and business was even worse. *We're No Angels* cost $22 million and took $5 million at the American box-office. De Niro's decision to play the part seems staggeringly ill-judged. His career was slipping again. However, he could not claim to be taking stock of his career as he had in his cameo period. This time he was making a conscious attempt to raise money; like a squirrel hoarding food for winter he needed the cash. He was firmly wedded to commerce not art, but commerce was spurning his advances. The simple fact was that De Niro was emerging once again as an actor with a reputation but no box-office appeal. *Midnight Run* was looking more and more like a fluke – a successful glitch in a ten-year run of box-office failure which stretched back to his last hit, *The Deer Hunter*. One source estimated that since *New York, New York* De Niro's movies had lost a cumulative total of $150 million at the American box-office. This could be disguised by bursts of activity taking him from film to film, keeping him one step ahead of the game, but clearly something would have to be done.

He would have to take control of his own fate, and quickly. But before then there would be help from two of his oldest friends.

28 TriBeCa

I T HAD BEEN SEVEN years since Scorsese and De Niro had been on a film set together. A lot of water had flowed under the bridge since *King of Comedy*. There was the abortive version of *The Last Temptation of Christ* for one thing. Their careers had diverged rapidly since they last worked together.

In those days De Niro had the box-office muscle and Scorsese the artistic vision. Now things had been subtly reversed. De Niro was the one whose career was in a trough while Scorsese, with hits like *The Color of Money* and *After Hours*, and critical acclaim for finally bringing *Last Temptation* to the screen, was on the crest of a wave. He had rightly been hailed, along with Woody Allen, as the greatest American director of his generation.

In those seven years they had, as Scorsese always promised, checked in with each other from time to time, not losing touch. Now they were back together again and, for both of them, it was familiar territory. *GoodFellas* was set on the streets of Little Italy. These were the streets where Scorsese was born and where De Niro hung out, in the world of the big men on Mott Street, the Wise Guys, the made men. Based on a book by Nicholas Pileggi, *GoodFellas* is the story of three decades of Mob life seen through the eyes of Henry Hill, a young man taken under the Mob wing when he is only a boy. De Niro would play Jimmy 'The Gent' Conway, a legendary figure in gangland circles. Conway masterminds a $6 million raid from the Lufthansa Airlines depot at Newark Airport in the early sixties and then promptly murders all his accomplices. The part was based on real-life gangster Jimmy Burke.

Scorsese saw the film as more than a simple gangster story. According to author and screenwriter Pileggi, he wanted to bring to the screen almost an anthropological study of a very small sub-culture which operated under its own rules, its own codes, and its own beliefs. Pileggi wrote the book because he believed this culture had never been properly depicted before.

Scorsese, who of course had known this environment from childhood, agreed, which is why he wanted to make it accessible to a wider audience.

If the seven years working apart had produced any strain or coolness in the relationship between De Niro and Scorsese it did not manifest itself on the set. De Niro seemed to be invigorated by the presence of his old friend in the director's chair. Watching De Niro play Jimmy Conway is a complete joy. His first scene in the film, as he bounces into the social club glad-handing everyone and stuffing twenty-dollar bills indiscriminately into breast pockets, is vintage De Niro. It is also seen from the point of view of the young Henry, which means that the audience shares his unalloyed admiration for this incredibly charismatic character. After the bizarre over-the-top performance of *We're No Angels*, De Niro's performance in *GoodFellas* is so convincing that, as one critic pointed out, at times he appears not to be acting at all.

'We're friends but we're best friends when we're working together,' says De Niro warmly of his favourite director. 'We have a very special relationship. Marty and I have a special way of communicating. He's very open and I can't tell you as an actor how important that is. If you work with certain directors you find yourself closing down and you don't want to do anything; you think whatever idea you come up with is not going to get a good response. With Marty it's the opposite – the more you come up with the more enthusiastic he gets and that's what makes it a joyous experience rather than just a job.

'I try not to get into situations with directors who I don't respect. I have to like and respect them and follow what they're doing otherwise there's no point in working with them. It's very arduous work and if you are not at least thinking you're with people you respect and are trying to help them realise a vision of one sort or another, there's no point. I'm proud of *GoodFellas*.'

De Niro's research for Jimmy the Gent came largely from Pileggi, whom he referred to as a fountain of information. He used Pileggi as a jumping-off point and then went on to talk to others who he thought might be useful. It was claimed at the time that the real Jimmy Burke was so tickled to have De Niro playing him that he phoned from prison to give him a few pointers. Pileggi denies this, saying the two men have never spoken, but admitting that there were men around the set all the time who knew all the principal characters. Conway is Irish rather than Italian, but he remains a middle-aged version of the characters that De Niro had played in his younger days. There are traces of Jon Rubin and Johnny Boy in Jimmy Conway.

'As a kid I didn't root for the bad guys,' says De Niro trying to explain the attraction. (Although, since he was fond of gangster movies as a youngster, he must have cheered on the bad guys at some stage.) 'I certainly know the difference between right and wrong but I think in our American tradition the bad guys get a lot of attention and you see that in the movies. There is a certain glamour, a certain allure that they have, but we always have to remember to put it in the right perspective of what they represent. Like a Robin Hood thing in reverse, but you always have to be aware of what the real world is too.

'I think *The Godfather* started it, popularised it in a very grand sense. It was a movie about the most typically reactionary type of people, set in a time where so much was going on. The bad guys are always more interesting than the good guys. The antagonist is more interesting than the protagonist. Because we're human beings, there's good and evil in all of us and these villains act out the worst part of ourselves.'

De Niro just missed out on cashing in on more *Godfather*-style popularity in 1989 when Francis Ford Coppola started work on the final part of his Mafia trilogy. *The Godfather Part III* would focus on the death of Michael Corleone and the passage of power to his nephew Vincent, the illegitimate son of his brother Sonny. Remarkably, De Niro said he was interested in the role and convinced Coppola he could play young. Coppola flirted for a time with casting him. De Niro went to the Napa Valley to read for the part and Coppola was so taken with him that he even considered rewriting the role to suit him. Things didn't work out, partly because De Niro's existing commitment to *Awakenings* would have pushed Coppola's picture back so far it couldn't have met its release date. In the end the role went to Andy Garcia after Val Kilmer, Nicolas Cage – Coppola's nephew – Charlie Sheen and Billy Zane had been considered. If De Niro had taken the role it would have meant him playing his own grandson, since he had played the young Vito Corleone in the second *Godfather* movie. Curiously he may not have had to play as young as he thought. De Niro was born in 1943 and, according to the *Godfather* chronology, Vincent was born around 1948.

While De Niro was in New York filming *GoodFellas* he was putting the finishing touches to his grand scheme. His apartment in Hudson Street is in the heart of the area known as TriBeCa – the abbreviation stands for the TRiangle BEneath CAnal (Street). TriBeCa was once an area of thriving warehouses but had lately fallen into disrepair. Many of the old warehouses had been converted into apartments and the area was slowly being gentrified. However, the process was not happening fast enough to stop many of these historic buildings coming under the wrecking-ball. De Niro did his civic duty and signed an open letter from the residents to the

Landmarks Preservation Association to try to maintain the character of the area.

'Hundreds of irreplaceable 19th Century cast iron and masonry buildings in TriBeCa are, as of now, unprotected and face certain destruction,' he wrote in the letter, which was distributed to other local residents, encouraging them to bombard the commission with a letter-writing campaign. De Niro had his eye on one building in particular, the former Martinson's coffee warehouse on the corner of Greenwich Street and Franklin Street. The elegant eight-storey building is only a block away from De Niro's own apartment.

'I used to walk past and think, What a beautiful building,' he said. 'It was kind of like a dream, to get a building, to get that building. The whole idea of a place where a lot of people can get together.'

De Niro turned his dream into a reality by acquiring the building with, as co-investors, developer Paul Stewart and Broadway producer Stewart Lane – De Niro took a 50 per cent share. The building alone cost them $7.5 million – it had changed hands for just over $4 million five years previously. He wanted to turn the dilapidated warehouse into a film production complex with a chic restaurant where he and his friends could hang out. This would be the TriBeCa Film Center, a $10 million eight-storey complex which in De Niro's eyes would serve as a Manhattan mecca for writers, producers and directors. To run the operation he brought in Jane Rosenthal as his executive vice-president. Rosenthal's background was in the development departments of Disney, Warner, Universal and CBS. She had experience in both television and film. She says that her reaction when De Niro approached her was one of excitement tempered with the feeling that the film industry was based in Los Angeles, so what on earth could he be talking about?

'People didn't believe that he could do this, that we could do this,' she told *Variety*. 'Even a lot of people who did believe us would kind of look at us. It's an investment in the future as far as he's concerned. He's not about to stop acting.'

Far from it. The start-up costs and the initial running costs of TriBeCa meant that De Niro would have to work virtually non-stop in a succession of high-earning roles just to keep his end up. The TriBeCa Bar and Grill, which occupies the ground floor of the building, cost just under $3 million. It requires an annual turnover of $1.2 million just to wash its face financially. De Niro admits that he found himself almost turning into a hustler in his quest to find co-investors.

'Literally I'd run into someone on the street,' he told *New York* magazine, 'and I'd think, Maybe I'll ask them. Maybe they'll do it, maybe they won't. It was very random.'

Eventually there were 23 signatures on the partnership papers, contributing $2.8 million. The investors included friends and former co-stars like Christopher Walken and Sean Penn, along with others like the ballet dancer Mikhail Baryshnikov and comedian Bill Murray. One famous name found the conditions involved just too much. Barbra Streisand was keen to be involved in TriBeCa but local by-laws dictated that in order to get a drinks licence all the partners had to be fingerprinted. Streisand, a notorious defender of civil liberties, decided that she could not subject herself to that and withdrew from the project.

De Niro supervised the conversion of the Martinson Building as though he were preparing for a movie role. He was involved in every aspect of the conversion, turning up at all hours of the day and night. Once he even turned up on Superbowl Sunday, when all right-thinking American males are glued to a television set – he found most of the workers watching the game in a nearby bar. The conversion did not proceed without problems. De Niro, who had earlier joined other residents in an open letter to the local authorities, now found himself the subject of such a letter. Residents who had been concerned about the effect that TriBeCa might have on their quiet arty community in terms of attracting in actors and yuppies had finally had as much as they could take. When the renovation work shattered the peace and quiet of their Sunday they took matters into their own hands. The following Sunday an 'open letter to Robert De Niro' was posted on lamp-posts throughout the area.

'Dear sir,' it said. 'You are disturbing hundreds of your new neighbours in the vicinity of your new building on Franklin and Greenwich Streets by operating your noisy demolition machinery on a Sunday. This noise is oppressive and if you do not have it stopped forthwith, it will only reveal the contempt you hold for the people of TriBeCa, the community you claim to "love so much".'

De Niro got the message. But there was another more persistent problem with rats. The fumigation and demolition work going on in the Martinson Building forced scores of the rodents out into the streets in search of new homes. The locals were less than pleased with the creatures, dubbing them 'Robertos', which by all accounts pleased De Niro even less than the rats pleased the residents. One TriBeCa local sat up all night with a baseball bat like Jack the Giant Killer. Once he had accumulated a suitable number of rodent corpses he deposited them outside the entrance to De Niro's Hudson Avenue penthouse.

But once residents' fears had been placated it was a proud De Niro who invited the media into his new building in October 1989. Work was still in progress, but evidence of what it would look like when it was completed was there to be seen. De Niro was resplendent in his blue-carpeted corner office on the eighth floor of the building. At 46 he was finally going into business for himself.

'I decided to go into business so that I could try my hand at producing and directing,' he explained. 'I never had full responsibility for a film before and I never wanted it. But now I do. I see this as a centre where writers, directors and producers can work in a great atmosphere.'

The TriBeCa Film Center, when it was completed, would boast an office complex, a 70-seat screening room, a private dining room, and the 150-seat public restaurant and bar. The eighth floor would be for De Niro's TriBeCa Productions, including his own private office complete with jacuzzi and steam room. Floors three to five were to be sold to film companies. Floors six to eight were to be rented out. Among the first occupants were Penny Marshall's *Awakenings*, which De Niro was currently filming, and Brian De Palma's *Bonfire of the Vanities*. Office space on these floors was also taken by De Niro's *Untouchables* producer Art Linson and Miramax Films, America's leading independent film company.

Although the acquisition of the building and the conversion had cost De Niro several million dollars, the actual running costs of his own company, TriBeCa Productions, were covered by an exclusive deal with TriStar Films. This 'housekeeping' deal meant that TriStar got first look at all TriBeCa's in-house output in return for meeting the company's overheads. TriStar also provided a discretionary fund for development finance.

Within weeks of opening its doors, TriBeCa had a slate of fourteen projects that it was developing in-house or at other major studios. The first to come to the screen was *Thunderheart*, a thriller set on an Indian reservation starring Val Kilmer. Other projects included *Tales of the Bronx*, based on the Chazz Palminteri play, which De Niro planned to direct himself; *The Battling Spumonti Brothers*, a comedy being prepared for De Niro and Danny De Vito, one of whom would also direct; *Gold Lust*, a movie that might one day star De Niro and Dustin Hoffman; *Mistress*, a low-budget Hollywood comedy that was to be the directing debut of De Niro's buddy Barry Primus; and a couple of scripts that had been commissioned, including one from *Midnight Run* writer George Gallo. It was an ambitious and enterprising raft of projects, some of which would have more success in coming to the screen than others.

TriBeCa has become in many ways De Niro's sword and his shield. It instantly establishes him as a player with his own mini-studio with which to develop and encourage talent. In addition it is a refuge from the vagaries of Hollywood modishness. It means that he no longer has to worry about whether or not a part might be right for him or whether or not he might need a co-star like Cher to open the picture. TriBeCa means that if De Niro wants to play a part then he can simply develop it for himself with his own company. On another level TriBeCa is a very conspicuous gesture of self-affirmation. It is his monument and his legacy, the equivalent of his father's paintings. But it goes one step beyond that. His father's work never hung in the galleries where De Niro believed it should. TriBeCa films would at least be seen and remembered.

One of the first movies to emanate from the TriBeCa Center was not a TriBeCa production. Columbia Pictures had taken office space there for six months for *Awakenings*, which was to star De Niro and Robin Williams. The two had been friends for years, but despite Williams's best efforts on *Midnight Run* this would be their first time working together. The film is based on the book by noted neurologist Dr Oliver Sacks. De Niro plays Leonard, a man who has been catatonic for 30 years as the result of a childhood neurological illness. Williams plays Doctor Malcolm Sayer, based on Sacks, who decides that, contrary to popular belief, Leonard and other victims are not necessarily vegetables although they appear to be in a vegetative state. Through painstaking experiments with the new drug L-Dopa, he manages to free them from their catatonic state. For some the transformation is permanent but for others, like Leonard, it is a frustratingly brief awakening. 'Learn from me,' he says hauntingly and poignantly to Sayer as he is about to lapse back into somnolence.

The story of Leonard L, as he was known, and his fellow patients had been told before in a television documentary by the British company Granada and in Harold Pinter's play *A Kind of Alaska*. Oliver Sacks was initially reluctant to allow it to be turned into a movie but was won over by the sincerity of producers Larry Lasker and Walter Parkes, and the sensitivity of Steve Zaillian's script.

'There is a wonderful scene in the film where De Niro as the revived Leonard L talks about the wonder of life and how we don't notice,' says Oliver Sacks, trying to explain the enduring fascination with this story. 'I think this is sort of true. We're not catatonic but I think we feel ourselves in a slightly dulled state and need to be awakened. Yet the awakening is so tantalisingly brief with these patients, it's like a revelation or falling in love. I think it's a deeply human story even though it seems so improbable.'

To prepare for the part De Niro met a great many of the surviving patients. He travelled to London at his own expense to meet some of them – there are nine patients in London who had been on L-Dopa for more than 20 years at the time. For Dr Sacks, who was a neophyte in the film business, the whole process was admirable and at the same time a little frightening.

'He spent hundreds of hours with patients and at a very deep level, beyond words,' he says admiringly. 'Bob is very intelligent but he doesn't feel like talking much. He often says "Shut up, let me feel it." This happened with one patient who is a very articulate, rather verbose Parkinsonian who said, "I have this freezing. I have seven different forms of freezing, let me enumerate." And he started to count and Bob said "No, I'll stay the weekend." And in fact he spent the next thirty-six hours non-stop with this man, observing all seven forms of freezing and observing him awake and asleep, alone and with others. This is the sort of concentration he brings.

'It was frightening at times and it didn't entirely disappear, or at least it didn't disappear instantly the minute he came off the set. Sometimes in the evening there would be fragments of the Leonard L character which still adhered to him. He would say things which belonged to Leonard L and not Bob De Niro. His foot would be turned a little bit, he might have a tic. I gather this occurs with other roles with him but here, since the role was one of neurological disorder, it was particularly disturbing.'

Dr Sacks is right up to a point. This sort of behaviour was characteristic of De Niro but it had not been happening of late. By his own admission he took short-cuts in preparing for *Stanley and Iris*, and judging by the evidence on screen his preparation for *We're No Angels* and *Jacknife* could hardly have been as thorough as he might have liked. He had been coasting in these films, but in *Awakenings* and *GoodFellas*, when his powers of concentration were fully engaged, he was once again a dramatic force to be reckoned with.

For De Niro, making *Awakenings* was a moving and frequently chastening experience.

'It was hard to play because it was so physical,' he says. 'Playing someone handicapped is difficult. It's not just being immobile but being blank. And finding the right position for the head and the hands and the feet. We were told to imagine we were stuck in glue.

'Seeing these patients who are totally immobilized, when you see this around you you realise how lucky you are. It's simple, you take things for granted. You realise you've got emotional problems or whatever; these people have real problems and they've got to overcome simple things like moving an arm.

'It gave me a whole sense of awareness of what it's like to be in that state and how beyond awful that must be. I don't know how to even describe it. That's part of it along with another idea – life and how precious it is. We take things for granted. If you get your faculties back – it was for one summer in the film – that's lucky enough, but when you lose them again, you realise how precious the time you had was. It must have been an incredible experience for everybody at that time, with Oliver Sacks, to appreciate that miracle. Temporary as it was.'

Filming of *Awakenings* went largely without a hitch. The two friends responded well to each other. De Niro was already cast and he suggested Williams after seeing *Dead Poets Society*. For his part Williams believed *Awakenings* allowed De Niro to show a genuine warmth that people had never seen on screen before.

The only hint of trouble came with press reports that Williams had become angry with De Niro and broken his nose.

'If that was true,' joked Williams at the time, 'I wouldn't be saying, "Let's talk," at least not with my own teeth.'

According to director Penny Marshall the incident was an unfortunate accident that happened while they were filming a scene together.

'There were no fits of temperament,' she explained. 'They were doing a scene and it was a scene where Bobby pushes Robin down. We had been rehearsing it and Bobby said to Robin, "I want you to hold my hands down as far as you can," because he wanted to be able to swing his arms up and push him away. And what it is, Bobby is stronger than Robin.'

According to Marshall's version, corroborated by Williams, when De Niro swung his arms up Williams's elbow crunched into his nose. There was apparently an audible crack which was picked up on the soundtrack of that day's rushes. De Niro continued with the scene even though there was blood streaming from his nose. After a preliminary clean-up he did nine more takes before finally going to hospital, where it was confirmed that the nose was broken.

'The thing is,' he said afterwards, 'my nose was broken once before and Robin knocked it back in the other direction. He straightened it out. It looks better than it did before.'

29 Enter Naomi

According to some sections of the press De Niro was going to mark the change in his professional life which the opening of TriBeCa had wrought by an equally significant change in his personal life.

Depending on your source, he was either going to marry Toukie Smith, thus cementing their four-year relationship, or he was going to ditch her altogether for the new woman in his life, supermodel Naomi Campbell. At the time the nineteen-year-old from Streatham in London was dating boxer Mike Tyson, who had just lost his world heavyweight title. Neither Tyson nor Toukie Smith was particularly happy with suggestions that De Niro and Campbell were a couple. The two had met a number of times at various up-market Manhattan parties and restaurants. The attraction for Campbell was obvious – De Niro was a powerful and internationally respected figure. If he was paying attention to her then she by extension acquired a kind of reflected respectability – no one can say you are just a model when you have Robert De Niro on your arm. For him the attraction was equally clear. Campbell is one of the most beautiful woman in the world – few middle-aged men would not be flattered by her attention. In many ways their pairing resembled the Marilyn Monroe–Arthur Miller marriage in which he was said to have given her brains while she gave him sex.

In the end De Niro did not choose Campbell or Toukie Smith; he tried to have both. The control freak in him plainly believed that he could continue to see both women. To be fair, he tried to keep the relationship with Campbell quiet, content to spend quiet nights with her at his Hudson Street penthouse or her Greenwich Village apartment. In the end, however, it was the youthful Campbell who was the less discreet of the two, confirming that they were indeed an item. Over the next three years their stormy relationship would occupy miles of film for paparazzi and acres of newsprint all over the world.

Campbell, like Diahnne Abbott, Toukie Smith, Helena Lisandrello, and Gillian De Terville, is black. De Niro appears to have a fondness for black women. But Helena Lisandrello believes it is more manipulative than sinister.

'I don't think it's racial,' she says. 'It's that black women aren't used to being courted by handsome, famous, rich white guys. So they don't say no to whatever the man wants. Black women take whatever the white man dishes out. We don't go public with these things.'

De Niro's view of relationships was almost certainly coloured by his own childhood. Here we have an interesting paradox. His own mother had a number of boyfriends over a long period, none of them lasting more than a few years. This would discourage him from forming stable relationships himself. But it was his opposition to his mother's suitors which prevented her from settling down with any of them, no matter how strongly she felt. In the end she always chose her son, and in a strange way, De Niro was instrumental in denying himself the domestic stability he may have craved.

When he started dating Naomi Campbell, De Niro was 46, and by even the kindest stretch of the imagination comfortably into middle age. His entire life had been characterised by rage and frustration. For the most part that had, in the early days at least, been sublimated in the characters he played, the angry young men who had defined his career. Now, in his middle years, when his skills were more practised and the parts less challenging, this rage would more and more often erupt into pointless and absurd violence. It was perhaps a shadow of the frustration-induced tempers his father endured.

Barry Norman has been presenting a weekly film review programme for the BBC for almost a quarter of a century. He is Britain's most popular and populist film critic, and throughout those 20-plus years has been scrupulously even-handed in his treatment of films, film stars, and directors. He is the last person you would expect anyone to lose their temper with, and certainly the last person you would expect to have a nose-to-nose confrontation with an angry movie star in the placid surroundings of the Savoy Hotel in London. The occasion was a brief publicity visit to London by De Niro in October 1990 to promote the UK release of *GoodFellas*. Norman had been told by Warner Brothers, the UK distributors of the movie, that De Niro was in London and had agreed to do one television interview.

'I had never attempted to interview him previously because people I knew had tried to interview him and said he was a very bad interview,' says Norman, taking up the story. 'I got the call from Warner Brothers and I thought, Fine, if he actually wants to be interviewed then he must have something to say. But it wasn't quite like that. We got to the Savoy Hotel and we sat around for an hour waiting for him to arrive. When he turned up he didn't seem particularly interested in talking to anyone or being introduced to anybody. He grudgingly met me and the producer, he didn't want to talk to the crew. Then he sat down on the edge of a sofa. I was on an armchair and I started asking questions. The camera was beside me but for some reason he kept addressing his answers to the far corner of the room which, to me, seemed not only to be stupid but also highly unprofessional.

'The answers were monosyllabic and almost inarticulate. After a few minutes I began to get angry because I was plainly wasting my time. Everyone was wasting their time and I, for one, had better things to do that day. Then at the very end I asked him a question – it was a genuine request for information – but it upset him. While I had been doing the research for the interview I had read several American magazines and in each of them there was this story about *Big*, that he had asked for the role and the producers had told him to shove off because they wanted a bigger star like Tom Hanks. At the time Tom Hanks wasn't even a household name in his own house and De Niro most certainly was, so I couldn't believe this. I decided I had to get to the bottom of it and that's what I asked him and that's what annoyed him. In the end he grudgingly gave a very garbled answer to the question. At the end of the interview when I said, "Thank you very much" I went to shake his hand but he wouldn't shake hands.

'He said, "You had to get that one in, didn't you?" I said, "What are you talking about?' But he simply turned on his heel and went out into the hotel corridor. By this time I was furious because I knew the interview was hopeless – I had been talking to him for half an hour and I was lucky if we had three minutes of usable material – so I followed him out. "What is your problem?" I said, and he said, "You know what my problem is." I didn't, of course, but the two of us stood there snarling nose to nose at each other. It was all very childish.

'It then transpired that he thought I had asked the question to stir up trouble. I tried to explain that this was not my intention, that I would have thought it was in his best interests to have this story refuted. It gave the impression, through repetition, that he was box-office poison. In fact the story, as he told it to me, was that the producers had approached him to do the role, he had been interested and he had agreed to do it. Then they started talking about where and when and how much money he would be paid and he walked away. Within a few days of him walking away from the whole enterprise the story started spreading that he had asked for the job and they had told him to go away. I believe his version, it makes much more sense. So we snarled a bit more and I said, "If it pleases you I won't use it in the interview." I wasn't going to anyway because it would have taken half the show to get the answer. He said, "Okay, fine," and he smiled and we shook hands and parted ostensibly amicably but I don't think either of us would wish to repeat the experience.

'Oddly enough the whole experience wasn't as uncomfortable as it might have been, but looking back I suppose it was a very stupid thing for me to have done. He is much fitter, younger, and probably more violent than I am because I am not a violent man. But I was so angry at the time that the adrenalin replaced any potential fear. I wasn't in any way anxious or afraid, I just wanted to let him know how annoyed I was that he had screwed up my entire day.

'That's why I now say, only half in jest, that I think Robert De Niro is from Mars. He doesn't seem to operate in the same way as anyone else. His attitude to a TV interview, indeed any kind of interview, is bizarre. His behaviour during the interview was even more bizarre, the monosyllabic mumbling and all those answers being addressed to the far corner of the room. It was all very strange.'

De Niro's rage was not simply confined to journalists asking awkward questions. On holiday in the Caribbean, an unfortunate tourist bore the brunt of his wrath. The *New York Daily News* reported that De Niro and Naomi Campbell were enjoying a romantic dinner in St Barts, dining at the elegant Lafayette Club, when he jumped up and bellowed menacingly at a woman with a camera. It wasn't clear whether she was trying to take a picture of the couple or whether, as she claimed, she was merely trying for a souvenir picture of her family at a nearby table. De Niro was not going to be mollified by her protestations and demanded that she give him the camera. When the woman refused De Niro reportedly told her, 'If that photo ever gets published I'll find out who you are.' He continued shouting oaths and profanities at the woman until Naomi Campbell eventually managed to calm him down.

While De Niro may not have been endearing himself to the BBC or to fellow tourists, he was still very much in favour with his fellow professionals.

'It's very interesting to see the way other American actors behave when De Niro's name is mentioned,' says Barry Norman. 'Screen actors in America behave towards De Niro the way stage actors in Britain behaved towards Olivier. They almost revere him, they talk about "Mr De Niro", which is really the nearest thing they could give as an accolade to a fellow thespian. He has a big reputation in America and, I think, deservedly so. He is also much admired by other actors and again I think deservedly so.'

Given that attitude, it was no surprise when in March 1991 the American Museum of the Moving Image paid tribute to De Niro at a glittering ceremony at the Waldorf-Astoria Hotel. The AMMI tributes had begun only five years previously, and honorees are among the cream of American cinema. It is a testament to the high regard in which De Niro – still the actors' actor – was held by his fellow professionals that he was chosen to receive this singular honour. The guest list was a virtual who's who of American cinema. Old friends like Martin Scorsese, Harvey Keitel, Joe Pesci and Christopher Walken were there. Co-stars like Sean Penn, Aidan Quinn and Jeremy Irons were there too. Other luminaries included Glenn Close, Spike Lee, Elia Kazan, Norman Mailer, Mayor David Dinkins and John F. Kennedy Jnr.

Some came to praise him. Jeremy Irons, his rival that year in the Best Actor Oscar stakes where he had been nominated for *Reversal of Fortune* and De Niro for *Awakenings*, described him as 'America's greatest living actor'. Penny Marshall, who had just directed him in *Awakenings*, said she had been 'obsessed' with the idea of working with him. Long-time friend and colleague Harvey Keitel said 'he has set a standard for generations to come', while Christopher Walken said: 'One of the things that made him a great actor is that he is also a great man.'

But, as is always the case on occasions like these, there were also those who came to roast Caesar, not to praise him. Once again Harvey Keitel contributed his explanation of how he had learned to evaluate film scripts from De Niro when they worked together on *Taxi Driver*.

'Bullshit,' Keitel began as he mimed turning pages. 'Bullshit,' turning a page. 'Bullshit,' turning a page. 'Bullshit,' turning a page. Then at last, 'My part,' he said with a huge smile. Robin Williams, who could not be there in person, contributed a videotaped insert with lots of in-jokes about De Niro and Toukie Smith. The mood was sustained by Charles Grodin, his co-star in *Midnight Run*

'I received the D.W. Griffith Award this week,' he told the audience, 'for best actor – for Bob! Tonight I'm here – for Bob! Tomorrow I'm flying to Anaheim to accept another award – for Bob! Then the Denver Film Society is honouring Bob as 'the actor who was won the most awards'. Bob has the Meryl Streep clause in his contract. He must be given at least seventy per cent of all awards.'

Grodin's comments were ironic since De Niro was in the Oscar race for the first time in more than ten years. His nomination for *Awakenings* ended a barren spell that had lasted since his win for *Raging Bull*. Normally De Niro would rather be smeared with honey and staked naked over an anthill than attend a ceremony like this, far less make a speech. But this was a special night that called for a special effort. He rose to his feet to a standing ovation and charmed the audience.

'I consider myself too young for these kind of tributes,' he began. 'They should be given to guys like Al Pacino or Dustin Hoffman. To me this is like the prom I never went to and the graduation I never had.'

As he had done unfailingly throughout his adult life, De Niro stopped to pay tribute to his father. He had always referred to him as 'the real star of the family'. On this occasion he told the crowd his father was 'a painter who wished his work would end up in a museum. I feel the same way,' he added, 'not just about my films but about the things from my films.'

As it happened, a few weeks later De Niro would lose out to Irons in the Best Actor Oscar race. Perhaps his marvellous performance came too close to Daniel Day-Lewis's portrayal of the handicapped Christy Brown in *My Left Foot*, which won the previous year. He might have had more success in the Best Supporting Actor category had the publicity machine focused its efforts there. As it was his *GoodFellas* co-star Joe Pesci won his first Oscar while De Niro's Jimmy Conway went unrecognized.

There was consolation from an unlikely source when De Niro was honoured by the French government. The French Minister of Culture, Jack Lang, named De Niro as a Commander of Arts and Letters and praised him for his commendable acting skills. The presentation came at the Cannes Film Festival in which De Niro's latest film, *Guilty by Suspicion*, was in competition. De Niro had been working hard to promote the film, a drama about the Hollywood blacklist, even making a rare chat show appearance on the BBC's *Wogan* show to talk about the film and his work. What he said was not earth-shattering but the fact that he said anything at all was. Only eighteen months previously he had cancelled what would have been his first American talk show – an appearance on the Arsenio Hall show – at the last minute, citing 'personal reasons'.

In *Guilty by Suspicion* De Niro plays David Merrill, a hot shot director whose career is put on hold by studio boss Darryl Zanuck. The studio is concerned about Merrill's political sympathies and wants him to get a clean bill of health from the House Un-American Activities Committee before allowing him to resume his career. Merrill is not a Communist but he is a fellow traveller, having attended a couple of meetings when he was younger. His lawyer advises him that the only way he can protect himself is to come clean and name names to the committee. He is then left with the dilemma of whether to protect his career or protect his friends.

The film was written by producer Irwin Winkler, who would also make his directing debut. He had known De Niro since producing *The Gang That Couldn't Shoot Straight* 20 years previously. He gave the actor the script of *Guilty by Suspicion* during the filming of *Raging Bull*, which he was also producing.

'I was just reading Irwin's script as a friend because I've known him a long time,' De Niro explains. 'I liked what it stood for. I thought it was a subject that very little had been done about. I had been aware of this period and curious about it for a while. The more I became involved as an actor and the more successful I became, the more curious I became. It happened to people I could very easily identify with and empathise with.'

De Niro then found himself in the strange position of having been given a script to read as a favour and then asking if he could play the part. Winkler had not written the movie with him in mind but with De Niro on board, things fell into place much more quickly. He was then able to assemble a cast that included Annette Bening, Patricia Wettig, George Wendt, Sam Wanamaker, Barry Primus and, in a small role, the other member of the *Raging Bull* trinity, Martin Scorsese.

Given their political sensibilities *Guilty by Suspicion* is a film that De Niro's liberal parents would have been proud to see their son in. But playing David Merrill put De Niro in a curious situation. On *The Gang That Couldn't Shoot Straight* he had worked with Lionel Stander, who had been blacklisted by the HUAC committee for not co-operating. It was Stander's first Hollywood film since then. On *The Last Tycoon* he had been directed by Elia Kazan, who did cooperate with the committee. This gave De Niro a somewhat unique perspective when the cast discussed the ethics of the situation in *Guilty by Suspicion*.

'I read a lot of material,' recalls De Niro. 'I looked at documentaries and I spoke to people who were involved in that period. Sam Wanamaker, who plays my attorney in the film, was blacklisted *in absentia* and he had to live and work in England for a long time. I had worked with Lionel, I guess he was the first person I had ever met who had really been involved with that period. I know that world, that period, and Irwin Winkler who wrote the script knows it too. As for Elia, he was really in a no-win situation and I feel sorry for anyone involved in that no matter what position they took.

'It was terrible for Kazan that he had to do what he did. I know him, he's a friend, and I have a great respect for him. And I know others who didn't co-operate and whose lives were ruined. People's lives were changed by the witch-hunt no matter what position they took.'

But what of De Niro? What position would he take?

'I really don't know how I would have reacted under that pressure,' he said, for once candid rather than evasive. 'It was a terrible thing and I hope that in my lifetime I never have to face those kind of choices; but you never know. The old things resurface with new faces.'

30 Burning Bridges

*G*UILTY BY SUSPICION was not a box-office success. De Niro, however, was managing to keep his career on an even keel. TriBeCa still needed to be fed, and that meant another high-priced cameo was in the offing.

He had chosen to play the part of Fire Inspector Donald Rimgale in *Backdraft*. Director Ron Howard's adventure epic about Chicago fire-fighters was one of the big summer hits of 1991. Although the stars of the movie were nominally Kurt Russell and William Baldwin, it was a strong ensemble piece which also included Scott Glenn, Donald Sutherland, Jennifer Jason Leigh, Rebecca De Mornay, J. T. Walsh, and of course, De Niro.

'It was just good luck,' says director Howard about how he persuaded De Niro to do his movie. 'It was an interesting enough character, the kind of stand-out supporting role that is not unusual for a major star to agree to do. I think our timing was perfect and I also think De Niro was paying off the buildings that he bought in New York so occasionally he would have to look around and take a job.

'It's really hard to identify what you really learn from any one movie. Hopefully you glean some knowledge but each project has its own set of problems and you feel a bit lost when you get into the next one and it's new territory again. But I actually learned something from De Niro and it had to do with preparation. I'm sure this was a money job for him and we were thrilled to have him. No one was forcing him to do anything, he could have phoned it in if he had wanted to. But he came down for a week of rehearsals and research and he requested an additional week at no additional compensation because he thought he was learning something.

'I watched him meet three different fire investigators, one of whom was the "real" Don Rimgale, and I slowly saw him build his character in front of me. He took on one guy's posture, another guy's phrasing, and a bit of another guy's attitude. He was just drawing from all of them. He doesn't do accents or things unless the part calls for it, he's just Robert De Niro – but he isn't really, there's something which is just a little different each time.

'I learned a lot from watching him and tagging along and watching the evolution of his character in terms of his research. I really had a lot of fun applying those principles to films like *The Paper* and then *Apollo 13*. I think working with him really changed forever the way I prepare for a movie.'

Thanks to *GoodFellas* and *Awakenings*, De Niro's career was finally on an upswing in box-office terms. But regardless of that he had never been short of producers who wanted him to sign on for their movies. The man who signed him for *Backdraft* was Ron Howard's long-time producing partner Brian Grazer. Together Howard and Grazer ran Imagine Films. Grazer is one of the sharpest and savviest negotiators in Hollywood and he knew this was a money job for De Niro. But he also knew what De Niro would bring with him to *Backdraft*.

'He elevates the entire cast of the movie,' says Grazer simply. 'Very definitely on a performance level because they are all nervous about working with Robert De Niro. Whether they are nervous or anxious or excited, any one or all of those things will make them better. They feel they are working with one of the great actors so it elevates their performance. It also helps in marketing the movie for a producer. If we didn't have De Niro then the other three or four star names wouldn't have added up quite as much, if you know what I mean.

'Everybody wants Robert De Niro. He hasn't had many hits but he represents quality and integrity and you want to be associated with that. Also, if you're a producer who actually cares about movies and really likes telling stories and loves film, then you want to be able to say, "I worked with Robert De Niro." You want to be able to say that to your kids, or your friends, or even to yourself in the mirror. It's kind of nice. He's a piece of film history and having him in your movie is like a hallmark, a seal of approval if you like.'

De Niro was very much a visiting fireman on the set of *Backdraft*. Most of his scenes were with William Baldwin, and there is the sense of a master class being conducted. De Niro takes fairly ordinary dialogue and elevates it in much the same way that even the corniest ballad can sound memorable if it's sung by Sinatra. As Kurt Russell, who was the notional star of the movie, points out, this was not *Raging Bull*, nor was it *The Deer Hunter*. This was simply a film where the actors served the script to the best of their abilities, and in some cases that ability is greater than in others.

Russell is one of the few child stars to make the grade as a genuine adult box-office draw. He is now in the $10 million a picture category. But he has been acting for enough years not to be impressed without good reason. Brian Grazer may have felt that having De Niro there would raise everyone else's game, but Russell was not about to be intimidated by anyone else.

'I just don't think of those things at all,' he says. 'I looked forward to being able to do my role with him doing his role. I liked him and we got along very well but I wouldn't say that I got to know him, it was not a job where he and I were spending three or four months together in an intimate fashion. He just showed up and did his work, it was not a case of him immersing himself in the role. He was trying to hit his marks and remember his lines and do his job, the normal things we all worry about.

'I've never had a situation with any actor in thirty-four years in the business that I would describe as intimidating. I'm not intimidating, I make sure I'm not. I started in this business when I was nine years old and the only one it would make sense for me to think of in those terms is Marlon Brando. But if someone said to me "Tomorrow you're working with Marlon Brando," then I'd say "Great." I'd go in there and hit my marks and do my stuff and I might say at the end of the day "Hey, that was fun." I don't mean to be flippant about his stature. He was a nice quiet guy who came in and did his work, he struggled with the lines a bit as I recall, but not to the point where he was in big trouble or anything like that.

'He's like a lot of other actors. When he is right for the role and in the groove, he's terrific. He's done enough roles to be memorable and he's done enough that were not memorable. That's okay. We make our living acting, we don't make our living being memorable.'

Before he made *Backdraft*, De Niro immersed himself in another macho lifestyle. He was preparing for a film he had agreed to do the following year for director John McNaughton which was being produced by Martin Scorsese. The film was *Mad Dog and Glory*, in which he would play a forensic photographer. To prepare for the role, he spent part of the summer of 1991 touring the streets of New York with homicide detectives. He turned out to a homicide in the Bronx, and a murder-suicide in Queens. The detectives accompanying him reported that De Niro was neither squeamish nor stand-offish, he liked 'to get right up close', they told reporters.

De Niro's role in *Backdraft* was, as Howard and Grazer speculated, a money job. It was a way of paying the bills. TriBeCa was about to put movies actively into production with *Thunderheart* and *Mistress*, and De

Niro was now no longer just an actor. His dream of a forum for independent film-makers meant that he had virtually become a one man corporation. He was a landlord, he was a producer, he hoped soon to be a director, and he was also rapidly becoming a superstar for hire. But despite all this there were still roles that excited him, still roles that got his juices flowing.

Although people like Barry Norman and the unfortunate tourist on St Barts had seen the dark side of De Niro up close and personal, it had been a long time since he had examined it on screen. Steven Spielberg had wanted to work with him for some time. In the late seventies Spielberg wanted him to star in a screen version of William Goldman's *Magic*. In the end, however, the film was made by Richard Attenborough with Anthony Hopkins. Now Spielberg had another project that looked as if it might be right for De Niro. He was planning a remake of the 1962 cult favourite *Cape Fear*, and thought De Niro would be perfect for the role of Max Cady.

Robert Mitchum had made Cady a study in sadism in the original version as an ex-convict who tormented the family of Gregory Peck, the lawyer who had put him in jail. De Niro would produce a Cady for the morally ambiguous nineties. He created a character who was more than simply a sadist; his Cady was an elemental, a force of evil.

Spielberg was becoming increasingly preoccupied with pre-production on *Jurassic Park* and *Schindler's List*, and it was obvious that he would not direct *Cape Fear* himself. Instead he wanted Scorsese to handle the directing chores.

'Bob De Niro and Spielberg asked me to read this while I was directing *GoodFellas*,' recalls Scorsese. 'By the time I had finished editing the film I had read the script three times. And three times I hated it. I mean really hated it. I thought the family was too clichéd and too happy. Then along comes the bogeyman to scare them. They were like Martians to me. I kept rooting for Max to come and get them.'

Despite Scorsese's reservations, De Niro was very keen to play the part, and this time round he had Steven Spielberg in his corner. Spielberg told Scorsese to get a rewrite done. Once the director took the script into his own hands, he turned it on its head. This time round the lawyer – originally considered by Robert Redford but finally played by Nick Nolte – has not simply testified against Cady. He has actively perverted the course of justice by suppressing evidence that kept Cady in jail. De Niro's version of Cady is more than just an avenging angel; he is a symbol of Nolte's own corruption come to take revenge on the family. These were familiar themes to Scorsese, and he set to work with a vengeance and – with $34 million to play with – the biggest budget he had ever handled.

De Niro transformed himself to play Cady as he had not done for years. He played a man consumed by thoughts of vengeance who worked out daily in prison to give him the strength to wreak his revenge. His body almost grotesquely muscled and ritually tattooed, he eventually sets off to ruin Nolte and his family. The muscles were real – De Niro, who had been in good shape since *Midnight Run*, simply stepped up his exercise regime – the tattoos were not. It would have been asking too much for any actor to permanently disfigure himself, no matter how much he wanted a role. But De Niro acknowledged that the look of the character would be extremely important in this film.

'Max is incessant,' he said, 'he just keeps coming and coming. What's terrifying is the idea that you can't stop someone no matter what you do. He's like the Alien or the Terminator. I feel if you are going to do certain parts, you really have to commit to them all the way to make them special.'

De Niro and his dialogue coach, Sam Chwat, also spent a lot of time with real-life prisoners. De Niro listened to tapes to find the voice he believed most closely approximated to that of Max Cady. Chwat says there was one in particular he decided on. Chwat never knew his name but did know that he had been convicted of a particularly savage assault. He described him as 'self-possessed, intelligent, judgmental, and with a strong air of personal conviction'. Exactly the qualities De Niro seized on to make Cady such a terrifying character.

At the end of the day the critics were divided over whether or not Scorsese had made a film that commented on America's moral ambivalence, or whether it was simply an up-market horror movie. More than one critic compared De Niro to Freddy Krueger, the anti-hero of the successful *Nightmare on Elm Street* series. Nonetheless his colleagues were impressed by what they saw as a return to form. The actor who hadn't received an Oscar nomination in ten years suddenly found himself with two back to back – Max Cady would join Leonard L in providing De Niro with another Best Actor nomination.

Despite his reputation, De Niro went into the Oscar race in March 1992 as a rank outsider. *Cape Fear* was deemed too bleak to win any awards, and he was personally suffering from what is known in Hollywood as the 'full trophy cabinet syndrome'. Not only had he previously won in the Best Actor and Best Supporting Actor category, but this would be his fifth Best Actor nomination. The final nail in De Niro's Oscar coffin was the absence of *Cape Fear* in the Best Picture or Best Director categories, normally a good indicator of where the acting awards will go. In the end Max Cady would lose out to a much more chilling villain. The Best Actor Oscar for 1991 would be won by Oscar débutant Anthony Hopkins for his stunning portrayal of Hannibal Lecter in Jonathan Demme's *The Silence of the Lambs*. Who knows what Lecter and Cady would have made of each other had they met, but on Oscar night at least it was the Cannibal who emerged victorious.

If he ever did care about acting awards, De Niro's thoughts could not have been on them much in the early part of 1992. His often turbulent private life was once again heading for heavy seas.

According to Helena Lisandrello, De Niro and relationships go together like oil and water.

'Bobby isn't really capable of a loving, devoted relationship,' she told the *New York Post*. 'He loves only his children – Andrina [Drina], Raphael, and Nina. He truly loves Nina. And she loves him. Bobby doesn't know how to give love to a grown-up. He can put it on and wear it in a film, but it's only make-believe.'

Toukie Smith was plainly coming to the same conclusion. She had put up with De Niro's non-exclusive relationships, she had given him his space, and now she was watching him with Naomi Campbell. He continued to insist that he and the supermodel were 'good friends', although he rather gave the lie to that hackneyed cliché when in January 1992 he faxed her a 22-page letter. It was ultimately Toukie Smith who decided that enough was enough. Eventually she gave him an ultimatum. It was either her or Naomi, and in the end he chose Naomi. Smith's decision was reported only a few weeks after the *Daily Mail* in London had carried an article with the headline 'I'm so in love with De Niro my GoodFella says Naomi'. De Niro may have been insisting that they were only friends, but Campbell was prepared to tell the world that she, at least, was 'very much in love' with the actor. The model went on to say that her dream was to marry and have children, 'and some day it will come true,' she added.

'His understanding,' she replied when asked what she most liked about De Niro. 'That he is a true friend and a support to me. I'm somebody who needs a great deal of love. With love I'm a much happier person. Love to me is the most important thing to have in life. I give everything when I am in love.'

De Niro and Smith split up in March 1992. Two months later Campbell again opened her heart, this time to the doyen of British show-business writers, Baz Bamigboye of the *Daily Mail*. Bamigboye had tracked the couple to Paris where they had spent a week at the Ritz Hotel, each wearing disguises in order to avoid being recognised.

'He is such a great actor and I admire him tremendously,' she told the journalist. 'Along with Marlon Brando he's about the best in the world, isn't he? I think he is a man who is passionate about what he does and that makes him a great actor. But a private life is a private life and it's difficult to talk about the man you love in public. My relationship should remain private because love is the most important thing to have in life and you fight so hard for it to work that you can damage it all by talking about it.'

One can only speculate about how the intensely private De Niro felt about Campbell's comments. For someone who wanted to keep her love a secret she seems to have had no problem talking about it. Campbell said that life with De Niro was never dull, which was one of the attractions for her. But for De Niro that never-dull life was about to become particularly interesting before the year was out.

31 A Talent Spread Thinly

IT TOOK DE NIRO ten years to make the most important movies of his career, from his breakthrough in *Bang the Drum Slowly* to *King of Comedy* – eleven films in all. As he approached the end of 1992 he had made eleven films in just five years. Not one of them would come close to the career-defining films he had made in the seventies.

Creatively the roles may not have been terribly rewarding – it's hard, for example, to imagine the younger De Niro contemplating a movie like *We're No Angels*. Financially he was raking it in.

A survey of Hollywood's richest entertainers by *Forbes* magazine in 1992 put De Niro 32nd on the list, having earned $25 million in 1991. That was a long way behind Bill Cosby, America's highest-earning entertainer of the time, who made $98 million, and Kevin Costner, who was the top-earning movie star with $78 million. However, for a man who must now have realised what the industry had realised for a long time, that he has no box-office clout on his own, $25 million is a highly satisfactory year's wage. Even allowing for taxes and overheads, De Niro still walks away with a comfortable income.

But he was spreading himself more and more thinly in the process. Creatively Hollywood was passing him by. The beginning of the nineties saw the emergence of wonder-boy Quentin Tarantino and his video-store generation of film-makers. These were young men who had idolised De Niro in his pomp. In many cases he was the inspiration for these men to make their way into the film business.

'De Niro was it,' says Tarantino, who had a brief and abortive career as an actor before finding fame as a director. 'He was who everyone in my acting class wanted to be. He was the ideal – to be Robert De Niro, that was the be all and end all. He was the focus the way Brando was the focus, and his work affected you in very much the same way. People idealised him, and the way young film-makers now want to be Scorsese, that's the way actors felt about De Niro. You ran to see his new movie.

'In his book *American Film Now* James Monaco makes the case that De Niro was probably the greatest American film-maker of the 1970s by his association with the talents that he worked with. Everybody wanted to work with him. This holds true for today – you know if De Niro is in your movie you've got prestige because he is the best out there. But in the 1970s he didn't work that often and the people that he worked with were at the forefront of the most interesting film-making of the time.'

Tarantino's praise for De Niro is a succinct summation of what was wrong with De Niro's career. He was no longer working, Scorsese excepted, with the best talent available. The man who prided himself as a young actor on taking the path less travelled was now taking a path that had been beaten bare by those who had gone before him. De Niro, it appeared, had stopped taking risks. The burden and the distractions that TriBeCa imposed on him meant that he could no longer afford the luxury of taking a chance. While Harvey Keitel could work with a new, untried director like Quentin Tarantino in *Reservoir Dogs*, or an edgy, uncommercial director like Abel Ferrara in *The Bad Lieutenant*, De Niro never allowed himself that luxury. He had to work with commercially proven directors like Ron Howard and Penny Marshall, both of whom are fine film-makers but neither of whom has anything like the edge of a Scorsese or a De Palma. The rewards for De Niro, in the shape of a $25 million pay packet, were very tangible, but the artistic satisfaction could not have been great. Unlike Keitel, he had not mastered the art of choosing one for the heart and one for the wallet. For every *Reservoir Dogs* and *Bad Lieutenant* that Keitel made he could also find a box-office hit like *Sister Act* or *Rising Sun*. De Niro was not in that position, and although he was regarded by Tarantino and the new generation of movie brats as a cinematic demi-god he had done little of late to confirm that reputation.

'I think that for a while De Niro was the best screen actor in the world,' says Barry Norman of the BBC. 'I don't think that applies any more. I think he is one of the top three. I don't think he's versatile enough and I don't think he's stretching himself enough. He's been doing a lot of cameo stuff which is really like standing on your head for someone like De Niro. So I think he's been overtaken by people like Gérard Depardieu and Anthony Hopkins. Depardieu stretches himself all the time and Hopkins too is challenging himself with a great variety of roles. I think De Niro has lost ground, not because he has lost any talent but because he isn't doing the hard work any more.

'In many ways I think Harvey Keitel is now catching him up, which is interesting considering their respective positions at the time of *Mean Streets*. But now if you're looking for the interesting work by that kind of actor, that specific sort of post-Brando Method actor, then the interesting stuff is all coming from Keitel rather than De Niro. I don't think Keitel is actually as good as De Niro – he doesn't have the power – but at least he tries.'

De Niro appears to have been running just to stand still. By the end of 1992 he had three films waiting to come out – *Night and the City, Mad Dog and Glory*, and *This Boy's Life*. He had also got *Thunderheart* off the ground for TriBeCa, receiving an on-screen credit as producer. He had also shepherded *Mistress*, a Hollywood comedy by his friend Barry Primus, to the screen under the TriBeCa umbrella. He found time to play a small part in *Mistress* as a Hollywood money man. Some critics liked the performance, others were less enthusiastic.

'Since TriBeCa Films produced *Mistress* it is not surprising to find him [De Niro] appearing in the film,' wrote *Boxoffice* magazine, 'but what is surprising is how singularly uninteresting his performance is. In the past, when De Niro has taken a supporting turn, there's been a certain gleefulness in his acting. We remember his performances in *Angel Heart* and *The Untouchables* as examples of the relish with which he performs when freed of the burdens of carrying a film. Here he is completely lifeless.'

Boxoffice merely set in print what others had been thinking. De Niro had not lost it – you can no more stop being a great actor than you can forget how to ride a bike. But great actors need great parts and if they were being offered there was no evidence of De Niro choosing them. He was showing a great deal of loyalty to his friends, which is admirable in itself, but his career was suffering. *Mistress* was directed by an old friend. *Mad Dog and Glory*, which he had just completed, was being produced by Scorsese. *Night and the City*, which was about to be released, was another directorial effort from Irwin Winkler, who had also directed *Guilty By Suspicion*. *Night and the City* would be a co-production between De Niro's TriBeCa Films and the Italian company Penta Pictures, which was in the midst of what would turn out to be a disastrous foray into Hollywood. Directing is not Irwin Winkler's forte. He is a fine producer but at best a journeyman director who could not be guaranteed to bring the best out of an actor like De Niro. Worse still, De Niro was doing another remake. Just as in *Cape Fear* he had been following in Robert Mitchum's footsteps, he would now be following in the footsteps of Richard Widmark.

Night and the City was originally a moody, atmospheric 1950 British movie made by Jules Dassin. Widmark made a big impression as an American low-life on the run in London's underworld. For the 1992 version Winkler had updated the story, and the central character, Harry Fabian, was now a hustling low-life lawyer in Manhattan. Harry is as faithless and disloyal as they come. He is cheating on his best friend Cliff Gorman by having an affair with his wife, played by his *Cape Fear* co-star Jessica Lange. In the end he will rip her off as well. Harry always has a scam going until the day he crosses boxing promoter Boom Boom Grossman, played by Alan King. Grossman publicly humiliates him and Harry decides to get even by becoming a boxing promoter himself. Up till this point he has always managed to tread water, but now he finds himself seriously out of his depth.

'Harry is accused of being an ambulance-chasing, shyster bastard, but he's also witty, gullible and good-hearted,' said De Niro of his character. 'Harry makes life hard for himself by always taking the easy way like a child seeking instant gratification. It's expedient morality. Whatever works, he'll take. But he's an innocent too – not insensitive, just insensitised. He's a person who's afraid to deal with himself, so he's always running, running, frantic to satisfy this emptiness inside himself. Harry's like somebody jumping across a creek, scampering from stone to stone and he can't afford to get wet or trip on any of those stones. He's flying.'

During publicity for *Night and the City* De Niro revealed one of the tricks of his acting trade in terms of getting into a character. Apparently he imagines the character he's playing as an animal and tries to take on some of its attributes. Previously, he said without specifying, he has seen some of his roles as a crab, a cat, a wolf, a rabbit, a snake, and an owl.

'I liken Harry to a chicken with its head cut off,' he elaborated. 'Or a rabbit darting through a maze, literally running amok. He's not a party animal, he's a city animal. He's a man who doesn't want to face himself so he keeps moving at a quick pace.'

Harry doesn't so much walk through the movie as dance. One character refers to him early on as 'Harry the Dancer'. To make sure he got the rhythm right, director Winkler had De Niro wear a tiny earpiece which would blare out the Chris Montez hit 'Let's Dance'. It didn't work. The film flopped and De Niro once again received the sort of reviews that wondered aloud whether he was past his best. Some actors claim not to read their reviews but all the signs point to De Niro being well aware of what was being said.

'You know the answer to that, so don't even ask the question,' he snapped testily at a *New York Times* reporter who had, quite reasonably, asked whether he might be working too hard as an actor to finance his ambitions as a producer.

While he was publicising *Night and the City* De Niro had also started work on his own directorial debut, *A Bronx Tale*. He had felt for some time that he should get behind the camera and, as he approached 50, he began to feel the time was right. It was another burden on an increasingly heavy workload.

'Workaholic? No, I don't think so,' he told one interviewer. 'There's enough time to get it all done. While I'm acting in one I prepare for the next. I don't feel pushed because I like to work but this isn't going to last forever. I'm going to slow down for more directing, writing and producing.

'When I'm directing the waiting makes me feel kind of helpless. I want it to go faster. But directing myself is a breeze. I have the writer, the first assistant, and the director of photography giving me feedback. I usually know when it's right and I have playback just to be sure.'

Other events in De Niro's life were reaching a conclusion at this period. Helena Lisandrello had finally decided formally to sue for paternity. The singer claims she had asked De Niro to submit to a blood test several times to try to settle the issue one way or another. De Niro said he had had the tests done by his own doctor and they proved that he was not the father. She then hired top-gun attorney Marvin Mitchelson, who claimed she was going ahead with the case because De Niro had been paying anywhere between $8000 and $10,000 a month in support for Nina Nadeja but had stopped earlier in the year. De Niro, according to Lisandrello, did not want any attorneys involved in the proceedings. De Niro's spokesman, Stan Rosenfeld, said the claims were absurd. He confirmed that De Niro knew Lisandrello but added that the claims were totally unfounded. Nonetheless the issue would finally be settled in court.

In the end De Niro did submit to a blood test which was taken on 4 October 1992. Lisandrello and Nina Nadeja – who was now ten years old – also had samples taken for DNA analysis and comparison. Previously the court had ordered that he pay $2500 in child support plus a further $1000 in schooling costs until the results of the tests were determined. When the results of the blood tests were made public in early November they showed that, despite Lisandrello's claims, De Niro was not the biological father of Nina Nadeja. But Mitchelson, who was known as the king of the palimony suit, because of his precedent-setting work in gaining settlements for couples who had lived together without being married, was not about to let matters rest there. He and Lisandrello were going to pursue the case.

Not surprisingly De Niro was less than pleased and issued a statement through his lawyer, Ronald Anteau.

'Mr De Niro had voluntarily submitted to two prior blood tests,' said Anteau, 'both of which also excluded him as the child's biological father. Mr Mitchelson and his client were always aware of the results of the first two blood tests. They have continually insisted on wasting not only Mr De Niro's time but that of the court.'

Mitchelson was not about to be put off by angry statements from opposing lawyers. He maintained that, right from the outset, they had proceeded on the assumption that De Niro may not indeed have been Nina Nadeja's biological father. The case, according to Mitchelson, was being pursued on the doctrine of estoppel, which is based on the fact that you cannot deny something if your previous actions have shown it to be contrary. In short, whether he was Nina Nadeja's biological father or not, Mitchelson was maintaining that he had acted as her father and could therefore not now deny it.

'De Niro said he was her father,' alleged Mitchelson. 'He called her his daughter. He named her Nina. He gave the mother fifty thousand dollars. He took the child on a vacation to Canada. She loves him. She feels he's her dad.'

Mitchelson also claimed that De Niro's relationship with Helena Lisandrello was more than just a casual fling. It was not a one-night stand, he insisted; they were involved for three years. After behaving like her father it was not fair to the child for him suddenly to decide that he was not her father.

'The man who could be the real father was killed in a car accident years ago,' Mitchelson told the *New York Daily News*. 'De Niro is lucky to have a beautiful daughter like this. He should be happy.'

While Mitchelson argued his case the Los Angeles Supreme Court ruled that De Niro would have to continue paying child support until a final disposition had been reached. The money was not an issue for De Niro by this stage; it scarcely made a dent in his income. However, after suspecting for some time that he may not have been the father of the child, he was keen to have the matter settled once and for all.

The final decision came the following April in the Los Angeles Supreme Court. Lisandrello was suing the actor for $5500 a month in child support plus some $70,000 in legal fees. De Niro, who has always avoided talking about his private life, spent three hours before Judge James Endman revealing details of his love life and his relationship with Lisandrello. The issue under consideration was based on Mitchelson's claim that De Niro had 'bonded' with his daughter, who was named in court as Nina Nadeja De Niro. After hearing the actor's evidence and deliberating over three blood tests, all of which proved negative, Judge Endman ruled in De Niro's favour.

The judge decided that he had indeed not formed a sufficient bond with the unfortunate child to be considered her father. He pointed out that he had not met her until she was three years old and then saw her no more than half a dozen times before the test proved that he was not her biological parent. He ruled that De Niro no longer needed to pay child support to Lisandrello.

The actor, who had given evidence in a marathon session, left the court without saying a word and flew home to New York.

32 Exit Naomi

A LTHOUGH APPEALS WOULD DRAG the procedure out, Judge James Endman had effectively removed Helena Lisandrello and Nina Nadeja from Robert De Niro's life. However his personal life was growing no easier. There was growing speculation that all was not well in his relationship with Naomi Campbell. In addition, De Niro now found himself linked with his co-star in *Mad Dog and Glory*, Uma Thurman.

In *Mad Dog and Glory* De Niro plays mild-mannered police photographer Wayne Dobie. So mild-mannered is he that the other guys in the squad room, with blinding originality, have nicknamed him 'Mad Dog'. Stopping off at a convenience store one night Wayne foils a robbery and in the process saves the life of mobster Frank Milo, played by Bill Murray. To show his gratitude Murray sends Uma Thurman, the 'Glory' of the title, to live with Wayne for a week. Wayne wants nothing to do with her at first but she points out that she is already working off a debt – her brother owes money to Milo – and things will go badly for both of them unless she does what Frank wants. By the end of the week Wayne and Glory have fallen in love and he refuses to hand her over, whatever the consequences.

When *Mad Dog and Glory* was released it turned out to be the latest in a string of movies which objectified women by presenting them as commodities. In *Pretty Woman* Julia Roberts had been bought for a week for $3000, in *Honeymoon in Vegas* Sarah Jessica Parker had been offered in exchange for a $65,000 bet, and in *Indecent Proposal* Demi Moore had been 'bought' for the night by Robert Redford for $1 million. Screenwriter Richard Price defended his script by claiming it was inspired by a real-life incident several years earlier when he had been on holiday and met a woman on a plane who was in exactly the same situation as Glory.

Mad Dog and Glory was directed by John McNaughton and was being produced by Martin Scorsese. McNaughton had become something of a

Scorsese protégé since Scorsese had championed his controversial debut film *Henry, Portrait of a Serial Killer*. *Mad Dog and Glory* would be McNaughton's first mainstream picture. The script was by Richard Price who had written *Night and the City*. Once again De Niro found himself in the semi-incestuous situation of working among friends. Certainly no one there was going to tell him that Wayne Dobie was yet another part that he could have done in his sleep. De Niro may have done the research and travelled with homicide cops but there was nothing in this film to stretch him.

Things might have been different had he and Murray swapped roles. The sharkskin-suited mobster with delusions of being a stand-up comic is the sort of part which might have been more challenging for De Niro. But the actor didn't see it that way, and as a consequence Murray walks away with the movie leaving De Niro virtually a guest star in his own movie.

'We had a reading of the movie with John McNaughton and Steve Jones, who was the producer, and Marty Scorsese, and people whose opinions we trusted for that reason,' De Niro says explaining his choice of roles. 'First I read the part of Frank and then I read the part of Wayne. I was leaning towards Wayne but I wanted to get some input on it and see what John felt. So we read the screenplay twice back to back and everyone seemed to feel that Wayne was the better part for me to do. Frank Milo is a great part, a lot of fun. He's ironic, he's a comedian, there was a lot of fun stuff. But I've done that before so it was actually better for me to do Wayne.'

With hindsight it seems a curious choice. De Niro could not honestly have been worried about repeating himself given that Rupert Pupkin, the only character he has played who is close to Frank, was more than ten years earlier. On the other hand he may have been aware that it was being remarked that the man who was once the most original actor of his generation had now done three re-makes – *We're No Angels*, *Cape Fear* and *Night and the City* – and two of them were virtually back to back. However, although he passed on playing Frank, De Niro retained his usual input and it was his inspired suggestion that led to Bill Murray being offered the role.

Mad Dog and Glory is notable for two things. De Niro sings on screen for the second time. He had managed a few bars of 'Blue Moon' with Mary Kay Place in *New York, New York*; this time it is 'Just A Gigolo'. De Niro would doubtless have been familiar with the Louis Prima standard from his days roaming the streets of Little Italy. De Niro says singing that particular song seemed like the most natural thing to do and it didn't pose him too many problems. The film is also notable for De Niro's first major love scene. Some of his other romantic films – especially *Falling in Love* – have been notable for their lack of on-screen consummation. Here Wayne and Glory make love in all their clumsy, fumbling splendour.

'It's always difficult to do a love scene in a movie,' says De Niro. 'Everyone is there, they're all watching and you get very self-conscious. I enjoyed doing the awkward love scene – the one that starts when they're watching television. That was one of my favourite scenes when it was written and it was pretty well realised too. That's kind of how the love scene later in the bed feels, the way the awkward love scene looks is actually how it feels to do the longer fluid love scene later in the movie.

'I've done love scenes before, although not so realistic. That was just the style of this movie. I've done love scenes in other films which were maybe a little more pretentious, but I thought this was a good love scene. I thought John did very well, I thought the realism was good. But they are very hard to do, they're very awkward.'

Uma Thurman had been married to actor Gary Oldman but had recently divorced. She and De Niro became friends and occasional partners after working together on *Mad Dog and Glory*. She would later tell *Vanity Fair* magazine that she and De Niro had been friends but were never an item. At the time it fell once again to *Daily Mail* show-business writer Baz Bamigboye to chronicle this latest episode in De Niro's tangled love life.

'Uma and Robert became very good friends while working together,' a spokesman for the actress told Bamigboye. 'They see each other when they are both in New York. They have never dated but they like to joke and pretend that they are lovers to confuse the press.'

De Niro has never come across as the sort of person who prefers to play jokes on the press and in the light of his frequent outbursts this explanation has to be taken with a very large pinch of salt. But no matter how serious his relationship with Thurman, by the time De Niro arrived at the Cannes Film Festival in May 1993 to promote the movie, his relationship with Naomi Campbell was over. In March of that year the *New York Daily News* had reported that De Niro and Thurman were 'just friends', the same expression that was used to describe his relationship with Campbell before splitting with Toukie Smith. Coincidentally, within weeks De Niro and Campbell had split up too. Campbell had been linked with Adam Clayton of the rock band U2, but the real stumbling block appears to have been De Niro's inability to appreciate Campbell's acting talents.

Campbell seemed determined to get a role in De Niro's *A Bronx Tale* which he had been directing in the winter of 1992 and the early part of

1993. She had gone to some length to prepare herself for the key role of the young black girl in the film. Campbell had been working with voice coach Sam Chwat – the man who had given De Niro Max Cady's voice in *Cape Fear* – to lose her British accent and sound convincingly like a young black girl from the Bronx. De Niro was not convinced and would not cast her. De Niro issued a statement saying his decision not to cast her in his film was based on 'a professional decision which had no bearing on their personal relationship'. Within days they had split up and she had flown to Ireland where, a short time later, she announced her engagement to Adam Clayton.

While they were together Campbell and De Niro enjoyed a tempestuous relationship. She was very possessive of her lover and would often take spectacular revenge if she suspected him of being unfaithful. New York columnist George Rush reported that she once called the fire department to De Niro's apartment because she suspected he was entertaining another woman.

But she insists their time together was a long-term relationship, not just the brief fling it has been painted.

'Being with Robert taught me a lot,' she said afterwards. 'He is a fantastic person and we were extremely close. We managed to keep our relationship quiet for a long time. Not many people realise that we were together for three years.

'I thought about settling down with him but I think every girl goes through that stage. But being with him was different from a lot of the other relationships I've been in because Robert isn't a showbizzy person. Robert steers clear of the parties and premières and I liked that.'

Once again the reviews for *Mad Dog and Glory* were poor, as they had been for De Niro's performances in *Night and the City* and his cameo in *Mistress*. De Niro was plainly getting tired of suggestions that he was spreading himself too thinly and when it was mentioned by the London listings magazine *Time Out*, De Niro went ballistic. De Niro had previously been on good terms with the magazine, granting them one of his rare full-length interviews in the days when he was rationing his media time. Obviously when they spoke again on one of his flying visits to London De Niro had had enough. Writer Stuart Jeffries pointed out that although the quantity of De Niro's output had increased in the past five years, the same could not be said of the quality. Was he perhaps spreading himself too thinly, wondered Jeffries?

De Niro exploded.

'Listen,' he began. 'Are we having a conversation that's nice and positive or are you just trying to get me to say things? I don't care to hear about

Time Out. Time Out's a fucking asshole magazine, OK? So I don't care for them to say that they think I'm doing too much. That's like a loaded question.'

Jeffries, reasonably, pointed out that the question was not in fact loaded. But De Niro would not be deterred.

'If you're not going to ask me productive, positive questions about the movie' – he was promoting *Night and the City* on its brief UK release – 'and you want to get personal in a sly way then, you know, goodbye. Don't be a fucking wiseguy, man. You know – talk straight or don't do it. Don't tell me negative stuff, I'm not interested in that. That's intended to get me to give you a certain answer and I don't like it. 'Cause I'll never give you a fucking interview again ... You wanna talk about the movies then, yeah, ask questions that are decent and not trying to get me annoyed and get a certain kind of answer out of me.'

Once again, as it had done with Barry Norman, a journalist's reasonable request for information had provoked De Niro seemingly beyond endurance. His response on both occasions was absurdly inappropriate and reflected very little credit on him either as an actor or as a man. De Niro's on-screen career and some of his off-screen behaviour has been characterised by frequent volatile explosions of an inner rage. In his fiftieth year, when you might reasonably have expected him to have some degree of self-control, there was so sign of the inner fire diminishing. Sadly none of that fire seemed to have been directed towards his performances which had become increasingly formulaic and uninteresting. The characters he played were less and less complex. The research took less and less time. For *Stanley and Iris* he even relied on someone else to do it for him – an unthinkable notion for the younger De Niro. And De Niro's responses to legitimate questions suggest that he was as aware of the situation as anyone.

'You get a little more confident as you get older,' he would later confide to the *London Evening Standard*, 'a little more relaxed about certain things. Anger? I guess I can still get quite angry in certain situations, if I feel I'm being taken advantage of or if a photographer pops a camera in my face. These days I try not to react and I've learned if a situation develops the best thing to do is wait until it passes and just let it go away. These things have a way of sorting themselves out.'

De Niro spoke to the *Evening Standard* in February 1994. The ink was barely dry on the paper when a few weeks later he turned on another photographer and roughed him up. He claimed the man had tried to sneak up on him and take a picture at Elaine's restaurant in New York. De Niro was attending a party for the première of the film *Jimmy Hollywood* starring his friend Joe Pesci, and had done his own share of sneaking by arriving at the party through the kitchen to avoid photographers. The man he accosted turned out to be a photographer for the *New York Daily News* who insisted that De Niro had got the wrong man. Either way it is an extraordinary way for a man to behave who has chosen a career in the public eye.

Robert De Niro had one more movie awaiting release in 1993. His friend and *Untouchables* producer Art Linson had brought to his attention the first volume of Tobias Wolff's autobiography *This Boy's Life*. Wolff had grown up with a peripatetic mother and a tyrannical stepfather who, perversely, believed he was doing the boy some good by giving him such a hard life. Linson felt the role of the stepfather, Dwight, would be perfect for De Niro. He gave him the book and De Niro was so impressed with it that he went to visit Wolff to continue his research. Wolff recalls the actor arriving at his house with a copy of his book and a thick notebook under his arm filled with hundreds of questions about Dwight. De Niro was impressed with Wolff's book and Wolff as it turned out was just as impressed with De Niro.

Having got De Niro on board Linson then had to find a director. He chose the young Scottish film-maker Michael Caton-Jones. Having got his big break with a thriller series for Britain's Channel 4, Caton-Jones had delivered three modestly successful films. His screen debut with *Scandal*, a film about the Profumo affair, was well received and made money on both sides of the Atlantic. He followed that up with *Memphis Belle* and *Doc Hollywood* which were also crowd-pleasers in America and Britain. Caton-Jones felt an affinity with the material since like Wolff he came from a small town which had seen better days. De Niro also felt an affinity with Caton-Jones. The Scot was hardly in the same category of edgy newcomers like Tarantino, but for De Niro at least it was a change from the safe decisions he had been making previously. As it turned out it was a change for better.

'I think once Bob signs off on doing a part that's it,' says Caton-Jones. 'He just does what he does. He's the hardest working actor I've come across by a long chalk. But whether that affects him in the choices of parts that he makes I don't know. I don't think he feels any necessity to have to fulfil any commercial criteria, he simply figures himself as an actor. He's not making the picture, he's doing his part in the picture. I think he's drawn to interesting characters as opposed to career choice characters.

'For him a lot of the problem is the things that we are pre-conditioned to because we know his body work. But working with him you discover there is a side to him that is really rather nice and sweet and soft. As far as I can make out all he's doing is exploring parts of his own character. If he's drawn to the darker ones it's because they are more interesting to play.'

Dwight Hansen in *This Boy's Life* was one of the most complex characters De Niro had had to play in some time. He could be a charming rogue when he was dealing with Wolff's mother, played by Ellen Barkin, or he could be a complete sadist when he had to deal with Wolff himself. One has to wonder whether De Niro saw perhaps Manny Farber or some of his mother's boyfriends when he came to think of Dwight. Caton-Jones chose newcomer Leonardo Di Caprio as the young Tobias and Di Caprio justified his faith with a stunning performance.

'Leonardo was not in the slightest bit in awe of Bob,' recalls Caton-Jones. 'Bob and Ellen had their own way of preparing, they're adults and they go through a lot of stuff. Leonardo asked me what he should do to prepare but I didn't really want him to do anything. I just wanted him to behave like a kid. I would wrestle and mess about with him on the set and the result was that he would come in completely spontaneous and natural – quite the opposite thing to what the others were expecting.

'He was so honest and so emotionally open that the other actors had to run to keep up with him. He went head to head with Bob and Ellen and they didn't pull their punches. But he was more than able to hold his own.'

De Niro was equally impressed with his young co-star although he admitted later that he may have given him a slightly rougher time than he intended.

'The father that I played in *This Boy's Life* is a stepfather, he had his own kids. I have three kids,' he told a press conference at Cannes in May 1993. 'I used certain things that I feel as a father in *This Boy's Life* and I would use them towards Leonardo. He's about the same age as my son and sometimes, like any father, I feel like killing my son so I transferred that to poor Leonardo.'

De Niro's claim at Cannes that he had three kids may have been a simple error or it may have been something of a Freudian slip. It was only a few weeks after all since a judge had ruled that he did not have three kids but only two.

This Boy's Life was made for Warner Brothers at a time when the studio was achieving colossal results in marketing blockbusters like both *Batman* films, the *Lethal Weapon* movies, and *The Fugitive*. A film like *This Boy's Life* was a much more difficult proposition. It was harder to market and although it got good reviews and did good business in its platform release in New York and Los Angeles, the film did not open widely. In Britain the film scarcely opened at all. It was ironic that De Niro had finally risen to a challenge and given his best screen performance in years and no one was there to see it.

33 The Third Eye

DE NIRO HAD REACHED a crisis in his career. His energies had been directed towards getting TriBeCa off the ground, but he had paid the price in his loss of status as an actor. He had lost ground to the likes of Harvey Keitel, and there is no doubt that he knew he was spreading himself too thinly. He has spent his life searching for the inner truth of the characters he plays, and he must have been aware that in most of his recent roles he hadn't found it, and in many of them it was scarcely worth looking for.

The very best actors, certainly on stage, are blessed with what for want of a better word some refer to as a 'third eye'. Various cultures believe that the pineal gland, which grows out of the brain, is the source of human foreknowledge and heightened awareness. Develop this gland and unlock its secrets, they argue, and we will greatly enhance our mental powers and perceptions. Again this is a trait that the best actors have evolved without the rest of us being privy to the process. They are able to distance themselves from their own performances. They have a sort of theatrical out-of-body experience which allows them to look down on their own performances in much the same way that patients undergoing surgery occasionally claim to have looked down on the doctors and nurses surrounding the operating table. When a scene is going well an actor knows it is going well. This third eye enables the performer to gauge the performance from the point of view of the audience. And it is only through the audience that an actor can tell whether or not the performance is real. If the audience accepts it, then it is real. It is, in that sense, not being faked.

In the theatre at least you cannot fake acting in the sense that you cannot hide the truth of your performance from the audience. On film the situation is completely different. Film is fake – it is founded on the principle that if an image is projected on to the human retina 24 times every second then thanks to a phenomenon called 'persistence of vision' the eye will retain the image and trick the brain into thinking that it is moving. Cinema survives on the suspension of disbelief. Film acting has to be fake – if it wasn't it would take days to get a single take in the can. Stuntmen and special effects teams would be redundant and the sort of fare on offer at the local multiplex would not have progressed much from the Lumière Brothers' films of trains arriving at railway stations. Movie acting is an elaborate optical illusion which the audience unconsciously indulges.

De Niro's third eye is probably more finely honed than anyone else's. It must have told him he was selling himself short. This, after all, was the man who insisted famously that he could not fake acting. Certainly there was nothing fake about his preparations for playing Travis Bickle or Jimmy Doyle or Jake La Motta. Whether driving a New York taxi cab, learning the correct fingering for saxophone passages no one would hear, or putting on 60 pounds to the endangerment of his health, De Niro's preparation has become his trademark. In *Raging Bull* he stayed in character as Jake and even taught the neophyte actress Cathy Moriarty to stay in character as Vickie La Motta. But *Raging Bull* was almost the last film for which De Niro required an extraordinary amount of physical preparation. With the exception of the role of the catatonic Leonard in *Awakenings*, most of De Niro's subsequent parts – including the cameos to finance TriBeCa – have involved what we might call intellectual preparation. Has he now learned to fake acting?

De Niro's stage experience is limited. He has not trodden the boards for the better part of ten years and shows no inclination to do so in the foreseeable future. However, what he does appear to have done is to have developed his cinematic third eye.

Michael Caton-Jones, who directed De Niro in *This Boy's Life* recalls that the actor's normal way of working is to go for take after take, each one slightly different from the one before. Each version of the line reading will have a different nuance, a different gesture, sometimes a different interpretation. The director, in this case Caton-Jones, will then have a number of choices, and the editor something of a headache. It was this technique which forced film editor Jim Clark to utter his famous quote about a De Niro performance being mined rather than edited.

Actor-director Kenneth Branagh had a similar experience when he was behind the camera and De Niro was playing the Creature in *Mary Shelley's Frankenstein*.

'He paid me the great compliment of trusting me as a director which, I gather, is something he likes to do. He likes to give himself over to the director so that he can be completely free as an actor and available to any suggestion. On *Frankenstein* this reached the point where we could keep the camera running so that we could repeat scenes and do them again.

We kept up to speed – there was no cutting and resetting. Bob would respond to that. You could just throw directions at him.

'If it was his close up then you could say, "Let's do another one slower, or angrier, or da de da de da." It was almost like directing a silent movie, and Bob was completely up for that and for what little bit of improvising we did. There's no superfluous small-talk. He doesn't agonise in a corner and stay crazily in character. He says it just wastes energy, if the camera isn't on you then there's no point in telling the rest of the set that you are still in character. If he did he would probably have been completely wasted when he went home and then – in his case – had to get up at two in the morning to get into another fifty pounds of make-up.'

De Niro did very little improvisation of his own in *Frankenstein* but that was a considered decision on his part. There would be very little point in the Creature doing a Travis Bickle routine in front of a mirror.

'*Frankenstein* demanded that kind of discipline,' he said. 'You can't be too contemporary, you have to watch every move that you make, every word has to be the right word. You can sometimes add a word here or there but you have to stick to what's written.'

But as De Niro also points out, there is really very little scope for genuine improvisation, in a film like *Mary Shelley's Frankenstein*.

'If you do something that appears to have been improvised,' he reveals, 'it will only be improvised slightly. There might be some ad libs and stuff but actually it's all been worked out beforehand.'

Branagh, like De Niro, is first and foremost an actor, which puts him in a rare position to gauge De Niro's performance. Ron Howard directed De Niro in what was little more than a cameo, albeit a showy one, in his fire-fighting action epic *Backdraft*. De Niro played a fire investigator who was on the trail of the arsonist who he suspected was setting the fires. For Howard, directing De Niro was a singular experience. And like Branagh, Howard, with a successful career as an actor behind him, is better placed than most of De Niro's directors to evaluate the performance.

'He doesn't really rely on any technique,' he recalls. 'In fact he doesn't appear to have developed any technique over the years. He seems to have ignored it because he seems to want to always be in the moment and apply whatever points of view he has gathered from his research on his character. And it's very effective even though in dailies – when we look at the previous day's footage after it has come back from the labs – it can sometimes be very awkward. But Bob likes to sit and watch the dailies, he really studies them.

'He's not embarrassed in the least by a series of awkward takes when he stumbles over the dialogue or takes when it's disjointed. There may be only one or two elements in those takes that are valuable, but that doesn't bother him in the least. He understands film and he understands that what is important is that for a few moments here and there he really connected with something which is truthful, and that was interesting. Occasionally of course he'll hit a scene where every take is perfect and amazing, so it's not like he's out to lunch or anything. He just has no fear.

'My theory after watching him on *Backdraft* is that he doesn't need to rely on technique, he doesn't make anything up. He does it all through the incredibly thorough preparation. He then applies this to the script in an artistic way and then merely gives the audience what he has learned. As an actor Robert De Niro is almost a reporter; it's like a journalistic approach to acting. He didn't stay in character but I bet that he's not faking it. I bet what he's learned is that he can do all this preparation and with his concentration he can just call it up whenever he needs to. He doesn't have to sustain it every minute to be truthful. I never discussed this with him and I don't know if he would perceive it this way or not. But that's what I think I saw.'

De Niro will do anything and use anything necessary to get the performance he demands of himself. Frequently, as he did with Joe Pesci in *Raging Bull*, he will say or do outrageous things to goad his co-stars into a response to give him the reaction he needs to play his part.

Perhaps what Ron Howard and Kenneth Branagh and Michael Caton-Jones all saw to a greater or lesser extent was a third eye in action. De Niro knows instinctively what is right and what is wrong. He knows when a scene is working and when it is not. Meryl Streep, his co-star in *Falling in Love*, described him as being as certain and unerring as a compass. He does the takes and is instinctively able to know which are good, which are bad, and which show promise.

But is it faking? It is in the strictest sense of the word, since all acting is. However, like any other actor, De Niro knows that acting has to have at least the ring of truth. Whether or not you have brought any of your own experience or memories to the role, it must appear truthful. De Niro, perhaps more than any other screen actor, has to believe in what he is doing. And if he believes it and it seems truthful to his third eye, then he is not faking.

'Each problem is individual,' he says. 'It really doesn't matter whether you spend a lot of time trying to prepare in a certain way. My way is not to worry about things until I have to. I know what I have to do when I'm there but I think that's just a way of conserving energy, only using it when it's necessary. I think that just from doing it so often I know what's really important and what's not. Some parts, like *Raging Bull*, were harder and more rewarding. That's what I mean about conserving the energy. If you conserve the energy until the moment you have to do it and then you do it, it's draining but maybe it's also satisfying.

'The thing with movies is that there is so much waiting until you get to the moment, and the moment isn't always when you think it's going to be. Quite often you're all ready but they're not ready.

'What I like in a role is if somebody says, "I never thought of you for this type of part but then I thought you'd be good for it for that very reason." That sparks something in me. Sometimes you need that from an outside source to get you inspired or revved up about doing something different.'

34 On the Streets of the Bronx

O N 17 AUGUST 1993 De Niro reached a landmark in his life when he celebrated his 50th birthday. In the past he had suggested that when he notched up the half-century it might be time to stop acting and earn his living on the other side of the camera. In fact his 50th birthday saw De Niro working harder than ever on both sides of the camera.

His private life had now settled down to occasional dates with Uma Thurman after the turbulent affair with Naomi Campbell. She was about to get married to U2 guitarist Adam Clayton, and De Niro had publicly wished her well. Professionally, his part in *This Boy's Life* seemed to have galvanised his interest in doing serious work again. The Michael Caton-Jones film gave him his first serious challenge in a long time, ending a run of parts that were at best indifferent and at worst eminently forgettable. Off screen his TriBeCa studio was up and running and De Niro no longer felt the pressure to do 'take the money and run' cameos to help fund it. In the year of his 50th birthday he had committed to doing three films almost back to back, and there were serious discussions about doing several others. But most important to De Niro, he was about to direct his first film.

At 50 De Niro was physically still in great shape. His fearsome regime of exercise and self-discipline had left him with a physique that would be the envy of men half his age. The years had added dramatic weight and gravitas to his features. The only outward sign of middle age was a touch of grey at the temples, but even that looked distinguished. However, the creative clock was ticking and De Niro felt strongly that the time had come for another challenge.

'I had reached a crossroads,' he acknowledged. 'Maybe you hit a certain age and it makes an impression. You see you are moving on, and if there is anything you have felt you should be doing in your life then maybe you should be getting on with it.

'It's a turning point, a change you can't avoid. Whatever you think you want out of life you must start thinking seriously about it because you know that time is running short. You become aware of your own mortality. You must take advantage of the things you want to do in your life and seize the moment. I always wanted to direct something. I would find a book or this or that over the years but never go fully forward with it. I started realising that I have to do something or it is not going to happen.'

A Bronx Tale started life as a one-man, one-act show called *Tales of the Bronx*, written by actor Chazz Palminteri. It reflected his own life growing up on the streets of the Bronx in New York. The key incident in the story is a small boy witnessing a man being shot from the vantage point of his own front stoop. Palminteri did indeed witness such a thing as a child.

'I was sitting on my stoop,' he recalls vividly. 'These two guys in their cars were fighting over a parking space. One guy got out, then the other guy got out and shot him. My father grabbed me by the arm and dragged me upstairs.'

This would not be the only time the young Palminteri would encounter death on the streets of his neighbourhood. On one occasion he turned a corner to find a local wiseguy dead in a car. Palminteri used that single act of violence he witnessed from his doorstep as the catalyst for his story of the battle for the soul of a young boy. The boy, Calogero Anello, is attracted to the flashy glamour and easy life of Sonny, the local hood. His father, Lorenzo, a bus driver, tries vainly to convince him of the error of his ways. There is nothing, he tells him, worse than wasted talent. For Lorenzo real courage comes not from carrying a gun but from submitting yourself to the numbing grind of the daily routine for the sake of your family. Ironically Sonny wants exactly the same thing for Calogero as Lorenzo does; he wants him to stay at school, educate himself, and make a decent life for himself. In the end Calogero learns from both men, especially from Sonny's pointless death, and we are left to assume that he will turn out to be possibly a better man than either of them.

'There was a fighter once in my neighbourhood,' says Palminteri going back to his own childhood. 'He was seventeen years old and he had fought for the welterweight championship of the world. He lost, but the next day they found him on the roof, dead of a heroin overdose. He was a good friend of my father's, my dad had actually trained him at one point, and this was my father's ultimate example of wasted talent. He always drove that into my head. "Don't waste your talent, don't waste your life, do something with it." He wrote it down on a little index card and stuck it in my room, and even as I grew older and moved to my own apartment, I took it with me. I could never throw it out, that would be sacrilegious. It has always been with me.

'Growing up in my neighbourhood I did idolise a lot of the wiseguys on the corner. I would watch them and talk to them. But at the end of the day my father would always tell me, "Look, it doesn't take much strength to pull a trigger. But try to get up every day and work for a living to feed a family – that's a tough guy. It's harder to do that." So here was an opportunity to have the working man and the Mafia meeting head on with the boy, whom they both love, in the middle.'

Palminteri's one-man show started life in a small theatre in Los Angeles in 1988. It was originally a five-minute monologue for a workshop. Every week Palminteri would write ten or fifteen minutes of new material to try out the following week. From that he would take perhaps the four or five minutes that worked and incorporate them into the body of the piece. After about a year of this kind of trial-and-error honing, he eventually had a one-man show that ran for about an hour and half. De Niro heard of *Tales of the Bronx* through his trainer and sent his TriBeCa partner Jane Rosenthal to the West Coast to see for herself. She was impressed and recommended that they try to buy the film rights. De Niro saw the play himself and agreed. What he didn't know was that *Tales of the Bronx* was in the middle of a Hollywood bidding war. He was not the only actor interested. Al Pacino was also sniffing around the project, and at one point it looked as though the two actors were racing to see who could get the rights. De Niro went to see the play twice, Pacino only once.

But there was studio interest too, possibly sparked off by the news that both De Niro and Pacino were seriously looking at the play. Palminteri was initially offered $250,000 for the rights to his property. He said he would sell it but only if he could play Sonny. Palminteri is now one of Hollywood's most respected actors with an Oscar nomination for Woody Allen's *Bullets over Broadway* to his credit. At this point, however, he was an unknown screen actor who was most frequently seen as the heavy standing in the background of gangster movies. The studios would simply not entertain the idea of him playing the leading role. The offers continued to rise but always on condition that someone else play Sonny. Palminteri turned them all down.

'In Hollywood when you say no they think you mean you want more money,' says an amused Palminteri. 'I had refused their initial offer of a quarter of a million, then two months later they offered me half a million dollars and again I said no. A month after that it went up to three-quarters of a million and they said they would do the best they could to get me the part. Believe me, once they said that I knew I was going to definitely get screwed so I said, "Absolutely not!" '

By this stage Palminteri had decided it wasn't working out for him in Los Angeles and decided to take the play to New York. That was when the studios upped their offer to a million dollars, but still Palminteri wouldn't play ball. De Niro, like the other potential buyers, was reluctant to make the commitment to Palminteri. Not because he had any doubts about his talent as an actor or writer, but simply because for his first directing project he wanted to start with a clean slate. He met Palminteri while he was working on the draft of a screenplay and made him an offer.

'Let me make this clear,' De Niro told him. 'If you give it to a studio, they'll pay you for it and other people will get involved and they'll give the Sonny part to another actor. If you give it to me now, I can guarantee you'll be in it and we'll set it up in our own way and I'll have more control, which is what I want. I don't want any producer getting in the way and telling me what to do.'

Palminteri was impressed with De Niro's clarity of purpose.

'Right from the beginning there had been a lot of directors who had been around for a long time who wanted to make *A Bronx Tale*, but there was something about Bob when I talked to him. I thought, My God, he just gets it. He told me the way he would shoot it, he told me how real he would make certain things, and for me he was the one. It didn't bother me that he hadn't directed before, we're not talking about a stranger, we're talking about the man who is, in my opinion, the greatest actor of our time. I really thought he could bring something to the table. We were at the Bel Air Hotel, and this is before I had decided where I was going to take it, and he said to me, "Chazz, you can take this to anybody you want." But this is the quote from him that I remember. He said to me, "If you let me make it, I'll make it right." And he had this look in his eyes. I'll never forget that look in his eyes, and I got into my car, drove home, and thought, This is the guy!

'That meeting in the Bel Air was the defining moment in our relationship but I knew in my heart I was going to go with him. He said to me first of all that he would protect me and he would let me star in the role and he would let me write the screenplay. But when he said, "I'll make it right," that's when I knew.'

Even so, both men continued to finesse the finer points of the deal. Palminteri's contract was initially what is known in Hollywood as 'pay or play'. That means that, provided they were willing to pay him his full fee, Palminteri could effectively have been fired at any time and TriBeCa would still be able to go ahead with the movie. Palminteri objected with sufficient force for the word 'or' to be substituted with the word 'and' in the pay or play contract. That effectively made him bomb-proof; once the contract was signed there was no way the film could go ahead without him. Although he agreed to Palminteri's final request, De Niro for his part thought Palminteri was a little young to play Sonny convincingly. So he had him put on a stone in weight to fill out his face and shave his hairline slightly to make Sonny look a little older.

'I knew Chazz would be good and I knew that I could direct him,' said De Niro. 'No one could have been better than Chazz, because nobody knows him, he's a very good-looking guy, a sexy leading man, and he's just terrific. Plus, he'd be around all the time, because he was the writer. He'd be there even when he wasn't required as an actor. We'd always be talking about a cut here or reworking a scene there, or making it more succinct.'

There is no doubt that what attracted De Niro most to *A Bronx Tale* was not so much its subject-matter as its subtext. While the film may be about a boy growing to manhood and making the right choices along the way, it is also about the nature of the relationship between fathers and sons. Lorenzo is Calogero's biological father while for a time Sonny becomes his surrogate father. De Niro could not possibly have read the piece without echoes of his own relationship with his estranged father coming to the surface. We can only speculate on how he felt when during the scripting process there was a reading of the material at TriBeCa and De Niro's own son Raphael, from whom he is estranged, read the role of Calogero.

De Niro's father left when he was only two years old, and although the two remained close in the intervening years he grew up without a father in the family home. However close they may have been, his father would not have been there on every occasion when De Niro needed him. Some of the warmest and most poignant moments in *A Bronx Tale* come when Lorenzo is sharing private moments with his son. It is unlikely that these father-son talks echoed any exchanges between De Niro and his own father. Perhaps because of that there is an added warmth to De Niro's performance in these scenes, both with the nine-year-old Francis Capra and the teenage Lillo Brancato. It is a warmth that goes beyond acting and verges on longing.

De Niro dedicated *A Bronx Tale* to his father, who died in May 1993, five months before the film opened.

'My father died while I was editing this film,' De Niro explained later. 'It's true my parents divorced early on. My father and I had a father-son relationship but not in a family situation. He lived downtown, near me, and we spent time together. I don't know whether this would have been his kind of movie but I would have liked him to have seen it.'

Although De Niro was born and raised in New York, in Greenwich Village and Little Italy, he never ventured as far as the Bronx, which shares a similar Italian-American background. In the days when he was known as 'Bobby Milk' he acquired plenty of experience of the street life that young Calogero has to face. On one occasion his own father chastised him in public when he found him hanging out with some local hoods. De Niro remembers that it was a long time before he spoke to his father again after that.

'I realised, though, that this wasn't the life for me,' he says. 'That's why I went in another direction and pursued acting. However, I did spend many years of my life hanging out with kids on the streets so I had an early sense of being streetwise. But I never became fascinated with violence the way some people did.'

His original intention was simply to direct *A Bronx Tale*. He had already promised the part of Sonny to Palminteri, but quickly realised that the film would get made more quickly and attract finance more easily if he were to appear in it. With Palminteri playing Sonny it made sense for De Niro to play Lorenzo, named after and based on Palminteri's own father. He also reasoned that he had played too many wiseguys of his own for the part of Sonny to hold any challenge. Lorenzo, however, was a type of role he had never played. The man who parted company with Mike Nichols all those years ago because he couldn't play 'warm' had never been required to be a supportive parent on screen. Dwight Hansen in *This Boy's Life* was a stepfather, a distinction De Niro drew himself in interviews. In any event, Dwight's mode of parenting could hardly be called supportive.

'Bob said to me, "I want to meet your father," ' Palminteri recalls. 'I said, "You're going to play my father but nobody knows who my father is. If you're playing a famous person then you have to come up with what that person was like, but nobody really knows my father." "No," he said, "I want to meet him anyway." '

So Palminteri made the call to a slightly incredulous and disbelieving Lorenzo Palminteri who duly came north from Florida to spend three weeks with De Niro.

'How did my dad feel?' asks Palminteri rhetorically. 'How do you think your father would feel if you wrote a movie and told him Robert De Niro was going to play his life story. He couldn't get over that and he couldn't get over it when I told him Bob wanted to meet him too.'

The meeting with De Niro had an upside for Lorenzo Palminteri other than simply giving him stories to dine out on. De Niro found out that he had once been a fight trainer. While he was preparing for *A Bronx Tale*, De Niro was also shooting *Night and the City*. When he found out about Lorenzo's background he told Palminteri to bring his father along to the shoot. Lorenzo then found himself playing a corner man and sharing a scene with De Niro in Irwin Winkler's movie.

'I can see now why Bob wanted to spend time with my dad,' Palminteri continues. 'My dad showed him how you drive a bus and how he would do all sorts of things. Bob's an observer, he just watches. But when we started filming I saw him doing so many of the things that my father did. He didn't have to, but there was a sense that he felt this was real. A man did this. This is the way he drove a bus, this is the way he handled change, this is the way he wiped the steering wheel. So he took all of those things and stored them away.

'One of the great things about Bob is that, even though this was his directing debut, he was so collaborative. He would allow ideas to go back and forth. He would say, "If you don't agree with me tell me why." Sometimes I would win, sometimes he would win, but for him all that mattered was the work. And that's important. The best people don't care where an idea comes from because it takes just as much talent to recognise an idea as it does to come up with one.'

De Niro was quick to realise that Palminteri's story, through its various evolutions from monologue to full-blown screenplay, would not require a great deal of work to bring it to the screen. He saw that Palminteri knew the people and places he was writing about and, as much as he could, he was willing to respect that. He was determined that, as far as possible, *A Bronx Tale* would be filled with real people.

'Other than Joe Pesci, who was perfect because he knows that world too, I didn't want to use any name actors,' De Niro explained. ' Mostly we worked with non-professionals. I told the casting director that I didn't want her to start calling agents. I told her to hit the streets a year before we started shooting. "You gotta get out there and look," I told her. "I know the people we want are out there. But I don't have time to teach them. It would take forever to do that, so we have to get the right people who have a flair and who understand what we are doing and then put them together.'

De Niro and casting director Ellen Chenoweth also enlisted the aid of Marco Greco, who runs the Belmont Italian-American Playhouse in the heart of the Bronx. Greco sent them as many tapes as he could of local people. Many of them were rejected, but De Niro brought some in to read for various roles. In the end most of the cast came from New York; some were even childhood friends of De Niro. Clem Caserta, who appears memorably as Sonny's right-hand man Jimmy Whispers, ran in the same street gang as De Niro when they were boys. But the casting net had also been spread to other urban areas like Philadelphia and Chicago, with ads in newspapers, radio stations, and community newspapers. De Niro was determined that he would find the right people for this film, even if he had to cast right up to the day the cameras started rolling.

Seventeen-year-old Lillo Brancato, who plays the key role of Calogero as a teenager, was discovered in the Bronx. Marco Greco found him at Jones Beach, a local hangout for Italian kids. According to De Niro, Greco spotted him as he came out of the water and started doing impressions of Joe Pesci and De Niro. Brancato apparently bears a striking resemblance to the teenage Robert De Niro. Francis Capra, who plays the younger Calogero, and Taral Hicks, who plays Calogero's girlfriend, both came from open casting calls.

'I love to find new people,' says De Niro. 'It's not for the sake of their being new. It's because if you find someone who perfectly fits a part, that's such a great thing.'

De Niro quickly saw the potential of his cast, especially Brancato, who has gone on to a solid movie career. Just as he had done more than ten years previously with Cathy Moriarty in *Raging Bull*, he took a proprietary interest in his young cast. He realised and had seen for himself what sudden fame can do to young people.

'I was concerned about Lillo because of the age he was at,' he says. 'I talked to his family about things that have changed for him. He has a good family support system so I think he will be okay. But it is a lot of attention and it kind of distorts reality. No one is really prepared for it.'

De Niro's preparation for playing the part of Lorenzo Anello was as thorough as always. Not only did he want to spend time with Lorenzo Palminteri, learning how a bus driver behaved, he also wanted to get a New York City bus driver's licence. The Motor Vehicle Building in New York is no respecter of title or personage, so De Niro had to go down there and queue like everyone else to get the learner's permit that is the first step on the route to becoming a bus driver.

'You have to go early before a line builds up,' he recalls. 'You go in there and you meet people who genuinely don't care about you. It's a nightmare. So I went up to the room and I studied the booklet, everything from axles to explosions. I was told there were seven parts to the test and I studied the whole book. It took me three hours to take the test. Then she goes out with the paper and comes back in and says, "You failed".'

De Niro was stunned. But he took the test again. He studied hard and failed once again. This time, shaken to the core, he asked the examiner to check the papers. She did and it turned out he had passed – both times. So now, armed with his bus driver's learner's permit, he was ready to get behind the wheel of his bus and drive through the streets, not of the Bronx, but of Queens, the neighbouring borough where the film would be shot. The permit didn't actually allow him to drive a bus on the streets of New York; it limited him to driving in confined spaces like a movie set. As added insurance Lorenzo Palminteri had been brought in to be on hand every time De Niro was behind the wheel.

One of the key subplots in *A Bronx Tale* revolves around Lillo Brancato's relationship with Taral Hicks. He is Italian, she is a young black girl. He has been brought up in an insular community where blacks were looked down on as a matter of course. Even his father shares the institutionalised racism of the rest of the community. As an Italian-American actor who has dated a succession of black women – from Diahnne Abbott to Naomi Campbell – De Niro may have felt there was a point to be made here.

'I liked the whole thing because it was so rich but of course that part interested me,' he told *Interview* magazine. 'You see these two people are from different worlds; Calogero from his and Jane from hers. Then they come together and to me that was very interesting.

'There was talk about cutting out the whole Calogero – Jane story. People would say, "Just make it between a father and his son – that's a story in itself," which it was. But I felt that to take away any one of those elements would be wrong. The part with Jane is the one that you don't expect, and for that reason alone I didn't want to take it out. There's a beginning, a middle and an end to this whole relationship. It happens fast. They meet and fall in love and boom! – something really happens.

'I don't want to preach. I don't know whether it can help [fight racism] or not. It depends on who sees it and what they want out of it.'

De Niro had already consulted his close friend Martin Scorsese before he started on *A Bronx Tale*. It seems natural for a man who has been so closely associated with Scorsese to elect to direct a New York urban rites-of-passage story himself. But it would be unfair to dismiss *A Bronx Tale* as simply the work of a Scorsese disciple. There is more humanity and warmth in this one film from De Niro than there is in the seven films he had made with Scorsese up to that point. He also talked to people like Danny De Vito and other actors who had directed themselves in preparing for the movie. In the end he found directing not so much stressful as uncomfortable because of the schizophrenic demands of trying to maintain the viewpoint of both actor and director.

But despite all the consultation, once the cameras rolled for the first time De Niro was on his own, and *A Bronx Tale* was not an easy shoot. There were reports of long delays and De Niro going for take after take. The *New York Post* quoted one 'insider' as claiming that De Niro had shot a near-record amount of film. The unnamed source was quoted as saying that De Niro would sometimes insist on shooting 40 or 50 takes of a single scene. A whole week's shooting was missed completely. A spokesman for TriBeCa insisted that this was simply because of rain. However, there is no denying that the film finished up behind schedule and over budget. *A Bronx Tale* was originally to be produced with MCA Universal but De Niro pulled it after the studio would not guarantee more than $10 million. In the end he worked out a deal with the new independent company Savoy Pictures. Savoy were keen to make a name for themselves in Hollywood and felt a De Niro picture would bring them the kudos they needed. His original financing had been for a $14 million picture, but Jane Rosenthal admitted that the final budget was $21 million. She also added that this was only slightly more than they had eventually estimated. Most films shoot for a maximum of twelve weeks whereas the *Bronx Tale* crew shot for almost five months, an inordinate length of time for a film with no big effects or difficult action set-pieces.

Speculation that the movie was in trouble intensified when De Niro was seen spending time with his *Godfather Part II* director, Francis Ford Coppola. It was claimed that De Niro was having difficulty editing the film into shape, and Coppola was providing much-needed advice. It was being suggested that De Niro was showing Coppola the rushes of *A Bronx Tale* and heeding his guidance. Jane Rosenthal was quick to quash such speculation on De Niro's behalf.

'That is a total and complete rumour,' she told the *New York Post*. 'Francis was in New York talking to Bob about *Frankenstein*. That was the only thing they were talking about.'

Indeed, in April 1993, Coppola announced that De Niro would play the creature in *Mary Shelley's Frankenstein*, his 'sequel' to the previous year's *Bram Stoker's Dracula*. This time Coppola would only produce the picture; the directing chores would be handled by Kenneth Branagh.

A Bronx Tale was a critical success for De Niro. It was also a modest commercial success, making money both for TriBeCa and Savoy. Afterwards De Niro looked back on his work with much the same satisfaction that Lorenzo Palminteri might have taken from an honest day's toil.

'I wish I had directed earlier,' he said wistfully when the film was completed. 'I always wanted to from my early twenties. What happens is the years go by before you know it. Now I want to do it on a more consistent basis, but the material will have to be right.'

'The thing that really makes him great is that he can concentrate harder than anybody I have ever seen,' says Chazz Palminteri of De Niro. 'He could simply suck away his own personality and become that other person, it's the most amazing thing I have ever seen. When he was playing Lorenzo he would talk to me, as the director, about the scene he was about to do. I would stand behind the camera and he would say, "Okay, Chazz, this is what we are going to do here," and block it all out. Then he would walk out the door and come back in and I swear to God it wasn't him, it was this Lorenzo character. It was so amazing.

'As an actor working with someone like that, I think it makes someone like me strive to get to that level. I remember acting with him and seeing those eyes again. They were like hands that came out and grabbed you by your head and held you and looked right at you. I thought, Hey, I'm fighting for my life here. If I don't equal this I'm gone. No one is going to even look at me on the screen.

'There's no doubt in my mind that working with Robert De Niro made me a better actor because I knew I had to take my acting up to another level. He forces you to take it up to another level because if you don't you're dead.'

35 Tributes

EDITING *A BRONX TALE* was proving to be something of a marathon task for De Niro. He was working round the clock pulling all-nighters at his state-of-the-art editing suite in TriBeCa trying to get the film finished. It was due for release in October 1993. The last thing to be done was mixing the sound, but even that was proving difficult, or so it seemed.

One Saturday in August, De Niro had intended to spend another long evening dubbing and mixing the sound on the finished print of the movie. Chazz Palminteri was going to be there as well, as he had been throughout most of the editing process. However, late in the day, Palminteri broke the news to De Niro that the editing machines had developed a fault, and therefore they would be unable to work that night.

Palminteri told him that although a repair crew was working on the machines they would be out of commission for hours. That being the case, why didn't they grab a bite of dinner and perhaps come back later and work through the night? De Niro agreed, especially when Palminteri suggested they might visit a new restaurant that had opened nearby and had been recommended by Irwin Winkler. When they walked in, De Niro thought the place would suit him perfectly – the ambience was marvellous, but more important for a privacy hound like himself, it was nice and quiet. Had he thought about it he might have realised that it was maybe too quiet for a Saturday night.

De Niro walked upstairs to his table on the second floor and was stunned by the reception. More than 70 people had taken over the restaurant to throw a surprise party for his 50th birthday, which was only a few days away. De Niro had been so wrapped up in trying to complete his directing debut that he had barely remembered that he would soon reach his half-century.

The guest list made up a who's who of the New York film and literary scene. Directors Francis Ford Coppola, Martin Scorsese, Brian De Palma,

Penny Marshall, Ulu Grosbard and Elia Kazan were there. Acting friends like Danny De Vito, Harvey Keitel, Raul Julia and Gregory Hines turned up. Writers like Nora Ephron and long-time friend Paul Schrader were there too, as was his *Frankenstein* director Kenneth Branagh with his then wife, actress Emma Thompson. And in a mark of respect, CAA superagent Michael Ovitz had flown in from California to wish De Niro all the best.

It seemed that everyone in the *Bronx Tale* crew had played a part. The props department had decorated the upstairs room to resemble a French château, a slightly bizarre environment for the toasts and roasts that followed. As he had at the American Museum of the Moving Image tribute, Robin Williams turned out to be the star of the show. He stood up to propose a toast and ended up doing a blistering stand-up routine in which his old friend and *Awakenings* co-star took a roasting. His obsession with secrecy was the order of the day. Paul Schrader recalled how once he and De Niro had been lunching and the actor insisted on changing tables twice for fear of someone eavesdropping. Schrader also pointed out that this had happened 20 years ago – just after *Mean Streets* – when scarcely anyone knew or cared what either of them had to say.

There was no sign of Naomi Campbell but Toukie Smith and Uma Thurman were at the party. It was a family event too. De Niro's children Raphael and Drina were there, as was his ex-wife, Diahnne Abbott.

'You were a lousy husband,' she reportedly told De Niro, 'but you're my best friend. You are a wonderful father to our children.'

De Niro's mother Virginia Admiral was there, and even though his father had died three months previously Robert De Niro Snr was represented in spirit at least. Before he died, De Niro Snr had been commissioned by Francis Ford Coppola to create a wine label for a special vintage from the director's Napa Valley vineyard. The design had been misplaced and only recently discovered in an attic. Coppola had it reproduced and put onto a special bottle of wine for everyone at the party to take home with them.

The wine label was a particularly poignant note in an evening that De Niro found both touching and heart-warming. His father had been 71 years old when he died in May 1993. For 48 years he and his son had lived apart, but even in his absence he was still a profound influence on his son's life. De Niro always referred to his father as the real talent in the family and never missed an opportunity to sing his praises. Many of his friends shared his enthusiasm for his father's talents. Almost two years after his death there was a major retrospective of his work at the Salander-O'Reilly Galleries on East 79th Street in New York. Many of the paintings on show came from the private collections of De Niro's friends and colleagues, including Liza Minnelli and Bill Murray.

With the death of his father De Niro had lost a touchstone in his life. Sorting through his personal effects was a particularly haunting task, and for many months De Niro chose to leave things as they were.

'For a long time I didn't want to touch his studio except to have it cleaned occasionally,' he wrote in an article in *Vogue* magazine to coincide with his father's retrospective. 'I wanted to photograph it and videotape it and now sometimes I just go there and sit.

'Everything is still the way he left it: the old chairs, the sketches tacked up here and there, the big wire bird-cage. There used to be a parrot named Dimitrios but he's gone too. Now there's a fake bird in his place.'

Earlier in his career the actor had been known as Robert De Niro Jnr to distinguish him from his then much more eminent father. Then, when his father privately published his collection of poetry, *A Fashionable Watering Place*, in 1976, it appeared with the inscription: 'These poems are by Robert De Niro, the painter, not to be confused with Robert De Niro the actor, his son.' The two men shared the same name but they had their differences.

'I also have his temper, his eccentricity, and his passion,' said De Niro in his *Vogue* appreciation. 'And a strong connection to the smell of oil paints and cigarettes and musty old sweaters.

'As a kid I wasn't really interested in art much the same way my son today doesn't care about acting. My parents separated when I was two and I lived with my mother in the Village, so I didn't see him on a day to day basis. He had these dank lofts in NoHo and SoHo at a time when nobody wanted to live in those areas.'

They went to the movies together frequently and many of the films he saw with his father had an abiding influence on his own career.

'There were some English films like the Karel Reisz film *Saturday Night and Sunday Morning* with Albert Finney,' he recalled in a subsequent interview. 'Or there was *This Sporting Life* with Richard Harris. Those films I remember. When I was a kid they were art films and they were not as much in the mainstream as European films are today. The actors that I thought were most interesting were James Dean, Brando, Montgomery Clift, Kim Stanley, and Greta Garbo.'

His father's fascination with Garbo is well known. He painted and sculpted her often, especially in his best-known series with the actress as Anna Christie. De Niro says he did not see a Garbo movie until he was in his thirties, but when he did he thought she was just great.

Although his father frequently took him to the movies, the De Niros – father and son – also visited museums or went to nearby Washington Square Park to roller-skate. Even though they lived apart, Robert De Niro

Snr was no dead-beat dad; he took as much of an interest in his son and his career as he possibly could – sometimes, as far as the boy was concerned, too much of an interest.

'He didn't entirely approve of my friends,' recalls De Niro. 'When I was about thirteen we ran into each other in Washington Square Park. I was with a group of street kids and he got fairly worked up going on and on about bad influences.'

In the end the son would eclipse the father in terms of fame and career success. The surest sign of this is that the father is now known as Robert De Niro Snr, rather than his son as Robert De Niro Jnr. For a man who knew he was talented and had watched his fame recede over the years, De Niro Snr must have had very ambivalent feelings about his son's success.

'He was proud of me,' wrote De Niro in *Vogue*, 'but in some respects it must have been hard for him.'

36 Thrilling Horror

F RANCIS FORD COPPOLA HAD struck a chord with the movie-going public with his screen version of the Dracula legend. Audiences jaded with gore and cheap schlock flocked to Coppola's Gothic romance with Gary Oldman as a nobleman searching through four centuries for lost love. The film was a commercial success and naturally Sony Pictures wanted another one. Just as Universal had done some 60 years before, Coppola turned from Dracula to Frankenstein.

Universal still owned the copyright on the titles so Coppola could not call his version *Dracula*. He had to come up with the more unwieldy *Bram Stoker's Dracula*; however, this did allow him to set out his stall by going back to the original source and not simply remaking the movie. It was the same with Frankenstein, which because of similar copyright restrictions would be known as *Mary Shelley's Frankenstein*. In her foreword to the novel Shelley promises '. . . a story which would speak to the mysterious fears of our nature and awaken thrilling horror. One to make the reader dread to look around, to curdle the blood and quicken the beating of the heart.'

That was a tall order by anyone's standards. No version of *Frankenstein* had achieved that since Boris Karloff first applied the make-up back in 1931.

Coppola was not directing; this time he would simply produce. He had a director in mind for the project in the shape of Kenneth Branagh, whose Shakespearian adaptations had been international box-office and critical hits. Branagh had never handled a film as big as this $40 million epic, but Coppola was convinced he could bring the right degree of theatricality and gusto to the finished product. But first there was the problem of casting. Branagh was used to directing himself in his films, and he could certainly play Victor Frankenstein. But the Creature was another matter. This was going to be a faithful adaptation of Shelley's novel, complete with a creature who could speak and think and hold philosophical discourses with its creator, not a muscle-bound giant inarticulately tearing up the scenery.

There were a number of suggestions from various sources. Some favoured John Malkovich while others favoured Jeremy Irons. However, the most likely choice appeared to be the French star Gérard Depardieu, who has building a large and growing following in America to match his enormous popularity in Europe. Coppola, however, had other ideas. He believed that De Niro would be perfect as the Creature, and spent many hours convincing him that he was right for the part. Eventually, after some juggling with schedules, De Niro committed himself to the project, which would require an arduous eighteen weeks of shooting in England, Wales and Switzerland. Branagh, for one, was delighted.

'We wanted someone who could act through the make-up,' he says. 'We also wanted someone who could come up with a make-up which was not a mask or a suit to hide behind. We very much wanted to see Robert De Niro's eyes, De Niro's soul – there and available. We see him grow before our eyes, we see this innocent born and then acquire language and be very eloquent. It needed an actor of some emotional size or whatever you care to call it, to make this basic plea that the creature makes. In the great scene where he confronts Frankenstein in the ice cave this outcast says to him that he just wants a friend. He wants some company, a companion. "For the sympathy of one human being I would make peace with all," he tells him.

'He tells Frankenstein that he left him to die, he gave him life and simply walked away. That rings a lot of bells and that basic need for companionship is simply awful. Frankenstein is forced by the creature to think of the consequences of his actions. It gets under the skin, it's a very difficult scene, and it is done beautifully by De Niro.'

De Niro's main reason for accepting was that the film was going to stay as close as possible to the original text. He was attracted by the notion of taking a more realistic view of the story. There was also the dramatic challenge that Branagh had hinted at. De Niro was used to changing his appearance to play parts – it had been his trademark, after all – but this time he would have to be made all but unrecognisable. Could he wear the make-up or would the make-up wear him?

'As good as prosthetics are these days they can mask you too much,' he said afterwards. 'I'm still not sure even now that I achieved it but we certainly tried. It is something I didn't worry about too much but I did understand what people were saying. I've been in other movies over the years where I wore prosthetics for ageing things and I realised afterwards that you couldn't see me. You really have to be able to see the expression through them.'

Before agreeing to do the film, De Niro had Branagh thoroughly checked out. He may have come highly recommended but he was not yet part of De Niro's charmed circle. But after he had watch his films Branagh eventually got the green light from De Niro and the two men met for the first time in incongruous circumstances.

'We were in the back of a taxi for that first meeting,' recalls Branagh. 'I was with Francis Ford Coppola in the afternoon and then we went to meet Robert De Niro. I was merely a bystander to this clash of the titans – actually there was no clash at all – they talked wine as I recall. Robert is very proud of his restaurant and film complex and Francis is very proud of his vineyard. I think my job on that first evening was to express profound interest in both things in the hope that an arrangement could be made where Robert would give his services to the film. In the end it turned out all right.

'Francis was very helpful in briefing Bob on my behalf and then we talked and we established some rapport. He liked the fact that I was Irish but I think to begin with he expected me to turn up in some sort of Elizabethan suit with a box of sonnets under my arm. He's a great mate of Liam Neeson and I'm from the same part of the world so that helped.'

The next major problem was designing the look of the Creature. The man responsible for the make-up was Daniel Parker, a second-generation movie make-up specialist, whose Animated Extras workshop was based at Shepperton Studios outside London where *Frankenstein* was to be shot. Parker and Branagh and De Niro collaborated closely on how the Creature would appear on the screen. Branagh and Parker shuttled back and forth across the Atlantic with sketches and models. De Niro shuttled in the opposite direction for make-up tests and in the end a look was achieved.

'I tried not to look at the Frankenstein make-ups that have been done over the years when I was doing my designs because we were all familiar with that look anyway,' says Parker. 'The overall concept for this make-up was that he wasn't a monster but a creature, a man made up of other men. This gave me a great opportunity because our starting point was different from what had been done previously. One of the things which surprised me doing the research was that surgical techniques really haven't changed all that much since then, which is a bit worrying, I suppose. We based all the operations on medical fact and once I had an idea what Victor might have done to revive his creature, I did loads of drawings to experiment with different looks for his make-up.

'One complication is that, once revived, the Creature actually heals over the course of the film. He starts off with open wounds which have no blood, but then the wounds become bloody, gradually close and the stitches fall out. By the end of the film these wounds have become scars, so we had to create six different stages that involved either colour changes or sculpting changes. In between these main stages we also created dozens of make-ups for specific shots, such as a close-up of a stitch falling out, to help show that progression.'

As a man who prides himself on his own research, De Niro was very impressed with Parker when he turned up with his sketches, his contact lenses, his false teeth and his wigs. He agreed enthusiastically with Parker's basic premise, even though he knew it would mean hours of tedium and occasional discomfort sitting in the make-up chair. The original shooting schedule called for 41 days of filming in make-up, but De Niro baulked at that. He wanted a day out of make-up in between each day in make-up to protect him from the effects of having the latex glue poured over him some 60 times in the course of the film. The number of days in the make-up chair would have to be reduced, he insisted. The only way to do that was actually to lengthen the time spent in make-up. Finally De Niro agreed to go through the discomfort for twice as long for half the number of days. In the end he spent 21 days in the make-up chair.

'We had some long days but that's the nature of the game,' he says of the role he described as the most terrifying of his career. 'We were concerned about keeping a balance between making the character distorted and letting people recognise me. I think it turned out okay.'

'At the start it took us almost nine hours to apply the full body make-up,' says Parker. 'We did manage to get it down to six and a half hours, which I was really pleased with. By the time we had it on him we were all exhausted and then we had to keep it looking good for ten or twelve hours at a time. For the beginning of the film his entire body was covered in prosthetics which, to my knowledge, has never been done before so that an actor still looks like a man.

'It was nerve-racking, because if any of those large prosthetic pieces had ripped we would have been in big trouble because they were so tight – they would just have torn along their entire length and the whole thing would have had to be done again. I'd never had a sleepless night before *Frankenstein* and I had a great many while I was working on the film. Fortunately the make-up held together amazingly well, even when Victor and the Creature are rolling around on the laboratory floor smashing into things.'

One of the first things Parker had to do was to take a thin rubber mould of De Niro's head so that the Creature's head could be modelled on it.

'When it was done and he saw it Robert said, "Daniel, one of the hairs on my eyebrow is wrong," ' recalls Parker. 'And he was right. It was.'

Parker and his team worked long hours making up not just De Niro but also his double, who was required to look like the Creature. But thanks to patience on everyone's part – especially De Niro's – there were no dramas or tantrums in the make-up department. De Niro was remarkably good-natured about it for most of the time. He claimed to have spent his time watching MTV, CNN, and catching up on the tabloids. His good nature extended onto the set as well. After weeks in full make-up he walked out onto the set without his grotesque facial embellishments – the shot required only that his arms be made up. When the crew saw him, effectively as himself, to a man they screamed in horror. De Niro saw the joke and was as amused as the rest of them.

'He was a pussycat really,' says Branagh. 'He had watched the things that I had done and he had asked around about me and he did agree to do it, even if it took him a while. But for nine or ten months we had meetings about costumes and make-up about once every three weeks. During that process we discovered that we shared a sense of humour and I have to say he is a very funny man. He liked the Celtic bit of me and that seemed to connect with the mad Italian-American thing.

'He was also extraordinarily generous as an actor. John Cleese was on the set on the first day that Robert worked. It's always a good sign from an actor when they give an equal or greater amount of energy off camera when it's the other person's close-up. And Robert gave miles more for John than he did on camera – although what he did on camera was perfect for his scene – which was a great help for John who was terrific in the part but also very scared. He was equally generous in his big scene with Richard Briers, who plays the blind hermit.'

Other co-stars, like Helena Bonham Carter, who plays Elizabeth Frankenstein, also spoke warmly of De Niro's on-set behaviour. She claimed he was 'fabulous' to work with.

'His reading of the Creature is radical and surprising,' she says. 'I don't think we've ever seen a portrayal quite like this one. He helped out on all my close-ups and was very generous with no self-involvement at all. Our scenes together were very tiring yet he never complained once or came out with any diva nonsense. It's nice to find out that some superstars don't have the attitude that's supposed to go with their performance.'

But at the end of the day the Creature is not all sweetness and light. He does after all rip out Helena Bonham Carter's heart at one point in the film, before brandishing it in front of Victor Frankenstein. And although Branagh had been looking for an actor who could convey the tortured soul of the Creature, De Niro had one other quality that made him absolutely indispensable.

'He appears to have a tremendous potential for violence,' says Branagh respectfully. 'He is one of the more frightening people I have met in my life and you seriously wouldn't want to cross him. So he was able to bring both aspects of that to his performance. What I think is really frightening is that power that you've seen him bring to bear in the movies. It's just that moment where perhaps you've said something and his eyes just go. It's not so much the physical threat as the potential for him to be very, very free with whatever aggression he might feel. You wouldn't want to get in the way of that. I've seen him in a couple of situations where the smile just drops and you really don't want to be there when that happens. You would imagine that you would basically just get thumped.'

There is no doubt that the sense of menace to which Branagh refers makes De Niro an extraordinary screen Frankenstein. The final touch came when his voice was digitally remastered in a hi-tech recording studio to make it sound more inhuman and in the process remove the last lingering traces of his New York accent. But the film was not the huge commercial success that everyone had hoped it might be. At the end of the day it barely covered its costs with grosses of $100 million worldwide.

There were a number of factors. The most obvious was that the film was released at virtually the same time as another big-budget horror movie. Tom Cruise was always going to be a bigger box-office draw than De Niro. But when you consider that this was Cruise in *Interview with the Vampire*, his most talked-about film in years, *Frankenstein* didn't stand a chance. Likewise Sony took the curious decision to open the film in America and Britain on the same day. This meant that the stars had to spread themselves around trying to do publicity for two territories at the same time – Branagh was tearing himself away from final mixing to do interviews. For his part De Niro said he would do only one television interview in Britain and that would have to be conducted by Branagh – a ploy used by Daniel Day Lewis the year before when he was interviewed by Martin Scorsese for *The Age of Innocence*. The result in both cases was deferential, incestuous interviews that left viewers with the notion that the stars had something to hide. The worst effect of this publicity dearth was felt in Britain, where even the poorest box-office performer stands some chance of publicity trickling over on the coat-tails of the American release. There was no trickle-down effect and the film failed in both countries.

The American release was particularly disappointing. It was in the United States that the film would be under most pressure from the Tom

Cruise picture. However, to counter that, the film was having a rare American royal première. The Prince of Wales, who was on a visit to the United States, had agreed to attend the Los Angeles première screening. De Niro, however, did not. His non-attendance, plus the lack of general publicity, was quickly seized on as a reflection on the film. It was also seen as a snub to Prince Charles, who is a friend of Kenneth Branagh. De Niro's office said no snub was intended – the actor was simply busy with night shoots on *Casino*, his new film for Martin Scorsese. Nonetheless the damage had been done in the eyes of the cinema audience, and the hoped-for publicity coup left everyone with egg on their faces.

37 Another Roll of the Dice

'W E ALWAYS HAVE A good time working together. It's always a special experience. No matter how well the film turns out or how it's received it will always be a special experience. If you are fortunate and lucky enough to have the money for that process there is nothing more you could ask for. It's not like working with a brother. We just have a very similar sensibility and – I wouldn't be so pretentious as to say artistic sensibility – but certainly a creative sensibility.'

That is as close as De Niro can come to distilling and defining the nature of his unique relationship with Martin Scorsese. There has never been a cinematic collaboration like it, nor is there ever likely to be another. The two men have marched in lock-step since Scorsese persisted in the belief that he recognised De Niro from the old days in the neighbourhood when they bumped into each other at Jay Cocks's Christmas party. Their latest film together, *Casino*, is their eighth as director and star in a little over 20 years. They have gone on to make other movies with other people, but always they come back to each other.

Casino is a culmination of all that the two men have been working towards since *Mean Streets*. The *Los Angeles Times* describes it as 'the film where Johnny Boy gets his wings – Icarus wings'. The film reunites Scorsese and De Niro with actor Joe Pesci and screenwriter Nicholas Pileggi, who wrote *GoodFellas*. The three-hour epic is the natural successor to *GoodFellas* and the conclusion of the loose trilogy that began with *Mean Streets*.

The relationship between the two men has blossomed over their eight movies together. You would be hard put to think of a film that either has made without the other which ranks with any of their collaborations; even the poorest of them, like *New York, New York*, is made fascinating by their relationship. The balance of power has swung back and forth but it now appears to be a genuine partnership. Almost fifteen years ago Steven

Spielberg compared Scorsese and De Niro to yin and yang; Scorsese is the thinker, De Niro the doer.

The director now says that Spielberg's analysis is probably closest to the mark.

'Bob gets to do the things I would like to do, I guess,' says Scorsese. 'I think he enjoys playing out those aspects of the character and, there's no doubt about it, it's almost like a catharsis of going through moments that he feels are emotional truth. It sounds very arty but when we work together we use the phrase "It feels right." If I ask if it's the right way to go he'll say, "Aahh, it doesn't feel right." Then he goes, "That's right, that's right, that feels right." It's very inarticulate. It's almost like a piece of primal behaviour on his part as an actor. It's very interesting. He'll hardly articulate anything.'

In the past De Niro has had to persuade and even coerce Scorsese into directing certain films. However, for *Casino*, Scorsese says they were in absolute agreement.

'What was in the character was very interesting for Bob,' he says. 'It was different from him acting out a lot. Rothstein had a control and would try not to let the emotions get in the way. The colder he could be the more he was able to test the temperature of the game as a handicapper, not to get emotionally involved. That appealed to Bob.'

It is easy to see how De Niro, who has been in control of his own life and whenever possible the lives of others since he was ten years old, would be attracted to a man like Rothstein, a man whose very control is what keeps his edge. Even when his wife is threatening to leave and take his child he never loses it. Ultimately it is his control which keeps him ahead of the game and enables him to avoid the tragic consequences that befall almost everyone else in the film.

Like *GoodFellas*, this was supposed to be a non-fiction book first and then become a movie. That's the way things were heading when Pileggi began researching the story of real-life Las Vegas gambler Frank 'Lefty' Rosenthal. De Niro and Scorsese had spoken about the project, but at that stage De Niro was more concerned with *A Bronx Tale* and Scorsese was preparing to film *Clockers*. As it happened Scorsese abandoned *Clockers* to Spike Lee and without a project to film he asked Pileggi to write the screenplay before the book.

De Niro's version of Lefty Rosenthal is Sam 'Ace' Rothstein, a small-time gambler whose talent for odds-making makes him a Las Vegas legend. He rises through the ranks, making millions for his bosses, until he eventually ends up running a high-profile casino on the Strip in Las Vegas. In his private life he marries cool blonde Ginger McKenna, played by Sharon

Stone. The marriage gives him a spurious credibility as a pillar of Vegas society and he even manages to join the country club. Joe Pesci is his oldest friend, Nicky Santaro, a Mob enforcer who arrives in town and leaves a trail of bodies in his wake. Rothstein's life and career turn to dust and he blames Santaro for all his ills. When he confronts him, it ends in tragedy.

Although the film may appear more mainstream than some of their other work, *Casino* is still firmly in the mould of *Mean Streets, Raging Bull* and *GoodFellas*. Rothstein remains solely responsible for his own downfall; as responsible as Johnny Boy was for his or Jake La Motta for his.

'This is the oldest story in the world,' said Scorsese. 'It's people doing themselves in by their own pride and losing paradise. If they handled it right they would still be here. Everybody would be happy. But it got out of hand. I think I learn more in a movie or a story when I see what a person does wrong and what happens to them because of that. It's also more interesting when they go about doing bad things, as antagonists. It's like a catharsis.'

Filming *Casino* was a gruelling experience. Shooting took almost five months, and since Scorsese had decided that the entire film would be shot on location that involved lengthy night shoots. Finding anywhere that looked like vintage Vegas – the film is set in the 1970s – proved almost impossible on today's theme park-style resort. Eventually the Riviera allowed them to film, but only in its quieter moments. This meant that De Niro and the rest of the cast and crew had to turn up in the dead of night every night for six weeks while the Riviera was reasonably quiet to get the shots they needed. By ten every morning their sets had to be struck and they had to be out to allow the casino to get on with the business of separating gamblers from their cash.

Las Vegas never really closes, so the gambling would continue just out of camera shot. The noise caused nightmares for the soundman, and Scorsese even recalls a set of dice flying across the room and landing on his video monitor. Even at those ungodly hours there were still large crowds of rubber-neckers and tourists who had come to see De Niro, Stone and Pesci. The film-makers were baffled until they discovered that, in a very Vegas-like bid to exploit another attraction, the Riviera had hung up a banner that said, 'Robert De Niro, Joe Pesci, Sharon Stone – Now filming inside!'

De Niro accepted the intrusion with as much good grace as anyone could under difficult circumstances. His usual private clowning with Scorsese also seemed likely to be upstaged this time with the presence of legendary Las Vegas lounge comedians like Don Rickles and Alan King in the cast. Rickles, playing a straight role as Ace's right-hand man, was particularly hard on De Niro. The actor was a frequent target for his barbed put-downs, but De Niro reacted only with bemused indulgence. With the experience of handling a crew in *A Bronx Tale* under his belt, he would appreciate that in such difficult circumstances any kind of laughter is welcome, no matter where it comes from. In any event Scorsese would never have allowed it if he hadn't discussed it with De Niro beforehand.

The De Niro-Scorsese partnership is also characterised by the presence of the statutory blonde. This time Sharon Stone follows in the footsteps of Cybill Shepherd in *Taxi Driver*, Cathy Moriarty in *Raging Bull*, and Jessica Lange in *Cape Fear*. Stone was one of a long line of 'A' list performers who read for the part of Ginger. She had two meetings with De Niro and Scorsese which, she thought, came to nothing. Then, to the surprise of Scorsese fans and almost everyone in Hollywood, she was offered the role. In the past De Niro and Scorsese have been accused of Italian laddishness, but Sharon Stone appears to have found no trace of anything like that. However, she did delight the tabloid press in an unguarded moment by revealing that De Niro is the best kisser she has ever come across. That, however, appears to have been strictly for media consumption.

'I had known Bob for a long time personally and he is such a wonderful gentleman,' she says. 'It was fun working with him but sometimes the movie was a bit like *Who's Afraid of Virginia Woolf?* meets *GoodFellas*. We had some scenes that were pretty hairy and we would cut and we'd just look at each other and giggle so much because we had been so out there.'

This is plainly not the De Niro who would remain in character throughout a movie. The notion of Travis Bickle collapsing in fits of laughter after a take is hard to accept. But again it suggests that with age and maturity De Niro realises that in some cases it's okay to fake it. Stone, however, like so many other De Niro co-stars before her, found herself running to stand still. And again like so many others, she was prepared to raise her game when she had to.

'Bob plays a character that is often really affected by this woman. She drives him crazy. I had to be courageous enough to do that. It can be a daunting consideration but there was no way I was going to get on set and not do it. I've been a long time prepping for this moment. I knew that I had abilities that I hadn't yet had an opportunity to demonstrate. But we went way beyond what I understood that I could do to things that

I had never guessed that I would be able to tackle. I surprised myself, I think I surprised everybody.'

Stone's character descends into alcoholism through the course of the movie and she is the catalyst for the decline of Ace's empire. When he was asked to characterise his films at the time of his successful attempt to make *The Last Temptation of Christ*, Scorsese said they were about sin and redemption. Here there is little redemption for Ace, only the sin of pride. And pride usually goes before a fall.

'It's almost for the slightest thing that everything gets undone,' the director told the *Los Angeles Times*. 'It seems like the slightest thing but it's his inability to give,' he added of Rothstein. 'There are certain scenes in this picture where he should have given in to certain people and doesn't. Whether it's behind his desk or in his bed he refuses. And people can only take that so much.

'The great sin is pride. It's the undoing of everyone. It's the sin that created Lucifer, because he was the angel that felt he would be as important as God and was cast into Hell. He was a favourite up to that point, but thought he could take over. So I'm very interested in a character who consciously makes the effort to deal with every problem with a solution in which his pride is ten steps ahead of him. It's the kind of story you like to hear over and over again.'

Working with Scorsese again appears to have revitalised De Niro, as it did when he emerged from a previous dry spell with *GoodFellas*. When *Casino* was finished he launched himself into no fewer than four films back to back – including one as producer – and hinted at the possibility of directing a fifth. And it has to be said that the choices appear to be good ones with 'A' list directors, none of whom he has worked with before.

After *Casino*, De Niro was again on the wrong side of the law with his next film, *Heat*. The movie is the work of Michael Mann, a former cult director who delighted critics with films like *Thief* and *Manhunter* before entering the mainstream with the TV series *Miami Vice* and the hit movie *The Last of the Mohicans*. In *Heat* De Niro plays career criminal Neil McAuley, who is preparing to hand everything over to his protégé, played by Val Kilmer. McAuley's nemesis is career cop Vincent Hanna, played by Al Pacino. De Niro and Pacino have never played a scene before in a movie – they played characters in separate time-frames in *The Godfather Part II* – and the prospect of seeing them together was tantalising. Mann knows just how tantalising it was.

'People ask me if it was difficult getting them together and the undramatic answer is no,' he says almost apologetically. 'When I started thinking about casting this film I thought of it as a duet and I put down pairs of actors – the first two I put down were Bob and Al. I sent scripts to each of them and they agreed within a couple of weeks. They have been friends for more than twenty years and have always sort of been looking for a project to do together.'

For the first time in a long time it seems, De Niro immersed himself in his preparation for this role. He could not meet the real McAuley – the film is based on an incident in 1963 in which a friend of Mann, Chicago detective Charles Adamson, pursued and killed McAuley – but he did as much as he could to immerse himself in his world. He met men like McAuley, he talked to the wives of men like him, he went into prisons, and he surrounded himself with detail.

De Niro has never looked more striking or more handsome on screen than he does in *Heat*. He is never less than immaculately dressed and coiffured in any of the scenes. This, according to Mann, is how De Niro found the character.

'It's a very additive process in a naturalistic way,' he explains. 'It will be how starched the collar and front is on the white shirt he wears throughout. It's not just that it will feel a certain way against his skin, it's the fact that everything is expressive of character. It's like saying, "Given who my character is he would wear a shirt like this." This is a regional thing but if you're in prison on the West Coast, like McAuley, and your realm of expression of your individuality is constricted to a narrow cell, the human need to express oneself and manifest a personality is not going to diminish. In fact it even becomes amplified and you use whatever is available to you. That frequently manifests itself in clothes where everything has to be pressed and immaculate – there's a great attention to hair too. There is also a remarkable amount of attention to one's physicality.

'That would manifest itself in life on the street too, so Bob would pay a lot of attention to his hair and his shirt. We spent a lot of time with some guys. One guy in particular was a very notorious bank robber who was out on parole. But when you went into this guy's modest three-bedroom apartment it was immaculate, just immaculate, there was an almost anal-compulsive order about it. This film is all about a man who has been in prison for a long time, so you pick up on these things. It's the significance of physical details which Bob accumulates in an additive way, almost like sedimentary rock.'

During the filming of *Heat* it was reported that Mann was keeping De Niro and Pacino apart deliberately to increase the attention. Mann says that this was not the case. As he points out, both men are good enough actors, and have been acting sufficiently long, not to insist on avoiding each other because their characters hate each other. The two men have only one dialogue scene together so there was no real need for them to be separated since they were almost never working at the same time.

The landmark scene in *Heat* – the one that will go down in the movie history books – is the on-screen coffee-shop meeting between Pacino and De Niro. It is the dramatic equivalent of Gene Kelly and Fred Astaire duetting on 'The Babbit And The Bromide'. The scene came halfway through the shoot, and Mann concedes that even a jaded film crew who had seen it all and done it all were excited at the prospect of the two best actors of their generation appearing in the same scene.

The set-up is that Hannah's character has had De Niro under surveillance. Spontaneously Pacino takes part in the tail operation himself. He eventually flags De Niro down and then invites him for a cup of coffee. In a secluded coffee shop the two protagonists declare a temporary truce and discuss their mutual respect for each other.

The scene was shot in thirteen takes.

'When we hit take nine, halfway through I knew this was the one,' says Mann. 'I knew we had just nailed the scene and I was surprised because I felt an elation as though one of the major hurdles in making this film had just been cleared. Then I shot four more takes because I wanted some variations. Take eleven had some nuances and harmonics that are almost impossible to describe, and that's the one I used the most – almost all of what you see on screen is take eleven. I shot both sides simultaneously, which is difficult to do in cinema, because the whole scene is carried in the faces and postures and body language of these two guys. Bob would throw a look to the side like he's evading Al but then he comes back suddenly with a little bit of aggression, and Al instead of backing up comes forward. All of these interplays made it like two spectacular musicians playing a duet and I didn't want to miss a note.'

The studio wanted more scenes between De Niro and Pacino but Mann stood his ground. One was all that was needed for the story, he claimed, and he was right. The last time De Niro went head to head with a serious rival he lost out to Jack Nicholson in *The Last Tycoon*. In *Heat* De Niro aces the whole picture. Pacino is the one left resorting to obvious tricks like yelling inappropriately to suggest his unbalanced inner nature. De Niro gives a magnificently controlled performance which seems to suck all the energy out of everything else on the screen. The eye of the audience goes to him in a way that it has not done for years. At last he is playing a character complex enough to justify his talents and engaging enough to command his full attention. The end result is one of his finest screen performances.

Regardless of how good he had been, *Heat* confirmed De Niro's assessment of Los Angeles as a place he only goes to when he gets paid. Once shooting in Los Angeles had finished he moved out of the house he had rented from Roger Moore for the duration and was heading back to New York to appear in another movie and get another TriBeCa project off the ground.

Lorenzo Carcaterra's novel *Sleepers* is one of the most controversial books to be published in recent years. It is the story of four New York teenagers sent to a state correctional facility when a prank goes tragically wrong. Once inside, the four boys are systematically raped and abused by their guards. In later life two of the boys – now career criminals – meet one of their tormentors in a bar and shoot him dead. The other two boys – one a lawyer, the other a journalist – conspire to have the prosecutor take the case in order to throw it. The film has attracted an all-star cast that includes Brad Pitt, Kevin Bacon, Dustin Hoffman and Robert De Niro. Director Barry Levinson persuaded De Niro to play the small but pivotal role of Father Bobby, the priest on whom the whole case turns. The script throws up the mouth-watering possibility of a scene between De Niro and Dustin Hoffman. De Niro was happy to be working in New York, but not so happy with pictures that showed him in an ecclesiastical dog collar with a very secular bodyguard to keep the fans at bay.

Sleepers has become controversial because Carcaterra has insisted that it is not fiction. He has sworn to protect the identities of all those involved – himself (the journalist) excepted – and has resisted all attempts to reveal his sources, even from De Niro.

'I've said all along that I wouldn't say who these people are, that's a promise I made them,' he says. 'But that hasn't stopped De Niro. He kept asking me if he could meet the real Father Bobby and I had to keep saying no.'

Although his role in *Sleepers* is basically a cameo, it allowed De Niro to move back to New York, where he was able to make a start on *Marvin's Room*, a TriBeCa Film that he is executive-producing. The family drama will reunite him with his co-stars from *This Boy's Life*, Ellen Barkin and Leonardo Di Caprio. But back in the Big Apple De Niro's temper got the better of him once more and he again found himself playing out a real-life drama as exciting as anything he has done on screen.

In October 1995 he found himself charged with assault after allegedly leaving a cameraman with a bloody nose. The video cameraman, Joseph Ligier, claimed that De Niro had grabbed his hair and punched his nose while he tried to take his picture outside the Bowery Bar. De Niro gave himself up peaceably to the police and was duly fingerprinted and charged with a misdemeanour. He was then bailed to appear in court the following month to answer the charges. However, Ligier's lawyer contacted him a few days after the assault and said the cameraman was prepared to let the matter drop if De Niro would hand over $150,000.

De Niro agreed to make the delivery but instead went to the police. They were sufficiently interested to involve De Niro in an undercover 'sting' to arrest Ligier. De Niro duly arrived at the appointed rendezvous in a stretch limousine carrying $110,000 in a carrier bag – Ligier had revised his figure downwards in the interim. Ligier got into the car, De Niro showed him the money in the bag, and they sped off. Ligier understood that the car would head for the office of the Manhattan district attorney where he would announce his intention of dropping charges against the actor. What he didn't know was that the car had been wired by detectives who had heard every word. When they arrived at the district attorney's office Ligier found himself being questioned and held with a view to pressing extortion charges.

Ligier turned out to be one of the new breed of paparazzi – known as 'videorazzi' – who specialise in provoking stars into a fight or some kind of abuse and then sell the tapes to tabloid television shows. The charges against De Niro were dropped for lack of evidence. Police later praised his involvement in the case. One detective said he was 'very gung ho' and had attacked the undercover operation with the enthusiasm he would bring to his movie roles.

De Niro's action-packed lifestyle continued when he began shooting *The Fan* for British director Tony Scott. *The Fan* will take him back into *King of Comedy* territory as an obsessive fan who stalks baseball player Wesley Snipes. However, Scott, whose work includes *Top Gun* and *Crimson Tide*, is likely to take a different tack on the material to Martin Scorsese. De Niro was involved in a bizarre incident early in filming when he became involved in what appears to have been a head-to-head confrontation with, of all things, a train. He drove a jeep across the railway track in San Francisco where they were shooting, despite warnings from railwaymen and safety officers that a train was on its way. He reportedly said, 'Fuck you, I'm in charge.' He was later apparently questioned by police, but no action was taken.

After completing *The Fan*, De Niro has hinted that he might like to direct again. Chazz Palminteri has a project in mind which they might do together following the success of *A Bronx Tale*. However, De Niro has been more immediately linked with a film tentatively titled *The Brothers Mitchell*. The film is based on the true story of two brothers who set up a porn empire in the United States before one killed the other. If De Niro does direct he seems unlikely to act as well. There is also the possibility that De Niro would direct and star in a $60 million version of *Moby Dick*. He is also to star with Sylvester Stallone in the police drama *Copland*.

The Fan started shooting on 21 October 1995, only the day before De Niro had become a father again in the most unconventional of circumstances. When they were together he and Toukie Smith had wanted nothing more than to have a child of their own. They did try to adopt a baby whose mother had died of AIDS after Smith miscarried their child. After that miscarriage both De Niro and Smith decided that she could not conceive children. But now, three years after they had ended their relationship, they became the parents of twin boys. The children were born through a test-tube surrogate mother. De Niro's sperm was used to fertilise one of Smith's eggs which was then implanted in the womb of the unnamed surrogate mother. The two healthy children were born on 20 October, but news of their birth did not emerge for a fortnight. The fact that they were now parents did not mean that Smith and De Niro would be getting back together again.

'The children were conceived with the assistance of modern fertility techniques and were carried to term and delivered by a surrogate,' said De Niro's spokesman, Stan Rosenfeld. 'De Niro and Smith will continue with their separate personal and professional lives. They look forward to sharing the parenting of the children.'

De Niro found himself at the centre of a row over his new babies. At a time when Hollywood was under attack for eroding family values, his decision seemed to fly in the face of conventional wisdom. He was heavily criticised for undermining the sanctity of the family by having children with a woman with whom he did not even intend to continue a relationship. It is worth remembering that his ex-wife Diahnne Abbott pointed out that he was a wonderful father to his children. However, just as he had done with his son Raphael when he left his wife, he was condemning two children to grow up as he had, without a father on hand. The experience may have coloured his perception of family life. Presumably he believes that his children can grow up as self-determinedly as he did if he is not around all the time.

The criticism that he faced over the birth of his twins is in keeping with the image De Niro has fashioned for himself. He has constantly cast himself as a Hollywood outsider. He is the man who works outside the system. He is the blue-collar superstar who lives life on his own terms and according to his own rules. As with most things in Hollywood there is an element of artifice in this. No one can be as moody as De Niro would have us believe he is – no one would want to work with him otherwise –

and much of what we see of him exists only as an image on the screen. Hollywood, however, is prepared to indulge him as it will indulge anyone provided they can deliver the goods. With De Niro the goods more often come in critical acclaim and artistic respect for a studio than money in the bank. But Hollywood is prepared to live with this, especially if the talent involved is on a hot streak, as De Niro was once again perceived to be with *Casino* and *Heat* making serious money at the box-office and with other major projects in the pipeline.

That is why De Niro and fellow 'outsider' Al Pacino walked onto the stage at last year's Oscar ceremony to present the award for Best Picture. Despite his early ambivalence about the Oscars, De Niro has subsequently shown he can play the Hollywood game and Hollywood is prepared to embrace him for it. So the man who was too shy to turn up for his own Oscar nominations walks out onto the stage carrying the most important envelope in the film business. Hollywood had bestowed its benediction and De Niro is now old enough and savvy enough to accept it.

'You have to be consistent and just keep going,' he said once of his career choices. 'One movie might do well, it might be received well with a lot of people seeing it, another might be received well but not do so well in terms of many people seeing it. The important thing is the process. You do the movies because you like them and you feel they're important and you want to be part of them.

'I have been fortunate enough to have been part of the whole thing and to be paid well. I have nothing to complain about.'

Epilogue

THE WITCH IS DEAD. Dorothy and her friends had killed the Wicked Witch of the West and were on their way back to the Emerald City to confront the Great and Powerful Oz. Surely now he would make good on his promise to give them their hearts' desire.

Back in the Emerald City they entered the castle of the Great and Powerful Oz. As always they were scared, but they had the witch's broomstick to prove they had succeeded. Great columns of orange flame spewed out of the main hall and plumes of thick green smoke filled the air. Through all this the massive green head of the Great and Powerful Oz could be faintly seen.

'Can I believe my eyes,' the voice boomed through the great hall. 'Why have you come back?' asked the autocratic ruler of Emerald City.

As they stood in the entrance, Scarecrow, Lion, Dorothy, Tin Man and even little Toto were quaking with fear. Dorothy, trembling in her enchanted ruby slippers, screwed up her courage and stepped forward. In a piping voice she announced that they had indeed killed the Wicked Witch as Oz had demanded. She now wanted to go home and her friends wanted the heart, the brain and the courage they had each been promised. Dorothy held the broomstick tightly. Its bristles had been burned off when the witch threatened Scarecrow. Nonetheless she thrust it forward like a talisman to ward off whatever retribution the Great Oz might deal out.

'Not so fast, not so fast,' roared Oz. 'I have to give the matter a little thought. Go away and come back tomorrow.'

This was too much even for Dorothy.

'I want to go home now,' she said, her voice full of anger and disappointment. Tin Man moved quickly to her shoulder, followed by Lion and Scarecrow. Emboldened by Dorothy's presumption, they too made noises of discontent.

'Do not arouse the wrath of the Great and Powerful Oz,' the voice roared again. 'I said come back tomorrow.'

As his voice echoed around the chamber, the four friends stepped back quickly, their courage momentarily deserting them. Toto weaved in and out of their legs looking for somewhere to hide. As he did so something caught the little dog's eye and he trotted across the floor to an emerald-green curtain concealing an alcove which looked a likely hiding place. Dorothy and her friends had not noticed where Toto had gone, but they stood their ground.

'Do you presume to criticize the Great Oz?' the voice came again. This time, though, it was accompanied by much rustling of the curtain.

As the Great Oz spoke, Toto ran from behind the curtain. The fabric was caught in the buckle of the dog's collar and as he trotted out the curtain was drawn open in its wake. There, behind the curtain, was an old man pulling levers, turning flywheels, and speaking into a microphone suspended from the ceiling to amplify his voice throughout the chamber. Dorothy and her friends saw him, and he knew instantly that he had been seen.

'The Great Oz has spoken,' he insisted but, as he had forgotten to speak into the microphone, his voice was much more plaintive now. He drew the drapes back quickly.

'Pay no attention to that man behind the curtain,' he said despairingly. 'The Great Oz has spoken.'

But it was too late. Dorothy, her friends, and everyone in the cinema had seen. The Great and Powerful Oz was human after all. Despite the sound and fury the man behind the curtain was just that – a man. A man capable of remarkable things in his time, but for all that only a man, with all the decency, faults and foibles of the rest of us.

Robert De Niro on Screen

The Wedding Party (1963/1968)

Director, producer, writer and editor Cynthia Munroe, Wilford Leach, and Brian De Palma; photography Peter Powell; music John Henry McDowell. Running time 92 mins.

Cast: Jill Clayburgh, Charles Pfluger, Valda Satterfield, Raymond McNally, Jennifer Salt, John Braswell, Judy Thomas, Robert De Niro, William Finley.

Made in 1963 but unable to secure a release for almost six years, this marital comedy of manners is De Niro's first significant film role. His name is spelled 'Robert De Nero' in the credits. Jill Clayburgh also makes her debut.

Trois Chambres à Manhattan (1965)

Director Marcel Carné; writers Jacques Sigurd and Marcel Carné; photography Eugen Schuftan. Running time 110 mins.

Cast: Anne Girardot, Roland Lesaffre, Maurice Ronet, Gabrielle Ferzetti.

Two lonely people are thrown together on the streets of New York. Robert De Niro has a walk-on appearance.

Greetings (1968)

Director Brian De Palma; producer Charles Hirsch; screenplay Brian De Palma and Charles Hirsch; photography Robert Fiore; editor Brian De Palma; music Children of Paradise. Running time 88 mins.

Cast: Jonathan Warden, Robert De Niro (Jon Rubin), Gerrit Graham, Richard Hamilton, Megan McCormick, Allen Garfield.

Improvisational satirical comedy about the late-sixties counter-culture. Originally rated 'X', later reduced to 'R'. Also known as *The Three Musketeers*.

Sam's Song (1969)

Director Jordan Leondopoulas; producer Christopher C. Dewey; screenplay Jordan Leondopoulas; photography Alex Phillips Jnr; editor Arline Garson; music Gershon Kingsley.

Cast: Robert De Niro (Sam), Jered Mickey, Jennifer Warren, Martin Kelley, Viva.

Low-budget effort about film editor's weekend with friends on Long Island. See also *The Swap* in 1979.

Bloody Mama (1970)

Director and producer Roger Corman; co-producers Samuel Z. Arkoff and James H. Nicholson; screenplay Robert Thon from a story by Thom and Don Peters; photography John Alonzo; editor Eve Newman; music Don Randi. Running time 92 mins.

Cast: Shelley Winters, Pat Hingle, Don Stroud, Diane Varsi, Bruce Dern, Clint Kimbrough, Robert Walden, Robert De Niro (Lloyd Barker), Alex Nicol, Pamela Dunlap, Scatman Crothers, Lisa Jill.

De Niro made his first big impression as 'Ma' Barker's psychotic son in this Roger Corman 'B' picture.

Robert De Niro: Untouchable

Hi, Mom! (1970)

Director Brian De Palma; producer Charles Hirsch; screenplay Brian De Palma from a story by De Palma and Hirsch, photography Robert Elfstrom; editor Paul Hirsch; music Eric Kaz. Running time 87 mins.

Cast: Robert De Niro (Jon Rubin), Allen Garfield, Lara Parker, Jennifer Salt, Gerrit Graham, Charles Durning.

Satirical sequel to *Greetings*. De Niro's Jon Rubin is now making blue movies and bombing buildings. Also known as *Confessions of a Peeping John* and *Blue Manhattan*.

Jennifer On My Mind (1971)

Director Noel Black; producer Bernard Schwartz; screenplay Erich Segal; photography Andy Laszlo; editor Jack Wheeler; music Stephen J. Lawrence. Running time 90 mins.

Cast: Tippy Walker, Michael Brandon, Lou Gilbert, Steve Vinovich, Peter Bonerz, Renee Taylor, Chuck McCann, Bruce Kornbluth, Barry Bostwick, Jeff Conaway, Robert De Niro (Mardigian), Erich Segal.

Robert De Niro is nineteenth in the cast list of this story of a romance between two junkies. Prophetically perhaps he is cast as a taxi driver!

Born to Win (1971)

Director Ivan Passer; producer Philip Langner; co-producers George Segal and Jerry Tokofsky; screenplay David Scott Milton; cinematographers Jack Priestly and Richard Kratina; editor Ralph Rosenbaum; music William S. Fisher. Running time 90 mins.

Cast: George Segal, Karen Black, Jay Fletcher, Hector Elizondo, Marcia Jean Kurtz, Irving Selbst, Robert De Niro (Danny), Paula Prentiss, Sylvia Sims.

De Niro is a tough policeman tracking down hairdresser Segal who commits a robbery to feed his habit. Also known as *Addict*.

The Gang That Couldn't Shoot Straight (1971)

Director James Goldstone; producers Robert Chartoff and Irwin Winkler; screenplay Waldo Salt; photography Owen Roizman; editor Edward A. Biery; music Dave Grusin. Running time 96 mins

Cast: Jerry Orbach, Leigh Taylor-Young, Jo Van Fleet, Lionel Stander, Robert De Niro (Mario), Irving Selbst, Herve Villechaize.

De Niro and Leigh Taylor-Young are the romantic leads in this film version of Jimmy Breslin's Mafia farce.

Bang the Drum Slowly (1973)

Director John Hancock; producers Maurice and Lois Rosenfield; screenplay Mark Harris from his own novel; cinematographer Richard Shore; editor Richard Marks; music Stephen Lawrence. Running time 96 mins.

Cast: Robert De Niro (Bruce Pearson), Michael Moriarty, Vincent Gardenia, Phil Foster, Anne Wedgwood.

De Niro is the simple-minded baseball catcher, dying of a terminal illness, who is befriended by star pitcher Moriarty. De Niro won the New York Critics Circle Best Supporting Actor Award.

Mean Streets (1973)

Director Martin Scorsese; producer Jonathan T. Taplin; executive producer E. Lee Perry; screenplay Martin Scorsese and Mardik Martin; photography Kent Wakeford; editor Sidney Levin. Running time 110 mins.

Cast: Harvey Keitel, Robert De Niro (Johnny Boy), David Proval, Amy Robinson, Richard Romanus, Cesare Danova.

De Niro's first collaboration with Martin Scorsese brings his breakthrough performance in this mould-breaking film about honour and redemption on the streets of Little Italy.

Robert De Niro: Untouchable

The Godfather Part II (1974)

Director and producer Francis Ford Coppola; co-producers Gray Frederickson and Fred Roos; screenplay Francis Ford Coppola and Mario Puzo; photography Gordon Willis; editors Peter Zinner, Barry Malkin, and Richard Marks; music Nino Rota with additional music by Carmine Coppola. Running time 200 mins.

Cast: Al Pacino, Robert De Niro (Vito Corleone), Diane Keaton, Robert Duvall, John Cazale, Talia Shire, Lee Strasberg, Michael V. Gazzo.

De Niro plays the young Vito Corleone, the part made famous by Marlon Brando, in this second part of Coppola's Mafia trilogy. The performance won him a Best Supporting Actor Oscar.

The Last Tycoon (1976)

Director Elia Kazan; producer Sam Spiegel; screenplay Harold Pinter based on the unfinished novel by F. Scott Fitzgerald; photography Victor Kemper; editor Richard Marks; music Maurice Jarre. Running time 122 mins.

Cast: Robert De Niro (Monroe Stahr), Tony Curtis, Robert Mitchum, Jeanne Moreau, Jack Nicholson, Donald Pleasance, Ingrid Boulting.

De Niro effectively plays tragic Hollywood wonder-boy Irving Thalberg in this 1930s period piece.

Taxi Driver (1976)

Director Martin Scorsese; producers Michael and Julia Phillips; screenplay Paul Schrader; photography Michael Chapman; editors Marcia Lucas, Tom Rolf and Melvin Shapiro; music Bernard Herrmann. Running time 114 mins.

Cast: Robert De Niro (Travis Bickle), Cybill Shepherd, Jodie Foster, Peter Boyle, Albert Brooks, Leonard Harris, Harvey Keitel, Martin Scorsese.

De Niro plays an embittered Vietnam veteran in Scorsese's riveting and disturbing story about alienation and dislocation. De Niro received his first Best Actor Oscar nomination for Travis Bickle.

1900 (1977)

Director Bernardo Bertolucci; producer Alberto Grimaldi; screenplay Franco Arcalli, Bernardo Bertolucci, Giuseppe Bertolucci; photography Vittorio Storraro; editor Franco Arcali; music Ennio Morricone. Running time 320 mins (versions also exist at 278 minutes and 245 minutes).

Cast: Robert De Niro (Alfredo Berlinghieri), Gérard Depardieu, Dominique Sanda, Burt Lancaster, Donald Sutherland, Sterling Hayden.

De Niro plays the son of a wealthy landowner as two families face upheaval in turn-of-the-century Italy. Also known as *Novecento*.

New York, New York (1977)

Director Martin Scorsese; producers Irwin Winkler and Robert Chartoff; screenplay Earl MacRauch and Mardik Martin; story Earl MacRauch; photography Laszlo Kovacs; editors Irving Lerner, Marcia Lucas, Tom Rolf, B. Lovitt, and David Ramirez; musical director Ralph Burns; new songs by John Kander and Fred Ebb; choreography Ron Field. Running time 153 mins (a 137-minute version was released in 1978 and the complete, restored 164-minute version was released in 1981).

Cast: Liza Minnelli, Robert De Niro (Jimmy Doyle), Lionel Stander, Barry Primus, Mary Kay Place, Georgie Auld.

Saxophonist De Niro and singer Minnelli bicker through the swing era in this musical drama. The film is based on the 1946 movie *The Man I Love*, which starred Ida Lupino and Robert Alda.

The Deer Hunter (1978)

Director Michael Cimino; producer Barry Spikings, Michael Deeley, Michael Cimino, John Peverall; screenplay Deric Washburn from a story by Cimino, Washburn, Louis Garfinkle, and Quinn K. Redeker; photography Vilmos Zsigmond; editor Peter Zinner; music Stanley Myers. Running time 183 mins.

Cast: Robert De Niro (Michael Vronsky), John Cazale, John Savage, Christopher Walken, Meryl Streep, George Dzundza, Chuck Aspegren.

De Niro is the linchpin of a trio of Polish-Americans who do their duty by their new home in this first epic film treatment of the Vietnam War. The role brought him another Best Actor Oscar nomination.

The Swap (1979) (see *Sam's Song*)

Director Jordan Leondopoulas; producer Christopher C. Dewey; screenplay Jordan Leondopoulas; photography Alex Phillips Jnr; editor Arline Garson; music Gershon Kingsley. Running time 90 mins.

Cast: As for *Sam's Song* with the addition of Sybil Danning, James Brown and Lisa Blount.

De Niro's fame prompted the re-release of *Sam's Song* with some additional footage turning it into a 'film within a film' as the strange death is investigated by the victim's ex-con brother. Director Leondopoulas is variously billed as John Broderick or Johnny Shade in different releases. The film is also known as *Line of Fire*.

Raging Bull (1980)

Director Martin Scorsese; producers Irwin Winkler and Robert Chartoff; screenwriters Paul Schrader and Mardik Martin based on the book by Jake La Motta with Joseph Carter and Pete Savage; photography Michael Chapman; editor Thelma Schoonmaker; music, Pietro Mascagni. Running time 128 mins.

Cast: Robert De Niro (Jake La Motta), Cathy Moriarty, Joe Pesci, Frank Vincent, Nicholas Colasanto, Theresa Saldana, Martin Scorsese.

De Niro plays charismatic middleweight prizefighter Jake La Motta in this tragic biopic. The performance won him a Best Actor Oscar. De Niro also undertook an uncredited rewrite on the screenplay with Scorsese.

True Confessions (1981)

Director Ulu Grosbard; producers Irwin Winkler and Robert Chartoff; screenplay John Gregory Dunne and Joan Didion from the novel by Dunne; photography Owen Roizman; editor Lynzee Klingman; music Georges Delerue. Running time 108 mins.

Cast: Robert De Niro (Monsignor Desmond Spellacy), Robert Duvall, Burgess Meredith, Charles Durning, Ed Flanders, Cyril Cusack.

De Niro is an ambitious and powerful priest whose brother, Duvall, is investigating a controversial murder case. Based loosely on a real-life murder case.

King of Comedy (1983)

Director Martin Scorsese; producer Arnon Milchan; screenplay Paul D. Zimmermann; photography Fred Shuler; editor Thelma Schoonmaker; music Robbie Robertson. Running time 108 mins.

Cast: Robert De Niro (Rupert Pupkin), Jerry Lewis, Diahnme Abbott, Sandra Bernhard, Shelley Hack.

De Niro's Rupert Pupkin is the ultimate talentless 'wannabe' who will go to any lengths to get his fifteen minutes of fame in this black comedy.

Falling in Love (1984)

Director Ulu Grosbard; producer Marvin Worth; screenplay Michael Christofer; photography Peter Suschitzky; editor Michael Kahn; music Dave Grusin. Running time 106 mins.

Cast: Robert De Niro (Frank Raftis), Meryl Streep, Jane Kaczmarek, George Martin, David Clennon, Dianne Wiest, Harvey Keitel.

De Niro and Streep are two prosperous married commuters who begin an ill-starred romance.

Once Upon a Time in America (1984)

Director Sergio Leone; producer Arnon Milchan; screenplay Sergio Leone, Leonardo Benvenuti, Piero De Bernardi, Enrico Medioli, Franco Arcalli, Franco Ferrini and Stuart Kaminsky; photography Tonino Delli Colli; editor Nino Baragli; music Ennio Morricone. Running time 265 mins (Italian TV version), 227 mins (European theatrical version), 143 mins (American theatrical version).

Cast: Robert De Niro (David 'Noodles' Aaronson), James Woods, Elizabeth McGovern, Treat Williams, Tuesday Weld, Burt Young, Danny Aiello.

De Niro and Woods are friends who move from small-time crime into big-time racketeering in Leone's epic homage to the American gangster film.

Brazil (1985)

Director Terry Gilliam; producer Arnon Milchan; screenplay Gilliam, Tom Stoppard and Charles McKeown; photography Roger Pratt; editor Julian Doyle; music Michael Kamen. Running time 131 mins.

Cast: Jonathan Pryce, Robert De Niro (Archibald 'Harry' Tuttle), Katherine Helmond, Ian Holm, Bob Hoskins, Michael Palin.

De Niro is a psychotic air-conditioning repairman in Terry Gilliam's surreal fantasy of a Kafkaesque future. His billing does not justify the role's cameo status.

The Mission (1986)

Director Roland Joffe; producers Fernando Ghia and David Puttnam; screenplay Robert Bolt; photography Chris Menges; editor Jim Clark; music Ennio Morricone. Running time 125 mins.

Cast: Robert De Niro (Mendoza), Jeremy Irons, Ray McAnally, Aidan Quinn, Liam Neeson, Cherie Lunghi, Ronald Pickup, Daniel Berrigan.

De Niro is a mercenary who becomes a Jesuit missionary in the Central American jungles to atone for killing his brother in a duel.

Angel Heart (1986)

Director Alan Parker; producers Alan Marshall and Elliott Kastner; screenplay Alan Parker from the novel *Falling Angel* by William Hjortsberg; photography Michael Seresin; editor Gerry Hambling; music Trevor Jones. Running time 113 mins.

Cast: Mickey Rourke, Robert De Niro (Louis Cyphre), Lisa Bonet, Charlotte Rampling.

De Niro contributes a Mephistophelean cameo as the shadowy figure who sends private eye Rourke on a mission to collect a debt.

Dear America (1987)

Director Bill Couturie; producers Bill Couturie and Thomas Bird; screenplay by Richard Dewhurst and Bill Couturie based on the book *Dear America, Letters Home from Vietnam*. Running time 87 mins.

Voice cast includes narration by Robert De Niro, Michael J. Fox, Ellen Burstyn, Kathleen Turner, Tom Berenger, Willem Dafoe, Sean Penn and many others.

De Niro is one of many star names whose voices contribute to this compelling and moving account of the Vietnam War through the newsreels and letters of those who fought there.

The Untouchables (1987)

Director Brian De Palma; producer Art Linson; screenplay David Mamet; photography Stephen H. Burum; editors Jerry Greenberg and Bill Pankow; music Ennio Morricone. Running time 119 mins.

Cast: Kevin Costner, Sean Connery, Charles Martin Smith, Andy Garcia, Robert De Niro (Al Capone), Richard Bradford.

De Niro contributes a compelling cameo as the nemesis of Kevin Costner's Elliot Ness in this epic gangster movie.

Midnight Run (1988)

Director and producer Martin Brest; executive producer William S. Gilmore; screenplay George Gallo; photography Donald Thorin; editors Billy Weber, Chris Lebenzon, and Michael Tronick; music Danny Elfman. Running time 122 mins.

Cast: Robert De Niro (Jack Walsh), Charles Grodin, Yaphet Kotto, John Ashton, Dennis Farina, Joe Pantoliano.

Bounty hunter and former cop De Niro is determined to bring bail-jumping Grodin from New York to Los Angeles, no matter who gets in his way.

Jacknife (1989)

Director David Jones; producers Robert Schaffel and Carol Baum; screenplay Stephen Metcalfe from his play *Strange Snow*; photography Brian West; editor John Bloom; music Bruce Broughton. Running time 102 mins.

Cast: Robert De Niro (Joseph 'Megs' Megessey), Ed Harris, Kathy Baker, Charles Dutton, Loudon Wainwright III.

De Niro is a veteran who has come to terms with his memories of Vietnam and is now trying to encourage Harris to do the same.

We're No Angels (1989)

Director Neil Jordan; producer Art Linson; executive producer Robert De Niro; screenplay David Mamet from the 1955 screenplay by Ranald McDougall; photography Philippe Rousselot; editors Mick Audsley and Joke Van Wijk; music George Fenton. Running time 108 mins.

Cast: Robert De Niro (Ned), Sean Penn, Demi Moore, Hoyt Axton, Bruno Kirby, Ray McAnally.

De Niro and Penn are a couple of convicts on the run who take refuge by pretending to be eminent theologians.

Awakenings (1990)

Director Penny Marshall; producers Walter F. Parkes and Lawrence Lasker; screenplay Steve Zaillian based on the book by Oliver Sacks; photography Miroslav Ondricek; editors Jerry Greenberg and Battle Davis; music by Randy Newman. Running time 121 mins.

Cast: Robert De Niro (Leonard Lowe), Robin Williams, Julie Kavner, Ruth Nelson, John Heard, Penelope Ann Miller, Dexter Gordon, Max Von Sydow.

De Niro plays a catatonic patient brought out of his living coma by

Williams's pioneering drug treatment. The role brought him his fifth Oscar nomination and his fourth in the Best Actor category.

Goodfellas (1990)

Director Martin Scorsese; producer Irwin Winkler; executive producer Barbara De Fina; screenplay Martin Scorsese and Nicholas Pileggi based on the book *Wiseguy* by Nicholas Pileggi; photography Michael Ballhaus; editor Thelma Schoonmaker. Running time 146 mins.

Cast: Robert De Niro (Jimmy 'The Gent' Conway), Ray Liotta, Joe Pesci, Lorraine Bracco, Paul Sorvino.

De Niro is the mentor for up-and-coming gangster Liotta in Scorsese's tale of three decades with the Mob.

Stanley and Iris (1990)

Director Martin Ritt; producers Arlene Sellars and Alex Winitsky; executive producer Patrick Palmer; screenplay Irving Ravetch and Harriet Frank Jnr from the novel *Union Street* by Pat Barker; photography Donald McAlpine; editor Sidney Levin; music by John Williams. Running time 102 mins.

Cast: Jane Fonda, Robert De Niro (Stanley Everett Cox), Swoosie Kurtz, Martha Plimpton, Harley Cross, Jamey Sheridan.

De Niro is an illiterate who realises his potential when the widowed Fonda teaches him to read in this blue collar romance.

Guilty by Suspicion (1991)

Director Irwin Winkler; producer Arnon Milchan; screenplay Irwin Winkler; photography Michael Ballhaus; editor Priscilla Nedd; music James Newton Howard. Running time 105 mins.

Cast: Robert De Niro (David Merrill), Annette Bening, George Wendt, Patricia Wettig, Sam Wanamaker, Martin Scorsese, Barry Primus.

De Niro is a successful movie director forced to choose between his friends and his career in this Hollywood blacklist drama.

Backdraft (1991)

Director Ron Howard; producers Richard B. Lewis, John Watson and Pen Densham; screenplay Gregory Widen; photography Mikael Salomon; editors Daniel Hanley and Michael Hill; music Hans Zimmer. Running time 135 mins.

Cast: Kurt Russell, William Baldwin, Jennifer Jason Leigh, Scott Glenn, Rebecca De Mornay, Robert De Niro (Donald Rimgale), Donald Sutherland, J.T. Walsh, Jason Gedrick.

De Niro contributes a cameo as a wounded fireman turned fire investigator in Ron Howard's drama about the Chicago Fire Department.

Cape Fear (1991)

Director Martin Scorsese; producer Barbara De Fina; executive producers Kathleen Kennedy and Frank Marshall; screenplay Wesley Strick from the original screenplay by James R. Webb; photography Freddie Francis; editor Thelma Schoonmaker; music Bernard Herrmann adapted and arranged by Elmer Bernstein. Running time 128 mins.

Cast: Robert De Niro (Max Cady), Nick Nolte, Jessica Lange, Juliette Lewis, Joe Don Baker, Robert Mitchum, Gregory Peck, Martin Balsam.

De Niro is a psychopath terrorising the family of the attorney who allowed him to go to prison by suppressing vital evidence. He received another Best Actor Academy Award nomination.

Mistress (1992)

Director Barry Primus; producers Meir Teper and Robert De Niro; screenplay Barry Primus and J.F. Lawton from a story by Primus; photography Sven Kirsten; editor Steven Weisberg; music Galt MacDermot. Running time 109 mins.

Cast: Robert Wuhl, Martin Landau, Jace Alexander, Robert De Niro (Evan M. Wright), Laurie Metcalf, Eli Wallach, Danny Aiello, Christopher Walken.

De Niro plays a money man in this Hollywood insider comedy. It is the first film produced by his TriBeCa Films.

Night and the City (1992)

Director Irwin Winkler; producers Jane Rosenthal and Irwin Winkler; screenplay Richard Price based on a script by Jo Eisenger; photography Tak Fujimoto; editor David Brenner; music James Newton Howard. Running time 104 mins.

Cast: Robert De Niro (Harry Fabian), Jessica Lange, Cliff Gorman, Alan King, Jack Warden, Eli Wallach, Barry Primus.

De Niro is hustling lawyer Harry Fabian who goes up against the local big-shot boxing promoter in a remake of a 1950 British movie directed by Jules Dassin. Richard Widmark played Fabian in the original.

Mad Dog and Glory (1993)

Director John McNaughton; producers Barbara De Fina and Martin Scorsese; co-producer Steven A. Jones; executive producer/writer Richard Price; photography Robby Müller; editors Craig McKay and Elena Maganini; music Elmer Bernstein. Running time 97 mins.

Cast: Robert De Niro (Wayne 'Mad Dog' Dobie), Uma Thurman, Bill Murray, David Caruso, Mike Starr, Tom Towles, Kathy Baker.

De Niro is a mild-mannered forensic specialist who is 'loaned' Thurman for a week after saving the life of gangster Murray.

This Boy's Life (1993)

Director Michael Caton-Jones; producer Art Linson; executive producers Peter Guber and Jon Peters; screenplay Robert Getchell from Tobias Wolff's book; photography David Watkin; editor Jim Clark; music Carter Burwell. Running time 115 mins.

Cast: Robert De Niro (Dwight Hansen), Ellen Barkin, Leonardo DiCaprio, Johan Blechman.

De Niro is a dysfunctional stepfather in this screen version of Tobias Wolff's autobiographical account of growing up in the fifties.

Robert De Niro: Untouchable

A Bronx Tale (1993)

Director Robert De Niro; producers Robert De Niro, Jane Rosenthal, Jon Kilik; screenplay Chazz Palminteri from his own play; photography Reynaldo Villalobos; editors David Ray and R. Q. Lovett; music Butch Barbella. Running time 122 mins.

Cast: Robert De Niro (Lorenzo Anello), Chazz Palminteri, Lillo Brancato, Francis Capra, Joe Pesci, Taral Hicks, Katherine Narducci.

De Niro makes his directing debut in this rites-of-passage story. A young boy has to choose between his stand-up father De Niro and local mobster Palminteri.

Mary Shelley's Frankenstein (1994)

Director Kenneth Branagh; producer Francis Ford Coppola; screenplay by Frank Darabont from the novel by Mary Shelley; photography Roger Pratt; music Patrick Doyle. Running time 123 mins.

Cast: Robert De Niro (The Creature), Kenneth Branagh, Helena Bonham Carter, Aidan Quinn, John Cleese, Thomas Hulce, Cherie Lunghi, Ian Holm, Richard Briers.

De Niro is almost unrecognisable under layers of make-up as Victor Frankenstein's creation in this lavish adaptation, the most faithful yet to the original novel.

Casino (1995)

Director Martin Scorsese; producer Barbara De Fina; screenplay Nicholas Pileggi and Martin Scorsese based on the book by Nicholas Pileggi; photography Robert Richardson; editor Thelma Schoonmaker.

Cast: Robert De Niro (Sam 'Ace' Rothstein), Sharon Stone, Joe Pesci, Don Rickles, Kevin Pollak, James Woods.

De Niro is a Mob-connected gambler undone by his own pride.

Heat (1995)

Director Michael Mann; producer Michael Mann and Art Linson; screenplay Michael Mann; photography Dante Spinotti; editor Dov Hoenig, Pasquale Buba; music Elliot Goldenthal. Running time 172 mins.

Cast: Robert De Niro (Neil McAuley), Al Pacino, Val Kilmer, Ashley Judd, Jon Voight.

De Niro plays a professional criminal hunted by his nemesis, Pacino.

Sleepers (1996)

Directed, written and produced by Barry Levinson; photography by Michael Ballhaus; editor Stu Linder.

Cast: Kevin Bacon, Billy Crudup, Robert De Niro (Father Bobby), Minnie Driver, Ron Eldard, Vittorio Gassman, Dustin Hoffman, Jason Patric, Brad Pitt, Brad Renfro.

De Niro plays another priest. This time he holds the key to the outcome of a murder case in which abused kids have taken their revenge on one of their abusers in later life.

Marvin's Room (1996)

Director Jerry Zaks; producers Scott Rudin and Jane Rosenthal; executive producer Robert De Niro; screenplay Scott McPherson; photography Piotr Sobocinski; editor Jim Clark.

Cast: Meryl Streep, Diane Keaton, Leonardo DiCaprio, Robert De Niro, Hume Cronyn, Gwen Verdon.

De Niro is a psychiatrist treating a dysfunctional family.

The Fan (1996)

Director Tony Scott; producer Wendy Finerman; screenplay Phoef Sutton; photography Darik Wolski; editor Chris Wagner.

Robert De Niro: Untouchable

Cast: Robert De Niro, Wesley Snipes, Ellen Barkin, John Leguizamo, Benicio Del Toro.

De Niro plays a baseball fan obsessed with star player Snipes.

Bibliography

Robert De Niro: The Hero Behind the Masks by Keith McKay, NEL, 1988.
The Films of Robert De Niro by Douglas Brode, Citadel Press, 1993.
Martin Scorsese: A Journey by Mary Pat Kelly, Secker & Warburg, 1991.
Scorsese on Scorsese, Faber and Faber, 1989.
Taxi Driver by Paul Schrader, Faber and Faber, 1990.
You'll Never Eat Lunch in This Town Again by Julia Phillips, Random House, 1991.
Jack's Life by Patrick McGilligan, Hutchinson, 1994.
Liza Minnelli: Born a Star by Wendy Leigh, NEL, 1993.
My Indecision is Final by Jake Eberts and Terry Illott, Faber and Faber, 1990.
David Puttnam: The Story So Far by Andrew Yule, Sphere, 1989.
The Godfather Companion by Peter Biskind, Harper Perennial, 1990.
The Oscars by Anthony Holden, Little, Brown, 1993.
Wired by Bob Woodward, Faber and Faber, 1985.
The Rolling Stone Interviews: The 1980s, St Martin's Press, 1989.

Index

Index

Index

Index

Index

BLACK C

STRANGLI

BLACK GOLD
STRANGLEHOLD

THE MYTH OF SCARCITY AND THE POLITICS OF OIL

Jerome R. Corsi, Ph.D.

Craig R. Smith, CEO, Swiss America

WND BOOKS

AN IMPRINT OF CUMBERLAND HOUSE PUBLISHING, INC.
NASHVILLE, TENNESSEE

2809367

Library of Congress Cataloging-in-Publication Data

Corsi, Jerome R.
  Black gold stranglehold : the myth of scarcity and the politics of oil / Jerome R. Corsi and Craig R. Smith.
        p.   cm.
  Includes bibliographical references and index.
  ISBN-13: 978-1-58182-489-6 (hardcover : alk. paper)
  ISBN-10: 1-58182-489-0 (hardcover : alk. paper)
  1. Petroleum industry and trade—United States. 2. Energy policy—Political aspects—United States. 3. United States—Foreign economic relations. 4. Energy consumption. 5. Petroleum products—Prices. 6. Deep-earth gas theory.
7. Petroleum—Geology I. Smith, Craig R., 1954– II. Title.
HD9565.C597 2005
338.2'7282—dc22   2005021551

Printed in the United States of America

1 2 3 4 5 6 7 8 9 10—10 09 08 07 06 05

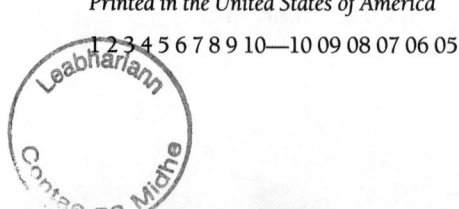

To the most important women in our lives:

Our daughters—

ALEXIS CORSI, HOLLY SMITH, and KATIE SMITH

*whose future depends upon America having
the energy to fuel us ahead*

Our mothers—

ALICE E. CORSI and JOAN L. SMITH

*who have had the patience and wisdom to listen
to our ideas and encourage us, even when
they did not necessarily agree*

Our wives—

MONICA CORSI and MELISSA SMITH

who have believed in us even when we doubted ourselves

CONTENTS

BLACK GOLD
STRANGLEHOLD

PREFACE

Any new interpretation of nature, whether a discovery or a theory, emerges first in the mind of one or a few individuals.

— THOMAS S. KUHN
The Structure of Scientific Revolutions (1962)

F YOU BELIEVE THAT oil is fossil fuel, then reading this book may well change your thinking forever. If you are convinced that human activity is warming up the earth and that disastrous climate change will occur unless we stop burning oil and gas, then what we say here will either anger you or cause you to reexamine the evidence for your opinion. If you believe the United States has no alternative but to slip backward in a world running out of oil, then we challenge you to consider our view that we in the United States have the opportunity to help give birth to a new generation of oil politics and economics that will eclipse in greatness what we have already experienced.

The genesis of this book began over fifty years ago. Jerry Corsi has never stopped thinking about a science article he read in the 1950s, that the Soviets were discovering oil deep below the surface of the earth. That thought stayed with him, along with the conviction that the fossil fuel theory for the origin of oil was probably not correct. For decades he wondered if he would ever find the time or the opportunity to explore this thought seriously.

For some twenty-five years, Craig Smith has run an investment business trading in numismatic-quality collectible gold coins. Craig and Jerry met during the 2004 presidential campaign. They were introduced by mutual friend and colleague Joseph Farah, the founder of WorldNetDaily and the principal creator of the Web site, the radio show, and the publishing company affiliated in the WorldNetDaily family of companies. Craig had worked with Joseph for many years, focusing largely on the Web site and the radio show. Jerry Corsi, the coauthor of *Unfit for Command: Swift Boat Veterans Speak Out Against John Kerry*, was considering working with Joseph on his next book.

Craig wrote the foreword to that book, *Atomic Iran: How the Terrorist Regime Bought the Bomb and American Politicians*. While working on that project, Jerry discussed with Craig his longtime fascination with the idea that oil was not fossil fuel. Craig too was fascinated. He added to the topic his many years of dealing with gold and his understanding of financial markets. For twenty-five years Craig has written a newsletter on geopolitical world and economic events. Craig also has extensive radio and television experience, having hosted both nationally syndicated coast-to-coast shows and having appeared as a guest on hundreds of radio and television interviews. Both Jerry and Craig felt they had the experience to develop this story and to bring it to the public.

Next Jerry and Craig discussed the idea with Ron Pitkin, the president and publisher of Cumberland House. Ron, who was then getting ready to publish *Atomic Iran*, liked the idea of a book on oil, so he checked with Joseph Farah to see if he bought into the concept. Joseph believed *Black Gold Stranglehold* would follow on the oil politics discussed in *Atomic Iran* and that the book could make a strong contribution on its own merit, so we proceeded to a contract to write this book. Ron and Joseph proposed adding the new book into the WND imprint at Cumberland House. Assistant publisher Stacie Bauerle agreed, and this project was born. As you will see in the following pages, much of what we learned in publishing *Atomic Iran* was also important here. Iran stands at the center of the next phase of developing world oil dynamics. Whatever happens with the radical Islamic theocracy ruling Iran will ultimately affect us all at the gas pump.

We have wondered if the book would get attention or if our natural critics would try to ignore us. We knew many of our arguments were supportive of the oil industry, but even here we were confident we would not win universal agreement from oil company executives, scientists, or engineers. Alternatives to the fossil fuel theory have been proposed for more than 150 years, yet the alternative theorists have always had to fight against conventional wisdom in order to be heard at all.

We also believed our politics would draw *ad hominem* attacks from our critics, as have our other books and political efforts. Personal criticism usually comes when critics have nothing else to say, otherwise they would focus on the ideas, arguments, and evidence directly. We do not mind the controversy; actually we will welcome it. We have written this book because we believe these arguments need to be heard. We did not receive financial support from any person or company within the energy industry as we researched and wrote this book. Yet we will not be surprised if our critics suggest differently.

Simply stated, we believe those who say we are running out of oil are wrong. We have plenty, maybe even an inexhaustible amount available deep within the earth. Nor do we believe the burning of hydrocarbon fuels is warming up the earth such that we are likely to experience catastrophic climate changes. There is solid scientific evidence and argument that back up these views. Please don't listen to those who try to discredit us, trying to discourage you from considering anything the environmentalists and conservationists don't want you to hear. We ask you to read the book and consider the evidence for yourself. Then make up your mind.

We have tried to write the science, economics, and politics in this book so that our meaning can be easily understood. More detailed, technical explanations are possible, but we believe the time for these is later, after the major ideas have been brought forth, hopefully, to a wide audience of readers. Understanding the science is important to seeing the power of the idea that oil cannot possibly be fossil fuel. The science sets the stage for exploring the economics and politics of oil. If we are not running out of oil, world politics need not be based on a scramble for a scarce resource. If global warming is a hoax, as we argue here, the politics

13

and economics of burning hydrocarbon fuels wisely takes on a new dimension, one that does not demand we simply use less oil to solve the supposed problem.

Many who read this book undoubtedly believe they are being robbed at the gas pump and by power companies over higher oil prices. They are worried that the wealth of America is being stolen by foreign interests who are extorting us for oil. Even though our view is optimistic, we agree that America today is in the grips of a stranglehold over oil. As we write this book, gasoline at five dollars or ten dollars a gallon is a real and frightening possibility on the horizon. Increasing U.S. dependence on foreign oil places us at the whim of corrupt and greedy foreign leaders. We also risk falling into the grasp of multinational oil corporations whose primary goal is to continue their ever-higher quarterly profits. Our oil money is also funding terrorists who are willing to attack us and our oil resources in order to destroy our economy and our way of life. This black gold stranglehold, we argue, threatens both our economic and our political futures. To break free we need to have a new understanding of the origin of oil, a new understanding of the true environmental consequences of burning oil, and a new understanding of the emerging alternatives to oil.

So hopefully the debate will begin with this book. With any luck, the main grounds of the debate will be substantive, especially because the substantive issues argued in these pages deserve our serious consideration. The future of oil is certain to remain center stage as a national and international concern, now as well as in the years and decades to come.

PART 1

THE MYTH OF FOSSIL FUELS

1

OIL, A FOSSIL FUEL?

The overwhelming preponderance of geological evidence compels the conclusion that crude oil and natural petroleum gas have no intrinsic connection with biological matter originating near the surface of the Earth. They are primordial materials which have been erupted from great depths.

—VLADIMIR B. PORFIR'YEV
Senior Petroleum Exploration Geologist for the USSR, 1956

FOSSIL FUEL" IS A term that has become synonymous with "oil." We all say "fossil fuel" when we mean "oil," whether we are scientists, professional writers, journalists, or average people. Oil comes from ancient plants and dinosaurs. Doesn't everybody know that? The statement that oil is fossil fuel has become an axiom. Nobody needs to explain anything when the term "fossil fuel" is used. The code does not need to be translated. Fossil fuel—that's the end of the story. Even university textbooks make the reference without further explanation.

Yet the story is anything but clear. There is a competing theory—that the origin of oil has nothing to do with rotting ancient plants or decaying dinosaurs. Don't worry that you may never have heard about the "deep, abiotic theory of oil." Not many people have heard what you are about to read—that oil may well be a natural product of the earth, that oil may still be in constant production by the earth, that oil may be readily available in abundant supplies at levels deep within the mantle of the planet.

Skeptical? Well, read on. We are about to challenge the generally unquestioned "truism" that oil is fossil fuel.

WORLD WAR II AND THE STRATEGIC IMPORTANCE OF OIL

The Allied nations had won World War II, but not without an enormous struggle. Europe was devastated, with most German cities reduced to rubble by relentless U.S. and British bombing attacks. The heaviest toll in human casualties was suffered by Russia, where some nineteen million civilians were killed. From 1937, when Japan invaded China, to 1945, when the war with Japan ended, more than sixty million people were killed worldwide, half of whom were civilians. Slaughter of this magnitude had never before been witnessed in human history.

As the war was drawing to a close, two Allied leaders, Franklin D. Roosevelt and Joseph Stalin, had the sense to call for important studies to be conducted. As we shall see, the United States learned little from the study ordered by Roosevelt. The Soviet Union, in sharp contrast, gained valuable strategic insight from the study Stalin commissioned.

Both studies focused on the strategic importance of oil, but the Soviets apparently learned much more than we did.

ROOSEVELT ORDERS THE STRATEGIC BOMBING SURVEY

On November 3, 1944, well before the end of the war, President Roosevelt issued a directive calling for a government study to determine whether or not all the bombing we had done in the war had served any purpose.[1] To many, the answer was obvious—the bombing reduced Germany and much of Europe to rubble. Why did we need a government study to prove that the bombing had contributed to our winning the war?

Yet, to Roosevelt, the question was more subtle. Granted, the bombing had destroyed some 3.6 million dwellings in Germany alone, leaving almost 7.5 million people homeless. But what precisely did dropping more than 2.7 million tons of bombs on the civilians of Europe accomplish? The bombing had helped the Allies to win the war. Still, had all the bombing been equally effective? Was it really necessary to bomb cities? This was a key question.

To some the answer was obvious. The scorched-earth model had been set in the American Civil War, when Gen. William T. Sherman burned a sixty-mile-wide path across central Georgia to the sea, beginning by incinerating Atlanta. In World War II we rained scorched earth from the sky. But the model was still total war, a concept approved by Abraham Lincoln, the Great Emancipator himself, a president revered for gentleness and sympathy even though his interior of steel called for the application of relentless violence to defeat the Confederacy. Citizens of the South were not spared the cruelty of the Union army as General Sherman pressed for victory, according to the plan Lincoln had approved.

Few after the Civil War had stopped to examine what exactly about Sherman's March to the Sea had been so effective. Was it the burning of Atlanta? Or was more accomplished by destroying the railroads? The Union army burning a bonfire of railroad ties and twisting the metal rails around trees, "Sherman's hairpins" as they were called, produced a powerful image. In that era, without the railroads, troops could not be moved or resupplied. The South came to a halt. Sherman and Lincoln had both worked for railroad companies, and so they understood what they were doing.

As World War II was drawing to a close, Roosevelt had the insight to ask the type of important questions that are rarely asked at the end of a successful war. The president's assumption was that all the bombing was not equally effective. Perhaps some of the bombing had been wasted effort or, even worse yet, counterproductive.

In 1944 these were daring questions to ask. America and Great Britain had been determined to crush the Nazis in defeat. We were incensed at the determination of the German people to start a second world war within the span of little more than two decades, angry at the bombing of

London, outraged at the inhuman genocide we were coming to see as the Holocaust. Bombing Germany into the Stone Age seemed a reasonable, almost satisfying solution to ending the war.

The report on the bombing in Europe was completed first, with the final report published on September 30, 1945, only one month after the atomic bomb attacks on Japan.

The answers Roosevelt's successor received were surprising. One of our most important targets was to knock out the German Luftwaffe, the goal being to achieve air supremacy over Europe.

The aerial bombing attack on the Nazi aircraft industry had begun in the summer of 1943. In the autumn of 1944 the tactics changed. The heavy losses suffered over Schweinfurt caused the U.S. Army Air Force to revise tactics away from daylight bombing accomplished by heavily armed but unescorted bombers flying in well-designed, tight formations. When the P-51 Mustang fighter became available in December 1943, bombing missions were redesigned to stay within range of the long-distance fighter escorts. Having fighter planes accompany the bombers reduced bomber losses substantially. The bombing attack on the German airplane industry culminated in the last week of February 1944, when 3,636 tons of bombs were dropped on airframe plants. In that week and the days following, every known aircraft factory in Germany was hit.

Still, the Nazis continued to produce planes. Surprisingly, in 1944 they accepted a total of 39,807 aircraft of all kinds, when the number accepted in 1942 before the bombing attacks began had only been 15,596. German aircraft production had actually increased despite the massive bombing of aircraft plants. Why? The bombing destroyed the buildings, but the machines "showed remarkable durability." The Germans reorganized the management of the aircraft plants and subdivided production into many small units that were immune to massive bombing raids.

As the aircraft manufacturing plants were being destroyed, the Germans adapted, learning how to recover the machinery and disperse the manufacturing. The result was clear—bombing the plants had not slowed down the Nazis' ability to make new airplanes.

The air attack on ball-bearing plants showed the same results. We focused attacks on these facilities slow down production of machinery that required ball bearings to move. Even heavy artillery pieces were generally built with wheels, so they could be moved around. If the German ability to produce ball bearings was destroyed, then the Germans would lose the ability to manufacture all forms of war vehicles that required wheels, including tanks and troop carriers, even airplanes.

Again the story turned on the bombing raids over Schweinfurt. On October 14, 1943, a devastating and pivotal bombing raid was conducted on the ball-bearing plants in and around Schweinfurt. More than 228 bombers were viciously and effectively attacked by German fighters as soon as the B-17s flew out of the range of their fighter escorts. The USAAF lost 62 bombers, and another 138 were damaged, many beyond repair. As a result, further attacks on the Schweinfurt ball-bearing plants were suspended for four months.

During this time the Nazis appointed a ball-bearing "czar" who had unlimited authority to requisition men and materials. Again the Germans realized that the machines had been much less damaged than had been the plants. They dispersed the industry and drew upon excess ball-bearing supplies. By the autumn of 1944 the bombing raids were back to previous levels. Still, the Strategic Bombing Survey concluded, "There is no evidence that the attacks on the ball-bearing industry had any measurable effect on essential war production."[2] Despite massive bombing and heavy losses, the Germans still had all the ball bearings they needed.

Bombing civilians produced equally unexpected results. We attacked German cities with high-explosive and with incendiary bombs, the latter of which were found to be four and five times more destructive given their ability to cause secondary damage from widespread fires that burned out of control. Still, the morale of the German population proved resilient. If anything, the bombing of civilian centers actually convinced the German people that the Allies were vicious, confirming Hitler's argument that Germany's enemies needed to be defeated at all costs.

Right to the end, the mental reaction of the German people "showed surprising resistance to the terror and hardships of repeated air attack, to the destruction of their homes and belongings, and to the conditions under which they were reduced to live."[3] German morale remained high, and the German people continued to be confident in ultimate victory. As long as the physical means of production remained available, the Germans continued to work in war production, even if they were reduced to living in the streets.

Surprisingly, the study concluded, the only bombing attacks that proved truly effective were those that targeted oil. By the end of the war, the Germans could produce Messerschmitts, but they had no fuel with which to fly them. The output of aviation gasoline from synthetic plants fell from 316,000 tons per month, when the air attacks began, in 1943 to 5,000 tons in September 1944, when every major plant had been hit.

The Germans viewed the attack on oil as catastrophic. Even when the Nazis appointed an "oil czar," nothing could be done. Synthetic oil plants were complex structures that could not be easily dispersed. Without fuel, the Nazi war machine came to a grinding halt. Panzers could not move, armies could not redeploy efficiently, airplanes could not get off the ground. Without oil, the *Wehrmacht* could not make war.

Of all the types of attacks analyzed by the Strategic Bombing Survey, including attacks on railroads and transportation centers, the attacks on the German oil industry proved to be the most effective. We might well have been better advised to have avoided attacking cities altogether, focusing virtually all our energy on bombing out the Nazi oil industry as our top priority. Bombing the cities only resulted in making the German people angry and more determined to continue fighting. Bombing the war-manufacturing industry scored no knockout blow. Yet, in sharp contrast, bombing oil-production facilities brought the Nazi army to a halt. Oil was the lifeblood the *Wehrmacht* needed to keep fighting.

Yet the U.S. military gained little insight from this study. Even as the Strategic Bombing Survey was completing its study of the bombing in Europe, President Harry S. Truman made the decision to drop atomic bombs on Hiroshima and Nagasaki. The trauma of losing two major cities, each with one bomb dropped from a solitary airplane, was enough to cause the Japanese emperor call off the suicidal defense of the homeland planned by the Japanese military.

The atomic bomb attacks on Japan were not the first time the Allies had killed massive numbers of civilians by bombing. The fire-bombing of Dresden and Tokyo was clear proof that the Allied air commands had mastered the techniques required to create a fire storm that could be relied upon to incinerate virtually all the residents of a city, including those who foolishly thought they could save themselves by jumping into rivers or fountains. With the atomic bomb, the order of magnitude was different. One bomb was dropped and one city was destroyed in an instant, a flash of light, and a mushroom cloud the only evidence an attack had occurred.

We brought Germany to her knees by depriving the Nazis of oil, not by bombing its cities. Yet the images of the atomic bomb attacks on Japan were too powerful for the mind to comprehend. Hiroshima and Nagasaki drowned out the core message of the Strategic Bombing Study. Instead, America learned Sherman's lesson all over again, that attacking civilians could end a war. The Japanese had shown in the island warfare of Iwo Jima and Okinawa that they were willing to fight from caves, with or without oil. The militarism of Japan was only blinded in the flash of the atomic bombs that destroyed Hiroshima and Nagasaki.

When the United States waged war in Vietnam, we bombed forests against an enemy that used no oil to move troops into battle. The Vietcong fought on pockets of rice, and the Ho Chi Minh Trail was more a footpath than an autobahn. Still, we bombed with the predictable result that we hardened the people of North Vietnam to resist us, convincing them that the communists were right in portraying us as inhumane imperialists, not a democracy fighting for their freedom. The light of the atomic flash had also blinded our thinking. We forgot important lessons about conventional bombing that could have saved us from the type of wasteful bombing in Vietnam that helped our enemies turn the tide of American public opinion against the war.

STALIN ORDERS A STUDY OF OIL

Stalin never lost sight of oil's strategic importance.

The Ploesti refineries in Romania, together with the oil refineries in

Hungary, were responsible for supplying about a quarter of the total oil available to the Nazis in 1943. In August 1943 the Allies attacked Ploesti with a daring and costly low-level bombing raid. One year later the Soviets had occupied the Hungarian oil fields, depriving the Germans of this vital supply. Stalin understood the importance of oil. The Russians had two advantages in defeating the Nazis—the severity of the Russian winter that had defeated even Napoleon and the likelihood that the Nazis would run out of oil, especially if the Allies continued to attack Nazi oil resources with a vengeance. Once the war was over, Stalin determined that the Soviet Union would never be vulnerable because of a dependence on foreign oil. He resolved that Russia would become oil self-sufficient as part of his plans for expanding communism and Soviet domination worldwide.

As World War II was coming to a close, Stalin was encouraged by a series of surprising scientific reports regarding oil production in the Soviet Union. Soviet oil explorers had begun discovering large oil reserves thousands of meters deep below the surface of the earth, at levels far below what would be expected according to the theory that oil was a fossil fuel. Stalin was no scientist, but he seized upon the idea that oil might be readily available at deep levels below the surface of the earth, far below where oil explorers generally looked.

Beginning in 1946, Stalin organized a scientific examination into studying every aspect of petroleum, including how it is created, why reserves are formed, and how the oil can best be discovered and extracted. The scope of the project was huge, virtually a Soviet-style Manhattan Project, but one focused specifically on oil.

Ruthlessness defined Stalin's resolve. In gaining power within the Soviet Union, he killed millions through purges and banned millions more to the Gulags in Siberia from which they never returned. During World War II he was willing to take massive civilian casualties to defeat the Nazis. At the end of the war, he had no hesitation to turn on the very Allies he had needed to win that war. Even as the U.S. Manhattan Project began, Stalin took steps to steal our atomic secrets through espionage.

In the 1950s the Soviet Union was considered a poor prospect for oil discovery. Yet Stalin thought better. If the Soviet Union could obtain a strategic advantage through exploring new theories about oil's availability, what could be better? Stalin was not interested in the pure pursuit of science as much as he was interested in a military and political advantage. He had no doubt that oil was a key resource of strategic importance.

By 1951 Professor Nikolai Kudryavtsev articulated what was to become known as the Russian-Ukrainian theory of deep, abiotic petroleum origins. Essentially, the theory rejected the contention that oil was formed from the remains of ancient plant and animal life that died millions of years ago. According to Kudryavtsev, oil had nothing to do with the unproved concept of a boggy primeval forest rotting into petroleum. The Soviet scientist ridiculed the idea that an ancient primeval morass of plant and animal remains was covered by sedimentary deposits over millions of years, compressed by millions of more years of heat and pressure.

The Soviet theory advanced by Kudryavtsev and dozens of Russian scientists who followed him was that the origin of oil was "a-biotic." In other words, oil did not come from the once-alive "biotic" material of ancient plants and animals. Instead, the Soviet scientists concluded oil should be seen as a primordial material that the earth forms and exudes on a continual basis.

The Soviet theory should have shaken the world in the 1950s. Here Russian scientists were proclaiming that oil required no connection whatsoever with biological agents in order to be formed. Oil was a natural product of the earth itself, manufactured at deep levels where there were no plants or animals. Oil was then pushed upward toward the earth's surface by the intense pressures of the earth's core and the influence of the centrifugal force that the rotation of the earth exerted upon the specific gravity of oil as a fluid substance. Abundant oil could be found if only we drilled deep enough.

Why did this theory not advance beyond the Soviet Union? First, Stalin had no reason to inform his enemies, especially not the Americans or the British. Second, most of the findings of the Soviet scientists were published in Russian, and few American or British scholars of the day read Russian. Besides, we were locked into the mind-set that oil is a fossil fuel. The Russian alternative theory had to be crackpot simply because it lay so far beyond our Western conventional thinking.

Over the past fifty years Soviet scientists in a wide range of disciplines have published academic articles advancing the theory of deep, abiotic petroleum origins. Several thousands of articles were generated by physicists, chemists, and geologists, all validating and expounding the theory that oil is generated naturally by the earth on a continuous basis. Today the theory is widely accepted by Russian science, even though the theory is largely unheard of in the rest of the world.

Few of the Soviet scientific papers have ever been translated into English. Yet the Soviets took these concepts and found abundant oil deep within the earth, advancing to become one of the world's largest producers of oil. As committed communists, the Soviets had no reason to see that their ideas were equally understood outside Russia. And Stalin had no reason to worry that his scientists had any inclination to do so. Scientists outside Russia were poised to ridicule any theory that offered any alternative to their nearly universal agreement that oil was fossil fuel. Why consider anything else, especially when everybody agreed oil came from ancient forests and decaying dinosaurs?

Why have so few Americans heard the theory that oil is an abiotic product, arising from deep levels within the earth? We should not be surprised. Our mind-set has been that oil is fossil fuel. This was what we have consistently thought since the earliest days, when in 1859 Edwin L. Drake successfully drilled for oil in Titusville, Pennsylvania.

Subsequent generations of Americans have been deeply invested in the idea that we are running out of oil, that our greedy oil companies are intent on making wild profits regardless what social or economic cost they bring to bear on the environment, as they use up with abandon our scarce and dwindling supply of hydrocarbon-based fuel. Any competing idea is so threatening it has to be ridiculed, not examined, lest it might be true. How else could radical environmentalists continue their attack on the oil companies, a pillar in their view of American capitalism at its corrupt worst?

The thought that oil might be naturally produced on a regular basis, that oil itself might be a renewable resource, is very threatening to those who have invested their minds into believing oil is fossil fuel. The logical consequence of the fossil fuel theory of oil has always been that we will run out of oil. After all, there could only be a finite number of ancient forests available to rot into oil. Ancient forests, even if once plentiful, are a finite resource that by definition will become exhausted after they are fully explored and their oil harvested. The logic of the fossil fuel theory is that inevitably we will run out of oil.

Yet the bet changes instantly if oil is produced by the earth, possibly even today, on a continual basis. Is it possible we might never run out of oil? Could it be that oil is abundant, nearly an inexhaustible resource, if only we drill deep enough? These turn out to be very threatening questions to anyone who has any kind of bias against "big oil."

Oil is running out. We are nearly at the "end of oil." What fool would dare doubt this?

THE RUSSIANS FIND OIL IN THE DNIEPER-DONETSK BASIN OF THE UKRAINE

The Dnieper-Donetsk Basin is in the eastern part of Ukraine. Today Ukraine is credited with having 395 million barrels of proven oil reserves, the largest part of which is found in the Dnieper-Donetsk basin.[4] In the 1950s this area had been abandoned after extensive study as not likely to produce oil. The region's rock had been geologically examined and determined to have "no potential for petroleum production," according to a Soviet scientific analysis that reported on the region. This study is available in English in large part because the scientific team included a rare American, J. F. Kenney, a Texas oil well driller who was affiliated with the Gas Resources Corporation in Houston.[5]

Specifically, geologists found the area contained no "source rock." Under the theory that oil is fossil fuel, those searching for petroleum typically look in sedimentary rock configurations. Sedimentary rock is generally softer, more porous earth formed in soft layers as soil deposits accumulate on the earth's surface. *Source rock* is so termed because geologists logically believe that ancient forests and the fossils of ancient animals such as dinosaurs lay on the ground and became sedimentary rock over thousands and millions of years. Source rocks then are sedimentary rock that contains evidence of oil deposits. The idea is that the oil is "sourced" from these very rocks, almost as if the rocks themselves produced the oil. When geologists examine sedimentary rock configurations and fail to find source rocks, they generally declare the area to be an unlikely prospect for oil exploration. Where there are no source rocks, there are unlikely to be ancient forests that have developed into oil, so the conventional theory goes.

In the early 1990s the Dnieper-Donetsk Basin was reexplored according to the principles of the abiotic theory, looking for oil and gas at great depths within the earth. The area was known to have active, strongly circulating artesian waters. To the geologists, the presence of artesian wells suggested a deep earth structure that permitted fluids to flow up from great depths, through the metamorphic and volcanic rock far below the surface, into the sedimentary layers closer to the surface.

Metamorphic rock is sedimentary rock that has been hardened under great pressure, for example, granite, as opposed to limestone or sandstone. Volcanic rock forms as the molten outflows from volcanoes harden. Volcanic rock generally does not derive from sedimentary or metamorphic rock. According to the abiotic theory, oil arising naturally from within the earth will be trapped in "basement" structures that are capped by the hardened crystals that form the underpinning of volcanic layers. Abiotic explorers expect to drill through the crystalline basements of volcanic rock to find hydrocarbon oil and gas trapped in deep reservoirs below. If fissures exist in the volcanic or metamorphic layers, then abiotic explorers expect that oil will have flowed upward into the sedimentary layers of later geological time.

Some sixty-one wells were drilled in the northern flank of the Dnieper-Donetsk Basin in the early 1990s, of which thirty-seven proved commercially productive, resulting in a successful exploration rate of 57 percent. A series of scientific tests run on the oil discovered confirmed the deep, abiotic theory. Paleontology analyses conducted on the oil showed microfossil traces of an earlier geological era than the geological era of the rocks where the oil was found. This finding confirmed to the geologists that the oil had migrated upward from deep within the earth, picking up microfossil traces from the sedimentary rock through which the oil passed.

For example, oil found in Permian era rock deposits (251–299 million years ago) contained fossil remnants from the Devonian era (416–359 million years ago) or the Cambrian era (542–488 million years ago). This could not have happened unless the oil trapped in Permian-era rock on its upward progress toward the surface of the earth had first passed through Devonian- and Cambrian-era deposits, picking up biogenic ("fossil") debris in the process. According to the fossil-fuel theory, oil found in Permian-era source rock would be expected to contain Permian-era fossil remnants.

What the scientists were examining was "micro-photo-fossil" debris in the oil—small or "micro" amounts of biogenic material that evidences photosynthesis, or "life," as would be evident in the ancient plants and animals, all of which depended on transforming the energy of the sun into living tissue, scientifically known as the process of photosynthesis.

The oil from the Dnieper-Donetsk Basin evidenced a considerable quantity of micro-photo-fossil deposits from many different ancient plants. Still, 70–75 percent of all the ancient spore pollens found in the oil were identified as Proterozoic micro-photo-fossils, regardless of which reservoir rock, depth, or geological age the oil came from. The Proterozoic era began 2.5 billion years ago and ended 543 million years ago.

This finding strongly supported the abiotic theory, because it suggested that all the oil in the basin, regardless where the oil was found in the 1990s trapped below the surface, had passed through the most ancient sedimentary deposits in the area. The living organisms of the Proterozoic era were mostly bacteria and relatively primitive plant structures. The oxygen buildup in the atmosphere that permitted the development of more sophisticated plants and animals did not begin until the middle and end of the Proterozoic era.

The types of ancient forests and primeval animals we imagine rotting into oil are generally thought to have been formed much later than the Proterozoic era. Dinosaur fossils do not appear until the Mesozoic era, some 245 to 65 million years ago. The oil in the Dnieper-Donetsk Basin may have contained microfossils, but it was not "fossil fuel" in the sense commonly meant.

Reporting in September 2001, J. F. Kenney and his coauthors noted that of the more than fifty commercially successful oil and gas fields in the Dnieper-Donetsk Basin, two were producing oil strictly from the "crystalline basement," the area defined as below volcanic rock, well out of range of the upper sedimentary rock layers from later geological eras. Surveying all the scientific analyses conducted on the oil from the Dnieper-Donetsk Basin, the authors were strong in their conclusion: "These results, taken either individually or together, confirm the scientific conclusions that the oil and natural gas found both in the Precambrian crystalline basement and the sedimentary cover of the Northern Monoclinal Flank of the Dnieper-Donetsk Basin are of deep, and abiotic, origin."

So, according the U.S. Department of Energy's most recent reports, the Dnieper-Donetsk Basin contains Ukraine's largest proven oil reserves even though explorers looking for "fossil fuel" had long ago abandoned the area, having failed to look deep enough. Oil had been there all along. Having the correct theories in mind with which to find the oil was the key that had been missing.

2

THOMAS GOLD AND
THE DEEP HOT BIOSPHERE

The suggestion that petroleum might have arisen from some transformation of squashed fish or biological detritus is surely the silliest notion to have been entertained by substantial numbers of persons over an extended period of time.

> —FRED HOYLE, astronomer, longtime friend and
> scientific coauthor with Thomas Gold (1982)

WHERE DID THE THEORY that oil is fossil fuel come from in the first place? How critically has the theory been demonstrated and defended by modern science?

These questions are rarely asked. Yet they are legitimate questions that deserve to be rigorously examined.

MIKHAIL V. LOMONOSOV AND FOSSIL FUEL

The theory that oil is fossil fuel traces back to an eighteenth-century Russian natural scientist who, in 1745, became the first professor of chemistry at St. Petersburg's Academy of Science. Lomonosov is regarded as Russia's first scientist of world importance. He was widely educated and worked in astronomy, geophysics, geology, and mineralogy as well as chemistry. A surviving portrait of Lomonosov shows him as middle-aged

31

and cherublike in his roundness, his beardless visage framed by a fashionable wig. He is shown wearing a stylish shirt with ruffles and a formal jacket, pensively holding a quill pen in his hand as he glances into the distance over his right shoulder, as if looking for his next thought to memorialize on the writing paper at his fingertips. In addition to his scientific achievements, Lomonosov was also known as an artist, poet, and student of Russian history.

The 1757 proceedings of the Imperial Academy of Sciences in St. Petersburg attribute to Lomonosov the conclusion that oil is fossil fuel. One sentence was sufficient to express the theory: "Rock oil originates as tiny bodies of animals buried in the sediments which, under the influence of increased temperature and pressure acting during an unimaginably long period of time, transform into rock oil."[1] That is evidently how the belief that oil is fossil fuel began. At the time Lomonosov stated the premise, the argument seemed reasonable enough to be generally accepted.

Even in the eighteenth century oil was known to contain microbes of a biological nature. From this Lomonosov evidently deduced that oil had been produced by biological processes. Under some leap of imagination, he tied together fossils that are biological remnants generally found beneath the surface of the earth with oil that contains biological remnants and is also found beneath the surface of the earth. Surely oil had to come from fossils, right? How else could oil contain traces of microbiological life? Lomonosov's process of deduction seems no more sophisticated than this leap of imagination and conjecture.

Lomonosov's hypothesis had early critics. An important one was Dmitry Mendeleyev, the Russian chemist who in 1896 first arranged the sixty-three known elements into a periodic table based on atomic mass. Mendeleyev also studied the origin of petroleum, but he rejected Lomonosov's contention that oil was fossil fuel. Instead, Mendeleyev was one of the first to suggest that oil is primordial material that arises from great depths from within the earth. He suggested that oil moves upward toward the surface of the earth along structures he theorized were "deep faults" within the crust of the earth. Mendeleyev's observations anticipated the later deep, abiotic theory developed by the Soviets. Still, both

Lomonosov and Mendeleyev were making at best theoretical deductions that seemed to them to be reasonable intuitively. Neither postulated any form of proof, other than the power of their personal experiments in thought.

Still, Lomonosov's fossil-fuel theory took hold, probably because the theory made intuitive sense. Petroleum is commonly found to contain fossil spores or pollen. How did this biological material get there? These traces are often categorized as "biomarkers," as if their presence evidenced the conclusion that the oil itself had arisen from biological material. Exactly how ancient forests and dinosaurs decomposed into oil at great pressures under the earth is typically assumed rather than demonstrated or proved in any scientific manner. We are left to imagine a rotting morass that is covered by a millennium of dirt to the point where the resulting subterranean intense pressure cooks the soup. Hundreds of thousands or even millions of years later, the goop transforms into oil. The scientific literature is deficient in demonstrations that anyone actually has produced oil from decayed biological material. Yet that has been overlooked, given the theory's near universal acceptance.

Perhaps the best explanation for the theory's persistence is deceptively simple. We have all seen swamps and can easily imagine the dark-colored slime that accumulates at the bottom of swamps. Crude oil has the same black slimy quality as pond residue, so why not assume that crude oil results from pond residue? Add into the equation the usual assumption that ancient plants and animals must have stewed around and rotted on the floor of some imagined forest primeval. Did the ancient plants and animals somehow become pond residue? Oil and pond slime look and feel alike, but did rotting dinosaurs and pond slime always look the same?

We have been told since we were children that oil is fossil fuel. So why bother questioning what everybody knows to be true?

The problem is that somehow many important questions never get asked. Let's be contrarian and pose a few of the puzzling questions just for fun. How many ancient forests and decaying dinosaurs were there that actually rotted as is usually imagined? Does it matter exactly how the forests and dinosaurs died or precisely where their corpses fell? For instance, did a whole group of dinosaurs all have to die at once, or was it okay if they died one at a time and were scattered about, one here and one there? Did it take a pile of dinosaurs before they started rotting into oil? Did dinosaurs go to a particular place to die, like we hear elephants do? Or did oil only get going when the supposed great comet hit the earth and killed virtually all of the dinosaurs once and for all?

Then why weren't these ancient debris piles evenly distributed around the world? Why, for instance, did so many ancient forests and dinosaurs die and decompose into oil in what is now the Middle East as compared to Florida? Was the prehistoric Middle East really that different from prehistoric Florida or New Mexico? How about the bottom of the ocean, maybe the North Sea for an example? How did the ancient forests and decaying dinosaurs get that deep under the ocean? What happened?

Let's continue for a minute. Today we unearth plenty of dinosaur bones in Montana. Why don't we find more oil in Montana? Why do we generally not find distinct isolated fossils in coal, with individual ancient animals in complete but singular preserve, a bird here or a fish there? Why instead don't we find great groups of ancient plant and animals all on top of one another in a pile, forming a virtual panorama of fossils filling the entire coal bed?

There is a lot of oil in the Middle East, but we never hear anything about dinosaur bones being discovered in Saudi Arabia. Why not? How about in Iraq or Iran?

Detailed questions such as these are rarely posed and virtually never answered. For most of us, the fossil-fuel theory is more an impressionistic suggestion than a rigorously demonstrated and proven scientific conclusion. Some 260 years after Lomonosov made his first suggestion, we still have little more to go on than the original one sentence observation he made, namely that oil must have come from prehistoric biological debris.

In truth, the fossil-fuel theory is so vague its proponents can easily hide behind ill-defined assumptions and readily fashioned explanations. Just consider, for a moment, the convenient answers available to fossil fuel theorists. Maybe oil did not form in Montana because the subsequent sediment laid on top of those particular piles of ancient debris was not quite right. Or maybe the ancient debris left lying on the floor of ancient Montana forests was not compressed under sufficient pressure.

Maybe the ancient debris in Florida rotted before it was covered over by sediment. After all, it's pretty humid in Florida. Maybe it was equally humid in Florida during prehistoric times, a million or so years ago. Who knows? That could be the ready explanation for why the dinosaurs that died in ancient Florida rotted there before dead ancient trees had a chance to fall and cover them over. So we don't have so much oil in Florida, not because there weren't any dinosaurs in ancient Florida, but because the temperature and humidity conditions weren't right to get the dinosaur-to-oil transformation process started.

When it comes to the fossil-fuel theory, tons of ground-shifting answers are available to prop up the hypothesis. Maybe in New Mexico there isn't much oil these days because the ancient sediment that covered the ancient debris in New Mexico was not the right type of sediment. So the explanation for ancient New Mexico is a little bit different than the explanation for ancient Florida—in ancient New Mexico the temperature and humidity conditions were right, but the conditions were wrong to have the dinosaurs die in ancient swamps and be buried by ancient trees. After all, it's pretty dry in New Mexico. Maybe it was also dry in New Mexico during the Mesozoic era when dinosaurs abounded.

Argument ground-shifting of this kind commonly results from less-than-rigorous scientific thinking. What was the exact ancient debris needed to form oil? What was the right sediment that had to be deposited on top of the decaying mess, the amount of pressure needed, over how many hundreds of thousands or millions of years? In other words, what is the scientific formula for getting from ancient goop to modern oil? That's what we want to know.

When paleontologists find a pile of ancient bones, we usually have a reasonable explanation—such as the ancient animals were all trapped in the same tar pit. As an aside, we should also stop to ask where the tar pits came from in the first place that trapped the ancient animals. We could almost get into an infinite loop here, like looking from a mirror into a mirror and seeing an endless regression of mirrors reflected back and forth. Which came first, the ancient tar pits or the dinosaurs that got trapped in them? If the tar pits were first, how did they get there? Did it take hundreds of thousands of years of dinosaurs dying before there were any tar pits around to trap the dinosaurs that came along later?

Somehow, when geologists discover oil, all we get is the assertion that oil is a "fossil fuel," not a convincing, detailed proof demonstrating exactly how those particular fossils transformed into precisely that oil field. We need to see specified the exact type of sediment required to cover the ancient debris for the fossil-to-oil transformation to take place. Why don't the textbooks show the oil transformation formulas specifying in equation form the amount of pressure that must be applied over what period of time. Where do we find the exact chemical formulae under which ancient leaves and bones became hydrocarbon petroleum? Where is the laboratory experimental proof?

Or maybe we're just nuts to ask these questions. But then if the only response left to the advocates of the fossil-fuel theory is to launch (ad hominem) attacks on anyone who questions the theory, that itself should be a flashing red light signaling the theory is weak.

ENTER THOMAS GOLD

Thomas Gold was a controversial professor of astronomy who taught at Cornell University and died in 2004 at eighty-four years old. In 1998, when he was seventy-eight, he published *The Deep Hot Biosphere: The Myth of Fossil Fuels,* a book that directly challenged the conventional wisdom.[2] Gold ventured into geology to argue that the Russian-Ukrainian deep, abiotic theory on the origin of oil was right despite being ignored by Western scientists and geologists.

Gold himself was an eccentric character.[3] He was born in Vienna in 1920 and studied in Switzerland before going to England to study at Cambridge University shortly before World War II broke out. For a year Gold was held in a British internment camp, because he was suspected of being an enemy spy. When he managed to talk his way out of that predicament, Gold ended up helping develop radar for the British Admiralty. From there he landed in the United States, at Harvard. In 1959 he was recruited by Cornell University where he chaired the astronomy department and directed the Center for Radiophysics and Space Research. He had to wait until 1969 to get his doctorate, when Cambridge University finally decided to bestow upon him an honorary degree.

A photograph of Gold in his laboratory at Cornell in 1986, a year before he retired, shows him to be the reasonably normal older-professor type—balding, wearing reasonably styled large-frame eyeglasses, dressed in a suit and a tie, scowling with just the right touch of "prove it to me" toughness in the lines of his face. His laboratory apparatus is framed nicely in the background over his right shoulder.

A 1968 photograph shows Gold with more of an Orson Wells flare. Here a man with a full head of dark hair sits at a table pointing at some kind of experiment; he has fire in his eyes and his mouth looks as if he is about to tell us some strange, startling theory. He looks like an oddball genius who is about to shake us with a new revelation. Behind him, framing his head and shoulders, is a large blown-up photograph of the moon that vividly displays the craters and lines of the moon's surface. Maybe he's H. G. Wells rather than Orson Wells, but in this photograph he sure looks like he's unlocked the secret of the war of the worlds.

Throughout his career, Gold espoused scientific theories that his peers tended to reject. Many of Gold's arguments proved to be valid despite being initially rejected by a nearly universal majority of more conventional scientific thinkers.

In 1946, when he was a graduate student in astrophysics at Cambridge University, he was intrigued with a problem that had stumbled auditory physiologists for years. How did the human ear manage to distinguish so finely the subtleties of musical notes? The conventional scientific wisdom then was a nineteenth-century idea first proposed by the German physicist Hermann von Helmoltz. The accepted theory was that the inner ear functioned as a series of "strings" vibrating at different frequencies. The ear was merely thought to be the rough instrument that took in the noises; it was the brain that distinguished between the tones so that we could identify individual notes and combinations.

Gold disagreed. His work on radar convinced him that the ear as a detecting instrument had to function more finely, truly adding something to distinguish the sounds. Gold believed the ear amplified incoming noise by adding energy to the detected frequencies before the signals were transmitted to the brain. Not until the 1970s did physiologists finally conclude that the inner ear contained a series of fine hairs that did act as amplifiers, exactly as Gold had suggested years earlier.

Then, in 1955, Gold suggested, contrary to conventional wisdom, that the surface of the moon was covered by a fine rock powder. Again he was vindicated, but not until Apollo 11 touched down on the moon in 1969, and the world watched as Neil Armstrong hopped around, kicking up a fine-grain powder of rock as he moved along. Gold was one of the 110 scientists worldwide who received samples of moon soil from the Apollo 11 mission to test.

In 1967 Gold advanced the theory of pulsars by suggesting that pulsars are neutron stars that spin out radio waves as they rotate. The theory was ridiculed by other astronomers until a pulsar was discovered in the Crab Nebula, and it turned out to be a neutron star that spun out radio waves as it rotated.

Not all Gold's scientific insights have been validated. In 1948 he and two fellow graduate students published a steady-state theory of the universe that flew in the face of the currently accepted big-bang theory that the universe was created at a single instant. Gold's steady-state model assumed the universe had no beginning and no end and that matter is being constantly created within the universe as we go along. Today big-bang theorists regard Gold's steady-state model as a brilliant mistake at best. Yet that argument is far from over.

Variously described as a gadfly or maverick, Gold considered himself a "scientific heretic," and he enjoyed annoying his fellow academicians with his unconventional views. When in 1998, in retirement, he published *The Deep Hot Biosphere,* the scientific community was not surprised that Tommy Gold, as he was known to friends and colleagues, was again taking them on—this time arguing that the theory of fossil fuel was a myth masquerading as a proven scientific hypothesis. The Cornell community knew Gold as an oddball who refused to take elevators, instead preferring to surprise students and fellow teachers alike by bounding up stairs two at a time. The world knew Gold as a brilliant but unconventional thinker whose opposing views more often than not had a bad habit of proving out right.

Gold's thinking about oil began with his primary discipline, astronomy. As an astronomer, he was aware that hydrocarbons are abundant in the universe. Since the early part of the twentieth-century, spectrographs that analyze wavelengths have permitted astronomers to determine with certainty that carbon is the fourth most abundant element in the universe, right after hydrogen, helium, and oxygen. Furthermore, among planetary bodies, "Carbon is found mostly in compounds with hydrogen—hydrocarbons—which, at different temperatures and pressures, may be gaseous, liquid, or solid. Astronomical techniques have thus produced clear and indisputable evidence that hydrocarbons are major constituents of bodies great and small within our solar system (and beyond)."[4]

In other words, hydrocarbons are not "organic chemicals" resulting from life processes on earth, as is commonly assumed by proponents of the fossil-fuel theory. Rather, hydrogen is a fundamental element readily available in the universe, one that combines with carbon to form hydrocarbons whether life is present or not.

What astronomers have known about the abundance of hydrocarbons in the universe unfortunately has not passed over to geologists who all too often continue to think of hydrocarbons as forming only through the activity of life—either in building life through photosynthesis or when life dies, such as when dinosaurs rot into oil. At his core, Gold was an astronomer. His study of radar during World War II came from his appreciation that astronomers used spectrography to read the optical and radio portions of the electromagnetic spectrum as they worked to identify the chemical composition of various bodies in the sky. This led him to puzzle about the structure of the inner ear, to wonder how we transformed sound vibrations into musical tones. He comprehended that pulsars produce radio waves.

As an astronomer, Gold knew that hydrocarbons were abundant in the universe, found in countless millions of heavenly bodies where there were no ancient decaying trees or dinosaurs. From this realization, his thinking turned to oil, where he suspected the accepted theories were once again poorly thought out. Gold understood all too well that geologists were not trained as astronomers and that this blind spot could be a fatal flaw when geologists tried to understand the origin of oil.

His observations about himself confirmed that Gold thoroughly understood why he was drawn to this project. "The earth is, after all, a planet, and thus geology should be regarded first and foremost as a subset of planetary science, but that view has been slow to take hold. Because I spent a good part of my working life as an astronomer, I was made aware of the importance and reliability of these observations early on."[5] Gold's study of astronomy told him that hydrocarbons were abundant in the universe, which meant to him that the earth did not need decaying ancient trees and dinosaurs to make oil. It was that simple. If fossils weren't needed to produce hydrocarbons in outer space, then why were they needed to produce oil on earth?

Astronomers continue to confirm Gold's observations that hydrocarbons are amply available in space. In 1986 scientists had a rare chance to study the makeup of comets when Haley's Comet passed. Several probes flew close enough to obtain detailed scientific readings on the chemical composition of the comet's core. What they found was that about 80 percent of the comet's nucleus was ice; some 15 percent of the remainder was frozen carbon monoxide; the remainder was frozen carbon dioxide, methane, and ammonia.[6]

Methane is a hydrocarbon product. Were there dinosaurs in outer space? No credible scientist yet has come forward to suggest that the methane found in comets was produced as a result of decaying protoplasm. This is the light bulb that went off in astronomer Thomas Gold's mind. As an astronomer, Gold felt it was nonsense to say that decaying ancient trees or dead dinosaurs were the reason we have oil on the earth. If hydrocarbons were in the earth before the dinosaurs, then the earth did not need the dinosaurs to produce oil. That was the insight that drove Thomas Gold to elaborate his theory.

We are going to venture one full paragraph from Gold directly. Even reading the paragraph may take some effort, Gold should be given the opportunity to make the point himself:

> It is therefore clear that the occurrence of hydrocarbon molecules within the earth is in no way an anomaly. It would be surprising indeed if the earth had obtained its hydrocarbons only from a source that biology had taken from another carbon-bearing gas—carbon dioxide—which would have been collected from the atmosphere by photo-synthesizing organisms for manufacture into carbohydrates and then somehow reworked by geology into hydrocarbons. All this, while the planetary bodies bereft of surface life would have received their hydrocarbon gifts by purely abiogenic causes. (Remember that carbon is an element, and no processes on earth—other than human-built nuclear reactors—can create it. I am sure there were no big stagnant swamps on Titan or Pluto).[7]

The parenthesis was Gold's own. The more he pondered the fossil-fuel theory, the more he found himself ridiculing the theory.

What made sense to Gold was that hydrocarbons in various forms, including crude oil and methane gas, were fundamental building blocks of earth as it formed and as it has continued to develop over millions of years. Gold fully realized his agreement with the Russians, his proposal (and that of his many Russian colleagues) was that petroleum is "abiogenic and ubiquitous deep in the earth."[8] In other words, go deep enough into the mantle of the earth, and you will find abundant oil everywhere.

So, according to Gold, the reason we find more oil in the Middle East than in Florida or Montana is because the deep subsurface structure of the Middle East is more sufficiently fractured to allow the oil to flow upward, the natural direction oil should be expected to flow given its specific gravity and the centrifugal force caused by the rotation of the earth. The reason we find oil in sedimentary rock is not that sedimentary rock is the source rock enclosing the rotting ancient forests and dinosaurs, but because sedimentary rock is porous enough for the oil moving toward the surface of the earth to pool into.

But Gold didn't stop here. He turned his attention to the curious phenomenon of ocean vents that were actively pumping gases and fluids into the sea from deep within the earth. Around these vents, marine scientists were discovering a wide variety of living creatures, including simple organisms (such as bacteria) to more advanced organisms (such as tube worms). How could these organisms live in seawater so deep no light could penetrate that far?

What fascinated Gold was this: the fossil-fuel theory had assumed that all life started with photosynthesis, the process by which plants and animals transform sunlight into energy and protoplasm, the cells that make up plants and animals. Life on earth is carbon based. We take in our food the building blocks of carbon compounds that we need to oxidize if we are to build our bodies. In simplified form, the basic chemical transformation of human life is that we breathe in oxygen, the oxygen transforms the carbon food we eat (replacing carbon molecules with oxygen molecules), and we exhale carbon dioxide, in the process retaining carbohydrates.

Granted, what we are presenting here is a great simplification of a very complex process that Gold studied in detail. But the point most relevant here is that, according to Gold, the deep-water living organisms without access to light are still able to transform hydrocarbons into the energy and tissue they need to live and grow. Gold's solution was that these deep-water creatures have learned to draw the carbon they need directly from the output of deep-water vents while drawing the oxygen they need for the transformation from the deep water itself and from the soil and rock nutrients available around them.

All of this is accomplished without light or the process of photosynthesis. "Because we are surface creatures," Gold wrote, "we are inclined to regard an ecosystem based on chemical energy rather than photosynthetic energy as a strange, if wonderful, adaptation of life. We marvel at the ecology of the deep ocean vents as a deft adjustment of surface life in an inhospitable environment. The evidence argues otherwise. Microbes and even animals are thriving at these vents; growth rates are thought to exceed those in even the most productive surface realms."[9]

Thomas Gold embraced the scientific discoveries being made in the

1970s, 1980s, and 1990s that deep realms of the ocean abounded in life that had never seen the light of day. He understood that deep-water vents allow gases and fluids to escape from within the earth's mantle. These gases and fluids provide the hydrocarbon chemicals needed for this life to exist. With this realization, Gold could explain the presence of microbes in petroleum. The microbes live directly off the oil, with no need of photosynthesis to provide them nourishment. Life is not confined to the surface of the planet. The deep earth is itself a biosphere, teeming with living organisms that have never seen the light of day.

Next, Gold deduced that oil, as it travels upward from deep within the earth's mantle, is able to pick up along the way various microbes and bacteria that live in the layers of rock through which the oil passes on its way to the earth's surface. These microbes are adapted to living directly off the hydrocarbons that constitute the oil itself, without need of sunlight or photosynthesis.

So oil could contain evidence of living organisms and still be a completely abiotic substance, one not requiring any form of living agent to be produced. Drawing from the huge microbial biosphere of living organisms that existed deep below the surface, the oil could simply pick up microbes that would be assimilated into the body of the oil. Many of these microbes would continue to live off the oil. With his theory of a deep, hot biosphere, Gold recognized that he was able to "resolve the petroleum paradox," explaining how it was possible for oil to be an abiotic substance that could yet contain strong evidence of biological activity.

DRILLING IN THE SILJAN RING

In 1985 Gold had a chance to test out his theory. The Swedish Parliament granted the State Power Board authority to drill 5 kilometers (3.1 miles) into what was known as the Siljan Ring, a large meteor-impact crater area in what was essentially volcanic rock. Two years earlier Gold had given a speech to the Swedish State Power Board, urging that it drill in the Siljan Ring. Here was his perfect test of the deep, abiotic oil theory. The Siljan Ring contained no sedimentary rock of the type traditional fossil-fuel geologists believed were good prospects as source rocks containing petroleum. The meteor-impact nature of the Siljan Ring suggested to Gold that the substructure of bedrock below the surface might be sufficiently fractured to allow the upward passage of oil from deep levels within the earth's mantle.

In explaining the project to the Swedes, Gold referenced the deep borehole that the Soviets had drilled on the Kola Peninsula in the far north of European Russia, near the city of Nikel. The Kola Peninsula region resembled the Siljan Ring in that the substructure was volcanic rock with a crystalline basement that trapped oil into reservoirs deep below the surface. After drilling down 11 kilometers (6.8 miles), the Soviets hit methane gas. As Gold explained to the Swedes, "No explanation in terms of a downward seepage of surface biological material"[10] would seem possible in an area like the Kola Peninsula. Finding methane in the Kola Peninsula at 11 kilometers below the surface of the earth appeared to be strong confirmation for Gold's theory.

Drilling at the Siljan Ring began in June 1986 and continued until June 1990. Drilling stopped largely because of funding limitations. The deepest hole drilled prior to the cessation of drilling reached 6.7 kilometers (about 4 miles). Even at this depth, the results indicated that "hydrocarbon gases from methane to penthane—as well as light, largely hydrogen-saturated oils—are indeed present deep in the granitic rock."[11] The area of the Siljan Ring selected for drilling had been chosen so as to rule out the possibility that any hydrocarbon products that might be found there had simply seeped down from the thin layer of Paleozoic limestone and sandstone that surrounded the meteor crater.

Granted, the exploration failed to find enough oil or gas to make the project commercially viable. Still, that any hydrocarbon products at all had been found at a level of 4 miles instead of the deeper 6.8 miles that had been drilled at Kola was considered confirmation of the abiogenic theory of petroleum formulation. A depth of 4 miles was still deep enough within the earth to rule out that petroleum found there was the product of fossils, especially when seepage from above had been ruled out. Gold strongly proclaimed that the test had supported "my view that enormous quantities of hydrocarbons were still streaming up from a primordial source in the deep crust and upper mantle."[12]

Near the end of his life, in 2001, when the paperback version of his book was published, Thomas Gold remained as confident as ever about the validity of his theory.

> Since the first publication of this book, in December 1998, I have only become more convinced that petroleum and black coal are not fossil residues that have worked their way down from the surface of the Earth into their subterranean resting places. This widely accepted view of their biogenic origin is, in my view, mistaken, and this book proposes an alternative—namely, that Earth's massive reserves of hydrocarbons are abiogenic, that they were part of the primordial "soup" from which our planet was created, and that to this day they exist in abundance deep within our planet and continue to upwell toward the surface.[13]

Even today, Gold's work on the origin of oil has remained largely unknown to the public. Though he took pains to write in a way that would be accessible to most readers, his book still requires a reasonably sophisticated scientific background, as well as a basic understanding of a range of scientific disciplines, including astronomy, geology, biology, and chemistry. Hopefully the explanation here makes the basics of Gold's theory more easily accessible.

What is at sake is a question important enough that it makes the intellectual effort worthwhile: Is it really possible that oil is a natural product of the earth, one that is abundantly available if we can find commercially viable ways to drill several miles below the surface of the earth? Gold says, "Yes, it is possible." Moreover, he argues that the deep, abiotic theory of petroleum is the only theory that stands up to rigorous analysis.

OIL, AN ORGANIC OR AN INORGANIC CHEMICAL?

Going back some two hundred years, chemistry was divided into two branches: organic and inorganic. The original idea was that chemicals derived from plants and animals were organic in that they contained some kind of vital force, a "life force" as it were. Inorganic chemicals were those derived from minerals. Like the minerals they came from, inorganic chemicals were considered devoid of life, lacking in the "vital life force" intrinsic to organic chemicals.

Oil was always considered an organic chemical, principally because oil was found to contain living microbes. Because the study of oil was assigned to organic chemistry, the assumption that oil derived from living creatures was reinforced. If oil had been considered an inorganic chemical, no one would have taken seriously the suggestion that oil was produced by decaying ancient trees and dinosaurs.

The distinction between organic and inorganic chemistry did not last long. In 1828 German chemist Friedrich Wohler accidentally synthesized urea from inorganic starting materials.[14] Urine is obviously produced by many animals, including humans. Wohler was trying to make ammonium cyanate from silver cyanate and ammonium chloride. What he got instead was a crystalline material identical to urea, a chemical that can easily be isolated from urine. This result blew up any theory that organic chemicals could only be derived from living organisms. Wohler clearly showed that no mysterious vital force was needed to synthesize organic chemicals. And this result destroyed the traditional basis for distinguishing organic from inorganic chemicals.

Still, scientists continued to study organic chemistry as if the chemicals assigned to that branch of inquiry were somehow different. Today organic chemistry has evolved to study primarily chemicals that contain both carbon and hydrogen. Again, the bias that organic chemistry deals with living things persists. Life on earth is carbon-based. So if we extend the traditional thinking, the chemistry studying hydrocarbon chemicals should logically be organic chemistry. But even with this new classification, the hidden assumption continues that organic chemicals somehow derive from living things. So organic chemistry shifts to study hydrocarbon chemicals without announcing that the "vital force" idea behind organic chemicals has been dropped. This result spills over to the study of oil, a hydrocarbon chemical, reinforcing the idea that oil must derive from living things such as ancient plants and dinosaurs. Else why would oil be considered an organic chemical? So goes the circular reasoning.

Still, the distinction that organic chemicals derive from living material is now largely abandoned by serious chemists. Compounds produced by biological agents have repeatedly been produced from inanimate materials in laboratories under controlled conditions. Modern chemists understand that organic chemistry studies carbon-hydrogen compounds simply because that is what organic chemistry studies, not because anyone really assumes there is a vital force intrinsic to hydrocarbons.

Yet the myth persists among geologists. Subconsciously the classification of oil as an organic chemical continues to reinforce the fossil-fuel theory. Hydrocarbons are organic chemicals, so they must somehow refer back to living things, else why continue to classify them as organic? Few modern chemists take the time to sort through all the historical associations that have ended up assigning hydrocarbons to organic chemistry. For all practical purposes, modern chemists make no significant deductions from the distinction between chemicals derived from living things and chemicals derived from minerals. Still, the myth of fossil fuels continues as strong as ever.

To attack the fossil-fuel theory directly, all that was needed was for scientists to synthesize from completely inorganic chemicals a form of hydrocarbon fuel in a laboratory under controlled circumstances. This is exactly what happened in 2004, when a group of American scientists did for methane what Friedrich Wohler did for urea.

SCIENTISTS CREATE METHANE IN A LABORATORY

In 2004 a group of scientists decided to test the abiotic theory to see if they could produce a form of hydrocarbon fuel in a laboratory. Henry Scott of Indiana University in South Bend, together with colleagues from Harvard University, the Carnegie Institute in Washington, and the Livermore National Lab, designed an experiment to test Gold's theory. The research team included Dudley Herschbach, a Harvard University research professor of science and recipient of the 1986 Nobel Prize in chemistry.

The research team decided to squeeze together iron oxide, calcium carbonate, and water at temperatures as hot as 500 degrees Celsius and under pressures as high as 11 gigapascals (one gigapascal is equivalent to the pressure of 10,000 atmospheres). Simply put, the scientists were trying to see if iron oxide, calcium carbonate, and water would produce oil if they were combined under pressures and temperatures comparable to those experienced in the earth's upper mantle.[15]

To conduct the experiment, the scientists designed a "diamond anvil cell" mechanism consisting of two diamonds, each about three millimeters high (about one-eighth inch). The tips of the diamonds were pointed together, allowing them to compress a small metal plate designed to hold the sample of iron oxide, calcite (the primary component of marble), and water that the scientists wanted to force together. The scientists then conducted a variety of highly accurate spectroscopic analyses on the sample material that resulted. Herschbach explained the diamonds were ideal material for the experiment because, as one of the "hardest substances on earth, they can withstand the tremendous force, and because they're transparent, scientists can use beams of light and X-rays to identify what's inside the cell without pulling the diamonds apart."[16]

The basic idea was to smash the iron oxide, calcite, and water together at the types of temperatures and pressures we would expect to see deep within the earth and stand back to see what happened. The diamond mechanism provided a reliable way to take the end product and submit it to spectrographic analysis so its chemical content could be analyzed accurately.

No decaying ancient fossils or dinosaur parts were added to the experimental mix. The goal was not to demonstrate that alchemy was possible, but to prove that a hydrocarbon of the petroleum family could be produced via simple inorganic reactions involving no biological agents whatsoever.

Remarkably, the experiment worked. The scientists found they could easily produce methane, the principal component of natural gas, at temperatures around 500 degrees Celsius and at pressures of 7 gigapascals or greater. The result was stunning, strongly suggesting that Gold was right, that an abiotic process deep within the earth could produce oil. Inorganic chemicals (iron oxide, calcium carbonate, and water) had been combined to produce an "organic" chemical, methane. So a nonbiological source of hydrocarbons may well exist within the earth's mantle such that a hydrocarbon fuel like methane could be produced through reactions between rock and water without involving any decomposition of living organisms. Laurence Fried of Livermore Laboratory's Chemistry and Minerals Science Directorate summed up the importance of these findings as follows:

> The results demonstrate that methane readily forms by the reaction of marble with iron-rich minerals and water under conditions typical in Earth's upper mantle. This suggests there may be untapped methane reserves well below Earth's surface. Our calculations show that methane is thermodynamically stable under conditions typical of Earth's mantle, indicating that such reserves could potentially exist for millions of years.[17]

So where is the proof that dead ancient trees and dinosaur corpses can rot into hydrocarbon fuels? Here we will let Thomas Gold have the honor of taking the floor to make the final point: "Nobody has yet synthesized crude oil in the lab from a beaker of algae or ferns."[18]

SCIENTISTS DISCOVER DEEP UNDERSEA ECOSYSTEM IN ANTARCTICA

Scientists are also establishing increasing proof for Gold's contention that living organisms abound at a level so deep under the sea that photosynthesis could not possibly be the principle by which they grow.

In 2002 a large section known as the Larsen B Ice Shelf broke free of the Antarctic Peninsula. The shelf collapse revealed a huge previously hidden glacial trough, lying half a mile down on the seafloor and measuring twice the size of Texas. The conditions in the trough were dark, without sunlight, and frigid. The trough below the Larsen B Ice Shelf had been undisturbed for some ten thousand years. Here scientists from the

U.S. Antarctic Program made a startling discovery. An ecosystem thrived here below the Larsen B Ice Shelf, a virtual community of clams and what amounted to a layer of bacterial mats. Eugene Domack of Hamilton College described the finding in *Eos,* the weekly newspaper of the American Geophysical Union: "Seeing these organisms on the ocean floor—it's like lifting the carpet off the floor and finding a layer that you never knew was there."[19]

The creatures living deep below the Larsen B Ice Shelf were not using photosynthesis to produce their energy. They couldn't, since no light could penetrate either the ice when the ice shelf was in place, or the water. Even more surprising to the scientists, these extreme creatures were living off methane. The methane, which originated deep within the earth, poured onto the seafloor through underwater vents. This type of ecosystem, described as "cold-seep" or "cold-vent," was first discovered in 1984 off the shore of Monterey, California. Similar finds were subsequently made in the Gulf of Mexico and the Sea of Japan.

The scientists made the discovery by accident. Reviewing a video of the seafloor, the scientists were surprised to notice the clams and bacteria growing around mud volcanoes. The find confirmed the prediction of Thomas Gold that a "deep, hot biosphere" would be found where organisms thrived by drawing energy directly from hydrocarbon sources pouring out of the earth. Hydrocarbons, as he hypothesized, could be found pouring from the earth as a primal material. Here, at the bottom of the sea, we find "extreme creatures" capable of living on methane, without any need of light. So, too, we could expect that bacteria and other microorganisms might well blend into the oil that for them was a source of food.

We should pause here to make an observation about how scientific disciplines work. Geoscientists are just now coming to realize that scores of living organisms can thrive without ever seeing the light of day. Somehow this is a new revelation, even as we proceed into the twenty-first century. Geophysicists should have consulted biologists or medical physicians. Louis Pasteur, working in Paris in the 1860s, established the science of microbiology, proving that infectious diseases are caused by microorganisms living within the human body. Even schoolchildren today know the basics of the germ theory of disease. Since Pasteur, biologists have studied hundreds of organisms that live within our bodies and feed off our bloodstream or intestines without benefit of photosynthesis.

These insights do not cross over to geologists who observe microbes in oil and deduce that oil must have been produced by decaying living organisms, such as ancient trees and dinosaurs, living creatures that grew by photosynthesis. Clearly, a biologist looking at oil passing through the earth could have drawn on the image of blood moving through the human circulatory system, or waste material moving through our intestines, to conclude that the microbes found within the human body can live off the blood or waste material itself without ever seeing the light of day. Hydrocarbon chemicals, such as oil or methane, attract living organisms that feed off the hydrocarbons themselves. Oil passing through the earth on the way to the surface will attract these very microorganisms as well as more advanced life forms, such as clams at the deep bottom of the sea. Thomas Gold was right. A deep biosphere does exist within the earth, probably all the way to the bedrock of the earth's mantle. Microbes feed off the soil or the nutrients in the deep sea, just as they can adapt to feed upon hydrocarbons when and where hydrocarbons are available.

The fossil-fuel theory, then, is a conventional hypothesis that may not be sustainable in light of scientific evidence to the contrary. If this is the case, we must seriously consider that the deep, abiotic theory of the origin of petroleum gives us a much more solid scientific base on which to proceed. There is considerable precedent in the history of science for understanding how old scientific theories are discarded when new, more robust theories come forward as superior explanations of the phenomena being observed.

THOMAS KUHN AND THE THEORY OF SCIENTIFIC REVOLUTIONS

In 1962 physicist Thomas S. Kuhn published *The Structure of Scientific Revolutions,* a watershed book that changed forever how the question of scientific progress is conceptualized and debated.[20] Kuhn's core argument

was that science advances not by the gradual progress of studies that refine major propositions but by revolutionary theories that disrupt and ultimately supersede previous, nearly universally accepted scientific
hypotheses that are shown to be inadequate in comparison.

According to Kuhn, accepted scientific theories form a "paradigm,"
defined as a series of propositions and theories that constitute the scientific theory. Ptolemaic astronomy, for instance, was a paradigm built
around the idea that the sun and planets revolved around the Earth. The
Copernican Revolution replaced Ptolemaic astronomy with the understanding that the Earth and other planets revolve around the sun. Paradigm shifts, according to Kuhn, involve revolutions in which new,
competing theories appear first as heresies and have to fight their way to
acceptance against a legion of established opponents who have invested
careers as well as their entire adult belief systems in a view of the world
that the new theory demands they abandon.

If this discussion sounds familiar to the argument presented here, it
should. Essentially, we are arguing that the fossil-fuel theory of the origin
of petroleum is an old, established idea that needs to be supplanted by a
more adequate explanation, namely the abiotic theory as described by
Soviet scientists since the 1950s and by Thomas Gold in the United
States. As explained by Kuhn, all revolutions in scientific thinking are
painful, especially to the established adherents of the scientific hypothesis that is being supplanted.

Yet paradigm shifts become unavoidable when new theories emerge
that more adequately explain puzzles, unexpected results that established
theories cannot explain. Thus if fossil-fuel theorists simply ignore the type
of contrary scientific evidence we have presented in this chapter, they do
so at their own risk. The abiotic theory is on the table, contending for the
lead position in the debate, advancing the argument that the fossil-fuel
theory cannot explain why methane can be produced from inorganic
chemicals in a laboratory or why an active biosphere that has never seen
the light of day can thrive deep beneath the Antarctic ice, living off
methane that arises into the sea from vents that open into the mantle of
the earth.

Listen to how Kuhn explains scientific revolutions:

Political revolutions are inaugurated by a growing sense, often restricted to a segment of the political community, that existing institutions have ceased adequately to meet the problems posed by an environment that they have in part created. In much the same way, scientific revolutions are inaugurated by a growing sense, again often restricted to a narrow subdivision of the scientific community, that an existing paradigm has ceased to function adequately in the exploration of an aspect of nature to which that paradigm itself had previously led the way.[21]

This is why we have focused on the Soviet science of the 1950s and on the work of Thomas Gold. Both sensed that the fossil-fuel theory of petroleum's origin no longer fits the data. Even worse, the fossil-fuel theory is limiting in that we are looking for oil in the wrong places, underestimating the availability of oil because we are locked into a belief that oil will have to run out. We, as authors, have not spent scientific careers locked in the belief that oil comes from decaying plants and dinosaurs. Kuhn would argue that this prequalifies us to argue the opposing point of view. Thomas Gold fancied himself a contrarian, and as an astronomer, he knew hydrocarbons were found on objects in space that never saw a tyrannosaurus rex or a brontosaurus. The Soviet scientists at the end of World War II had no choice—Russian geologists had already found oil deep within the earth, and Stalin was in no mood to hear that Russia was deficient in source rock.

How long can the fossil-fuel theory last when credible scientific evidence continues to surface that hydrocarbons such as methane may have an abiotic origin? This is not simply a scientific question. As we will see, important political and economic issues will be seen very differently if and when the world begins questioning our long-held prejudice that oil comes from decaying ancient forests and dinosaurs.

In these first two chapters we have strongly suggested that now is the time for the scientific paradigm to shift—oil is not fossil fuel. There is already far too much evidence to the contrary. Next, let's take a close look at a necessary conclusion of the fossil-fuel hypothesis, namely, that sooner or later we must run out of fuel. Because we reject the fossil-fuel theory, we are also going to reject the idea that running out of oil is a scientific necessity. Traditional scientific thinking about oil has caused us severe economic and political limitations. We want in this book to move forward toward the economics and the politics of an energy policy that is founded on solid scientific grounds, not "junk science" thinking.

3

HUBBERT'S PEAK AND THE RUNNING-OUT-OF-OIL SCARE

The eleven major and one giant oil and gas fields here described have been discovered in a region which had, forty years ago, been condemned as possessing no potential for petroleum production."

—VLADILEN A. KRAYUSHKIN,
chairman of the department of petroleum
exploration, Institute of Geological Sciences,
Ukrainian Academy of Sciences, Kiev (1994)

PREDICTIONS THAT WE ARE running out of oil are not new. The scare began virtually from the first moment we found commercially useful purposes for oil.

We are going to argue here that the running-out-of-oil scare is built into the myth that oil is fossil fuel. Here is the point: there only were so many ancient forests and dinosaurs—there was no endless supply. So when we run through all the oil these decaying ancient residues produced, we're done. Only a finite number of dinosaurs ever lived; so there's a finite amount of oil. Built into the logic of the scientific paradigm that has become the "fossil-fuel theory" is the concept that sooner or later we have to run out. We don't have to find any political conspiracy or bias to explain the fear. That we will run out of oil is a necessary conclusion built into the implicit logic of the fossil-fuel theory itself.

As we will see in this chapter, the abiotic, deep-earth theory has no such necessary conclusion. If the earth produces oil as a natural substance, then very possibly the earth has never stopped producing oil. In other words, we may never run out of oil. Let's see how the competing logics play out against one another. Remember, the consequences of this debate are both economic and political. If we are inevitably running out of oil, then our industrial society is threatened—unless we develop alternative fuels or conserve oil. Alternative fuels and conservation are the only alternatives allowed if we follow the logic of the paradigm of the fossil-fuel theory to its necessary conclusions. As we shall see, the abiotic, deep-earth theory permits alternative conclusions that are not doomsdaylike in nature.

HUBBERT'S PEAK

Probably the most famous formulation of the running-out-of-oil scare is known as "Hubbert's Peak."

In 1956 M. King Hubbert, a geophysicist working in the Shell Oil research lab in Houston, Texas, published a graph that predicted U.S. oil production would peak in the 1970s. Hubbert's graph looked like a normal bell-shaped distribution curve—in other words, the graph showed almost no production of oil in the early 1900s, then the curve rises to a top point in the early 1970s, from where it drops off gradually until there is no more U.S. oil production at all by 2050. Because the graph rises on the page like a mountain, the analysis has become known as Hubbert's Peak. The name also stuck because "peak" suggests we will reach a highpoint of oil production from which we will inevitably fall back to zero, the same place were we began prior to 1859 and the historic Drake well in Pennsylvania.

Hubbert became famous for his prediction that U.S. oil production would peak in the early 1970s. The problem was that U.S. oil production did not peak as predicted. New oil finds in Alaska and in the Gulf of Mexico actually boosted oil production far beyond any limit envisioned by Hubbert's model. One would have thought that these new finds that proved Hubbert's projections were wrong would also have proved Hubbert's assumptions and theory were wrong. But that is not what happened. His supporters have revised, not abandoned, Hubbert's model. Any other conclusion was incomprehensible to the theory's adherents. Believers insist that their revisions are minor corrections and that Hubbert's basic concept is inevitable—U.S. production of oil does not have much longer to go. After all, we are eventually going to run out of fossil fuel, so what difference does it make if we find a few last oil fields. The logic still dictates that we have no option but to run out of oil sooner or later.[1]

Even though Hubbert's Peak generated false predictions, his graph continues to be accepted as biblical truth to the adherents of the fossil-fuel theory. Countless books and articles cite Hubbert's Peak as proof that the world is running out of oil. We are reminded of the type of debate that went on among medieval theologians. To win an argument, all a theologian had to prove was that the argument had been made by Aristotle— *Aristotle ipse dixit,* which translates as "Aristotle said it himself." Any theologian who could add *Aristotle ipse dixit* at the end of his argument won the debate, it was about that simple. The same is true today. To prove the world is running out of oil, all a geologist has to do is cite Hubbert's Peak. Everybody is then supposed to throw up their arms in agreement. "We must be running out of oil—just take a look at Hubbert's Peak."

That the Hubbert's Peak argument is circular seems to escape the notice of these adherents. In logic, tautologies are meaningless because they merely state in other words an assumption implicit in the original argument without actually proving anything. Looked at this way, Hubbert's Peak is a tautology, an assumption implicit in the fossil-fuel theory itself, not a separate proof. How do we know this? It's obvious. When actual data counters the predictions of Hubbert's Peak, the predictions are simply revised. Believers act as if they cannot contemplate an alternative explanation, namely, that Hubbert's Peak has to be wrong, because we are not running out of oil. New oil finds are being made worldwide, and today we have more proven oil reserves than ever before. There is no empirical evidence that these trends will ever stop. The world is not running out of oil. That is the alternative hypothesis, the one supporters of Hubbert's Peak never contemplate seriously.

The Hubbert's Peak graph for the United States has been reworked to make the same argument for the world. No matter how much oil we find around the globe, eventually explorers worldwide are bound to find all of it. Remember, there were a finite number of ancient trees and dinosaurs to start with, so there can only be a finite amount of oil worldwide. No matter what the world does, sooner or later we will have drilled for it all, and the planet will simply have no more oil. Unless we stop using oil right now, we are doomed regardless of what we do. Yes, supporters of Hubbert's Peak argue that we should slow down our use of oil. Yet oil conservation just postpones the inevitable. If we cannot find acceptable alternative fuels, then we must remain oil-dependent to the bitter end. The final act of the fossil-fuel play is built into the very statement of the fossil-fuel theory itself. If we remain oil-dependent, as we are today, then we're doomed sooner or later, regardless of how much oil we find in the last chapters. Eventually we have to face the end of this dismal drama. Eventually there will be no more oil, the theory inevitably concludes.

Looking closely, we see that Hubbert's original suggestion was basically a back-of-the-envelope drawing. The scientific literature is filled with articles by oil experts and economists who argue whether the statistical evidence agrees or disagrees with Hubbert. Even how Hubbert developed his famous graph is unclear. Consider this explanation given by Kenneth Deffeyes, who worked at Shell Oil's research lab in 1958, when Hubbert was there as the "star of the show":

> The numerical methods that Hubbert used to make his predictions are not crystal clear. Today, 44 years later, my guess is that Hubbert, like everybody else, reached his conclusion first and then searched for raw data and methods to support his conclusion. (Despite sharing roughly 100 lunches and several long discussions with Hubbert, I never had the guts to cross-examine him about the earliest roots of his prediction. Lunch discussions were more cheerful when Hubbert chose the topic.) Guessing the answer first and then searching for supporting arguments is a common scientific procedure; it is not cheating. Hubbert had a message; he packaged his message in a format that he found convincing.[2]

And this statement was by one of Hubbert's closest associates and strongest supporters. Do we need further proof that Hubbert was jamming the data into his graph with his mind set to "prove" what he already believed, namely, that the world is running out of oil. Yet, evidently, nobody at Shell Oil dared to argue with him. As Deffeyes explains: "His belligerence during technical arguments gave rise to a saying around the lab, 'That Hubbert is a bastard, but at least he's our bastard.' Luckily I got off to a good start with Hubbert; he remained a good friend for the rest of his life."[3]

Yet today, despite the arguments made to the contrary, Hubbert's Peak is almost universally accepted among petroleum geologists as a true and established law. Usually, after stating as a truism that the United States has no choice but to increase its dependency on foreign oil, professional oil experts turn to lament that in a short period of time, maybe two hundred years, we will have exhausted what nature took millions of years to create. Consider this statement in the thirty-year update of the famous 1972 MIT study entitled *Limits to Growth,* a generally pessimistic evaluation that world economies are outgrowing available resources:

> Optimists and pessimists differ by a few decades in the timing of its [oil's] production peak. But there is substantial consensus that petroleum is the most limited of the important fossil fuels, and its global production will reach a maximum sometime during the first half of this century.[4]

The 1972 *Limits to Growth* edition predicted that we would exhaust oil reserves by 2003. That didn't happen. Countless dire predictions have turned out to be wrong. Still, the fossil-fuel adherents of the Hubbert's Peak logic insist the day will come.

Simply put, oil is typically considered a nonrenewable energy source. Moreover, we are blamed for an irresponsible burning of fossil fuels. Consider this observation from an analyst who is convinced our burning of oil contributes to global warming:

> Nature took about a million years to lay down the amount of fossil fuel that we now burn worldwide every year—and in doing so it seems that

we are causing rapid change of the Earth's climate. Such a level of exploitation is clearly not in balance, not harmonious and not sustainable.[5]

Another pessimist is the noted oil exploration geologist Colin J. Campbell, founder of the international Association for the Study of Peak Oil and Gas (www.peakoil.net). Campbell notes the extraordinary advance of human beings since "the fossil-fueled heat-engine was developed into the internal combustion engine," an invention that "transformed the world during the short span of a single century."[6] Looking back over the two million years since humanlike creatures first appeared on the face of the earth, Campbell laments the short period of time we have left to enjoy a civilization based on petroleum:

> Now, as the twenty-first century dawns, we face the onset of the natural decline of the premier fuel that made all this possible, and we do so without the sight of a substitute energy that comes close to matching the utility, convenience and low cost of oil and gas. It remains to be seen if we will be the only species in over 500 million years of recorded history to evolve backward, from complexity to simplicity. Don't hold your breath, but there is little time left to adjust, as we have about as much oil left as we have used so far. Our challenge is to maintain demand in pace with or below the depletion rate. The first step in that direction is to determine what the depletion rate is, and to inform ourselves better about the resources with which nature has bestowed us.[7]

Peak oil statements fill today's literature on oil. The only real change is that believers have to constantly project further into the future the doomsday date when oil runs out. Somehow worldwide oil reserves have a nasty habit of increasing despite the projections. Still, believers continue to revere Hubbert as their prophet while they portray his peak-production graph as established science: "Just as no one will ever repeal the Second Law of Thermodynamics, almost nobody can seriously challenge M. King Hubbert, although heroic efforts have been made."[8] Citing various statistical arguments, these authors declare that worldwide oil and gas reserves will be depleted or exhausted in a profile similar to Hubbert's Peak, with a probability of 95 percent or more. Our future, according to these analysts, is dire indeed:

> Consumers of any petroleum product or of natural gas around 2035 will really be a dying species, somewhat like the entire class of reptiles and amphibians in Europe, whose species numbers are decreasing about 4 percent every year. This will also be the likely annual falloff or "average decay rate" for oil production and use through about 2008–35. Preceding this, there may well be sharper annual declines (perhaps well above 6 percent) for several years, slowing as the curve flows outward and downward. Fast decay rates will then return near the end. By around 2035, oil production will be down by around 75 percent from today's levels of about 78 million barrels/day, and through unstoppable demographic growth the per capita consumption of oil, oil products and natural gas will have fallen by about 95 percent, and at least 65 percent for gas, compared with today. Compressed into less time than from when the first Concord thundered into the stratosphere, burning up to nine liters per second of kerosene, to 2003, the wipeout of cheap oil and gas will be dramatically rapid.[9]

What choices do we have but to slow down our burning of hydrocarbon fuels and to scale back our economies and lifestyles? If the peak-production theorists are to be believed, we must now all start demanding new legislation that mandates fossil-fuel alternatives. The only solution left is government control, since consumers and markets obviously cannot solve the problem on their own. We are surely going to burn our way back to the Stone Age, unless Big Brother steps in to clamp down on the fossil-fuel abusers (namely us), aided and abetted by the big oil companies that greedily gobble up windfall profits as we proceed merrily along the inevitable spiral downward.

What happens when we get to 2035 and we still have plenty of oil? Will the peak-production theorists simply revise their models to show that we are still running out of oil, but maybe the date will be 2050? 2075? Locked into a tautology, the fossil-fuel advocates cannot be expected to break free from their preconceived notions, no matter how much evidence is produced to the contrary. As Kenneth Deffeyes, the longtime friend of M. King Hubbert, readily admitted, the peak-production theory began as a preconception in Hubbert's mind. The famous "peak graph" was devised subsequently, created by jamming the available data into an easy-to-understand math picture that could more easily be presented to the public.

Reading book after book predicting gloom and doom, we are left with the conclusion that the fossil-fuel advocates are locked into the type of thinking best characterized by Thomas Robert Malthus, whose famous 1789 essay predicted that population would ultimately outstrip our ability to produce food, resulting in a series of crises such as war and famine, which in turn would cut back populations to more manageable levels. Malthus proposed this as a mathematical law that governed and restricted population growth. Since population growth proceeds at a geometric rate (i.e., 2, 4, 8, 16, etc.) and food production proceeds at an arithmetic rate (i.e., 1, 2, 3, 4, 5, etc.) there was no way the success of population growth could not result ultimately in disaster to those very populations that had managed so successfully to grow.

Malthus is famous not because his theory was right but because human experience proved him wrong. Malthus failed to anticipate adequately the human genius for adaptation, invention, and technological advancement. Populations have grown widely beyond all the limits Malthus thought possible. Yet we have somehow avoided all the disastrous consequences he envisioned as necessary. His doom-and-gloom analysis proved alarmist in retrospect.

Still, Malthusian analysis persists today. In his famous four-volume compendium of important mathematical writings through history, James R. Newman included a selection from the treatise entitled "Mathematics of Population and Food," by Malthus. Introducing the selection, Newman observed astutely that Malthusian reasoning still had an audience: "For a time in the nineteenth century, as new lands and resources were developed, the Malthusian doctrine fell into disfavor. Today, with the world's population sharply rising and with a scarcity of new frontiers, the truth of his basic assertion is again very much in vogue."[10]

When we discuss the issues of the "greenhouse effect," global warming, and climate change in the next two chapters, we will have more reason to agree that Malthusian-like thinkers continue predicting even today that human behavior contains the seeds of our own destruction. Today's conventional mind-set regarding oil locks into the fundamental premise that, since oil is fossil fuel, we are bound to run out. There is no alternative. After all, there never was an infinite supply of rotting trees or dinosaur corpses.

The problem with this doomsday analysis is that, worldwide, we are now sitting on more proven petroleum reserves than ever before, despite the increasing rate at which we are consuming petroleum products. Moreover, new and gigantic oil fields are being discovered at an increasing rate in places the fossil-fuel theory would never have predicted as possible. Let's examine the evidence and see if it doesn't sound a lot more like the deep, abiotic theory is the more appropriate model.

KAZAKHSTAN

If you have heard about Kazakhstan and know where it is, you are probably ahead of most Americans. After the terrorist attacks of 9-11 and the U.S. war against the Taliban, most Americans know something about Afghanistan. Yet there are several countries whose names end in *stan*, about which Americans know very little. The ending *stan* essentially means "state," so Afghanistan is the state of the Afghan people. This area of the world has a tribal history that continues today to dominate the politics and social structure of the region. Kazakhstan is one of the stans that received its independence after the breakup of the Soviet Union.

Kazakhstan is a mountainous area about four times the size of Texas. It is bordered by Russia to the north, China to the east, the Caspian Sea to the west, and a bunch more stans to the South—Turkmenistan, Uzbekistan, and Kyrgystan to be specific. The country is 47 percent Muslim and 44 percent Russian Orthodox. Kazakhstan is interesting here because it turns out the country has a lot of oil, something very few outside Russia expected, at least until the country gained its independence.

In 2000 oil was discovered in what is today Kazakhstan's largest known oil reserve, at an area named Kashagan, just off the coast in the Caspian Sea. The Kashagan oil field poses many difficulties. Extracting the oil requires sophisticated offshore drilling technology. Moreover, the oil field is in very shallow waters that are difficult to reach; in winter, the area freezes and shipping requires icebreaker ships to clear the way. Moreover, the oil field contains a vast amount of poisonous hydrogen sulfide gas under extremely high pressure. The oil lies at a depth of 13,000 to 16,500 feet (4,000 to 5,000 meters, or about 3 miles deep). The good part about the Kazakhstan oil field is that it is enormous.

Current estimates are that the Kashagan oil field holds thirty-eight billion barrels of oil. This would make the find the second largest oil field in the world, nearly twice the size of all the North Sea oil fields put together.[11]

Kazakhstan's second largest oil field was discovered in 1979, at Tengiz, in the western part of the country. In 2001 additional exploration at the Tengiz site upped estimates of total reserves from an earlier estimate of eight billion barrels to a current estimate of around nineteen billion barrels.[12] Reserve estimates in 2004 were again increased to a total of twenty-five billion barrels. Add to the list a giant oil field at Karachaganak in the western part of the country, a 1979 discovery that is proving to be one of the largest natural gas reserves in the world.

Much of Kazakhstan is unexplored. Still, we have to ask the question: Should we be finding this much newly discovered oil and natural gas if the assumptions of the Hubbert Peak are correct? Kazakhstan contains some two hundred known oil and gas fields, and petroleum exploration within the republic is by no means complete. The politics of Kazakhstan are best defined by corruption; bribes to government officials have been essential to get anywhere to explore for oil or natural gas in the country. Yet what seems to be emerging is an understanding that beneath Kazakhstan is a huge reserve of oil and natural gas, a reserve that was completely unknown to Hubbert when he predicted in 1956 that oil production would peak very soon.

The Kazakhstan experience seems to indicate that our proven reserves of oil worldwide are increasing. Yet if you are locked into the fossil-fuel model, new finds of oil reserves in Kazakhstan cannot be expected to shake your view of oil. After all, no matter how much oil we continue to find, oil is still fossil fuel, and eventually we will have to find it all. Since there were only a finite number of ancient trees and dinosaurs, we must be getting close to the end. How much more could we possibly find?

If Kazakhstan is such a good prospect, maybe we should pay a little more attention to the other stans. How about Turkmenistan? Turkmenistan also borders the Caspian Sea, and everybody who looks for oil in the Caspian Sea seems to find oil. Then there's Uzbekistan, which shares the Aral Sea region with Kazakhstan. Oil prospecting around the Aral Sea has turned out to be a good deal for Kazakhstan, maybe it would work out for Uzbekistan as well.

IRAN

We all know about Iran. The clerics ruling Iran who have been exporting terror since their 1979 revolution are now pursuing a clandestine weapons program. The mullahs are dangerous, and they have a huge quantity of oil lying under their soil. Even more interesting, Iran is another country where estimates of oil and natural gas reserves continue to go up.

Since 2002 estimates of proven oil reserves in Iran have increased dramatically. In 2003 Iran's oil reserves were estimated at 90 billion barrels; in January 2004 the number went up to 125.8 billion barrels, an estimate that lasted only lasted seven months. In July 2004 new oil discoveries were announced in Iran, and the reserve estimate increased to 132 billion barrels.[13] Only Saudi Arabia, with an estimated 260 billion barrels of oil reserves, holds more than Iran.

In February 2004 a Japanese consortium announced a deal with Iran to explore the Azadegan oil field, which was first discovered in 1999. Azadegan, in southwest Iran, near the border with Iraq, is already recognized as Iran's largest oil discovery in thirty years. Current estimates are that Azadegan contains 26 billion barrels of oil reserves, but that number is probably low, given the determination of the Japanese that more oil can be found there.[14] The Azadegan oil field is considered to be geologically complex, and the likelihood is that the reserve estimate will increase, perhaps dramatically, as the Japanese more fully develop the find.

In 2004 Iran announced that oil had been discovered in the Aran and Bidgol regions in central Iran. Previously, most Iranian oil had been found in the south, especially in the Caspian Sea area. Encouraged by these finds, the National Iranian Oil Company (NIOC) declared its goal to find every oil and gas field in the country. To accomplish this goal, Iran identified fifty-one new exploratory blocks, which were then put out to international bid. Eskandar Bavarian, a senior NIOC adviser, boasted that Iran was looking forward to the discovery of 500 million barrels of recoverable oil as well as an additional 84 billion cubic meters of natural gas.[15]

Looking at Iraq, Kuwait, Iran, Kazakhstan, and Saudi Arabia, one can almost imagine the whole region sits atop an enormous underground ocean of oil and natural gas. Again, we pose the question. If the Hubbert's Peak model is correct, why do we continue to make so many new finds of enormous oil and natural gas reserves in the Middle East?

Still, not to worry. Diehard adherents of the fossil-fuel theory will not be dissuaded, no matter how many new oil and natural gas fields are found. Regardless of how high the worldwide proven oil and natural gas reserves grows, the foregone conclusion remains the same—sooner or later we will find it all and use it all and have nothing left. Then the Hubbert's Peak model will certainly prove right. No one cares if the model is wrong by fifty or a hundred years or two hundred years? What difference does it make? The result remains the same.

The one possibility that advocates of the Hubbert's Peak model cannot consider is that the supply of oil and natural gas may be so vast that we will never run out.

THE DRAMATIC INCREASE IN OFFSHORE OIL DRILLING

After the success of the North Sea oil project developed by the British, oil explorers began to turn increasing attention to offshore drilling as an attractive prospect. By the 1980s oil prospectors had begun exploring what the U.S. Department of Energy initially defined as "deep waters," namely any offshore well beyond thirteen hundred feet. Today, aided by 3-D seismic imaging that helps detect oil reserves below the ocean floor, "ultradeep" wells are being drilled under as much as ten thousand feet of water (approximately two miles down).[16]

Ultradeep drilling that begins at two miles below sea level has several important ramifications when it comes to exploring the theory of fossil fuel. First, by going through that much ocean, ultradeep offshore wells get a lot closer to the mantle of the earth without having to drill through dirt. Granted, there are a lot of technical problems to solve in running a rig that doesn't start boring into soil until the drill first gets two miles down. Yet the two miles of water permit the drilling to start at depths below those where conventional wells generally stop.

Besides, how did the ancient forests and dinosaurs get that far down and below the ocean floor? Granted, the earth has made a lot of changes since the Mesozoic era. But do the fossil-fuel theorists really have the evidence to argue that offshore areas two miles or more below the surface of today's ocean surface were ever above ground where ancient forests could grow and dinosaurs could roam?

Offshore drilling is one of the fastest growing emerging sectors in the oil industry worldwide. In the time period 1999–2003, one major industry database listed a total of 81 deepwater discoveries of oil. In 2003 alone, 57 new deepwater discoveries were announced. Now the database lists 185 deepwater discoveries slated for development between 2004 and 2008, estimated to yield forty billion barrels of oil reserves.[17] Additionally, the 2005 database listed for the first time ultradeep projects, noting that 27 ultradeep oil wells were slated for exploration between 2004 and 2008, with an anticipated yield of five billion barrels of oil.

Moreover, the deep and ultradeep oil exploration businesses are both drawing new competitors and significant new investment worldwide. In 2004 some twenty-four operators were involved in producing deepwater fields, with an expected sixteen additional competitors expected to enter the field over the next five years. Twenty years ago deepwater drilling was only getting started. Today companies are investing annually as much as $20.9 billion on floating production systems and fixed-platform facilities, with another $35 billion being scheduled for subsea structures needed for underwater drilling.

Offshore drilling is yet in its infancy, still waging war against determined environmental enemies. Until the past few years, however, an implicit assumption of all oil exploration was that oil would be found beneath ground—after all, ancient forests and dinosaurs required terra firma, so why look anywhere except below the ground we stand on today.

Yes, we are sure the argument will be attempted that some land currently submerged was above sea level in prehistoric times. Yet with some 70 percent of the world's geography currently under the water, we might reasonably assume that prospecting for oil and natural gas will bear surprisingly important results.

We might especially assume this if we think for a moment from the deep, abiotic model. If oil produced within the mantle of the earth seeps upward naturally, why not assume the deep sea throughout might have fissure substructures that would facilitate oil reserves under their crystalline basements below? Today we are finding oil at deep levels below ground. Why not develop the technology to go farther? Perhaps submerged platforms might today enable us to start looking for oil where the ocean floor is already many thousands of feet deep.

THE EUGENE ISLAND BLOCK 330 FIELD—EVIDENCE OF OIL AS A RENEWABLE RESOURCE?

In 1999 the *Wall Street Journal* published a surprising article about an offshore oil field in the Gulf of Mexico off the coast of Louisiana. The well, known as Eugene Island 330, began producing in September 1972. Production had peaked out at fifteen thousand barrels a day; by 1989 the production was down to four thousand barrels a day. Everything was proceeding as projected. Then suddenly, as noted by the *Wall Street Journal*, production jumped to thirteen thousand barrels a day. Reserves that had been pegged at sixty million barrels were now estimated at more than four hundred million barrels.

Journal staff reporter Christopher Cooper summed up the mystery:

All of which has led some scientists to a radical theory: Eugene Island is rapidly refilling itself, perhaps from some continuous source miles below the Earth's surface. That, they say, raises the tantalizing possibility that oil may not be the limited resource it is assumed to be.

"It kind of blew me away," says Jean Whelan, a geochemist and senior researcher from the Woods Hole Oceanographic Institution in Massachusetts. Connected to Woods Hole since 1973, Dr. Whelan says she considered herself a traditional thinker until she encountered the phenomenon in the Gulf of Mexico. Now, she says, "I believe there is a huge system of oil just migrating" deep underground.

Conventional wisdom says the world's supply of oil is finite, and that it was deposited in horizontal reservoirs near the surface in a process that took millions of years. Since the economies of entire countries ride on the fundamental notion that oil reserves are exhaustible, any contrary evidence "would change the way people see the game, turn the world upside down," says Daniel Yergin, a petroleum futurist and industry consultant in Cambridge, Mass. "Oil and renewable resource are not words that often appear in the same sentence."[18]

Eugene Island 330 proved to be a highly successful well, pumping more than a billion barrels of oil, despite the controversy that geologists struggled to understand. The Woods Hole Oceanographic Institution finally concluded that Eugene Island 330 did "support the possibility that reservoirs are being replenished by current migration of oil and gas from deeper depths." What was also clear was that the oil replenishing the original came from "source rock: of an earlier geological era, the Jurassic–Early Cretaceous era, not the Pleistocene era, which characterized the sedimentary rock from which the original oil flowed.[19]

The Woods Hole Oceanographic Institution concluded that oil flow from Eugene Island 330 was better characterized as "steady state" rather than a "fixed resource." The institution commented that the phenomenon of replenishing wells was being witnessed not only in the deep waters drilling in the Gulf of Mexico but also in oil-producing areas as diverse as the North Sea, the Niger Delta, the Mahakam Delta in Indonesia, the Trinidad Basin, the Taiwan Basin, and the Alaskan North Slope.

A geological report published on the Eugene Island Block 330 field confirmed that the area of the well was defined by a complex network of faults. The report also contained a highly technical explanation that oil from deep levels within the earth did move up along fault lines ("significant vertical migration," as the report termed the flow) to replenish the top reservoir as the initial oil was drilled out. These results were noted to be consistent with other scientists who had concluded that "most Gulf of Mexico oils originated 2,438 to 3,350 meters (8,000 to 11,000 feet) deeper than their reservoirs, from source beds 5 to 9 million years older than their reservoirs."[20]

Reading the technical reports, it appears that the geologists explained the phenomenon by reasoning that a second reservoir of oil lay underneath the originally discovered reservoir of oil. But analyzing the microbiological evidence in the oil, they concluded only that the lower lying oil was still fossil fuel, although of an earlier geological epoch.

What was not considered was the possibility that both reservoirs of oil had been filled, not with fossil fuel, but with abiotic fuel that came from very deep layers within the earth and moved upward along fault lines, very possibly originating from deep mantle depths within the earth. As we noted earlier, the microbiological evidence contained in the oil could simply be residue the oil accumulated on the way up, as microbes from the surrounding soil moved into the oil and continued to derive nourishment from the oil.

THE RUSSIANS HELP THE VIETNAMESE TO FIND DEEP, BASEMENT OIL OFFSHORE

In 1981 the Russians teamed up with the Vietnamese to form a joint venture oil company named Vietsovpetro (PetroVietnam). Together they headed into the South China Sea off Vietnam and drilled deep wells into the crystalline basement structure of the sea bottom.

As a result, seven production oil fields were discovered, the largest of which is known as White Tiger, which is on the continental shelf of Vietnam. The main reserve of the White Tiger oil field is "concentrated in fractured granite basement that is unique in the world oil and gas production practice."[21] Western oil companies expect to find oil only in sedimentary rock; generally Western oil companies refuse to drill unless they find source rock suggesting the sedimentary rock contains oil reserves. That the Soviets and the Vietnamese have found oil in granite structures is revolutionary, unless, of course, you think from the perspective of the deep, abiotic theory.

From the granite basement offshore Vietnam, the White Tiger oil field produces almost 280,000 barrels of oil a day. A second oil field, known as Black Lion, currently produces 80,000 barrels of oil per day, but within three years PetroVietnam expects to increase that output to 200,000 barrels per day.[22]

The White Tiger oil field is about five thousand meters (roughly 3 miles) deep, four thousand meters (about 2.5 miles) of which is fractured granite basement. How can the fossil-fuel theory explain finding oil at these deep levels in granite rock? The Russians and the Vietnamese have discovered huge reservoirs of oil offshore, where no one would have looked before. Maybe we should consider abandoning the idea that oil can only be found in sedimentary rock. How many continental shelves (or sea bottoms farther out) might possibly have deep-fracture underground structures into which abiotic oil may have seeped to form ready reservoirs? Right now, we don't know. Perhaps we should investigate it more.

THE RUSSIANS CHALLENGE SAUDI ARABIA IN OIL PRODUCTION

How do we explain this? Maybe there were a lot more Russian dinosaurs than anyone ever knew about. Or maybe the Russians are getting a lot farther by pursuing their abiotic theory than we are with our fossil-fuel mind-set.

In 2004 Russia produced approximately 9.27 million barrels a day of oil, whereas Saudi Arabia, the world's largest producer of oil, produced around 10.4 million barrels a day.[23] From March to May 2004, Russian crude oil production actually topped that of Saudi Arabia. Among non-OPEC nations, Russia is the number-two producer. And don't forget, in the 1950s few fossil-fuel theorists considered Russia to be a good prospect for oil exploration at all.

As the surge in Russian oil production was noticed worldwide, Yuri Shafranik, the head of the Russian Union of Oil and Gas Producers, stated that Russia had almost reached its maximum level of production. That statement should have reassured peak-production theorists, at least until he added the qualification that Russia's oil production could rise if world prices continued to rise.[24] How could the Western world ever be certain any estimates given by the Russians of their proven reserves would be accurate and not simply politically motivated? Who knows how much oil the Russians have actually found?

ESTIMATES OF WORLDWIDE PROVEN OIL AND NATURAL GAS RESERVES INCREASE

If we are running out of oil, why are worldwide oil reserves today at historically high levels? The truth is that we have never had as much oil and natural gas in proven reserves worldwide than we have right now.

Let's look at the facts. According to the Energy Information Administration of the U.S. Department of Energy, worldwide proven reserves of crude oil in 2005 total 1.28 trillion barrels.[25] That is an enormous supply of crude oil proven reserves. Since 1980 the trend line has been directly up. Again, look at the figures. In 1980 the worldwide proven oil reserves were 645 billion barrels; in 1985, 670 billion barrels; in 1990, 1 trillion barrels; in 1995, 999 billion barrels; and in 2005, 1.28 trillion barrels. The data represents virtually an unbroken progression of increasing numbers over the last quarter century.

The same upward trend holds true for worldwide proven reserves of natural gas. Here is how the Energy Information Administration of the U.S. Department of Energy defined the situation:

Since the mid-1970s, world natural gas reserves have generally trended upward each year. In 2004, worldwide reserve estimates increased for the ninth consecutive year. As of January 1, 2004, proved world natural gas reserves, as reported by Oil & Gas Journal, were estimated at 6,076 trillion cubic feet—575 trillion cubic feet (10 percent) more than the estimate for 2003.[26]

Despite these statistics, scholars and the U.S. government continue to generate "peak" tables under the assumption that eventually we will find all the oil and natural gas, so we will have to run out sometime, even if the date when the graph goes to zero has to keep being pushed back. Yet the truth is that we keep finding more oil and natural gas. We are now counting natural gas reserves in measures of zillions of cubic feet. Whoever thought we would be counting reserves of anything valuable in zillions? Yet this data does not shake the shared mind-set of the fossil-fuel and peak-production theorists.

At some point, we have to seriously entertain the possibility that the core assumptions are wrong, even though we have been told since we were children that we are running out of oil. Maybe the earth does have an available supply of oil and natural gas that is dramatically more abundant than we ever dared imagine. Possibly the earth may continue to manufacture oil and natural gas on a never-ending basis, such that the oil flowing to the surface never stops. Fossil-fuel theory leads logically to peak-production conclusions, and those assumptions are very hard to shake, even in the face of overwhelming data to the contrary.

Let's try to get a handle on just what having oil at over 1 trillion barrels of worldwide proven reserves means. In 2004 the world used approximately 82 million barrels of oil each day. This translates into approximately 30 billion barrels of oil used worldwide each year. Alarmists misrepresent these numbers into a scare. They reason if we are using about 3 percent of the worldwide proven oil reserves each year, then in 30 years we will run out of oil. Why is this reasoning wrong?

First, the worldwide reserve estimate is not a fixed number. Moreover, net worldwide oil reserves are increasing, even after we subtract for increasing consumption. Look at the numbers. Since 2000 worldwide proven oil reserves have increased at an annual rate of approximately 1.25 percent. Worldwide proven reserves have continued to increase after factoring in the increasing demand. Since 2000, worldwide use of oil has increased about 2.5 percent annually. So the reality is that newly found oil had to increase approximately 3.75 percent annually to show a net increase of 1.25 percent per year, after factoring in that demand had increased 2.25 percent. Otherwise, if use of oil had increased at a rate greater than our rate of finding oil, overall worldwide totals of proven oil reserves should have decreased, which they did not. So what the numbers indicate is that we are finding more oil all the time, more than enough to outstrip increasing demand. Why won't this trend continue?

Alarmists cannot get their thinking around the reality that we are finding more oil all the time. Nor do they acknowledge that their running-out-of-oil predictions have always proven wrong. The history of the Hubbert's Peak analysis is that proponents have to constantly revise their projections outward, always extending to later dates (and then later dates again) their estimates of the year in which the world will finally run out of oil. That year has never come, and we argue here that it never will.

There are so many predictions that we will run out of oil, it is hard to select the best example. In a televised speech on April 18, 1977, President Jimmy Carter addressed the nation about energy. His pessimism was characteristic: "The world now uses about 60 million barrels of oil a day and demand increases each year about 5 percent. This means that just to stay even we need the production of a new Texas every year, an Alaskan North Slope every nine months, or a new Saudi Arabia every three years. Obviously, this cannot continue."[27] He added: "World consumption of oil is still going up. If it were possible to keep it rising during the 1970s and 1980s by 5 percent a year as it has in the past, we could use up all the proven reserves of oil in the entire world by the end of the next decade."

But Carter was wrong. We did not run out of oil in the 1970s or 1980s. If anything, we have more oil then ever. Yet he could only see a grim future: "Each new inventory of world oil reserves has been more disturbing than the last. World oil production can probably keep going up for another six or eight years. But some time in the 1980s it can't go up much more. Demand will overtake production. We have no choice about that."

Despite Carter's prediction, demand did not overtake production in the 1980s. That point has still not been reached. The evidence of available proven reserves suggests we are still nowhere near the point of dire disaster Carter saw as imminent in 1977, almost thirty years ago.

We probably have not yet found the world's largest oil reserve. If Thomas Gold is right, the earth's mantle may contain more oil than we can ever imagine. What Kazakhstan and Iran prove is that the more we explore previously unexplored areas, even with traditional methods and conventional thinking, the more oil we find. What if our thinking embraced the deep, abiotic model? We might find that we can discover more oil than perhaps even our expanding worldwide markets could absorb.

Still, peak production theorists will put up a stiff fight to maintain their position, regardless of available evidence to the contrary. Oil geologist Colin Campbell, for instance, argues that world oil reserves are more like 853 million barrels, not 1.28 trillion barrels. Why the discrepancy? Campbell argues that many countries inflate their oil reserves to position themselves to get higher production quotas from the Organization of Petroleum Exporting Countries (OPEC). Moreover, Campbell maintains that about half of all known reserves have already been consumed and that future discoveries will not keep pace with demand.[28]

As Campbell sees the world, we have already burned through some 944 million barrels of oil. We only have "realistic" proven reserves of 853 million barrels, and only about 142 million barrels remain to be discovered. He expects world oil production to peak as soon as 2006, and that from there we will simply exhaust all oil available until we have no more left anywhere. Why Campbell believes we have only a limited number of barrels of oil yet to discover goes unexplained, unless we were simply to expect that conclusion as logically necessary rather than empirically proved. As his critics assert, Campbell's fault may be that he does not adequately support his claims and assertions with convincing empirical evidence.[29] How could he? We have only just begun to explore the earth for oil, at least according to the deep, abiotic theory.

The numbers tell a different story. As we noted at the start of this chapter, despite increased worldwide usage, we have never had oil and natural gas reserves so huge. The risk we face is not that we will run out of oil, but that if we maintain current exploration levels, we may end up with a worldwide glut of oil.

IS SAUDI ARABIA RUNNING OUT OF OIL?

As we noted earlier, Saudi Arabia has proven reserves of 260 million barrels and is currently the world's leading exporter of oil. Still, in 2005, Matthew Simmons, the head of a Houston-based investment bank that works heavily in the oil industry, argued that the Saudi oil industry was about to enter a sudden and irreversible decline. Why? Because the Saudis are lying about their reserves, their wells are underproducing, and pretty soon even the Saudis will be out of oil.

Simmons establishes his argument by reviewing approximately two hundred technical reports detailing the production activities at Saudi oil wells and production facilities. He concludes the Saudi oil industry is a mature industry, whose "peak production" has already been reached. Here's how Simmons summarizes his study of the technical reports:

> Collectively, these reports map out a lengthy paper trail documenting the growing severity of the problems and challenges affecting all of Saudi Arabia's major fields. Reading this paper trail in chronological order poignantly reveals how these problems have mushroomed in complexity over the last three decades. During this period, erratic production patterns not only drained an ever-growing amount of Saudi Arabia's proven, commercially recoverable oil reserves, but also, perhaps, diminished through over-production the extent to which these reservoirs can be produced without resorting to down-hole pumps.[30]

Simmons believes the day is almost over when the Saudis can pour more water into the giant Saudi oil fields in order to boost production. He believes the Saudis are lying, afraid to admit to the world that the oil in their giant fields is being pumped dry and that their exploration efforts to find more oil are failing. He publishes graphs showing that production in the eight Saudi "super-giant" oil fields is diminishing.[31] Not surprising, each of the graphs looks just like a Hubbert's Peak graph—each oil field starts out slow, builds to a high point, then levels off to near nothing—the classic bell-shaped curve that was characteristic to Hubbard's first drawing of the concept in 1956.

Simmons's thinking focuses on the importance that giant oil fields play in delivering the world's oil supply. "The 116 fields that produce over 100,000 barrels per day provided 47 percent of the oil used worldwide in 2000. The 4,000+ smaller fields contributed 53 percent."[32] Simmons buys fully into the peak-production logic of the fossil-fuel theory. All giant oil fields are bound to run dry. He writes:

> The litany of excellent case studies presented in the remainder of this chapter amply illustrates the grim fact that all giant oil fields ultimately peak. Once peaking occurs, most soon experience sharp production declines. The rate of decline obviously varies according to the volumes each field was producing when it peaked, along with various other factors. But despite all the variances that can be observed, the commonality among giant oil fields is unmistakable. They do deplete. And at some point on every field's depletion curve, hydrocarbon output begins to decline as encroaching water and gas simply crowd out the oil.[33]

Simmons argues this despite producing a table that shows a near doubling of world oil reserves between 1973 and 2000. According to data complied from BP's statistical review of world energy, Simmons shows that worldwide oil reserves in 1973 were just over 600 trillion barrels; yet in 2003 the table shows worldwide oil reserves at just under 1.2 trillion barrels.[34] If all the world's giant wells are depleting to zero, why do oil reserves continue to increase? Nowhere in the book does Simmons suggest we have a lot of oil yet to discover. His entire tone is that we have already discovered most of the oil and natural gas that exists and that we are rapidly depleting the giant fields that the world's oil supply depends upon.

The production-peak theorists seem locked into what logicians call the fallacy of composition. The mistake is made when we reason fallaciously from the properties of the parts to the property of the whole itself. "A particularly flagrant example would be to argue that since every part of a certain machine is light in weight, the machine 'as a whole' is light in weight."[35] Because individual oil fields deplete as they are pumped does not mean the oil supply of the world is diminishing as a consequence.

We have shown in this chapter that new, unexpected discoveries of oil are being made constantly. If we apply the principles of the deep, abiotic theory of petroleum's origin, we should expect to find even more oil at depths rarely explored. Proving that we have found all the oil there is to find is almost a logical impossibility—unless, of course, there was some way we could know for sure how much there was to find. The abiotic theory suggests our whole concept of oil's supply might change if only we explored for oil at deeper levels.

What about the evidence that oil fields might replenish or that below reservoirs, close to the earth's surface, there may be deeper, more extensive reservoirs that were the source of the oil initially found above them? We simply have not investigated where the oil comes from because we have assumed all reservoirs are the residue of decaying ancient forests and dinosaurs, so they must have been deposited just where those ancient fossils first fell. Why bother looking below or asking where the oil came from? There was nothing below, and the oil came from ancient detritus, so goes the fossil-fuel theory.

The fossil-fuel theory assumes we already know everything there is to know about oil. So most available oil has been found and pretty soon it will all be gone. The abiotic theory assumes we have not even begun to develop the right questions, let alone answer them. Moreover, if the abiotic theory is correct, the earth generates oil on a constant basis. There may never be a reason to stop looking for it, no matter how many giant wells we deplete in the process.

PART 2

THE POLITICS OF OIL

4

THE GLOBAL-WARMING HOAX

Yet in spite of the clear evidence available all around us, there are many who still do not believe that Global Warming is a problem at all.

—AL GORE,
Beacon Theater, New York, January 12, 2004

EVEN IF OIL WERE infinitely available, environmentalists would still have a problem with our using it freely. Why? Global warming. Environmentalists are convinced that our burning of fossil fuels is warming up the earth. We are creating a "greenhouse effect" with the result that the climate is going to change with disastrous results.

Once again we are going to dare to ask some tough questions and to examine the evidence. If you have guessed that we are going to argue that global warming makes about as much sense as the fossil-fuel theory, you're right. Environmentalists would like us to make their conclusions set in stone, maybe as firmly rooted as the fossil-fuel theory has become. The goal is to condition everyone's mind so that as soon as you hear *oil, natural gas,* or some other supposedly evil term, such as *gasoline,* you immediately think of it in terms of global warming and hear alarm bells in your head.

Look at the success conventional wisdom has had with the term *fossil fuel*. Right now when you say fossil fuel, everybody knows you mean oil, natural gas, gasoline, or their by-products, and you think immediately that we are soon going to exhaust the earth's finite resources. You're conditioned to think in that way without having to explain the logic or translate the terms. Environmentalists are looking forward to the day when we all equally agree that human activity is causing the planet to get warmer. Once this becomes an undisputed axiom, their social and political agenda will follow without objection.

Of course, the only reason we are going to question the global-warming assumptions is because we are right-wing reactionaries—at least that is how environmentalists react whenever their assumptions are challenged. Or that we've been paid millions by the oil companies to spread their lies—that's what the political Left believes, regardless what we say. Al Gore suggests we should look at the evidence. We are going to do that, but our suspicion is that the global-warming theory may have some difficulty sustaining itself under critical analysis. Still, we don't expect an appeal to rationality will win us any favors in the court of public opinion, where environmentalists want everyone to believe they alone are the only ones on the planet who care about life.

We will return to politics at the end of this chapter, where we will suggest that a primary reason the radical environmentalists care about global warming is because they have an underlying economic and political agenda. As we will see, the theme of global warming has come to have important economic and political implications. We are going to argue that global warming is one of the major political themes of the anti-oil forces that are gaining strength on the political Left. The environmentalists have joined with the political Left to push ahead their radical agenda. That agenda is not only anti-oil, it is also anti-industry, judging from what the radical environmentalists do, not just what they say.

WHAT IS THE GREENHOUSE EFFECT?

We can keep the science to a minimum if we concentrate on a few important concepts. The greenhouse effect begins with an understanding of the basics of how the earth absorbs sunlight.

First, the sun's energy radiates to the earth in a variety of ways. About a third of this energy is absorbed directly into the earth, another third is reflected back into space (largely by clouds), and the remaining third is absorbed by the atmosphere itself. If the earth and the atmosphere were only capable of absorbing solar energy and not releasing it, the earth would eventually burn away. Thus much of the solar energy absorbed by the earth is eventually emitted back into space in the form of thermal or infrared radiation.

Anyone who has spent any time in a desert knows that the area cools off dramatically at night, even in summer. Yes, the nighttime cooling of the desert intensifies because the earth at night is radiating energy back to the sky, something that occurs even though we never see the infrared rays going back into space. Because desert skies are generally cloudless, the nighttime cooling effect is more apparent than in cities, which are typically built in more humid settings where the nighttime clouds themselves trap and reflect back some of the escaping infrared waves.

Now let's focus on the atmosphere. The majority of the atmosphere is made up of nitrogen (78 percent) and oxygen (21 percent). Because nitrogen and oxygen are both two-atom molecules, they are bound so tightly together they cannot absorb sunlight. For this reason, nitrogen and oxygen, which together make up approximately 99 percent of the atmosphere, are not part of the greenhouse effect. The analysis of the greenhouse effect tends to concentrate on carbon dioxide, a chemical that makes up less then one-tenth of 1 percent of the atmosphere (0.1 percent).

Carbon dioxide is a three-atom molecule, which is bound together loosely enough that it can absorb sunlight. The sunlight absorbed in a carbon-dioxide molecule causes the molecule to vibrate. The vibrating carbon-dioxide molecule in turn radiates heat, which is identified by environmentalists as the primary culprit in the greenhouse effect. When we burn fossil fuels, we increase the amount of carbon dioxide being emitted into the atmosphere. If the greenhouse effect were a purely natural process that involved no human activity, then the environmentalists would have nothing to complain about. Maybe we could lament the problem, but we couldn't blame it on ourselves.

So environmentalists argue that we burn gasoline in our cars, for instance, and as a result we increase the amount of carbon dioxide in the air. The carbon dioxide absorbs sunlight and as a result emits heat. With more carbon dioxide in the air as a direct result of human activity, the earth warms up. The process is called a "greenhouse effect" because the environmentalists see additional carbon dioxide in the atmosphere as producing a filter that intensifies the heating effect of the sun, much as the glass of a greenhouse produces a like effect. Environmentalists use the term *greenhouse effect* as a code word for global warming, the result that they see as harmful.

We should note that when the term *greenhouse effect* is nothing new. When the idea of the greenhouse effect was first introduced in the 1800s, the term was not considered negative. If all the sun's energy were reflected back by the clouds or lost through the infrared rays reemitted by the earth back into space, then the earth would be about 60 degrees Fahrenheit colder than it is. The atmosphere naturally acts like a blanket that keeps all the sun's warmth from escaping back into space. We depend on our atmosphere to trap sunlight so it can radiate heat, and we need the clouds to bounce back to earth some of the escaping infrared rays being sent back into space, especially at night. If the atmosphere did not function like a blanket, or create a greenhouse effect, a much colder earth could probably not grow the plants that animals, like us, rely on for food.

Now let's examine the carbon dioxide in the air, because carbon dioxide is the environmentalist's culprit chemical. Carbon dioxide is a very small percentage of the atmosphere, as we have noted, less that one-tenth of one percentage. The accusatory rhetoric of the environmentalists is that we are throwing tons of carbon dioxide into the air. Their charge makes it sound as if we are pouring a huge quantity of a noxious chemical into the air simply by burning fossil fuels. So how much more carbon dioxide are we throwing into the air?

This is the first problem the environmental argument encounters.

The incremental addition of carbon dioxide to the atmosphere attributable to human activity is remarkably small. The carbon dioxide in the air is measured in terms of carbon "petagrams." One petagram equals one billion metric tons. So the atmosphere is said to contain some 730 petagrams of carbon (PgC), or 730 billion metric tons. The net annual addition of carbon dioxide contributed to the air by human activity is estimated to be 3 PgC, an increase of only about four-tenths of 1 percent (0.4 percent).

We are talking about a miniscule percentage of the total atmosphere here. Carbon dioxide itself only constitutes 1 percent of the atmosphere. Human beings burning hydrocarbon fuels increase the carbon dioxide by only 0.4 percent. So the annual increment of carbon dioxide we are concerned about constitutes a miniscule .0004 percent of the atmosphere, four one-thousands of 1 percent. All the dire effects environmentalists attribute to human activity would have to be the direct causal result of this very small contribution we make to the total atmosphere every year by burning petroleum products and throwing a small amount of additional carbon dioxide into the air.

To make the argument work, extreme environmentalists virtually have to identify carbon dioxide itself as a harmful chemical. This is absurd when we realize that plants need carbon dioxide to survive. Human beings breathe in oxygen and exhale carbon dioxide. Plants are just the reverse. Plants absorb carbon dioxide and throw out oxygen. This is another reason why plants and human beings are so compatible. Just because carbon dioxide is something human beings exhale doesn't mean carbon dioxide is a noxious chemical to other living things on the earth. Plants love carbon dioxide. Carbon dioxide is not a noxious chemical; plants and human beings both depend upon it for life. Environmentalists have to make an impossible stretch to argue that carbon dioxide is an intrinsically harmful chemical. Still, environmentalists push legislators to include such definitions in global-warming laws.

When we realize that plants take in carbon dioxide in the process of photosynthesis, we have an obvious solution to any supposed problems resulting from the greenhouse effect. Why not just to plant more trees.

Environmentalists generally favor planting trees, unless of course the suggestion is raised in this context. With more trees and plants on the surface of the earth, the net addition of carbon dioxide to the air resulting from human activity could be reduced significantly. As noted by the climate specialist John Christy:

> Each year the nonhuman world (forests, oceans, etc) releases about 210 PgC to the atmosphere but in turn absorbs about 213 PgC. What this means is that human activity actually produces about 6.3 PgC each year, because the natural world is pulling about 3 more PgC out than it is putting in. There is very strong evidence to show that the plant world (which includes agricultural production) is thriving as a result of this additional CO_2 (carbon dioxide) and is helping to remove half the portion humans are producing.[1]

So if we are throwing more carbon dioxide into the air, let's just grow more food and plant more trees. The additional green life on the earth will need more carbon dioxide to thrive. Christy continues:

> Is increasing CO_2 a harmful pollutant? The answer is absolutely no. In simple terms, CO_2 is the lifeblood of the planet. The green world we see around us would disappear if not for atmospheric CO_2. Plant life largely evolved at a time when the atmospheric CO_2 concentration was many times what it is today. We are, from the plants' point of view, putting more of their food into the air, and they are gobbling it up. If plants (and animals that like plants) could vote to offer awards, producers of CO_2 would win in a landslide. So the increasing of CO_2 does not pose a toxic risk to the planet. Efforts to designate CO_2 a pollutant by the U.S. government have not considered the plants' point of view.[2]

Thinking through the argument, we realize that environmentalists are relying on us to project our own human reactions onto the earth, assuming that the earth as a whole reacts the way we react as human beings. We exhale carbon dioxide out of our bodies. Plants demand carbon dioxide. What may be seen as noxious to us as human beings is seen by plants as the air they must breathe. If environmentalists wanted to be fair and not merely political, we could start worrying that thriving plants may take too much carbon dioxide out of the air. Would removing carbon dioxide from the atmosphere bring on global cooling? Yet environmentalists never raise this question.

We should also be careful to clearly distinguish the global-warming argument from the argument about a growing hole in the ozone. The issues are distinct. Ozone depletion has been linked to chlorofluorocarbons compounds and halon compounds, the types of chemicals that are typically used in industrial solvents, refrigeration, and air-conditioning systems and as aerosol propellants. Halons are also used as fire suppressants. Ozone depletion has not been linked to having a greater quantity of carbon dioxide in the air. Some may argue that the ozone depletion contributes to global warming. Even if that were true, we would not solve the problem of ozone depletion by burning fewer hydrocarbons. The burning of fossil fuels does not release into the air chlorofluorocarbons or halon compounds, the types of chemicals identified as the culprits causing holes in the ozone.

The most rabid environmentalists must wish they could hitch their wagon on a chemical other than carbon dioxide. Too bad that burning hydrocarbon fuels doesn't throw into the air something that is truly obnoxious to human life and to plant life, maybe even carbon monoxide. In the final analysis, carbon dioxide is beneficial to life.

But at this point the environmentalists shift the argument. The real problem evidently is not that human activity increases the amount of carbon dioxide in the air per se but that the increase in carbon dioxide generates more heat. So let's test this link. Is the earth warming up because of human activity?

ARE HUMANS HEATING UP THE EARTH?

An assertion the environmentalists want to translate into a truism is the presumption that the earth is heating up because we humans burn too many fossil fuels. Our industrial machine, the cars we drive, the structure of our suburbs, the affluence of our lifestyle—all these are dependent on petroleum. So if the earth is heating up, we're to blame. "The earth is warming up and it's our fault" is the mantra that environmentalists want to make an axiom, and "everybody knows that . . ." type of statement. Yet before we just roll over and quit, let's examine the proposition to see whether it is valid or just another example of junk science.

The idea that chemicals in the atmosphere could cause the earth to heat up traces back to another old idea, one first proposed by the Swedish chemist Svante Arrhenius. At the end of the nineteenth century scientists were debating why the ice age had ended in prehistoric times. In 1896 Arrhenius wrote a paper that examined the effect of carbonic acid in the atmosphere on the temperature of earth.[3] In the early 1900s his attention turned to carbon dioxide. Arrhenius became convinced that the ice age existed because the earth at that time had significantly less carbon dioxide in the atmosphere.

Greenhouse-effect theories begin around that time, when Arrhenius and his colleagues began to speculate that the coal being burned to fuel the Industrial Revolution would throw more carbon dioxide into the air, causing the temperature of the earth to heat up considerably.[4] Arrhenius was not alarmed. He figured that at the current rate industry was then burning coal, it would take three thousand years for carbon dioxide to rise sufficiently in the atmosphere to cause any real problems.

At any rate, the global warming idea took hold, as well as the suggestion that human beings burning fuel could heat up the earth. We have already established that carbon dioxide makes up a very small percentage of the atmosphere. We have shown that burning petroleum products contributes very little additional carbon dioxide to the atmosphere. We have suggested that growing more plants might itself be enough to absorb the carbon dioxide we contribute to the atmosphere. Now let's question whether or not the earth is in a warming cycle that can be attributed to human activity.

The analysis of historical data involves one of the most difficult applications in statistics. "Time series analysis," to use the technical term, is complicated because you are always trying to identify trends in data points created over time, and you want ultimately to attribute any identified trend to a cause. From the statistician's point of view, we first have to ask whether the trend in temperature observations over time permits us to conclude reliably that the world is warming.

The first problem with time series analysis is to identify the appropriate time period for the analysis. For instance, when a mutual fund claims to be the top performer in its category over the last five years, we can always question if that was a correct or meaningful time period to select for analysis. Maybe if we had looked at the same mutual fund over a six-year period, instead of a five-year period, the mutual fund turned out to be one of the poorer performers in its category.

Arrhenius and his nineteenth-century colleagues were right to wonder why the ice age happened. What we generally think of as the ice age is scientifically identified by geologists as the Pleistocene era, beginning some 1.8 million years ago and ending just 8,000 years ago. Most of us know that glaciers covered most of Europe and North America. The Great Lakes were supposedly dug out by North American glaciers of the great ice age. Mammoths wandered North America, and Neanderthals resided in Europe.

Perhaps the most appropriate time interval for analysis does stretch back to the ice age. Looked at objectively, the intense cold of then and the relatively moderate temperatures of today are distinct enough to be considered as statistically significant differences. What statisticians look for are differences that disprove hypothesis. A minor variation is not enough to be statistically significant. By statistically significant we mean a difference that lies outside the expected variation, outside what is defined as a standard deviation.

Besides, accurate temperature readings are relatively modern inventions; we do not have accurate temperature readings going back hundreds of years, unless we use reasonably unreliable historical human reports or try to impute temperature from other observations such as measuring tree rings as a gauge of temperature.

Has the earth warmed up since the ice age? Yes. Is the earth warming up now because we are burning gasoline in our automobiles? In truth, that's a much more difficult question to answer with a reasonable degree of scientific certainty.

Yes, we can see a significant difference between the cold needed to produce glaciers over most of the northern world during the ice age versus world temperatures today, when the ice cap is confined predominately to the global poles. But are we sure a warm winter this year means the earth is getting hotter? Does a cold, snowy winter next year mean we are headed back to an ice age? Which reading is the aberration? These are much more difficult questions. Any variation we experience might be just that—a variation, but not an aberration—in other words, an observation that differs from the true underlying pattern but not a determinative reading we ought to rely upon.

Let's take a look at the swings between glacial cold periods and interglacial warm periods experienced during the Pleistocene epoch, stretching back some 1.8 million years and ending only 8,000 years ago. We will focus on the last part of that cycle, where there are more than enough major fluctuations in temperature to make the point.

Around 130,000 years ago, the earth was going through a warm period between glacial periods. Geologists have termed this time the Eemian interglacial stage. They have studied the climate during the Eemian interglacial stage by examining ice core samples bored out of the Greenland ice cap. The earth's climate then was very much as it is today, maybe a little moister in certain regions. During the Eemian interglacial stage, there were several sudden but brief cold spells. Geologists estimate that ending the Eemian interglacial warm period took around 400 years.

At any rate, around 110,000 years ago, the earth became colder and drier—drier because when the earth cools dramatically, less water evaporates from the oceans to fall back as rain. Even in areas not covered by ice, the aridity caused forests to die, giving way to grasslands that require less water to survive. As the cold reached its low point around 70,000 years ago, much of the grasslands worldwide retreated and gave way to deserts. By this time much of Europe and Canada were buried deep under thick ice sheets.[5]

Then, around 60,000 to 55,000 years ago, the world began to warm. The ice melted, and the world entered a new interglacial period. This ended around 30,000 years ago, when the world went back into a deep freeze. Deserts again expanded and the ice sheets expanded. This period is known as the Late Glacial Cold Stage, sometimes called the Upper Pleniglacial. Pleniglacial clearly signifies what was going on—the world was literally "full of glaciers."

The ice covering the world reached its maximum point around 21,000 years ago, entering what has been called the Last Glacial Maximum. Now deserts and semidesert land occupied huge areas of all the continents as the forests world died and fell back. Glaciers and deserts covered the relatively treeless world during this time. We are now very possibly in the interglacial period coming out of this last great ice age. So within the Pleistocene epoch there have been several distinct periods when the cold and glaciers advanced, with the cold periods punctuated by the intervening warmer interglacial periods.

Looked at from this perspective, we can argue that the global temperature trends we are experiencing today need to be analyzed not over the last 100 years but stretching back to when this interglacial warming period began, some 21,000 years ago. Minor temperature fluctuations observed today pale in comparison with the trend of extreme cold as the last glacial period ended to the relatively warm conditions we experience today. We have observed swings between glacial and interglacial periods observed for the earth over the last 1.8 million years. Unless this trend has for some reason come to an end, we should expect the earth to begin cooling as we prepare to enter the next ice age.

A joke is circulating on the Internet involving a retired geologist who sent a friend and colleague a note from Mount Rainer. The note read: "Watch out, Al Gore. The glaciers will get you!" The point was appended to a report documenting that the best-measured glacier in North America, the Nisqually on Mount Rainer, has been growing since 1931. If the greenhouse-effect ecologists are right, we should burn more carbon dioxide into the air, hoping that perhaps we can hold back the next ice age. If the global warming the environmentalists attribute to the burning of fossil fuels is true, maybe we should burn even more gasoline in our cars to put off the day when the ice begins to return.

Why did the earth warm up since the ice age? Clearly the answer cannot be that human beings burned too many petroleum products, unless someone wants to suggest that the campfires of cavemen made the last great glaciers recede. Stretching back 1.8 million years, a lot of glaciers came and went before human beings ever walked the face of the earth.

Scientists debate whether the cause of the swings between glacial and interglacial ice ages involves a change in the earth's orbit around the sun or possibly a change in the intensity of the sun itself. All we can surmise is that the cause had to require a major system shift. Even if the cause was carbon dioxide, something greater than human beings had to be involved. When human beings weren't around to remove carbon dioxide from the atmosphere or to put more carbon dioxide into the atmosphere, the earth still hung in the pendulum somewhere between ice ages and warming spells. At any rate, the fluctuations of temperature we are experiencing today may be relatively minor, certainly not of the magnitude to constitute statistical significance, especially if we are headed toward a glacial period.

Also, huge forces must be necessary to cause the earth to go through such dramatic changes as to go from ice age to warming period and back again. Even if human beings detonated all the nuclear weapons in the world over a single city, the impact on the earth's rotation or orbit would be minimal.

Remember, humans tend to exaggerate their own importance. The distance to the center of the earth is approximately four thousand miles. No practical project has ever been devised to drill that deep, let alone to survive the pressures and heat we would encounter there. How do we know that the earth does not generate hydrocarbons below or within the mantle on a constant basis? We don't. We really have only a limited appreciation of the forces at the center of the earth. Yet we project a theory based on the concept of limited fossil fuels, and we are confident in our own knowledge, even though we haven't tested any competing theories empirically.

The point is that we tend to exaggerate our importance, to be so confident in our theories, even when our knowledge is admittedly limited. So, too, we project that we are the cause of global warming. Again, we generally do not appreciate the magnitude of the issue nor the limits of our understanding. The distance from the earth to the sun is ninety-three million miles, yet the sun heats us up fairly intensely as is. Energy generated by human beings pales in comparison. Moreover, the number of years involved to see real changes in temperature trends may well number in the thousands or hundreds of thousands of years. Human beings have no experience of time frames this long; we even have difficulty imagining such long time periods, except in a fairly cursory or intellectual way. We live on earth, yet we know very little about the deep ocean, and we have had almost no direct experience with the inner core of our own planet.

The environmentalists have the causal argument exactly reversed. Human activity has expanded because the earth in the current interglacial period has gotten warmer. But the earth has not gotten warmer because of human activity. We humans may be no more than a blip on the radar screen of a much more powerful trend that began tens of thousands of years ago, when the last glacial period began to come to an end. The earth would most likely continue to warm, with or without human beings, until the next glacial period begins and the earth starts cooling off once again. This has been the geological record over the last 1.8 million years. Human beings would not have thrived had the earth itself not begun warming, independent of any cause exerted by human beings or our activity.

Human beings have a hard time appreciating that what we do may actually be of minor importance, or possibly no importance at all, at least in geological terms, or in comparison to the scope of the true magnitude of power exerted by forces that impact the earth or our solar system. Remember, some 70 percent of the earth is occupied by oceans and sea water. Human beings, despite numbering today some six and a half billion people, probably occupy only 10 percent of the world's surface. Still, we think of ourselves as crowded in cities like New York or Tokyo, and we imagine that we are a blight on the earth simply because there are so many of us.

Let's conduct some additional thought experiments to get the impact of human beings into perspective. For instance, if all six and a half billion people came into North America and began jumping up and down at the same time, would that change the rotation or the orbit of the earth? Hardly. It took a magnitude 9.0 earthquake that struck off Sumatra in December 2004 to cause a vertical displacement of enough water and earth debris to produce a slight variation in the earth's rotation, measured as shortening the twenty-four-hour rotation of the earth by a miniscule amount. In other words, the earthquake of that huge magnitude decreased the length of the day by 2.68 microseconds by causing the earth to spin ever so slightly faster.[6]

Environmentalists develop computer models to project the effect of so-called greenhouse gases on global warming. Depending upon which model we reference, projections indicate that, at current rates of burning petroleum products, we can expect a warming of the earth of as much as ten degrees over the next one hundred years. The problem with these computer models is that the earth is not a controlled laboratory setting. The earth is a very complex system that has multiple ways of adjusting.

Yes, in a laboratory, if more carbon dioxide is added to a given volume of air, the temperature will rise above previous levels when the air is heated. How the earth will deal with increased carbon dioxide is not as predictable. What if there are more trees planted? What if the added carbon dioxide causes fewer clouds to be created? With fewer clouds, more infrared radiation will escape from the surface of the earth, and the net effect might be cooling rather than warming.

But what if the world is getting warmer? We don't really want to move into a new ice age, do we? If the earth is warming, why don't we all just put on some sunglasses and head to the beach? What's the problem?

You may have guessed it. To respond, the environmentalists shift ground once again. The problem, they say now, is not the global warming per se, but that global warming causes climate shifts that are detrimental to life or to the balance of the earth or to some other natural state.

The environmentalists, to win their argument, have a chain of deductions to prove. First, they must prove that human beings contribute enough carbon dioxide into the air to produce a statistically significant larger amount of net carbon dioxide in the air, beyond what we might correct by simply planting more trees. Then they must prove that more carbon dioxide in the air will cause statistically significant global warming, not just minor variations in a trend that is really better defined as interglacial and seen over thousands of years. Next they must prove that global warming will cause climate changes, and then that the resulting climate changes will in some way be harmful. Otherwise, what's wrong with burning fossil fuels?

According to environmentalists, there is plenty wrong. Remember, environmentalists are working toward a moral conclusion: namely, that it's wrong to burn fossil fuels at the current rate. The corollary is a political argument: namely, the fault rests with modern industrial society, and the worst offenders are Americans because we burn more fossil fuels than proportionately belong to us, all as a consequence of our lavish, selfish, materialistic lifestyle.

IS THE CLIMATE REALLY CHANGING?

No less an expert than former President Bill Clinton has jumped into the battle. Evidently, he buys hook, line, and sinker into the theory that human activity burning fossil fuels has caused global warming, which will cause climate change that will cause great harm to human beings. Clinton has just formed a new foundation to save the world, naming the foundation of course after himself—the Clinton Global Initiative—with a Web site that also puts the former president's name out front, www .clintonglobaliniative.com. In the foundation overview, Clinton embraces the global-warming hoax as true beyond reasonable doubt. Just read the first sentence of the Web site section devoted to climate change:

> Since the late 1800s, industrialization has caused the average temperature of the Earth's surface to rise by 0.8 degrees Celsius. Left unchecked, the by-products of human activity could raise global temperatures an additional 5.8 degrees Celsius by century's end. This alarming trend is expected to cause severe storms, floods, and droughts.[7]

95

Right, Clinton links industrialization (i.e., the burning of fossil fuels) to global warming and to horrible climate change, all causal connections resulting in severe harm to living creatures. Note how Clinton presents his suppositions as certainties, virtual laws of nature, fully proven axioms. Any doubter would have to be either a fool or (like us) one of those right-wing conspiracy nuts the Clintons love to hate. Global-warming believers are true believers, and doubters are certainly to be castigated and demonized, not reasoned with.

Let's persist in our determination to examine the logic. Is there any hard scientific evidence that the global climate is changing for the worse?

Here are the climate effects environmentalists like to cite: sea levels are rising because the polar ice caps are melting and severe weather conditions—such as prolonged droughts—and more intense events—such as hurricanes, tornadoes, or severe storms—are seeming commonplace. We can now add tsunamis to the list, because those buying into the global-warming theory are certain to include such events as the December 26, 2004, tsunami as another unnatural natural event in the list of global-warming indicators. As a rule, we can postulate that any extreme weather condition will be attributed by environmentalists to human activity that causes global warming. Let's say we have an exceptionally hot summer. Why? Global warming. Yet the environmentalists will be silent if we have an exceptionally cold winter. Or let's assume a hurricane season is especially severe. Once again, global warming is blamed as the culprit.

Environmentalists have a much harder time proving the causal link. For starters, we simply lack good long-term data on basic climate observations, including records of precipitation, humidity, winds, and atmospheric pressure. Going back over a period as short as one hundred years, few accurate databases of historical climatic information exist, and those that do exist are not often reliable. We can impute some measures by examining data that may be contained in tree rings or core ice samples, but the result is broad measures, not detailed daily records on the fundamentals we would need to make an analysis. Are the average temperatures today in Cleveland, Ohio, or any other U.S. city, measuring hotter or colder than one hundred years ago? two hundred years ago? three hundred years ago? We simply don't know, not with any degree of scientific certainty.

If real climatic trends can only be seen over hundreds or thousands of years, we have no choice but to go to inferential scientific measures. We can take ice-core samples or measure tree rings. Yet these measures always involve our inferences, a process very distinct from having precisely recorded contemporaneous readings. As we have already seen, we have good reason to believe that the fundamental global temperature and climate effects may be related to a swing between glacial cold and interglacial warming periods that the earth has been going through for about 1.8 million years. What we see as fluctuations in winds or storms today may be simply the normal variations expected in time series data, not readings that truly indicate the planet's climate has taken a fundamental change in direction.

Still, we should expect that any extreme weather condition we experience from now on will be cited by global-warming theorists as proof of their concept. If several bad tornadoes hit Kansas in rapid succession, we will all be expected to grasp the connection between the tornadoes and our use of gasoline. Yet we can readily cite instances to make impressionistic arguments that the climate has improved during the last century. The 1930s Dust Bowl involved one of the most severe droughts experienced in twentieth-century America. Because we don't have the Dust Bowl around anymore in states like Oklahoma and Kansas, does that mean the U.S. climate is getting better? For every severe hurricane today, historical records can be found for another. The same is true for tornadoes, floods, and even tsunamis.

Sea and ocean levels in various interglacial periods over the last 130,000 years have been higher than today. Those effects of rising waters were not due to any man-made industrial activity. Prior to 1850 human beings were not burning fossil fuels in any significant quantity. Nor was there an industrial revolution to blame for rising seas. Changes in sea level appear to occur naturally, apparently in response to whether the earth is in a glacial or interglacial period. The impact the greenhouse effect has on sea appears minimal at best, especially in comparison with ice-age effects.

The attention of the environmentalists seem for some reason always to be focused on water events—amounts of rain, levels of snow, hurricanes, or the level of the sea. Why is this? Why don't advocates of the greenhouse effect claim that our burning of fossil fuels cause more volcanoes to erupt or earthquakes to happen? We never see arguments that the warming up of the earth causes more volcanoes and earthquakes. Maybe the explanation is that, psychologically, environmentalists just project from (a) carbon dioxide in the air, to (b) temperature variations that show warming trends, to (c) the thickness of the polar ice, or measurements of sea levels, or the severity of droughts and the violence of storms. Yet volcanoes and earthquakes are environmental phenomenon. Are they simply outside the greenhouse effect?

Moreover, the scientific evidence is that the oceans are not rising. The mean sea level was established in 1841 at the Isle of the Dead, Port Arthur, Tasmania, Australia. Exact measurements show at most the sea level rose no more than 1.6 centimeters, less than two-thirds of an inch, during all of the twentieth century. A good argument can be made that the measurements actually show a slight lowering of the mean sea level since measurements were first taken. Given that the seas in Southern Hemisphere oceans contain nearly two-thirds of the world's ocean waters, accurate measurements taken in Australia over more than a 160-year period should carry great weight for all but the most determined of the greenhouse-effect advocates.[8]

Nor does the scientific data support an easy conclusion that the world's glaciers are melting. The data is conflicting. Some glaciers are advancing, others are retreating.

The World Glacier Monitoring Service in Zurich has determined that 55 percent of the glaciers in high altitudes are advancing; in 1950, only 5 percent were advancing.[9] Let's cite just one more example that seems both fair and typical. Researchers from the U.S. Geological Survey have documented that ten large calving glaciers in Alaska are advancing while the majority of Alaska glaciers are losing volume. Calving glaciers generally terminate at the sea, and they loose material when ice breaks off into the sea. Photographs of calving glaciers are often deceptive in that the glacier may actually be growing, even though the visuals of ice breaking into the sea give a dramatically different picture. The calving glaciers that are growing in Alaska include some of the larger ones, such as the Hubbard Glacier, the Meares Glacier in Prince William Sound, and the Harvard Glacier, which has a well-documented period of advance that began between 1905 and 1911 and continues today.[10]

The hype generated by the global-warming theorists has given birth to a worldwide climate study industry funded worldwide at an amazing level of around $5 billion per year.[11] International organizations such as the World Meteorological Organization (WMO), the United Nations Environmental Program (UNEP), and the Intergovernmental Panel on Climate Change (IPCC), despite their huge funding, have generated nothing but dire warning after dire warning. Few stop to notice that their predictions are predictably wrong and their climate models are always being readjusted as a result.

Consider this commentary made by Dr. Theodor Landscheidt of the Schroeter Institute for Research in Cycles of Solar Activity in Nova Scotia, Canada:

Precise forecasts that prove correct are a sharp criterion for efficient science. The protagonists of global warming remain empty-handed in this respect in spite of great material and personal expense. In the eighties S. Schneider from the National Center for Atmospheric Research in Boulder, Colorado, predicted in his book Global Warming a huge jump in temperature, polar ice melting away, seas surging across the land, famine on an epidemic scale, and ecosystem collapse. Today this is no longer taken seriously. Yet other climatologists, too, made forecasts in the eighties they no longer maintain. C. D. Schönwiese, usually critical and cautious in his statements, still predicted in 1987 a 4.5° C rise in temperature until 2030, though only as an upper limit. He thought the sea level in the German Bay could rise by 1.5 m until 2040 and in the ocean around India even 2 to 3 m. A projection of his temperature forecasts yields 11.8° for the year

2100. At the climate conference in Villach [Austria] in 1985 similar predictions were presented to the public. The IPCC still predicted in 1990 and 1992 that global temperature would rise 1.9°–5.2° until 2100 and thought that a rise in sea level by 1.10 m was possible.

All these predictions have turned out to be untenable.[12]

Determining with precision whether or not we are experiencing climate change is another complex scientific problem. What is required is the creation of a computer model that both accurately accounts for historical climate observations and predicts future climatic events. Let's say we want to know whether we have more or less rainfall in a given geographical area. The question is relevant because global-warming activists may charge that the earth is experiencing more drought because increased levels of carbon dioxide thrown in the air by the burning of fossil fuels is warming the atmosphere to the point where less rain is falling on certain areas of the globe. To answer this question, scientists have to be able to construct a computer model that accurately turns out numbers that reflect the historical data pattern. Then the computer model must be tested to see if future predictions of rainfall levels are correct. If future predictions are wrong, which generally they are, then the scientists have to revise the model.

Scientists are far from having a reliable model to predict climate change. First there are too many variables. Consider for a moment the scores of variables involved: variations in solar energy output (including the frequency of sun spots), effects of ocean currents, wind variation, changes in urbanization or land mass occupied by human beings, forestation levels, changes in ground vegetation, and cloud levels and density, to name just a few. As we have mentioned, climate changes may occur over hundreds or thousands of years, and reliable data is simply not available. Even if data were available, the computing task is enormous and far beyond the range of today's most advanced supercomputers.

What generally happens is that scientists take a minimalist approach to constructing what are known as climatic global circulation models. Rather than attempt to model climate changes on some global scale, scientists try for a reduced approach, limiting their analysis to a particular geographical area and a single climate phenomenon—perhaps rainfall, snow levels, or even temperature readings themselves—in one city, state, or region. When their predictions fail, the scientists refigure the variables, working until the model fits the data. Even then, the models rarely work reliably. The method is inductive, not deductive. Scientists get to the point where they don't really care why the variables in the model work just so the historical results can be turned out with some degree of accuracy.

The scientific models for explaining and predicting climatic change are so notoriously inaccurate that the U.S. Environmental Protection Agency has issued warnings about even using the computer-generated results:

> Virtually all published estimates of how the climate could change in the United States are the results of computer models of the atmosphere known as "general circulation models." These complicated models are able to simulate many features of the climate, but they are still not accurate enough to produce reliable forecasts of how the climate may change; and the several models often yield contradictory results. For the time being, however, these models are about all we have to say how the climate may change in particular areas.
>
> Given the unreliability of these models, researchers trying to understand the future impacts of climate change generally analyze different scenarios from several different climate models. The hope is that, by using a wide variety of different climate models, one's analysis can include the entire range of scientific uncertainty. For all these reasons, EPA reiterates the warning provided by all climate modelers to people considering the impacts of future climate change: the projections of climate change in specific areas are not forecast but are reasonable examples of how the climate might change.[13]

Radical environmentalists may dismiss the above caution simply because it was issued by a government agency. The challenge should then be issued back: show us a reliable scientific computer model of the climate that accurately explains historical data and predicts future data. We have yet to see such a model in the scientific literature. The challenge should be easy to test. Bring forth the computer model and churn out some predictions about future climate. How much rain will fall on Massachusetts next summer? next year? How much snow will we see in New York next winter? What will be the average temperature in Georgia next summer? Let's take the predictions and see how accurate they are. The problem is that weather changes have so much variability that accurate specific predictions like these are nearly impossible. Even trend analyses are difficult. A historically hot summer or a historically cold winter does not necessarily predict the next summer or winter. A historically hot summer is as likely to be followed by a cold winter as by a mild winter. That's the problem.

This is why environmental activists are reduced to pointing out extreme weather events and claiming they are a result of global warming, whether causality can be proved or not, forgetting about predicting anything about future events from that one extreme event. This type of reasoning is easy to refute. Let's look back to historical records more than three hundred years old, back to the time when human beings were burning virtually no hydrocarbon fuels, and find some extreme weather events. We will not have to look far to find very old accounts of extreme droughts and catastrophic rainfalls. The explanation of these extreme climactic events cannot possibly be global warming caused by human activity. How about changes such as the expansion of the Sahara Desert that has been going on since ancient Carthage fell to the Roman Gen. Scipio Aemilianus and the city was burned to the ground in 146 BC? Was the expansion of the Sahara caused by the greenhouse effect? by global warming?

In the 1970s environmental alarmists were concerned that the earth was cooling off. Now we hear global-warming activists argue that the climate changes caused by global warming might actually cause global cooling, even possibly bringing on a new ice age.[14] This was the theme of the 2004 Roland Emmerich film *The Day After Tomorrow*, in which we see global warming trigger a new ice age. Tornadoes flatten Los Angeles, a tidal wave hits New York City, and the entire Northern Hemisphere is

covered by the thick ice of a rapidly forming glacier. The film was produced during the 2004 presidential election campaign, possibly with the
intention to embarrass President Bush. The movie audience seemed less
than impressed and far from convinced. Nor did the film achieve any apparent adverse electoral effect on the Republican presidential and vice
presidential candidates.

The point is that the predictions made by global-warming advocates
do not have to be true or necessarily credible for them to be advanced in
an effort to gain public acceptance. A supportive and uncritical press
continues to give global-warming advocates extensive media coverage.
Our conclusion here can be stated clearly and firmly: global-warming
theory is not a scientific hypothesis whose validity can be demonstrated
by rigorous, indisputable evidence. The global-warming theory has become a political statement whose advocates seem to believe their predetermined conclusions regardless of critical argument to the contrary.

THE UNDERLYING POLITICAL AND ECONOMIC
AGENDA OF THE KYOTO TREATY

Nowhere is the environmentalist agenda clearer than in the blind determination with which they have pushed for U.S. adoption of the Kyoto
Treaty. In March 2001 the Bush administration decided not to pursue ratification. Specifically, the Kyoto Protocol is an amendment to the U.N.
Framework Convention on Climate Change (UNFCCC) designed to be a
legally binding agreement under which the industrialized nations of the
world, including the United States, are expected to pledge specified reductions in greenhouse gases by targeted dates. The Bush administration
concluded that an underlying agenda of the Kyoto Protocol was to punish the United States. The United States emits some 5,410 million metric
tons of carbon dioxide (some 20.1 tons per capita) compared with the
European Union, which emits approximately 3,171 million metric tons
of carbon dioxide annually (8.5 million tons per capita).

China, the world's second-largest emitter of carbon dioxide, was not
initially intended to be a signatory. The target reductions for the United

States were among the largest reductions specified as a percentage of current emissions to be eliminated. The Bush administration objected not only to the larger burden the United States would have to bear in hitting the targets but also the absolute cost of the reductions and the subsequent burden these costs would place upon American business and the U.S. economy in general. Other issues involved the loss of sovereignty that was viewed as intrinsic to the treaty's assumption that the United States would submit to a legally binding agreement whose ultimate arbiter was the United Nations. Nor was the Bush administration convinced that the case had been built with sufficient scientific certainty so as to require such costly steps be taken now.

In July 1997 the U.S. Senate voted unanimously (95–0) to oppose any international treaty that would damage the U.S. economy by restricting energy usage or by raising the costs of fuel. Those voting for the resolution included John Kerry (D-MA) and Joseph Lieberman (D-CT) as well as John McCain (R-AZ). The Kyoto Protocol was signed, however, by the insistent initiatives of then Vice President Al Gore. And President Clinton never submitted the treaty to the Senate for ratification. As a result of this history, Gore became one of the principal political spokespersons for the Kyoto Protocol.

On January 15, 2004, Gore gave one of his typical speeches on global warming. He showed the audience pictures of glaciers one hundred years ago and compared them with photographs of the same glacier today. "In Glacier National Park, ninety years ago, the Grinnell Glacier looked like this. With one of my daughters, I hiked to the top of it in '98. It looks like this now. Twenty-seven of the thirty-eight glaciers in the park have melted. This was a popular one earlier in the century and now it's completely gone. And within fifteen years, this could be called 'The Park formerly known as Glacier.'"[15]

The U.S. Geological Survey (USGS) agrees with Gore that the Grinnell Glacier has melted significantly. But unlike Gore, the USGS documents that all thirty-seven of the glaciers in Glacier Park "have receded dramatically since the mid-nineteenth century, the end of the Little Ice Age in the Western United States." The USGS points out that the Little

Ice Age comprised "a fairly long cool period during which glaciers expanded until the climate began to warm after the mid-1800's."[16]

Gore's "evidence" is typical of the type of evidence cited by radical political extremists. Just because a glacier is diminishing does not mean we can reliably attribute the cause to the burning of hydrocarbon fuels by U.S. citizens in their automobiles on interstate highways. The phenomenon viewed scientifically is more likely attributable to swings in temperature over many decades, swings that may be sufficiently dramatic as to be described as moving from a Little Ice Age when the glaciers were formed.

Gore punctuated his rhetoric by taking what even he admitted was a cheap shot at the Bush administration:

> And you know there's a—well, I'll tell this personal story. When I was in the sixth grade, I had a classmate in geography who pointed to the outline of South America and the outline of Africa and he asked the teacher: "Did they ever fit together?" And the teacher said: "Of course not! That's the most ridiculous thing I've ever heard!" That child went on to become a drug addict and a ne'er do well. The teacher became Science Advisor in the current administration.[17]

The Gore speech was also highlighted by the typical demonizing of those who saw the issue of global warming differently than he did:

> Now in spite of the clear evidence available all around us, there are many who still do not believe that global warming is a problem at all. And it's no wonder because they are the targets of a massive and well-organized campaign of disinformation lavishly funded by polluters who are determined to prevent any action to reduce the greenhouse gas emissions that cause global warming out of a fear that their profits might be affected if they had to stop dumping so much pollution into the atmosphere.
>
> And wealthy right-wing ideologues have joined with the most cynical and irresponsible companies within the oil and coal and mining industries to contribute large sums of money to finance pseudoscientific front groups that specialize in sowing confusion in the public's mind about

global warming. They issue one misleading report after another, pretending that there is a significant disagreement in the legitimate scientific community in areas where there's actually a broad-based consensus.[18]

Gore did not stop there. He went on to call up another straw man, the tobacco industry, playing to the sentiments of his audience that tobacco companies would do anything to keep people smoking, even if smoking caused heart attacks and death, just as long as the tobacco companies could continue to make a profit by selling cigarettes. Here is how Gore phrased the rhetoric:

Now focus on these pseudoscientific groups that take money from the coal companies and mining and oil companies. The techniques that they use were pioneered years earlier by the tobacco industry in its long campaign to manufacture uncertainty in the public's mind about the health risks caused by tobacco smoke. You know, that's an industry that kills one out of every five of its customers. Not a good business plan unless they can find a way to recruit massive numbers of what they call "replacement smokers." All right? And so—and it's interesting—if you look at the names of the people who took money from the tobacco companies, laundered through law firms often—some of the same scientific campfollowers who took money from the tobacco industry as part of that effort are right now taking money from the coal and oil companies in return for their willingness to say with a straight face that global warming is not real. It is a fact.[19]

Demagoguery like this suggests that Gore is less interested in scientific evidence than he is determined to make political points that deride and diminish anyone who disagrees with him. The tactics of radical environmentalists have been to push for media and general public acceptance of the basic global-warming arguments, regardless of legitimate scientific questioning or refutation. By repeatedly putting the topic on the agenda, the advocates of the Kyoto Protocol believe that ultimately opponents will simply give in. A key strategy has been to push for top public officials, including President Bush, to make fundamental admissions, such as agreeing that the earth is getting warmer or admitting human activity is a culprit.

At the G8 meeting scheduled for Scotland in July 2005, environmentalists pressed their agenda again. A great victory was scored when the president, on his way to the meeting, commented as he traveled from Denmark to Scotland in a manner that suggested he had caved in and accepted all the principle radical environmentalist articles of faith. Bush was quoted as saying, "I recognize the surface of the earth is warmer and that an increase in greenhouse gases caused by humans is contributing to the problem."[20] A principle of propaganda that would have been recognized by the twentieth-century masters of the art was in evidence here: repeat a lie often enough and it becomes truth, regardless of the evidence to the contrary.

If the Kyoto Protocol, or any international agreement like it, is implemented, we face a number of major costs—not just the economic impact of implementing measures to reduce emissions of carbon dioxide, but also the establishment of a large government bureaucracy to supervise the enterprise. In the darkest scenario, the government bureaucracy would be an international bureaucracy with legal authority to intervene directly within the borders of the United States to impose compliance with its dictates.

In pushing to make carbon dioxide a noxious chemical in the minds of Americans, radical environmentalists have joined forces with the extreme political Left. Imposing economic costs upon American business, even if the costs were to slow the economy significantly, might just be seen as a price worth bearing. Moreover, the imposition of the penalty may actually be the real goal sought for its own merit. If American consumers and American businesses are seen as somehow "morally evil" for burning "fossil fuels" in excess of some proportionate standard, then imposing economic penalties upon us may well be viewed as a justifiable remedy. The economic harm we suffer could well be perceived by such radical environmentalists and extreme leftists as just retribution for our lavish lifestyle and our selfish abuse of the earth's resources. As we maintained earlier, the underlying agenda is not the protection of the environment but the imposing of a moral and political cost upon the United States.

GLOBAL WARMING, JUST ANOTHER MALTHUSIAN SCARE?

Environmentalists have conducted an emotional, highly charged political campaign to press their agenda that human activity has caused global warming with disastrous climate change consequences. As Patrick Michaels, professor of environmental studies at the University of Virginia in Charlottesville, has pointed out, this highly charged, emotional agenda has dominated the attention of the mainstream mass media, many prominent politicians, and the public even though the science behind the idea of "anthropogenic global warming" is nowhere near conclusive.

It is doubtless that large-scale environmental changes known popularly as the "Greenhouse Effect" or "Global Warming" have commanded as much public attention as any environmental issue in recent history. As an example, *Time* painted the following picture in its 1988 "Man of the Year" issue, featuring Planet Earth: If left unchecked, anthropogenic alterations of the atmosphere will bring, by the years 2030–2050, a global temperature rise of 4°C, ecological chaos including famine, related civil strife, and tidal waves crashing through a Manhattan landscaped with palm trees. As a rhetorical vehicle, I will refer to this scenario as the "Popular Vision" throughout this article.

Such scenarios also abound in the writings of politically active environmental scientists, environmental lobbyists, and newswriters. United States elected officials have compared the current situation to that of fascist Germany, where several events, such as Kristallnacht, presaged the holocaust. Those that do not recognize this have been labeled modern Neville Chamberlains. Draconian interventionist legislation has been proposed, and the implementation of policies to counter "global warming" is now a touchstone of US foreign policy.[21]

Once global-warming theses become conventional wisdom, opponents can be labeled "right-wing kooks" in an attempt to discredit their arguments before anyone can seriously consider the validity of their criticism.

Bjørn Lomborg, an associate professor of statistics in the department of political science at the University of Aarhus in Denmark, has developed an interesting economic analysis of the global-warming issue. Lomborg is a former member of Greenpeace and generally supportive of the argument that human activity has increased carbon-dioxide emissions to the point where the earth is warming up. He considers himself a "skeptical environmentalist," however, in that he is not convinced the climate changes resulting from global warming are likely to be dramatic or terribly harmful. Moreover, he considers the cost of reducing carbon dioxide to be too high given the low likelihood that we will experience climate changes that we cannot manage. This is Lomborg's central argument, namely that "we should not spend vast amounts of money to cut a tiny slice of the global temperature increase when this constitutes a poor use of resources and when we could probably use these funds far more effectively in the developing world."[22]

In other words, Lomborg argues that the cure proposed is more costly than the danger warrants spending.

> To give a feel for the size of the problem—the Kyoto Protocol will likely cost at least $150 billion a year, and possibly much more. UNICEF estimates that just $70–80 billion a year could give all Third World inhabitants access to the basics like health, education, water and sanitation. More important still is the fact that if we could muster such a massive investment in the present-day developing countries this would also give them a much better future position in terms of resources and infrastructure from which to manage a future global warming.[23]

This type of cost-benefit analysis is rare among thinkers sympathetic to the environmentalist movement. Generally, radical environmentalists write in alarmist tones, suggesting we should spend whatever it takes to reduce carbon-dioxide emissions resulting from the burning of hydrocarbon fuels. If we do not heed their advice, the radical environmentalists act as if we are destroying the potential for future human life on the planet. Critics such as Lomborg add a perspective to the debate, reminding us that "it is not true that global warming has made us experience or will make us experience great increases in hurricanes and storms, and likewise the claim of an unprecedented and ever stronger El Niño seems weak and theoretically unsubstantiated."[24] If we are not facing the brink of disaster, as the radical environmentalists argue, more measured steps to deal with carbon dioxide emissions might be wiser, especially when weighed against the trade offs where the dollars invested to reduce carbon-dioxide emissions might be better spent.

Julian Simon, a professor of business administration at the University of Maryland, wrote at length about the "seductiveness of the Malthusian logic."[25] Simon's perspective was that humans have made dramatic advances since the eighteenth century. He asked, "Why is there so much false bad news about the subjects of the environment, resources, and population?" Even more important, he wondered, "Why do we believe so much false bad news about the environment, resources, and population?"[26]

Simon was perplexed that the mainstream media buys so completely the dire predictions advanced by the radical environmental movement, especially when the scientific basis for dire conclusions is less than solid:

> The current gloom-and-doom about an environmental crisis is all wrong on the scientific facts. Even the Environmental Protection Agency acknowledges that U.S. air and water have been getting cleaner rather than dirtier in the past few decades. Every agricultural economist knows that the world's population has been eating better ever since World War II, defying simplistic Malthusian reasoning. Every resource economist knows that all natural resources have been getting more available rather than scarce, as shown by their falling prices over the decades and centuries. And every demographer knows that the death rate has been falling all over the world; life expectancy almost tripled in the rich coun-

tries in the past two centuries and almost doubled in the poor countries in just the past four decades.[27]

It is almost as if the radical environmentalists are playing off the idea that hydrocarbon fuel is "dirty." People feel oil is "oily," not appealing to the touch, or that gasoline spilled on your hands feels nasty and stains clothes. We think of carbon as the dirty ashes and cinders that result from a fire. All these are distasteful images, so hydrocarbons must be bad. Yet, again, projecting human reactions onto nature is not necessarily justified. Trees breathe carbon dioxide; humans exhale carbon dioxide. Diamonds are pure carbon. Why don't we think of diamonds when we think of hydrocarbon fuels?

Lomborg warns us that if we take major steps to reduce carbon-dioxide emissions, the economic cost we will bear may be disproportionately large, as much as $5 trillion:

Global warming will not decrease food production, it will probably not increase storminess or the frequency of hurricanes, it will not increase the impact of malaria or indeed cause more deaths. It is even unlikely that it will cause more flood victims, because a much richer world will protect itself better. However, global warming will have serious costs—the total cost is about $5 trillion.[28]

Lomborg cautions that $5 trillion would be better spent developing the Third World, especially since credible science indicates the climate change effects will be minimal and manageable.

Radical environmentalists like to charge that anyone who has optimism about the ability of human beings to solve Malthusian problems are "cornucopia-thinkers" who blindly believe in abundant resources and no limitations on human creativity. What we have stressed here is the need to keep in perspective the scientific difficulties with concluding that the burning of fossil fuels generates enough carbon dioxide to cause such a magnitude of global warming that we will inevitably suffer disastrous climate changes. A radical environmental movement characterized by the type of rhetoric championed by Al Gore should give us all reason for pause. We have more proven reserves of oil and natural gas today than we have ever had in our history. The earth is sufficiently inhabitable to accommodate 6.5 billion people. In the scope of human problems, putting global warming at the top of the list is far from justified.

SCIENTISTS BET ON GLOBAL COOLING

In August 2005, as this book was going to press, Matt Drudge featured a series of articles that highlighted a global heat wave that was causing discomfort in major cities all over the world. Because Drudge's Web site (www.drudgereport.com) is a major destination for news professionals, what he posts on a daily basis tends to impact the new cycle in the media generally. On August 19, Drudge ran a story about Senators John McCain and Hillary Clinton, who were among a group of senators touring Alaska. Evidently the senators met with a group of Native Americans on Alaska's northern coast, where Native Americans were complaining about the melting permafrost and coastal erosion as evidence of global warming.

The Alaska trip produced a media photo opportunity where the senators could be filmed wearing light coats, walking under umbrellas in a drizzle. The theme coming out of the event was that anybody trekking to Alaska in the summer could obviously see that the earth was warming up. Senator Clinton commented: "I don't think there is any doubt left for anyone who actually looks at the science. There are still some holdouts, but they are fighting a losing battle. The science is overwhelming, but what is deeply concerning is that climate change is accelerating." The senators were appreciative of the Alaska guides who took the time to show them how "climate change" is affecting Alaska. Clinton was convinced: "I don't think anyone who has talked to these individuals as well as the scientists would have any doubt that this is a real and growing problem."[29] Many who have spent summers in Alaska were not convinced, having experienced many Alaskan summers when much of the state is warm. What seemed clear from the senators' jaunt to Alaska was that the issues of global warming and climate change are likely to become issues in the

2008 presidential campaign. McCain and Clinton seemed anxious to position themselves on the liberal side of the argument.

After we read Drudge's posts, we e-mailed him a caution not to be taken in by the environmental hype on these issues. We sent him a draft of this chapter. Typically, we received no response, but within the next few days he posted an article from the other side of the issue. That article reported that Russian solar physicists Galina Mashnich and Vladimir Bashkirtsev had wagered a British climate expert, James Annan, ten thousand dollars that the earth would cool over the next decade. The Russian solar physicists believe that the earth's temperature is affected more by the sun than by burning hydrocarbon fuels. According to their research, changes in the number and size of sunspots have a measurable effect upon temperature changes. Because they believe the sun is going into a less active phase in the next decade, the Russian solar physicists believe the earth will cool, experiencing a measurable drop in temperatures.[30] We will have to see who wins, since the bet will be determined by a series of agreed-upon temperature measurements to be made between 2012 and 2017. Still, Drudge's decision to post the article was positive. His readers should know that the scientific evidence is still far from settled. Evidently credible scientists still believe it is reasonable to wager one another over whether the earth is warming up or cooling off.

5

THE FOLLY OF OIL CONSERVATION

It is no program simply to say "use less energy."
—RONALD REAGAN,
November 13, 1979

GLOBAL-WARMING ACTIVISTS INEVITABLY propose three solutions. First and foremost, they encourage oil conservation. Second, they admonish us to use alternative fuels, such as wind technology and hydrogen-powered cars. Third, they press for government regulations to force oil conservation, mostly because they believe we will have to be coerced into making the right choices for our own survival. None of these approaches have worked to date. Yet that doesn't stop the environmental crowd. As we have seen, their underlying agenda is a political agenda. No true-believing fossil-fuel theorist or global-warming alarmist is going to be dissuaded from the cause by scientific or behavioral evidence to the contrary.

In this chapter we are going to focus on the first two proposed solutions. Why don't we embrace the call for energy conservation? Why don't we get enthusiastic about using alternative fuels? The answers are simple. We don't believe either approach has a chance of working. Why not? We are going to make an argument here that economic behavior is motivated by market forces, plain and simple. Appeals to conserve energy may sound good, but they don't work. Alternative fuels sound interesting, but they have not been proven to be economically viable or able to stand without the artificial support of government tax incentives. The only available technology that has a chance of making a major contribution is nuclear energy. We will explore this alternative, fully aware that the environmental Left can be expected to oppose any expansion of America's nuclear power plant system as virulently as it did in the 1970s.

Passing laws to enforce a conservationist agenda may be satisfying to true-believers, but our history when government attempts to regulate energy economics is not very encouraging.

Remember when Jimmy Carter had solar panels installed on the White House while he attempted to preach energy conservation to America. Ronald Reagan had the solar panels removed as he engineered a new era of market deregulation. Under Jimmy Carter we saw one oil disaster after another, from the shock of gas lines and high prices to the 1979 revolution in Iran, which has managed to keep Iranian oil off the U.S. market for more than a quarter century. Even today Carter remains a hero to environmentalists, despite the fact that none of his energy conservation proposals ever worked.[1]

Maybe this time around we should make sure we understand market forces before we start legislating.

OIL CONSERVATION, A KNEE-JERK REACTION?

When faced with the oil crisis of his day, Jimmy Carter gave us a great example of his natural impulse to blame us for our profligate ways and to demand conservation. In an April 18, 1977, speech televised to the nation from the White House, Carter listed ten principles that were supposed to save us from running out of oil, a crisis he said was unavoidable by the middle 1980s unless we followed this advice. If you guessed that conservation was his sixth and most important principle, you are right. He said the cornerstone of his policy was "to reduce the demand through conservation."

Our emphasis on conservation is a clear difference between this plan and others which merely encourage crash production efforts. Conservation is the quickest, cheapest, most practical source of energy.[2]

In the 1970s we did not end the oil crisis with conservation. Why should we believe conservation is the solution today?

AMERICANS KEEP PUMPING GAS

In the first months of 2005, oil increased to $50 a barrel and held there. Then oil advanced to $60 a barrel and once again held there. We heard many dire predictions that Americans would stop driving, that our economy would come to a grinding halt. Again, the predictions were wrong.

Americans keep driving their cars because, even at these higher prices, the marginal economic decisions made by motorists are such that they continue to drive their cars. A twenty-five-gallon tank costs $37.50 to fill when gasoline costs $1.50 per gallon. The same gas tank costs $55.00 to fill when gasoline costs $2.20 per gallon. The increase of $18.00 is clearly noticeable, but not so noticeable that people quit driving. If the vehicle gets fifteen miles per gallon, a twenty-five-gallon tank of gas will take you approximately 375 miles. At $1.50 per gallon, that comes to about ten cents a mile. If the gas costs $2.20 per gallon, you are paying about fifteen cents a mile. For a great majority of drivers, that is still a bargain.

Looked at another way, adjusted for inflation, the 1981 price for a barrel of oil today would be more like $85 per barrel. This was calculated by an oil analyst for Oppenheimer and Company, when oil future prices were around $56 per barrel.[3] The American Automobile Association (AAA) maintains that the increased cost of gasoline is almost offset by lower costs for auto maintenance, registration, tires, and taxes. The per-mile cost of driving a car in 2005 is estimated to be 56.2 cents in 2005, compared to 56.1 cents in 2004, after taking into consideration all costs, including the cost of buying the car.[4]

The second quarter of 2005 showed continued strong growth in the

117

U.S. economy. The Commerce Department reported that gross domestic product (GDP) expanded at an annual rate of 3.4 percent. This was the ninth consecutive quarter that GDP grew by 3 percent on a year-to-year basis. Granted, the first quarter GDP numbers showed a 3.8 percent growth, yet the second quarter numbers were supported by strong economic indicators suggesting the economy was still in an expansion mode.[5]

At some point, increases in gasoline prices will cause a slowdown in the U.S. economy, possibly if gasoline should hit $3.00 a gallon, almost certainly if gas were to hit $5.00 a gallon. Still, gas prices cannot be examined in isolation. In 2005, when Americans looked at the dramatically increasing prices of the homes they own, the overall psychology was to feel better off financially. The financial decisions that constitute our economy are made by millions of consumers who each calculate their own particular advantage. Consumers willing to pay the price don't care about somebody else's judgment that driving their cars is environmentally unsound or morally wrong because they use too much gasoline.

In the 1970s, under Jimmy Carter, when gasoline was in short supply and long lines clogged the gas stations, Americans did adapt their behavior by moving toward smaller, more gasoline-efficient automobiles. These decisions, however, were market-driven, not politically mandated. If gasoline prices were to rise today to a point where the economy is hurt, there will certainly be political consequences, but the fundamental adjustments will be made by individual consumers who alter their driving and car-purchasing behavior as they adjust to the higher prices. Economists can argue about the exact price where gasoline costs will adversely harm the economy. Still, in the final analysis, any conservation that results will be consumer-driven, not government-mandated.

AMERICA AND SAUDI ARABIA:
TWO SIDES OF THE SAME OIL COIN

In the last twenty-five years, U.S. dependence on foreign oil has increased dramatically, a subject we will discuss fully in the next chapter. Fossil-fuel theorists, global-warming alarmists, and environmentalists all point to this trend as a serious problem. Here we want to introduce a single theme: the move to import more oil is market-driven, and so far the market appears ready and able to supply America's need. At present there has been more than enough oil internationally to supply our need for foreign fuel. Let's examine here just how the international market works.

In 1973 oil imports accounted for about one-third of all U.S. petroleum needs. In 2005 imports supply nearly 60 percent of our petroleum needs. So the volume of oil imports has increased dramatically, nearly doubling from the 1991 total of 6.8 million barrels imported per day to a 2004 total of 11.8 million barrels imported each day. Today we import more oil than we produce domestically.

This is not just a function of increasing domestic demand; U.S. oil production has decreased in absolute terms as well. In 1985 U.S. domestic oil production was averaging 10.6 million barrels of oil a day. Data for the first ten months of 2004 showed that U.S. oil production was averaging only 5.4 million barrels per day, a five-year low.[6] Conventional theorists, as we have already explained, are convinced that U.S. oil production has peaked and there is no prospect that any significant new amount of U.S. oil will ever be found. Believing that oil is fossil fuel, the common wisdom is that America has already used up the majority of the oil that lies within our territory. From here on, conventional analysts see America's future as one where our dependence on foreign oil will only increase

We have already disagreed with this premise. With sufficient political resolve, we believe the U.S. domestic production of oil could increase dramatically. The three remaining U.S. oil-producing areas of any significance are the Gulf of Mexico, Texas, and Alaska's North Slope. We will return to this topic in the last chapter, when we recommend opening up U.S. oil exploration to reduce our dependence on foreign oil. Right now, let's continue with the market analysis.

Today about 70 percent of U.S. oil imports come from five countries, three of which are in the Western Hemisphere. In the first months of 2005 we imported about 1.5 million barrels of oil a day from Canada, Mexico, and Saudi Arabia each. An additional 1.3 million barrels a day comes from Venezuela, and 1 million barrels from Nigeria. Of these, our most flexible international supplier has been Saudi Arabia, a country that has been responsive to U.S. requests to increase production to maintain world supplies at a level consistent with the growth of demand.

From a point of view of pure economics, we have to ask what is wrong with this. We are still getting all the oil we need, even if some of it comes from overseas. We also spread our risk by drawing from as many as twenty countries to import the oil we need. Note also that we are not dependent upon Saudi Arabia for our foreign oil. If we drew no foreign oil from Saudi Arabia, we could draw more from others to get the oil we need.

Let's look at this from the viewpoint of Saudi Arabia. A considerable amount of wealth is transferred every day from the United States to Saudi Arabia. We will assume the price of oil stays at $50 per barrel. With 1.5 million barrels each day being exported from Saudi Arabia, each day $75 million goes from the United States to Saudi Arabia, for an annual total of $27.4 billion dollars.

Many Americans look at this outflow as dollars taken from our pockets and sent via the gasoline pumps to Saudi Arabia. Yet when the dollars get to Saudi Arabia, the problem becomes one of where to invest them. Many of the dollars shipped to Saudi Arabia for oil end up returning to the United States. Between October 2004 and March 2005, Saudi Arabia and the other oil-exporting countries have reinvested approximately $43.3 billion in U.S. assets. Many of these dollars went into U.S. Treasury bonds, helping to finance the U.S. debt. The rest went into U.S. equity markets, buying the stock offerings of U.S. companies listed on U.S. exchanges.[7]

Other dollars are going into Saudi Arabian real estate and the Saudi Arabian stock market. In the first seven months of 2005 the Shuaa Capital Arab composite index, an important Saudi Arabian index tracking 254 companies in 12 Arab nations, rose approximately 67 percent after two years in which the index had gained 60 percent each year. Since 2001 the market capitalization on the six stock exchanges of the Persian Gulf's main oil exporters (including Bahrain, Kuwait, Oman, Qatar, Saudi Arabia, and the United Arab Emirates) has nearly tripled to about

$875 billion. Construction is also booming, especially in the emirate of Dubai, a resort destination for many Arab nations of the Middle East.[8]

In the 1970s surging oil prices also sent windfall oil profits to the Middle Eastern oil-exporting countries. Then, too, their investment in the United States increased dramatically. Recently, the political Left has portrayed Saudi Arabian investment in the United States as a frightening scenario. Michael Moore, in his anti-Bush film *Fahrenheit 9/11* represents that the Saudis have approximately $860 billion invested in the United States, primarily in equities. Moore contends the Saudis have made major investments in blue-chip stocks, including Citibank and AOL Time Warner. The Saudis own approximately 7 percent of America, Moore claims, as a result of these investments. Moore also suggests the Saudis have $1 trillion in U.S. banks, and he comments that a huge blow would be done to the U.S. economy if the Saudis were to withdraw these funds suddenly.[9]

His point is to scare Americans that George H. W. Bush and George W. Bush have "sold out" the United States to the Saudis in return for oil. Moore also tries to establish that George W. Bush has exploited a "special relationship" with the House of Saud, whereby he and his father have continued to receive favorable investments and business opportunities from the Saudi royal family. In return, Bush supposedly has favored the Saudis, allowing the bin Laden family to escape America immediately after 9/11 and taking active steps to prevent any government investigation of 9/11 that could be embarrassing to the Saudi royal family.

The conspiracy nature of this thinking is extreme and largely established only by innuendo. Regarding any investments the Saudis have made in the United States, there is another side to this story. Foreign investment in the United States makes foreign investors more dependent upon the reality that the United States remains economically strong. When stock prices decline broadly on U.S. markets, all investors lose money, regardless of whether they are U.S. or foreign investors. The same holds true for real-estate investments. When prices decline broadly in U.S. real-estate markets, all real-estate investors lose money, including the foreign investors. In the 1980s Japanese investors suffered enormous loses from investing in overpriced U.S. real estate, especially in Hawaii.

When the bubble burst in these real-estate markets, the Japanese suffered huge losses that compounded simultaneous losses in Japan's domestic real-estate market.

If the Saudis were to take any steps calculated to harm the United States or to damage the U.S. economy, they would in effect be taking steps against themselves, putting their own valuable investments and assets within the United States at risk.

And just because foreigners invest in U.S. markets does not mean they are always winners. The reality is that foreign investment makes U.S. markets and foreign markets more interdependent. We must also remember that U.S. investors buy stocks and real estate in foreign markets as well. In July 2005 Saudi Arabia announced a series of measures designed to make Saudi Arabia more friendly to foreign investors.[10] Why do this when Saudi Arabia is realizing a nearly unprecedented increase in U.S.-dollar foreign reserves resulting from increasing oil prices? In today's international economy, the move by nearly all nations is to become more involved in foreign trade and foreign investment—not less.

There has never been greater pressure from a wide range of countries to join the World Trade Organization. Regional trade agreements are being pursued around the globe in ever-increasing numbers. The world market is growing, and nations are becoming more economically interdependent whether we like it or not. In January 1994 Canada, the United States, and Mexico formed the world's largest free-trade area by entering into the North American Free Trade Agreement (NAFTA). On August 2, 2005, President Bush signed a trade agreement with five Central American countries (Costa Rica, El Salvador, Guatemala, Honduras, and Nicaragua). Known as the Central American Free Trade Association (CAFTA), the agreement expands what has been accomplished with NAFTA, possibly setting the stage for additional Western Hemisphere agreements that could reach from Canada to Argentina. The development of regional and worldwide free-trade markets is clearly under way, with the likely result of international cross-investment among participating countries.

Let's consider another economic dimension of surging oil prices.

Money flowing overseas for higher gasoline prices in the United States may also reduce consumer domestic spending. Some economists calculate that for every one-cent rise in the price of gasoline at the pump, consumer spending declines $1.3 billion.[11] As we have pointed out, even with gasoline prices dramatically increasing to more than two dollars a gallon, consumers have continued spending, and the U.S. economic numbers have continued to advance generally. In short, the economy has absorbed the increasing oil prices. But we have also noted that adverse impacts on the U.S. economy are likely should U.S. gasoline prices continue to increase, possibly to three or five dollars a gallon and almost certainly at ten dollars a gallon. The U.S. economy cannot endlessly absorb gasoline price increases without suffering an adverse effect. As we have just seen, however, that adverse effect will also boomerang on the oil-exporting nations to the extent they have reinvested U.S.-dollar foreign reserves into U.S. investments, including Treasury bonds.

Let's also remember that many U.S. oil companies and gas-station operators have benefited from these higher prices. Second-quarter 2005 earnings for U.S. oil companies reached record levels. ExxonMobil posted second-quarter 2005 earnings of approximately $8 billion, the second highest in the company's history. ConocoPhillips posted a 51 percent gain in second-quarter 2005 profits, to report $3.1 billion in earnings.[12] In the 1970s, when U.S. oil companies reflected large gains in profit from rising oil prices, the Carter administration sought a windfall-profits tax, as if the oil companies had done something wrong. The U.S. economy is still a capitalistic system, and making profits in business is not yet a crime. The profits realized by the oil companies is invested back into the economy in many forms, including dividends and additional resources for expanded oil exploration within the United States. Profits, even large or unexpected profits, realized by U.S. oil companies have a positive effect on the U.S. economy, not a negative effect.

Besides, if higher oil prices should depress the U.S. economy, the resulting drop off will set in motion economic forces that will most likely put a brake on the upward movement of gasoline prices. Very little is certain in economics, but prices always seem to change direction when the economic forces that have led them to go up (or down) have sufficiently played out, and countervailing economic forces build and move the markets in the opposite direction. The market itself will adjust to higher oil prices when they reach a sufficiently high level that the overall impact on the U.S. economy is negative. At that point, oil companies and oil exporters will realize that prices must come down if their market share is to be maintained.

Again, when we look at the other side of the coin, we realize that the Saudi Arabian economy is dependent on oil exports. Currently oil-export revenues are estimated to make up 90–95 percent of total Saudi export earnings. Between 70–80 percent of the Saudi Arabian state revenues depend on oil-export revenues. Moreover, oil-export revenues make up about 40 percent of Saudi Arabia's gross domestic product. With 40 percent of the Saudi GDP coming from oil, the Saudis stand to be whipsawed by dramatic changes in oil prices and oil demand.

With oil prices surging, the Saudis are estimated to have received a windfall increase of $30 billion in oil revenues in 2004. Total gross revenue from oil exports in 2004 was estimated to have earned them some $100 billion per year, which translates into roughly $274 million daily. Originally, when Saudi Arabian economists prepared their economic forecasts for 2004, the expectation was that the government would experience a budget deficit. That calculation, however, was predicated on the assumption that oil would stay at $19 per barrel. In mid-2004, however, the Saudi Finance Ministry expected a huge budget surplus of $26.2 billion, due almost entirely to the dramatic 2004 increase in the cost of oil.[13] Saudi Arabia will not want to see this revenue stop, even if investing it wisely, as we have seen, requires both skill and good luck.

The majority of Saudi Arabia's oil exports (about 60 percent) go to China, India, Japan, and South Korea. Yet Saudi Arabia wants to increase its market share in the United States. Why? The United States is by far the largest market for oil. Currently we consume about one-fourth of the world's oil, and that market dominance is not likely to diminish for some considerable time. Granted, China and India are emerging oil consumers of major significance. Still, their industrial economies and their lifestyles have a long way to go. Today the United States consumes roughly 20 million barrels of oil daily. By comparison, China consumes about 6.83 million barrels a day, and India about 2.3 million. We are confident that one hundred years from now China and India will have closed these gaps considerably.

Today Saudi Arabia is happy to have an increasing share in providing oil to America. What has happened is not that Saudi Arabia has won and the United States has lost simply because we are importing 1.5 million barrels of oil a day from the Saudis. We want to stress that what has happened is that the United States and Saudi Arabia have become more *interdependent*, whether the political pundits realize it or not. We could each do without the other, but working together still continues to make sense for both.

The concept of world interdependence is not a right-wing conservative idea. The principle was first articulated by John F. Kennedy in an address he gave at Independence Hall in Philadelphia on July 4, 1962. His words that day were directed to the Atlantic partnership his administration was then seeking to establish with Europe:

> But I will say here and now, on this Day of Independence, that the United States will be ready for a Declaration of Interdependence, that we will be prepared to discuss with a united Europe the ways and means of forming a concrete Atlantic partnership, a mutually beneficial partnership between the new union now emerging in Europe and the old American Union founded here 175 years ago.
>
> All this will not be completed in a year, but let the world know it is our goal.
>
> In urging the adoption of the United States Constitution, Alexander Hamilton told his fellow New Yorkers "to think continentally." Today Americans must learn to think intercontinentally.[14]

Kennedy's vision is now being realized as world markets are growing in importance, supplanting in importance the economic effects that in previous generations would have been confined to the borders of individual countries. The emerging international oil market demands that we grasp this vision of interdependence if we are truly to understand the dynamics at play.

We have also begun to create interdependency with our other major oil suppliers, including Canada, Mexico, Nigeria, and Venezuela. Each side of the oil coin, importer as well as exporter, has a monetary stake in the economic health of the other. In today's world economy, international trading partners are having to realize the fundamental equation that their relationship is mutually dependent whether they like it or not. The adjustments we see in the world economic markets may not be as easy if oil reaches seventy or eighty dollars a barrel. Yet we should avoid responding emotionally. Projecting our preconceived notions on markets or predicting what we would like to see happen can be very embarrassing if investments made on those prejudices turn out to be losers. Markets tend to be very uncaring about the emotions of investors.

This thinking is in direct contradiction with the defeatism at the heart of fossil-fuel, global-warming, and much environmentalist thinking. Let's return once more to Jimmy Carter's April 18, 1977, televised address. What Carter said that day nearly thirty years ago could easily be said today by the pessimists who dominate much of the debate in the mass media:

> The oil and natural gas we rely on for 75 percent of our energy are running out. In spite of increased effort, domestic production has been dropping steadily at about six percent a year. Imports have doubled in the last five years. Our nation's independence of economic and political action is becoming increasingly constrained. Unless profound changes are made to lower oil consumption, we now believe that early in the 1980s the world will be demanding more oil that it can produce.[15]

As we have pointed out, Carter was wrong—we did not run out of oil. Moreover, we did not need to impose government-mandated conservation or even depend on the willingness of American consumers to use less gasoline because that was the "right thing" to do. In the 1970s Americans

126

moved to smaller, more gas-efficient cars and pumped less gas for market reasons. Gas cost more. That alone was enough for the market to impose the corrective needed. When gas prices came down, consumers bought more gas. In the 1990s, when gas was once again relatively cheap, consumers bought bigger cars, including SUVs, and drove even more. There was nothing "wrong" with that behavior—it reflects how rational consumers should be expected to behave in a relatively free-market economy.

What should be obvious is that Carter had almost no understanding of how world oil markets work. When commodities hit higher prices, new opportunities for competition open up. Oil that is left in the ground at twenty-five dollars per barrel may be worth drilling for at sixty dollars per barrel. Markets don't give up just because politicians do.

WHY ARE WE SAVING THE OIL ANYWAY?

So let's ask a fundamental question. If we're running out of oil, what point is there in trying to preserve it? At best, that logic only prolongs the inevitable. Why don't we use what we have right now? As supplies decrease, the price should increase. Increasing prices will either cause conservation or stimulate alternatives. Either way, the market will drive the adjustment, not politicians articulating platitudes.

Environmentalists have fought tooth and nail repeated attempts to grant oil exploration leases off the shores of Florida and California. The same is true for the Arctic National Wildlife Refuge (ANWR) in Alaska. We could also look to the Gulf of Mexico to expand oil-exploration efforts. Producing wells continue to indicate that we have extensive oil reserves that have not yet been tapped in all these areas. The American public is being whipsawed between the concerns generated by the fossil-fuel theorists, greenhouse-effect alarmists, and environmentalists. We don't know which is worse: a fear that we are running out of oil or a concern that we will wreck the environment if we look for more oil.

Again, environmentalists pursue with an emotional pitch that borders on hysteria the argument that oil exploration will destroy the environment. Yes, an oil spill off the shores of Southern California in 1969

127

did harm thirty miles of beach near Santa Barbara. Yes, in 1989, the *Exxon Valdez* oil tanker did run aground on Bligh Reef in Alaska, spilling some eleven million gallons of crude oil into Prince William Sound. In both cases, the news coverage and resulting photographs produced disturbing images that remain even today in people's minds. What is not appreciated is that oil exploration has continued off the California coast since 1969, and we have continued drilling oil in Alaska since 1989. These environmental disasters were rare occurrences, not inevitable and unavoidable consequences of oil production off the shores of California or in the ANWR. Besides, when we return today to the site of both incidents, we see clean water, abundant wildlife, and a pristine environment. Still, many people persist in seeing only the image of the damage, not the restored environment there today.

In the years since 1969 we can recall many instances where airliners have crashed, killing dozens or hundreds of passengers. We have not closed down commercial airlines. Even after 9-11, we implemented increased precautions and kept flying. Why is the same not true with oil exploration? Each catastrophe suffered by human beings causes extreme suffering and loss for those involved and for their loved ones. All people of good will suffer over the hurt of these incidents. The images linger in our collective memory and cause renewed pain whenever they are revisited. Yet we continue.

No one would argue that increased environmental precautions need to be taken with oil exploration and production. Radical environmentalists, however, want all drilling stopped because some harm might occur. Extreme environmentalists often appear to have no sense of balance. If we harm one bird, is that too much a price to pay for producing oil? Sometimes extreme environmentalists sound as if their goal is to stop industrialized society altogether, so the world can return to some idealized image of nature without human beings. Yes, we are told that man can live in "harmony with nature," but somehow for extreme environmentalists that means we must give up or dramatically reduce our use of carbon-based fuels and all the industry and lifestyle advantages we derive from the use of those carbon-based fuels.

President George W. Bush has spoken eloquently about the need to pursue oil production in Alaska:

> By far the most promising site for oil in America is the Arctic National Wildlife Refuge in Alaska. Technology now makes it possible to reach the oil reserves in ANWR by drilling on just 2,000 of the 19 million acres. Developing this tiny area could eventually yield up to a million barrels of oil every day—and that million barrels of oil a day would be—would make us less dependent on foreign sources of energy. Thanks to technology, we can reach ANWR's oil with almost no impact on the land or local wildlife. To make America less dependent, Congress needs to pass a pro-growth, pro-jobs, pro-environment development of ANWR. It makes sense. It is an important part of a comprehensive strategy.[16]

Think about it for a moment. The area the president wants to drill in Alaska is about the size of a postage stamp on a football field—the same footprint of two thousand acres on nineteen million acres, only about 0.01 percent (one one-hundredth of 1 percent) of the total area in the Alaska National Wildlife Reserve. Still, environmentalists fight a battle to the death to prevent any oil exploration in ANWR. They argue that even if the production from ANWR reaches one million barrels a day by 2010, that would only put a dent in our continuing dependency on foreign oil. They argue that "the tiny fraction of U.S. imports potentially accounted for by ANWR would only grow smaller with each passing year."[17]

The environmental lobby insists upon negative thinking. Why not look at the marginal increase in U.S. production made by ANWR as a positive, a step in the direction away from depending on exports? What if oil-production technology has advanced to the point where the environment remains protected by oil companies operating with a goal to protect the environment? What if the ANWR is only a small indication of the total quantity of oil available in Alaska? Ironically, there might be a huge quantity of oil under Alaska. That may well be the underlying but unspoken reason environmentalists argue so hard to prevent any oil exploration in Alaska. The underlying objective of the radicals sometimes seems as if their goal is to stop all oil production in the United States, maybe even worldwide, rather than encourage oil exploration to proceed under environmentally responsible preconditions.

Advocates of conservation tend to focus on one side of the argument: we must use less oil. They refuse to consider the other side of the equation: we must find more oil. We could start by allowing oil companies to explore and develop areas where we know there is more oil, namely offshore and in Alaska. Then, if the argument presented in this book is correct and oil is truly an abiotic product, we might find extensive oil still available to us yet on the continental United States—if only we were to explore deeper, not simply looking for oil where we find source rocks in sedimentary soil relatively near the surface. Who knows how much oil lies beneath the large wells we have already drilled out?

Conservationists just want to prolong what they see as inevitable. Beginning with a fossil-fuel orientation, conservationists are locked into peak-production thinking: since there only ever was a finite quantity of fossil fuel, sooner or later we have to find and use up whatever quantity of oil there is. Conservationists want us to ration out what is available so it lasts longer. But that isn't the conservationists' real point. Deep down, they believe we use too much carbon-based fuel. In this sense, the underlying agenda of the conservationists ends up agreeing with the radical environmentalists. Conservationists are calling for government intervention in markets, one way or another. At a minimum, the addition of tax incentives in legislation to promote the development and use of alternative fuels is an agenda conservationists can be counted on to support.

The idea of rationing out what is seen as a diminishing supply of oil reflects no serious understanding of markets. If we continue to use oil at our current pace, and we start running out of oil, then the price should go even higher. At higher prices, the market itself will force conservation and the pursuit of alternative fuels. From a market perspective, the problem right now is that oil is still cheap. At this cost, why bother conserving? Alternatives that might deliver substantial energy, such as nuclear power, are still expensive, even when oil reaches more than sixty dollars a barrel. When and if the price of oil gets sufficiently high, nuclear alternatives are going to start making sense economically. Until then, conservationists can preach to us all they want. Yet if the market forces are going in a different direction, we should not expect many people to be listening.

Moreover, despite decades of admonitions that we are running out of oil, we must point out once again that today the world has more proven reserves of oil than ever before in history. We return to ask why anyone listens to environmentalists or conservationists when their fundamental premises continue to be undermined by empirical evidence to the contrary? Maybe propaganda theorists do have the answer. When we do not think critically, emotional arguments sound persuasive, especially if the arguments are repeated often enough and firmly enough. Environmentalists and conservationists always present their arguments as truths only an idiot would disagree with, regardless of the evidence to the contrary. Proof of assertions presented as propaganda is not required unless the people listening continue to reason logically and demand evidence.

MOST ALTERNATIVE FUELS DON'T PRODUCE ENOUGH ENERGY

For decades conservationists implored us to utilize alternatives to carbon-based fuel—everything from windmills to solar cells to hydrogen-powered automobile engines are pushed as solutions. Billions of dollars in federal taxpayer revenue have been wasted by providing economic incentives to pursue energy alternatives. To date, the sad result is that none of these alternatives has taken hold with the consuming public. None of the fuel alternatives has successfully competed with hydrocarbon fuels, except on a small scale and only with massive tax incentives. Hydrocarbon fuels remain more commonly available, more convenient to use, and still reasonably cheaper in price than anything else. Let's review the alternative fuel landscape.

WINDMILLS KILL BIRDS

At first consideration, windmills should be an attractive alternative energy technology. Windmills throw off no carbon dioxide, and the wind is

free. The problem is that large quantities of windmills are needed to produce electricity on a commercially viable basis. The windmills are unat-
tractive, and they take up a lot of land. Windmills don't operate when
there is no wind. Moreover, they kill birds.

Windmill farms sprang up all over California during the last twenty
years, a phenomenon driven largely by a myriad of tax-incentive
schemes. Few places in the country have been more productive in using
windmill technology than Altamont, California, a stretch of rolling hills
about fifty miles east of San Francisco. The more than five thousand
windmills that line the hilltops of Altamont Pass generate some 820 million kilowatt hours of pollution-free electricity annually, enough to
power 120,000 homes a year.[18]

The downside is that the windmills have become a "death trap for
thousands of birds that get chopped up in fast-rotating turbine blades as
they fly through or hunt for prey or fly on migration through the mountainous region between the San Francisco Bay area and the San Joaquin
Valley."[19] Experts estimate that as many as forty-seven hundred birds are
killed each year in the fifty square miles that make up the Altamont Pass
Wind Resource Area. The dead birds include as many as thirteen hundred federally protected raptors, including burrowing owls, red-tailed
hawks, and even golden eagles, according to a study completed last year
by the California Energy Commission. Ironically, with so many endan-
gered birds being killed, the "pollution-free" Altamont Pass windmills
became an environmental nightmare.

Instead of ending the windmill experiment, the Altamont County supervisors came up with a different solution: they changed the regulations. In July 2005 the county supervisors ruled to phase in a new
generation of windmill turbines designed to spin higher, hopefully outside the birds' flight plan. To meet these requirements, the operating
windmill companies will be required to spend an estimated $540 million
over the next thirteen years to upgrade the old windmills.[20]

The supervisors also mandated moving the windmills to areas that
are considered out of the more prolific raptor breeding areas and out of
the middle of the major raptor migratory flight paths. Over the last two

decades the current windmills have probably killed twenty-six thousand raptors. Providing conventional electricity to the homes in the Altamont Pass area would probably have been a cheaper solution to the bird-kill problem, but then that solution would not have met legislative mandates to utilize alternative energies, regardless of their economic efficiency.

Windmill technology in California has had a checkered history. First introduced when gasoline prices were high during the Carter administration, windmills were encouraged by federal and California state tax breaks that only covered the construction of the windmills. Tax incentives were never consistent or strong enough for maintaining the windmills after they were built. So the craze to put up windmills led to "tax scheme" investing by many who had no serious long-term interest in the technology. When the windmills broke down, many were simply abandoned.[21] Driving along California highways today you can see eerie landscapes of broken-down windmill farms consisting of towering structures that may originally have cost hundreds of thousands of dollars to construct and now are towering testimonials to a now-abandoned alternative fuel technology.

Denmark has been the most enthusiastic country in the world in terms of adopting windmill technology. Estimates claim as much as 20 percent of Denmark's overall electricity needs are fueled by windmills. Still, the Danish government has to pay some $300 million a year in subsidies to keep the windmill industry going.[22] Without the subsidies, many of the windmills in Denmark would go the way of the California windmills. The Danes have advanced the technology, learning to produce lighter, less expensive windmills that can generate more electricity than the 1970s models. Yet even in Denmark, the windmills can be a noisy eyesore that kills birds.

One of the major downfalls to windmill technology is simply the amount of land that has to be devoted to windmills to generate any large amount of electricity. One estimate examined how large an area would have to be devoted to windmill technology if New York City were to abandon coal and natural gas to generate 60 percent of the city's needs for electricity. The answer was 10.6 square miles, an area larger than southern Manhattan, from the tip of the island through Greenwich Village. It would have to hold some sixty-eight hundred turbine windmills, each capable of generating 1.5 megawatts of electricity. Yet we should be encouraged. To deliver the same amount of electricity with solar power would take an area of seventy-four square miles, an area stretching from about Fifty-ninth Street north to the tip of the island in a square block that would reach across to New Jersey on the west and include the Bronx on the east. The installation would involve more than 145 million solar panels, each delivering 175 watts of power. By comparison, that quantity of electricity would take four nuclear reactors capable of delivering 1,000 megawatts each, with each plant taking up about two square miles.[23]

Still, when the wind does not blow, windmill technology is no more effective than a sailboat in a race caught in a doldrums. A giant modern windmill, standing about 150 meters (about 500 feet) high, with a blade diameter of about 100 meters (328 feet, slightly more than one football field), can generate about ten megawatts of electricity when the wind blows hard, about ten miles per hour. But when the wind blows moderately, say at one mile per hour, the windmill hardly produces any electricity at all, not even enough to power a dishwasher. Even in the windiest locations in the world, windmills rarely produce significant electricity more than half the time. Electricity in large quantities is hard, if not impossible, to store. Electricity when generated has to be delivered. Windmills, when they are working, can end up generating excess electricity. But when the wind is not blowing, windmills are next to useless. Because of this deficiency, windmill systems need conventional hydrocarbon-fuel backup, unless they are applied to very small applications (fueling an individual home, for instance) and don't have to work all the time.[24]

HYDROGEN CARS ARE NOT YET PRACTICAL

In July 2005 General Motors announced the results of a nationwide research study it had funded to investigate public perceptions of U.S. energy policy. The results indicated that energy security should be a top priority, with respondents voicing strong support for a "moon shot" effort to develop a hydrogen economy. Presenting the survey to the automotive press, GM Vice President for Environment and Energy Elizabeth Lowery lamented how little credit GM gets from the public for the investment the company is making to pursue hydrogen energy alternatives: "But while the survey shows that Americans support the same goals that are at the heart of GM's overall advanced technology strategy for improving efficiency, it's troubling what little credit we're getting."[25]

That major U.S. automotive manufacturers even have vice presidents for energy and environment shows that the car companies have heard the drumbeat from the political Left. Hydrogen cars are the current alternative energy fad. Why not? Hydrogen is abundant. Water molecules consist of one hydrogen atom bound with two oxygen atoms. Hydrogen is a powerful fuel, and burning it in an automobile engine throws off water as a by-product, not carbon dioxide. There are, however, several major problems. Releasing hydrogen from water requires the expenditure of considerable hydrocarbon energy to accomplish the task, so much so that burning the hydrogen in a car may not be a net savings in carbon-dioxide emissions. Moreover, with current technology, hydrogen is difficult to compress, and the resulting hydrogen fuel tank adds an enormous additional weight to the car.

Pressurized storage tanks can hold compressed hydrogen at around one hundred times the atmospheric pressure (1500 PSI, pounds per square inch). To match the energy efficiency of a fifteen-gallon gasoline tank would take around sixty high-pressure storage tanks (each tank holding about twenty-nine cubic feet of highly compressed hydrogen). Hydrogen storage tanks must be massive simply to withstand the pressure. And they weigh as much as one hundred pounds empty; only about a quarter of a pound in weight is added by the compressed hydrogen when the tanks are filled. Sixty of these tanks would add six thousand pounds to the twenty-eight hundred pounds the average American car now weighs. The vehicle would have to be about three times the average current size of automobiles, just to hold the hydrogen tanks.

So if you are getting ready to imagine driving what amounts to a large trailer weighing about nine thousand pounds, consider the safety risk. If a tank gets damaged in an accident, the pressurized hydrogen would rush out with a strong and potentially dangerous force. Anybody who has let go of a balloon only to see it fly around as the compressed air escapes should get the idea. Now imagine the extreme hazard of a nine-thousand-pound vehicle the size of a trailer having a major collision on a highway, with the resulting explosion of dozens of compression tanks jetting out hydrogen and flying around dangerously loose.[26]

When hydrogen cars are as easy to use and as cheap as gasoline-fueled cars, then we won't need surveys to show us what the public supports. Up until that point, the surveys and press releases from automobile manufacturers look more like public relations than advertising. Granted, car manufacturers want the public to understand that they are exploring energy alternatives. If any government tax breaks are forthcoming, car manufacturers want to be positioned in the receiving line. Besides, all good corporate citizens want ready answers to counter the commentary of the industry's inevitable conservationist and environmentalist critics. Burning hydrogen in an internal compression engine sounds like a good idea, but don't expect to be driving one anytime soon.

ETHANOL IS NOT FUEL EFFICIENT

The 2005 federal energy bill allocated approximately $6 billion in federal funds to assist in the development of ethanol plants around the country. Ethanol is a "biofuel," a gasoline substitute made from plants, generally corn. Proponents argue for ethanol both to reduce the emissions of carbon dioxide caused by burning hydrocarbon fuels and to provide substitutes for gasoline, addressing fears that we are running out of oil. A $20-billion market worldwide has developed around the production and marketing of ethanol.[27] Drug companies as well as major oil companies are involved as producers of ethanol and, in the case of the oil companies, as distributors. Ethanol can be mixed with gasoline or used as a complete substitute for gasoline, provided the internal combustion engine is adapted to burn ethanol-only fuel. Ethanol is clearly a boon to corn farmers. Environmentalists are also enthusiastic at finding a biological substitute for oil that is both cleaner and renewable. Sounds like a perfect, sustainable substitute for hydrocarbon fuel, at least as far as transportation is concerned. What's the downside?

For starters, the production of ethanol may burn up more hydrocarbon fuel than it saves. Consider the different uses of hydrocarbon fuels needed to convert corn into ethanol. An analysis conducted by David Pimentel, professor of ecology and agriculture at Cornell University, and Tad Patzek, professor of civil and environmental engineering at the University of California, Berkeley, came to this conclusion by taking into account the production of pesticides and fertilizers needed to grow the crops, the running of farm machinery and irrigation, the grounding and transporting the crop, and the fermenting and distilling of ethanol from the water mix. Their conclusions were that corn requires 29 percent more hydrocarbon energy than the fuel produced; switch grass requires 45 percent more, and wood biomass requires 57 percent more. The same conclusions held for plants that produce biodiesel fuel from soybeans (27 percent more hydrocarbon fuel used than produced) or sunflowers (118 percent more hydrocarbon fuel used). The analysis did not factor in the additional costs in federal and state subsidies that are passed on to consumers in the form of taxes.

"The United States desperately needs a liquid fuel replacement for oil in the near future," Pimentel said, "but producing ethanol or biodiesel from plant biomass is going down the wrong road, because you use more energy to produce these fuels than you get out from the combustion of these products." He added: "The government spends more than $3 billion a year to subsidize ethanol production when it does not provide a net energy balance or gain, is not a renewable energy source or an economic fuel. Further, its production and use contribute to air, water and soil pollution and global warming." Pimentel had nothing positive to say about the endeavor: "Ethanol production requires large fossil energy input, and therefore, it is contributing to oil and natural gas imports and U.S. deficits." He further added that the vast majority of tax benefits and subsidies went not to farmers but to large ethanol-producing corporations.[28]

Blending ethanol with gasoline also increases the emission of nitrogen oxide and other smog-forming chemicals. If you modify your car's engine to take an ethanol blend, you may violate the car's warranty so as to remove any future engine problems from coverage. Finally, a 10 percent ethanol-blend in gasoline reduces gas mileage by 3 to 5 percent; a 20 percent blend reduces gas mileage 6 to 10 percent. Higher corn prices resulting from government subsidies to support corn production increase the cost of corn grain supplied to beef and poultry producers, adding an estimated $1 billion to the cost of beef production annually. Still, ethanol is a biological product and carbon dioxide emissions are reduced, enough reason for global-warming enthusiasts to support government subsidies regardless of the efficiency of the fuel or the resulting economic side effects.

NUCLEAR POWER ON THE UPSURGE

In the 1970s the United States led the world in nuclear power plant technology. That was brought to an abrupt halt by the accident that began on March 28, 1979, at Three Mile Island. The partial core meltdown that occurred in that reactor also began a partial meltdown for the nuclear power industry in the United States. The second shoe fell on April 25, 1986, when the Russian nuclear power plant at Chernobyl exploded, throwing high radiation into an area within twenty miles of the plant. The American public never fully recovered from these images. The impact was reinforced by a politically motivated movie whose timing could not have been worse for the nuclear power industry. *The China Syndrome* was released just prior to the Three Mile Island accident and was playing in theaters as the public was reeling from the shock of the disaster.

Still, the nuclear power industry has continued, though at a slowed pace. Today 103 nuclear power plants operate in 31 states, generating approximately 20 percent of the nation's electricity. Surprisingly, Vermont—one of the country's most politically liberal states—leads the list with 73.7 percent of its electricity powered by nuclear plants. Nuclear power supplies more than 25 percent of the electricity in 18 states. South Carolina follows Vermont on the list (with 54.5 percent of the state's electricity produced by nuclear power plants). Other leading nuclear power states include Connecticut (54.4 percent), New Jersey (51.9 percent), Illinois (50.1 percent), and New Hampshire (43.0 percent).[29]

The construction of nuclear power plants requires considerable public funding to be feasible. Still, nuclear power has several major advantages. Nuclear power reactors are in the fourth generation of development. The newer-generation reactors have simpler, safer designs that reduce capital cost and use less fuel to obtain equivalent power output.[30] Today more than thirty countries are operating nuclear power reactors, generating approximately 20 percent of the world's electricity. In 2000 nuclear energy produced as much electricity as was produced worldwide in 1961 by all energy sources.[31]

The 435 nuclear reactors operating worldwide use some 180 million pounds of uranium annually. Currently only about 100 million pounds of uranium are being mined each year. With growing demand, more than 8,500 mining claim permits were filed in the first six months of 2005 in eight uranium-rich counties in Colorado and Utah. The Department of Energy has decided to put 13,500 acres of uranium-laced Colorado lands up for bid in 2006, the first time this has happened since 1974. Some 75 million pounds of uranium are estimated to remain in the Colorado plateau. All this activity evidences a move to reexamine the long-term viability of nuclear power as an alternative to burning hydrocarbon fuels.[32] Worldwide, resources of uranium appear abundant. Moreover, breeder reactors actually generate plutonium, which can itself be used as fuel.

Even when the cost of carbon-based fuel makes nuclear energy economically attractive, we should not expect an easy acceptance of expanding nuclear energy. Environmentalists hate nuclear energy worse than they hate the burning of fossil fuels. When nuclear power gains ground, we may not have as many global-warming arguments to face, but we are certain to hear a lot more about the environmental hazards involved in the disposal of spent nuclear fuel. A whole risk of hazards, from cancer to radiation dangers to spent-fuel disposal, will certainly return to the center once environmentalists begin to fear that the move to develop more nuclear power plants is under way. Ironically, environmentalists may regret that they pushed global warming so hard, especially if the ultimate result is that the public returns to favoring the construction of more nuclear power plants.

Technological innovations and inventions that truly succeed have market-driven advantages that propel them. Government will undoubtedly continue to mandate the exploration and development of dozens of otherwise economically untenable alternatives to carbon-based fuel. Someday we may even see nuclear batteries capable of powering everything from flashlights to automobiles. The serious innovations, however, will only take hold when they deliver power competitive with carbon-based alternatives at a price that is the same or cheaper.

6

THE GROWING U.S. DEPENDENCE ON FOREIGN OIL

Large amounts of oil and natural gas lay beneath our land and off our shores, untouched because the present administration seems to believe the American people would rather see more regulation, taxes and controls than more energy.

Ronald Reagan, July 18, 1980

EXPERTS ESTIMATE THAT AMERICANS consume more than 25 percent of the world's oil but have control of less than 3 percent of its proven supplies. This unbalanced pattern of consumption makes it possible for foreign governments, corrupt political leaders, terrorist organizations, and oil companies to hold the economy and the citizens of the United States in a virtual stranglehold. There is no greater proof of this than the direct relationship between skyrocketing gas prices and the explosion of wealth among those who control the world's supply of oil.

FIFTY YEARS FROM INDEPENDENCE TO DEPENDENCE

During World War II the United States derived a great strategic advantage by being able to produce all the oil it needed to fight a war across both the Atlantic and Pacific Oceans. We faced two foes, Nazi Germany

141

and Imperial Japan, both of whom were dependent on other nations for the oil they needed to run their industrial societies and to wage war.

Daniel Yergin, in his epic study of the oil industry, stressed how important America's oil independence was to our World War II victory:

> If there was a single resource that was shaping the military strategy of the Axis powers, it was oil. If there was a single resource that could defeat them, that, too, was oil. And as the United States almost single-handedly fueled the entire Allied war effort, putting an unprecedented drain on its resource, a fear of shortage began to grow. It was another of those periods of pessimism about the American oil position, similar to that at the end of the First World War, but etched, because of this war, in much greater urgency. What would a pervasive and lasting shortage mean for America's security and for its future?[1]

As the war progressed, planners within the Roosevelt administration became concerned that the rate at which new oil discoveries were being made in the United States was slowing down. Secretary of the Interior Harold Ickes wrote a disturbing article titled "We're Running Out of Oil!" which was published in December 1943, before the tide of war had turned in the Allies' favor. If America was destined to become a net importer of oil, experts knew that our attention would turn to the Middle East. Herbert Feis, an economic adviser to the State Department, understood America's coming oil predicament: "In all surveys of the situation, the pencil came to an awed pause at one point and place—the Middle East."[2]

Could the United States forever remain strategically independent if it was forced to import the bulk of the oil on which the economy and military strength depended? This was the question strategic planners were asking as World War II approached a successful conclusion. Today we are faced with the necessity to answer that question.

WHERE DO OUR IMPORTS COME FROM?

The United States consumes approximately 21 million barrels of oil a day. Each day we import some 12 million barrels of oil, about 60 percent of all the oil we consume. About 20 percent of our oil imports come from Persian Gulf countries, averaging about 2.4 million barrels a day. At $50 a barrel, this means we are sending more than $600 million a day overseas for oil, of which $120 million a day goes to Persian Gulf countries. At $60 a barrel, we are sending $720 million a day overseas for oil, of which $144 million goes to the Persian Gulf. With oil at $60 a barrel, we are sending overseas nearly a quarter of a trillion dollars each year just to buy oil.

We have never before in our history experienced this massive a transfer of our national wealth overseas. The political ramifications are enormous as we bleed dollars to the world so we can buy oil. In 2005 our largest amount of oil was imported from Mexico (approximately 1.75 million barrels a day), followed by Canada (about 1.72 million barrels a day), and Saudi Arabia (1.4 million barrels a day). The next two major importers on the list are Venezuela (1.3 million) and Nigeria (1.1 million).[3]

As Americans, we have traditionally focused on domestic politics. American soldiers have died in many foreign lands that many Americans could not readily find on the globe. Avoiding foreign entanglements has been an American watchword since George Washington published his Farewell Address on September 17, 1796. Whether we realize it or not, this situation has changed. We can no longer afford to ignore our oil-importing partners. Their internal politics can directly affect us by their willingness to open up or shut down the oil spigot. Today we have to have foreign entanglements because we have to import foreign oil. The trend of that dependency is increasing, not decreasing. If nothing is done to reverse this tendency, we will be importing 70 percent of the oil we use, perhaps as soon as 2010.

With so much of our imported oil coming from the Persian Gulf, the United States is constantly attuned to the ever-present potential for turmoil in that region. The Iranian Islamic Republic has continued to press forward with a clandestine nuclear-weapons program. The clerics ruling Iran have exported terrorism for more than a quarter century, funding Hezbollah in Lebanon and working hand-in-hand with al-Qaeda to kill

Israelis and Americans. The prospect of a nuclear-armed Iran providing a nuclear umbrella to cover its terrorist activities is frightening along many dimensions. One only has to think back to the 1980s tanker-war Iran fought against Iraq in the Persian Gulf to realize how quickly Iran could shut down oil transport through the Straits of Hormuz, quickly placing a stranglehold on the flow of oil worldwide. The minute the mullahs resume enriching uranium, we should expect oil prices to spike. Any move the Iranians make toward nuclear-weapons development will have an immediate negative impact on worldwide oil prices as markets price the commodity with an eye to the risk of a new wave of terrorism or even nuclear blackmail.

We have to realize that American oil policy has developed Western Hemisphere partners, including Canada, Mexico, and Venezuela, in part to reduce the risk of political or military instability in the Middle East. As long as the conflict continues between the Israelis and the Palestinians, the potential of terrorism or war in the region remains an alarming and ever-present danger. To keep downward price pressure on world oil markets, America must develop strong sources of oil supply elsewhere. To protect against the possible disruption of oil flow from the Middle East, we have no choice but to cultivate alternative oil-importing partners, even if there are serious political complications and risks given the relatively small selection of available international alternatives.

ILLEGAL IMMIGRANTS FLOOD ACROSS THE MEXICAN BORDER

Our top-fifteen oil-importing countries include several from south of the border. In addition to Mexico, we are importing oil from Brazil, Colombia, and Venezuela in South America and Ecuador in Central America. Understanding this lends a new perspective to the immigration invasion we are currently experiencing from our Spanish- and Portuguese-speaking neighbors. As of 2004 some 13.9 million illegal immigrants are estimated to be within our borders, including 4.7 million minor children who are U.S. citizens by birth, even though they are living in "mixed status" families where their parents are illegal immigrants.[4] More than half of the illegal immigrants entering the United States come from Mexico (59 percent), an additional 25 percent come from other Latin countries, including El Salvador, Ecuador, and Colombia.

The draw for illegal immigrants typically begins with economics—jobs and economic opportunity. Then the flow continues, drawn on by families wanting to reunite within the United States. The Center for Immigration Studies in Washington DC gives an excellent summary of the dynamics in play:

> The two "magnets" which attract illegal aliens are jobs and family connections. They typical Mexican worker earns one-tenth his American counterpart, and numerous American businesses are willing to hire cheap, compliant labor from abroad; such businesses are seldom punished because our country lacks a viable system to verify new hires' work eligibility. In addition, communities of recently arrived legal immigrants help create immigration networks used by illegal aliens and serve as incubators for illegal immigration, providing jobs, housing, and entrée to America for illegal-alien relatives and fellow countrymen.[5]

Nearly one-quarter of all illegal immigrants settle in California, followed by Texas (14 percent), Florida (9 percent), and New York (7 percent). Growing illegal immigrant populations are forming in Arizona, Illinois, New Jersey, and North Carolina—part of a trend whereby foreign-born communities have grown from a relatively small presence simply by families and relatives communicating, making it easier for additional family members to join them in the United States.[6]

Once here, illegal immigrants are very difficult to deport. Communities of Spanish-speaking foreigners are easy to recognize, even in states such as Illinois and North Carolina. In a state like New Jersey, some urban centers, such as Elizabeth, Morristown, Patterson, and Union City, end up with many thousands of Spanish-speaking residents. Still, authorities face a dilemma. Roundups to examine immigration papers are certain to arouse the ire of civil liberties groups such as the ACLU. Lawsuits would be certain to block any major law-enforcement attempt to identify and deport large numbers of illegal immigrants in such towns. Then, too, family situations are complex. Could authorities deport the parents and leave the children in the United States? Any children born here would be U.S. citizens and have a right to stay, even if their parents do not. Serious practical problems of this nature make law-enforcement efforts to deport illegal immigrants nearly impossible once the individuals are here and have joined or formed families.

Since 1990 more than 75 percent of the immigrants entering the United States from Mexico have been illegal, numbering somewhere between 400,000 to 485,000 illegal immigrants from Mexico annually. While most of these Mexican illegal immigrants stay in Arizona, California, and Texas, an increasing number are dispersing to other Spanish-speaking population centers throughout the country. In 2005 the U.S. Border Patrol reports an increase in OTM (Other Than Mexican) detainees who are illegally crossing the border, a number growing to an estimated 150,000 annually, mostly coming from Brazil and Central America. Mixed into the OTM total was a small but dangerous group not from Brazil, Central America, or Mexico, but from so-called countries of concern that may include countries with terrorist connections.

The U.S. government has not been able to stop this flood of immigrants from Mexico, as evidenced by the citizen group Minuteman Civil Defense Corps (http://www.minutemanhq.com/). The Minuteman group has been assisting in the capture and arrest of illegal immigrants attempting to cross a twenty-three-mile stretch of Arizona's border with Mexico. In August 2005 the group claimed it has prevented more than sixty thousand cases of illegal immigration from Mexico, at least 20 percent of whom had criminal records.[7] Mixed in with the illegal immigrants coming from Mexico is an increasing number from other countries, including Middle Eastern countries with terrorist connections. U.S. Border Patrol officers are overwhelmed; they lack sufficient resources and do not have the determined support of the federal government.

Typically, Mexicans caught at the border are only turned back, with no one knowing if or when they might make another attempt to cross later. Even more serious, many OTMs captured by the Border Patrol are not detained, simply because imprisonment facilities are already over-crowded. OTMs are given a court summons and told to appear in court in three months; more than 85 percent never show up. T. J. Bonner, presi-dent of the National Border Patrol Council, an organization that repre-sents more than nine thousand agents, pointed out the ridiculous nature of what amounts to a catch-and-release policy that he believes has allowed some 465,000 non-Mexican illegal immigrants to enter the United States: "It's an insane policy which encourages OTMs to come into the country il-legally, and we shouldn't be shocked that they are coming in record num-bers." Many OTMs actually flag down agents or walk up to them and surrender, knowing they will be released. "The word is out. They know that as soon as they are caught, they will be free to roam at will."[8]

Why doesn't Washington have more resolve to stem the flood of im-migration coming in from Mexico? Oil imports are a ready first answer. The U.S. government finds it difficult to take a systematic, hard look at the nearly free flow of illegal immigrants coming across our southern border.[9] Instead, we have been determined to expand free-trade areas by adding the Central American Free Trade Association (CAFTA) to the pre-vious NAFTA agreement we signed with Mexico and Canada, yet another of our oil-importing partners. The 2000 U.S. Census recorded the His-panic population of the United States at more than thirty-five million persons, nearly a 58 percent increase since the 1990 Census. Spanish today is virtually America's "unofficial" language. This trend shows no sign of stopping or even slowing.

Mexico has the third-largest proven reservoirs of crude oil in the Western Hemisphere, behind Venezuela and the United States. The United States imports virtually all the oil Mexico exports. As a hedge against instability in the Middle East, the U.S. government has to calcu-late our oil needs when considering any steps we take regarding Mexico or illegal immigrants. With such a large number of illegal immigrants coming from Mexico, any crackdown on illegal immigration would have an immediate impact on Mexico.

Mexican illegal immigrants send an enormous amount of money

back to their families. Illegal immigrants earn some $60 billion working illegally in the United States, of which some $17 billion a year is sent back home to their families in Mexico. Facilitated by U.S. banks and payment systems such as Western Union, these "remittance" payments sent back home by Mexicans working illegally in the United States rival the oil industry itself as Mexico's number-one revenue producer.

Family is extremely important in the Spanish culture. The ties back home continue long after a family member has emigrated to the United States. Whether the immigrant is legal or illegal, the same cultural influences keep thoughts of home foremost in mind. Plans are made to bring wives, children, parents, and relatives to the United States, working with the first family member to make it here as the person who establishes a "beachhead." The flow of money back home never stops, if only because there are always family members who cannot for one reason or another come here, or maybe just not yet.

Attacking the remittance industry by cracking down on illegal immigration would deal a severe blow to Mexico's economy. As mentioned earlier, the U.S. and Mexican economies are increasingly interdependent, even if the risk we take is to allow our southern border to be an immigration sieve across which flows not only illegal Mexican immigrants but very likely terrorists using the cover of Mexico to conceal their illegal entry from terror-supporting rogue states. Mexico's gross domestic product depends on America's allowing large numbers of illegal aliens to come here and stay here so they can get jobs in the United States and send money home.

VENEZUELA, LEFTIST REVOLUTIONARIES, AND NARCO-TRAFFICKERS

Venezuela has the Western Hemisphere's largest proven reserves of oil, nearly 78 billion barrels as of January 2004. As we saw above, the United States gets about 10 percent of its imported oil from Venezuela; in turn, about 60 percent of all Venezuela's oil exports come directly to the United States, not counting the crude oil Venezuela sends to the Caribbean to be refined there and then reexported to the United States. This flow of oil occurs despite the political enmity that has developed between the United States and the extreme leftist socialistic government of Venezuela's president Hugo Chavez. The economic benefit to Venezuela is obvious. With oil at $50 a barrel, Chavez takes in some $65 million a day for the 1.3 million barrels of oil shipped to the United States; at $60 a barrel, Venezuela daily rakes in $78 million in petrodollars.

What does Chavez do with this revenue? Reports suggest that he is financing the new Bolivarian army created by Daniel Ortega, who is still the head of the communist-sympathizing Sandinista Party. The Bolivarian army is supposedly constituted of soldiers from throughout Latin America uniting to resist the spread of American imperialism—what else? Chavez sports a Fidel Castro–style uniform. At the same time, Chavez reportedly offers refuge to the Colombian FARC (Revolutionary Armed Forces of Colombia), narco-terrorists who have been at war with Alvaro Uribe, the pro-American president of Colombia, yet another of America's top-fifteen sources of imported oil.[10] So importing oil from Venezuela and Colombia puts the United States at the center of Latin America's continuing struggle with leftist revolutionaries and narco-traffickers. Sarcastically, we could comment, "Why not? We need the oil."

But seriously, we face a nightmare in contemplating a Castro-Chavez-Ortega Axis of Evil combining forces with narco-terrorists and sending foot soldiers through Latin America and into the United States. Socialist political activists, criminal narco-traffickers, Latin American terrorists, and who knows how many other criminals could easily get lost in the growing river of OTM illegal aliens mixing in with the thousands of Mexican illegal immigrants who have been crossing our borders every day for some fifteen years or more. This is in addition to the destabilization of Latin America and South American countries that Chavez is empowered to continue engineering with ample financing available from our petrodollar windfall. Our purchase of oil from Venezuela finances the demise of democracy in our hemisphere and threatens us at home by opening the back door to Spanish-speaking terrorists and drug dealers.

In February 2005 reports circulated that Chavez was using his oil riches to buy weapons such as Kalashnikov rifles and attack helicopters from the Russians. Also reported were discussions about a possible $4 billion purchase of MiG jets from Russia.[11] But can the administration in Washington afford to take too hard a line against Chavez? Obviously not, unless we want to threaten the continued flow of oil and lose yet another hedge against the potential of instability in the Middle East and any interruption that might result in the flow of oil from the Persian Gulf.

CANADA, THE NEXT SAUDI ARABIA?

Canada has quietly come from nowhere to become one of the America's leading sources of imported oil. Most Americans have no idea that Canada has become a major exporter of oil. Yet the reality is that Canada's oil reserves in the arctic bordering Alaska may well prove to be one of the world's richest untapped resources of oil and natural gas, with reserves rivaling even those of Saudi Arabia, the country everyone thinks of first when the subject of proven oil reserves is mentioned.

The United States and Canada have had political tensions for decades, tensions that became exacerbated as forces in Montreal pushed forward with their French separationist efforts. Also, since the Vietnam War, liberal forces in Canada have opposed U.S. war initiatives around the globe, often warmly welcoming Americans who sought political refuge in Canada as an alternative to serving in the U.S. military forces. With so much oil coming available in Canada, the United States may well find it increasingly necessary to come some considerable distance toward hearing out what are typically leftist Canadian political sentiments.

When we appreciate how much oil is involved, we begin to contemplate that the Untied States has placed Canada onto our oil-importer list under the radar to set the stage for what could well expand in the coming years into major trade partnerships. NAFTA, which included Canada as a signatory, could well be a first step toward a more comprehensive, though little announced, plan to expand into a Western Hemisphere free trade market. CAFTA is the next step forward toward a plan to ultimately form a Free Trade Area of the Americas (FTAA), ultimately designed to include all countries in the Western Hemisphere—with the exception of Cuba. Even within the United States, any move toward FTAA is certain to be countered by strong political and economic opposition from many sides once the direction of the initiative is fully appreciated.

Yet what is at stake is a huge amount of oil and natural gas. Though most Americans know very little about Canada's potential to be a major oil supplier, the dimensions of the project are truly staggering. The Mackenzie Delta is in the extreme north of Canada's Northwest Territories, a large wilderness in the upper tier of Canadian provinces, above Alberta. The Mackenzie Delta turns out to be not only rich in natural gas but also contains a "huge but hard-to-tap supply of petroleum dispersed in underground gravel formations. These so-called oil sands hold petroleum reserves that are second in size only to Saudi Arabia's, and analysts say they could supply a large portion of U.S. energy needs for decades to come."[12]

The oil sands are rich in bitumen, a superheavy oil that has to be extracted by a process resembling strip mining. The scooped-out sand is then cooked at very high temperatures to extract oil from the sludge. Alternatively, steam can be pumped into the sands to dissolve the bitumen, a process that allows the oil to be pumped to the surface. Fortunately, the area already contains the natural gas that could fuel these complex processes. The thick oil extracted by these methods has to be refined to commercial grades of crude oil before it can be carried by pipeline to customers, most of which are in the western United States. Some two tons of sand have to be dug up and refined to make one forty-two-gallon barrel of oil.

Still, the Mackenzie Delta area is thought to contain 174 billion barrels of oil, which would place these reserves at second worldwide, only behind Saudi Arabia's 260 billion barrels of proven reserves. In contrast, Alaska's Arctic National Wildlife Refuge (ANWR) reserves, while also huge and largely untapped, holds only an estimated 10 billion barrels of reserves. Oil output from the Mackenzie Delta is expected "to reach 2 million barrels per day by 2010, rising to 3 million by 2020 and as much as 5 million for many decades to come."[13]

A $6 billion Mackenzie Pipeline Project has been organized by a group of major oil companies, including ConocoPhillips, Shell Canada, and ExxonMobil. The group plans to build a 1,220-kilometer pipeline (about 760 miles) connecting the Mackenzie Delta to the northern border of the United States. Initially, the pipeline would carry an estimated 800 million cubic feet per day of natural gas, a flow expected to grow quickly to 1.2 billion cubic feet per day. As the oil field is developed, the pipeline would be available to carry the oil into the United States through Montana.[14]

As might be expected, environmental groups have launched intense efforts to block the development of the Mackenzie Delta. Also, the Deh Cho First Nations, an Indian tribe of about forty-five hundred people who live in about 40 percent of the territory crossed by the pipeline's southern route, filed lawsuits to block the project. Elizabeth May, the executive director of the Sierra Club in Canada, issued a statement on April 15, 2005, expressing extreme concern that the pipeline project was about to begin: "This deal means that the sole function of the Mackenzie pipeline is to supply natural gas to extract oil from the Athabasca tar sands, the world's dirtiest source of oil. Canada could blow its chance of meeting its Kyoto targets if it allows tar sands productions of greenhouse gas emissions to increase from 17 megatonnes in 1990 to the projected 70 megatonnes in 2010. Tar sands projects would then represent the largest total single addition to Canada's greenhouse emissions, representing 9 percent of Canada's total in 2010."[15] The Sierra Club went on to emphasize what it saw as the extreme environmental risks involved:

> The Mackenzie Gas Project itself has important environmental issues including fragmentation of wilderness, loss of biodiversity, increased greenhouse gas emissions, reduction of boreal carbon sequestration capacity, and effects relating to permafrost melting and frost heaving. Once the gas starts to flow south, the 60 or more significant natural gas finds in the Mackenzie Valley and Delta, and Beaufort Sea will also likely be brought into production within 25 years. The conversion of Canada's largest, wildest watershed to yet another industrial landscape will then be well-advanced.[16]

At $50 or $60 a barrel, one million barrels a day in production generates the type of revenue Canada may find impossible to pass up. And the oil companies developing the area will undoubtedly be held to very tight standards of environmental concern. Still, barring any environmental disasters of an *Exxon Valdez* magnitude, the environmentalists are unlikely to win, not in the face of these economics.

Already a deal has been reached with the Deh Cho First Nations. On July 11, 2005, Indian and Northern Affairs Minister Andy Scott and Herb Norwegian, grand chief of the Indian nations, announced that an agreement had been reached with the Mackenzie Gas Project. In the agreement, Canada pledged a considerable range of consultation with the Indians regarding future energy development plans in their territory. Additionally, Canada promised $15 million in economic development funding to assist the Indian nations in pursuing economic and business opportunities. Scott was enthusiastic about the future: "With this agreement, Canada's discussions with the Deh Cho First Nations on land, resources, and governance are back on track and will proceed with renewed vigour—and we in turn generate greater certainty in the Mackenzie Valley. We are committed to ensuring effective and meaningful participation in the Deh Cho in both the environmental assessment and regulatory review of the Mackenzie Gas Project."[17] The Indians in turn agreed to drop all litigation to block the oil companies from proceeding.

The good news about the Mackenzie Delta energy resources is that once again we have strong evidence countering the "running out of oil" scare promoted by the fossil-fuel theorists and conservationists. The bad news may be that once again the United States is in a position of having to compromise national political agendas to meet the political objectives of yet another important oil importer. Even though Canada stretches across our longest border, few Americans have ever visited Canada and even fewer know much about Canada, other than perhaps to hear the Canadian national anthem played before a hockey or baseball game or at an international sporting event such as the Olympics.

Also, efforts to tighten border control to prevent illegal immigrants and drugs from crossing into the United States will be harder to achieve, as is the case with Mexico, to the extent that our oil dependence on Canada increases. For the past decade U.S. drug authorities have identified Canada as a major entry point for high-grade marijuana and heroin, much of which originates in Asia. Drugs are driven across the border or transported by ship on the connecting waterways, especially over the Great Lakes. In some cases, individual entrepreneurs simply walk backpacks of the drugs across the border's hundreds of unguarded miles. Consider this statement from a 2001 National Drug Intelligence Center threat assessment produced by the U.S. Department of Justice:

> The principal illicit substances smuggled into the United States through Canada are marijuana, heroin, and precursor chemicals. Canada increasingly is becoming a source country for high-grade marijuana, and organized Asian criminal groups as well as outlaw motorcycle gangs control facets of production and distribution. Higher purity heroin, primarily Southeast Asian, is transshipped through Canada to the United States where ethnic Chinese criminal groups operating on both sides of the border control distribution. Criminal groups divert precursor chemicals, which are currently unregulated in Canada, to facilitate their production of synthetic drugs, primarily methamphetamine, in the United States; however, regulations to address this are forthcoming.[18]

A 2004 threat assessment jointly published by U.S. and Canadian law-enforcement authorities made clear that drug trafficking across the Canadian border remains a problem: "Despite our best efforts, drug trafficking still occurs in significant quantities in both directions across the border. The principal illicit substances smuggled across our shared border are marijuana, cocaine, precursor chemicals and steroids."[19] The United States' border with Canada is nearly twice as long as the border with Mexico. Even today, much of the border is undeveloped and unwatched.

Despite regulations, the economics of the drug trade has its own compelling logic. Moreover, in a post 9-11 world, an open border across which ample supplies of drugs are transported is an invitation to terrorists seeking to slip unnoticed into the United States. This problem is intensified when we realize that Canada has immigration and visa regulations that in many instances are more relaxed than similar laws in the United States, especially involving nations where Canada has better relations, largely because we perceive the foreign nation involved as constituting a terrorism risk whereas Canada does not. Foreign nationalists who may not be able to meet Homeland Security objections to their entry directly into the United States may be able to enter more easily into Canada. Once in Canada, potential terrorists can assimilate into the population in an effort to "get lost" in a local community, a first step toward a planned illegal crossing of the U.S.-Canadian border.

In concluding this section, we have to wonder once again just how much oil and natural gas there is in Alaska. Now that we see these huge reserves under the Mackenzie Delta, we have to wonder if a huge underground reservoir stretches from ANWR through Canada's Yukon Territory across to the Northwest Territories, just like we have seen in the Middle East, stretching from Saudi Arabia through Iraq and Iran and into Kazakhstan? Environmentalists will fight hard to keep exploration out of the northern wilderness territories. We may yet find plentiful supplies of undiscovered oil right here in Alaska and Northwest Canada, possibly enough to supply our needs for another hundred years, even allowing for considerable increased usage.

U.S. OIL SUPPLY HELD HOSTAGE TO FOREIGN POLITICAL INSTABILITY

King Fahd of Saudi Arabia died on July 31, 2005. In truth, he had been incapacitated since suffering a stroke in 1995. His half-brother, Crown Prince Abdullah, who had been de facto ruler since 1995, officially took over control of Saudi Arabia. None of this was unexpected. Still, on the day after King Fahd's death, crude oil futures hit a new record high of $62.30 on the New York Mercantile Exchange. This marked a 40 percent increase in the price of oil during 2005 and a doubling in price over the previous two years. The hint of instability was enough to send oil markets higher, despite the low probability that King Fahd's death would change anything. Abdullah has been controlling Saudi oil markets since he effectively took over in 1995. What was more disconcerting about the price movement was how skittish oil markets are over any change in the Middle East. Abdullah himself is eighty-two years-old. Serious questions about instability may rise to the surface once he passes away.

Divisions within the ruling family could easily emerge in the next succession opportunity. The House of Saud quickly named Crown Prince Sultan as next in line to accede to the throne. Future succession is more problematic. Saudi Arabia faces severe challenges in attempting to balance the need to reform the country in a more democratic manner that is open to the growing ranks of emerging younger Saudi professionals. Some 60 percent of the Saudi population is eighteen years old or younger.[20] At the same time, the country maintains a deeply conservative Muslim heritage, one dominated by Wahhabism, perhaps the most extreme sect in traditional Islam. In recent meetings with top U.S. officials, the Saudis have asked Washington to relax the pressure to reform. If the Saudis press too hard for democracy within their country, they will be directly at odds with Wahhabi clerics who would prefer to see an Islamic theocracy established.

Saudi Arabia is currently the world's leading exporter of oil, one of the top three countries the United States depends upon for foreign oil. Moreover, the United States looks to Saudi Arabia to help maintain stability in OPEC and within the Middle East generally. Any disturbances within Saudi Arabia will almost assuredly send oil prices immediately higher. A recent role-playing exercise was conducted in Washington with top former government, military, and cabinet officials participating. One scenario proposed a simultaneous terrorist attack against oil facilities in the United States and in Saudi Arabia. As the exercise played out, oil prices hit $120 a barrel, doubling to $5,214.00 the average annual energy bill for the typical U.S. household. Economic forecasts projected an imminent collapse of the current economic recovery in the United States and a loss of more than two million jobs, the largest drop since 1945.

The price reactions in the exercise were prepared by John Down, an analyst at Sanford Bernstein, who clearly understands the implications being role-played by the experts: "With only 2.2 million barrels a day of spare capacity, which is enough capacity to meet a little more than one year of demand growth, the oil markets are at the mercy of political stability in Venezuela, Nigeria, and Iraq, as well as potential terrorist acts."[21] Nor are the U.S. strategic reserves a long-term answer. Even with a maximum reserve of 770 million barrels, the U.S. government maintains the equivalent of only about two months of imports. Besides, if the United States were to tap into these strategic reserves, a panic signal could be communicated to world oil markets, with the result that oil prices would only surge higher.[22]

Few events in international politics or economics are as well foreseen as was the death of King Fahd. Generally, events that cause political instability are sudden and unanticipated, the type of news that interrupts news programming worldwide and produces alerts. Devising immediate and effective responses to sudden, unpredictable events is something that cannot be relied upon with any degree of dependability. Unfortunately, our dependence on foreign oil is pushing U.S. government foreign policy into this corner. Our government has to respond instantly to adverse news that affects our oil-importing partners. Failure to follow initial responses with carefully devised long-term solutions runs the risk of adding momentum to what otherwise might be a temporary spike in oil prices. Even when oil supplies remain relatively stable and strong in world markets, uncertainty over economic or political developments can vault oil prices to new plateaus—plateaus that are only justified because of the uncertainty itself, not because any concrete action has actually depressed or disrupted world oil flows.

As we have mentioned, approximately 20 percent of our oil imports come from the Persian Gulf region. This puts great pressure on the United States to make sure its policy toward Israel includes strong recognition for the Palestinians. We should never forget that OPEC imposed the 1973 embargo specifically to punish the United States for assisting Israel. Our Arab oil-exporting partners in the Middle East want to see Israel make continued concessions to the Palestinians as the world moves toward establishing a Palestinian state. Even should the United States want to hold the line against certain concessions, oil pressure remains available to counter the argument. To the extent the United States remains dependent upon foreign oil, the Islamic Middle Eastern countries will continue to have a strong say on U.S. policy regarding Israel. When we have to calculate that the hint of political instability itself is enough to send oil prices higher, we have to proceed very cautiously in our support of Israel, especially if that support encounters strong objections from Persian Gulf oil exporters. In the final analysis, we are forced to consider that Persian Gulf oil has always been anti-Israel oil.

THE EMERGENCE OF NATURAL GAS IN WORLD ENERGY MARKETS

While attention has largely focused on oil supplies, another development has been taking place just below the public's level of attention. Natural gas deposits typically accompany major oil finds. For decades, natural gas was seen as a worthless product. Lacking a ready market, many oil developers simply allowed natural gas to burn off to get rid of it. With growing concern that the world was running out of oil, interest has been building in natural gas. Over the past few years many important energy demands have been switched not just from coal to oil but now from coal and oil to natural gas. Looking at the statistics, we should realize that natural gas is rapidly becoming an oil alternative of major importance.

In the 1970s natural gas played virtually no role in America's energy profile. Today, natural gas supplies about 20 percent of the country's energy needs.[23] The good news is that while 60 percent of our oil is imported, nearly 83 percent of our natural gas supply comes from domestic sources.

In the last decade electric-power generation has shifted dramatically away from coal and toward natural gas. Nearly all new electricity-generating facilities under construction are using more efficient gas-powered designs. Moreover, natural gas now heats more than 60 percent of all U.S. households, and some sixty million residential customers use natural gas. Natural gas provides almost half the energy for commercial facilities in the United States and nearly 38 percent for industrial operations. More than 130,000 buses, taxis, and delivery trucks in the United States are powered by natural gas. At some level, we are all aware that these changes are taking place, yet few of us realize how many fewer applications are oil-dependent. The only major energy application that remains almost exclusively oil-dependent in the U.S. economy is transportation. We still fill our cars with gasoline even though increasingly we tend to heat and air condition our homes with natural gas.

A major development in the natural gas market has involved advancements in the technology needed to produce liquefied natural gas (LNG) economically. LNG is pressurized and chilled so it can be stored and transported conveniently, advantages that increase greatly the commercial applications to which natural gas can be put. LNG costs have come down by as much as 30 percent over the past six or seven years, due largely to technological advances in liquefaction and shipping. Right now LNG supplies only about 2 percent of all natural-gas needs, but that percentage is growing. By 2020, projections indicate that LNG could provide somewhere between 25 to 30 percent of America's total natural gas needs.[24] We turn again to oil historian Daniel Yergin, who estimates that a capital investment of somewhere in the range of $200 billion will be needed for LNG to reach its full potential. He believes this investment will come from oil companies such as ExxonMobil, BP, and Royal/Dutch Shell, companies who, he observes, "have the financial heft to absorb the risk to the balance sheet and to absorb the volatility" of the marketplace.[25]

Natural gas is also more plentiful than oil. Chemically, natural gas is composed mostly of methane. Natural gas is still considered a fossil fuel, one that, like oil, has traditionally been thought to derive from ancient trees and dinosaurs. Yet methane is commonly available. The truth is that natural gas is not only plentiful, we easily know how to generate it without any need to go dig up ancient bogs. Any major garbage landfill will produce a large quantity of methane gas that can be captured and used as fuel. Even conservative estimates of natural gas availability project that we have adequate reserves to last sixty years or more at current consumption rates. According to the Energy Information Administration of the U.S. Department of Energy, technological improvements have made "unconventional production" techniques the largest source of U.S. gas supplies.[26] Translated into ordinary terms, we are now getting more of our natural gas from places other than the wells in which we also find oil. Instead, technological improvements and rising energy prices have made economical the recovery of natural gas from our abundant sources of tight sands, shale, and coal-bed methane contained in rocks. This has been good news for many mines in the Rocky Mountains that were previously closed because they were uneconomical to operate.

Moreover, natural gas is considered a "cleaner energy" in that burning natural gas does not generate the feared greenhouse gas of carbon dioxide. Not to worry, environmentalists can be expected to identify some other harmful gases that are emitted if burning natural gas begins to look like a possible solution to the so-called oil shortage. Besides, a lot of natural gas reserves are known to be in federal lands, so that should give environmentalists and conservationists plenty to fight over, even if they lose some carbon dioxide ground in the coming national debate over tapping more of our natural gas reserves. As Federal Reserve chairman Alan Greenspan likes to warn, we must be mindful not to allow environmental rules and regulations to become de facto energy policy without thoughtful and substantive debate on the energy issues themselves, not just the environmental concerns, something the radical environmentalists and conservationists have worked for decades to achieve.

OIL COMPANIES AND THE NEED FOR GREED

As we have pointed out, making a profit in America is not yet a crime, even if the profit is large. We have also noted that the dramatic rise in oil prices since the beginning of 2004 has given oil companies what critics like to characterize as "windfall profits," profits that are unexpectedly large and sudden. We very quickly forget 1998, when oil prices bottomed out at less that ten dollars a barrel. At that time many oil executives must have been feeling suicidal, as were many oil company board members and shareholders. If we look back over a long enough perspective, the history of the oil industry has been one of peaks and valleys, strong shifts between high and low prices, shifts that are often not explainable simply by reference to the expected dynamics of supply and demand economics.

Economics professor William J. Hausman, in studying long-term energy prices in the United States since 1800, makes the point that the history of oil prices has been unstable, with no clear long-term trend toward price increases. His observations are certain to surprise those who feel alarm that the current spike in oil prices is irreversible:

> It is actually difficult to make generalizations about the long-term trend in oil prices (and it certainly cannot be said that there has been a secular upward trend). Perhaps the most remarkable feature of the oil industry has been its relative price instability, which is especially evident in the energy price shocks of the 1970s. We remain heavily reliant on oil (both domestic and imported) as a source of energy. It is conceivable that the oil market may remain unstable, and thus it is likely that energy users in the United States will continue to move toward more diversity in sources of fuel.[27]

Hausman notes that several major shifts in the U.S. consumption of energy have occurred since the early 1800s. For the first three quarters of the nineteenth century, wood was the primary fuel used in America for all basic uses. Between 1870 and 1910 the amount of energy consumed in America increased tremendously, and a shift occurred away from wood and toward coal as the dominant fuel. Through the course of the twentieth century another shift occurred as oil and gasoline became America's dominant fuel sources. Now, Hausman believes, a further shift is occurring, away from relying primarily upon oil and natural gas toward a diversity of fuels, a mixture that would allow for the emergence of new fuel sources into the mainstream, including oil. Hausman further notes that the price of particular fuels has increased, but as the mix of fuels used adjusted, the "price of energy," as opposed to the price of particular fuels, has remained relatively stable over the more than two hundred years he studied. Applying Hausman's logic, a mix of fuels that uses more natural gas and nuclear power might well create the pressures that would keep the price of energy stable, even should the price of oil and gasoline continue increasing.

Thinking about nuclear power and natural gas together may open up an interesting new vista on how the composition of U.S. energy supply may be filled in the years ahead. If we move toward more reliance on natural gas and nuclear power to generate electricity for our businesses and homes, we may be able to take substantial demand off our use of oil. As we have mentioned, the only remaining application that depends almost exclusively on petroleum is transportation. Using more nuclear power and natural gas should create more net energy supply; so simply by diversifying our energy applications, we will be able to relieve the extent to which the United States is dependent upon foreign countries to import the oil we need to continue our industrial plant and maintain our lifestyles.

We need to import 60 percent of all the oil we currently use, a percentage that shows every sign of growing toward importing even a larger proportion of the oil we consume. With natural gas, we need to import only 20 percent, and domestic supplies remain abundant. All our nuclear power is produced right here. Changing our mix of fuels to include more natural gas and nuclear power holds the possibility of reversing current trends so that we might be able to reduce the percentage of oil we have to import. Moreover, the global-warming alarmists should be encouraged that neither natural gas nor nuclear power put any significant quantity of carbon dioxide into the atmosphere.

We can also reduce our dependence on foreign oil by exploring more of Alaska and by opening up our substantial continental shelf for increased offshore exploration. Reducing our dependence on foreign oil must remain a long-term goal of U.S. foreign policy for national security reasons, if not for reasons of pure economics. Even if the world market could supply all our oil needs for decades to come, we cannot count on favorable politics to ensure our steady supply. Our constant vulnerability to political instability within the borders of our foreign oil-importing partners opens up a ripe field for terrorists and other enemies of the United States to inflict harm upon us, harm that begins by developing a crisis in which oil prices spike. If we become almost totally dependent on imports to get the oil we need, we will never be rid of oil threats by corrupt political leaders and oil extortion by terrorist organizations.

As we work through all these issues, oil companies must take care that large profits received when oil prices spike are reinvested in continued oil exploration and continued technological innovation. Employees, officers, shareholders, and board members all deserve economic reward when oil companies experience profits. The image of windfall profits is one that must be carefully managed. Politicians from the Left tend to be less enthusiastic about large corporate profits, seeing them as a ready-made opportunity to impose wealth redistribution to their favored clients, typically those who are less economically advantaged, who can be argued to be bearing a disproportionate burden when oil prices increase. The higher oil prices go, the more likely it is that consumers will begin to feel gouged by greedy profit-takers. Money from the pocket of the consumer to the pocket of the shareholder only feels justified to some unspecified point; beyond that, the oil industry should be greatly concerned. Eventually, consumers will react negatively, sometimes angrily.

The Consumer Federation of America (CFA) places the blame on the wave of mergers that has allowed considerable consolidation within the oil industry as well as the support of a pro-oil Bush administration. In a CFA report subtitled "Price Spikes, Excess Profits and Excuses," Mark Cooper noted:

> While the operation of the domestic oil market is complex and many factors contribute to pricing problems, one central characteristic of the industry stands out—it has become so concentrated in several parts of the country that competitive market forces are weak. Long-term strategic decisions by the industry about production capacity interact with short-term (mis)management of stocks to create a tight supply situation that provides ample opportunities to push prices up quickly. Because there are few firms in the market, prices hold above competitive levels for significant periods of time. With an administration in Washington that is very unlikely to criticize or restrain the oil industry (both the President

and Vice President came out of the oil industry), oil companies have the opportunity to flex their pricing power. [28]

We may be asking too much to expect oil company executives to restrain price increases when supply and demand configurations show the market will absorb higher prices. Quarterly performance measures and annual bonuses all work in favor of getting the largest revenue returns the markets will allow. Still, consumers who believe gas prices are high because a sympathetic Republican president has not strictly enforced antitrust laws will demand answers both from the oil companies and from the politicians. In the 1970s when consumer anger boiled over, Congress passed a retributive windfall-profits tax on the oil industry. If energy prices continue to rise, pressure for legislation to tax what are seen as unjustified oil company profits could easily happen again.

As prices at the gas pump skyrocket, consumers will feel an increasing economic stranglehold. As huge amounts of money transfer from the paychecks of average Americans to large oil company conglomerates and foreign nations, consumers will need no further proof that a play is on by those who control oil to move substantial wealth to their side of the table.

How much of our national wealth can we send off to other nations in search of oil? Every dollar we send overseas is gone forever, to the benefit of the foreign country supplying us with oil. We are swapping the satisfaction of our current needs for our future economic well-being and security. If we move to become 100 percent dependent on foreign oil, we will lose our sovereignty. Every day that our dependence on foreign oil increases, we are putting ourselves more at risk. Even minor instances of instability in distant lands can send shock waves through a U.S. economy that is dependent on foreign stability for our flow of oil. How many of our petrodollars end up in the hands of terrorists whose ultimate goal is to use our dollars against us? Terrorists planning our destruction are more than happy to have us fund them as we purchase oil with blinders on.

We can no longer avoid these questions. America won World War II in large part because it was able to fuel the allied armies in their campaign to defeat Nazi Germany and Imperial Japan. Only some sixty years later, have we already forgotten the strategic importance of oil? As we become ever more dependent upon foreign oil, we are putting ourselves at increasing risk, not only for our continued economic well-being, but for our national security as well. What if our oil-supplying nations decide to cut off our oil because they do not want us to go to war? How do we make a decision to deploy the American military when we need foreign oil to supply our tanks, planes, and warships? We must never reach a point where we are dependent on the blessing of other nations to keep open the supplies we need to fight a war we believe is essential to our national defense and others believe is ill-advised. The black gold stranglehold we are placing on ourselves is one we can avoid.

We must renew our efforts to search for oil domestically, determined to reduce the percentage of oil we must import. We must consider energy alternatives that show promise, such as natural gas and nuclear power. As the price of crude oil continues to increase, natural gas and nuclear power become increasingly attractive and economic alternatives. If we are determined to switch the municipal generation of electricity to natural gas and nuclear power sources, we can reserve our oil supplies for use primarily in transportation. These are steps we can take now. Over the coming decades, inventions may open up other alternatives, but we cannot afford to wait. If we can scale back the percentage of foreign oil we import from 60 percent to 50 percent, we are headed in the right direction. Only if we are capable of thinking like this do we have the possibility of removing the black gold stranglehold we have placed around our own throats. Our economic security as well as our sovereignty may well depend on our moving away from continued dependence upon foreign oil. The stakes are that high.

7

WHY GOVERNMENT OIL PLANS FAIL

In nearly seven years of operation, the Oil-for-Food Programme has been required to meet an almost impossible series of challenges, using some 46 billion dollars of Iraqi export savings on behalf of the Iraqi people.
— U.N. Secretary-General KOFI ANNAN,
November 20, 2003

A S WE NOTED IN the last chapter, governments are tempted to think we can best regulate oil markets with legislation, administrative measures, and other forms of government-designed market intervention. Governments may be required to make sure markets remain free and robust. We want to eliminate criminal activity and prevent rogue states from disrupting the international free flow of oil. But when governments decide that their intervention is needed to direct markets or to determine a particular configuration of supply and demand, that is when we tend to get into trouble.

Put simply, U.S. legislators are typically lawyers who have become politicians. Rarely have legislators had extensive business careers before they enter politics. Even more rarely are legislators professionally trained economists. Still, we have seen in the United States continued attempts by our politicians to intervene directly into energy markets to predetermine results. Typically these efforts fail. Often the unintended consequences of government intervention are worse than the energy-market problem the politicians were trying to solve in the first place.

Nor is the problem limited to the United States. The attempts by the United Nations to regulate oil economics have been equally ill-fated. We would argue here that politicians worldwide would be best advised to limit their energy-market involvement to careful steps aimed predominately at maintaining open and unlimited access to oil markets. Politicians attempting to control or direct energy markets frequently end up where they never anticipated being.

We must be especially watchful today when the political enemies of oil have lined up to pressure governments to enforce statutes that embrace fossil-fuel thinking, enforce global-warming fears, and codify the wishes of conservationists and environmentalists to punish the continued unbridled exploration, production, and use of carbon-based fuel products.

Governments have a role to play in oil markets, but that role properly defined is very limited.

WHY DON'T WE HAVE ENOUGH
OIL REFINERIES?

If we were to find a huge quantity of oil in the continental United States tomorrow, the problem of excess demand would not be solved. More supply of crude oil today is not sufficient to lower gasoline prices.

Why not? The answer is that the United States simply does not have the oil-refining capacity to turn out any more gasoline than we are currently producing. For thirty years, no new gasoline refineries have been built in America.

That startling reality can only be understood when we realize that since the mid-1970s economic factors have mitigated against the decision to build new refineries. The last new refinery in America was constructed in 1976. Without more refineries, we are stuck right where we are, regardless how much crude oil is available to refine.

So the increasing demand for gasoline we are experiencing in the

United States must continue to outpace the ability of American refiners to put more gasoline in the pumps. As we entered 2005, American refineries are operating at 96–98 percent capacity in peak times and 90 percent capacity with normal operations. That is estimated to be about full capacity at the present time.[1] Without additional refinery capacity, more demand for gasoline inevitably means higher prices. With no excess refining capabilities available, there is no other alternative.

In 1981 there were 324 refineries in the United States, and refining capacity was at 17.9 billion barrels per day. In 2004 there are only 149 refineries in the United States. Still, refining capacity has held at 16.9 million barrels per day, down from 1981, but nowhere in proportion to how many refineries have closed.

Why? Since 1981 many small refineries have simply closed. The profit margins in oil refining are small, and since 1981 many independent refineries have found that their operations were not large enough to meet the economies of scale. Many closed between 1981 and 1996 when oil-refining capacity in the United States exceeded demand. Gasoline prices were simply not high enough to meet the increasing costs of operation.[2]

In the past ten years U.S. refiners have invested an estimated $47 billion to make environmentally mandated changes to their refineries. Many of those changes have been made to produce the cleaner, low-sulfur fuels that have been mandated by legislation.[3]

Oil companies like to build refineries near coastlines in large part to economize on fuel transportation costs. Approximately 50 percent of all Americans live near coasts, and few people welcome new refineries with the same enthusiasm with which they greet beach homes. Nationwide, the idea of a new refinery is certain to generate a NIMBY response—Not In My Back Yard.

Refineries are obtrusive and smelly. People worry about environmental impacts, including more truck traffic carrying hazardous materials. In California, the fear of harmful leaks in the event of an earthquake is an added worry. The California Energy Commission reports that ten refineries, representing 20 percent of the state's refining capacity, were closed in the decade between 1985 and 1995.[4]

President George W. Bush has proposed offering closed U.S. military bases as available sites for new oil refineries. Yet years of neglect have left substantial environmental cleanup costs at the closed bases. Problems range from unsafe ammunition disposal to harmful contaminants, such as leaking storage tanks that have contaminated groundwater. The Pentagon has already spent $8.3 billion to clean up contamination at closed military bases, and another $3.6 billion is scheduled for the ongoing effort.[5] Oil companies might still face additional costs preparing the land to meet the environmental requirements of operating an oil refinery.

Using closed military bases might help solve the issue of location, but the economics remain difficult. The cost of building a 150,000-barrel-a- day refinery is estimated to cost about $2.4 billion.[6] Unless gasoline prices remain relatively high, this capital cost may be difficult to recover. One industry joke asks, "How do you make $1 million in the refining business?" The punch line: "Spend $6 billion." Average industry profits in the refining industry have averaged less than 6 percent since the last refinery opened twenty-nine years ago in Garyville, Louisiana.[7]

To meet increasing demand, the industry has gone the route of expanding existing refineries rather than building new ones. This type of incremental growth is less costly; still the result expected is far less than what is needed. Between 2005 and 2007 industry internal expansion plans are expected to grow refining capacity at an annual rate of 1 percent, half the anticipated pace of demand for the same period.[8]

Industry critics frequently charge that the major oil companies have forced smaller refineries out of business. Limiting the number of refineries is seen as a way for large oil companies to keep gasoline prices high. Today the largest five oil refiners in the United States (BP, ConocoPhillips, ExxonMobil, Royal Dutch Shell, and Valero) control more than half (52.4 percent) of the domestic refinery capacity. Ten years ago these same top five oil companies controlled only one-third (34.5 percent) of the domestic refinery capacity. Here is a typical charge from the environmental Left:

This dramatic increase in the control of just the top five companies makes it easier for oil companies to manipulate gasoline supplies by intentionally withholding supplies in order to drive up prices. Indeed, the U.S. Federal Trade Commission (FTC) concluded in March 2001 that oil companies had intentionally withheld supplies of gasoline from the market as a tactic to drive up prices—all as a "profit-maximizing strategy." These actions, while costing consumers billions of dollars in overcharges, have not been challenged by the U.S. government.[9]

The government probably brought no charges against the oil companies because maximizing profits is not yet a crime. If an oil company engaged in practices that made its gasoline unreasonably expensive, the market itself would have solved the problem. Collusion between oil companies, if it had occurred, would have been a crime. But maximizing profit was probably a good idea in an oil-refinery business where the profits are relatively thin even in the best of times.

Oil companies seeking to build refineries also face a variety of hurdles: getting public approval of the land purchase, obtaining the required environmental permits, investing substantial capital in plant and equipment, and the added risk that, should they actually succeed in making a dollar, critics will unfailingly charge that the oil companies have intentionally manipulated supply so as to artificially raise the price of gasoline to the detriment of the consumer.

We might consider that the higher prices we are paying for gasoline today are putting into play the very forces we need to advance the market. Oil companies can be counted upon to fight the battles needed to find the land and work through the required environmental permits, provided a reasonable profit can be anticipated from building new refineries. Until that point is reached, a limit on refinery capacity will remain the bottleneck restraining a greater supply of gasoline from meeting the increasing demand of an ever-growing market.

Imported gasoline from foreign sources is now at 10 percent of supply, up from a negligible amount only a few years ago. Even here there are problems. After the *Exxon Valdez* disaster, many U.S. oil companies divested themselves of tanker fleets rather than face the embarrassment of another oil spill. Independent tanker operators simply do not have

171

enough of the double-hulled tankers needed to import gasoline into the United States in compliance with current environmental regulations.

If we are unwilling to reduce the burden of meeting these environmental requirements, we will have to wait until the price of gasoline becomes sufficiently high that the investment risk of opening new refineries once again makes sense to the major oil companies. Today the market economics of the oil-refinery business are not yet at that point. Oil companies must answer to investors. Even though oil-company profits today are reaching record numbers, stock buy-back plans probably make more stockholder sense than would decisions to build more refineries. Who knows where oil prices will be tomorrow?

Stock buy-back programs increase stockholder value right now. Costly investments in constructing new refineries would incur substantial economic risk even in an unregulated market. Faced with large and growing environmental-protection costs, the intrinsic investment risk of building a new refinery makes doing so an even more difficult decision to reach. Oil company executives must first justify their decisions to a board of directors. A board that is properly doing its job will be protecting the economic welfare of the shareholders—regardless of what politically motivated critics from the environmental Left may charge.

To appreciate the amount of investment capital needed to build new refineries and to understand how the world considers the risk involved, note this: In 2005 the United States is expected to refine approximately 17.125 million barrels of oil per day, approximately 25 percent of the world total of 82.8 million barrels per day. The next largest oil refinery competitor is Russia, which is expected in 2005 to refine only 5.4 million barrels per day. Only thirteen other countries refine more than 1 million barrels per day, the largest of which is Japan, at 4.7 million barrels per day. Even Saudi Arabia and the United Kingdom each only refine 1.8 million barrels of oil a day.

The oil-refinery business is costly, and making a profit is risky. That we have retained such a large oil-refining capacity at all is a testament to the great size and strength of the U.S. marketplace.

Still, conservationists and environmentalists regularly blame the

United States for consuming too large a proportion of the world's natural resources in relation to the size of our population. This criticism fails to realize that much of the development of the oil market worldwide continues to benefit from the size and capital strength of the U.S. marketplace. Our increasing imports drive profits in other nations, stimulating international capital structures to emerge more strongly outside the United States. Viewed from the perspective of interdependence, gains in the U.S. marketplace are not losses experienced in other nations. If the U.S. marketplace remains strong, gains in the oil market here should be reflected by gains in the oil market worldwide.

All of this depends on the daily activity of the international oil marketplace, not on central-planning government bureaucracies. Governments would be best advised to limit their involvement in the oil marketplaces to making sure those marketplaces function in an open and free way, not in devising central-planning bureaucracies or in enacting restrictions that limit trade for narrowly conceived advantages for favored countries.

OUR GREAT FAILURE WITH OIL PRICE CONTROLS

As 1971 progressed, President Richard M. Nixon became increasingly obsessed with winning reelection in 1972. In retrospect, this concern seems almost silly. In 1972 Nixon won a landslide victory against Democratic Party challenger George McGovern. When the final results were tallied, Nixon won every state except Massachusetts. The nation solidly rejected McGovern's "peace-now" campaign, which was predicated on the argument that the Vietnam War was fundamentally an unjust war that the United States could not win. If any president was ever given a mandate, Nixon received one in 1972, endorsing even the nation's continued involvement in Vietnam.

Yet in 1971 Nixon was beset with ghosts and worries. He never shook the idea that he had lost the 1960 presidential campaign to John F. Kennedy in large part because of the 1958 recession that haunted the last years of the Eisenhower administration. Sure, Nixon also believed that

Mayor Richard J. Daley stole the election for Kennedy by withholding Cook County votes until the last minute, when Daley knew for sure just exactly how many fraudulent votes were needed to tip the scale for Kennedy. Yet, deep down, Nixon believed he could not go into the election of 1972 and win if the country were in a recession.

This, of course, was not the only fear Nixon had; also, in retrospect, Nixon had a dark side that could appear paranoid about almost any aspect of domestic or foreign policy. The Watergate break-in occurred before the 1972 election, but the cover-up Nixon and his top aides put in place held until after the election. Watergate did not force Nixon's resignation until 1974, two years after his reelection.

Throughout 1971 Nixon held a series of meetings with his top advisers, exploring what steps he could put in place to make sure the economy would be booming on November 7, 1972, election day. Nixon came up with two bold moves. First, he put in place a set of wage-and-price controls designed to hold inflation in place. Second, he closed the gold window, completely taking the United States off the gold standard and ending the ability of foreign holders of U.S. currency to redeem dollars for gold. Each of these steps had far-reaching and continuing effects on the world petroleum market.

Most of Nixon's wage-and-price control scheme was declared a failure and was abolished relatively quickly. The price controls on oil, however, remained in place until 1980. At the end, there were different prices set for ten different types of crude oil. The lowest-price crude cost $6 per barrel, while the most expensive "stripper oil" sold for about $15 per barrel. Robert E. Litan, vice president and director of economic studies at the Brookings Institute, and Philip Verleger, a private economist, observed: "The patchwork system contained many perverse incentives. Rich producing wells were left to expire because producers had no incentive to maintain them, while investments poured into many small wells that would never make a difference to the nation's energy future."[10]

The same was true of natural gas, where the price-control scheme ended up with thirty-two different prices for natural gas. Daniel Yergin and Joseph Stanislaw noted, "The whole enterprise was an elaborate and confusing system of price controls, entitlements, and allocations. It was esti-mated that just the standard reporting requirements for what became the Federal Energy Administration involved some 200,000 respondents from industry, committing an estimated five million man-hours annually."[11]

What would have happened had we instead applied those five mil-lion man-hours to the exploration and harvesting of oil instead of filling out reports about oil prices? Still, adherents of peak-production theories would have thought the result would have been no gain, since practically all the oil in America had already been found.

Nixon pursued what he thought was a good idea—government in-tervention could maintain prices so as to control inflation and stimulate economic growth. There was only one problem: it didn't work. The mar-ket economy was too complex to regulate simply. The resulting confu-sion produced a myriad of conflicting regulations that ultimately failed to comprehend the nuances of dynamic market forces. The result was a mountain of paperwork that businesspeople had to fill out for bureau-crats while mismatches in supply and demand were the everyday result in the oil economy worldwide.

An argument can be made that the 1973 oil shortage began not with the Arab oil embargo but with the mismanagement inherent to the price-control debacle. On January 11, 1973, what was known as phase-three price controls were put in place. Unlike the previous two phases, these involved a voluntary phase. Given the opportunity to resume market-driven pricing, the oil companies increased the price of winter heating oil by 8 percent and stepped up production, anticipating a cold winter and increased demand. This left oil refineries in an awkward position to read-just output to generate sufficient gasoline for summer travel demand.

Seeing how the oil companies were taking advantage of this rare mar-ket opportunity, the Cost of Living Council retaliated with Special Rule No. 1 in March 1973, an order that reimposed mandatory price controls on 95 percent of the domestic petroleum market. The first signs of the gas shortage began, then, in the summer of 1973. Special Rule No. 1 ended up punishing consumers more than the oil companies. By freezing the price of petroleum for all but independent refiners, the Cost of Living Council prevented gas prices from reaching a market-based supply-and-demand equilibrium.[12] As a result, oil companies produced less gas than market conditions absent government intervention would have dictated.

It was not until October 17, 1973, that the Organization of Petroleum Exporting Countries (OPEC) decided to punish America for supporting Israel in the Yom Kippur War. Five months before the embargo, by May 1973, some one thousand U.S. gasoline service stations had already shut down because of lack of fuel. Many other service stations were forced to cut back on the hours they were open, or they began placing limits on the amount of gasoline motorists could purchase at each stop.[13]

The Arab members of OPEC took many steps to curtail production to the United States. The original idea was to cut their exports to the United States by 5 percent each month until Israel pulled out of the territories it occupied at the end of the war. Then, on October 20, 1973, President Nixon approved a $2.2 billion aid package for Israel, and Saudi Arabia cut off all oil exports to the United States. Between January and December 1973, OPEC increased oil prices 470 percent, further deepening the crisis. Any American who lived through the period remembers vividly the long lines at the gas stations, the panic and hot tempers that resulted, and the overall damage done to the U.S. economy.

What we fail to realize is that much of the fault was our own. Government price controls had set an artificial ceiling, demanding that a gallon of gasoline cost no more than 46 cents. This gave very little incentive to refiners to shift production to gasoline in an effort to meet the obviously greater demand created by the OPEC embargo.

Had we allowed oil to seek a market price, perhaps around 55 or 60 cents a gallon (prices that look ridiculously low given today's prices), perhaps then the refineries would have shifted gears, determined to produce as much gasoline as fast as they could. A price set by the market may have been all that was needed to remedy the shortage. Yet at the artificially low price set by bureaucrats, oil companies had no incentive to invest in added capacity. At 46 cents a gallon, oil companies may even have taken losses if exceptional moves were made to flow gas into the market to meet the crisis.

Would consumers have paid the higher price for gasoline in 1973? Without doubt, consumers would have jumped at the chance. During the oil embargo, price was not the issue—availability was the problem. At most gas stations throughout America, operators didn't have any gas to sell at any price.

Still, the lesson most Americans learned during the 1973 oil embargo was that the Arabs had discovered an oil weapon to which we were vulnerable because we are so dependent on foreign oil. Even this supposed conclusion is probably wrong. Oil is fungible, which means simply that this oil can easily be substituted for that oil. Once oil is in the tanker, nobody knows where the oil came from, except for the records of the tanker and the word of the crew. OPEC oil shipped to another nation, perhaps in Europe where there was no embargo, could simply be resold to the United States as European oil. Experts analyzing the 1973 oil embargo have argued that the United States suffered very little net effect: "Supply routes were shuffled, but import volumes remained steady."[14]

Markets are very adaptable and flexible, especially if they are unrestricted by governments. The truth is that nobody can tell where the gasoline you pump ultimately came from. There are several reasons for this. To begin with, the Energy Information Administration of the U.S. Department of Energy openly admits that it collects no data on the source of gasoline sold at retail outlets.[15]

Nor does the company name on the service station tell the whole story. Gasoline is sold at about 167,000 outlets in the United States today. About one-third of these gas stations are unbranded dealers that sell gasoline of any brand. The remaining two-thirds of all gas stations are branded, but even here the gasoline sold may not come from that company's refineries. Gasoline from different refineries is often combined for shipment by pipeline. Different companies owning branded service stations in a particular geographical area may all be buying their gasoline from the same pipeline terminal.

Yes, you could attempt to examine the small amounts of additives placed by particular companies in their gas in an attempt to trace that gas back to a particular company's refineries. By the time the gas is mixed in the pipelines, however, the additives are generally mixed together as well. Most refineries buy crude from different sources, not just the crude imported by the company that owns the refinery. So from the first moment oil goes into the refinery system, we find a mix of suppliers, with the refineries make their purchases depending on the relative cost and the availability of crude oil from different sources at different times. Remember, oil is fungible. Oil from many different sources can be mixed and interchanged with no appreciable impact on the final result.

WHY DOES THE U.S. GOVERNMENT RESTRICT OIL EXPLORATION LEASES?

On July 12, 1998, President Bill Clinton signed an executive order extending a moratorium on the leasing of oil drilling sites on the outer shelf of the U.S. continental shelf to June 30, 2012.[16] This moratorium affected virtually all the coasts of California, Washington, Oregon, New England, the North Atlantic, the Mid-Atlantic, and the Northern Aleutian Basin off Alaska. Also included were the eastern Gulf of Mexico off the coast of Southwest Florida, an area extending more than eight hundred miles from Baldwin County, Alabama, southward to the Florida Keys.

Clinton's motivation was obvious. He signed the executive order against the background of scenic Monterey Bay in California. In a speech before the National Ocean Conference, he made his environmental sympathies clear: "Our oceans are the key to the life-support system for all creatures on this planet."[17]

Clinton further challenged Congress to fund a $2.3 billion cleanwater plan to reduce pollutants running from the land into the rivers and oceans. What Clinton was implying was hard to miss—oil exploration inherently and inevitably wrecks offshore environments. The only responsible steps we can take must involve cleaning up pollution, not advancing oil exploration. Environmentalists were disappointed that Clinton did not make the offshore leasing ban permanent, as they had requested. Vice President Al Gore accompanied the president at the Monterey Bay signing of the moratorium. Both made sure they were photographed while examining the tidal pools in the rocks on the Monterey coast, surrounded by jeans-clad admirers of the natural setting.

On June 6, 2005, Florida's two senators, Republican Mel Martinez and Democrat Bill Nelson, announced that a deal had been reached with the Senate Energy Committee leaders that would block any drilling in federal waters off the shore of Florida. The senators declared that the offshore drilling could endanger the state's $50 billion tourism industry as well as the environment. They were also concerned that the offshore drilling might get in the way of space shuttles launched over the Atlantic Ocean.[18]

The U.S. Department of the Interior concludes that "a significant source of oil and gas for the Nation's energy supply, lies in the Outer Continental Shelf (OCS). At the end of 2002, the OCS supplied more than 25 percent of the U.S. natural gas production and more than 30 percent of the total domestic oil production. The Department of the Interior estimates that 60 percent of the oil and 59 percent of the gas to be discovered in the United States are located in the OCS."[19] That may be the case, but environmentalists will fight to the death against any effort to explore for oil anywhere off the U.S. continental shelf.

Objections to drilling in Alaska remain equally strong. When the George W. Bush administration proposed in 2004 to open up the 23.5 million acre preserve in Western Alaska known as the National Petroleum Reserve—Alaska (NPR-A), all the Wilderness Society asked for was a "balance" that protected the region, which "is home to myriad wildlife and waterfowl, and is a vital subsistence hunting and fishing ground for native Alaskans."[20]

Don't be confused—this rhetoric is easily translated as a warning to oil companies to stay away. Terms like *rational balance* are not meant to include any room in the equation for oil exploration. What groups like the Wilderness Society would like to see is a permanent ban on virtually any area that today does not already have an oil well on it. Anywhere else where drilling is proposed is certain to be important to some bird, fish, animal, or native group—or to be pristine earth that should never be violated by anything as foul as the oil business.

Let's take a look at group called the Porcupine Caribou Management

Board (PCMB). The group was established in 1985 by six signatories—the Government of Canada, the Government of Yukon, the Government of the Northwest Territories, the Inuvialuit Game Council, the Gwinc'in Tribal Council, and the Council of Yukon First Nations. The PCMB is dedicated to manage the porcupine caribou herd in its native Canadian and Alaskan habitat and to preserve the continuity of the herd for subsistence use by the natives who harvest the herd. The PCMB objects to increased oil exploration in the Arctic National Wildlife Refuge (ANWR) because this land comprises "much of the concentrated calving grounds" of the porcupine caribou herd.[21]

We have no doubt a convincing argument can be made for the preservation of the porcupine caribou herd in its natural habitat. We have only a few considerations. Do we have to accept as a predetermined conclusion that no matter what oil companies do, their oil exploration and production efforts must be detrimental to the animals? Couldn't we consider for a moment the possibility (remote as it may seem to groups like the Porcupine Caribou Management Board) that oil companies might be able to understand the habitat of the porcupine caribou and possibly even that the oil companies might be able to improve that habitat for the betterment of the herd?

Somehow, we fear that the PCMB will argue that only the PCMB is capable of understanding the herd and the only steps that can be taken to improve the herd involve leaving the natural habitat exactly as it is, regardless what any of the subsistence users may have previously done in their efforts to harvest the herd. Besides, how many people benefit from the porcupine caribou herd compared to the people who might benefit from the oil produced from the ANWR? Most people would not be able to identify a porcupine caribou even if they saw one in its natural habitat. Most people have never been to the ANWR, and the PCMB most likely wouldn't want too many of them to visit.

We are led to the conclusion that environmental groups are organized and determined to oppose all new oil exploration or production in the United States. Consider this 2003 decision of the federal courts in California. The Minerals and Management Service of the U.S. Department of

Interior had given out thirty-six oil and gas exploration leases offshore San Luis Obispo, Santa Barbara, and Ventura counties. On December 9, 2003, Judge Claudia Wilkin of the U.S. District Court for the Northern District of California issued an order that essentially mandated the federal government to submit the leases to the California Coastal Commission for review and public hearings before they could be given out. The decision effectively blocked the leases from ever being granted.

The law firm bringing the case is known as the Environmental Defense Center (EDC, Web site www.edcnet.org). The EDC represented a long list of clients in the lawsuit, including the Sierra Club, Friends of the Sea Otter, California Coast Keeper, and an activist group known as Get Oil Out! The leases in question could have doubled the historic oil production off the coastline in question, something the EDC viewed as a threat rather than an opportunity, one that posed "increased risks of oil spills, air and water pollution, and toxic gas releases." For more than two decades the EDC has represented clients opposed to drilling off the California shore.[22]

Reading through the huge volume of literature and litigation generated by the environmental and conservation movements, one comes to the conclusion that they are politically invested in maintaining the "truth" of the fossil-fuel and global-warming theories together with all the subsequent conclusions of these theories. In other words, it almost seems as if the environmentalists and conservationists want us to run out of petroleum because they can only see petroleum as harmful to the environment when we explore for it, extract it, and burn it.

Extreme environmentalists and conservationists sound virtually like socialists. Just below the surface is a leftist bias that oil is bad because it fuels industrial society. If we are running out of oil—their thinking sounds like they have concluded that there is a justice here, that the earth is getting even by punishing us. So our industrial society will have to scale back—which seems okay with the radicals. If we can't conserve now, maybe we will be forced to conserve in the future, simply because there will be no more oil and we haven't developed alternatives—that too seems okay with the radicals.

Nowhere in the literature or litigation efforts of these environmental and conservation radicals do we find a glimmer of possibility that oil companies might act responsibly, that they could find more oil offshore and in Alaska *and* actually improve the environment. To the radicals, joining the terms *oil companies* and *environmental improvement* results in an unavoidable oxymoron. To the radicals, the term *oil company* signifies only environmental degradation, maybe even imperialism. After all, oil companies are capitalistic by nature, and capitalism results inevitably in imperialism, exploitation of the poor, and the exhaustion of all natural resources to serve the self-centered interests of the rich.

We wonder how many environmental and conservation lawyers drive to court in BMWs or Mercedes-Benz automobiles versus hybrids or hydrogen cars? Radical groups always need financial supporters, and those who contribute large sums to radical environmental and conservation groups are rarely themselves poor. Putting this contradiction aside, we challenge the logic of the radicals. The environmental record of the oil companies operating off the shores of the continental United States and in Alaska has been admirable overall, even when it comes to cleaning up the few accidents that have occurred over the last forty or fifty years of oil exploration and production in those areas.

The underlying goal then of radical environmentalists and conservationists is not to allow the granting of oil leases in a so-called balanced manner but to make sure they apply enough political pressure so politicians have no choice but to buy into their agenda and block all future oil exploration leases. Politicians ultimately depend upon voters to remain in office. Radical environmentalists and conservationists understand this political reality. Until those who support responsible oil exploration and production realize that they are locked in a political battle with extremists on the other side, we will remain in an oil-and-natural-gas stranglehold from which we are unlikely to emerge.

THE UNITED NATIONS OIL-FOR-FOOD SCANDAL

Extensive government involvement in regulating the oil business also creates ample opportunities for scandal. Nothing illustrates this better that the oil-for-food corruption that came to light from captured documents found in Iraq when Saddam Hussein was deposed by the U.S. military in 2003. International politics may well prevent the investigation from ever being complete. Still, the U.S. Government Accounting Office has already estimated that Saddam Hussein had a pay-off system in place that raked in some $10 billion as percentage payoffs to a wide range of international trading partners and friends, including officials linked with the United Nations. Repeatedly there have been suggestions that the scandal might reach as high as the office of Kofi Annan, the Secretary-General of the United Nations.[23]

In the buildup to Operation Iraqi Freedom, President Bush repeatedly urged the United Nations to enforce the dozens of resolutions passed over the years in the attempt to restrain the criminal activities of Saddam Hussein. When the United States finally ran out of patience and took military action, together with a "coalition of the willing," Secretary-General Annan took a potshot at the president, claiming that the U.S. military action was "illegal." Some fifty-one days before the 2004 presidential election in the United States, Annan told the BBC that the decision to take military action contravened the U.N. charter and should have been made by the Security Council, not unilaterally.[24] The statement was widely interpreted as an attempt by Annan to influence the election in favor of the Democratic Party candidate, John Kerry, a candidate who had been critical of President Bush's decision to invade Iraq.

The oil-for-food crisis highlights the danger of international control. The original idea of the United Nations was to provide an international forum where conflicts could be resolved according to principles of justice before wars broke out. The concept sounds correct in the abstract. All too often, however, the United Nations appears to be nothing more than an anti-American debating society. An underlying issue in the 2004 presidential campaign was President Bush's strong statement that he would never hold American security interests hostage to the decision making of international bodies such as the United Nations.

As illustrated by the oil-for-food scandal, the United Nations is not a pristine body, part of a harmonious "new world order" where peace and human justice are the determining standard. How many Security Council resolutions were influenced by member states where officials of the countries involved were receiving oil-for-food payoffs? To what extent was Saddam Hussein buying time by making sure enough officials world-wide were being paid sufficiently so they would have a strong financial interest in making sure he remained in power? These considerations un-dermine any illusion that the United Nations can be given the benefit of the doubt that the decision process will be unbiased or fair. Greed fueled by money under the table cannot be the basis upon which a new world order of universal freedom and human justice will result.

We should draw the lesson here that governmental processes, even international governmental processes, can be susceptible to corruption. What we are learning from the U.N. oil-for-food scandal is that bureau-cratic decision making and the implementation of oil-related programs may reflect more the desire to protect those at the core of corruption rather than the impulse to administer an objective or fair standard to the benefit of all.

While there may be corruption in a market economy, an interna-tional market economy still affords countless opportunities for individual decision making across and within hundreds or thousands of corporate structures. Market collusion, while possible in the international oil busi-ness, is difficult to implement and maintain over time, especially where companies who break ranks can anticipate deriving important competi-tive advantages, particularly in a business as complex as the international oil business. Once again, we see that when governments get extensively involved in the oil business, the net result is likely to be negative to mar-kets and consumers alike.

PART 3

BLACK GOLD STRANGLEHOLD

8

THE DIMINISHING U.S. PETRODOLLAR

There is enough oil to service the global economy for decades to come and perhaps well into the second half of this century. . . . For the world at large—but particularly for the emerging economies of Asia, Africa and Latin America—there is enough oil to support their growth, in the same way that this important hydrocarbon fuelled the economic growth of today's industrialized countries in the last century.
— Sheikh AHMAD FAHAD AL-AHMAD AL-SABAH,
Minister of Energy for Kuwait, January 27, 2005

Deficit spending is simply a scheme for the confiscation of wealth. Gold stands in the way of this insidious process.
— ALAN GREENSPAN, 1966

In the 1970s the OPEC countries could reasonably believe that their decisions controlled oil prices.

Since then, we have seen the emergence of a world oil market in which the increasing predominance of oil spot and futures markets have become determinative not only for oil pricing but also to determine exactly how world supply and demand get matched together. As we proceed through the first decade of the twenty-first century, world oil economics, not geopolitics, are the determinant factor in how much a barrel of crude oil costs and where that barrel of crude oil will ultimately end up. Today the futures markets price into the cost of oil the impact of a hurricane or war far quicker than any nation, legislator, or bureaucrat can comprehend the market or the political dynamics of what is going on.

Regardless what peak-production theorists say, the world oil supply has today reached record levels. The growth of oil reserves shows every sign of increasing indefinitely, not slowing down and diminishing to the point where we run out of oil. Because our mind-set has been dominated by defeatist thinking, we have not truly appreciated the changing dynamics of the expanding marketplace we are experiencing worldwide.

As we will see, the United States today is less in control of world oil markets than it was in the past, not more in control. We are in an increasing economic and political stranglehold, especially as we allow the dollar to be free floating and completely divorced from any backing by gold. The world oil market has grown dramatically over the last thirty-five years, and its dynamics have moved into new dimensions we are only beginning to understand. Still, notions persist that governments are able to control the direction of the world oil markets. We see this idea persisting in the charge that the United States invaded Iraq in 2003, not to fight terrorism, but to seize oil.

WHY THE POLITICAL LEFT SEES THE IRAQ WAR AS A GRAB FOR OIL

As the political Left sees geopolitics, President George W. Bush attacked Iraq to control oil, regardless what other justifications the administration may have articulated. Michael Klare, a professor at Hampshire College in Amherst, lays out the charge from the Left in his book *Blood and Oil*. He begins the analysis by expressing his view that the United States has no alternative but to rely increasingly upon the Middle East for the oil we need to keep our industrial economy and perpetuate our lavish lifestyle:

> Our biggest problem, of course, is our growing reliance on the oil kingdoms of the Persian Gulf. No matter how hard the United States tries to diversify its energy imports by turning to producers in other regions, it

will *still* need to acquire more oil from the Gulf, the only region whose reserves are large enough to satisfy the U.S. and international demand.[1]

Klare's reference to international demand includes China and India, two countries whose oil demands are surging, putting pressure on the world oil supply, thereby squeezing the United States' ability to get cheap oil reliably into the future. Klare, of course, buys wholeheartedly into the idea that the world must eventually run out of oil:

Experts disagree as to when the world's oil fields will attain maximum (or "peak") production and begin an irreversible decline—some say this will occur by 2010, others in the second and third decade of this century—but *all* acknowledge that the planet's original petroleum inheritance has been substantially exploited and a reduction in output is inevitable.[2]

Although we disagree that the world's running out of oil is inevitable, we do admire Klare's adherence to conventional wisdom.

Klare then argues that military intervention in the Middle East, ultimately by Russia and China, as well as the United States, is also inevitable because each country will want to protect its claim on the last available reserves of oil as the supply dwindles to zero. He foresees a coming era in which the United States, Russia, and China compete militarily in the Middle East, generally avoiding a direct clash but fighting through surrogates, each fanning the "flames of regional conflicts" in a way that will increase "the potential for major conflagrations."[3] His solution: we should change our mind-set and use less oil, just as we have decided that smoking tobacco is bad for our health.[4]

A central point of Klare's book is that our military involvement in the Persian Gulf region has been motivated not so much by a desire to attack terrorism but to secure our continuing oil flow. Klare says as much directly: "In fact, it is getting harder to distinguish U.S. military operations designed to fight terrorism from those designed to protect energy assets." Moreover, he expands the argument to contend that our desire to protect oil flow also explains U.S. policy in Latin America and around the world.

American forces will speed overseas to protect oil fields, pipelines, re-fineries, and tanker routes more and more frequently, and they will often encounter enraged local populations. The American military can help deter attacks on vital oil facilities and ensure the continuing flow of pe-troleum, but it can never guarantee that our rising demand for imported oil will be satisfied. All that is certain is that we will pay for it with an in-creasing sacrifice of blood.[5]

Thus the title of Klare's book, *Blood and Oil,* accurately expresses his core thesis—America is a military power acting worldwide not in defense of freedom but in pursuit of oil.

The argument of the Left is based upon the fossil-fuel and peak-production arguments we have challenged throughout this book. The Left has repeated this argument so often and with such conviction that its as-sumptions have been accepted as conventional wisdom. The argument goes like this: America is addicted to oil. But since oil is bound to run out, we are locked in a battle we can never win. Still, we cannot stop ourselves from exercising our military might to secure our hold on the world's last remaining oil reserves. We don't care that our military intervention in the Middle East to seize oil means that the Islamic world has no choice but to hate us. So we bring terrorism upon ourselves. By intervening militarily in the Middle East, we invite the hatred of Americans by radical Muslims.

The self-defeatism in the argument is exceeded only by the argument's self-blame. Since the war in Vietnam began some forty years ago, the political Left has been trying to demonstrate that America is an imperialis-tic power seeking colonial gains. In criticizing the 2003 war in Iraq, the political Left acts as if it has finally found its ultimate proof.

Nowhere does the Left explain why the world now has more proven oil reserves than ever before in history. Nor will the Left relax its extreme attack against the U.S. oil business. The Left is locked into arguing that any expansion of oil drilling offshore or in Alaska will have completely unacceptable environmental consequences. If oil is truly abundant, as we suggest, and if responsible exploration can be conducted without causing environmental damage, then the United States does not need to invade foreign countries for oil. The Left needs to block oil exploration and production in the United States in order to self-fulfill the core argument against oil.

But the Left cannot tolerate those who argue that oil might be abundant or that the United States might be able to discover enough new oil to decrease significantly our oil dependency. What is the global-warming hoax all about if not a plea to stop burning carbon-based fuels? Conservation to the political Left equates with using less energy, which in turn translates to a reduction in what the Left sees as an indulgent and selfish materialistic lifestyle made possible by industrial enterprises that burn carbon-based fuels. The Left operates with a political understanding of oil.

The reality is that U.S. oil companies have not moved into Iraq to seize and operate the oil fields. While the political Left will probably discount all Bush administration statements to the contrary, the goal was to fight terrorism, not to seize oil fields. Since Saddam Hussein was deposed from power, the United States has worked to reestablish a self-determined Iraqi government that is sovereign over Iraqi politics. The United States does not have a history of establishing colonies, and the day is approaching when American military forces will begin withdrawing from Iraq. Should the Iraqi government decide that U.S. forces should leave Iraq, we will most certainly pull out, just as we did recently in Saudi Arabia. Still, the Left continues with its political agenda, pressing forward with determination to argue that the only reason we attacked Iraq was for oil and that all statements to the contrary are subterfuges.

Iraqi oil production in January 2003, before the war, averaged 2.6 million barrels per day. This dropped sharply in the period between March and July 2003, when the war was at its most intense level. The 2004 production level for Iraq averaged just over 2 million barrels per day, not quite back to the prewar level, but recovering. After the 2003 war, we resumed importing oil from Iraq. In 2004 we imported about 652,000 barrels of oil per day from Iraq, somewhat more than half of the 1.16 million barrels of oil per day Iraq was exporting worldwide. Iraq in 2004 exported to a large number of countries in addition to the United States, including Canada, England, France, Germany, Italy, Japan, and South Korea.[6]

If the United States attacked Iraq for oil, why didn't we just stabilize Iraq's oil industry and ship all the oil to the United States? Or, with our technology, why didn't we simply drill out as much Iraqi oil as possible and ship it to the United States as fast as we could? After all, peak-production believers would argue that Iraq is going to run out of oil sooner rather than later. So taking all Iraq's oil now, while we have the opportunity, and shipping it back to the United States would seem to be the logical consequence if the United States were really just an imperialistic power after colonial conquest and gain. Following the argument of the Left to its logical conclusion, the United States should have drilled Iraqi oil to the last drop, sent it to America, then brought home the troops. Who would care what would happen in Iraq after the oil was gone? Isn't that the point the Left wants us to believe?

IRAN'S SUCCESS DESPITE SANCTIONS

The United States has had Iran under economic sanctions virtually since the 1979 revolution, sanctions even maintained by the Clinton administration. For this reason, we import no oil or natural gas from Iran. This has not stopped Iran, however, from marketing its available oil and natural gas to others. Iran has found ready buyers in many countries, including China, India, and Japan.

After the 1979 revolution, Iran's oil industry was nationalized under the control of the state-owned National Iranian Oil Company (NIOC). Foreign investment in Iran since 1979 was hampered by the Iranian constitution, which prohibits granting direct equity stakes in oil production activities to any individual person or corporation. Then, in 1987, a new petroleum law permitted the Ministry of Petroleum to get around this provision by allowing buy-back contracts that confer what amounts to ownership over oil fields where investors provide capital to develop the resources. But relying on the word of the mullahs has proven problematic. Iran is a theocracy, and if the ruling clerics change their mind, there is no legal recourse. Still, over the last two years, China, Japan, and India have made a series of deals to develop Iranian oil fields.

Currently, Iran is producing about 3.9 million barrels of oil a day, down from the pre-revolution 1974 high of 6 million barrels per day. Iran's oil industry suffers greatly from outmoded equipment and low levels of capital investment, but in the last two years the clerics ruling Iran have grasped a great international opportunity. Realizing that oil demand was surging in countries such as China and India, the mullahs have negotiated deals with an eye toward attracting additional investment. Since 2003 the mullahs have inked a number of oil deals, not only with China and India, but also with Japan, a country with virtually no oil reserves of its own. In her March 2005 trip to India, Secretary of State Condoleeza Rice appealed to Indian Foreign Minister Natwar Singh to drop plans to build a $4 billion pipeline designed to bring natural gas to India from Iran by crossing over Pakistan. Singh rejected Rice's request, noting that India needed the natural gas.[7] So far the White House has been unsuccessful in discouraging other countries from dropping planned oil or natural gas investments in Iran.

The mullahs are heavily dependent upon oil-export earnings to prop up their otherwise failing economy. Oil represents approximately 80–90 percent of total export earnings and some 40–50 percent of the government budget. With oil prices surging, Iran has benefited from these windfall prices. With oil at $50 per barrel and with Iran exporting some 3.9 million barrels per day, the mullahs' state-owned oil company is raking in nearly $200 million a day in gross oil revenue. This revenue is not shared broadly with the Iranian people, who suffer from unemployment and underemployment, a suffering made more oppressive given the mullahs' brutal suppression of internal dissent.[8] Any capital the Iranians receive to develop their oil and gas markets gives them additional resources with which to enrich themselves, to prop up their failing economy, to fund terrorism, and to pursue their nuclear ambitions.

In 2001 the state-owned Japan Bank of International Cooperation gave Iran a $3 billion loan despite strong objections from the U.S. Department of State. Several Japanese companies have also made major private investments to claim a stake in the development of Iran's abundant oil fields. The U.S. government argued with Japan to no avail that Iran was supporting international terrorism by funding groups such as Hezbollah in Lebanon and that the mullahs were conducting a clandestine nuclear weapons program. In the end, Japan's need for oil overrode any international security concerns, and the mullahs received a huge capital investment to enrich themselves further and to keep their failing economy afloat. By 2004 the Iranians had completely drawn down on the first $3 billion loan from Japan and were negotiating a second loan.[9]

Iran and China have also signed several multibillion-dollar deals in which China has agreed to purchase oil and liquid natural gas from Iran. Deals have been negotiated between the two countries by which China has agreed to pay as much as $100 billion for oil and gas purchase contracts for as long as twenty-five years. This Tehran-Beijing axis sits alongside Iran's growing relationship with Russia.[10] In 2004 the Russians completed the construction of Iran's first nuclear reactor, at Bushehr, some 750 miles (1,200 kilometers) southwest of Tehran, on the Persian Gulf. In 2005 the Russians are expected to supply the Iranians with the necessary nuclear fuel to make the Russian-built reactor operational. Arguably, the major accomplishment of the U.S. embargo against Iran has been to remove U.S. companies from the competition for Iran's abundant oil and natural gas reserves.

What is emerging is a set of Iranian alliances that tie the mullahs increasingly into the mainstream of world economics. With some $200 million a day in oil revenue, the Iranian theocracy has abundant resources to buy the world's top economic, legal, and public relations talent. Despite their continued pleas that the only purpose of their nuclear program is for peaceful purposes, the U.N.'s International Atomic Energy Agency (IAEA) has found repeated violations. The U.S. government's concerns that Iran is sponsoring terrorism worldwide and that the mullahs intend to have the capability of building nuclear weapons are unfortunately well founded. We must face the reality, however, that a U.S. oil embargo against Iran has had almost no economic impact on Iran, given the current development of the international market for oil and natural gas.

China, India, and Japan have more than enough demand to purchase all the oil Iran can supply. Even more important, China, India, and Japan have sufficient capital resources to sustain the mullahs in power for years to come. Thus Iran is not suffering a shortage of oil revenue, despite the U.S. embargo. Moreover, the mullahs have established an intricate network of offshore contracts for their own benefit. Through these offshore contracts, they rake percentages of oil contracts into their bank accounts in Syria and Switzerland. If we could investigate these payments directly and honestly, we should not be surprised to find an oil-for-food type scandal through which the mullahs reward their international trade partners and fellow terrorists around the world. Nor should we be surprised to find the names of prominent Europeans included on the list.

While the United States has not been able to shut Iran out of the world's oil markets, Iran ironically can still affect the price of oil in the United States, even though we buy no oil from Iran directly. As Iran sells to foreign buyers, that oil flows into the world market, increasing the overall supply. Without Iranian oil, international supply would be less than it is now. And one result of that diminished supply would be an increase in price as the Chinese, Indians, and Japanese would be forced to look elsewhere for oil.

As Iran's position in the world oil marketplace grows, we should expect its political influence to grow as well. As we saw with Mexico and Canada, their national political agendas became increasingly important to the United States as we imported more oil from them. Unless Iran renounces its support for terrorist groups and reverses its determination to spread the radical Islamic revolution worldwide, we may well see in Iran the emergence of the world's first terror-supporting nation as a superpower in the oil and natural gas marketplaces. If Iran's oil and natural gas superpower status is strengthened with a nuclear-weapons capability, the consequences should be frightening for all free countries, including the United States and Israel. We and Israel have already been attacked by radical Islamic extremists whose determination to attack us shows no sign of letting up. In 2004–5 we have seen terrorist attacks in Egypt, Great Britain, Saudi Arabia, and Spain. Radical Islamic extremists will gain considerable strength if they receive additional support from a nuclear Iran, especially if Iran has countries like China, India, and Japan investing substantial amounts in its energy industry infrastructure and buying the oil and natural gas that are produced as a result. Will Iran be able to impose its political agenda on the world to an increasing extent as its importance as an oil exporter grows in the world marketplace? Unfortunately, the answer is probably yes.

With Iran having close ties to both China and Russia, its alliances with India and Japan take on a new dimension. Iran is quietly using oil resources to build an Asian network of relationships that exclude the United States. Therefore, every drop of oil that Iran pumps has a geopolitical impact that can reach well into the next several decades, continuing to tighten the stranglehold we Americans face. Our increasing dependence on foreign oil makes us more vulnerable to disruptions in the world oil marketplace. And Iran today is the second largest producer of oil among the OPEC nations. With virtually unlimited investment coming from countries like China, India, Japan, and Russia, and with more Iranian oil and gas being discovered by new methods of exploration, what is the limit for increased production of oil and natural gas in Iran? Iran's emergence as a major supplier of oil and natural gas has dramatically changed the world's energy market, with the United States positioned on the sidelines, objecting but unable to stop the market forces from moving ahead to the advantage of the mullahs and their oil-importing partners.

The mullahs' abysmal human rights record at home and their documented support of terrorism abroad may be morally abhorrent, but these records are no barrier to the mullahs engaging in the international oil and gas business. Short of war, the mullahs may be unstoppable. The conclusion again is clear: the world oil marketplace, not the political wishes of the United States, determines what Iran can accomplish economically, possibly even politically.

THE WORLD OIL MARKET DOUBLES IN SIZE

Since the early 1970s the world marketplace has increased more than 60 percent, despite constant warnings that we have hit peak oil production and that we are running out of oil. In 1970 the world produced approxi-

196

mately 49 million barrels of oil per day; in 2004 the world average was approximately 83 million barrels per day.[11]

We have a tendency to think that a larger market operates just like a smaller market, only on a grander scale. Here we risk ignoring yet again an often overlooked mathematical principle: a difference in scale is often a difference in phenomenon. A simple illustration will make the point. A bumblebee is able to fly because of the particular aerodynamics of the animal. If you increase the size of the bumblebee by a great factor, making the bumblebee maybe ten times larger, or perhaps one hundred times larger, the bumblebee cannot lift off the ground. Even if every part of the bumblebee is increased proportionately, the wings at ten times or one hundred times larger are not sufficient to lift the greater mass of the bumblebee's larger body. There are many illustrations of the principle. The "Spruce Goose" that Howard Hughes built was barely able to lift off the ground. Even with more propellers, an airplane this large could not fly. Huge cargo aircraft required a totally different design, one that had to await the invention of jet engines and lighter metals that could be used in the body construction of the aircraft.[12]

If a difference in scale is a difference in phenomenon, then a world oil market that has increased more than 60 percent in the past thirty-five years may well be a market whose dynamics and internal laws of operation are significantly different than those which operated in 1970. No nation today, not even the United States, can control worldwide oil markets.

In 1973 the OPEC nations imposed an oil embargo with a reasonable expectation that by reducing the supply of oil available, they would cause a severe shortage that would bring the United States to its knees and force it to abandon Israel. As we have seen, the price controls imposed by Nixon were probably the main reason we experienced long gasoline lines in 1973. The Arab oil embargo removed some 5 million barrels of oil a day from the world's supply; only about 1 million barrels a day were made up by increased production from other nations. Oil jumped dramatically in price. In 1972 the price of crude oil was about $3 per barrel, and by the end of 1973 the price had increased to $12 per barrel. One analyst observed correctly: "If there was any doubt that the ability to control oil

197

prices had passed from the United States to OPEC it was removed during the Arab Oil Embargo. The extreme sensitivity of prices to supply shortages became all too apparent when prices increased 400 percent in six short months."[13]

The main effect of the Arab oil embargo was that the OPEC nations themselves lost revenue they could not afford to lose. The Arab oil embargo officially began on October 16, 1973, when Abu Dhabi, Iran, Iraq, Kuwait, Qatar, and Saudi Arabia decided to raise oil prices 17 percent to $3.65 a barrel and also to cut production. On March 17, 1974, only some five months later, the OPEC countries announced the end of the embargo. The embargo had virtually no impact on the U.S. policy of support for Israel.

Looking at the U.S. oil import data from 1973 and 1974, the oil embargo had an impact on overall U.S. imports. In October 1973 the United States imported approximately 6.6 million barrels of oil per day; in December 1973 the figure was 6.3 million barrels per day. From January through March 1973 the figure was more like 5.3 million barrels per day, but by April the number was back to about 6 million barrels a day, and by May the number was back to 6.5 million barrels.[14] Had the embargo lasted longer, additional suppliers would have entered the market. The U.S. recession that followed the oil embargo also had an impact in keeping oil prices relatively stable through the remainder of the 1970's.

Never again was OPEC able to exert such a major impact on oil prices. The next big spikes in oil prices occurred around political events, the disruption in Iranian oil caused by the exile of the Shah and the rise to power of Ayatollah Ruhollah Khomeini during the Iran revolution of 1979, followed by the Iran-Iraq war which began the next year. Through the 1980's, oil decreased in price as world oil production increased and futures markets such as the New York Mercantile Exchange (NYMEX) were formed. The next oil spikes awaited more political events, such as the invasion of Kuwait by Iraq in 1990, the 9/11 attack on the World Trade Center and the Pentagon, and the 2003 invasion of Iraq. Even as the second Iraq war started in 2003, oil was still averaging under $30 per barrel.

In the 1980's and 1990's OPEC made many different decisions to increase or decrease production, yet without any clear demonstration that changes in OPEC policy could directly influence world oil prices. Looked at in retrospect, many of the OPEC decisions in this period appear reactive, more an attempt by OPEC to boost their profits than a clear ability of OPEC to determine oil pricing directions. Since 1973, OPEC "has seldom been effective at controlling prices."[15]

The oil price spike of 2004 seems more related to political uncertainty than to fundamental changes in the world configuration of supply and demand. What this reflects is the dynamics of a world oil marketplace that has grown to such a dimension that no one government of group of governments can fundamentally impact price by taking unilateral action to increase or restrict supply. As we have seen, refinery limitations in the United States are the restraint that today will keep U.S. gasoline prices high, even if OPEC were to dramatically increase the production of crude oil.

Today's world oil marketplace is sufficiently large and complex that futures markets can be determinative of pricing. Futures markets can factor a whole range of market impacts into price within a matter of moments. Hurricanes, political disasters, uncertainties due to labor strikes, terrorism attacks, decisions by governments to increase or reduce oil production—all these and many more variables are weighed instantly in the oil prices quoted by futures markets. The efficiency of the NYMEX and London's International Petroleum Exchange (IPE) to determine oil prices is virtually unchallenged in today's oil markets. OPEC, the U.S. government, and oil producers worldwide all key off NYMEX and IPE prices, the same way industries and governments key off New York Stock Exchange (NYSE) prices to value corporations, large and small, and to monitor major market movements.

A change in scale is a change in phenomenon in the world oil markets. We should note here that the NYMEX and IPE are not behaving as if our running out of oil were imminent. We may have seen rising oil prices in the 2004 and 2005, but we have not seen panic increases. Nor is the increase in world oil prices necessarily bad. At higher price levels, oil that may otherwise be left in the ground may economically be able to be developed. Besides, the United States has alternatives. If we want to see oil prices decrease, we should open up domestic oil exploration in an effort to increase available supplies. Any dramatic increase in U.S. oil reserves due to the discovery of new oil fields would most likely decrease world oil prices.

Higher world prices for oil will certainly stimulate new oil production somewhere; ultimately that production will enter the world market, where the result most likely will be to place downward pressure on the price of oil. At higher prices, alternatives to hydrocarbon fuels also become more attractive. The cost of alternative energy sources, such as nuclear power, may today not be able to compete economically with the still relatively low price of oil and natural gas. The same may not be true if oil and natural gas become much more expensive in the future.

The stranglehold we feel from world oil dependence is largely one we have imposed upon ourselves. The solution is not conservation or the reduction in our industrial economies. The solution lies in attacking the arguments of the conservationists and environmentalists directly on the basis of scientific evidence and in proceeding to develop our oil supply capabilities at home as well as worldwide. We have passed the point where government decrees or price controls will do anything but make us look foolish. At the risk of repeating ourselves, the empirical evidence is that the world today has more proven reserves of oil and natural gas than ever before. Despite the cry from the political Left, we are nowhere near running out of oil. The world oil market is larger, more robust, and more dynamic than ever.

THE GROWING IMPORTANCE OF THE OIL
SPOT AND FUTURES MARKETS

Prior to 1970, negotiations among the major private sector companies such as Standard Oil of Jersey (Exxon), Standard Oil of California, the Texas Company, and Royal Dutch Shell set the price of oil. Beginning in the 1970s the power to control supplies and determine prices moved from private companies to the governments of major oil-producing countries.[16] Today, control of oil prices has largely passed to the internal dynamics of the world oil market itself. Oil companies and governments, even OPEC, are all increasingly subject to the laws of supply and demand as played out on international markets.

In the last few years the spot transactions and futures markets have become increasingly important.[17] A spot transaction is a one-time agreement to buy a particular quantity of oil at a specified price with no requirements that any future purchases ever be made. Oil refiners, for instance, go into the spot market to purchase additional crude oil when gasoline prices are high. Spot markets have developed over various types of oil: crude oil as distinct from gasoline, or low sulfur crude oil as distinct from high sulfur crude oil. Spot markets have also developed for different geographical markets, such as New York Harbor for the Northeast, or Chicago for the Midwest, Rotterdam for Northwest Europe, and Singapore for Southeast Asia. Any oil company or refinery can go to the spot market to buy or sell oil.

A futures market operates as a complex set of contracts to buy and sell a specified commodity at a specific time at a specified price. A futures oil contract involves a promise by the seller to deliver a quantity of oil to the buyer at a particular date for a specific agreed-upon price.

In addition to futures contracts, the oil market has also developed options contracts. Oil is not actually delivered under a options contract. Instead, third parties buy and sell options contracts. A losing options contract is one that bets incorrectly on the market price for oil at the expiration date; a winning options contract bets correctly on the market price at the expiration date. Options contracts act as speculative financial bets and are traded actively by third parties before expiration. The holders of the oil futures contracts make or lose money depending on their positions; the writing of futures contracts is a way for oil producers to hedge their positions.

The New York Mercantile Exchange (NYMEX) and the International Petroleum Exchange (IPE) in London are the largest worldwide markets for the trading of oil futures contracts. And recently oil has become the most actively traded commodity in the world. The price of oil is set today by oil futures trading on the IPE and NYMEX, not in OPEC meetings, not in ExxonMobil boardrooms, not in price-control committees established by the U.S. government. When oil prices are quoted, the quotes come from the futures exchanges, and all world buyers and sellers of oil use the futures exchanges to determine price.

With spot transactions and futures contracts becoming an active part of the oil business, the market has changed. In the past, specific oil producers sold to specific oil buyers. Today oil trading has moved into the hands of investors and speculators. Much like the shares of any company, such as IBM or even ExxonMobil, prices are determined by the buying and selling of stock on Wall Street. In the same way, the price of oil is determined by investors and speculators buying and selling futures contracts on the NYMEX and the IPE.

In simple terms, oil is fungible—once it enters the system, we have a hard time telling where it came from. Oil in a particular tanker may end up being bought and sold several times before it actually hits a gas pump. Financial intermediaries, more than governments or even the oil companies themselves, set oil prices based on their ability to shuffle oil supplies to meet demand wherever that demand is found. Oil companies anywhere in the world can find buyers in the world market, just as refiners can buy or sell oil depending on the grades of oil they need, what they have in supply, and what type of oil product they currently believe will be the most profitable to refine. Undoubtedly, despite the U.S. embargo, some Iranian oil enters the United States due to this fungible nature. Once oil enters the world market, it is difficult to determine its origin. Spot contracts purchased on the world market can conceivably be delivered even to the United States with supplies that originated in Iran. Very possibly no one, not even the U.S. government, could trace that oil back to Iran with a degree of certainty.

One way to understand this is to realize that while the United States is now a net importer of oil, we still continue to export oil. According to data from the Energy Information Administration of the U.S. Department of Energy, the United States in 2004 exported more than 1 million barrels of oil per day, even though our net imports averaged approximately

11.851 million barrels per day.[18] Why would we export oil when we import so much oil? The answer derives from the many individual decisions made by U.S. oil companies and refiners operating on the world oil market. When U.S. oil companies have an excess supply of oil, or when price opportunities present themselves on the spot market, U.S. companies are happy to sell oil abroad, even though at the same time they are also buying oil from overseas.

Increasingly, we are all in a world oil market. Political arguments that we went to war in Iraq to gain control of Iraqi oil miss the point. U.S. oil companies buy and sell oil on the world market. If a U.S. oil company can get more profit by selling its oil to someone else, then the sale is a rational decision. When that same oil company stops buying from a foreign producer because domestic sources of production are cheaper, the result becomes a pressure on the international oil market for overall prices to fall. When worldwide oil prices go up, virtually all buyers of oil suffer and virtually all sellers of oil benefit. The consequences on buyers and sellers reverse when the price of oil goes down. The development of the NYMEX and the IPE has virtually set this rule in stone such that markets rule, not oil companies or governments.

THE U.S. DOLLAR IS A COMMODITY
JUST AS OIL IS A COMMODITY

When President Nixon in 1971 closed the gold window at the U.S. Treasury Department, he took the dollar completely off the gold standard, completing the process that began with Franklin D. Roosevelt in 1933. The result was that the U.S. dollar became a commodity.

Traditionally, the world oil market has traded in dollars. As we continue to import an increasing amount of oil, our international suppliers are being forced to receive an increasing amount of U.S. dollar reserves. The value of these foreign currency reserves depends in turn upon the value of the dollar. As a result, we are seeing increased anxiety worldwide that the quantity of dollar holdings currently in the foreign exchange balances of our oil exporting partners may be getting uncomfortably large.

In turn, financial problems may be looming for the U.S. dollar in the immediate future.

Since the dollar can no longer be exchanged for gold, the dollar's value is independent of the price of gold. Today the dollar is a commodity, just like oil, wheat, copper, and pork bellies. Thus the price of a dollar is determined every day by the currency markets. The dollar is primarily traded on a market known as *forex*, an abbreviation of *foreign exchange*. The forex market is not a formal market like the New York Stock Exchange (NYSE). Instead, the forex consists of a network of "over the counter" traders from major commercial and investment banks, all of whom are networked. A wide range of parties trade currencies on the forex—importers and exporters, managers of major investment or pension portfolios, mutual fund managers, and foreign exchange brokers, even private speculators—all these constitute the complex group of participants who enter the forex every day to buy and sell money.[19]

More than $1.5 trillion in various currencies around the world are traded every day. Still, the exchange has "no central trading floor where buyers and sellers meet. Most of the trades are completed by commercial banks and forex dealers in the U.S. and abroad using telephones and computers."[20] The forex operates twenty-four hours a day, beginning at 00:00 GMT (Greenwich Mean Time) on Sunday afternoon until 10:00 p.m. GMT on Friday—a period that roughly stretches in the United States from Sunday afternoon until Friday afternoon. Every day worldwide currency traders make and lose millions of dollars on the forex, depending upon the skill and luck with which they trade their currency positions.

Here is how the Federal Reserve Bank of Chicago describes the daily international operation of the forex:

> The forex market operates worldwide, 24 hours a day. Traders in Australia and the Far East begin trading in Hong Kong, Singapore, Tokyo, and Sydney at about the time most workers in San Francisco are going home for supper the previous evening. As the business day in the Far East closes, trading in Middle Eastern financial centers has been going on for a couple of hours, and the trading day in Europe is just beginning. By

the time the New York business day gets going in full force, it is almost time for early afternoon tea in London. Some of the large U.S. banks and brokerage houses have an early shift to minimize the time difference of 5 to 6 hours with Europe. To complete the circle, West Coast financial institutions extend "normal banking hours" so they can trade with New York or Europe on one side, and with Hong Kong, Singapore, or Tokyo on the other.[21]

Currency is traded for many business reasons. A company doing business in a particular country may has a need to purchase the currency of that country. A government may not want to hold reserves obtained through foreign trade balances in a particular currency, so it trades that currency for another currency. Many traders also use this market effectively to hedge against future declines of any given currency.

Speculators also trade currencies, trying to capture small pricing differences that may exist only for seconds between one exchange or another. This speculative trading is termed *arbitrage,* and with skill, millions can be made by recognizing these minor inefficiencies that exist in the instants it may take for one exchange to adjust the price of a currency to reflect the price of that currency on other exchanges. The entire process is complex, expert, and fast. Huge amounts of money move around the globe electronically with no paper currency ever changing hands.

A very active options market has developed for foreign currency exchange. The Chicago Mercantile Exchange has created an options market in forex, so participants in forex can buy and sell options contracts to exchange a specified currency at a specified price on a specified date. These options contracts were developed to allow major institutional currency exchange participants to hedge their positions on current currency exchanges by going long or short with bets on the future value of a particular currency.

Only experts are advised to participate in forex options contracts. The nature of options transactions is not common sense, simply because most ordinary consumers are accustomed to buying or selling today, but they are not accustomed to buying and selling an option to buy or sell in the future. As we saw with oil options, few forex options contracts ever result in currency actually changing hands. A forex option is "in the money" if the future bet made by the purchaser turns out to be right. An "in the money" options contract can be sold to another investor at a gain in price prior to the delivery date specified. An options contract that is not "in the money" is worthless, so it generally expires with no consequence other than the investor loses whatever sum of money was paid to purchase the options contract.

About half of all forex transactions (including future transactions and options transactions) are made in dollars. The dollar is the most actively traded currency in the world. Moreover, nearly all other currencies are quoted in dollars, so the dollar becomes the "pegging" currency by which all others are measured. Still, the dollar either increases in value or decreases in value depending upon how much of another currency the dollar is able to buy. Thus, when the dollar buys 100 yen, it is worth less than when the dollar buys 120 yen. Even at 120 yen, the dollar might be considered weak, for instance, if the historical high of the dollar (or at the high in recent months) bought 125 yen.

The key point is that the value of the dollar on the forex is floating. Each instant of trading is an opportunity for the dollar (and all other currencies) to be repriced simultaneously, depending upon the estimates traders are making of the currency's underlying strength. Even measuring a currency's underlying strength is problematic. Currency traders have to anticipate the purchasing power of the dollar (or any other currency). Estimating a currency's purchasing power demands making judgments about whether the underlying domestic economy of that currency is in economic boom or recession, whether the country is experiencing inflation or turmoil. Terrorism, war, and many other factors may affect the purchasing power of a currency. The value of a currency, including the dollar, depends to a large extent upon the confidence the international market has in the dollar. To a large extent, confidence has replaced gold as the key element backing the dollar.

Many foreign countries end up holding dollars because the United States buys more from that country than we export to them. If we import

15 million barrels of oil a day at a price of $50 per barrel, then $750 million goes overseas every day to the countries that sell us oil. Exporting countries end up holding large amounts of U.S. currency. Ultimately, oil exporters ask the all-important question, "What are these dollars worth?" Since the dollar has become a commodity, there is no fixed value of the dollar. The value of the dollar fluctuates moment to moment through the trading day as its price in relation to other currencies goes up or down. Nor can the dollar be turned in to the U.S. Treasury and redeemed for gold. The dollar today is worth only as much of another currency as the dollar will buy right now. Tomorrow may be dramatically different.

This puts the foreign holders of U.S. dollars at considerable risk. When the dollar was pegged to gold, the U.S. Treasury could only print up as many dollars as our current gold reserves permitted. With the dollar removed from the gold standard, as it is today, the U.S. Treasury has no fixed limit regarding how many dollars it can issue. The U.S. Treasury may simply decide to issue additional billions of debt, such as Treasury notes, which in turn are sold to institutions and foreign holders of dollars. If the U.S. Treasury takes the path of issuing more debt, we risk devaluing the dollar, making it worth less in relation to other currencies.

Oil is a commodity in that its value changes daily. Likewise the dollar is a commodity whose value changes daily in relation to other currencies.

Oil is not sold today for money that can ultimately be traded for gold. Gold and money are not interchangeable. Oil is sold for dollars, which has a floating value that depends on price fluctuations of the dollar on the forex. One commodity (oil) is exchanged for another commodity (dollars). If the dollar decreases in value, exporters of oil take a loss in their dollar currency holdings. Simply put, the exporters of oil are at a constant risk because they sold their oil for dollars that could become worth less than the dollar was worth when their oil was sold. When foreign exporters sell their oil to the United States, they receive dollars that hold no promise they can be redeemed for any fixed value, because redemption of dollars in gold is no longer permitted. And that is the problem: oil exporters take a risk the moment their oil is sold. One commodity, oil, is a tangible product that is being exchanged for another commodity, dollars, that is neither tangible nor fixed in value.

Historically, the dollar has lost value dramatically. A standard measure of value is the Consumer Price Index (CPI), which measures a bundle of goods and services in terms of price over time. The U.S. Bureau of Labor Statistics, the government department that is responsible for the CPI, pegs the period 1982–84 as the standard CPI measure of what $100 would buy. According to this measure, in 1913 it only cost $9.90 to buy what in 1982–84 cost $100.00. Clearly the dollar depreciated over the seventy years between 1913 and 1982–1984. Moreover, the rate of depreciation since 1982–84 has increased. Some twenty years later, in 2004, it took $189.00 to buy what in 1982–84 cost only $100.00. Consider this: In 1971, the year the United States closed the gold window, it took only $40.50 to buy the same bundle of goods and services that cost $100.00 in 1982–84. By 2004 the cost was $189.00—an increase from $40.50 to $189.00 only thirty-three years after we closed the gold window.[22]

Let's look at the data from a slightly different angle. How much was a 1971 dollar (the year the United States closed the gold window) worth in 2003? Measured against the CPI, you would have to have $4.55 to buy in 2003 what $1.00 bought in 1971. Measured against the gross domestic product per capita, you would have to have $6.97 in 2003 to have what you had with $1.00 in 1971.[23] Again, the result is the same. While the dollar has lost significant purchasing power over time, a strong argument can be made that the dollar has depreciated at an exponential rate since 1971 when the United States closed the gold window.

Since 1971 the U.S. Treasury has also been issuing debt at an increasing rate. The national debt in 1919 at the end of World War I was $27.4 billion. In 1971 the national debt was $449 billion, about sixteen times greater than the 1919 debt fifty-two years earlier. By 2003 the national debt was $6.8 trillion, about fifteen times greater, this time accomplished in only thirty-two years.[24] In August 2005 the national debt had risen to $7.85 trillion, up more than $1 trillion in less than two years. As we issue more debt, the supply of dollars available on the world market grows dramatically. We are setting up a system where anyone who holds U.S.

currency as a foreign reserve will inevitably see the purchasing power of those dollars diminish, just as anyone who holds foreign debt will most certainly get paid back in dollars that are worth far less than the dollars borrowed in the first place. To put the point even more bluntly: anyone who holds dollars ends up losing.

In contrast, before we closed the gold window in 1971, the official price of gold was $35.00 an ounce. In 2004 gold traded as high as $428.00 an ounce. In 1975 gold became a tradable commodity in America, with the price fluctuating according to the gold market. The increase in the price of gold reflects a key point. Dollars are anything but scarce, and their value has decreased dramatically. Gold remains truly scarce, and its value has increased in terms of dollars.

One could argue that the buying power lost by the dollar has remained constant in gold. What one hundred ounces of gold bought in 1975 is virtually what one hundred ounces of gold will buy today. Gold is a fixed value whose buying power remains constant. In 1920 a twenty-dollar paper bill or a twenty-dollar gold piece would purchase a good suit, shirt, and tie in a men's store. In 2005 a twenty-dollar bill would barely buy a new tie, but a twenty-dollar gold piece in any condition is worth five hundred dollars, which would still buy a good suit, shirt, and tie. The dollar has depreciated in value. Gold has not.

In August 1976, one year after gold was made available for purchase by American citizens, gold traded at $105 an ounce. In January 2005 gold was as high as $428 an ounce (as low as $420 an ounce). So gold increased about 4.2 times in value from 1976 to 2005. Viewed against the dollar in the same time period, gold maintained its buying power—the price of gold went up because the buying power of the dollar went down. Gold price increases functioned to offset the losses in purchasing power suffered by the dollar. An ounce of gold in 2005 still bought what an ounce of gold bought in 1976, even though the dollar prices of goods increased (as a function of the dollar's diminishing purchasing power).

Prior to 1971 oil exporters were hedged (protected) because their international settlements in dollars were ultimately backed by gold. Now oil exporters must factor in additional costs to hedge their foreign currency holdings in dollars. The hedge can be accomplished through a variety of sometimes complex strategies, including purchasing other currencies as a portion of the portfolio and possibly purchasing futures and options contracts in an attempt to insure their positions against adverse movements in the currency markets. All these hedging strategies bring added costs to the managers of foreign currency reserve portfolios that accumulate in dollars from oil exports.

Gold, a truly scarce commodity, functions as a constant when measured in terms of purchasing power. The dollar, separated as it is now from gold, has had its purchasing power eroded. In contrast to gold, dollars are not rare or in short supply. We increase the supply of dollars every time the U.S. Treasury issues debt, and there is no set limit anymore on how much debt the Treasury can issue. Gold reserves no longer cap the dollar supply the Treasury can issue. By law, we have a debt ceiling; however, Congress continues to raise the debt ceiling every time we hit it.

In recent years the buying power of the dollar has decreased 40 percent on the average against all major foreign currencies. Is it any wonder that real commodities (such as housing, copper, steel—all tangible assets) have exploded in price relative to dollars? Oil is no different and has increased accordingly. No wonder foreign exporters of oil have grown increasingly anxious about the future of the dollars they currently hold.

THE MOVE TO SETTLE OIL TRANSACTIONS IN EUROS

In 2003–4, while the price of oil was increasing dramatically in terms of the dollar, the price increase of oil in euros was much less dramatic. Since November 2003 oil prices in dollars have been increasing dramatically; oil prices in euros did not begin to increase until February 2004. By May 2004, oil prices in dollars had increased by 54 percent while oil prices in euros had increased only 31 percent.[25]

In 2004 the Switzerland-based Bank for International Settlement, often called the world's central bank, reported that U.S. dollar-denominated deposits of OPEC countries fell from 75 percent of their total deposits in the third quarter of 2001 to 61.5 percent by the end of 2003. In the same period, the share of euro-denominated deposits of OPEC countries rose from 12 percent to 20 percent. In December 2004 the *Washington Times* reported, "At the end of June 2004, OPEC members Euro denominated deposits reached 44 billion Euro nearly doubled compared to 23.5 billion Euro held in the third quarter of 2001. By comparison, OPEC dollar denominated deposits stood at $132.1 billion, down from $145.3 billion in the third quarter of 2001."[26]

In part, the move to hold more euros represents a decision by OPEC countries to diversify their foreign currency holdings, reducing the proportion of dollars. Since different currencies are not expected to vary in the same direction, gains might be realized in the euro portion of a foreign currency portfolio when the euro goes up in value if, at the same time, the dollar goes down in value. Also, ironically, when a currency is strong, the foreign currency managers might shy away from holding more dollars if they are worried that if the dollar is high now, it will fall in value soon. Too great a shift out of dollars by foreign currency managers could precipitate the dollar's falling in a crisis manner, making it even more difficult for the U.S. Treasury to continue financing U.S. debt with the sale of Treasury bonds.

In 2000 Saddam Hussein convinced the United Nations to allow him to sell Iraqi oil for euros instead of dollars. Saddam even received permission from the U.N. to convert the $10 billion oil-for-food reserve fund from dollars to euros. The idea of switching to the euro for oil settlements is not new; variations of the idea have been circulated since at least 1973, when the Arab oil embargo was under way. Then the idea was floated to move toward settling oil in a basket of some sixteen different currencies in order to weaken the hold of the dollar on the international oil market.[27]

Saddam Hussein profited from the strength of the euro vis-à-vis the dollar, though he would have begun to suffer if he had been able to continue the policy into 2004 and 2005, when the dollar began to strengthen against the euro. Saddam might have responded that since the dollar floats in value, there would be times when the dollar is up, but still the long-term trend of the dollar is down. From time to time government officials in Iran and Russian have made statements suggesting a switch toward the euro and away from the dollar as the denomination in which they want to settle their international oil transactions.[28] Moving to the euro to hurt the United States only makes sense if the euro remains strong. We have repeatedly pointed out that politically motivated moves in the current world oil market are only justified if the moves also make economic sense. Moving oil transactions to euro settlement at a time when the euro is about to weaken in value would ultimately be self-defeating. The real damage might ultimately be done to the exporter now holding lower-valued euros.

Hedging oil foreign currency portfolios by reducing the percentage of dollar holdings probably makes sense as the world market evolves. Currently about two-thirds of the world's foreign exchange reserves from oil sales are held in dollars. Some slippage in that percentage would probably not affect the U.S. Treasury's ability to sell Treasury bills in the volume needed to continue financing the U.S. debt. That picture could change if the percentage of the world's foreign exchange reserves from oil sales drops to 50 percent or less held in dollars.

Did President George W. Bush decide to attack Iraq because Saddam Hussein was threatening to move away from the dollar? Probably not. Did Bush decide to attack because Hussein was encouraging OPEC and Russia to follow his lead and move to the euro? Again, probably not. Yet the United States could not afford to ignore the threat. Saddam's move was clearly aimed at harming the United States. Still, the amount of oil we were importing in 2003 from Iraq was relatively small. Nor did it make sense to calculate that the euro would forever remain relatively strong. OPEC and Russia were not following Saddam's lead. In 2003 there was no mass conversion of foreign exchange portfolios from dollars to euros. Still, OPEC and Russia took note. Other Muslim countries did not follow Saddam's lead; he remained alone in his move to settle oil transactions in euros.

If Bush was trying to protect the dollar, all he needed to do was wait, not attack Iraq. At the end of 2004 the inability of the European countries to ratify the European Union's constitution was clear. The continuing validity of the European Union itself was being called into question as a result of the votes being registered against the constitution in Europe. War against Iraq was never Bush's only option. Had he merely decided to express confidence in the dollar, instead of invading, he would have pleased America's political Left. Ultimately, the market itself would have punished Saddam for moving toward euros. Granted, in 2003 the EU political problem over ratifying a European constitution was not foreseen. Still, even in 2003, when the euro was strong, the idea that the euro would only continue to strengthen was foolish. In a free-floating system, the values of all currencies fluctuate. A strong euro today may not be a strong euro tomorrow. The same is true for the dollar.

The dollar is strong today in large part because of the continued strength of the U.S. economy. The U.S. economy is certainly larger and more resilient than the combined economies of the EU countries. The movement we are seeing in international foreign exchange portfolios is to hedge portfolios by marginally reducing dollar positions, not to fundamentally change portfolios by dumping major dollar holdings. Continuing disagreements over the European Union's proposed constitution raises serious international concern that the EU may never become the political or economic powerhouse once envisioned. Still, all this could change. When Saudi Arabia's King Fahd died in July 2005, rumors circulated worldwide that Saudi Arabia had begun to move its foreign-currency holdings away from the dollar and into the euro. Even though the world expected no change in Saudi Arabia's oil policy, the uncertainty over the transition caused the price of gold to jump, a market movement that gained impetus from the rumors that the Saudis were moving toward the euro.

We ourselves are concerned that the long-term trend of the dollar is down. A dollar not backed by gold runs the risk that oil will continue to be expensive for Americans and that those foreign nations who sell us oil will have increasing reserves of dollars that they hold nervously. An oil-currency war launched against the dollar remains a theoretical possibility. In reality, the nations participating in such an attack would have to be careful not to damage themselves in the process. If countries holding dollar reserves decide to diversify their holdings away from the dollar, the U.S. Treasury will have to respond quickly. What is at risk is our continuing ability to finance our growing national debt by selling Treasury bonds at affordable rates. If confidence in the U.S. dollar begins to fade, we will face a crisis that will demand serious retrenchment in our economy at home.

Our international trade partners are already making serious efforts to hedge their foreign-currency portfolios against the dollar, seeking to minimize their risk by holding fewer petrodollars. Over time, the U.S. position may erode to the point where hedging against the dollar takes up increasing proportions of the foreign-currency portfolios of our trading partners. Then what is a small impact today could well become a serious problem tomorrow. What if foreign-exchange portfolios from oil sales drop to 60 percent being held in dollars—would that cause a crisis in the U.S. economy? Or would it take 55 percent? All we know today is that hedging against the dollar already makes sense to foreign-exchange portfolio managers. We should expect even more hedging against the dollar to occur if the long-term trend to a weakening dollar persists.

This discussion points in one major direction: producers of foreign oil are exploring other areas in which to hold their money, something other than classic dollar deposits that have been proven to devalue over time. This is a trend we are not likely to reverse as long as we keep printing dollars freely while increasing our levels of debt without limit.

The supply of dollars cannot continue to grow at an unrestrained pace without adverse international effects. The exporting oil countries are clearly thinking about this issue actively. All of us would be thinking about it if we were oil exporting countries. All we would have to figure out is that the large dollar holdings we have accepted as value for the delivery of our oil aren't worth what we thought they were worth.

When a hard commodity like oil is sold for a commodity of decreasing value, namely dollars, the buyer takes serious risks. Let's say oil sells for $50 a barrel, but then the dollar depreciates by 20 percent while you are still holding the dollars from the sale in your reserves. It turns out you sold the barrel of oil not for $50 a barrel but for $40 (a 20 percent depreciation). If the dollar devaluates by 40 percent, you effectively sold the oil for $30 a barrel.

This is the problem we discussed earlier. Oil is a hard, tangible commodity sold for dollars that are an intangible commodity with no fixed values. Since dollars can no longer be exchanged for gold, no hard, fixed commodity stands behind U.S. international payments, including oil purchases. Unless the dollar remains strong, we run a constant risk that foreign nations holding dollar-currency reserves could get nervous and move out of the dollar. When we depend upon foreign nations to buy our currency bonds, we again are in a form of dependency, a financial stranglehold. If we have to raise the price of U.S. Treasuries in order to sell them on international institutional markets, we may price ourselves beyond the ability to finance our staggering national debt at reasonable levels. This is a time bomb waiting to harm the U.S. economy when we can least afford the damage. In other words, the problem of a weakening dollar will be compounded by the problem of more expensive financing of the national debt.

The trend since 1913, when we formed the Federal Reserve, has been a continued increase of the federal debt and a continued long-term devaluation of the dollar. Unless steps are taken to reestablish some gold backing for the U.S. dollar used in international trade, we see nothing in place to get us out of this financial stranglehold.

MUSLIM NATIONS CONSIDER THE GOLD DINAR

Former Malaysian prime minister Mahathir Mohamad has championed a move for the Muslim nations of the world to reinstate the gold dinar for use as a currency of international trade. "The value of one gold dinar is one gold dinar no matter what the exchange rate of a currency is against the gold dinar. If the value of goods or services is expressed in gold dinar, the value remains the same no matter which country is involved in the trade," explains Mohamad correctly.[29] The gold dinar was used as currency throughout the Muslim world prior to the collapse of the Ottoman caliphate in 1924. Prime Minister Mohamad has pressed for the reintro-duction of the gold dinar since the Asian financial crisis of 1997–98, which he blames largely upon currency speculators who benefited themselves by betting against various Asian countries, including those of Malaysia and Indonesia, both countries with strong Muslim populations.[30]

But his idea is not to reinstitute the gold dinar as the common cur-rency for day-to-day transactions. Rather, the gold dinar would exist as an international currency to settle international transactions. The goal would be to denominate international trade in dinars. By fixing the dinar as a standard unit of weight in gold, exporters would be paid in their respec-tive national currency by their central bank on the due date of exports based on the dinar exchange rate at the time of the transaction. Thus bilat-eral international imports and exports within the Muslim world would be standardized by settlements made only in reference to the value in gold di-nars. As a result, the Muslim nations would reestablish the gold standard at a time when we have abandoned the gold standard.[31]

Gold dinars would not have to exist in physical form. An electronic dinar would be sufficient. Central banks involved in the program would settle differences in bilateral trade every three months by transferring gold between their custodian accounts at an international bank such as the Bank of England. The gold would not physically have to move from one country to another, but the beneficial ownership of the gold in the selected international bank would be reassigned according to the adjust-ments made every three months to settle the international trade accounts in dinars between participating nations.[32]

The idea of the Islamic gold dinar is traceable to Professor Ibrahim Fadillo, the founder of the Morabeteen International Organization in 1983 in South Africa. The organization believes that unity in the Muslim world must be achieved through economic unity. If the gold dinar be-comes the standard of international trade throughout the Islamic world, much progress would be made toward this goal.[33] This is no longer a the-oretical discussion; the gold dinar currently exists. In November 2002 the gold dinar was reissued by the West Malaysian Royal Mint and is available now in physical form throughout the Middle East. The gold dinar is equivalent to 4.3 grams at .916 fineness (22 carat), or 4.22 grams of "four-nines" gold (0.14 troy ounces), virtually pure gold. In 2003 the gold dinar began to be privately used in twenty-two Islamic countries and is minted in four countries.

Use of gold dinars in this manner could represent a strong challenge to the dollar simply because the gold backing of the dinar reestablishes in international trade the central role of gold as a fixed value, challenging all market-floating currencies, which by their very nature cannot have a fixed value. The United States should consider reestablishing some gold backing to the dollar used in settling international payments. The Islamic oil-producing world sees the wisdom in having a gold-backed currency, one that can be used for settling international payments, a direct challenge to the free-floating U.S. dollar.

In January 2004, at an economic conference in Saudi Arabia's Red Sea city of Jeddah, Prime Minister Mohamad advised the Islamic world to sell oil for gold, not dollars, to avoid being "short-changed" by a decline in the U.S. economy: "The price of oil is $33, but the U.S. dollar has declined by 40 percent against the euro, so you're effectively getting $20. You're being short-changed." He suggested that the Islamic oil-producing nations should tally their annual imports and exports, settling the difference at the end of the year in gold dinars.[34] The wisdom of Mohamad's advice was to hedge the bet against the dropping dollar. What happens if the oil-producing nations in the Middle East move toward the gold dinar as the basis for settling international gold sales? How then does the U.S. Treasury finance the ever-growing growing U.S. debt? This is not an abstract economics lesson. The point here could well be felt by every American in very painful terms that could dramatically affect the U.S. economy.

The system proposed by Mohamad could well become the standard for dealing with Muslim countries. Some fifty-six countries, members of the Organization of the Islamic Conference (www.oic-oci.org), including Iran, have indicated an interest in exploring the idea with the intent to establish the gold dinar as the standard of international trade for all goods and services moving between Iran and Malaysia. The ultimate goal is to establish the gold dinar as the alternative to the dollar in all international trade engaged in by Muslim countries throughout the world. This would mean that the U.S. Treasury market would be competing with a gold-backed currency. In other words, we would have to use U.S. dollars to buy gold dinars to settle our oil purchases. A weakening dollar at the time of such gold purchases would make the oil we purchased from the Middle East even more expensive.

At present the United States is losing ground in the world's oil markets. Continuing to depend on the Middle East for our foreign oil supplies is a risky policy. The strategy becomes even shakier when the Muslim world begins to take serious steps to back with gold their international-exchange currencies while we do not. The United States will remain vulnerable as long as no gold stands behind the dollar. We should never forget that we are in a continuing war against radical Islamic terrorism, and that war has serious economic dimensions.

9

HOW HIGH THE PRICE OF OIL?

A billion here, a billion there, and pretty soon you're talking about real money.

—U.S. Senator Everett Dirksen

WILL WE SEE GAS costing five dollars or even ten dollars a gallon? Very possibly we will. The configuration of the world's petroleum supply and demand is shifting right before our eyes.

U.S. dependency on foreign oil has pushed us into alliances with countries whose interests are not necessarily our own. We have accepted a flood of immigrants from Mexico, taking virtually no steps to reverse the tide or return the illegal immigrants, even though we know terrorists are also slipping across the border by mixing in with the rising tide surging north. We have tolerated the leftist Hugo Chavez regime in Venezuela so we can buy oil, knowing full well that the petrodollars shipped to Caracas will be used to fund socialist revolutionary activity and narco-trafficking in Central and South America. We rely heavily on oil shipped from the Middle East while we fight a war against radical Islamic terrorism that has deep roots within one of our longer-term, more stable oil partners, namely Saudi Arabia.

Meanwhile, anti-American oil alliances are forming, orchestrated by the rogue state of Iran. Europe is scrambling to find a reliable oil supply at affordable prices, and that price advantage is being secured by the willingness of Europeans to form anti-American alliances with oil-producing nations. China and India are also searching to lock up the oil they will need to meet the demands of their exploding populations and rapidly developing economies. Against this background, Russia continues to calculate the advantages that can be won through oil alliances. We should never assume that Russia has quietly accepted that the cold war has been permanently lost.

These are the scenarios that make gas at five or ten dollars a gallon a reasonable possibility, one that we cannot afford to ignore. We return to the mathematical principle that a difference in scale is a difference in phenomenon. We have already pointed out that the world oil market has doubled in size since the early 1970s. As a consequence, the market has become more complex, not simply larger. The oil alliances that are forming now may well shape the structure of international politics and economics for decades to come. We cannot assume that the international structure that emerges will be necessarily favorable to the United States.

We may well see the development of a two-tier pricing structure in the oil market. A lower price structure could be available from oil suppliers such as Iran to such nations as China, India, and the European nations that are willing to invest in the development of Iran's oil infrastructure and struggling economy. If the United States is shut out from such favorable pricing through the formation of anti-American alliances emanating from Iran, we may find ourselves scrambling on the spot markets to find foreign oil at less-than-favorable prices.

IRAN HAS OIL AND WANTS NUKES

In 2005 the world has a clear opportunity to see just how important Iranian oil is to Europe. We also saw the lengths to which Europeans were willing to go to preserve for themselves favorable access to Iranian oil. Understanding how this plays out will require a look at the negotiations regarding Iran's nuclear-weapons program that took place in the critical months after the 2004 U.S. presidential election.

The clerics ruling Iran have pursued a secret nuclear-weapons program for more than two decades. In November 2004 the mullahs agreed to suspend the enrichment of uranium as part of an agreement with France, Germany, and Great Britain (known as the EU-3) to further negotiate the development of Iran's nuclear industries. Iran has long claimed that its only purpose in pursuing nuclear power is to generate electricity, not bombs. Prior to the 2004 presidential election, the United States, had been moving toward a confrontation with Iran. Vice President Dick Cheney had even suggested that Israel might launch a preemptive strike against Iran, one that the United States could well see as within Israel's legitimate rights of self-defense.[1] Then, after the election was over, a newly reelected President Bush traveled to Europe, having first sent his new secretary of state, Condoleezza Rice, to prepare the way.

As a result of discussions in Europe, the Bush administration changed the course of its Iran policy. A decision was reached to support the EU-3 negotiations to see if Iran might be persuaded to drop its nuclear-weapons program in a clear and verifiable manner. The United States agreed not to take military action until the outcome of these negotiations was final. There were some conditions placed as this new direction was being set. The United States insisted that Iran would abandon all efforts to enrich uranium. Given the history of Iran's clandestine weapons program, the Bush administration believed the word of the mullahs could not be trusted. Thus the Iranian plant at Isfahan, which was used to process yellowcake uranium to uranium hexafluoride gas, would have to remain closed. Iran would also have to agree to keep closed its uranium-enrichment facility at Natanz. Here the mullahs have built a huge underground facility housing thousands of sophisticated centrifuges that are used to process uranium hexafluoride gas into weapons-grade uranium 235. The EU-3 agreed that this bright-line distinction would be a negotiating point. The Iranian heavy water plant at Arak would also have to be closed. The facility at Arak would give the Iranians the ability to produce weapons-grade plutonium.

In return for allowing the EU-3 time to work out a deal with Iran, the Europeans agreed that the Iranian question would go to the U.N. Security Council for the imposition of further sanctions should Iran refuse to negotiate an agreement the Europeans and the Americans would accept. Why did the Bush administration back off its hard-line position after the 2004 election victory? Second terms for U.S. presidents have proven difficult since the ratification of the Twenty-Second Amendment to the Constitution. Presidents reelected to second terms are by definition "lame ducks" who cannot seek reelection. Politicians who cannot run for reelection have difficulty holding together their own political party, let alone setting the agenda for the opposition party. Second terms proved disastrous for Richard M. Nixon, who was forced to resign under the shadow of Watergate, for Ronald Reagan, who was severely limited by the Iran-Contra scandal, and for Bill Clinton, who was impeached for perjury, having lied under oath regarding his sexual activity with White House intern Monica Lewinsky.

During the election campaign, Bush had been strongly attacked over the failure to find stockpiles of weapons of mass destruction in Iraq after the United States had invaded and deposed Saddam Hussein. The controversy over the failure of U.S. intelligence before the Iraq War could easily have cost him reelection. After the 2004 election, the administration faced the same difficulty with regard to Iran. Now even the International Atomic Energy Agency (IAEA) of the United Nations openly admits that Iran has been deceitful about its nuclear research and development program.[2] Still, no one had incontrovertible evidence that Iran actually had an atomic bomb. Thus, invading Iran at this point would amount to launching another preemptive war. In a lame-duck second term, Bush would run the risk of impeachment should he go to war unilaterally against Iran to prevent that country from developing a nuclear weapon. By playing out the EU-3 negotiations, the administration might get the desired result. If not, the Europeans have agreed to join the United States in bringing the issue before the United Nations.

No one had any illusions that the Security Council would take strong steps against Iran. China and Russia are both permanent members of the

Security Council. Russia had just completed building Iran's first nuclear reactor at Bushehr, on the Persian Gulf. China was in the midst of negotiating rights to develop Iranian oil fields with the intent of using the oil in China. Both countries would be expected to support the mullahs. Still, advancing the case through the United Nations with the support of the Europeans was a way for the Bush administration to lay the case on the table, not only to the world, but more importantly to American voters.

The Europeans made a series of very generous offers to get the mullahs to agree not to enrich uranium. Many of the proposals directly involved oil. They offered to make Iran the main transit route for oil and natural gas moving from Central Asia. This would allow crude oil and natural gas to move from the huge reserves in Kazakhstan to world markets without having to move this oil through the American-supported rival pipeline through Turkey.[3] The proposed route across Iran would move oil into Europe quicker than the traditional pipeline route via the Caspian Pipeline Consortium to a terminal near the Black Sea port of Novorossiik. The EU-3 proposed to the mullahs that Iran would be positioned in the coming decades to be the main oil and natural gas supplier to Europe. By also making sure all pipeline routes crossed through Iran before the oil moved out of Central Asia, the Europeans were making sure that Iran had a strategic hold on a huge quantity of Middle Eastern oil. They would be positioned to derive revenue whether Iran produced the oil and gas supplying Europe or merely served as the geographical conduit for the passage of the oil to Europe from other suppliers.

The EU-3 proposals also contained guarantees of sovereignty, promising that Iran would not be invaded by other nations, including the United States. These assurances were designed to resemble the types of assurances John F. Kennedy's administration gave the Soviet Union to end the Cuban missile crisis, when the United States gave its word that it would not invade Cuba to depose Fidel Castro.

A bundle of additional economic incentives were packaged together by the EU-3, including substantial commitments to help the mullahs develop their extensive oil and natural gas resources. Since the 1979 revolution, much of Iran's oil industry infrastructure has fallen into disrepair and become obsolete. By propping up Iran's oil industry, the Europeans would give the mullahs the revenue to maintain their personal lavish lifestyles and to keep their subsistence economy above the point where the oppressed people of Iran might rise up en masse to demand regime change and reform. The EU-3 even offered to supply Iran the enriched uranium needed to operate peaceful nuclear power plants, provided the Iranians promised not to develop their own uranium enrichment capabilities.

All these proposals missed the mullahs' main point. As a signatory to the Nuclear Nonproliferation Treaty (NPT), Iran insisted it had the right to develop the "full fuel cycle." This language contained code words for Iran's insistence it had the right to enrich uranium and to develop weapons-grade uranium as long as no atomic bomb was actually produced. Although the original intent of the NPT was to prevent additional nations from pursuing nuclear weapons, the mullahs had turned the treaty's intent upside-down, claiming the NPT justified their pursuit of the full fuel cycle as long as they stopped "a turn of the screw away" from actually developing a bomb. This is why the United States demanded that Iran take clear and verifiable steps to dismantle their existing uranium-enrichment facilities. Anything less would give the mullahs all the room they needed to continue cheating, producing nuclear weapons clandestinely, while insisting publicly that their intents were peaceful and that they had stopped just short of actually producing a bomb.

The mullahs knew that the world would come to them for oil whether or not they agreed to the conditions of the EU-3. What the mullahs saw was that a nuclear-armed Iran, or one that could become nuclear armed in a short time, was the strategic advantage they were seeking. With nuclear-weapons capability, the mullahs would buy themselves a "stay in power" form of insurance they could get no other way. Dislodging by military force an Iranian regime armed with nuclear weapons would be a major feat far more difficult and dangerous than the Iraq War. If the mullahs could put a nuclear-weapons umbrella over their support for terrorist organizations such as Hezbollah, which they created and funded in Lebanon, then their desire to spread the Islamic revolution worldwide would take great leaps forward. Moreover, armed with nuclear weapons, the Iranian government could take a central place on the world stage, demanding more-advanced nations listen to the mullahs' demands or face a form of nuclear extortion that could easily be aimed at stopping or impairing the world's needed flow of oil.

The reasons the EU-3 were determined to prolong negotiations with Iran, desperate to scramble for any solution that would be acceptable by both Tehran and Washington, can be more easily understood when we appreciate the extent to which EU-3 oil companies are already active in Iran. Some 31 French companies are currently developing the oil industry in Iran. The list also includes 80 German companies, plus an additional 48 from the United Kingdom. Clearly, each of the EU-3 countries already have substantial economic involvement in Iran's oil economy. The Eleventh International Oil, Gas, Petrochemicals Exhibition (IOGPE) is scheduled for Tehran on April 20–23, 2006. A list of 442 international companies in the oil and natural gas industries are already listed on the IOGPE as exhibitors and participants. In addition to companies from the EU-3, the list also includes participants from Australia, Austria, Belgium, China, Denmark, India, Italy, Japan, Kuwait, Malaysia, Monaco, the Netherlands, Norway, Poland, Russia, Saudi Arabia, Singapore, South Korea, Spain, Switzerland, Turkey, and the United Arab Emirates. About the only major nation not involved is the United States, and that is only because of U.S. sanctions currently in place against Iran.[4]

The minute Iran moves to enrich uranium, the price of oil will spike. Should the world become convinced that the only way to stop Iran from enriching uranium is to take military action, the price of oil might not only spike, it might settle in at a new, higher plateau. The world oil markets are extremely sensitive to political or economic instability. While Iran might claim its intents are entirely peaceful and that the mullahs would stop short of making nuclear bombs, the world oil markets can be expected to price themselves as if the mullahs are lying. If Iran begins enriching uranium, the country will reach a point of no return very soon. The point of no return is defined as the moment Iran has everything necessary to make an atomic weapon, the point where Iran's nuclear-weapons industry is so advanced that not even a military attack would be able to

225

take out the country's ability to make a bomb. Reports continue to surface that Iran already has a bomb or that it has purchased on the black market all the components needed to make a bomb, including enriched uranium.

Gasoline in the United States at five dollars or ten dollars a gallon becomes very likely as soon as the world oil market determines that international diplomatic efforts to stop Iran's progress toward the bomb have failed. A war with Iran, should it occur, would boost prices even higher.

CHINA EMERGES EVERYWHERE IN WORLD OIL MARKETS

In July 2005 China's foreign-currency reserves hit a record high of $711 billion, boosted largely by the lopsided favorable balance of trade that China enjoys with the United States.[5] This huge war chest has prompted the Chinese to look worldwide for oil and natural gas deals. One of the most controversial was the bid by the China National Offshore Oil Corporation (CNOOC), China's third-largest government-controlled oil company, to purchase the California-based Unocal for $18.4 billion. The bid drew intense political criticism from U.S. critics who believed the deal might severely compromise U.S. national security interests. The acquisition would have gained for the Chinese not only a U.S.-based oil company but substantial reserves. Even though Unocal is considered a third-tier or midsized U.S. oil company, it still commanded oil reserves estimated at 211 million barrels.[6] Valued at $50 a barrel, the value of Unocal's reserves alone could exceed $10.5 billion; at $60 a barrel, $12.6 billion.

Those who believed the merger should proceed argued that market forces would be determinant of the ultimate wisdom of the purchase. If the Chinese used Unocal to capture oil reserves that could be sent at below-market prices back to China, they might undermine the value of their investment in Unocal. As an investor, China should be motivated to maximize Unocal's profits, not just secure for China cheap oil. Opponents argued that the United States should not allow foreign nations to buy U.S. oil companies that held such substantial reserves. Given our dependence on foreign oil, we could face a national security problem if China decided to ship the Unocal oil to China, even if doing so meant taking a market loss for Unocal. Critics believed we should not empower any foreign nation with the ability to deal that kind of blow to the U.S. economy. On August 2, 2005, CNOOC withdrew its bid for Unocal, giving in to the intense adverse U.S. political pressure the proposal had generated. The withdrawal of the bid allowed ChevronTexaco to acquire Unocal for a lower bid of $17.6 billion. On a purely economic basis, those in the United States who had supported the CNOOC acquisition noted that the political fallout had been costly to the shareholders of Unocal.

China's consumption of petroleum exceeded 6.84 million barrels a day in 2004, placing it third in the world after the United States and Japan. China currently has six nuclear power plants in operation, with a generation capacity of 8.8 million kilowatts, accounting for 1 percent of the country's total power output. The Chinese government is planning to increase nuclear power generation to 20 million kilowatts by 2010, expanding to the point where nuclear power can account for 5 percent of China's total power output by 2020.[7] Also, China is making major efforts to shift from using coal as its major industrial energy source to using oil and natural gas. Before the opening of the Beijing Summer Olympics in 2008, China wants to reduce substantially the amount of urban air pollution caused by burning coal. To fuel an economy whose GDP grew at a staggering rate of 9.1 percent in 2003 and 9.5 percent in 2004, the Chinese government has launched a worldwide search for oil.

China is able to offer international partners a comprehensive deal. Nothing illustrates this better than the visits China's President Hu Jintao made to South America at the end of 2004,[8] including Argentina, Brazil, Chile, and Venezuela. Given China's tremendous need to import a variety of goods, from Brazilian chicken and beef to Argentinean soybeans to Chilean cooper, Hu Jintao could offer each country appropriate exporting opportunities of mutual benefit. Moreover, the Chinese were willing to make infrastructure deals with countries willing to be trade partners, looking to develop roads, telecommunications, and seaports. In Venezuela, President Hugo Chavez offered to put at China's disposal the development of many of its oil facilities. Chinese firms will be allowed to develop fifteen mature fields in eastern Venezuela, which together are capable of yielding more than 1 billion barrels of oil. Chavez offered to give China a favored position in the bidding for natural gas exploration contracts in the western part of the country that Venezuela is planning to offer for bid in 2006. In return, China offered to invest heavily in the development of Venezuela's agriculture, railways, mining, and telecommunications. China and Venezuela discussed plans to build a pipeline across Colombia, or possibly through Panama, to facilitate an easier passage to move Venezuela's oil and natural gas to the Pacific Ocean for export to China.

Hu Jintao ended his swing through the southern Western Hemisphere by visiting Fidel Castro. He promised that China would invest in Cuba's nickel mines with the goal of doubling the shipments of nickel from Cuba to China. The Havana visit communicated to South America that China was an open political alternative to the United States, one willing to invest in its development without objecting to its leftist politics. The approach was similar to the type of deals the Chinese were willing to make with the radical terror-supporting Islamic mullahs in Iran. Lest anyone miss the point, China was clear to communicate that an enemy of the United States could find a friend in China, one with plenty of dollars in foreign currency that the Chinese were willing to invest for the benefit of their friends. These overtures were well received, especially as the Chinese emphasized the contrast to what all too often is perceived as decades of economic neglect and second-class status suffered at the hands of the United States, South America's self-satisfied and self-focused neighbor to the north. China has now acquired oil exploration and production rights in Azerbaijan, Canada, Indonesia, Iran, Iraq, Kazakhstan, Sudan, and Venezuela.[9]

In 1998 the Chinese government reorganized the state-owned oil and natural gas operations into two vertically integrated firms: the China National Petroleum Corporation (CNPC) and the China Petrochemical Corporation (Sinopec). These two megastructures sit alongside the China National Offshore Oil Corporation (CNOOC), the entity that tried to purchase Unocal, the structure in China charged with the primary responsibility for offshore oil and natural gas exploration and production. Between 2000 and 2002 all three entities—CNPC, Sinopec, and CNOOC—successfully carried out initial public offerings (IPOs) on foreign stock markets, an initiative that brought in billions of dollars of foreign capital to develop China's oil and natural gas industries. PetroChina, a subsidiary of CNPC, sold a minority interest on both the Hong Kong and New York stock exchanges in April 2000. The IPO brought in $3 billion, with BP, the largest purchaser, acquiring 20 percent of the shares offered. Then, in October 2000, Sinopec raised $3.5 billion by offering a minority stake of 15 percent on the Hong Kong and New York stock exchanges. About $2 billion of this was purchased by ExxonMobil, BP, and Shell.[10]

China obviously can afford to purchase top worldwide investment banking expertise. What is also obvious is that the world's major oil conglomerates in both Britain and the United States are more than willing to invest substantial amounts in the development of what promises to be ultimately the world's largest market for oil and natural gas consumption. In none of these foreign investments did the U.S. government or the government of China raise any national security concerns. The dynamics of the world oil marketplace were in full swing here as the opportunity for economic gain looked across borders, inviting the willing participation of major oil conglomerates whose interests were for their stockholders, not the specific national interests of the countries where they are headquartered. If China rises economically and politically to the detriment of the United States, oil conglomerates based in the United States will have assisted it substantially.

China has for decades been considered oil-poor. This classification, however, has been no detriment to the Chinese. Within the past five years, major oil and natural gas discoveries have been made in China. After twenty years of exploration, Sinopec has announced that it has discovered large amounts of oil and natural gas in the country's northwest Tarim Basin. This one find added some 8 billion barrels of oil to proven reserves, which before the find had been estimated at no more than 23.5 billion barrels for all of China.[11] So far, fifteen oil fields and fourteen natural gas fields have been found in the Tarim Basin.[12] Exploration there is continuing while new exploration efforts are being planned across China. The experience in China seems to be repeating the experience in countries such as Iran, Kazakhstan, and Russia—geological estimates were wrong. All the oil had not been found. Previous estimates are giving way to higher estimates as new resources are being found.

China appears to be following a policy of investing in oil and natural gas exploration and development in order to secure for itself virtually exclusive production rights for the oil and natural gas that is produced as a result. The calculation seems to be that the investment required to acquire and develop these rights, either domestically or in foreign countries, will be economically sound if future production is thereby insured today at prices lower than market prices would have demanded in the future. Thus, oil secured by China through this invest-and-own methodology may never enter the world marketplace except to the extent that its availability keeps China off world markets in search of future imports where no rights have been secured. We could see, as a result, the development of a two-tier marketplace where China has oil it owns coming in at cheaper prices, and countries like the United States must still go to the world market to buy the oil they need at then current prices.

As China continues to buy up oil and natural gas reserves worldwide, we should expect continued pressure on the price of oil. The marketplace can be expected to price oil higher today, anticipating that China's buying more oil rights for itself today will mean less oil will be available to others—including the United States—tomorrow. No matter how much oil China acquires in foreign countries or discovers at home, there is no reason to expect that China will become a net exporter of oil. China's historical perspective has always been long-term, which contrasts sharply with U.S.-based companies that can rarely see beyond quarterly profit objectives. China is patient enough to expect that the size of its population and the strength of its economy will ultimately overtake all others, even if reaching that objective takes another hundred years.

RUSSIA PLAYS BOTH SIDES AGAINST THE MIDDLE

In 2004 Russia's GDP grew by 7.1 percent, easily beating the growth rates of all other G8 countries. This expansion was driven largely by increased oil prices worldwide. The U.S. Department of Energy estimates that a $1 boost in the price of oil increases Russian revenue by $1.4 billion.[13] The impact of oil prices on the Russian economy is huge; Russia's oil-and-gas sector account for more than 25 percent of the country's GDP. When oil prices were bottoming out at around $10 a barrel in 1998 (something we find hard to remember when oil hits new highs over $70 a barrel in August 2005), the Russian economy suffered. The spike in oil prices since the 2003 invasion of Iraq has breathed new life into the Russian economy.

China and Russia are working now to develop the most efficient rail or pipeline routes to bring oil out of Russia and into China. Other transportation routes are being examined to bring Russian oil to ports where it can be shipped via the Barents Sea to the United States or via the Baltic Sea to Europe. Other pipeline projects would carry oil from Russia into Europe through Poland or south into Turkey. The point is that Russia intends to expand its ability to get oil and natural gas into world markets from its extensive oil fields in Siberia. The U.S. Department of Energy estimates that Russia has 60 billion barrels of proven oil reserves. Oil production has increased to 8.8 million barrels a day, of which 70 percent is exported to foreign markets. As we noted earlier, experts considered Russia to be oil-poor decades ago. Today Russia rivals Saudi Arabia as the world's largest oil exporter.

The United States would like to think that Russia lost the cold war when the Berlin Wall fell and the Soviet Union broke apart. We should never forget that Russia continues to have strong national interests, whether they are communist or not. In many instances, Russia pursues goals that are at odds with U.S. national interests. As we have pointed out, Russia has built a nuclear reactor for Iran, even though the United States continues to impose sanctions on Iran. We are very concerned that an atomic Iran will destabilize the Middle East, giving reason for Turkey and Saudi Arabia to consider whether they, too, need to pursue nuclear weapons, if only for their national defense. Russia has moved to center stage, offering needed economic assistance to Iran at a time when the United States continues to charge that Iran supports terrorism worldwide. These interests could not be more at odds. In August 2005 Russia and China staged joint military exercises. At various points in the cold war, Russia and China were often at each other's throats. Now, the military in the two countries cooperate in military exercises, reflecting an emerging alliance in which oil is probably at the unspoken center.[14]

So, too, Russia has supplied missiles to Syria, another regime the United States considers supportive of terrorism and a national security risk to our ally Israel. In April 2005 Israel objected to a Russian deal to sell advanced SA-18 antiaircraft missiles to Syria. These missiles would make it more difficult for Israeli airplanes to fly over Syria. Russian President Vladimir Putin had backed off an earlier plan to sell Syria a shoulder-held version of the SA-18 because of American and Israeli pressure. Still, Israeli military experts objected that the vehicle-mounted SA-18 could easily be adapted to be shoulder-held. Israel also expressed concerns that Syria might well supply the Russian-made SA-18 missiles to insurgents in Iraq who are destabilizing efforts to establish democracy and attacking U.S. troops, or to Hezbollah operatives in Lebanon who have been supporting terrorist attacks against Israel.[15]

Each of these geopolitical developments affects the price of oil. World oil prices could further spike if the futures markets begin to conclude that Russian oil deals are moving to position their available supply with selected trading partners at special pricing, a move that would take huge quantities of Russian oil off the open world market. Again, we have suggested that America's dependence on foreign oil places us in a position where the formation of anti-American political alliances may have immediate repercussions on the price of oil. The moment futures markets sense that the U.S. supply of foreign oil might be restricted, the market will reprice upward to factor in that uncertainty.

U.S. OIL CONGLOMERATES CONSOLIDATE POWER AND SIT ON HUGE RESERVES

Since 2000 a wave of mergers has hit the oil and natural gas industries in the United States. The U.S. Department of Energy maintains a system called the Federal Reporting System (FRS) that tracks major U.S.-based energy companies. Following the recent mergers affecting oil and gas producers, FRS identified a total of thirty-four companies that merged into thirteen from 1997 to 2002.[16] The U.S. oil and gas industry is consolidating, with a few huge conglomerates emerging. A report by the Consumer Federation of America was quick to identify this trend with energy price increases: "The big got bigger and domestic prices started ratcheting up soon thereafter."[17]

Industry observers concluded that a major strategy was "to acquire reserves through mergers and acquisitions, rather than exploration."[18] A look at the reserves of several of the newly emerged major oil conglomerates confirms this. Chevron and Texaco merged in 2000 in a $35 billion transaction to form ChevronTexaco. The resulting conglomerate became the world's fourth largest in terms of oil and natural gas production. The U.S. Department of Energy estimates that ChevronTexaco owns 2.9 billion barrels of oil and national gas reserves, about 9.6 percent of the U.S. total.[19] When Exxon and Mobil merged in 1998 in an $80 billion transaction, the end result was about the same. ExxonMobil also commanded 2.9 billion barrels of oil. So between ChevronTexaco and ExxonMobil, the two companies have about 6 billion barrels of oil reserves, about 20 percent of the U.S. total.[20]

The oil industry strategy to consolidate through mergers and capture reserves proved very profitable. The U.S. Department of Energy reported that 2003 earnings for FRS consolidated oil companies exceeded $57 billion in 2003, nearly triple the earnings of 2002 and the highest net income (in constant dollars) since 1980. The earnings resulted almost entirely from the rising energy prices in 2003, a trend that continued throughout 2004 and into 2005. Undoubtedly, the period of spiking oil prices since the United States invaded Iraq has been one of the most profitable periods in history for the U.S. oil industry. The oil industry has largely used these increased profits to reduce debt, repurchase stock, and pay dividends to shareholders. The industry has not expanded exploration efforts or opened new refineries.

As we stressed earlier, even if U.S. oil companies decided to increase immediately the supply of oil onto the market, they would face a barrier. The bottleneck remains: oil reserves must be refined before they can be put onto market. U.S. oil refineries are operating at or near capacity right now, and no new refineries have been built in the last thirty years, and no new refineries are scheduled to be built in the immediate future. The refinery part of the oil business has traditionally been a low-margin part of the industry, and the environmental regulations enacted over the last three decades have been compounded by the desire of most communities to keep refineries out. If tomorrow the major oil conglomerates increased dramatically the amount of crude oil put on the market, the increase in the flow of gasoline to the pumps would be negligible at best. The commitment that needs to be made is long-term.

If the oil industry made a commitment, for instance, to increase oil-refining capacity dramatically, perhaps by 10 or 15 percent, that might have an impact on pricing. Industry pricing could adjust to the greater possibility of supply. The exact impact on pricing would depend on many factors, including increase in demand that an increase in supply might stimulate. Yet in an environment of high gasoline prices, the public is looking for effective responses from oil conglomerates that are enjoying record profits. A move to expand refining capacity would demonstrate the determination of the oil industry to break the stranglehold that limited refining capacity has on the flow of more gasoline to the market in times when demand is outpacing supply. An unwillingness to add refinery capacity leaves American consumers vulnerable to continued strangleholds whenever we face dramatic increases in crude oil prices that cannot be countered by oil companies responding by increasing gasoline supplies at the pump.

Today the U.S. oil industry is sitting on a quantity of oil reserves that have never been higher. The picture that emerges is one of major oil industry conglomerates simply sitting on huge reserves and waiting for oil prices to go even higher. This is an industry profile that is certain to cause consumers to complain loudly, especially if gasoline prices continue to spike. Shareholders might like to see oil go to five dollars a gallon, but consumers may not be able to tolerate an increase of that magnitude without suffering severe economic pain. In market terms, these pressures should lower demand, which ultimately will result in lower oil and gasoline prices. Politically, however, scenarios such as these are disastrous—both to oil companies and to politicians in office.

The oil companies would be well advised to take immediate steps to increase refinery capacity, even if most of those steps can only be expected to have longer-term market impacts. Building refineries or adding capacity to existing refineries takes time. Still, the public must be able to see that the oil companies are doing everything possible to get more oil and gas to the market when price increases continue to rise to unacceptable levels. It may be hard to determine in advance what the exact tolerance for increasing prices will be. Consumers have weathered gasoline prices as they have passed two dollars a gallon, but will the same hold true as gas prices get higher, to five dollars a gallon or ten dollars a gallon? This is a calculated risk both oil company executives and incumbent politicians must take. The problem is that many of the conditions that affect oil prices are beyond immediate control. Another series of terrorist bombings in the subways of London, or possibly New York, could be all we need to see the price of crude oil spike even higher.

The range of imaginable political scenarios capable of causing oil prices to rise is almost limitless, but the steps oil companies can and should take to avert further price increases are fairly obvious. In markets where the pressures on oil prices are higher, oil company executives would be well advised to make sure the public sees that they are using windfall profits on efforts to increase supply. Where are the new oil exploration efforts? the increased refinery capacity? These are the questions the media and the public will want answered. Yes, reducing corporate debt, repurchasing stock, and paying dividends are all responsible corporate governance, but not at the risk that the public feels gouged in the process. Reinvestment in increasing supply is mandatory for good corporate governance when increased oil prices look like they have no ceiling. Otherwise, the public may conclude that the oil conglomerates are content simply to sit on their huge reserves and wait until the price of oil rises to their liking before any of their ample supplies are released for the benefit of a demanding public.

Oil company mergers and acquisitions can arguably position the industry for greater achievements. Larger companies should be able to achieve operational efficiencies by consolidating operations. A stronger capital base should position U.S. oil conglomerates to access the world investment and banking capital markets to obtain the resources needed to remain competitive in the world marketplace. Yet consumers will have to see more than record profits, especially if energy prices continue to climb. It will not be enough for oil company executives to run for cover under newspaper and television public-relations campaigns replaying the tired theme Are We Running Out of Oil? Instead, the oil companies should take the lead in explaining to Americans how we can end our dependence on foreign oil. Conservation will not be the answer. Using less energy is not a solution. The theme of scaling back represents an even bigger problem to consumers who want to maintain their lifestyles in an economy that should continue to lead the world.

Oil conglomerates will have to be in the lead to show America how we can explore for more oil domestically without risking unacceptable environmental damage. Oil companies should explain to the public their plans to expand the usage of natural gas or show how they plan to be constructively involved in the development of energy alternatives, including nuclear power. If our mix of energies needs to shift, the American consumer will expect the oil conglomerates to lead the way. We need to see active involvement by oil company executives explaining to the public how they intend to transform themselves from being oil companies to being energy providers. Otherwise the picture presented to America and world is one of fat-cat oil conglomerates content to play out an end game, milking record profits down to the last drop of oil as long as the oil flows.

The U.S. economy continued to expand through 2004 and into 2005 even as the price of gasoline went over two dollars a gallon and headed toward three dollars a gallon. At some point, increased gasoline prices become an inevitable drag on economic expansion as higher fuel transportation costs impact a range of businesses from trucking companies to airlines. Industries hit by fuel-cost increases must eventually pass those costs onto consumers. The U.S. economy works off confidence. Nobody ever knows for sure what magic number will be too high a price for gasoline before consumers feel the pinch. That price always comes in times of rising markets. Increasing energy prices may not be an immediate cause for panic, but certainly they are a long-term basis for concern. Stable energy costs create confidence, which is an essential condition for the continued growth and development of the American economy.

THE PRICE OF OIL AND THE FUTURES MARKET

Today the price of oil is largely a function of the futures market. Just as the U.S. economy works off consumer confidence, the world oil market is sensitive to any disruptions or potential disruptions that can cause uncertainty. The range of variables that can cause oil prices to increase on futures markets is almost infinite: shutdowns because of labor problems in U.S. refineries, hurricanes in the Gulf of Mexico that disrupt offshore drilling, terrorist attacks anywhere in the world, changes of government within countries, or statements by oil-producing nations that they are going to increase or decrease production. These and countless more variables affect oil prices on the world futures markets. Essentially, buyers of futures contracts are making a bet on what the price of oil will be at a specific date in the future. When those buyers feel more uncertainty, the price of futures contracts goes up. When futures prices go up, the current market for crude oil—including the world spot markets—suffers upward pressure as a result.

World oil-pricing markets tend to be spirals of cause and effect, both in upward and downward directions. With the greater political uncertainty we are experiencing today due to international terrorism, the pressure on worldwide oil markets is likely to continue in an upward direction. Unless we can break the stranglehold of U.S. dependence on foreign oil, we will have an ever-weakening hold on our own destiny. Our dependence on Middle Eastern oil has increased since the end of World War II, as many government planners at that time predicted it would. Today we are at a crisis point. Nothing in the Middle East will be stable as long as fundamental conflicts persist, yet resolving the conflict between Israel and the Palestinians remains problematic at best. With Iran holding strong oil reserves and gaining increasing economic assistance from a wide range of countries, including China, India, Japan, and Russia, as well as Europe, we are likely to face constant challenges from the commitment of the Iranian regime to Islamic fundamentalism and the spread of their Islamic revolution.

We cannot stress enough that oil at five dollars or ten dollars a gallon is a clear and present danger, if not for today then certainly in the immediate future. As we have noted repeatedly, oil prices have been extremely volatile since the early 1970s. Yet we should not expect to see anytime soon a return to the 1998 low of ten dollars a barrel. The challenge America faces today is how to evolve a new oil independence while maintaining continued economic growth at home and fighting to secure our national security as the war against terrorism continues. Reaching out to understand the Islamic world, as critics on the Left constantly implore, are necessary steps to a peaceful future. Understanding alone, however, will not be sufficient in a world where radical Islamists are resolved to destroy America and Israel. The attack on Western economies launched by radical Islam cannot be won without economic strength. That alone necessitates our continued drive for ending our dependence on foreign oil. If we are held hostage to increasing oil costs, our economy will soon run out of the fuel we need at a price we can afford.

10

TERRORISM AND THE THREAT TO OIL

*You steal our wealth and oil at paltry prices because of your
international influence and military threats. This theft is indeed the
biggest theft ever witnessed in the history of the world.*

—OSAMA BIN LADEN,
"Letter to the American People,"
November 24, 2002

AN ECONOMIC ARGUMENT IS central to Osama bin Laden's war against America. He believes that we have stolen the oil of the Muslim world. "Whoever has stolen our wealth, then we have the right to destroy their economy," was a key statement in bin Laden's November 24, 2004, letter to the American people.

Bin Laden's statement should be taken as a thoughtful expression of a serious concern. At the core of the issue is bin Laden's perception that America has paid for oil, a hard commodity, with paper dollars that are no longer backed as they once were by the hard commodity of gold. Bin Laden is astute to realize that America could at any time reduce even more the price we have paid for the oil by devaluing our currency. Devaluation can occur at any moment on a free exchange where the value of the dollar floats in relationship to other currencies. If the world's currency traders lose confidence in the dollar, a resultant sell-off of dollars could easily constitute a de facto devaluation, whether the U.S. government wanted it to happen or not.

Make no mistake: America is in an economic war with radical Islamic extremists. The World Trade Center was targeted for attack on 9-11 in large part because of its importance as a symbol of American capitalism. So, too, the masterminds behind the 9-11 attack realized that a physical blow to New York City could quickly become an economic blow not only to New York City but, even more important, to the U.S. economy. Moreover, the psychological damage from the attack would be suffered by Americans across the nation, with further economic harm likely to result.

What were the consequences of 9-11? Airlines were grounded, the New York Stock Exchange was closed, even major league baseball games were cancelled. America came to a standstill as people all over the country canceled travel plans and retrenched, worried about their jobs and their safety. The Patriot Act, one of the most severe laws ever debated, was passed, and the nation prepared for war against the Taliban in Afghanistan. The economic downturn after 9-11 showed that the terrorists had calculated correctly. After more than 1 million jobs lost, several trillion dollars of equity evaporated from the stock market, and an increase of $1.6 trillion to our national debt, no one can say 9-11 was anything short of financially devastating. Terrorist attacks upon industrial nations have serious and immediate adverse economic consequences.

Radical Islamic extremists view the economic advantages of America as having been derived in large part because we have stolen from Islamic countries the oil we need to fuel our industrial economies. Islamic extremists may easily conclude that America's final moves away from the gold standard were in response to the steps taken by OPEC during the 1973 oil embargo, even though those steps were begun by President Nixon in 1971. Still, the charge is not only that we have paid too little for the oil, but also that the dollars we have exchanged in the purchase are potentially worth less tomorrow than they are today.

TERRORISTS AND ROGUE STATES

The admonition to follow the money is fundamental to law enforcement investigations of criminals. The same holds true for terrorists. Without money, terrorists are dead in the water. Terrorism itself is not a business, so terrorists have no sales revenue. Terrorists do not run any governments, at least not openly. So terrorists cannot finance themselves by levying taxes. And without money, terrorists can create no organizations, finance no sleeper cells, purchase no airplane tickets to travel internationally, buy no bombs to give to suicide bombers. Without money, terrorists cannot plan or recruit for future attacks. The point is simple but important: without money, terrorists can do nothing.

Where do terrorists get their funding? Terrorist organizations and their supporters engage in various forms of organized crime, including the worldwide drug trade. Radical Islamic terrorists also run fraudulent charities that are really front organizations whose primary purpose is to fund terrorist activities, not to distribute money to the needy.[1]

Yet much of the support terrorists receive depends upon the active cooperation of rogue states. Frank Gaffney and the Center for Security Policy in Washington DC has launched a project called Divest Terror (www.DivestTerror.org) to investigate public and private pension plans, college endowments, individual retirement account managers, 401(k) plans, and other investment vehicles to identify investments in publicly traded companies that operate in terror-supporting states.

> In a united front, we should all be saying "This is my money and it will not go to support terror." DivestTerror.org is a nationwide campaign aimed at some 400 public companies worldwide that are providing revenues, technology and moral cover to governments that sponsor terrorism.[2]

The goal of the campaign is to give terror-supporting governments a choice between losing important investment income or cease to give financial support and refuge to terrorists. The model of the campaign is the boycott and divestiture campaign that forced South Africa to end apartheid in the 1980s.

Radical Islamic terrorist organizations depend upon sympathetic governments to provide the money they need to send suicide bombers to attack the World Trade Center and the Pentagon, to bomb trains in Spain, and to attack subway cars and buses in London. Iran is the leading rogue state supporter of terrorism in the world. Even Saudi Arabia, supposedly one of our major allies in the Middle East, is a culprit. Without direct funding from the Saudi Arabian government, the Wahhabi sect of Islam, one of the most virulently radical, anti-United States, anti-Israel sects of Islam, would have a hard time existing.

The economies of both Saudi Arabia and Iran are heavily dependent upon oil revenue. The thought is frightening: even though we buy no oil from Iran directly, we may ultimately be funding terrorism every time we buy gas. Ironically, radical Islamic terrorists depend upon us to keep filling our gas tanks so their cash flow can continue. So just by driving automobiles in our everyday life we may well be sending money indirectly to the terrorist enemies who have sworn our destruction.

Radical Islamic extremism is at the core of the geopolitics of many Middle Eastern governments. Wahhabism is the sect of Islam at the core of Saudi Arabian society. The Saudi Arabian government has begun to realize that appeasing Wahhabism by funding their radical schools and supporting their clerics may be self-defeating. Still, it is problematic to reject the Islamic sect that is at the core of the Saudi faith as Sunni Muslims. The House of Saud is linked to the House of Wahhab through the marriage of the son of Muhammad ibn Saud with the daughter of Muhammad ibn Abd al Wahhab in 1744. The conservative principles of Wahhabism are virtually impossible to separate today from the identity of the family ruling Saudi Arabia.

Iran represents a somewhat different problem. Even though we do not buy oil directly from Iran, we are a key component of the consumer demand in the worldwide oil market. Our oil requirements expand the market to the economic benefit of the Iranians, whether we buy oil from them or not. Since 1979 the religious clerics ruling Iran have sworn to expand their radical Islamic revolution worldwide. The mullahs continue to fund Hezbollah with $100 million or more each year. And Hezbollah has worked hand-in-hand with the Palestinian terrorist organizations Hamas and Islamic Jihad to train and send suicide bombers into Israel. Refer to pages 240–241 of the *9-11 Commission Report* for documentation regarding how Hezbollah worked with al-Qaeda to bring the 9-11 terrorists into the United States via Iran.[3]

We cannot assume that all Islamic countries have identical interests simply because they are Muslim. There are important nationalistic differences that distinguish the interests of Iran from Saudi Arabia. Moreover, even within Islam there are differences. The Iranians are predominately Shi'ites, whereas at Saudis are Sunnis. The dispute between Shi'ites and Sunnis goes back hundreds of years; ultimately their differences involve determining the legitimate line of authority within the religion stretching back to the death of the Prophet Mohammed himself. National, economic, and religious differences have caused the Islamic nations to fight among themselves, including controversies about even the oil that lies under their various lands.

With oil hitting more than $60 per barrel, Iran and Saudi Arabia are enjoying huge windfall oil profits that will ultimately flow to the benefit of terrorists and terrorist organizations. We will recommend in the conclusion of this book that the United States take measures to expand domestic oil and natural gas exploration and production despite the anticipated objections of environmentalists. Expansion of the world oil supply can be expected to make a substantial impact on reducing oil prices worldwide. Moreover, reducing U.S. oil dependence on foreign oil imports will reduce the extent to which our dollars end up funding terrorists who in turn intend to attack us.

Still, international terrorists understand the importance of oil to the world industrial economy. Despite their dependency on oil revenue to fund their activities, terrorists nonetheless plan to attack the world oil infrastructure, both to boost the price of oil and to harm the industrial West, specifically the United States.

TERRORISTS ATTACK THE OIL INFRASTRUCTURE

The sabotage witnessed in the continued domestic violence following the 2003 war in Iraq show how easily oil pipelines can be attacked. The Institute for the Analysis of Global Security has created an Iraq Pipeline Watch that has identified 248 separate attacks on Iraqi pipelines between June 12, 2003, and July 8, 2005.[4] Terrorists have also attacked oil refineries and port terminals in Iraq. Their goal has been to hurt the Iraqi economy by blocking efforts to restore Iraq's oil industry. One analyst has noted:

> Such attacks also have a corrosive influence on the morale of the Iraqi people and their attitude toward the presence of U.S. forces in their country. Iraqis are growing increasingly vexed by the coalition's slow progress in the reconstruction effort and its inability to guarantee a reliable supply of electricity, which is primarily derived from oil. Worse, the sabotage campaign has created an inhospitable investment climate in Iraq and scared away oil companies that were supposed to develop its oil and gas industry.[5]

Estimates are that pipeline sabotage has cost the Iraqi economy an estimated $10 billion in revenues.[6]

Protecting Iraq's pipelines and restoring the country's oil industry is a top priority in Iraq. In 2003 the Coalition Provisional Authority authorized Operation Task Force Shield and employed some fourteen thousand security guards along the pipelines and at critical oil installations.[7] But even this did not stop attacks. Copycat terrorists have emulated the success of the Iraqi saboteurs by attacking pipelines in Chechnya, India, Sudan, and Turkey. Pipelines stretch thousands of miles, making it difficult for security forces to secure every available opportunity for sabotage.

To the extent that terrorists can attack pipelines or refining facilities in the Middle East, they destabilize both the world oil markets and moderate Arab regimes. Writing for the Cato Institute in 2001, Jerry Taylor and Peter VanDoren quantified the threat:

> In the short run the relationship between supplies and price in oil markets is about 0.1. That is, a 1 percent reduction in supplies induces a 10 percent increase in price. In 1990 after the Iraqi invasion of Kuwait, world oil production decreased from 61 million barrels a day (mbd) to 56.5 mbd, or by about 7.4 percent. Oil prices increased from $18 to al-

most $31, or about 72%. World output is now 68 mbd, with the Mideast accounting for 21 mbd (30.9 percent) and Saudi Arabia accounting for 8 mbd (11.8 percent). So a complete Saudi shutdown would produce at least 120 percent increase in price (from $19 to almost $42) while a Mideast shutdown would produce over a 300 percent increase (from $19 to $76).[8]

The fundamental analysis applies even with today's larger oil numbers. Oil and currency markets immediately jump in times of uncertainty or disruption. A terror attack on oil-production facilities anywhere in the world could drive oil prices up and push the dollar down. Even the anticipation of such an attack could adversely affect markets. The cost of uncertainty and disruptions is the upward repricing of oil, a kind of terror premium on oil. This can also lead to a downward cycle where the ripple effect of higher oil prices depresses the U.S. economy, with further damage being done to the dollar.

TERRORISTS AND THE WORLD OIL MARKETPLACE

Earlier we made the point that government attempts to regulate and control the oil marketplace have largely been counterproductive. We have repeatedly argued that government's most effective role is to ensure the continued operation of a free and open worldwide oil market, where economic forces have the opportunity to best drive forward the critical issues of supply and demand. Terrorists, like governments determined to impose price controls on oil, act to disrupt free markets. In doing so, they clearly understand the economic harm they can inflict.

As noted above, Osama bin Laden fully recognizes the economic impact of terrorism. In a speech on November 1, 2004, bin Laden claimed that al-Qaeda spent $500,000 on the 9-11 attack, but "America, in the incident and its aftermath, lost—according to the lowest estimate—more than $500 billion."[9] In a statement to the Saudi rulers on December 16, 2004, bin Laden called for terrorist attacks on Saudi oil. He again complained that oil was being stolen from the Muslim lands:

You have to realize that our enemy's biggest incentive in controlling our land is to steal our oil. So, do not spare any effort to stop the greatest robbery in history. This [oil and other resources] is the treasures of our current and future generations. They [the West] plot with their allies and puppets in the area to buy our oil at a very low price. All products have gone up in prices several folds except oil itself, which is the basic component of the whole industry. Oil prices do not reflect market reality. Oil was sold for USD 40.00 a barrel, two decades ago, but it went for USD 9.00 a barrel, last decade. A fair price for oil at the present time is a minimum USD 100.00. Oh you Mujahideen, do your best to prevent them stealing it. Focus your operations on it, especially in Iraq and the Gulf. This will choke them.[10]

Terrorists clearly see the opportunity to inflict major economic harm by attacking oil resources. In the terrorists' view, disrupting oil markets has the added dimension of preserving Muslim natural resources from theft by the industrial West. Bin Laden's sense of justice, though, continues to appreciate economic bounds. He sounds as if oil at $100 a barrel would be a fair price. Yet at that price, he would probably begin complaining that we were simply buying the oil with devalued dollars in our continuing determination to rob the Muslim nations of oil resources that were rightfully theirs.

The continued operation of free worldwide oil markets depends upon the ability of governments to defeat terrorism. This will not be an easy battle to win, nor will it be won without extensive cost, time, and determination. Radical Islamic terrorism has already inflicted an economic price on the industrialized West. Had Iraqi oil been flowing freely and at the increased volumes we first projected at the conclusion of the war, we might never have seen oil hit prices ranging between $60–$70 a barrel.

AL-QAEDA ATTACKS SAUDI ARABIA

Saudi Arabia is also vulnerable. On the Persian Gulf, the Saudi terminal of Ras Tanura is the world's largest offshore loading facility, one through which approximately one-tenth of the world's oil supply passes every day. Former CIA Middle East field officer Robert Baer estimates that a terrorist cell hijacking an airplane and crashing into an oil facility such as Ras Tanura could take a large proportion of Saudi oil off the market for as long as six months: "Such an attack would be more economically damaging than a dirty nuclear bomb set off in midtown Manhattan or across from the White House in Lafayette Square, enough to bring the world's oil-addicted economies to their knees, America's along with them."[11] Again, just because Saudi Arabia is a Muslim state does not mean that Saudi oil resources are safe from attacks by terrorists. Because the Saudis are exporting oil to the United States, radical Islamic terrorists see Saudi oil resources as fair game for attack.

Saudi Arabia has a complex relationship with radical Islamic terrorists. As we have noted, the ruling family of Saudi Arabia, the House of Saud, has a long relationship with the House of Wahhab, the root of Wahhabism, an extremist sect of Islam that is at the center of the Saudi Arabian Sunni faith. Worldwide, approximately 90 percent of all Muslims are Sunnis. The Saudis have funded Wahhabi religious schools, known as *madrassas,* in Saudi Arabia and around the world. The *madrassas* have been charged with being a breeding ground for terrorists, given the extreme Islamic fundamentalism that is at the core of education in the *madrassas.* The Saudi ruling family has been under increasing pressure from the United States to open up Saudi society to more democratic practices. To the extent that the Saudis move in this direction, they face intense opposition from conservative Wahhabi believers who are determined to keep Saudi Arabia on a fundamentalist religious path.

In April 2002 Saudi Arabia held a telethon that raised approximately $100 million for the Palestinians. Critics worldwide claimed that the real intent of the telethon was to raise funds for the families of suicide bombers. The Saudi government denied these charges, arguing that the campaign was intended for humanitarian purposes and that the charitable donations would go to providing emergency aid to the two hundred thousand Palestinians whose West Bank homes were being besieged by Israeli forces who were reacting to violence against Israel launched by

Palestinians as part of the Intifada that was under way at the time. The Saudis also argued that the telethon allowed Saudi citizens to vent their anger against the United States and Israel on television rather than in the streets. The event, however, remained controversial. Reportedly a six-year-old boy wearing fake explosives strapped around his waist and carrying a plastic machine gun walked into a donation center during the telethon and made a gift of his plastic toy explosives.[12]

Osama bin Laden was born in Saudi Arabia to a father of Yemeni origins, and much of his anger has been directed against the Saudi ruling family. Prior to the start of the war against Iraq, the United States in 2003 made a decision to pull all U.S. forces out of Saudi Arabia. This was largely in response to intense pressure from bin Laden and Al-Qaeda that U.S. forces on Saudi territory defiled the Muslim holy sites of Mecca and Medina, both situated within Saudi borders. Bin Laden has called for the overthrow of the Saudi ruling family as a necessary step toward establishing a Muslim caliphate that would liberate Jerusalem and unite the Muslim world.

The Saudi government has been torn between a strong alliance with the United States on the one hand and the appeasement of radical Islamic extremism on the other. Saudi Arabia remains the world's largest exporter of oil and is consistently one of the top three importing countries to the United States. Some six million expatriates work in Saudi Arabia, primarily to support the oil industry. Many of these expatriates are Americans who are increasingly targets of terrorism.

On May 12, 2003, Al-Qaeda launched a major terrorist attack in Riyadh, simultaneously detonating three car bombs within three Western housing compounds. Nine U.S. citizens were killed, and fourteen more Americans were among the hundreds who were wounded. In response, Saudi officials arrested Al-Qaeda suspects. By November 2003 Saudi foreign affairs adviser Adel al-Jubeir announced that more than six hundred Al-Qaeda suspects had been arrested and that terrorist cells had been destroyed throughout Saudi Arabia. Then on November 8, 2003, a truck bomb in an Arab residential compound in Riyadh killed seventeen people, including five children, in an attack aimed at Arabian managerial classes working alongside American nationals in Saudi Arabia. On June 18, 2004, Al-Qaeda terrorists beheaded American hostage Paul Johnson, a forty-nine-year-old specialist on Apache attack helicopters, who worked for Lockheed Martin in Saudi Arabia. An intense search failed to find the terrorists before Johnson's decapitated body was found. Saudi security forces stormed a central Riyadh neighborhood, claiming they had killed the Al-Qaeda leader who had organized Johnson's kidnapping and beheading. Photographs of Johnson's severed head and body appeared on Islamic Web sites to show that he had received just punishment for having trained Saudi security forces on how to use Apache helicopters in antiterrorist efforts.[13]

On December 6, 2004, Al-Qaeda terrorists mounted an assault on the U.S. consulate in Riyadh. Five consular employees, four local staff members, and a contract guard were killed; four other local staff members were wounded. This was the first time a hard target had been attacked, not soft targets such as residence compounds. The attack made clear that Saudi efforts to eradicate or control Al-Qaeda cells had failed. The attack also underscored the continuing threat faced by Western expatriates working in the Saudi oil industry. The significance of this attack was not missed in Israel. Here is how the Jerusalem Center for Public Affairs summed up the incident:

> Moreover, when it turned out that nearly all the victims of the consulate attack were local or foreign Muslims, many Saudis, who were at first pleased by the U.S. humiliation, strongly condemned al-Qaeda for disrupting the kingdom's stability. Even the families of the four terrorists killed in the consulate's courtyard (the fifth was wounded and arrested) were denounced by their kin who, despite the custom, did not hold a wake for them.
>
> However, the U.S. embassy spokesman in Riyadh told the news media that al-Qaeda's attacks on Western experts in Saudi Arabia, as well as attacks on Saudi and American installations, were far from over, and that attempts to sabotage the Persian Gulf oil industry should not be ruled out, despite President Bush's assurance on December 7, 2004,

about the Saudi regime's stability and ability to participate in the war against international terrorism.[14]

On December 6, 2004, the day of the attack, the U.S. Embassy in Riyadh issued a travel warning advising U.S. citizens in Saudi Arabia to "exercise utmost security precautions" given the heightened threat of terrorist attacks.[15]

Some ten days after the attack on the U.S. consulate in Riyadh, a new bin Laden tape surfaced on Arabic Web sites. He claimed the attack demonstrated the instability in Saudi Arabia as a direct result of the corrupt nature of the Saudi regime: "While the struggle in Saudi Arabia appears to be internal, it is part of the struggle between believers and nonbelievers" of Islam. Bin Laden called those who died in the attack "martyrs." He called the Saudi rulers "puppets of a crusader-Zionist alliance led by America," and he called for their overthrow, claiming the Saudi royal family was stealing the wealth of the nation while millions of Saudis were "suffering poverty." The timing of the tape made clear that bin Laden had not lost his focus on causing instability in Saudi Arabia with the ultimate goal of overthrowing the current regime.[16]

The radical Islamic extremists target any Muslims they believe are working with the United States or Israel. The terrorists view themselves as involved in a religious war. Any person or state supporting the United States or Israel is a target, whether or not the target is Muslim. Bin Laden's many taped messages make clear that he sees himself involved in an international war. Destabilizing Saudi Arabia and disrupting the oil flow from the Middle East remain top priorities for Al-Qaeda.

OSAMA BIN LADEN ON ECONOMICS

Reading through Osama bin Laden's speeches can be tedious. The rhetoric is very stylized, with much "Allah be praised" language interspersing his attacks against what he sees as the moral corruption of America and our "crusade" to steal from Islam the holy lands of the Middle East. Still, the exercise is important, especially if we ferret out his economic thinking. Bin Laden watches America very closely; often it seems as if he is watching our television or reading our news media. His commentary is especially pointed when it comes to his appreciation that he is fighting an economic war against the United States. Let's consider a few of his pronouncements.

On October 19, 2003, bin Laden taped a message for the people of Iraq. In this statement, he referred again to the economic harm inflicted upon the United States by the 9-11 attack. From there, bin Laden goes immediately to the huge deficits America has been running, tying the size of the deficits to our need to support a huge war effort in the Middle East. In speaking about America, bin Laden says:

> Never be afraid of their multitudes, for their hearts are empty while their strength has begun to weaken—militarily and economically. This was particularly true after the blessed day of New York, by the grace of Allah, when their losses reached more than one trillion dollars, following the attack and its aftermath.
>
> Moreover, they have had a budget deficit for the third consecutive year. This year, the deficit reached a record peak of more than US $4.5 billion. Praise be to Allah.
>
> Never be scared of their multitudes, for their hearts are empty while their strength has begun to weaken—militarily and economically.[17]

Since this speech, our deficits have only increased by more than one hundred times what bin Laden estimated.

In October 2004 bin Laden sent another videotape to Aljazeera. In this video, he promised to bankrupt America, drawing the comparison to how the Soviet Union was economically destroyed by its war in Afghanistan. Bin Laden brags about how easy it is for him to bait the Bush administration into losing more money fighting Al-Qaeda:

> All that we have mentioned has made it easy for us to provoke and bait this administration. All that we have to do is send two Mujahideen to the furthest point East to raise a piece of cloth on which is written al-Qaida,

in order to make the generals race there to cause America to suffer human, economic, and political loses without their achieving for it anything of note other than some benefits for their private companies.

This is in addition to our having experience in using guerrilla warfare and the war of attrition to fight tyrannical superpowers, as we, alongside the Mujahideen, bled Russia for ten years, until it went bankrupt and was forced to withdraw in defeat. All Praise is due to Allah.

So we are continuing this policy in bleeding America to the point of bankruptcy. Allah willing, and nothing is too great for Allah.[18]

Bin Laden understands the importance of oil to the U.S. economy. One of his constant themes is that we steal the oil of the Middle East to fuel our corrupt lifestyles. Bin Laden was patient in fighting against the Soviet Union; we can expect he will be equally patient with us. Bin Laden is willing to bet that the United States will not be able to afford politically or economically a protracted global war against radical Islamic terrorism. He knows the true expense involved in occupying both Afghanistan and Iraq may be more than the American public is willing to bear for long. Bin Laden has made clear that he believes we have stolen oil from the Islamic Middle East. He believes in retribution; for bin Laden, terrorism against the United States is economic payback. Bin Laden's calculation is that the United States will run out of patience and money just as the Soviet Union did. He knows that the terrorism exacts an economic price, especially when the world's number-one economic power has become so dependent upon foreign oil, much of which is shipped from the Middle East.

THE THREAT OF ECOTERRORISM

Terrorism from radical Islamic terrorists is not the only form of terrorism that represents a threat to oil. Radical environmentalist groups on the political Left are also capable of targeting oil interests to pursue their political goals. "Ecoterrorists" have pursued an extreme form of politics designed to protect what they consider a pristine natural environment.

Their interests can extend to the protection of animals in their natural settings. To the extent that oil interests are preserved to be inherent "enemies of the environment," ecoterrorists might well target oil facilities to make their political point. Attacks of this nature are even more likely if the United States pursues the type of policies we recommend here, to expand domestic oil exploration and open new refineries.

The FBI defines ecoterrorism "as the use or threatened use of violence of a criminal nature against innocent victims or property by an environmentally-oriented, subnational group for environmental-political reasons, or aimed at an audience beyond the target, often of a symbolic nature." In particular, the FBI has characterized the Animal Liberation Front (ALF) and the Earth Liberation Front (ELF) as serious criminal threats. The FBI estimates that ALF and ELF have committed at least six hundred criminal acts in the United States since 1996, with resulting damages estimated at more than $43 million.[19]

Other groups, such as the radical Earth First! innovated with "tree spiking"—the practice of inserting metal or ceramic spikes in trees to damage chainsaws or the loggers who were attempting to cut down trees. ELF has pioneered with "monkey wrenching"—acts of sabotage and property damage against industries that are viewed as causing environmental damage. ELF has also attacked SUVs at car dealerships, igniting jugs of gasoline under vehicles and writing slogans such as "Fat Lazy Americans" on others.

Pipelines, refineries, even gasoline stations are all potential targets in the United States either by radical Islamic terrorists or ecoterrorists. Since 9-11, key oil facilities are better protected, though the lessons of terrorism are that few targets are truly well protected until an attack prompts the full awareness of their vulnerability.

Ecoterrorists fully understand their compatibility with radical Islamic terrorists. Consider this statement by Mike Roselle, an Earth First! radical and self-proclaimed revolutionary, describing the dimensions of his radical environmentalism: "This is Jihad, pal. There are no innocent bystanders, because in these desperate hours, bystanders are not innocent. We'll broaden our theater of conflict."[20]

Hopefully, we will never see ecoterrorists reach the level of sophistication where they could successfully attack major oil facilities in the United States. But their rhetoric and determination to use extreme measures could be tested should oil companies ever receive authorization to begin serious offshore oil exploration or should oil exploration and production activities proceed out of the few small areas in Alaska where oil companies have been permitted to go.

We should have no doubt, however, that responsible environmental groups are well organized and well funded. Choosing to do combat via lawyers, environmentalists continue to take strong, well-calculated steps to block oil companies at every step. We need more refineries. Should we build them? Not until we factor in the costs of fighting the environmentalists who want the refinery situated someplace else. The same logic impacts oil companies who want to expand their U.S. domestic oil exploration and production efforts.

The environmental lobbies can be counted on to work hard to make sure that the U.S. oil marketplace develops no more than it is already developed today. Environmentalists will undoubtedly fight hard to hold on to their myths—that oil is fossil fuel, that we have already hit peak production, that all the oil in the United States has already been found, and that global warming presents such a threat of climate change that we shouldn't be burning hydrocarbon fuels anyway.

If America is to take steps to move from dependency on foreign oil, environmentalists offer us no solutions except to stop driving our cars, stop using carbon-based fuels, and to cut back on our lifestyles—or to start using alternative fuels, none of which have yet proved to be cost-effective substitutes for oil, natural gas, coal, or gasoline.

We move to conclude this book fully aware that the arguments we have presented here are likely to be hotly contested. Environmentalists and conservationists cannot afford to allow Americans to believe that oil might actually be a natural product of the earth, that oil and natural gas are readily available. Many Americans today are about to accept uncritically the conclusion that the energy stranglehold we are facing is inevitable, a concession the radical environmentalists hope our society will make. Because of this, we feel the arguments we have expressed in this book are essential to establishing a counterview.

Environmentalists and conservationists who permit no debate on their predetermined conclusions are acting every bit as political terrorists—radicals whose ideology has taken such hold of their minds that no room is left for scientific evidence or rational debate to the contrary. Make no mistake about it—environmentalists and conservationists present a clear and present threat to free and open oil markets. This is ultimately a threat to the economy as we know it in America today and to the lifestyle that is enjoyed in the industrial nations around the world. We do not believe that economic advancement is somehow politically or morally wrong. Nor do we believe that industrial society must abuse or exhaust the resources of the earth. Our view is that together we can advance, both materially and spiritually, within industrial society, seeking to embrace science and technology for the betterment of the human species and the earth worldwide.

Fortunately the First Amendment remains in place and conservative books are not yet banned from print. What we urge here is open minds, especially as we proceed to make recommendations that we know environmentalists and conservationists are likely to ridicule, particularly if they feel at a loss to make effective logical refutation.

CONCLUSION

TOWARD U.S. OIL INDEPENDENCE: AN ACTION PLAN

Our dependence on foreign oil is like a foreign tax on the American Dream—and that tax is growing every year.
George W. Bush, June 15, 2005

I
F WE BEGIN WITH the assumption that markets anticipate future developments, we have to ask a fundamental question: Why don't industries around the world act as if we are running out of oil? Automobile manufacturers make plans to introduce new models of internal-combustion gasoline-fueled cars. Hybrid automobiles are being developed, but they are yet a novelty, and the verdict is not in on their real costs of operation and maintenance. We continue to put millions into the maintenance of our local roads and interstate highways. Quite simply, the alarmist cries of environmentalists and conservationists have not translated into panicked reactions within the automobile industry, one of the key mainstays of the U.S. economy.

We are told that America is addicted to oil and natural gas. Yet if we carry forward the analogy of drug addiction, we can again ask the same question. Any drug addict who has reason to believe his drug supply is coming to an end has only one driving purpose that begins to dominate his life, namely, How do I get more drugs? The American consumer has heard all the rhetoric that we are running out of oil, yet we continue to calmly drive to the gas station and pay increasing prices to fill our gas tanks. Yes, we grumble about the price. Still, Americans are not hoarding gasoline, nor are they demanding from Congress answers regarding where the next fill-up is going to be found.

If we assume that markets and consumers are good barometers of future economic developments, we could reasonably conclude that the arguments of the environmentalists and conservationists have been heard but not fully believed. The rebuttal from the political Left would be that Americans are too lazy or too comfortable to care. Moreover, the political Left all too often lectures us from their ocean-front homes in Malibu while they drive around in their BMWs to their private jets, talking all the while on their cell phones—all of which ultimately depends on hydrocarbon fuels in one way or another. If Americans truly felt that a shortage of oil was on the verge of adversely affecting our economy or our lifestyles, the outpouring of concern would be immediate and loud.

In this final chapter, we are going to call for seven steps that we believe will allow us to focus attention on the arguments we have raised in this book. We see our seven steps as an action agenda that will allow the alternative theories expressed here to be taken seriously. First, however, we are going to ask a seldom-asked question—Why is the oil industry today the industry Americans love to hate?

WHY DOES THE OIL INDUSTRY FACE SUCH HOSTILITY TODAY?

In the early days of the oil business in the United States, less than one hundred years ago, wildcat explorers were seen as American heroes. We admired their willingness to risk everything as they drove into fields and drilled for black gold. If the wildcatters were lucky, they got rich. If not, they lost everything. We admired their daring and benefited from the oil they found.

Even the popular culture at the mid-twentieth century continued to admire oil people. We saw how *The Beverly Hillbillies* came to California and enjoyed a Hollywood lifestyle because black gold came bubbling up from their country backwater fields. We admired J. R. in *Dallas* because of his bold thinking and oilman ways. Yet today we have come full circle.

Imagine if an oil executive on vacation went hunting in Alaska. What if he shot at a wild animal and missed it? If the errant bullet struck the ground and up bubbled oil, there probably would be no end to the trouble. His hunting license would be investigated. The Animal Liberation Front (ALF) and People for the Ethical Treatment of Animals (PETA) would rush to the scene to defend the animals. Lawyers representing environmentalists would file briefs in court blocking any serious oil exploration, arguing that the environment would be destroyed if any oil finds were to be developed commercially. The network media would go into a feeding frenzy, blaming the oil companies for their irresponsibility in hiring executives who supposedly hunted wild animals while slyly looking for oil. Needless to say, the oil executive's career would be destroyed.

We may not believe the alarmist cries of the political Left that we are running out of oil and that any series of storms and other natural phenomena are because our burning of hydrocarbon fuels has dangerously warmed up the earth. Still, environmentalists and conservationists have managed to reframe our view of the oil industry. We now think of carbon as dirty, not remembering that plants view carbon dioxide as the life-giving element they need to breathe. We think of oil as spills that contaminate beaches, not the fuel that keeps us going.

In almost every aspect of life, Americans depend upon carbon-based fuels. We can drive on our highways from one end of the country to another or simply get on an airplane and be anywhere we choose to go within a few hours, regardless of distance. Our homes and schools are heated in the winter and air-conditioned in the summer. Trucks drive groceries to the stores where we casually shop for food. The list goes on endlessly. Almost every aspect of modern life depends in one way or another upon our burning hydrocarbon fuel. Yet oil company executives are reluctant to proclaim their professions at public meetings for fear they might be attacked as spoilers of the earth.

Subconsciously, we have bought into the propaganda. Yet today our beaches are cleaner than ever, our air is more breathable, and our rivers run with purer water. Even in Cleveland, Ohio, the heart of the U.S. Rust Belt, fish again live in Lake Erie, the beaches along the waterfront are available for swimming, and the Cuyahoga River no longer catches fire from pollutants.

We have advanced to the point where we burn more hydrocarbon fuel than ever while our environment continues to make substantial gains in health and vitality. American industry, including the oil business, has embraced modern technology, including incorporating reasonable environmental protections that have become part of today's responsible business operations. For these achievements, the oil business receives no acknowledgment. Great progress has been made in the last fifty years. Still, radical environmentalists and conservationists sound like they will not be satisfied until we quit using hydrocarbon fuels altogether.

We are conservatives politically, and we believe that America should advance to maintain a strong position in the world. We continue to see American economic, religious, and political freedoms as standards that continue to benefit us at home and profit countless others around the world. We are proud to proclaim our confidence in America, and we share President Bush's enthusiasm that economic, religious, and political freedoms live within the heart of every human being, not just Americans.

Radical environmentalists and conservationists have become opponents of oil. Their arguments end up placing us in a stranglehold. Consider how they have sought to position oil in our thinking: oil is fossil fuel, we are running out of oil, all the oil in the United States has been found, we are at peak production, half of all the oil the United States ever possessed has already been burned, we are becoming dependent upon foreign oil. Next they move to make sure we see the use of hydrocarbons as noxious: we are throwing too much carbon dioxide into the air, this creates a greenhouse effect, the earth is warming up, our climate is changing, the ice caps are melting, the seas are rising, we are suffering increasingly violent storms as worldwide temperatures get hotter and hotter.

Environmentalists want us to harm no animals, move no trees. The "balance" they want with nature is one in which human beings play a minimalist role—maybe there are even too many people. After all, the earth would be better of with fewer of us. We should use wind power, solar power, hydrogen power—none of which has proved to be as powerful or as cheap as hydrocarbon fuel. But, of course, we shouldn't use nuclear power, because spent nuclear fuel harms the environment. There really are no alternatives but to reduce our lifestyle. Should we go back to horses for transportation? Maybe, unless we are inherently cruel to horses by placing saddles on them and riding them.

We have countered this thinking throughout this book. Our approach is positive. We believe we can have a strong oil industry and still benefit the environment.

We believe we have paid our foreign partners fairly for the oil we have bought. The billions of dollars we have sent overseas to buy oil have provided ample resources for those countries to advance for the betterment of all their citizens. Since World War II we have been involved as peacekeepers to resolve countless wars and political crises in the Middle East, including supporting the peace process over the last two decades in the effort to resolve conflicts between the Palestinians and the Israelis. We are on record for decades as encouraging Middle Eastern countries to introduce more democratic political and economic processes that would share their oil wealth broadly within their societies. We see no credible evidence that America intends to establish permanent armies in the Middle East so we can confiscate oil.

We believe the earth contains abundant oil, enough to meet all our needs as the world industrializes and moves to improve lifestyles around the globe. We do not see the oil business as exploitation, colonialism, or imperialism. We believe that human beings can enjoy material possessions and still be religiously strong.

THE SEVEN STEPS

Our agenda for moving forward centers on the following seven action steps. If these steps are followed, we believe we can restore America to energy independence while also strengthening the international oil markets for the benefit of the developed and emerging countries around the globe. We believe the recommendations we make here will advance the cause of energy for the benefit of all. We invite debate with our critics.

1. PROMOTE SCIENTIFIC RESEARCH TO INVESTIGATE ALTERNATIVE THEORIES.

The National Science Foundation (NSF) should fund an aggressive program of scientific research to investigate the deep, abiotic theory of the origin of petroleum. NSF should explore Thomas Gold's hypotheses that a deep, hot biosphere exists within the mantle of the earth, that oil is a natural product of the earth, one that seeps up toward the surface of the earth along natural fault lines at very deep levels. We invite scientific research to determine if oil truly is fossil fuel, as has become conventional wisdom, or if the alternative abiotic theory can be proven with sufficient scientific rigor as to merit widespread public acceptance.

We would invite similar NSF research designed to explore the fundamental premises of the greenhouse effect, global warming, and climate change. Research grants should be awarded fairly, with grants going equally to opponents of the conventional views advanced by environmentalists and conservationists, not just those scientists on the political Left. Unfortunately, science itself has become politicized within our universities today, largely due to grants and subsidies that have made their science departments dependent on a growing federal government; so the NSF will have to take specific steps to invite participation from scientists who are political conservatives.

Science should be open-minded and nonpartisan, but today liberal thinking dominates our universities. To get a balance of views, specific steps will have to be taken to recruit conservative scientists to the task. Hopefully, the NSF can encourage an environment in which the studies proceed as objectively as possible and the results are presented to the American people as fairly as possible.

2. EXPEDITE LEASES OFFSHORE AND IN ALASKA TO ENCOURAGE OIL EXPLORATION.

The federal government should make a concerted effort to grant new oil exploration leases in Alaska and offshore on both coasts and the Gulf of Mexico. Fast-track criteria should be established to review oil company applications where the applicant can demonstrate a prior history of safe and environmentally sound operations offshore or in Alaska. New applicants should be provided clear and simple criteria, possibly in the form of a checklist that will facilitate the approval process.

We should instruct the Department of Energy to cut through administrative barriers. We should be prepared to introduce legislation to reduce the impact of harassment lawsuits launched to block any of these new leases from being awarded.

Special consideration should be given to advance the lease applications of oil companies that propose to explore deep within the earth, through the process of drilling ultradeep wells, according to the hypothesis of the deep, abiotic theory of petroleum's origin. These exploration efforts will provide additional information as we explore the scientific evidence to support or refute the abiotic theory.

Our goal should be to identify as quickly as possible the quantity of oil that lies offshore and throughout Alaska. We wonder if environmentalists and conservationists have resisted granting leases because they do not want the American public to realize that America still has available huge, possibly unlimited reserves of oil yet to be discovered. Let's explore for additional oil in a responsible fashion, realizing that much oil offshore and in Alaska remains yet to be found.

3. PROVIDE TAX CREDITS FOR DEEP-DRILLING OIL EXPLORATION.

As the second point above expresses, deep and ultradeep well drilling efforts should be encouraged. Tax credits can be established to offset the additional costs of developing environmentally safe deep-drilling techniques and machinery. We should encourage oil companies to return to previously developed sites to see if any additional oil reserves not previously discovered lie at deeper levels below. Very possibly wells that have been considered exhausted might be revitalized if only drilling efforts had continued below the initially discovered oil reservoirs. As has been the case in America, a well thought-out formula of economic rewards to compensate risk has been proven to stimulate important corporate initiatives to explore new dimensions even in well-established industries.

These tax credits should be provided for deep and ultradeep drilling oil exploration wherever the technology is applied within the continental United States, offshore, or in Alaska. Should the deep-drilling efforts prove successful, we might return the United States to oil independence.

The example of Russia is illustrative here. Once considered oil-poor, the deep-drilling techniques applied by the Russian scientists and oil companies have positioned Russia as one of the leading oil suppliers in the world. Today few have any doubt that Russia is oil self-sufficient. The United States should take pains to see if the science and technology of deep-drilling that the Russians have applied since the end of World War II might also produce similar results in the United States.

4. CREATE AN OIL RESEARCH INSTITUTE TO SERVE AS A CLEARINGHOUSE OF OIL INDUSTRY INFORMATION.

We propose the establishment of an oil research institute to serve as a public clearinghouse of oil-industry information. We should encourage information to be placed in the database by oil companies who want the public to understand modern oil industry exploration and production technologies that are environmentally friendly. The database should include comprehensive information on oil reserves, exploration, and production worldwide, building upon the extensive information already made available by the Energy Information Administration of the U.S. Department of Energy.

Oil industry funding for the oil research institute should be encouraged. The board of directors should be drawn broadly, including scientists and independent experts in addition to oil company executives.

The institute can also commission additional research studies designed to supplement the National Science Foundation grants proposed in our first point. The oil research institute data should be readily available on the Internet. An institute headquarters could serve as a site for scheduling frequent industry and scientific conferences open to the public.

The idea is not to launch a public-relations effort to promote the oil industry but to create an open and unbiased repository for comprehensive oil industry information. We should not be afraid to show the oil industry in a positive light when unbiased information supports positive conclusions. Americans should be reminded that the oil industry has been the bedrock of our strong and lasting economy.

Today the oil industry has no forum outside commercial advertising to tell its story to the public. The oil research institute will be that forum, balanced by criticism and concerns that can be presented fairly and examined critically, with judgments resulting as much as possible from scientific, objective evidence, not politically motivated predetermined conclusions.

5. DEVELOP A PUBLIC BROADCASTING TELEVISION SERIES DEVOTED TO THE OIL INDUSTRY.

We propose the development of a PBS television series devoted to educating the public about the oil industry. Few of us have actually seen the advanced technologies that are being applied in modern oil exploration and production. All of us remember the few environmental disasters attributable to the oil industry over the last fifty years. We are generally unaware, however, of the advanced technologies that are currently being applied in environmentally aware offshore oil drilling or in Alaska.

Again, the series should not be designed as an oil industry public-relations effort. Instead, we should invite oil industry experts and executives to tell the positive side of the story, the side the public rarely hears. The series should be designed to explore the scientific theories and countertheories we have advanced here. Is oil a fossil fuel? What is the evidence that hydrocarbon fuels have caused global warming? Are we in an interglacial period, one that is more responsible for our current world temperatures than is human activity? The public has been hammered with political opinions, but the scientific questions are rarely explained, nor are the relevant data and arguments examined in a way that is comprehensible to a person who is not an expert or a scientist.

Public education should be a top goal in a discussion as vital to America as the future of the oil industry. A PBS series that goes to oil exploration sites, that sees into oil production, that visits gasoline refineries, should be interesting to a public that wants facts, not simply opinions. All sides can be presented in this show. Environmentalists and conservationists should have time to explain their viewpoints as long as their critics are also heard fairly. Television is an important and powerful visual media that needs to supplement information that is available in printed publications or on the Internet.

6. REESTABLISH A GOLD-BACKED INTERNATIONAL-TRADE DOLLAR.

The U.S. government should reestablish a gold-backed dollar that is designed to be used only in the settlement of international trade transactions. This international-trade dollar would be designed as a separate currency. We would be returning to the advice of our Founding Fathers who believed that gold-backing was critical to any U.S. currency that would have enduring strength.

The gold-backed international-trade dollar would be an electronic media, not necessarily a printed currency. Still, the international-trade dollar would have a fixed value expressed in a specified quantity of gold, to be held at Fort Knox, or at participating international banks in various cities around the world.

International settlements could be settled by changing the beneficial ownership of U.S. gold held in the participating international banks to reflect payments to countries whose exports to the United States makes their international balance of payments favorable to them. We would be taking serious steps to keep our currency as the dominant currency in which international trades are settled worldwide. The goal would be to move toward a more reliable standard so that our international trading partners could once again hold U.S. currency reserves in a fixed-standard international-trade dollar.

We believe that establishing a gold-backed international-trade dollar is an important step to preserving stability and value in the world's international trade market for all commodities bought and sold worldwide, including oil.

7. ESTABLISH TAX INCENTIVES FOR OPENING NEW REFINERIES IN THE UNITED STATES.

We need additional refineries in order to remove an important bottleneck with the U.S. oil industry. Right now, even if we found huge additional oil reserves that are readily available, we would be limited in getting the additional oil to market simply because our refineries are already running at or near full capacity.

Tax incentives should be established to encourage the construction of new refineries in the United States. Again, we should establish an expedited approval policy for those oil companies that have a proven track record in operating environmentally safe refineries. As we suggested before, a checklist should be developed for new business entrants to demonstrate their capability to perform important requirements specified for oil refinery operation.

The goal would be to get enough new refineries built so that adequate supplies of various grades of oil products, ranging from gasoline to heating oil, can reach the market as demand increases. Once again, tax incentives may be important in providing sufficient financial rewards to motivate oil companies to make the substantial investments required and to take the economic risks involved in developing new refinery capacity.

Similar tax incentives should be established for oil companies that seek to expand existing refineries since the goal is to increase the overall refining capacity, not just to build new facilities.

CONCLUSION

The black gold stranglehold we are facing is largely one of our own making. We do not expect oil company executives to embrace immediately the concept that oil is not fossil fuel. Many of the ideas presented in this book are certain to jolt minds that have accepted uncritically, almost as articles of faith, the understanding that we are running out of oil or that our burning of hydrocarbons is bringing on climate changes with disastrous effects.

We strongly believe that we have within our means the ability to increase our supply of readily available oil. If we allow the oil industry to develop creatively, we should be able to meet our growing demand for hydrocarbon fuels well into the foreseeable future. We have been able to institute measures that allow us to burn hydrocarbons today more efficiently, with less environmental damage, than was the case only a few decades earlier. The economies of America and the world are far stronger and more resilient than critics allow. So, too, is the world more abundant in resources than we generally think.

Some one hundred years ago our major forms of transportation were horses and railroads. Some one hundred years into the future will we still be driving internal-combustion gasoline-fueled engines? Possibly. Yet the history of human innovation strongly suggests that new, economically efficient alternative technologies will develop. Tomorrow we may understand the physics of nuclear batteries, and we may all be driving nuclear cars. We are encouraged by the trends we have discussed to see increased usage of natural gas and a return to explore the potential of nuclear power. As we have discussed, if we can increase our use of natural gas and nuclear energy to power electricity to our homes, offices, and cities, then we can increasingly reserve the use of oil to provide gasoline for transportation. This shift in the mix of energies we use can assist us as we move once again toward energy independence.

Right now, even with oil prices increasing, petroleum fuels are still reasonably affordable alternatives. We challenge readers to reexamine many preconceived ideas. What if oil has nothing to do with decaying ancient forests or dead dinosaurs? What if the probabilities are actually more in favor of a new ice age beginning, and it is unlikely that the ice caps will melt because we are causing global warming? What if we truly have all the oil we will ever need if we just look deep enough within the earth?

We continue to observe that the world has never had as large a quantity of proven oil reserves as we have today. Even the most radical environmental skeptic is still able to fly comfortably across country to give a speech attacking the oil industry, having published the speech in advance on the Internet, while counting on being driven in a taxicab to a heated and air-conditioned hotel, where the television will show dozens if not hundreds of channels, while planning to call home to the family by cell phone to say good night. How much of this would be possible without burning hydrocarbon fuels or using petroleum products?

ACKNOWLEDGMENTS

NOTES

INDEX

ACKNOWLEDGMENTS

We would like to acknowledge Dr. Thomas Gold for his courage and vision to look beyond conventional wisdom for an answer so critical to the future of our nation. Scientists like Thomas Gold challenge each of us to not accept at face value anything that has not been thoroughly examined and proven.

At *WorldNetDaily.com,* Joseph Farah continues to have the courage and conviction to bring forth reporting and news that tackle the controversial issues of our day. Ron Pitkin, the president of Cumberland House Publishing, and Stacie Bauerle, the assistant publisher at Cumberland House, believed in this book and encouraged us from the beginning. We are grateful both for their moral support and for their guidance as we completed the manuscript. Ed Curtis once again helped us complete the manuscript with thoughtful and intelligent editing.

Moving through the twenty-first century, we will need scientists, economists, and politicians who are willing to think creatively as together the nation works to meet our ever more difficult challenges. We hope this book will encourage all who read it to add their voices to the debate we have tried to stimulate within these pages.

NOTES

CHAPTER 1: OIL, A FOSSIL FUEL?

1. The United States Strategic Bombing Survey. The European War report was the first completed, published by the Government Printing Office on September 30, 1945. The original report can be read on the Internet at http://www.anesi.com/ussbs02.htm#page1.
2. Ibid., 6.
3. Ibid., 16.
4. "Ukraine: Country Analysis Brief," Energy Information Administration, U.S. Department of Energy. This analysis was updated in January 2005. See http://www.eia.doe.gov/emeu/cabs/ukraine.html.
5. "The Drilling and Development of the Oil and Gas Fields in the Dnieper-Donetsk Basin," a research report coauthored by V. A. Krayushkin, T. I. Tchebanenko, V. P. Klochko, and Ye. S. Dvoryanin of the Ukrainian Institute of Geological Sciences at Kiev in the Ukraine, together with J. F. Kenny, who is listed as affiliated with the Russian Academy of Sciences, Joint Institute of the Physics of the Earth in Moscow and also with Gas Resources Corporation in Houston, Texas. See http://www.gasresources.net/DDBflds2.htm.

CHAPTER 2: THOMAS GOLD AND THE DEEP HOT BIOSPHERE

1. J. F. Kenney, "Considerations About Recent Predictions of Impending Shortages of Petroleum Evaluated from the Perspective of Modern Petroleum Science," Energy World (1996): 16–18. See http://www.gasresources.net/. This site reprints a number of articles that relate to the Russian-Ukrainian theory of deep, abiotic petroleum origins.
2. Thomas Gold, The Deep Hot Biosphere: The Myth of Fossil Fuels (New York: Copernicus Books, 1998).
3. See Cornell news release, "Thomas Gold, Astronomer and Brilliant Scientific Gadfly, Dies at 84," June 22, 2004, http://www.news.cornell.edu/releases/June04/Thomas_Gold_obit.hrs.html. See also, "Thomas Gold: 1920–2004," June 23, 2004, http://www.physicsweb.org/articles/news/8/6/13/1.
4. Gold, Deep Hot Biosphere, 44.
5. Ibid.

6. See, for instance, the article "Comet" published online by the National Aeronautics and Space Administration at http://www.nasa.gov/worldbook/comet _worldbook.html.
7. Gold, *Deep Hot Biosphere*, 46.
8. Ibid., 39.
9. Ibid., 19.
10. Ibid., 107.
11. Ibid., 111.
12. Ibid., 112.
13. Ibid., 209.
14. "Encyclopedia: Friedrich Wohler," http://www.nationmaster.com /encyclopedia/Friedrich-Wohler.
15. "Petroleum Under Pressure," *PhysicsWeb.org*, September 14, 2004, http://www.physicsweb.org/articles/news/8/9/9/1. The final results of the research have been published in Henry P. Scott et al., "Generation of Methane in the Earth's Mantle: *In Situ* High Pressure-Temperature Measures of Carbonate Reduction," *Proceedings of the National Academy of Sciences*, 101, no. 39 (September 28, 2004), http://www.pnas.org/cgi/content/abstract/101/39/14023 ?maxtoshow=&HITS=10&hits=10&RESULTFORMAT=&fulltext=her-schbach&searchid=1120925532834_2225&stored_search=&FIRSTIN-DEX=0&journalcode=pnas.
16. Erin O'Donnell, "Hydrocarbon Heresy: Rocks into Gas," *Harvard Magazine* (March-April 2005), http://www.harvardmagazine.com/on-line/030573.html.
17. Quoted in Lawrence Livermore National Laboratory, "Methane in Deep Earth: A Possible New Source of Energy," September 13, 2004, http://www .energybulletin.net/2093.html.
18. Gold, *Deep Hot Biosphere*, 85.
19. Quoted in Bjorn Carey, "Ice Shelf Collapse Reveals New Undersea World," July 18, 2005, http://www.livescience.com/animalworld/050718_antarctic _life.html. This description is drawn from this source.
20. Thomas S. Kuhn, *The Structure of Scientific Revolutions*, 3rd ed. (Chicago: University of Chicago Press, 1962).
21. Ibid., 92.

CHAPTER 3: HUBBERT'S PEAK AND THE RUNNING-OUT-OF-OIL SCARE

1. Kenneth S. Deffeyes, *Hubbert's Peak: The Impending World Oil Shortage* (Princeton, NJ: Princeton University Press, 2001). See the chart on page 3

for evidence that Hubbert's peak prediction in the early 1970s was wrong. Yet Deffeyes was not deterred from "fixing" the failed theory. He "corrects" Hubbert's original 1956 graph, showing actual U.S. oil production for 1956 through 2000 at higher levels than Hubbert originally predicted.

2. Ibid., 135.

3. Ibid., 2–3.

4. Donella Meadows, Jorgen Randers, and Dennis Meadows, *Limits to Growth: The 30-Year Update* (White River Junction, VT: Chelsea Green, 2004), 87.

5. John Houghton, *Global Warming: The Complete Briefing*, 3rd ed. (Cambridge, England: Cambridge University Press, 2004), 199.

6. Colin J. Campbell, "The Assessment and Importance of Oil Depletion," in *The Final Energy Solution,* ed. Andrew McKillop and Sheila Newman (London, England: Pluto Press, 2005), 29–55, 54.

7. Ibid., 55.

8. Andrew McKillop and Sheila Newman, "Depleting Energy and Bioresources: The Fossil-Fuel Key," in Houghton, *Global Warming,* 5.

9. Ibid., 6–7.

10. James R. Newman, "Commentary on Thomas Robert Malthus," in *The World of Mathematics,* ed. James R. Newman (New York: Simon and Schuster, 1956), 2:1190. Newman's commentary is followed by the treatise, Thomas Robert Malthus, "Mathematics of Population and Food," 2:1192–99.

11. Michael Blackman, "Abundant Oil Makes Kazakhstan a Country to Watch," *The Age,* December 1, 2004, http://theage.com.au/news/Business/Abundant-oil-makes-Kazakhstan-a-country-to-watch/2004/11/30/1101577481456 .html?from=storylhs&oneclick=true.

12. For the 2001 estimate, see "Chevron Doubles Estimate of Tengiz Oilfield Reserves," *Alexander's Gas and Oil Connections,* April 24, 2001, http://www .gasandoil.com/goc/company/cnc12258.htm. The 2004 estimate comes from Blackman, "Abundant Oil."

13. "Iran: Country Analysis Brief," U.S. Energy Information Administration, U.S. Department of Energy, http://www.eia.doe.gov/emeu/cabs/iran.html.

14. Ibid.

15. "Iran Discovers New Oil Field in Central Region," Scandinavian Oil-Gas Magazine Online, January 5, 2004, http://www.scandoil.com/moxie/news /world_news/iran-discovers-new-oil-fi.shtml.

16. "Big Oil Wields Ultra Deep Influence: Legislators Push for Energy Industry Tax Breaks, Regulatory Changes to Hunt for Oil at the Bottom of the Sea," July 10, 2005, http://www.public-i.org/oil/report.aspx?aid=436.

17. "Deep and Ultra-Deepwater Oil and Gas Market Update 2004/08," Infield,

Energy Data Analysts, see http://www.infield.com/Deep_and_Ultra-Deepwater_Annual_Market_Report.htm.

18. Christopher Cooper, "Odd Reservoir Off Louisiana Prods Oil Experts to Seek a Deeper Meaning," *Wall Street Journal,* April 16, 1999, http://www.oralchelation.com/faq/wsj4.htm.
19. Kathy Blanchard, "Oil and Gas—'Renewable Resources'?" ER News, U.S. Department of Energy's Office of Energy Research, http://www.pnl.gov/er_news/08_95/er_news/oil1.kb.html.
20. David S. Holland, John B. Leedy, and David R. Lammlein, "Eugene Island Block 330 Field—U.S.A. Offshore Louisiana," Search and Discovery Article #20003, 1999, AAPG Treatise of Petroleum Geology, Atlas of Oil and Gas Fields, Structural Traps III, 103–43, http://www.searchanddiscovery.com/documents/97015/eugene.htm.
21. "About VIETSOVPETRO," Vietsovpetro, http://www.vietsov.com.vn/wps/portal/!ut/p/.cmd/cs/.ce/7_0_A/.s/7_0_GC/_s.7_0_A/7_0_GC.
22. "Prospects in Vietnam: Roaring Young Lions," American Association of Petroleum Geologists, http://www.aapg.org/explorer/2005/02feb/vietnam.cfm.
23. "Russia: Country Analysis Brief," U.S. Energy Information Administration, U.S. Department of Energy, http://www.eia.doe.gov/emeu/cabs/russia.html.
24. "Russia's Oil Exports Reach Maximum, Decline to Start in 2 Years—Official," November 9, 2004, http://www.mosnews.com/money/2004/11/09/oilproduction.shtml.
25. The data are taken from spreadsheets published by the Energy Information Administration, U.S. Department of Energy. See http://www.eia.doe.gov/emeu/international/petroleu.html#IntlReserves.
26. Ibid., see http://www.eia.doe.gov/oiaf/ieo/pdf/nat_gas.pdf.
27. Jimmy Carter, April 18, 1977, http://www.pbs.org/wgbh/amex/carter/filmmore/ps_energy.html. The next two quotes come from this same speech.
28. Ciaran Ryan, "Does the Earth Re-fuel Itself?" *Australia Sunday Times,* May 3, 2005, http://www.suntimes.co.za/zones/sundaytimesNEW/business/business1115100901.aspx.
29. Michael C. Lynch, "The New Pessimism About Petroleum Resources: Debunking the Hubbert Model (and Hubbert Modelers)."
30. Matthew R. Simmons, *Twilight in the Desert: The Coming Saudi Oil Shock and the World Economy* (Hoboken, NJ: John Wiley, 2005), 92.
31. Ibid., 288.
32. Ibid., 286.
33. Ibid., 287.
34. Ibid., 270.

35. Irving M. Copi, *Introduction to Logic,* 4th ed. (New York: Macmillan, 1972), 96.

CHAPTER 4: THE GLOBAL-WARMING HOAX

1. John R. Christy, "The Global Warming Fiasco," in *Global Warming and Other Eco-Myths: How the Environmental Movement Uses False Science to Scare Us to Death,* ed. Ronald Bailey (Roseville, CA: Prima Publishing, 2002), 2.

2. Ibid., 10–11.

3. Svante Arrhenius, "On the Influence of Carbonic Acid in the Air upon the Temperature on the Ground," *Philosophical Magazine,* 41 (1896): 237–76. See http://web.lemoyne.edu/~giunta/ARRHENIUS.HTML.

4. Spencer R. Weart, "The Discovery of Global Warming. The Carbon Dioxide Greenhouse Effect," http://www.aip.org/history/climate/C02.htm. See also Weart, *The Discovery of Global Warming* (Cambridge, MA: Harvard University Press, 2003).

5. Environmental Sciences Division of the Oak Ridge National Laboratory, "A Quick Background to the Last Ice Age," http://www.esd.ornl.gov/projects/qen/nerc130k.html.

6. Data from NASA, reported in *Planetary Times,* January 12, 2005, http://news.space-explorers.com/display.asp?v=3&i=1&a=1.

7. Clinton Global Initiative, "Climate Change: Business Challenge, Business Opportunity," under the Initiative Goals section of the foundation's Web, http://www.clintonglobalinitiative.com/home.nsf/pt_climate_change.

8. The Bunderheim Rural Electric Association (REA; a member of the Alberta Federation of Rural Electric Associations, Alberta, Canada), "Global Warming Explained: Melting Glaciers, Shrinking Polar Ice and Rising Oceans?" http://www.fathersforlife.org/REA/warming10.htm.

9. Ibid.; see "Global Warming Explained: What Is Wrong with the Forests?" http://www.fathersforlife.org/REA/warming3.htm#Surfacetemps.

10. D. C. Trabant, R. S. March, and B. F. Molnia, "Growing and Advancing Glaciers in Alaska," *Eos Trans. AGU,* 83 (47), Fall Meeting Supplement, 2002, http://ak.water.usgs.gov/glaciology/hubbard/reports/200212_agu_poster/200 2.12_AGU_Calving_Glaciers.pdf.

11. Zbigniew Jaworowski, "The Global Warming Folly," http://mitosyfraudes.8k .com/INGLES/Warm.html.

12. Theodor Landscheidt, "Solar Activity: A Dominant Factor in Climate Dynamics," http://www.john-daly.com/solar/solar.htm.

13. "Global Warming—Climate. US Climate, Climate Models," Environmental

Protection Agency, http://yosemite.epa.gov/oar/globalwarming.nsf /content/ClimateFutureClimateUSClimate.html#models.

14. See, for instance, Thom Hartmann, "How Global Warming May Cause the Next Ice Age," January 30, 2004, http://www.commondreams.org/views04/ 0130–11.htm.

15. Al Gore, "Global Warming and the Environment," January 15, 2004, http://www.algore-08.com/index.php?option=com_content&task=view&id =94&Itemid=123&mosmsg=Thanks+for+your+vote%21.

16. "Glacier Retreat in Glacier National Park, Montana," http://www.nrmsc.usgs .gov/research/glacier_retreat.htm.

17. Gore, "Global Warming and the Environment."

18. Ibid.

19. Ibid.

20. Caroline Daniel in Copenhagen and Fiona Harvey in Gleneagles, "Bush Admits to Role of Humans in Global Warming," *Financial Times,* July 7, 2005, http://news.ft.com/cms/s/cb0c3b94-ee84–11d9–98e5–00000 e2511c8.html.

21. Patrick J. Michaels, "The Greenhouse Effect and Global Change: Review and Reappraisal," in *The State of Humanity,* ed. Julian L. Simon (Oxford, England: Blackwell, 1995), 544.

22. Bjørn Lomborg, *The Skeptical Environmentalist: Measuring the Real State of the World* (Cambridge, England: Cambridge University Press, 2001), 322.

23. Ibid.

24. Ibid., 299.

25. Julian L. Simon, *Hoodwinking the Nation* (New Brunswick, NJ: Transactions, 1999), 31.

26. Ibid., 1.

27. Ibid., 7–8.

28. Lomborg, *Skeptical Environmentalist,* 317.

29. Dan Joling, "Senators Attest to Alaska Climate Change," Associated Press, August 17, 2005, http://news.yahoo.com/news?tmpl=story&u=/ap/20050818 /ap_on_go_co/climate_change_alaska_2.

30. David Adam, "Climate Change Skeptics Bet $10,000 on Cooler World," *Manchester Guardian,* August 19, 2005, http://www.guardian.co.uk/uk_news /story/0,3604,1552092,00.html.

CHAPTER 5: THE FOLLY OF OIL CONSERVATION

1. Jennifer Jacobson, "US: Renewable Energy Remains Elusive," Energy Bulletin, September 3, 2004, http://www.energybulletin.net/1895.html.

2. Jimmy Carter, Speech, April 18, 1977, http://www.pbs.org/wgbh/amex/carter/filmmore/ps_energy.html.

3. Reuters, "Motorists Keep Driving Despite High Gas Prices: Americans Not Likely to Change Transportation Habits During Shortages," MSNBC.com, March 22, 2005, http://www.msnbc.msn.com/id/7267497/.

4. Ibid.

5. Paul J. Lim, "Chugging Along," *U.S. News & World Report,* posted July 29, 2005, http://www.usnews.com/usnews/biztech/buzz/archive/buzz050729.htm

6. Oil production and supply data are drawn from the Web site of the Energy Information Administration of the U.S. Department of Energy. See in particular, "U.S. Country Analysis Brief," http://www.eia.doe.gov/emeu/cabs/usa.html.

7. Dean Calbreath, "Soaring Home Prices Worldwide Driven by a Variety of Factors Such as Asian Financial Crisis, Rising Oil Prices, Shifts in Capital," *San Diego Union Tribune,* July 11, 2005, http://www.signonsandiego.com/news/metro/20050711–9999-lz1n11warming.html.

8. Roula Khalaf, William Wallis, and Gillian Tett Aabar, "Oil Money Makes Good Times Roll Again in Middle East," July 7, 2005, http://www.resourceinvestor.com/pebble.asp?relid=11095.

9. Michael Moore, *Fahrenheit 9/11,* Lions Gate Films, 2004. Moore relies heavily upon Craig Unger, *House of Bush, House of Saud: The Secret Relationship Between the World's Two Most Powerful Dynasties* (New York: Scribner, 2004).

10. Maha Akeel, "New Incentives to Woo Foreign Investment," July 3, 2005, Arab News, http://www.arabnews.com/?page=1&section=0&article=66334&d=3&m=7&y=2005.

11. David Rosenberg, quoted in Lou Dobbs, "The Party's Over: With Interest Rates Rising, Gas Prices Up and Wage Growth Tepid, Consumers Face Strong Headwinds," June 16, 2004, http://money.cnn.com/2004/06/16/commentary/dobbs/dobbs/.

12. Elliot Blair Smith, "Huge Oil Profits Go for Exploration," *USA Today,* July 26, 2005, http://news.yahoo.com/news?tmpl=story&u=/usatoday/20050728/bs_usatoday/hugeoilprofitsgoforexploration.

13. Ibid. The analysis of this section is drawn largely from the Saudi Arabian Country Analysis, http://www.eia.doe.gov/emeu/cabs/saudi.html.

14. John F. Kennedy, address, Philadelphia, Pennsylvania, July 4, 1962, http://www.jfklibrary.org/jfk-independencehall-1962.html.

15. Jimmy Carter, address, April 18, 1977, http://www.pbs.org/wgbh/amex/carter/filmmore/ps_energy.html.

16. George W. Bush, Sixteenth Annual Energy Efficiency Forum, June 17, 2005,

http://www.h2cars.biz/artman/publish/article_749.shtml. The Web site www.h2cars.biz is dedicated to promote hydrogen-fueled cars.

17. Michael T. Klare, "Artic Drilling Is No Energy Answer: Tapping ANWR Wouldn't Help Much with the Most Pressing Problem: American Dependence on Foreign Oil," *Los Angeles Times,* April 3, 2005, http://www .commondreams.org/views05/0403–26.htm.

18. Terence Chea, "Wayward Windmills: Altamont Pass Turbines Deadly to Rare Raptors," *Los Angeles Daily News,* July 9, 2005, http://www.dailynews.com/ Stories/0,1413,200~20954~2958434,00.html.

19. Ibid.

20. Guy Ashley, "13-Year Timetable Set to Reduce and Replace Altamont Wind-mills," *San Jose Mercury News,* July 8, 2005, http://www.mercurynews.com/ mld/mercurynews/news/local/states/california/counties/alameda_county/ 12083488.htm.

21. "Denmark Inherits the Wind," Business Week Online, April 30, 2001, http://businessweek.com/magazine/content/01_18/b3730108.htm.

22. Ibid.

23. Michael Parfit, "Future Power: Where Will the World Get Its Next Nuclear Fix?" *National Geographic,* August 2005, http://www7.nationalgeographic .com/ngm/0508/feature1/fulltext.html.

24. "Calculation of the Power Produced by a Windmill," http://www.ecolo.org /documents/documents_in_english/WindmillFormula.htm.

25. "Survey Finds Americans Support Energy Independence, Hydrogen-Based Economy," http://www.h2cars.biz/artman/publish/article_757.shtml.

26. "Hydrogen as a Fuel for Automobiles," http://mb-soft.com/public2/hydrogen .html.

27. Stefan Theil, "The Next Petroleum: With Oil Prices Going Through the Roof, So-Called Biofuels Are at Last Becoming a Viable Alternative to Gaso-line and Diesel," *Newsweek,* August 8, 2005.

28. Reported in Susan S. Lang, "Cornell Ecologist's Study Finds That Producing Ethanol and Biodiesel from Corn and Other Crops Is Not Worth the En-ergy," Cornell University News Service, July 5, 2005, http://www.news.cor-nell.edu/stories/July05/ethanol.toocostly.ssl.html.

29. Kathy Kiely, "U.S. Nuclear Power Industry Working on Quiet Comeback," *USA Today,* May 19, 2005, http://www.usatoday.com/news/washington/ 2005–06–19-nuclear-energy_x.htm.

30. "Advanced Nuclear Power Reactors," Nuclear Issues Briefing Paper 16, May 2005, Uranium Information Centre, Melbourne, Australia, http://www.uic .com.au/nip16.htm.

31. Web site of the World Nuclear Association (www.world-nuclear.org), http://www.world-nuclear.org/education/whyu.htm.

32. Nancy Lofholm, "Plans for Increased Nuclear Power Sparking a Demand for Uranium," *Denver Post*, July 31, 2005, http://www.baltimoresun.com/news/nationworld/bal-te.uranium31ju131,1,2900024.story?coll=bal-nationworld-headlines&ctrack=1&cset=true.

CHAPTER 6: THE GROWING U.S. DEPENDENCE ON FOREIGN OIL

1. Daniel Yergin, *The Prize: The Epic Quest for Oil, Money, and Power* (New York: Simon & Schuster, 1991), 395.

2. Ibid., 396.

3. Unless otherwise indicated, the energy data in this chapter are drawn from the Energy Information Administration of the U.S. Department of Energy, www.eia.doe.gov.

4. Jeffrey S. Passel, "Unauthorized Migrants: Numbers and Characteristics," briefing paper, Independent Task Force on Immigration and America's Future, June 14, 2005, http://usconservatives.about.com/gi/dynamic/offsite.htm?zi=1/XJ&sdn=usconservatives&zu=http%3A%2F%2Fpewhispanic.org.

5. Center for Immigration Studies, "Illegal Immigration," http://www.cis.org/topics/illegalimmigration.html.

6. Passel, "Unauthorized Migrants."

7. "Invasion USA: Minutemen Aid in Arrest of 21 Illegals," August 2, 2005, WorldNetDaily.com, http://www.worldnetdaily.com/news/article.asp?ARTICLE_ID=45569.

8. Kris Axtman, "Illegal Entry by Non-Mexicans Rises," *Christian Science Monitor*, July 26, 2005, http://www.csmonitor.com/2005/0726/p01s01-usfp.html.

9. Michelle Malkin, *Invasion: How America Still Welcomes Terrorist Criminals and Other Foreign Menaces to Our Shores* (Washington DC: Regnery, 2002).

10. Oliver North, "Venezuela's Chavez Seeking to Create 'Bolivarian Army' to Counter 'U.S. Imperialism,'" *Human Events OnLine*, February 25, 2005, http://www.humaneventsonline.com/article.php?id=6690. The phrase "Castro-Chavez-Ortega Axis of Evil" comes from this article.

11. "The Iron Fist of Hugo Chavez," FoxNews.com, February 4, 2005, http://www.foxnews.com/story/0,2933,146472,00.html.

12. Robert Collier, "Battle for Canada's Underground Resources," *San Francisco Chronicle*, March 24, 2005, http://sfgate.com/cgi-bin/article.cgi?file=/chronicle/archive/2005/03/24/BUG8MBTQPS1.DTL&type=business; also available at http://sfgate.com/cgi-bin/article.cgi?file=/chronicle/archive/2005/03/24/BUG8MBTQPS1.DTL&type=business.

13. Ibid.

14. See the Mackenzie Gas Project homepage, www.mackenziegasproject.com. The Web site describes the project in considerable detail, including presenting a summary of the project's environmental impact statement.

15. Elizabeth May, "Mackenzie Valley Pipeline and Alberta Oil Sands," April 28, 2004, http://www.sierraclub.ca/national/programs/atmosphere-energy/energy-onslaught/campaign.shtml?x=307.

16. Ibid.

17. "Mackenzie Pipeline Agreement Signed," July 27, 2005, http://www.globe-net.ca/news/archiveview.cfm?type=2&newsID=1044.

18. U.S. Department of Justice, National Drug Intelligence Center, Executive Summary, "United States-Canada Border Drug Threat Assessment," December 2002, Document ID: 2002-R0423–001, http://www.usdoj.gov/ndic/pubs07/794/.

19. Canadian version published by Public Safety and Emergency Preparedness Canada, "United States–Canada Border Drug Threat Assessment," October 2004, http://www.psepc.gc.ca/publications/policing/drug_threat_e.asp#3.

20. Richard Beeston, "Dynasty Faces Enormous Challenges in Years Ahead," TimesOnLine.com, August 2, 2005, http://www.timesonline.co.uk/article/0,,251–1717321,00.html.

21. Carola Hoyos, "Simulation Shows US Held over a barrel," Financial Times, August 4, 2005, http://news.ft.com/cms/s/1a76b890–0518–11da-97da-00000e2511c8.html.

22. Ibid.

23. Unless otherwise noted, the statistics regarding natural gas use are drawn from "Factsheets," http://www.naturalgasfacts.org/index.html.

24. "The Quest for a New Energy Prize: Daniel Yergin Talks About the Critical Role Liquefied Natural Gas Is Destined to Play," Business Week Online, March 1, 2004, http://www.businessweek.com/magazine/content/04_09/b3872106_mz009.htm.

25. Ibid.

26. "Market Trends—Natural Gas Demand and Supply," Annual Energy Outlook 2005, Energy Information Administration, U.S. Department of Energy, http://www.eia.doe.gov/oiaf/aeo/gas.html.

27. William J. Hausman, "Long-Term Trends in Energy Prices," in The State of Humanity ed. Julian L. Simon (Oxford, England: Blackwell, 1995), 280–86.

28. Mark Cooper, "Spring Break in the U.S. Oil Industry: Price Spikes, Express Profits and Excuses," Consumer Federation of America, October 2003, http://www.consumerfed.org/pdfs/gasoline1003.pdf.

CHAPTER 7: WHY GOVERNMENT OIL PLANS FAIL

1. Kevin G. Hall, "U.S. Refineries Straining: Nation Becomes More Dependent on Foreign Gasoline," *Detroit Free Press,* June 7, 2005, http://www.freep .com/money/business/refineries7e_20050607.htm.

2. Ibid.

3. Jocelyn Parker, "Gas Prices May Be High, But New Refineries Cost Even More," *Alexander's Gas & Oil Connections, News & Trends: North America,* August 4, 2004, http://www.gasandoil.com/goc/news/ntn43140.htm.

4. Daniel Gross, "The Great Refinery Shortage: America Needs Oil, You'd Rather Have a Beach Condo," *Slate,* June 8, 2004, http://slate.msn.com/id/2102031.

5. Government Accounting Office, "Military Base Closures: Updated Status of Prior Base Realignments and Closures," GAO-05–138, January 2005, http://www.gao.gov/highlights/d05138high.pdf.

6. William Roberts, "Bush to Propose Using Old Bases for Refinery Sites," www.bloomberg.com, April 27, 2005, http://www.bloomberg.com/apps /news?pid=10000103&sid=aKyjUhrmV2m0&refer=us.

7. Hall, "U.S. Refineries Straining," http://www.freep.com/money/business /refineries7e_20050607.htm.

8. Richard Valdmanis, "U.S. Refiners Shun Call for New Refineries," Reuters UK, June 23, 2005, http://today.reuters.co.uk/news/newsarticle.aspx?type =summitNews&summit=UtilitiesSummit&storyid=2005–06–23T184531Z_ 01_N2357145_RTRIDST_0_SPECIALEVENTII-ENERGY-SUMMIT -REFINERIES-DC.XML&archived=true&show=all.

9. Protecting Health, Safety and Democracy, "Myths and Facts About Oil Re- fineries in the United States," http://www.citizen.org/cmep/energy_enviro _nuclear/electricity/Oil_and_Gas/articles.cfm?ID=11829.

10. Robert E. Litan and Philip Verleger, "Energy Price Controls: Been There, Done That," *Washington Post,* May 21, 2001, http://www.brook.edu/views /op-ed/litan/20010521.htm.

11. Excerpt from Daniel Yergin and Joseph Stanislaw, *The Commanding Heights : The Battle Between Government and the Marketplace That Is Remaking the Modern World* (New York: Simon & Schuster, 1998), 60–64.

12. Benjamin Kohlmann, "A Detriment of the Public Service," Federal Reserve Bank of Minneapolis, June 2000, http://minneapolisfed.org/pubs/region/ 00–06/essay.cfm. The article was selected from more than 260 entries in the Federal Reserve Bank of Minneapolis's twelfth annual essay council for Ninth District high-school juniors and seniors. Unfortunately, what high- school juniors and seniors correctly perceive today was missed entirely by a

group of our supposedly best politicians and bureaucrats who from 1973 through 1980 believed falsely that their decisions and actions would "fix" an otherwise "broken" free market. Unfortunately, many areas of social and political life remain where we still place far too much reliance on bureaucrats to make informed, unbiased decisions in the best interests of the public good.

13. Jerry Taylor and Peter Van Doren, "Time to Lay the 1973 Oil Embargo to Rest," Cato Institute, October 17, 2003, http://www.cato.org/dailys/10–17–03–2.html.

14. Ibid.

15. Energy Information Administration (EIA), U.S. Department of Energy, "Primer on Gasoline Sources and Markets," http://www.eia.doe.gov/neic/experts/contactexperts.htm. The analysis in the next two paragraphs is drawn from this source as well.

16. Bill Clinton, "Memorandum for the Secretary of the Interior," June 12, 1998, http://www.eia.doe.gov/oil_gas/natural_gas/analysis_publications/ngmajorleg/moratorium.html. The rest of this paragraph is drawn from the Energy Information Administration Web site.

17. "Clinton Extends Moratorium on Offshore Oil Drilling," CNN.com, June 12, 1998, http://www.cnn.com/TECH/science/9806/12/offshore.drilling.pm/.

18. "Deal Reached to Extend Ban on Fla. Offshore Drilling," Associated Press, June 16, 2005, http://www.cnn.com/TECH/science/9806/12/offshore.drilling.pm/.

19. U.S. Department of the Interior, Offshore Minerals Management, http://www.mms.gov/offshore/.

20. Wilderness Society News Release, "Administration Signs 'Unbalanced' Plan for National Petroleum Reserve—Alaska. Decision to 'Drill It All' Ignores Public, Scientists Who Called for Balance," January 22, 2004, http://www.wilderness.org/NewsRoom/Release/20040122.cfm.

21. Porcupine Caribou Management Board, "Updates: The Arctic Refuge and American Politics 101: What Happens Next?" http://www.taiga.net/pcmb/updates_06.html.

22. Linda Krop, "Court Orders Federal Government to Comply with Judgment Directing State Review of Offshore Oil Leases," December 11, 2003, http://www.edcnet.org/ProgramsPages/PressReleases/121103.htm.

23. David Asman, "Oil-for-Food Scandal Draws Scrutiny to U.N.," Fox News Channel, September 20, 2004, http://www.foxnews.com/story/0,2933,132832,00.html. See also Jed Babbin, "The U.N. vs. Iraq: Kofi Annan Treats Allawi's Government Worse than He Treated Saddam's," *American Spectator*

(November 2004): 14; Jed Babbin, *Inside the Asylum: Why the United Nations and Old Europe Are Worse than You Think* (Washington DC: Regnery, 2004).

24. "Iraq War Allies Rebuff UN Chief," BBC, September 16, 2004, http://news .bbc.co.uk/2/hi/middle_east/3661736.stm.

CHAPTER 8: THE DIMINISHING U.S. PETRODOLLAR

1. Michael T. Klare, *Blood and Oil: The Dangers and Consequences of America's Growing Dependency on Imported Petroleum* (New York: Metropolitan Books/Henry Holt and Co., 2004), 20.

2. Ibid., 23.

3. Ibid., 146.

4. Ibid., 188.

5. Ibid., 73.

6. Drawn from the Energy Information Administration, "International Petroleum Monthly Oil Imports," http://www.eia.doe.gov/emeu/ipsr/imports.html.

7. David J. Lynch, "Iran Unlikely to Drop Pipeline Deal with Iran," *USA Today*, March 1, 2005, http://www.usatoday.com/news/world/2005–03–16 -rice-india_x.htm.

8. The issues of Iranian oppression and economic suffering under the brutal rule of the mullahs is covered extensively in Jerome R. Corsi, *Atomic Iran: How the Terrorist Regime Bought the Bomb and American Politicians* (Nashville, TN: WND Books, 2005).

9. "Japan Plans Second Iran Loan to Secure Oil Amid U.S. Protests," Bloomberg, February 23, 2004, http://www.iranexpert.com/2004/japan23february.htm.

10. Frederick Stakelbeck, "The Growing Tehran-Beijing Axis," *In the National Interest*, http://www.inthenationalinterest.com/Articles/January%202005 /January2005stakelbeckPFV.html.

11. Data from the Energy Information Administration, U.S. Department of Energy, contained on the EIA Web site as an excel spreadsheet labeled t44, "Total Oil Supply (Crude Oil, Natural Gas Plant Liquids, Other Liquids and Refinery Processing Gain)—United States, Persian Gulf, Total OPEC, and World Total 1970–2003 (Thousands of Barrels)," http://www.eia.doe.gov /emeu/international/petroleu.html#ProductionA.

12. This often overlooked mathematical principle is expressed eloquently in J. B. S. Haldane, "On Being the Right Size," in *The World of Mathematics*, ed. James R. Newman, 4 vols. (New York: Simon & Schuster, 1956), 2:952–57.

13. WTRG Economics, "Oil Price History and Analysis," http://www.wtrg.com /prices.htm.

14. Energy Information Administration, U.S. Department of Energy,

http://www.eia.doe.gov/pub/oil_gas/petroleum/analysis_publications/oil
_market_basics/Price_transactions.htm.

15. WTRG Economics, "Oil Price History and Analysis," http://www.wtrg.com
/prices.htm.

16. New York University, Leonard Stern School of Business, "The Petroleum
Market: 1970–2001," August 28, 2002, http://pages.stern.nyu.edu/
%7Elcabral/teaching/oil.pdf.

17. Spot contracts and the futures market in international oil markets are explained on the Web site of the Energy Information Administration, U.S. Department of Energy, http://www.eia.doe.gov/pub/oil_gas/petroleum
/analysis_publications/oil_market_basics/Price_transactions.htm.

18. This spreadsheet is listed as "mer_data.asp-4" on the Energy Information Administration Web site. See "Overview of U.S. Petroleum Trade, Total Petroleum (Thousand Barrels per Day)" as "All Months, January 1973–Present,
and Annual Averages for 1973–Present": http://www.eia.doe.gov/emeu/
international/petroleu.html#USTradeExports.

19. See, for instance, the description on www.greekshares.com, a Web site
managed by Evangelos G. Haramis, the new business development managing director for Proton Investment Bank in Greece. See Currency
Trading—FOREX, http://www.greekshares.com/currency_trading_
forex.asp.

20. An excellent description of the forex can be found on the Web site of the
Federal Reserve Bank of Chicago, "Strong Dollar, Weak Dollar: Foreign Exchange Rates and the U.S. Economy," http://www.chicagofed.org/consumer_
information/strong_dollar_weak_dollar.cfm.

21. Ibid.

22. Consumer Price Index, U.S. Bureau of Labor Statistics, ftp://ftp.bls.gov/pub
/special.requests/cpi/cpiai.txt.

23. The Economic History Series Web site (www.eh.net) provides a calculator to
determine the depreciation of the dollar over time. See What Is Its Relative
Value in U.S. Dollars, http://eh.net/hmit/compare/.

24. A U.S. National Debt Clock is available on the Internet at http://www.toptips
.com/debtclock.html.

25. A. F. Alhajji, "The Impact of Dollar Devaluation on the World Oil Industry:
Do Exchange Rates Matter?" *Middle East Economic Survey*, August 16, 2004,
http://www.mees.com/postedarticles/oped/a47n33d01.htm.

26. John Zarocostas, "OPEC Boost Euro Deposits over Dollars," *Washington
Times*, December 7, 2004, http://washingtontimes.com/upi-breaking
/20041207–031853–3224r.htm.

27. Lawrence J. Joyce, "OPEC Will Switch from the Dollar to the Euro: A Reemergence of the Ancient Roman Empire?" April 16, 2002, http://www.888webtoday.com/joyce8.html.

28. See, for instance: Catherine Belton, "Putin: Why Not Price Oil in Euros?" October 11, 2003, http://www.defencetalk.com/cgi-bin/news/exec/view.cgi/2/142/printer.

29. Mahathir Bin Mohammed, "Seriousness of the Gold Dinar," http://www.taxfreegold.com/gold-dinar.html.

30. Sonia Kolesnikov, "Gold Dinar Could Soon Be Reality," November 15, 2002, http://www.upi.com/view.cfm?StoryID=20021115–051010–4184r.

31. Ibid.

32. Ibid.

33. Khaled Hanafi, "Islamic Gold Dinar Will Minimize Dependency on U.S. Dollar," IslamOnline.net, http://www.islam-online.net/english/news/2003–01/08/article08.shtml.

34. "Sell Oil for Gold, Mahathir Tells Saudi Arabia," Reuters, January 18, 2004, http://www.forbes.com/business/newswire/2004/01/18/rtr1216007.html.

CHAPTER 9: HOW HIGH THE PRICE OF OIL?

1. Jim VandeHei, "Cheney Warns of Iran as a Nuclear Threat," *Washington Post*, January 21, 2005, http://www.washingtonpost.com/wp-dyn/articles/A24677–2005Jan20.html.

2. See, for instance, "Mohamed El Baradei: The Head of the United Nations Organization Charged with Stopping the Nuclear Proliferation of Nuclear Weapons Had an Upbeat Message About Iran: Progress Was Being Made," BBC, March 3, 2004, http://news.bbc.co.uk/2/hi/programmes/newsnight/3529253.stm. In an interview with the BBC diplomatic editor Mark Urban, El Baradei acknowledged that Iran had not "come clean" regarding important details of its nuclear program.

3. "EU Offers to Back Iran Oil Pipe Routes from Central Asia," *New Zealand Herald*, August 6, 2005, http://www.nzherald.co.nz/index.cfm?c_id=2&ObjectID=10339451.

4. Eleventh International Oil, Gas, Petrochemicals Exhibition exhibitor list, http://www.iran-oilshow.com/En/list_exhibitors.aspx.

5. Barrie McKenna, "China's Foreign Reserves Balloon to Record," GlobeAndMail.com, July 15. 2005, http://www.theglobeandmail.com/servlet/ArticleNews/TPStory/LAC/20050715/IBYUAN15/TPBusiness/International.

6. "Aspects of ChevronTexaco's Proposed Acquisition of Unocal," Energy Information Administration, U.S. Department of Energy, April 5, 2005, http://www.eia.doe.gov/emeu/finance/mergers/ctuindex.html.

7. "China to Care for the Earth, Conserve Energy," *Beijing's People's Daily,* August 26, 2002, http://english1.people.com.cn/200208/26/eng20020826_102097.shtml.

8. See William R. Hawkins, "China Pursues 'Manifest Destiny' Through Mercantilism and Imperialism," AmericanEconomicAlert.com, February 3, 2005, http://www.americaneconomicalert.org/view_art.asp?Prod_ID=1246.

9. "China: Country Analysis Brief," Energy Information Administration, U.S. Department of Energy, http://www.eia.doe.gov/emeu/cabs/china.html.

10. Ibid.

11. Press Release, "Sinopec Oil Discovery Could Lift China Reserves by Third," OilVoice.com, January 4, 2005, http://www.oilvoice.com/South_East_Asia/3083.htm.

12. "China's Tarim Basin Becomes Major Oil and Gas Supplier," August 2, 2005, http://news.tradingcharts.com/futures/2/7/68926972.html.

13. "Russia: Country Analysis Brief," Energy Information Administration, U.S. Department of Energy, February 2005, http://www.eia.doe.gov/emeu/cabs/russia.html. The statistics in the following paragraph also come from this source.

14. "Preparations for Russian-China Military Exercises Begin," Itar-Tass News Agency, August 8, 2005, http://www.tass.ru/eng/level2.html?NewsID=2299200&PageNum=0.

15. "Putin: Russian-Syrian Deal Completed," *Jerusalem Post,* April 20, 2005, http://www.jpost.com/servlet/Satellite?pagename=JPost/JPArticle/ShowFull&cid=1113963509285.

16. For the most current version of this report, see "Performance Profiles of Major Energy Producers 2003," Energy Information Administration, U.S. Department of Energy, http://www.eia.doe.gov/emeu/perfpro/index.html.

17. Mark N. Cooper, *Fueling Profits: Industry Consolidation, Excess Profits and Federal Neglect, Domestic Causes of Recent Gasoline and Natural Gas Price Shocks* (Washington DC: Consumer Federation of America, 2004), 25, http://www.consumerfed.org/pdfs/oilprofits.pdf.

18. Ibid., 32.

19. "Aspects of the Merger of Chevron and Texaco," Energy Information Administration, U.S. Department of Energy, http://www.eia.doe.gov/emeu/finance/mergers/ctindex.html.

20. Ibid.

CHAPTER 10: TERRORISM AND THE THREAT TO OIL

1. Loretta Napoleoni, *Terror Incorporated: Tracing the Dollars Behind the Terror Networks* (New York: Seven Stories Press, 2005). See also, Rachel Ehrenfeld, *Funding Evil: How Terrorism Is Financed—And How to Stop It* (Chicago: Bonus Books, 2005).

2. Operation Divest Terror, "Empowering Americans to Defeat Terrorism: Mission Statement," http://www.divestterror.org/.

3. The National Commission on Terrorist Attacks Upon the United States, *The 9-11 Commission Report* (Washington DC: U.S. Government Printing Office, 2004), 240–41.

4. Institute for the Analysis of Global Security, "Iraq Pipeline Watch: Attacks on Iraqi Pipelines, Oil Installations, and Oil Personnel," July 12, 2005, http://www.iags.org/iraqpipelinewatch.htm.

5. Guy Luft, Institute for the Analysis of Global Security, "Energy Security: Pipeline Sabotage Is Terrorist's Weapon of Choice," http://www.iags.org /n0328051.htm.

6. Ibid.

7. Guy Luft, "Iraq's Oil Sector One Year After Liberation," Saban Center Middle East Memo no. 4, June 17, 2004, http://brookings.edu/fp/saban/luftmem 020040617.htm.

8. Jim Taylor and Peter VanDoren, "Oil Weapon Myth," December 6, 2001, http://www.cato.org/research/articles/taylor-011206.html.

9. Osama Bin Laden, speech transcript, November 1, 2004, http://256.com /gray/blog/2004/11/09_1.html. Also available at: http://english.aljazeera.net /NR/exeres/79C6AF22–98FB-4A1C-B21F-2BC36E87F61F.htm.

10. "Osama Bin Laden, Statement to the Saudi Rulers: Part 4, December 16, 2004, http://www.jihadunspun.com/newsarchive/article_internal.php?article=101052&list=/newsarchive/index.php&. Phrasing, spelling, and the expression of the dollar are from the original translation with the exception that "chock" in the last line was changed to "choke."

11. See, for instance: "Terrorists Are Now Targeting Saudi Arabia's Oil Infrastructure. How Bad Could Things Get?" *Economist*, May 27, 2004, http://www.economist.com/business/displayStory.cfm?story_id=2705562. Robert Baer's scenario is quoted in Safe Money Report, June 1, 2004, www.martinweiss.com.

12. Associated Press, "Saudi Telethon Raises Over $100 Million for Palestinians," FoxNews.com, April 13, 2002, http://www.foxnews.com/story/0,2933 ,50260,00.html.

13. See "Al-Qaeda Organization in the Arabian Peninsula," GlobalSecurity.org, http://www.globalsecurity.org/military/world/para/al-qaida-arabia.htm.
14. Mordechai Abir, "The Al-Qaeda Threat to Saudi Arabia's Oil Sector," *Jerusalem Center for Public Affairs* 4, no. 13, December 28, 2004, http://www .jcpa.org/brief/brief004–13.htm.
15. "Travel Warnings and Warden Messages: U.S. Consulate Attack," U.S. Embassy, Riyadh, Saudi Arabia, December 6, 2004, http://riyadh.usembassy.gov /saudi-arabia/Warden_Messages.html.
16. "CIA: New bin Laden Tape Likely Al-Qaeda Leader," CNN.com, December 17, 2004, http://www.cnn.com/2004/WORLD/meast/12/16/bin.laden.tape /index.html.
17. See Utah's Independent Media Source, "Osama Bin Laden—Full Text of Message to Iraqis," October 18, 2003, http://utah.indymedia.org/news/2003 /10/6566.php.
18. See Information Clearing House, Osama bin Laden, speech, November 1, 2004, http://www.informationclearinghouse.info/article7201.htm.
19. James F. Jarboe, domestic terrorism section chief, Counterterrorism Division, FBI, in testimony before the House Resources Committee, Subcommittee on Forests and Forest Health, *The Threat of Eco-Terrorism,* February 12, 2002, http://www.fbi.gov/congress/congress02/jarboe021202.htm.
20. Quoted at http://www.envirotruth.org/ecoterrorism.cfm.

INDEX